THEORIES OF MYTH

*From Ancient Israel and Greece
to Freud, Jung, Campbell,
and Lévi-Strauss*

Series Editor

ROBERT A. SEGAL

University of Lancaster

A GARLAND SERIES

Series Contents

VOLUME

3

PHILOSOPHY, RELIGIOUS STUDIES, AND MYTH

Edited with introductions by

ROBERT A. SEGAL

University of Lancaster

GARLAND PUBLISHING, Inc.
New York & London
1996

Library of Congress Cataloging-in-Publication Data

Philosophy, religious studies, and myth / edited with introductions
by Robert A. Segal.
    p.   cm. — (Theories of myth ; v. 3)
    Includes bibliographical references.
    ISBN 0-8153-2257-7 (alk. paper)
    1. Myth.   2. Myth—Study and teaching—History.   3. Religion—
Philosophy.   4. Religion—Philosophy—Study and teaching—
History.   5. Religion—Study and teaching.   6. Religion—Study
and teaching—History.   I. Segal, Robert Alan.   II. Series:
Theories of myth ; 3.
BL304.P45   1996
291.1'3—dc20   95-43178
                                                                    CIP

Printed on acid-free, 250-year-life paper
Manufactured in the United States of America

CONTENTS

SERIES INTRODUCTION

The modern study of myth is already more than a hundred years old and is the work of many disciplines. This six-volume collection of 113 essays brings together both classic and contemporary analyses of myth from the disciplines that have contributed most to its study: psychology, anthropology, folklore, philosophy, religious studies, and literature. Because myth has been analyzed for so long by specialists in so many fields, knowledge of the range of sources and access to them are difficult to secure. The present collection provides a comprehensive and systematic selection of the most important writings on myth.

All of the essays in this collection are theoretical. All are concerned with myth per se, not with a single myth or set of myths. Many of the essays make explicit claims about myth generally. Others use individual myths to make or to test those claims. Most of the essayists are proponents of the theories they employ. Some are critics.

By no means has each of the disciplines considered here developed a single, unified theory of myth. Multiple, competing theories have arisen within disciplines as well as across them. The leading theories from each discipline are represented in the collection.

Theories of myth are never theories of myth alone. Myth always falls under a larger rubric such as the mind, culture, knowledge, religion, ritual, symbolism, and narrative. The rubric reflects the discipline from which the theory is derived. For example, psychological theories see myth as an expression of the mind. Anthropological theories view myth as an instance of culture. Literary theories regard myth as a variety of narrative. Within a discipline, theories differ about the nature of myth because they differ about the nature of the rubric involved. At the same time, theorists qualify as theorists of myth only when they single out myth for the application of the larger rubric. Writings that completely subsume myth under its larger rubric—discussing only religion or symbolism, for example—fail to qualify as writings on myth.

Theories of myth purport to answer one or more of the fundamental questions about myth: what is its origin, what is its function, what is its subject matter? Theories differ, first, in the answers they give to these questions. For most theorists, myth originates and functions to satisfy a need, but that need can be for anything—for example, for food, information, hope, or God. The need can be on the part of individuals or on the part of the community. Similarly, the subject matter, or referent, of myth can be anything. It can be the literal, apparent subject matter—for example, gods or the physical world—or a symbolic one—for example, human beings or society.

Theories differ even more basically in the questions they seek to answer. Few theories claim to answer all three of the major questions about myth. Some theories focus on the origin of myth, others on the function, still others on the subject matter. The answer a theory gives to one question doubtless shapes the answer it gives to another, but most theories concentrate on only one or two of the questions. Writings that merely describe or categorize myths fail to qualify as theories, as do writings that are skeptical of any universal claims about myths.

Still more basically, theories differ in the definition of myth. By some definitions myth can be a sheer belief or conviction—for example, the American "myth" of the frontier or of the self-made man. By other definitions myth must be a story. By some definitions the agents in a story can be humans or even animals. By others the agents must be either gods or extraordinary humans such as heroes. Theories employ definitions that reflect the disciplines from which they come. For example, theories from literature assume myth to be a story. Theories from religious studies assume the agents in myth to be gods or other superhuman figures.

Theorizing about myth is as old as the Presocratics. But only since the development of the social sciences in the last half of the nineteenth century has the theorizing become scientific. Some social scientific theories may find counterparts in earlier ones (see Burton Feldman and Robert D. Richardson's introduction to *The Rise of Modern Mythology* [Bloomington: Indiana University Press, 1972]), but social scientific theorizing still differs in kind from earlier theorizing. Where earlier theorizing was largely speculative and philosophical in nature, social scientific theorizing is far more empirical. The anthropologist John Beattie best sums up the differences, which apply to all of the social sciences and to the study of more than myth:

> Thus it was the reports of eighteenth- and nineteenth-century missionaries and travellers in Africa, North America,

the Pacific and elsewhere that provided the raw material upon which the first anthropological works, written in the second half of the last century, were based. Before then, of course, there had been plenty of conjecturing about human institutions and their origins; to say nothing of earlier times, in the eighteenth century Hume, Adam Smith and Ferguson in Britain, and Montesquieu, Condorcet and others on the Continent, had written about primitive institutions. But although their speculations were often brilliant, these thinkers were not empirical scientists; their conclusions were not based on any kind of evidence which could be tested; rather, they were for the most part implicit in their own cultures. They were really philosophers and historians of Europe, not anthropologists. (*Other Cultures* [New York: Free Press, 1964], 5–6)

By no means do all of the theories represented in this collection come from the social sciences. But even theories from philosophy, religious studies, and literature reflect strongly the impact of these fields.

The first four volumes in this collection are organized by disciplines. The selections in each volume typify the nature of the theorizing in the discipline. By far the most influential psychological theories of myth have been Freudian and Jungian. Anthropological theories have proved both more numerous and more disparate, with no one theory dominating the field. Folklorists have been particularly concerned with distinguishing myth from other verbal genres. Many theories of myth from philosophy and especially from religious studies grow out of attempts to decipher the classics and the Bible. Literary critics have understandably been preoccupied with both the similarities and the differences between myth and literature.

The final two volumes of the collection are grouped by theories rather than by disciplines. While the number of essays written on any major theory would readily fill a volume, the number written on the myth-ritualist theory and more recently on structuralism has been so large as to necessitate individual volumes about them. The burgeoning of writing on these theories stems in part from the array of disciplines that have adopted the theories. The myth-ritualist theory originated in the fields of classics and biblical studies but soon spread to the study of myth everywhere and, even more, to the study of secular literature. As a theory of myth, structuralism began in anthropology but has since been incorporated by many other fields.

Space does not permit inclusion in this collection of any essays that survey the field of theories of myth. Some useful surveys in

English are the following:

Campbell, Joseph. "The Historical Development of Mythology," *Daedalus* 88 (Spring 1959): 234–54.

Cohen, Percy S. "Theories of Myth," *Man*, n.s., 4 (September 1969): 337–53.

Dorson, Richard M. "Theories of Myth and the Folklorist," *Daedalus* 88 (Spring 1959): 280–90.

———. "Current Folklore Theories," *Current Anthropology* 4 (February 1963): 93–112.

Eliade, Mircea. "Myth," *Encyclopaedia Britannica*, 14th ed. (1970), vol. 15, 1132–40.

———. "Myth in the Nineteenth and Twentieth Centuries," in *Dictionary of the History of Ideas*, ed. Philip P. Wiener (New York: Scribner, 1973–74), vol. 3, 307–18.

Farnell, L. R. "The Value and the Methods of Mythologic Study," *Proceedings of the British Academy* (1919–20): 37–51.

Fischer, J. L. "The Sociopsychological Analysis of Folktales," *Current Anthropology* 4 (June 1963): 235–73, 292–95.

Georges, Robert A. "Prologue" to *Studies on Mythology*, ed. Georges (Homewood, IL: Dorsey, 1968), 1–14.

Halpern, Ben. "'Myth' and 'Ideology' in Modern Usage," *History and Theory* 1 (1961): 129–49.

Herskovits, Melville J. and Frances S. *Dahomean Narrative* (Evanston, IL: Northwestern University Press, 1958), 80–122.

Kaines, J. "The Interpretation of Mythology," *Anthropologia* 1 (1873–75): 465–75.

Kluckhohn, Clyde. "Recurrent Themes in Myths and Mythmaking," *Daedalus* 88 (Spring 1959): 268–79.

Larson, Gerald James. "Introduction: The Study of Mythology and Comparative Mythology," in *Myth in Indo-European Antiquity*, ed. Larson (Berkeley: University of California Press, 1974), 1–16.

MacIntyre, Alasdair. "Myth," *Encyclopedia of Philosophy* (1968), vol. 5, 434–37.

Maranda, Elli Köngäs. "Five Interpretations of a Melanesian Myth," *Journal of American Folklore* 86 (January-March 1973): 3–13.

Patterson, John L. "Mythology and Its Interpretation," *Poet Lore* 37 (Winter 1926): 607–15.

Puhvel, Jaan. *Comparative Mythology* (Baltimore: Johns Hopkins University Press, 1987), 7–20.

Reinach, Solomon. "The Growth of Mythological Study," *Quarterly Review* 215 (October 1911): 423–41.

Rogerson, J. W. "Slippery Words: V. Myth," *Expository Times* 90 (October 1978): 10–14.

Segal, Robert A. "In Defense of Mythology: The History of Modern Theories of Myth," *Annals of Scholarship* 1 (Winter 1980): 3–49.

Simon, Ulrich. "A Key to All Mythologies?" *Church Quarterly Review* 117 (1956): 251–61.

INTRODUCTION

Much of the theorizing about myth in philosophy and religious studies grows out of efforts to understand the classics and the Bible. In the case of the classics, the presence of myth has been taken for granted, and conclusions reached about Greek and Roman mythology have spurred generalizations about myth. In the case of the Bible, however, the existence of myth has been contested. In fact, Judaism and Christianity are regularly praised for their nonmythic outlook. Conclusions reached about the presence or absence of myth in either the Hebrew Bible or the New Testament have led to generalizations about myth per se. Many of the essays in this volume apply theories of myth to classical, biblical, and ancient Near Eastern cases, but in so doing they draw conclusions about the nature of myth itself. Those essays that criticize past applications make generalizations as well.

By no means has all theorizing about myth from philosophy and religious studies centered on the ancient world, and this volume contains selections from theories in both disciplines that stem from reflections on the nature of science, language, knowledge, and reality.

MYTH AND SYMBOL IN CONTEMPORARY PHILOSOPHY AND THEOLOGY: THE LIMITS OF DEMYTHOLOGIZING

R. F. ALDWINCKLE*

Ever since Rudolf Bultmann spoke of "demythologizing" the Christian gospel, the term "myth" has become the occasion of increasing debate and ambiguity.[1] Until the meaning of this term has been defined with greater precision, it is doubtful whether much progress can be made. Bultmann has not himself given much assistance in this process of clarification, but in other quarters the problem is being tackled with more success. For the English-speaking thinker, certain initial prejudices must be overcome. The popular identification of myth with the legendary and the fictional must obviously be abandoned completely if the term is to be used helpfully in theological and philosophical reconstruction. One wonders whether this is not an impossible undertaking now, in view of the associations of the term. Professor W. M. Urban, however, believes that it can be done. Let us summarize briefly the arguments he uses.

He claims that the modern disparaging use of the word "myth" is a product of the eighteenth-century *Aufklärung*

* A graduate of the University of London, Russel F. Aldwinckle studied theology at Regent's Park, Oxford, and at the University of Strasbourg (D.Th., 1938). His doctoral thesis was published under the title, *The Object of Christian Worship—a Study of the Notion of Objectivity in Relation to Religious Experience*. Articles recently published include "After Humanism, What?" (*Crozer Quarterly*, 1951) and "How Did Existentialism Become Atheistic?" (*Review and Expositor*, 1954). In 1947 Dr. Aldwinckle became a member of the faculty of McMaster University, where he is associate professor of systematic theology.

and that this does justice neither to the classical use of it by Plato nor to the more modern use of it by critical minds, for whom the term has once again become neutral.[2] "A myth is a story, the spontaneous product of unreflective and uncritical consciousness in which the forces of nature are represented in personal or quasi-personal forms and as performing supernatural or superhuman functions."[3] The two great classes of nature myths—the sun and the life myths—do not simply treat of fertility and sex in a merely human context. The supernatural world is depicted in terms of dramatic representations taken from those aspects of human knowledge and experience. What is being asserted in these myths is the real presence of the divine in the world of time and space, the immanence of the transcendent reality. Bultmann seems to use the word to describe two different things. The three-storied pre-Copernican universe of the biblical writers is for him mythology, in the sense that it involves a cosmology now thoroughly discredited from the scientific point of view and which can never be reinstated. "Das Weltbild des Neuen Testaments ist ein mythisches." Here he seems to be talking of myth in the loose, popular sense. On the other hand, he speaks of myth when he is thinking of stories or descriptions of events in which the transcendent touches time and God breaks into this spatio-temporal world. This latter view, if carried through consistently, would agree with Urban's use of the term.

1

If we work with this second meaning, an important distinction must be made. There are "myths" which have to do with events considered to have "happened" in some sense within the temporal process, and there are myths which describe the mystery of creation and the last things at the end of history of which no man has ever had direct experience. It is well known that when Plato came to deal with eschatology, he had recourse to the story or myth. In this sense, the eschatological forms of the New Testament serve a similar purpose as a description of the last events. It is this use of myth which raises in its clearest form the fundamental metaphysical question, What purpose exactly does the myth serve, and does it give men knowledge which can be regarded as intellectually valid? This compels us to ask what the validity of the higher anthropomorphism is; and this, in turn, raises the whole problem of symbol and its significance both in religion and in philosophy.

Professor Urban seems to the writer to have dealt more convincingly than anyone else with this aspect of the question. Myth is not pseudo-science,[4] nor is it the "illusion of primitive mentality";[5] it is a "unique way of apprehending the world with its own character and presuppositions."[6] Nevertheless, religion and myth must not be identified. They are not the same either in form or in spirit. In the religious consciousness, myth becomes symbolic. Pictures and signs taken from the sensible world are used to point to transcendent reality. The mythical is used to express the nonmythical, the phenomenal to symbolize the noumenal. What, then, is the nature of the religious symbol? It is not literally true, since it purports to suggest the transcendent by reference to that which

is sensuous. On the other hand, literal truth in this sense does not exhaust the meaning of truth. The symbolism provided by myth to the religious consciousness is to be taken seriously. It differs from every other type of symbol, in that it always stands for that which transcends the intuitive and the perceptible, as far as these words refer to the sensuous order. The religious consciousness, however, always considers the symbol to contain a nonsymbolic element, i.e., it refers to a transcendent reality which exists. Hence "the religious symbol is, then, in its essence—and epistemologically—metaphysical in character, although psychologically it is more akin to poetry."[7] Now this does not mean that we can strip away the symbol and intuit the reality apart from it. The religious symbol remains for our human mode of apprehension the inevitable and indispensable means of expression. The Christian use of "father" would come in this category. This argument, however, depends for its validity upon another, namely, that "analogical predication is a true form of predication, even when applied to the noumenal or metempirical."[8] So much for Professor Urban's contention.

Let us apply it to the biblical mythology and see whether it helps us to elucidate its significance and value. It must be conceded to Bultmann that some myths in the Bible are dead, i.e., they presuppose a world view, a cosmology, which is described in symbols now totally inadequate for the purpose. Such, for example, would be the Hebrew view of the earth as flat, resting on the abyss of waters, surmounted by a physical dome through whose windows the rain is poured. The idea of a local heaven to be reached by jet plane or a hell literally beneath the earth, showing evidence of its existence in volcanoes, is mythical in this sense. Some demythologizing would seem to be essential here if the gospel is to be made not only relevant but meaningful at all to modern man. When engaged in this kind of thing, Bultmann seems to appear in the guise of a nineteenth-century liberal Protestant adapting Christianity to modern thought. And, indeed, he is not original in this, and the now despised liberals of the previous century deserve some credit for grappling with the problem.

Surely, Emil Brunner is right in detecting here a basic ambiguity in Bultmann's thought, an unwarranted confusing of myth and world view. To link the admittedly obsolete science of the biblical writers with the fundamental Christian tenets about the sending of the Son of God, his pre-existence, the atoning death, the coming judgment, and the Holy Spirit, and regard them both as mythical is to cause unnecessary confusion. The reason why the theological statements just mentioned often constitute an offense to modern man is not because they are obsolete science but because they run counter to modern man's understanding of his nature and destiny—and on this point modern man may very well be mistaken. So Emil Brunner, and with justice.[9]

Few outside the ranks of the fundamentalists would deny the necessity for some demythologizing in regard to biblical science. Nevertheless, in this attempt to rid biblical thought of obsolete science, the limitations of science itself must be recognized. It is Bultmann's failure to make this clear that sometimes gives the impression that he is dismissing as myth in the sense of fiction anything which does not fit into the modern scientific view of the world, if there is such a thing as a coherent world

view generally accepted by all scientists. M. Casalis pertinently comments that Bultmann's description of modern man, lucid and master of himself, conscious of his scientific power and of his responsibility, reads rather strangely as coming out of Germany after the Hitler adventure and its aftermath.[10] Even if it were true that science holds the position which Bultmann thinks it does, by what right and according to what intelligible principle do we erect modern science into an absolute, by which the forms of New Testament thought are dismissed as "myth"? This in turn demands a definition of science, its methods and limitations. Perhaps we need to demythologize Bultmann's thought at this point.

Can we really accept without further ado Bultmann's claim that the scientific world view is not mythical? If we rigorously exclude from the scientific account of the world's origins or from the various descriptions given of the evolutionary process all those elements which contain symbolic imagery worked up into some kind of story of events, what have we left? Surely nothing that can be called a scientific Weltanschauung. Julius Schniewind justifiably calls attention in his reply to Bultmann to the contention of both Karl Heim and Oswald Spengler that our scientific concepts are really myths.[11] Atomic research has only strengthened the conviction that all pictorial descriptions of natural and cosmic happenings are inadequate, if not untenable; yet no scientist can abjure them if he wants to suggest a scientific world view. "In Bohr's model of the atom there is none of this picturesque language. Science no longer speaks the language of common-sense experience; it speaks the Pythagorean language. The pure symbolism of number supersedes and obliterates the symbolism of common speech."[12] Cassirer speaks of the vanishing of figurative illustration from the latest scientific language. This dominance of the symbolism of number in modern scientific description certainly removes it a long way from the earlier idea that a mechanical model could be made of all natural processes and events. It is certainly not myth in the sense of pictorial story-telling, but this does not support without further argument the assumption that this scientific description of the world in terms of number is more true than the "mythical" language of religion. The philosophical significance and validity of number still remain an open question, as well as the problem of whether this kind of description is the only one that can claim to give us real knowledge by contrast with religion.

Nor must we allow to pass uncontested the claim that the biblical world view remains mythical in the crudest and most unrefined sense. Cassirer has pointed out that a theory of myth encounters insuperable difficulties for the simple reason that "myth is non-theoretical in its very meaning and essence."[3] He also points out that philosophy could never take the myth-making function at its face value but sought to find within it a meaning philosophically intelligible and valid. He might, however, have added that religion, at least biblical religion, could not take over myth at its face value either. One can see, for example, how the Babylonian creation myth has undergone a profound and refining change under the influence of the prophetic conception of Yahweh to bring it into line with a more ethical and spiritual understanding of his will. It might still be answered that the Genesis account is still myth and not science. This is true as far as scientific detail is concerned; but if Professor Urban is right in claiming

that the divorce of being and value leads to meaninglessness and unintelligibility, then the Genesis account of the source and ground of creation in terms of intelligent will directed toward the good is more rational than a scientific account of the world in terms of a symbolism of number abstracted from all considerations of value. This contention would not be touched by the admission that Genesis is not a textbook of geology or astronomy.

Professor Urban, following Cassirer, maintains that science itself is one among several forms of symbolism. The positivist scientist, if he is logical, must exclude all cosmological statements about nature as a whole, since such generalities, no less than those in religion, are incapable of being empirically verified in the normal sense. This is not an attempt to reduce science to a subjective play of symbols with no reference to reality. The contention simply is that science, when it makes pronouncements about the whole of reality, is as "mythical" as religious thought and that the validity of its myths must be subject to the same test of fundamental intelligibility and coherence as that demanded in religion. The scientist must not be allowed to get away with the assumption that his myths are scientifically "proved," whereas religious myths are an illegitimate leap into the realm of fantasy. Granted, however, that, even with the recognition of the true nature of scientific symbolism, some demythologizing is necessary, what are we to say of those religious myths which seem to be inextricably bound up with all known forms of historical Christianity?

Let us take first a Christian belief which does not involve the vexed question of historical actuality. New Testament scholars today are agreed that one fundamental idea, present in the thought of Jesus and universal in the New Testament, is that of the parousia of the Son of Man, linked with final judgment and the consummation of the ages. Here we have a dramatic expression, a myth, if you like, expressing the belief that God will ultimately rule in his universe in and through Christ. How would Bultmann go about demythologizing this? If Professor Urban is right, it is impossible anyhow. It would only be a case of substituting one myth for another and saying, with Plato, something like this must be true. It is only fair to Bultmann to concede that his intention is not simply to eliminate at one stroke the mythology of the New Testament but rather critically to interpret it; nor must the reinterpretation be simply a forcible imposition of the modern world-view upon the New Testament meaning. "Nur müsste dann das Kriterium nicht aus der modernen Weltanschauung, sondern aus dem Existenzverständnis des Neuen Testaments selber erhoben werden."[14] "Der Mythos will nicht kosmologisch, sondern anthropologisch-besser existentiel interpretiert werden."[15]

What, then, is this existential core of meaning? What is meant by "existential" in this connection; and, even if it were possible to strip it of all the mythological forms of the New Testament, would there be anything left, or would it leave us, as with the peeling of an onion, with nothing in the center when the stripping process is completed? Professor Henderson has suggested that Bultmann may be doing what Aquinas did in his day, namely, attempting a *rapprochement* between Christianity and current philosophy.[16] Now this, despite some modern theological reluctance, is a perfectly necessary and legitimate activity. Theological and philosophical activity cannot be kept in water-tight compartments. What needs to be kept in mind is that philosophy itself cannot dispense with various forms of symbolism in its delineation of reality, and therefore it cannot write off the religious myths which supply it with that symbolism.[17]

Let us return to the problem of the parousia and the consummation of the ages. What is the existential core behind this myth, and can it be expressed when the New Testament form of it is completely abandoned? It poses a special difficulty for Bultmann, since he is concerned with the present act of decision demanded by the confrontation of Jesus as Saviour with modern man in his sin and guilt. The New Testament eschatology, while involving the individual's decision, is also concerned to say something significant about the whole temporal process and its relation to God's final rule within his universe. "He [i.e., the Christian believer] is now in Christ and yet expects His coming again. He has already died with Christ and risen with him, yet he looks forward to the resurrection at the last day. Justice must be done to both aspects of salvation."[18] How far can we allow such a statement to stand? Does it not involve a view of the future course of events which, for the modern man, is "mythological" in the bad sense? Must we not rigorously "detemporalize" the eschatology completely and say that modern man no longer needs to retain a futurist reference in his Christian thinking at this point? The parousia then means nothing more than a present existential decision when confronted with Jesus. This is a drastic procedure, because, if Oscar Cullman is right,[19] the New Testament writers certainly did not think in this way, and we must be prepared for an overhauling of the whole New Testament eschatological framework, which will look startlingly different when the task is completed. But why should we detemporalize the New Testament eschatology in obedience to modern existentialism or, for that matter, in deference to Hellenic mysticism or to any philosophy which has a defective understanding of the actuality of history and its significance for God. Will our demythologizing really make the gospel more intelligible to modern man? Is not Professor Henderson right in contending that what modern man really objects to is the activity within history of the transcendent God,[20] and is this made any more congenial to the modern mind in the Bultmann form than in the existing forms of New Testament eschatology?

This does not mean that we are committed to every detail of apocalyptic or eschatological imagery in the New Testament or to the various forms of millennialism based on Rev. 20:1–6 which have been imposed on the eschatology of Jesus, from which it is entirely absent. It does mean, however, that the criterion of selection and judgment in regard to New Testament eschatology is the character and purpose of God, given in Jesus, which can be applied without detemporalizing the thought. Nor must this be interpreted in such a way as to suggest that the biblical categories are incapable of being expressed in philosophical terms, since philosophy by its very nature is concerned with the timeless and not with the temporal. May not the philosopher hold with very good reason that "the fundamental categories of thought which we employ in historical and existential thinking—reason and purpose, freedom, will and love—must also be the fundamental categories of metaphysical thought."[21] Are there not

definite limits, therefore, to this process of demythologizing in regard to such a fundamental tenet of New Testament teaching as the parousia?

It may be contended that the eschatological materials of the Gospels have a real significance for Bultmann, since faith for him not only liberates man from his past through a present existential act but also delivers him to the future. "This is what is meant by 'faith': to open ourselves freely to the future."[22] Unfortunately, what this means is not too clearly elucidated. Faith delivers a man to the future only in the sense of enabling him to achieve complete inner detachment from the world and therefore inner freedom. It does not seem to mean for Bultmann the belief in a divine purpose which is being worked out in and through the historical process to a final consummation, despite his insistence on historic actuality. Eschatological existence does mean being a new creature; but in the New Testament this is never separated from the conviction that the new creation in Christ is a participating in a dynamic process, the fulfilment of which is not yet. Bultmann concedes that to believe means to be traveling along the road between the "already" and the "not yet," always to be pursuing a goal; but the goal does not recede forever. The New Testament never denies that it will be reached when the divine purpose in history is achieved. "The New Testament gospel without the Parousia, or (second) Coming, would be as impossible as Marxism without the classless society."[23] There is always the uneasy feeling that Bultmann is detemporalizing the eschatology in a radical sense, despite his clear recognition that the New Testament never speaks of the training of the soul in mystical experience but lays the stress rather on faith.

Wilder appears to be justified in claiming that "Bultmann and Dodd have granted the early Christians and ourselves a D-day, but seem to think that we can be content with that. No V-day or Victory day is necessary."[24]

Bultmann appears to believe in a transcendent God and therefore is not on the side of those who would treat some element of man's own nature as absolute. In this sense, he is Christian as against all the relativities of modern humanism. It is also true that the biblical notion of transcendence is bound up with spatial conceptions; but Bultmann seems hardly to be aware of the philosophical problem of symbolism which this raises, or at least he makes no mention of it. There are two questions which arise here: How far are the biblical writers themselves working with spatial conceptions which they apply uncritically in terms of crude physical analogy? and How far are they aware of the symbolic element in their thought? Is it making them too sophisticated to suggest that they are aware that they are using symbols taken from the sensuous and the intuitable, i.e., from space and time, to describe what Professor Urban calls the "metempirical"? If a symbol is not literally true in the ordinary sense, it does not mean that it is untrue, as we have already seen. It certainly seems odd, as Edwyn Bevan said, to think of moral and spiritual worth as increasing or decreasing according to the distance outward from the earth's surface.[25] Yet this appears to be implied in the almost universal belief among mankind that the sky is the abode of the Supreme Being.[26] It is hardly possible to doubt that primitive man did locate his god up there in the sky, and this has left its effect upon the early strands of the biblical record; but did not the men of the

Bible themselves move beyond this level of thinking?

No doubt the process from the cruder anthropomorphic conception to one more consciously symbolic was a long one, but there is good reason to believe that it had been accomplished within the biblical period itself. A somewhat long quotation from Edwyn Bevan is justified because of its great interest in this connection:

> We may say at any rate that by the time that the constituent of the book of Genesis, which modern critics call the "Priestly Code," and which they believe to belong to a time near that of Ezra, was composed, a conception of God as locally circumscribed by His sitting in the sky had given place to a more worthy one. The first chapter of Genesis is assigned to the Priestly Code and in its first verse it demolishes in a single phrase any idea of God as coinciding with the idea of the sky. "In the beginning God created the heavens." If God created the heavens, He must have existed in almighty power before there was any heaven there at all. Perhaps one does not easily realize in the case of a verse so familiar what a breach it meant with the conception hitherto almost universal in the religious traditions of mankind.[27]

If this comment is just, then the notion of spatial transcendence has already been demythologized, and this some centuries before Christ! If Bultmann replies by asking why the spatial language is still used, the answer must be that the choice is between utter silence or the use of symbols taken from the sensuous and the intuitable. That certain symbols have become charged with transcendent meanings and implications because of the role they have played in mankind's increasing apprehension of God fits them for, and justifies their continued use in, religious language.

Let us now consider another element in the Christian kerygma, which does involve reference to an event in history and which in some sense was apprehended by man. Bultmann describes the Resurrection as a "typically mythical event." "Die Auferstehung Christi aber—ist sie nicht ein schlechthin mythisches Ereignis?"[28] Does he mean that it has no historical or factual basis? The Resurrection, he suggests, cannot be dated in history, only the disciples' faith in the Resurrection and their witness to it. Does this mean that no historical value can be given to the empty tomb? Further, if the answer is Yes, does it mean that the Resurrection appearances, separated from the empty tomb, are not patient of the interpretation which sees in them evidence of the approach of the "risen Christ" to the disciples in any sense other than that which would reduce them to the "psychological" experiences of the disciples?

The apostolic testimony, which is the vital thing according to Bultmann, is the means whereby the "saving event" becomes situated in time and space and thereby becomes the present eschatological fact which demands of contemporary man an existential decision. The task of the church is to make sure that modern man's refusal of the gospel is not his refusal of the false stumbling block due to the mythological form in which the gospel is expressed, but is a real refusal of the true scandal of the Cross. Bultmann does not believe that the gospel can ever be so reduced as to make it easy for modern man to accept it without experiencing any sense of offense. This, however, does not absolve us from the necessity of continually seeking a more faithful translation of the gospel into terms which will give offense at the proper point, and not an offense which the modern man may rightly resent because of the form in which it is presented to him.

We may agree with Bultmann that the gospel can never be exhaustively expressed in scientific and historical categories as these are commonly understood. The truth of the Resurrection has never been accepted by any man simply on the basis of a careful weighing of the historical data. Nor need we refuse to admit that such an event contains implications and an element of mystery which escape satisfactory intellectual formulation. Yet surely the act of faith, which says Jesus is Lord, is not divorced from some intellectual conviction that this event, however much it defies full explanation, is rooted in the actuality of history. If, of course, we approach our historical investigation with the assumption that "nature" is ruled by a rigid uniformity of natural law and that we know the precise limits beyond which there can be no modification of this uniformity, then are we not again victims of myth, but this time of scientific myth? Here again is ambiguity. Does Bultmann describe the Resurrection as mythical because it runs counter to the dogma of the uniformity and unbreakableness of natural law? And, if so, must not this dogma itself be subject to critical appraisal?[29] Or does he regard it as the supreme case of the activity of the transcendent God in history, in which case modern man's difficulty with it is not scientific at all but religious, a consequence of his refusal to face the reality of God and his relation to history and man.

It is no doubt useful to distinguish between *historisch*, by which is meant the occurrence of an event at a particular place and time in history, and *geschichtlich*, which describes the eschatological significance of the event for man here and now.[30] "Eschatological" is not here a futurist reference to the last things but the "existential" import of the event evoking human decision in the present. What is unsatisfactory is that Bultmann never seems to make clear the application of these terms in regard to such an event as the Resurrection. While most Christians would agree that the Resurrection is *geschichtlich* and eschatological in the sense that the believer may meet the risen Christ here and now in the Spirit-guided community or *koinonia,* nevertheless it is also *historisch* in the first sense; otherwise the believing community would never have come into existence at all. It is therefore not adequate to say "Das Osterereignis als die Auferstehung Christi ist kein historisches Ereignis; als historisches Ereignis ist nur der Osterglaube der ersten Junger fassbar."[31] This is to reduce the Resurrection once again to psychology and thereby implicitly to question the early disciples' interpretation of this event, which was emphatically not merely psychological. We must still insist that the Resurrection is *historisch* in a sense other than merely the apostolic conviction that Christ was risen. Otherwise we can give no intelligible account of how that conviction arose and therefore of the rise of the Christian church. This means that any existential decision I may make here and now in the presence of Christ cannot be intelligibly related to those events which have made my decision possible. Or it gives us a faith rooted in a kind of irrationalism from which even Kierkegaard, with all his greatness, is not free.

Karl Barth's criticism of Bultmann's treatment of the Resurrection is here surely justified. He rightly insists that the Easter event is not the arising of the belief in Him as risen, but rather His manifestation to them, i.e., the disciples. Otherwise, the disciples' belief would have no object other than its own peculiar psychological reality. The act of God in the Resurrection would be identical with the fact that they believed. Bultmann's rejection of the forty days is based on the assumption that no event can take place in space and time which cannot be proved by modern historical methods; but these methods themselves contain silent presuppositions as to what can and cannot happen, assumptions which are not binding for a view of the world which does not exclude from the beginning the possibility of action by the transcendent God. Thus, says Barth, in spite of Bultmann, we must still continue "die Auferstehung Jesu und seine Erscheinung als Auferstandener unter seinen Jungern als eine wirkliche, zu ihrer besonderen Zeit geschehene Geschichte zu verstehen."[32]

This is not affirming that the event of the Resurrection is *historisch* on the basis of faith. While it is true that no man can say Jesus is Lord save by the Holy Spirit, this cannot be construed to mean that the evidence which convinced the disciples that Jesus was risen was wholly unrelated to the normal criteria by which a valid experience of an objective reality is judged. It is no doubt true that the distinction between hallucination and the normal perception of the external world is more complex than the ordinary person believes, but persistence, congruity, and agreement remain the foundations of our acceptance of an external world.[33] Apart from solipsism, which no sane man has ever made the basis of his actual behavior, the reality of the external world has never been seriously questioned, not even by idealism. But what has this to do with the Resurrection of Jesus? After all, he did not appear to everyone, but only to disciples; nor does he continue to appear to men in this way with the same persistence as the objects of the physical world. Persistence, congruity, and agreement can, therefore, in the case of the Resurrection appearances, be referred only to a comparatively limited number of men and women in whom the conditioning factor of faith was present. That the reality of the Resurrection could be proved only if all men had seen him involves a test not even applied to our knowledge of the external world. All I know of the top of Mount Everest is given to me through the testimony of men who have had firsthand experience of this physical reality. I believe what I hear about Everest because I have reasons for believing that Col. Hunt and his party were honest men in recording what they saw. I can hear them lecture, read their books, see their pictures. The weight of testimony, which leads me to believe that they actually undertook this expedition and were successful, is so great that seriously to doubt it would imperil my rational understanding of the world in which I live. It may be objected that this is a false and misleading analogy. After all, I can test the reality of their testimony by climbing Mount Everest myself or by flying over it in a plane or both. It is hardly likely that I shall ever do either of these things; yet I shall still believe. I can actually hear them speak, it may be said, whereas the Christian can no longer question the original eyewitnesses of the Resurrection. This is true, but the church still exists as the living historical witness to the truth which the early disciples attested. The church is a contemporary witness linked in the unbroken tradition of Christian life and worship. The scientist may still insist that if I put myself in the same place and set of conditions as Hillary and Tensing, I can have the same knowledge of Everest as they had, where-as I cannot put myself in the same position as the first eyewitnesses and see the risen Christ as they did. That is true if we agree that the appearances of the New Testament cannot be equated with mystical experiences of the risen Christ which later generations have enjoyed. Such a distinction the evidence compels us to make, however much we may discover some common characteristics, as Dr. Selwyn does, for example, in his essay on the Resurrection.[34] Yet when all has been said, it is the sense of rational congruity and essential trustworthiness which constitutes the most compelling reason for my belief in the Resurrection of Christ and in certain things about the summit of the highest mountain in the world.

These early disciples certainly believed that the risen Jesus had appeared to them in the spatiotemporal continuum in a way which they themselves distinguished from faith. Rightly or wrongly they believed that they had "seen" him. Their faith becomes inexplicable apart from this evidence, which seemed convincing to them; and, apart from their faith, the emergence and continuance of the Christian church become likewise inexplicable. It is true enough that belief in the Resurrection of Jesus presupposes a certain world view as to what may or may not happen in the kind of world in which we live. It further refuses to substitute without inquiry an explanation of the course of events other than that which seemed compelling to the earliest disciples. This, however, is not to say that faith creates the fact of the Resurrection; otherwise the reference to historic evidence would be superfluous, which was the case neither for the first believers nor for those who come after them.

There are some not hostile to the

Christian faith who would no doubt claim that the problem can be solved at a stroke by adopting a "veridical vision" theory of the Resurrection appearances.[35] This, it is asserted, gets rid of many perplexing problems of historical interpretation; it does not rest the Christian case exclusively on the empty tomb; and it is more reasonable to believe that God can manifest himself to men in a way congruous with the psychological laws which govern the mind than by a miracle which seems to involve a suspension of all known laws. This at first sight is plausible and attractive, except for the haunting doubt that the early believers in the Resurrection did not interpret their experience of the risen Lord in this way. Furthermore, as A. E. Taylor persuasively maintains, if the uniformity of law runs through the psychic as well as the personal worlds, which seems to follow inevitably from the very concept of uniformity, a psychological miracle becomes as improbable as a physical one.[36] On the other hand, if uniformity of law is not absolute in the psychological realm, why make it so in the physical on the basis of an unproved dogma? But if the dogma of uniformity is questioned, the way is open for factors in the Resurrection of Jesus which affected the minds of the disciples not only from within in psychological terms but also from without in physical terms, however puzzling this interaction of physical and psychical may be. Perhaps we should remind ourselves, too, that this miracle is an everyday occurrence in the workings of the human mind in and through the organ of the body.

It is not suggested that Bultmann is a naïve apostle of the natural sciences or that he is unaware of the limits of the scientific world view. Despite this,

however, he does in practice seem to find the criterion of the possible in this same method. Otherwise why should he make this dogmatic assertion: "An historical fact which involves a resurrection from the dead is utterly inconceivable."?[37] Why? Presumably because Bultmann is working, Schniewind charges, with the closed world view of modern science which makes any action of the transcendent God in nature and history antecedently impossible, long before any question of historical evidence is raised. One can hardly escape the feeling that Bultmann is himself aware of an inconsistency in his thought here. He admits that some people will regard all language about an act of God as mythological, even when it has been stripped of all supernatural and miraculous elements which appear to contradict the scientific world view.[38] When he speaks of an "act of God," what kind of God does he mean? Does he mean a God limited by natural laws regarded as absolute in themselves, which is a kind of deism, or the biblical conception of God, which regards nature as plastic to his will. The latter cannot simply be dismissed as unscientific myth, because it can be stated and defended in terms of a rational philosophy. Behind Bultmann's treatment of the Resurrection is not so much the problem of myth versus science as it is a fundamental clash of basic assumptions concerning the nature of the world and its relation to its creative ground and source.

What is evidently needed is a more precise definition of "myth" and the range of its application. Bultmann's criticism of some conceptions of the Holy Spirit or of grace as quasi-natural forces mechanically mediated would evoke sympathy from many Christians who are far removed from his general position in other respects. John Oman told us long ago that grace cannot be the mere might of omnipotence:

What is a moral personality and how is it succoured? To consider instead the coruscation of omnipotence as resistless might and of omniscience as undeflected fixity of plan, is as if an engineer could only prove his power by making engines weighty enough to break all the bridges. Real power, on the contrary, is never violent, and real wisdom never rigid.[39]

Inadequate conceptions of the Holy Spirit are not infrequent in Christian history and are justly subject to attack. Some conceptions of original sin do make impossible that true moral autonomy which, Oman again rightly insisted, must exist if there is to be a truly "religious dependence" on God. Bultmann is right to demand a rethinking of many of these issues, but it is highly doubtful whether the introduction of the word "myth" is of much help in this direction.

When, however, we have stripped away the obsolete science, which is an unnecessary stumbling block to modern man, and rethought our conception of freedom, grace, and the Holy Spirit so that they more truly express the Christian understanding of God and man and their relationship, we are left with myth in Professor Urban's sense as that dramatic element in the gospel record which furnishes those symbolically valid ideas which constitute the essential truth and express it in a way which neither science, philosophy, nor poetry can adequately do. The major problem, therefore, is not one of demythologizing the gospel in Bultmann's sense to make it fit the scientific world view but rather of finding those "myths" which provide the symbols which most adequately express valid metaphysical insights about the nature and activity of God. Nobody is as yet in a position to say what elements of the New Testament are absolutely necessary

for this purpose. It might be possible to express the significance of the Cross for the redemption of men without employing any of the terms which derive from the Jewish conception of sacrifice. Dr. H. Wheeler Robinson in his last book, commenting on the use of sacrificial metaphors in Christian thinking, wrote:

But the metaphor in itself does not satisfy our thought, when we try to turn it into a theory; or rather, shall we say, true as far as it can take us, needs completion from a wider range of thought, and all the more because the practice from which the metaphor is drawn is no longer with us, to actualize the intensity of the spiritual meaning.[40]

As long as the Bible is read, it is doubtful whether such metaphors will ever be dispensed with; but we cannot deny offhand the possibility of effectively presenting the Cross to men without the necessary use of sacrificial metaphors.

What is obviously needed is a careful study of the various religious symbols provided by the New Testament "mythology" and their metaphysical validity. This involves a philosophical justification of what has been called the "higher anthropomorphism." The revival of biblical theology has made this an urgent necessity, since we seem to be in grave danger of a "demythologizing" which distorts or an authoritative demand for the acceptance of the kerygma on a take-it-or-leave-it basis, with no reasons given. The assumption that the modern biblical emphasis has rendered philosophical theology unnecessary is one that will not stand examination. "There can be no religion of mere humanity," says Professor Urban, "but there can also be none of mere deity. Doubtless man without God is not man, but it is equally true that, while God without man would still be God, he would not be the God of any city that man has yet seen or ever will see."[41]

NOTES

1. H. W. Bartsch, *Kerygma und Mythos* (Hamburg: Herbert Reich Ev. Verlag, 1941).

2. W. M. Urban, *Language and Reality* (New York: Macmillan Co., 1951), pp. 587 ff.

3. *Ibid.*, p. 587.

4. *Ibid.*, p. 587.

5. N. Berdyaev, *Freedom and the Spirit* (London: Geoffrey Bles, 1935), p. 70.

6. Urban, *op. cit.*, p. 587.

7. *Ibid.*, p. 581.

8. *Ibid.*, p. 600.

9. Emil Brunner, *The Christian Doctrine of Creation and Redemption*, trans. Olive Wyon (Philadelphia: Westminster Press, 1953), pp. 264 ff.

10. G. Casalis, "Le Problème du mythe," *Revue d'histoire et de philosophie religieuse*, 31e Année 1951, No. 3, pp. 330 ff.

11. H. W. Bartsch, *Kerygma and Myth*, trans. Reginald H. Fuller (London: S.P.C.K., 1953), pp. 48-49.

12. Ernst Cassirer, *An Essay on Man* (New York: Doubleday & Co., 1953), p. 270.

13. *Ibid.*, p. 99.

14. Bartsch, *op. cit.* (German), p. 24.

15. *Ibid.*, p. 22.

16. Ian Henderson, *Myth in the New Testament* (London: S.C.M., 1952), p. 22.

17. Urban, *op. cit.*, p. 455.

18. *The Second Report of the Advisory Commission on the Theme of the Second Assembly of the World Council of Churches* (New York: World Council of Churches, 1953), p. 12.

19. Oscar Cullmann, *Christ and Time*, trans. F. V. Filson (Philadelphia: Westminster Press, 1950).

20. Henderson, *op. cit.*, p. 53.

21. J. V. L. Casserley, *The Christian in Philosophy* (London: Faber & Faber, 1949), p. 226.

22. Bartsch, *op. cit.* (English), p. 19.

23. J. A. T. Robinson, *The Christian Hope in Christian Faith and Communist Faith*, ed. D. M. Mackinnon (London: Macmillan & Co., Ltd., 1953), p. 210.

24. A. N. Wilder, "Mythology in the New Testament," *Journal of Biblical Literature*, LXIX (June, 1950), 126.

25. E. Bevan, *Symbolism and Belief* (London: Allen & Unwin, 1938), p. 30.

26. *Ibid.*, p. 48.

27. *Ibid.*, p. 46.

28. Bartsch, *op. cit.* (German), p. 44.

29. F. R. Tennant, *Miracle and Its Philosophical Presuppositions* (Cambridge: At the University Press, 1925).

30. Henderson, *op. cit.*, p. 42.

31. Bartsch, *op. cit.*, pp. 46-47.

32. K. Barth, "Die Lehre von der Schöpfung," in *Die Kirchliche Dogmatik*, Vol. III, Part II (Zurich: Evangelischer Verlag A. G. Zollikon, 1948), pp. 537 and 531 ff.

33. H. W. Robinson, *Redemption and Revelation* (London: Nisbet, 1942), p. 13.

34. E. G. Selwyn, "The Resurrection of Christ," in *Essays Catholic and Critical* (London: S.P.C.K., 1930).

35. C. J. Cadoux, *Catholicism and Christianity* (London: Allen & Unwin, 1928); *The Historic Mission of Jesus* (London: Lutterworth, 1941).

36. A. E. Taylor, *The Faith of a Moralist* (London: Macmillan & Co., Ltd., 1930).

37. Bartsch, *op. cit.* (English), p. 39.

38. *Ibid.*, p. 43.

39. J. Oman, *Grace and Personality* (4th ed.; Cambridge: At the University Press, 1942), p. 41.

40. Robinson, *op. cit.*, p. 257.

41. W. M. Urban, *Humanity and Deity* (London: Allen & Unwin, 1951), p. 26.

THE MEANING OF „MYTHOLOGY" IN RELATION TO THE OLD TESTAMENT *)

BY

JAMES BARR
Edinburgh

This paper is intended to contribute towards the clarification of a term which is to-day enjoying frequent use in reference to Bible, religion and theology. The continuing need for such clarification may be indicated by the following two points:

1. We are becoming increasingly aware that the study of the facts or phenomena cannot be separated from the terminology which we apply to them. When we work with detail on a small scale this problem of terms is less serious and the danger of error more remote. But when we attempt to relate facts and their significance over a wider area we may by inappropriate use of terms lay our study open to misconstruction, and much more serious, lead ourselves into actual errors of interpretation. We may take as an example the difficulties into which we may have been led by terms like "monolatry" and "Monotheism", and still more by "animism" or "polydae-monism"—each of which has no doubt been used with good intention to express something in some of our texts, but which has carried other connotations going beyond the Old Testament texts and has thus become a mould forcibly applied to a reluctant material.

2. The recent discussion of "mythology" has been to a great extent dominated by New Testament studies and general philosophy and theology. It seems to me however that the basic problem of faith and mythology is one hammered out in the Old Testament, and that discussions which evade this fact miss a great deal of the point. This has not been unrecognised, e.g. by ALAN RICHARDSON in his paper "Gnosis and Revelation in the Bible and in Contemporary Thought" (*Scottish Journal of Theology*, vol. 9, no. 1, 1956). It is very largely ignored however by the essays translated from German in the volume *Kerygma and Myth*, by HENDERSON in his *Myth in the New Testament*, and by MacQUARRIE in his *An Existentialist Theology*—three

*) A paper read to the Society for Old Testament Study, Cardiff, July 1956.

of the most influential expositions of the problem in English. In the
discussion it has too often been imagined that mythology could be
identified for some purposes at least with the First-Century view of
the universe. It will be part of the thesis of this paper that this First-
Century cosmology is only a part of an approach to myth which is a
theme of the whole Bible, and which is indeed more consciously a
central concern of ancient Israel than it is of the New Testament
Church. For this reason I suggest that Old Testament scholarship
has a special contribution to make to this study.

We may begin by admitting that in a sense we are discussing a
problem of definition. What do we mean by "mythology"? We
have here the same difficulty that appears in other terms like "eschatology", "animism", etc., namely that we are abandoning actual
Biblical language and seeking to find other terms to express Biblical
thought. So far we might say that the terms can be used in any sense
we wish, provided always that we define them clearly in advance.
This would appear to avoid one of the commonest causes of confusion.

But we cannot be satisfied with this as a solution. In fact it is
impossible for language to carry *any* sense by an arbitrary act of
definition. Words carry a certain connotation of content; definition
must be appropriate, in a sphere of this kind, to the entities studied;
the division between words must, if error is to be avoided, be made
to correspond as closely as possible with the division between
relevant actualities. If this is true, the following appears to be true
also:

1. A definition of myth for the purposes of Old Testament study
would not be built upon universal theoretical considerations, or
even upon the universal phenomenology of religion at all times and
in all places. Definition would begin from example. Thus we could
say, "By myth we mean, in this context, the sort of thing we find in
Ugarit, or in the Enuma Elish, or in other expressions of culture
which in fact impinged upon Israel with some directness." We would
thus leave for the moment undecided whether in fact such myth
universally existed, or whether other types existed elsewhere which
would also within their own sphere of relevance require to be designated as "myth".

2. The most serious fault in much recent discussion has been
that the sense of the word "myth" has been tacitly or deliberately
fixed not in reference to myth as it actually existed in cultures in

contact with Israel but by its position in more or less modern philosophic usage. BULTMANN's original essay defines myth as follows:
"Mythology is the use of imagery to express the otherworldly in
terms of this world and the divine in terms of human life, the other
side in terms of this side." This is perhaps not an impossible definition
in itself, though open to criticism in many ways. But in its context
in BULTMANN's thought it is clear that the *content* attached to myth
is drawn from the opposition of myth to modern science rather than
from the study of a mythology in its actuality.

3. It is not my concern here to deny that the word "myth" may
be properly used in a general philosophical sense as opposed to, or
even as a part of, natural science or epistemology. But it does seem
true that such usage when applied to the Biblical and extra-Biblical
cultural data introduces considerations completely foreign to the
subject.

On this basis we can go on to say the following:

1. Myth has to be seen as a totality within the relevant cultural
group. It is true that within a single civilisation we have myths of
different strata and of different degrees of importance, and myths
which appear to bear little relevance to one another. Historical and
phenomenological study may for certain purposes have to isolate
these elements and see them separately. None the less the effect of
myth upon the consciousness of a people is seen only when we
realise that it was the mythology as a totality which both shaped and
expressed its mind.

It is a totality first of all because mythological thinking is a striving
for a total world-view, for an interpretation or meaning of all that is
significant. Mythology is not a peripheral manifestation, not a
luxury, but a serious attempt at integration of reality and experience,
considerably more serious than what we loosely call to-day one's
"philosophy of life." Its goal is a totality of what is significant to
man's needs, material, intellectual and religious. It has then its
aspects which correspond to science, to logic, and to faith, and
and it would be wrong to see myth as a distorted substitute for only
one of these. Egyptian mythology, for example, has its insights into
the configuration of the land of Egypt, the nature of truth, and the
dealings of the gods with one another and with men. Myth is then a
total worldoutlook; not an outlook brought to expression only on
certain solemn occasions, rather one which informs and inspires
with meaning the daily business of living. Where new interests and

needs emerge, myth will expand to comprehend the new and greater totality of what is now relevant. This is not to say that mythology was always or ever fully successful in comprehending the totality for which it strove; hard facts can be awkward for myth as they can for any world-outlook; yet to claim the comprehension of such a totality was its nature.

On the other hand man influences and is influenced by the totality of myth as he knows, believes and enacts it. Elements in mythology may come and pass away; but at any point of time and place there is a totality of myth as it is then and there known, which in one way moulds and controls the minds of men and in another way equally is expressing them or being moulded by them. One mythological form or pattern may infiltrate into another and finally replace the other; but man does not see himself in this as surveying two alternatives and choosing between them; rather throughout the process of infiltration, from the beginning to the end of the change, he is moved by the totality as it then exists.

This does not mean that myth is a totality in the sense of a logical system. On the contrary, the attempt to make myth intelligible by a logical systematisation usually distorts it. On the other hand myth may have a logical background; rationalisation does not necessarily abolish myth, but alters it. In late times we have such a phenomenon as post-rational myth, such as the Gnostic mythology, with the rationality of Greek philosophy lying behind it. But in general the totality of myth consists not in its logical organisation but in its grasp of what is significant and its recognition as such by man.

Being such a totality, myth is not a substitute for or a distortion of merely *one* of our forms of knowledge, scientific, philosophical or religious. It is not merely a pre-scientific attempt to understand the world of nature, sun and moon, plant and animal. Nor is it simply the philosopher's quest for a Logos or ultimate reality, a quest which lacking the instrument of rational logic has fallen into inextricable symbolic confusion. Nor is it merely a kind of religion which, unable to know God in his spiritual reality, has cultivated the creator under the guise of the creature. And it is not just the projection of the human subconscious, important as the psychological aspect must be for understanding the hold which myth has upon the mids of men.

2. Secondly, myth is not really a symbolic knowledge. In fact it is only within limits and with some reserve that we can look upon

myth as symbolic at all. MALINOWSKI (speaking however of "primitive" culture) can say, "Studied alive, myth, as we shall see, is not symbolic, but a direct expression of its subject matter; it is not an explanation in satisfaction of a scientific interest, but a narrative resurrection of a primitive reality, told in satisfaction of deep religious wants, moral cravings, social submissions, assertions, even practical requirements" [1]).

This would seem to apply equally well to the mythological culture of the Near East contemporary with the Old Testament. This myth was not the symbolism to which we may turn when we reach the rationally incomprehensible, when our logical concepts fail to take us farther; nor was it the symbolism which uses pictures for the sake of the impression they give, for the extra tones of their colouring. In ancient times myth was not a picture language. We cannot translate it element by element into another type of language, as if we could say, "This stands for this and that represents that." When we consider myth functionally, in its actual working within a society of mythological culture, we cannot understand it as essentially symbolic in nature.

If this is true, one or two consequences must be drawn. In particular, and this should surely be obvious, it is entirely confusing to treat myth and metaphor as things of the same kind. All language is symbolic in one sense, but this does not make it myth. Some language is metaphorical, but even then it is not myth. It is not myth to say that somebody is a worm. It has sometimes been argued against BULT-MANN's plans to get rid of mythology that mythology is indispensable to human discourse, since all language, especially when it goes beyond the description of familiar tangible things, is symbolic. This argument is entirely misleading and unsuccessful. Even if the position I have just been maintaining were denied, and it was held that myth was a kind of symbolism, even so it would not mean that all symbol was myth.

3. Thirdly, the centre of mythology, or at any rate its characteristic which is specially significant in relation to the Biblical material, is its doctrine of correspondences. Myth always maintains a secret correspondence or hidden harmony of some kind between gods and

---

[1]) MALINOWSKI, *Myth in Primitive Psychology*, London, 1926, p. 23. Also in *Magic, Science and Religion*, Doubleday ed., p. 101. The quotation of this passage should not be taken to imply an approval of MALINOWSKI's remarks on methodology in the same essay.

man, gods and nature, man and nature, the normative primeval and the actual present. The correspondence is, as we have said, not merely figurative but ontological. Tammuz dying and the vegetation dying are not merely like one another but are one another. The correspondence is not only believed but enacted. Not only does myth teach the existence of the harmony, but ritual ensures that the harmony will in fact exist. In Enuma Elish there is a correspondence between gods and man because both had their origin ultimately from the same monsters of chaos; and there is a correspondence between the salvation of the universe from chaos and the prosperity and fruitfulness of the existing state. The recital and re-enactment of the story at the festival not only relates these correspondences but brings them into renewed being. We believe then that this correspondence doctrine is fundamental to myth as we find it in the ancient Near East.

This is not to say that in every sentence or element of myth we can trace a direct correspondence to something in the present world. It is rather in the totality of myth, and not in each component part, that we find the necessary connecting link somewhere, which makes the whole relevant to life in this world, and it is in the form of a correspondence that the link exists.

The place of ritual makes clearer to us the unitary type of apperception which lies behind the correspondences. The King of Egypt succeeding his dead father *is* Horus succeeding the dead Osiris, and myth and ritual celebrate not one of these two things but both, for both are one. Zeus is the rain. Mythology does not perceive Zeus and then symbolise him as rain, nor see rain and then personify it as Zeus, but it sees Zeus-rain, as it can also see Zeus-thunder, or Zeus-meteorite (Zeus Kappotas). The perception is essentially unitary. We might ask what is characteristic of Zeus as separate or abstracted from these unitary relations, but mythology proper sees no meaning in such a question.

The importance of the correspondences is above all functional. They express the fact that myth is not a mere story or fiction but an integral and essential instrument for the maintenance of actual human life in the world. When it is related that the world of the gods was defended successfully against the attack of chaos this is significant because this world of the gods has a connection of origin or other correspondence with the world of men, and its successful defence guarantees corresponding prosperity for the farmer or shepherd or merchant. The provision of this guarantee is the function of myth and ritual in society. Without the correspondences myth could not provide anything of value.

We are now in a position to approach Israel's special position among the mythological cultures which surrounded it.

1. In Israel we have a very radical departure from the characteristic mythical thought in terms of harmony or correspondence. The thinking out of this change may well have been slow and gradual; perhaps its clearest example is the creation story in Gen. i, where the old creation story is very thoroughly demythologised. The very sharp distinction between God and his creation here carried out seems to be characteristic of the central currents of Hebrew thought from early times also. It is not too much to say that the main battle of the Hebrew faith is fought against the confusion of human and divine, of God and Nature. The historical Sitz im Leben of this movement in thought may well be the problem of Canaanite Baalism, in which the confusion of God and nature was a basic principle. Against this background, so well illustrated in an earlier form from Ugarit, we can see the significance of another Israelite affirmation— namely that Yahweh alone is God, and that (in pure forms of Israelite faith) he has no female goddess with him—in its full contrast with the Canaanite interest in the divine sexuality and the sexual aspects of human worship which are here part of the correspondence theme. The 'Asherah was more offensive to reformers than the maṣṣebbah, of which many innocent traditions remain.

The main thesis of this paper is, then, that in Israel the correspondence pattern of mythology was broken.

2. We must return however to our point about totality. Israelite thought is a totality with its own centre, and its various peripheral manifestations have their place in relation to that centre. It is clear that many fragments of traditional near-Eastern mythology survive in Israel. In a sense they remain mythology. But whether they are so called or not, they now have to be understood in their relation to a totality which is shaped largely by its repudiation of the characteristic mythological pattern of correspondence. Fragments of mythology are no longer mythology in the full sense. This, we may remark in passing, seems to be one of BULTMANN's errors here; he exemplifies what he calls mythology from the concept of the "three-decker universe", which is not really living mythology in any full.

21

sense, but rather a residual and sterilised fragment, on the cosmo-logical side, of what was once myth [1]).

3. It will probably be agreed that the importance of history in the Israelite mind was the greatest factor in enforcing the diffe-rences from the mythological environment. It is thus perhaps pos-sible to say that the central position in Israelite thought is occupied by history rather than myth, and that such survivals of myth as exist are controlled by the historical sense. It is perhaps too much to say, as has sometimes been said, that myth by its own nature is in principle unhistorical and uninterested in history. But it is certainly true that for the most part myth has in fact tended to an interest in the cyclic or the permanent rather than in the moving stage of history. If we ask how this Israelite interest in the historical arose, we are probably forced back on Israel's own confession to the centrality of the Exodus and the events surrounding it. This is independent of any question of the exact accuracy of the Exodus narratives as we have them.

4. Perhaps the most difficult problem at this point lies in the understanding of the Israelite cult in its double aspect of action and word, as we see it in the Psalms for example, or in the kingship as a focus of that cultic life. Is this not "ritual and mythology" in the sense of the surrounding cultures? Does this not include certain themes of divine-earthly correspondence, as in the Messianic attri-butes of the king, or elements of that functional purpose of ritual and myth, to keep the world going on and society prosperous? It is important here not to see the cultic elements in isolation from the historical; on the one hand the historical basis of the Israelite consci-ousness going back to the Exodus; on the other hand the historical realities of the Israelite kingship from David on. From early times a tendency to pure culticism, to cultic myth in the Canaanite sense, was balanced and restricted by the old traditions of the people. The functional idea of the cult, where the cult stabilised society by re-producing the primaeval divine event, was checked in Israel by the understanding of the transcendence of God, evidenced in the Exodus and contradicting a simple harmony picture of God and the world. Under this influence the central position of the king, which seems to me now to have been well established, and the ideas related to his person of the renewal of creation and the establishment of justice,

---

[1]) BULTMANN, "New Testament and Mythology", ap. BARTSCH, *Kerygma and Myth*, English edit., London 1953, p. 1.

take on a new colour as gracious acts of God. In so far as they refer to the great acts of the past (and this past is a real past, not the unhistorical primeval time of mythology), celebrate and re-enact them in the present, and bear also a future reference, they carry a certain sense of movement in time which we might designate as eschatological.

This leads us on to the question of myth and eschatology; and in this we may make special reference to the paper of S. B. Frost read before this society some years ago [1]). He says there, following Mowinckel, that "fundamentally, myth is opposed to eschatology by its very nature". This is a statement which the writer would also be prepared to make, but which seems to have rather different ramifications in his thinking from what it has in Frost's. For Frost agrees with Mowinckel that "while the cult maintained its hold upon men's thinking, eschatological thought could not arise; only in the mythological mother's death could the eschatological child come to life" [2]). We have just argued, however, in effect that while mythology in the usual sense of the near East is opposed to eschatology, cult as such is not. There is no reason to think that the Israelite cult from David's time was dominated by these static and therefore anti-eschatological features; more likely, indeed, it was the cult, and not only the breakdown of the cult, which under the influence of the history of God's acts in time, transmitted to later generations the impulses towards eschatology. It seems impossible that the Israelite eschatology arose from disillusionment under the pressure of political deterioration and disaster, which broke the mythological idealisation of the *status quo* and forced men's interest into the future. Mesopotamia and Egypt also had their times of disaster but produced no eschatology; their mythology remained relatively stable through it all.

This is important in its consequences; for I am unable to agree with Frost that at the time of the Exile there was a re-mythologising of Israelite eschatology, and that Apocalyptic represents the completion of this process of mythologisation. He writes as follows: "It was this fusion of myth and eschatology which produced what we call apocalyptic. In fact, we may define apocalyptic as the mythologizing of eschatology" [3]). What I take it Frost is pointing out here

---

[1]) S. B. Frost, "Eschatology and Myth", *VT*, vol. 2, 1952, pp. 70-80.
[2]) *Ibid.*, p. 72.
[3]) S. B. Frost, *Old Testament Apocalyptic*, London, 1952, p. 33.

is the extensive use in later prophecy and in apocalyptic of themes like the conquest of the dragon or the return of the Golden Age, in other words the use of themes with a mythological origin. He is not saying that the philosophy of the *status quo*, the *rationale* of mythology, is now being revived and integrated with eschatology. But he does not make it quite clear that he is not saying this. The following points in particular should be made:

1. It is somewhat artificial to argue that the early stages of eschatology were not expressed in mythological terms, while later stages were [1]). Can we really draw so sharp a distinction in nature between the fire which ate up *tehom rabbah* in Amos and the prophecies of the Golden Age?

2. It seems unlikely that the situation of the Exile was a sufficient cause for the alleged upsurge of mythology among the Jews. Is it not an attempt at learned explanation, rather than a credible account of reality, with a basis in evidence, to suggest that in Babylon Jews suddenly came to hear of the Dragon, the Flood or the Golden Age, and at once began to use these new terms as their natural idiom?

It seems more likely that from early times the cult in Israel, while using motifs from mythology, had already under the influence of the Exodus traditions broken away from the real underlying mythical view of life; and that with the development of eschatology under the prophets this movement took on a new impetus.

3. Why then did late prophecy and apocalyptic enter so much more deeply into symbolic and difficult language? This is not, I think, either a revival of mythological ideals, or a new injection of mythological language. It comes rather from the basic fact that these later writers had a greater sweep of history before their consciousness. The earlier prophets made no great effort to clarify the sequence or the arrangements of the things which were "coming". But when the prophetic tradition becomes temporally longer its interpretation of God's activity requires something closer to a philosophy of history, a discerning of the divine purpose through the ages. But such a total view is necessarily a view δι' ἐσόπτρου ἐν αἰνίγματι, a discerning of a veiled purpose. Hence Daniel has as principle that "there is a God in heaven who unveils secrets" [2]). It is the natural outgrowth of classical prophecy in the fullness of time.

---

[1]) S. B. FROST, *VT*, vol. 2, p. 75, 79.
[2]) Dan. ii 28.

Myth and the New Testament[1]

The Greek Word μῦθος

By the Reverend C. K. Barrett, D.D., The University of Durham

In the present article I propose to examine, by means of an outline study of the Greek word μῦθος, the use made of myths, first by Gentiles, then by Jews, in the period in which the New Testament and primitive Christianity were evolving. This study will lead to a brief account of the uses of the word μῦθος in the New Testament. In the second article I shall discuss more generally the questions raised by myth and the New Testament.

The early history of the word μῦθος is simple. It is closely parallel to the word λόγος, and means *word*, *speech*. This meaning is quite common in Homer and the tragic poets. We find μῦθος contrasted with ἔργον as speech with action ; in special contexts it can mean conversation, a public speech, a threat, a piece of advice, or even thought, the unspoken word.

A natural, and very early, development of this primitive meaning is *story*, or *tale*. In the early period nothing whatever is implied about the historical truth of the story, and μῦθος is still used interchangeably with λόγος. Thus in the *Odyssey* (iii. 94) Telemachus asks Nestor to tell him about the fate of his father, Odysseus, whether he has witnessed it himself, or heard the story (μῦθος) from some one else. Telemachus is, of course, wrong in supposing his father to be dead ; but this does not affect the issue. What he wants is a plain account of what happened. This use of μῦθος continued in later Greek poetry.

At the same time, however, in Greek prose, the word μῦθος was taking on a new meaning, in which it is contrasted, sometimes explicitly, with λόγος. The development is easy to understand, especially in the light of developing Greek rationalism and scepticism, when it is remembered that most of the μῦθοι—the stories—upon which the Homeric epics and the great tragedies were based were (in the popular sense of the word) myths, stories, that is, of gods and men which only primitive or credulous man believes actually to have happened. Criticism of the myths is practised with complete freedom by Plato. I need only refer to the well known passage at the end of *Republic*, ii., where Socrates is discussing the education of the young.

It is necessary, he says, to tell them stories, and stories are of two kinds, false and true (376 E). It is necessary to use both kinds, the true and the false, but we begin with the false. This causes surprise. But it is true : we begin by telling children μῦθοι, and these on the whole are false, though there are elements of truth in them (ἔνι δὲ καὶ ἀληθῆ ; 377 A). From this follows a more detailed criticism, and examples of harmful myths which should be rejected.

Plato has, however, another use of μῦθος. A μῦθος provides the basis for one kind of demonstration, just as λόγος, or rational argument, provides another. When some point is raised, Socrates asks (*Protagoras*, 320 C), ' Shall I prove it to you by telling you a μῦθος, or by going through a λόγος ? ' ' Please yourself,' says the company. ' Well, I think it would be nicer (χαριέστερον) if I told you a myth.' And a story about the gods follows.

Thus you can argue to a truth, or you can express the same truth—sometimes, it may be, more convincingly—in a myth. The best definition of the word μῦθος in this stage of its development—and for us it is the crucial stage—is that of Suidas : μῦθος is λόγος ψευδής, εἰκονίζων τὴν ἀλήθειαν—a story which is not itself true but represents the truth pictorially.[2] From the time of Plato onwards there was a strong and growing tendency to look upon the ancient traditional stories about the gods and their relations with men in this way. At the same time, as part of that ' failure of nerve ' which marked the post-classical, Hellenistic, age, there was a growing preference for μῦθος over λόγος as a means of expressing truth. This preference is characteristic of gnosticism : the saving gnosis is often cast in the form of a myth.

It will thus be seen that, as we approach the New Testament period, we meet with two kinds of myth. There are the traditional Greek stories of the gods, the stock of mythology which is familiar to us chiefly from Homer and the great tragedians ; these received interpretations which made them media for the expression of theological or philosophical or moral truth. The more they were interpreted, the less they were believed to be historically

---

[1] This article and a second which will follow next month contain the substance   General Lecture delivered at King's College, Newcastle, on 7th February 1957.

[2] Cf. the motto drawn by H. Jonas, in *Gnosis und spätantiker Geist*, from Sallustius, 4 : ταῦτα δὲ ἐγένετο μὲν οὐδέποτε, ἔστι δὲ ἀεί (These things never happened, but eternally *are*.)

'true.' There are also myths which owe their origin to the desire to elucidate or propagate some particular truth. These myths were not freely invented, for they were often based upon ancient religious convictions conceived from the beginning in mythological form, or upon the cycle of Nature with its recurring process of life, death, and resurrection. Indeed, it would perhaps be better to speak not of 'two kinds of myth,' but rather of two different processes into which mythological material was taken up. In the one, the myth is the primary datum, and the reader says, 'Let us find some means—allegorical or other—of getting acceptable truth out of it.' In the other, the primary datum is the truth, which the believer has reached, in all probability, not by ratiocination but by revelation. He now says, 'Where can I find suitable mythological material to commend this truth to my contemporaries ? '

Perhaps the best illustration of the work of those who begin with mythology is the careful and systematic analysis of myth made by that Sallustius who wrote *On the Gods and the Universe*, and may have been the friend of Julian. Sallustius is, it is true, a rather late author, but much of what he says can be paralleled in earlier writers ; he was a systematizer rather than an innovator. Here is one example of the way in which he deals (4) with a well-known myth.

'At the banquet of the gods Strife (῎Ερις) threw a golden apple and the goddesses, vying with one another for its possession, were sent by Zeus to Paris to be judged ; Paris thought Aphrodite beautiful, and gave her the apple. Here the banquet signifies the supra-mundane powers of the gods, and that is why they are together, the golden apple signifies the universe, which, as it is made of opposites, is rightly said to be thrown by Strife, and as the various gods give various gifts to the universe they are thought to vie with one another for the possession of the apple ; further, the soul that lives in accordance with sense-perception (for that is Paris), seeing beauty alone and not the other powers in the universe, says that the apple is Aphrodite's.'

The analysis and interpretation of myths is a very complicated matter. Here is more from the same chapter of Sallustius. 'Of myths some are theological, some physical ; there are also psychical myths and material myths and myths blended from these elements.' This is what Sallustius says, but it is not quite all that he means, for, as he shows by example, one myth may be treated as theological and physical and psychical and material. The example he gives is the tale of the god Cronus, who is said to have swallowed his own children. If we take this as theology, then, since the god is intellectual

(νοερός), and all intellect is directed towards itself, we learn something about the essential nature of god. The physical interpretation works from the common identification of Cronus with χρόνος (time) ; time as a whole swallows up its parts. The psychical interpretation looks at the human soul, and teaches that the thoughts of our souls, even if they go forth to others, still remain in their creators. The material interpretation involves the equating of gods with material substances, as Cronus with water.

It is hardly open to doubt that in all this theologizing Sallustius has taken the mythological material as it came to him and done his ingenious best to make something out of it. But now we must look at the other side of the picture.

We may take, for example, the story of creation in the Hermetic tractate *Poimandres*.[1] The essence of it lies in its account of the origin and nature of man. Before the emergence of man as we know him the supreme God produced an essential or archetypal man, quite free from the taint of matter. This Man looked out from heaven and saw himself reflected in the watery chaos below. He fell in love with his own image and Nature fell in love with him. He fell out of heaven and found himself in Nature's arms. From the marriage of these two sprang the human race, and it follows from this their mixed origin that they themselves are compounded of Mind and matter. Out of this cosmological myth arises the gnostic message. Men must recognize their mixed nature, and side with Mind against matter. In no other way can they find salvation.

So much for the gospel based upon the myth ; where did the myth come from ? It is not itself a *creatio ex nihilo*, for it owes much to traditional Oriental accounts of the Creation and of the first man—and among these we must reckon the Genesis story. But it was not taken over ready-made. Whoever may have been responsible for the story as we read it to-day put together the pieces that he used in the light of the truth he wished to convey. He *knew* that men were made of Mind and matter ; he knew that their only hope of returning to the heavenly life they had lost lay in turning their backs upon matter and cultivating the world of Mind ; and he believed that this truth could best be conveyed in the form of a myth.

In this account of the word μῦθος and of the development and use of myth, I have been discussing what myth meant to the pagan mind. I must now narrow the circle and ask what myth meant to the Jews.

We may begin with Philo, as the representative

[1] For the details see my *The New Testament Background : Selected Documents* [1956], 84–87.

of Alexandrian Judaism. There is no simple answer to our question. At least three points must be made.

(1) Philo shows complete impatience with the pagan myths, and can hardly find language severe enough to castigate them. The heathen myths are bound up with idolatry and altogether to be rejected.[1]

(2) But this is not the whole truth about Philo ; he does not always act upon the principle just enunciated. He could on occasion use the heathen myths, at least as illustrations. Thus in *Quod Det. Pot.*, 178, he says of Cain that ' nowhere in the book of the Law has his death been mentioned. This shows in a figure that, like the Scylla of fable (ἡ μεμυθευμένη Σκύλλα), folly is a deathless evil.' This incidentally is almost a verbal quotation from Homer (*Odyssey*, xii. 118). Again in *de Opificio Mundi*, 133 : ' The earth, as we all know, is a mother, for which reason the earliest men thought fit to call her " Demeter," combining the name of " Mother " with that of " earth " ; for, as Plato says [*Menexenus*, 238 A], earth does not imitate woman, but woman earth. Poets quite rightly are in the habit of calling earth " All-mother " and " Fruit-bearer " and " Pandora " or " Give-all," inasmuch as she is the originating cause of existence and continuance in existence to all animals and plants alike.'

(3) Philo sharply distinguishes between the myths and the Bible—in *de Opificio Mundi*, 2, he says that Moses ' refrained from inventing myths himself (μύθους πλασάμενος) or acquiescing in those composed by others.' Yet in fact he accords to the Bible the same allegorical treatment that his contemporaries gave to the myths. This scarcely needs illustration ; Philo's works consist of prolonged allegories, which are justified by the conviction that the anthropomorphisms of the Old Testament simply cannot mean what they say.

So much for Philo. It is worth noting briefly that the three observations I have just made about him could also be made, *mutatis mutandis*, about the Rabbis. Like him, they abominated polytheistic mythology ; yet like him, though probably to a smaller extent, they knew and could on occasion use the myths.[2] Further, they too sometimes applied to the Old Testament the methods of allegorical exegesis ; up to a point this may have been a native product, but it has been argued, with much plausibility, that even the exegetical *middoth* were derived ultimately from principles of Hellenistic rhetoric.

These are all contacts of a superficial kind. More important perhaps is the fact that Jewish

[1] See *e.g.*, *de Praemiis et Poenis*, 8.
[2] See Strack-Billerbeck, iv. 408 ff.

apocalyptic seems to be not without contact with non-Jewish mythology. I am here referring not to the popular stories of the Greek pantheon, but to the cosmological speculation, and speculations about the first man, or about a primal, heavenly man, which seem to have been current in the ancient East, and to have affected the Old Testament here and there. This is hardly the place to develop this theme ; it will suffice to quote Professor H. H. Rowley (*The Relevance of Apocalyptic* [1944], 38). We need not ' doubt that ancient mythological material was used by the apocalyptic writers. In treating of great cosmic events they would find the figures of cosmic myths appropriate to their purpose.' What we have to do with here is not, of course, the taking over of myths as if they were history, but the use of myth in theology, and in the setting forth of Israel's hope of salvation and the renovation of the world.

We must now turn to the New Testament. The word μῦθος itself occurs in several New Testament passages, and these will provide for us an objective starting-point, from which we may be able to move on to deal with the question in a more general way.

One passage stands by itself : 2 P 1[16] : οὐ γὰρ σεσοφισμένοις μύθοις ἐξακολουθήσαντες. It is not hard to see the point of this disclaimer. It stands over against the claim that we ' were eye-witnesses of his majesty' (ἐπόπται γενηθέντες τῆς ἐκείνου μεγαλειότητος). A specific reference to the Transfiguration follows, and this event was no doubt chiefly in mind ; but it is clear that what the author intends to do here is to claim that the stories of the gospel tradition were not artificially created myths but were historically veracious and trustworthy, and depended upon the recollections of eye-witnesses.

All the remaining passages are in the Pastoral Epistles, and are as follows :

1 Ti 1[3f.] : . . . μὴ ἑτεροδιδασκαλεῖν' μηδὲ προσέχειν μύθοις καὶ γενεαλογίαις ἀπεράντοις.

4[7] : τοὺς δὲ βεβήλους καὶ γραώδεις μύθους παραιτοῦ.

2 Ti 4[4] : ἀπὸ μὲν τῆς ἀληθείας τὴν ἀκοὴν ἀποστρέψουσιν, ἐπὶ δὲ τοὺς μύθους ἐκτραπήσονται.

Tit 1[14] : . . . μὴ προσέχοντες Ἰουδαϊκοῖς μύθοις καὶ ἐντολαῖς ἀνθρώπων ἀποστρεφομένων τὴν ἀλήθειαν.

What are these myths, which are to be summarily rejected ? Where did they come from ?

There is a clear pointer in the words which occur, in the passages I have quoted, along with ' myth.' In two the word ' truth ' is mentioned : to turn to myths is to turn away from the truth. Parallel to giving heed to myths is ἑτεροδιδασκαλεῖν, to teach strange doctrines. In one passage the myths are linked with γενεαλογίαι ἀπέραντοι ('endless genealogies') ; in another they are Jewish ; in a third they are βέβηλοι and γραώδεις ('profane and old wives' fables '). What do these facts tell us about their origin ? The adjective Jewish seems at first decisive, and the view has been held that Rabbinic myths and speculations about the genealogies found in the Old Testament are meant. Others, however, believe that the material taken as a whole points to gnostic speculations. The myths are cosmic myths of the gnostic kind, and the genealogies are the lists of divine and semi-divine emanations which are characteristic of several second-century gnostic systems. These different lines of interpretation are not incapable of reconciliation. We have the excellent evidence of Colossians for the existence of a movement at the same time Jewish and gnostic, and I see no reason why it should not have developed, after Paul wrote Colossians, in such a way as to produce myths and genealogies which could constitute a serious danger to the Church in Asia.

The danger was so serious that the author of the Pastorals felt himself obliged simply to stand in the old ways and have nothing to do with the application of mythology to Christianity ; but we must not conclude that this was the only attitude that sincere Christians could take. Indeed we have no reason to think that those who made the myths were not sincere Christians, trying, however misguidedly, to work out systematically the truths of the Christian faith. Christianity is, at least from the intellectual point of view, a system of truths about the relation between God, man, and the universe ; in an age, therefore, when men's beliefs about these relations were frequently set forth in mythological form, nothing could be more natural than that advanced Christian thinkers should set out their beliefs in the same way.

The Pastoral Epistles, then, show us a situation in which Christian speculation is beginning to develop, and to develop in a mythological direction. This does not mean that completely new myths are being created, but that Christians are drawing upon the body of mythological material already in existence, no doubt modifying it in the process. *One* reaction to this dangerous process was that of men like the author of these Epistles, who utterly refused to budge ; the only safe course was to stand fast by the old faithful sayings. But was this the only possible line for a Christian to follow ?

RUDOLF BULTMANN

NEW TESTAMENT AND MYTHOLOGY

The Mythological Element in the Message of the New
Testament and the Problem of its Re-interpretation

I

THE TASK OF DEMYTHOLOGIZING THE
NEW TESTAMENT PROCLAMATION

A. The Problem

1. *The Mythical View of the World and the Mythical Event of Redemption*

THE cosmology of the New Testament is essentially
mythical in character. The world is viewed as a three-
storied structure, with the earth in the centre, the heaven
above, and the underworld beneath. Heaven is the abode of
God and of celestial beings—the angels. The underworld is hell,
the place of torment. Even the earth is more than the scene of
natural, everyday events, of the trivial round and common task. It
is the scene of the supernatural activity of God and his angels on
the one hand, and of Satan and his daemons on the other. These
supernatural forces intervene in the course of nature and in all
that men think and will and do. Miracles are by no means rare.
Man is not in control of his own life. Evil spirits may take
possession of him. Satan may inspire him with evil thoughts.
Alternatively, God may inspire his thought and guide his
purposes. He may grant him heavenly visions. He may allow him
to hear his word of succour or demand. He may give him the
supernatural power of his Spirit. History does not follow a
smooth unbroken course; it is set in motion and controlled by
these supernatural powers. This aeon is held in bondage by

Satan, sin, and death (for "powers" is precisely what they are), and hastens towards its end. That end will come very soon, and will take the form of a cosmic catastrophe. It will be inaugurated by the "woes" of the last time. Then the Judge will come from heaven, the dead will rise, the last judgement will take place, and men will enter into eternal salvation or damnation.

This then is the mythical view of the world which the New Testament presupposes when it presents the event of redemption which is the subject of its preaching. It proclaims in the language of mythology that the last time has now come. "In the fulness of time" God sent forth his Son, a pre-existent divine Being, who appears on earth as a man.[1] He dies the death of a sinner[2] on the cross and makes atonement for the sins of men.[3] His resurrection marks the beginning of the cosmic catastrophe. Death, the consequence of Adam's sin, is abolished,[4] and the daemonic forces are deprived of their power.[5] The risen Christ is exalted to the right hand of God in heaven[6] and made "Lord" and "King".[7] He will come again on the clouds of heaven to complete the work of redemption, and the resurrection and judgement of men will follow.[8] Sin, suffering and death will then be finally abolished.[9] All this is to happen very soon; indeed, St Paul thinks that he himself will live to see it.[10]

All who belong to Christ's Church and are joined to the Lord by Baptism and the Eucharist are certain of resurrection to salvation,[11] unless they forfeit it by unworthy behaviour. Christian believers already enjoy the first instalment of salvation, for the Spirit[12] is at work within them, bearing witness to their adoption as sons of God,[13] and guaranteeing their final resurrection.[14]

[1] Gal. 4. 4; Phil. 2. 6ff.; 2 Cor. 8. 9; John 1. 14, etc.
[2] 2 Cor. 5. 21; Rom. 8. 3.
[3] Rom. 3. 23–26; 4. 25; 8. 3; 2 Cor. 5. 14, 19; John 1. 29; 1 John 2. 2, etc.
[4] 1 Cor. 15. 21f.; Rom. 5. 12ff.
[5] 1 Cor. 2. 6; Col. 2. 15; Rev. 12. 7ff., etc.
[6] Acts 1. 6f.; 2. 33; Rom. 8. 34, etc.   [7] Phil. 2. 9–11; 1 Cor. 15. 25.
[8] 1 Cor. 15. 23f., 50ff., etc.   [9] Rev. 21. 4, etc.
[10] 1 Thess. 4. 15ff.; 1 Cor. 15. 51f.; cf. Mark 9. 1.
[11] Rom. 5. 12ff.; 1 Cor. 15. 21ff., 44b, ff.
[12] Ἀπαρχή: Rom. 8. 23, ἀρραβών: 2 Cor. 1. 22; 5. 5.
[13] Rom. 8. 15; Gal. 4. 6.   [14] Rom. 8. 11.

2. *The Mythological View of the World Obsolete*

All this is the language of mythology, and the origin of the various themes can be easily traced in the contemporary mythology of Jewish Apocalyptic and in the redemption myths of Gnosticism. To this extent *the kerygma is incredible to modern man, for he is convinced that the mythical view of the world is obsolete.* We are therefore bound to ask whether, when we preach the Gospel to-day, we expect our converts to accept not only the Gospel message, but also the mythical view of the world in which it is set. If not, does the New Testament embody a truth which is quite independent of its mythical setting? If it does, theology must undertake the task of stripping the Kerygma from its mythical framework, of "demythologizing" it.

Can Christian preaching expect modern man *to accept the mythical view of the world as true?* To do so would be both senseless and impossible. It would be senseless, because there is nothing specifically Christian in the mythical view of the world as such. It is simply the cosmology of a pre-scientific age. Again, it would be impossible, because no man can adopt a view of the world by his own volition—it is already determined for him by his place in history. Of course such a view is not absolutely unalterable, and the individual may even contribute to its change. But he can do so only when he is faced by a new set of facts so compelling as to make his previous view of the world untenable. He has then no alternative but to modify his view of the world or produce a new one. The discoveries of Copernicus and the atomic theory are instances of this, and so was romanticism, with its discovery that the human subject is richer and more complex than enlightenment or idealism had allowed, and nationalism, with its new realization of the importance of history and the tradition of peoples.

It may equally well happen that truths which a shallow enlightenment had failed to perceive are later rediscovered in ancient myths. Theologians are perfectly justified in asking whether this is not exactly what has happened with the New Testament. At the same time it is impossible to revive an obsolete view of the world by a mere fiat, and certainly not a mythical view. For all our thinking to-day is shaped irrevocably by modern science. A blind acceptance of the New Testament

mythology would be arbitrary, and to press for its acceptance as
an article of faith would be to reduce faith to works. Wilhelm
Herrmann pointed this out, and one would have thought that his
demonstration was conclusive. It would involve a sacrifice of the
intellect which could have only one result—a curious form of
schizophrenia and insincerity. It would mean accepting a view of
the world in our faith and religion which we should deny in our
everyday life. Modern thought as we have inherited it brings
with it criticism of *the New Testament view of the world.*

Man's knowledge and mastery of the world have advanced to
such an extent through science and technology that it is no
longer possible for anyone seriously to hold the New Testament
view of the world—in fact, there is no one who does. What
meaning, for instance, can we attach to such phrases in the
creed as "descended into hell" or "ascended into heaven"?
We no longer believe in the three-storied universe which the
creeds take for granted. The only honest way of reciting the
creeds is to strip the mythological framework from the truth they
enshrine—that is, assuming that they contain any truth at all,
which is just the question that theology has to ask. No one who
is old enough to think for himself supposes that God lives in a
local heaven. There is no longer any heaven in the traditional
sense of the word. The same applies to hell in the sense of a
mythical underworld beneath our feet. And if this is so, the
story of Christ's descent into hell and of his Ascension into
heaven is done with. We can no longer look for the return of the
Son of Man on the clouds of heaven or hope that the faithful
will meet him in the air (1 Thess. 4. 15ff.).

Now that the forces and the laws of nature have been discovered, we can no longer believe in *spirits, whether good or evil.*
We know that the stars are physical bodies whose motions are
controlled by the laws of the universe, and not daemonic beings
which enslave mankind to their service. Any influence they may
have over human life must be explicable in terms of the ordinary
laws of nature; it cannot in any way be attributed to their
malevolence. Sickness and the cure of disease are likewise
attributable to natural causation; they are not the result of

daemonic activity or of evil spells.[1] The *miracles of the New Testament* have ceased to be miraculous, and to defend their historicity by recourse to nervous disorders or hypnotic effects only serves to underline the fact. And if we are still left with certain physiological and psychological phenomena which we can only assign to mysterious and enigmatic causes, we are still assigning them to causes, and thus far are trying to make them scientifically intelligible. Even occultism pretends to be a science.

It is impossible to use electric light and the wireless and to avail ourselves of modern medical and surgical discoveries, and at the same time to believe in the New Testament world of spirits and miracles.[2] We may think we can manage it in our own lives, but to expect others to do so is to make the Christian faith unintelligible and unacceptable to the modern world.

The mythical eschatology is untenable for the simple reason that the parousia of Christ never took place as the New Testament expected. History did not come to an end, and, as every schoolboy knows, it will continue to run its course. Even if we believe that the world as we know it will come to an end in time, we expect the end to take the form of a natural catastrophe, not of a mythical event such as the New Testament expects. And if we explain the parousia in terms of modern scientific theory, we are applying criticism to the New Testament, albeit unconsciously.

But natural science is not the only challenge which the mythology of the New Testament has to face. There is the still

---

[1] It may of course be argued that there are people alive to-day whose confidence in the traditional scientific view of the world has been shaken, and others who are primitive enough to qualify for an age of mythical thought. And there are also many varieties of superstition. But when belief in spirits and miracles has degenerated into superstition, it has become something entirely different from what it was when it was genuine faith. The various impressions and speculations which influence credulous people here and there are of little importance, nor does it matter to what extent cheap slogans have spread an atmosphere inimical to science. What matters is the world view which men imbibe from their environment, and it is science which determines that view of the world through the school, the press, the wireless, the cinema, and all the other fruits of technical progress.

[2] Cp. the observations of Paul Schütz on the decay of mythical religion in the East through the introduction of modern hygiene and medicine.

B

more serious challenge presented by *modern man's understanding of himself.*

Modern man is confronted by a curious dilemma. He may regard himself as pure nature, or as pure spirit. In the latter case he distinguishes the essential part of his being from nature. In either case, however, *man is essentially a unity.* He bears the sole responsibility for his own feeling, thinking, and willing.[1] He is not, as the New Testament regards him, the victim of a strange dichotomy which exposes him to the interference of powers outside himself. If his exterior behaviour and his interior condition are in perfect harmony, it is something he has achieved himself, and if other people think their interior unity is torn asunder by daemonic or divine interference, he calls it schizophrenia.

Although biology and psychology recognize that man is a highly dependent being, that does not mean that he has been handed over to powers outside of and distinct from himself. This dependence is inseparable from human nature, and he needs only to understand it in order to recover his self-mastery and organize his life on a rational basis. If he regards himself as spirit, he knows that he is permanently conditioned by the physical, bodily part of his being, but he distinguishes his true self from it, and knows that he is independent and responsible for his mastery over nature.

In either case he finds *what the New Testament has to say about the "Spirit"* ($\pi\nu\epsilon\tilde{\upsilon}\mu\alpha$) *and the sacraments utterly strange and incomprehensible.* Biological man cannot see how a supernatural entity like the $\pi\nu\epsilon\tilde{\upsilon}\mu\alpha$ can penetrate within the close texture of his natural powers and set to work within him. Nor can the idealist understand how a $\pi\nu\epsilon\tilde{\upsilon}\mu\alpha$ working like a natural power can touch and influence his mind and spirit. Conscious as he is of his own moral responsibility, he cannot conceive how baptism in water can convey a mysterious something which is henceforth the agent of all his decisions and actions. He cannot see how physical food can convey spiritual strength, and how the unworthy receiving of the Eucharist can result in physical sickness and death (1 Cor. 11. 30). The only possible explanation is that it is

---

[1] Cp. Gerhardt Krüger, *Einsicht und Leidenschaft, Das Wesen des platonischen Denkens*, Frankfort, 1939, p. 11 f.

due to suggestion. He cannot understand how anyone can be baptized for the dead (1 Cor. 15. 29).

We need not examine in detail the various forms of modern *Weltanschauung*, whether idealist or naturalist. For the only criticism of the New Testament which is theologically relevant is that which arises *necessarily* out of the situation of modern man. The biological *Weltanschauung* does not, for instance, arise necessarily out of the contemporary situation. We are still free to adopt it or not as we choose. The only relevant question for the theologian is the basic assumption on which the adoption of a biological as of every other *Weltanschauung* rests, and that assumption is the view of the world which has been moulded by modern science and the modern conception of human nature as a self-subsistent unity immune from the interference of supernatural powers.

Again, the biblical doctrine that *death is the punishment of sin* is equally abhorrent to naturalism and idealism, since they both regard death as a simple and necessary process of nature. To the naturalist death is no problem at all, and to the idealist it is a problem for that very reason, for so far from arising out of man's essential spiritual being it actually destroys it. The idealist is faced with a paradox. On the one hand man is a spiritual being, and therefore essentially different from plants and animals, and on the other hand he is the prisoner of nature, whose birth, life, and death are just the same as those of the animals. Death may present him with a problem, but he cannot see how it can be a punishment for sin. Human beings are subject to death even before they have committed any sin. And to attribute human mortality to the fall of Adam is sheer nonsense, for guilt implies personal responsibility, and the idea of original sin as an inherited infection is sub-ethical, irrational, and absurd.

The same objections apply to *the doctrine of the atonement*. How can the guilt of one man be expiated by the death of another who is sinless—if indeed one may speak of a sinless man at all? What primitive notions of guilt and righteousness does this imply? And what primitive idea of God? The rationale of sacrifice in general may of course throw some light on the theory of the atonement, but even so, what a primitive mythology it is, that a divine Being should become incarnate, and atone for the sins of men through his own blood! Or again, one might adopt an analogy from the law courts, and explain the death of Christ as a transaction between God and man through which God's claims on man were satisfied. But that would make sin a juridical matter; it would be no more than an external transgression of a commandment, and it would make nonsense of all our ethical standards. Moreover, if the Christ who died such a death was the pre-existent Son of God, what could death mean for him? Obviously very little, if he knew that he would rise again in three days!

The *resurrection of Jesus* is just as difficult for modern man, if it means an event whereby a living supernatural power is released which can henceforth be appropriated through the sacraments. To the biologist such language is meaningless, for he does not regard death as a problem at all. The idealist would not object to the idea of a life immune from death, but he could not believe that such a life is made available by the resuscitation of a dead person. If that is the way God makes life available for man, his action is inextricably involved in a nature miracle. Such a notion he finds incomprehensible, for he can see God at work only in the reality of his personal life and in his transformation. But, quite apart from the incredibility of such a miracle, he cannot see how an event like this could be the act of God, or how it could affect his own life.

Gnostic influence suggests that this Christ, who died and rose again, was not a mere human being but a God-man. His death and resurrection were not isolated facts which concerned him alone, but a cosmic event in which we are all involved.[1] It is only with effort that modern man can think himself back into such an intellectual atmosphere, and even then he could never accept it himself, because it regards man's essential being as nature and redemption as a process of nature. And as for the pre-existence of Christ, with its corollary of man's translation into a celestial realm of light, and the clothing of the human personality in heavenly robes and a spiritual body—all this is not only irrational but utterly meaningless. Why should salvation take this particular form? Why should this be the fulfilment of human life and the realization of man's true being?

[1] Rom. 5. 12ff.; 1 Cor. 15. 21ff., 44b.

B. The Task before Us

1. Not Selection or Subtraction

Does this drastic criticism of the New Testament mythology mean the complete elimination of the kerygma?

Whatever else may be true, we cannot save the kerygma by selecting some of its features and subtracting others, and thus reduce the amount of mythology in it. For instance, it is impossible to dismiss St Paul's teaching about the unworthy reception of Holy Communion or about baptism for the dead, and yet cling to the belief that physical eating and drinking can have a spiritual effect. If we accept *one* idea, we must accept everything which the New Testament has to say about Baptism and Holy Communion, and it is just this one idea which we cannot accept.

It may of course be argued that some features of the New Testament mythology are given greater prominence than others: not all of them appear with the same regularity in the various books. There is for example only one occurrence of the legends of the Virgin birth and the Ascension; St Paul and St John appear to be totally unaware of them. But, even if we take them to be later accretions, it does not affect the mythical character of the event of redemption as a whole. And if we once start subtracting from the kerygma, where are we to draw the line? The mythical view of the world must be accepted or rejected in its entirety.

At this point absolute clarity and ruthless honesty are essential both for the academic theologian and for the parish priest. It is a duty they owe to themselves, to the Church they serve, and to those whom they seek to win for the Church. They must make it quite clear what their hearers are expected to accept and what they are not. At all costs the preacher must not leave his people in the dark about what he secretly eliminates, nor must he be in the dark about it himself. In Karl Barth's book *The Resurrection of the Dead* the cosmic eschatology in the sense of "chronologically final history" is eliminated in favour of what he intends to be a non-mythological "ultimate history". He is able to delude himself into thinking that this is exegesis of St Paul and of the New Testament generally only because he gets rid of everything mythological in 1 Corinthians by subjecting it to an interpretation which does violence to its meaning. But that is an impossible procedure.

If the truth of the New Testament proclamation is to be preserved, the only way is to demythologize it. But our motive in so doing must not be to make the New Testament relevant to the modern world at all costs. The question is simply whether the New Testament message consists exclusively of mythology, or whether it actually demands the elimination of myth if it is to be understood as it is meant to be. This question is forced upon us from two sides. First there is the nature of myth in general, and then there is the New Testament itself.

2. The Nature of Myth

The real purpose of myth is not to present an objective picture of the world as it is, but to express man's understanding of himself in the world in which he lives. Myth should be interpreted not cosmologically, but anthropologically, or better still, existentially.[1] Myth speaks of the power or the powers which man supposes he experiences as the ground and limit of his world and of his own activity and suffering. He describes these powers in terms derived from the visible world, with its tangible objects and forces, and from human life, with its feelings, motives, and potentialities. He may, for instance, explain the origin of the world by speaking of a world egg or a world tree. Similarly he may account for the present state and order of the world by speaking of a primeval war between the gods. He speaks of the other world in terms of this world, and of the gods in terms derived from human life.[2]

Myth is an expression of man's conviction that the origin and purpose of the world in which he lives are to be sought not within it but beyond it—that is, beyond the realm of known and tangiblereality —and that this realm is perpetually dominated

[1] Cp. Gerhardt Krüger, Einsicht und Leidenschaft, esp. p. 17f., 56f.

[2] Myth is here used in the sense popularized by the 'History of Religions' school. Mythology is the use of imagery to express the other worldly in terms of this world and the divine in terms of human life, the other side in terms of this side. For instance, divine transcendence is expressed as spatial distance. It is a mode of expression which makes it easy to understand the cultus as an action in which material means are used to convey immaterial power. Myth is not used in that modern sense, according to which it is practically equivalent to ideology.

and menaced by those mysterious powers which are its source and limit. Myth is also an expression of man's awareness that he is not lord of his own being. It expresses his sense of dependence not only within the visible world, but more especially on those forces which hold sway beyond the confines of the known. Finally, myth expresses man's belief that in this state of dependence he can be delivered from the forces within the visible world.

Thus myth contains elements which demand its own criticism —namely, its imagery with its apparent claim to objective validity. The real purpose of myth is to speak of a transcendent power which controls the world and man, but that purpose is impeded and obscured by the terms in which it is expressed.

Hence the importance of the New Testament mythology lies not in its imagery but in the understanding of existence which it enshrines. The real question is whether this understanding of existence is true. Faith claims that it is, and faith ought not to be tied down to the imagery of New Testament mythology.

3. The New Testament Itself

The New Testament itself invites this kind of criticism. Not only are there rough edges in its mythology, but some of its features are actually contradictory. For example, the death of Christ is sometimes a sacrifice and sometimes a cosmic event. Sometimes his person is interpreted as the Messiah and sometimes as the Second Adam. The kenosis of the pre-existent Son (Phil. 2. 6ff.) is incompatible with the miracle narratives as proofs of his messianic claims. The Virgin birth is inconsistent with the assertion of his pre-existence. The doctrine of the Creation is incompatible with the conception of the "rulers of this world" (1 Cor. 2. 6ff.), the "god of this world" (2 Cor. 4. 4) and the "elements of this world" στοιχεῖα τοῦ κόσμου, Gal. 4. 3). It is impossible to square the belief that the law was given by God with the theory that it comes from the angels (Gal. 3. 19f.).

But the principal demand for the criticism of mythology comes from a curious contradiction which runs right through the New Testament. Sometimes we are told that human life is determined by cosmic forces, at others we are challenged to a decision. Side by side with the Pauline indicative stands the Pauline imperative. In short, man is sometimes regarded as a cosmic being, sometimes as an independent "I" for whom decision is a matter of life or death. Incidentally, this explains why so many sayings in the New Testament speak directly to modern man's condition while others remain enigmatic and obscure. Finally, attempts at demythologization are sometimes made even within the New Testament itself. But more will be said on this point later.

4. Previous Attempts at Demythologizing

How then is the mythology of the New Testament to be re-interpreted? This is not the first time that theologians have approached this task. Indeed, all we have said so far might have been said in much the same way thirty or forty years ago, and it is a sign of the bankruptcy of contemporary theology that it has been necessary to go all over the same ground again. The reason for this is not far to seek. The liberal theologians of the last century were working on the wrong lines. They threw away not only the mythology but also the kerygma itself. Were they right? Is that the treatment the New Testament itself required? That is the question we must face to-day. The last twenty years have witnessed a movement away from criticism and a return to a naïve acceptance of the kerygma. The danger both for theological scholarship and for the Church is that this uncritical resuscitation of the New Testament mythology may make the Gospel message unintelligible to the modern world. We cannot dismiss the critical labours of earlier generations without further ado. We must take them up and put them to constructive use. Failure to do so will mean that the old battles between orthodoxy and liberalism will have to be fought out all over again, that is assuming that there will be any Church or any theologians to fight them at all! Perhaps we may put it schematically like this: whereas the older liberals used criticism to *eliminate* the mythology of the New Testament, our task to-day is to use criticism to *interpret* it. Of course it may still be necessary to eliminate mythology here and there. But the criterion adopted must be taken not from modern thought, but from the understanding of human existence which the New Testament itself enshrines.[1]

To begin with, let us review some of these earlier attempts

[1] As an illustration of this critical re-interpretation of myth cf. Hans Jonas, *Augustin und das paulinische Freiheitsproblem*, 1930, pp. 66–76.

at demythologizing. We need only mention briefly the allegorical interpretation of the New Testament which has dogged the Church throughout its history. This method spiritualizes the mythical events so that they become symbols of processes going on in the soul. This is certainly the most comfortable way of avoiding the critical question. The literal meaning is allowed to stand and is dispensed with only for the individual believer, who can escape into the realm of the soul.

It was characteristic of the older liberal theologians that they regarded mythology as relative and temporary. Hence they thought they could safely eliminate it altogether, and retain only the broad, basic principles of religion and ethics. They distinguished between what they took to be the essence of religion and the temporary garb which it assumed. Listen to what Harnack has to say about the essence of Jesus' preaching of the Kingdom of God and its coming: "The kingdom has a triple meaning. Firstly, it is something supernatural, a gift from above, not a product of ordinary life. Secondly, it is a purely religious blessing, the inner link with the living God; thirdly, it is the most important experience that a man can have, that on which everything else depends; it permeates and dominates his whole existence, because sin is forgiven and misery banished." Note how completely the mythology is eliminated: "The kingdom of God comes by coming to the individual, by entering into his *soul* and laying hold of it."[1]

It will be noticed how Harnack reduces the kerygma to a few basic principles of religion and ethics. Unfortunately this means that *the kerygma has ceased to be kerygma*: it is no longer the proclamation of the decisive act of God in Christ. For the liberals the great truths of religion and ethics are timeless and eternal, though it is only within human history that they are realized, and only in concrete historical processes that they are given clear expression. But the apprehension and acceptance of these principles does not depend on the knowledge and acceptance of the age in which they first took shape, or of the historical persons who first discovered them. We are all capable of verifying them in our own experience at whatever period we happen to live. History may be of academic interest, but never of paramount importance for religion.

[1] *What is Christianity?* Williams and Norgate, 1904, pp. 63–4 and 57.

But the New Testament speaks of an *event* through which God has wrought man's redemption. For it, Jesus is not primarily the teacher, who certainly had extremely important things to say and will always be honoured for saying them, but whose person in the last analysis is immaterial for those who have assimilated his teaching. On the contrary, his person is just what the New Testament proclaims as the decisive event of redemption. It speaks of this person in mythological terms, but does this mean that we can reject the kerygma altogether on the ground that it is nothing more than mythology? That is the question.

Next came the History of Religions school. Its representatives were the first to discover the extent to which the New Testament is permeated by mythology. The importance of the New Testament, they saw, lay not in its teaching about religion and ethics but in its actual religion and piety; in comparison with that all the dogma it contains, and therefore all the mythological imagery with its apparent objectivity, was of secondary importance or completely negligible. The essence of the New Testament lay in the religious life it portrayed; its high-watermark was the experience of mystical union with Christ, in whom God took symbolic form.

These critics grasped one important truth. Christian faith is not the same as religious idealism; the Christian life does not consist in developing the individual personality, in the improvement of society, or in making the world a better place. The Christian life means a turning away from the world, a detachment from it. But the critics of the History of Religions school failed to see that in the New Testament this detachment is essentially eschatological and not mystical. Religion for them was an expression of the human yearning to rise above the world and transcend it: it was the discovery of a supramundane sphere where the soul could detach itself from all earthly care and find its rest. Hence the supreme manifestation of religion was to be found not in personal ethics or in social idealism but in the cultus regarded as an end in itself. This was just the kind of religious life portrayed in the New Testament, not only as a model and pattern, but as a challenge and inspiration. The New Testament was thus the abiding source of power which enabled man to realize the true life of religion, and Christ was the eternal symbol for the cultus of the Christian Church.[1] It will be noticed how the Church is here defined exclusively as a worshipping community, and this represents a great advance on the older liberalism. This school rediscovered the Church as a *religious* institution. For the idealist there was really no place for the Church at all. But did they succeed in recovering the meaning of the Ecclesia in the full, New Testament sense of the word? For in the New Testament the Ecclesia is invariably a phenomenon of salvation history and eschatology.

Moreover, if the History of Religions school is right, the kerygma has once more ceased to be kerygma. Like the liberals, they are silent about a decisive act of God in Christ proclaimed as the event of redemption. So we are still left with the question whether this event and the person of Jesus, both of which are described in the New Testament in mythological terms, are nothing more than mythology. Can the kerygma be interpreted apart from mythology? Can we recover the truth of the kerygma for men who do not think in mythological terms without forfeiting its character as kerygma?

5. An Existentialist Interpretation the Only Solution

The theological work which such an interpretation involves can be sketched only in the broadest outline and with only a few examples. We must avoid the impression that this is a light and easy task, as if all we have to do is to discover the right formula and finish the job on the spot. It is much more formidable than that. It cannot be done single-handed. It will tax the time and strength of a whole theological generation.

The mythology of the New Testament is in essence that of Jewish apocalyptic and the Gnostic redemption myths. A common feature of them both is their basic dualism, according to which the present world and its human inhabitants are under the control of daemonic, satanic powers, and stand in need of redemption. Man cannot achieve this redemption by his own efforts; it must come as a gift through a divine intervention. Both types of mythology speak of such an intervention: Jewish apocalyptic of an imminent world crisis in which this present aeon will be

[1] Cp. e.g. Troeltsch, *Die Bedeutung der Geschichtlichkeit Jesu für den Glauben*, Tübingen, 1911.

brought to an end and the new aeon ushered in by the coming of the Messiah, and Gnosticism of a Son of God sent down from the realm of light, entering into this world in the guise of a man, and by his fate and teaching delivering the elect and opening up the way for their return to their heavenly home.

The meaning of these two types of mythology lies once more not in their imagery with its apparent objectivity but in the understanding of human existence which both are trying to express. In other words, they need to be interpreted existentially. A good example of such treatment is to be found in Hans Jonas's book on Gnosticism.[1]

Our task is to produce an existentialist interpretation of the dualistic mythology of the New Testament along similar lines. When, for instance, we read of daemonic powers ruling the world and holding mankind in bondage, does the understanding of human existence which underlies such language offer a solution to the riddle of human life which will be acceptable even to the non-mythological mind of to-day? Of course we must not take this to imply that the New Testament presents us with an anthropology like that which modern science can give us. It cannot be proved by logic or demonstrated by an appeal to factual evidence. Scientific anthropologies always take for granted a definite understanding of existence, which is invariably the consequence of a deliberate decision of the scientist, whether he makes it consciously or not. And that is why we have to discover whether the New Testament offers man an understanding of himself which will challenge him to a genuine existential decision.

[1] *Gnosis und spätantiker Geist. I. Die mythologische Gnosis*, 1934.

DEMYTHOLOGIZING IN OUTLINE

A. The Christian Interpretation of Being

1. Human Existence apart from Faith

WHAT does the New Testament mean when it talks of the "world", of "this world" (ὁ κόσμος οὗτος), or of "this aeon" (οὗτος ὁ αἰών)? In speaking thus, the New Testament is in agreement with the Gnostics, for they too speak of "this world", and of the princes, prince, or god of this world; and moreover they both regard man as the slave of the world and its powers. But there is one significant difference. In the New Testament one of these powers in conspicuously absent —viz., *matter*, the physical, sensual part of man's constitution. Never does the New Testament complain that the soul of man, his authentic self, is imprisoned in a material body: never does it complain of the power of sensuality over the spirit. That is why it never doubts the responsibility of man for his sin. God is always the Creator of the world, including human life in the body. He is also the Judge before whom man must give account. The part played by Satan as the Lord of this world must therefore be limited in a peculiar way, or else, if he is the lord or god of world, "this world" must stand in a peculiar dialectical relation to the world as the creation of God.

"This world" is the world of corruption and death. Clearly, it was not so when it left the hands of the Creator, for it was only in consequence of the fall of Adam that death entered into the world (Rom. 5. 12). Hence it is sin, rather than matter as such, which is the cause of corruption and death. The Gnostic conception of the soul as a pure, celestial element imprisoned by some tragic fate in a material body is entirely absent. Death is the wages of sin (Rom. 6. 23; cf. 1 Cor. 15. 56). True, St Paul seems to agree with the Gnostics as regards the effects which he ascribes to the fall of Adam as the ancestor of the human race.

17

But it is clear that he later returns to the idea of individual responsibility when he says that since Adam death came to all men "for that all sinned" (Rom. 5. 12), a statement which stands in formal contradiction to the Adam theory. Perhaps he means to say that with Adam death became possible rather than inevitable. However that may be, there is another idea which St Paul is constantly repeating and which is equally incompatible with the Adam theory, and that is the theory that sin, including death, is derived from the flesh (σάρξ, Rom. 8. 13; Gal. 6. 8, etc.). But what does he mean by "flesh"? Not the bodily or physical side of human nature, but the sphere of visible, concrete, tangible, and measurable reality, which as such is also the sphere of corruption and death. When a man chooses to live entirely in and for this sphere, or, as St Paul puts it, when he "lives after the flesh", it assumes the shape of a "power". There are indeed many different ways of living after the flesh. There is the crude life of sensual pleasure and there is the refined way of basing one's life on the pride of achievement, on the "works of the law" as St Paul would say. But these distinctions are ultimately immaterial. For "flesh" embraces not only the material things of life, but all human creation and achievement pursued for the sake of some tangible reward, such as for example the fulfilling of the law (Gal. 3. 3). It includes every passive quality, and every advantage a man can have, in the sphere of visible, tangible reality (Phil. 3. 4ff.).

St Paul sees that the life of man is weighed down by anxiety (μεριμνᾶν, 1 Cor. 7. 32ff.). Every man focuses his anxiety upon some particular object. The natural man focuses it upon security, and in proportion to his opportunities and his success in the visible sphere he places his "confidence" in the "flesh" (Phil. 3. 3f.), and the consciousness of security finds its expression in "glorying" (καυχᾶσθαι).

Such a pursuit is, however, incongruous with man's real situation, for the fact is that he is not secure at all. Indeed, this is the way in which he loses his true life and becomes the slave of that very sphere which he had hoped to master, and which he hoped would give him security. Whereas hitherto he might have enjoyed the world as God's creation, it has now become "this world", the world in revolt against God. This is the way in which the "powers" which dominate human life come into being, and as such they acquire the character of mythical entities.[1] Since the visible and tangible sphere is essentially transitory, the man who bases his life on it becomes the prisoner and slave of corruption. An illustration of this may be seen in the way our attempts to secure visible security for ourselves bring us into collision with others; we can seek security for ourselves only at their expense. Thus on the one hand we get envy, anger, jealousy, and the like, and on the other compromise, bargainings, and adjustments of conflicting interests. This creates an all-pervasive atmosphere which controls all our judgements; we all pay homage to it and take it for granted. Thus man becomes the slave of anxiety (Rom. 8. 15). Everybody tries to hold fast to his own life and property, because he has a secret feeling that it is all slipping away from him.

The Life of Faith

The authentic life, on the other hand, would be a life based on unseen, intangible realities. Such a life means the abandonment of all self-contrived security. This is what the New Testament means by "life after the Spirit" or "life in faith".

For this life we must have faith in *the grace of God*. It means faith that the unseen, intangible reality actually confronts us as love, opening up our future and signifying not death but life.

The grace of God means *the forgiveness of sin*, and brings deliverance from the bondage of the past. The old quest for visible security, the hankering after tangible realities, and the clinging to transitory objects, is sin, for by it we shut out invisible reality from our lives and refuse God's future which comes to us as a gift. But once we open our hearts to the grace of God, our sins are forgiven; we are released from the past. This is what is meant by "faith": to open ourselves freely to the future. But at the same time faith involves obedience, for faith means turning our backs on self and abandoning all security. It means giving up every attempt to carve out a niche in life for ourselves, surrendering all our self-confidence, and resolving to trust in God alone, in the God who raises the dead (2 Cor. 1. 9) and who calls the things that are not into being (Rom. 4. 17). It

[1] Terms like "the spirit of the age" or "the spirit of technology" provide some sort of modern analogy.

means radical self-commitment to God in the expectation that everything will come from him and nothing from ourselves. Such a life spells deliverance from all worldly, tangible objects, leading to complete detachment from the world and thus to freedom.

This detachment from the world is something quite different from asceticism. It means preserving a distance from the world and dealing with it in a spirit of "as if not" (ὡς μή, 1 Cor. 7. 29–31). The believer is lord of all things (1 Cor. 3. 21–3). He enjoys that power (ἐξουσία) of which the Gnostic boasts, but with the proviso: "All things are lawful for me, but I will not be brought under the power of any" (1 Cor. 6. 12; cf. 10. 23f.). The believer may "rejoice with them that do rejoice, and weep with them that weep" (Rom. 12. 15), but he is no longer in bondage to anything in the world (1 Cor. 7. 17–24). Everything in the world has become indifferent and unimportant. "For though I was free from all men, I brought myself under bondage to all" (1 Cor. 9. 19–23). "I know how to be abased, and I know also how to abound in everything, and in all things I have learned the secret both to be filled and to be hungry, both to abound and to be in want" (Phil. 4. 12). The world has been crucified to him, and he to the world (Gal. 6. 14). Moreover, the power of his new life is manifested even in weakness, suffering, and death (2 Cor. 4. 7–11; 12. 9f.). Just when he realizes that he is nothing in himself, he can have and be all things through God (2 Cor. 12. 9f.; 6. 8–10).

Now, this is eschatological existence; it means being a "new creature" (2 Cor. 5. 17). The eschatology of Jewish apocalyptic and of Gnosticism has been emancipated from its accompanying mythology, in so far as the age of salvation has already dawned for the believer and the life of the future has become a present reality. The fourth gospel carries this process to a logical conclusion by completely eliminating every trace of apocalyptic eschatology. The last judgement is no longer an imminent cosmic event, for it is already taking place in the coming of Jesus and in his summons to believe (John 3. 19; 9. 39; 12. 31). The believer has life here and now, and has passed already from death into life (5. 24, etc.). Outwardly everything remains as before, but inwardly his relation to the world has been radically changed. The world has no further claim on him, for faith is the victory which overcometh the world (1 John 5. 4).

The eschatology of Gnosticism is similarly transcended. It is not that the believer is given a new nature (φύσις) or that his pre-existent nature is emancipated, or that his soul is assured of a journey to heaven. The new life in faith is not an assured possession or endowment, which could lead only to libertinism. Nor is it a possession to be guarded with care and vigilance, which could lead only to asceticism. Life in faith is not a possession at all. It cannot be exclusively expressed in indicative terms; it needs an imperative to complete it. In other words, the decision of faith is never final; it needs constant renewal in every fresh situation. Our freedom does not excuse us from the demand under which we all stand as men, for it is freedom for obedience (Rom. 6. 11ff.). To believe means not to have apprehended but to have been apprehended. It means always to be travelling along the road between the "already" and the "not yet", always to be pursuing a goal.

For Gnosticism redemption is a cosmic process in which the redeemed are privileged to participate here and now. Although essentially transcendent, faith must be reduced to an immanent possession. Its outward signs are freedom (ἐλευθερία), power (ἐξουσία), pneumatic phenomena, and above all ecstasy. In the last resort the New Testament knows no phenomena in which transcendent realities become immanent possessions. True, St Paul is familiar with ecstasy (2 Cor. 5. 13; 12. 1ff.). But he refuses to accept it as a proof of the possession of the Spirit. The New Testament never speaks of the training of the soul in mystical experience or of ecstasy as the culmination of the Christian life. Not psychic phenomena but faith is the hallmark of that life.

Certainly St Paul shares the popular belief of his day that the Spirit manifests itself in miracles, and he attributes abnormal psychic phenomena to its agency. But the enthusiasm of the Corinthians for such things brought home to him their questionable character. So he insists that the gifts of the Spirit must be judged according to their value for "edification", and in so doing he transcends the popular view of the Spirit as an agency that operates like any other natural force. True, he regards the Spirit as a mysterious entity dwelling in man and guaranteeing his resurrection (Rom. 8. 11). He can even speak of the Spirit as if it were a kind of supernatural material (1 Cor. 15. 44ff.).

Yet in the last resort he clearly means by "Spirit" the possibility of a new life which is opened up by faith. The Spirit does not work like a supernatural force, nor is it the permanent possession of the believer. It is the possibility of a new life which must be appropriated by a deliberate resolve. Hence St Paul's paradoxical injunction: "If we live by the Spirit, by the Spirit also let us walk." (Gal. 5. 25). "Being led by the Spirit" (Rom. 8. 14) is not an automatic process of nature, but the fulfilment of an imperative: "live after the Spirit, not after the flesh". Imperative and indicative are inseparable. The possession of the Spirit never renders decision superfluous. "I say, Walk by the Spirit and ye shall not fulfil the lust of the flesh" (Gal. 5. 16). Thus the concept "Spirit" has been emancipated from mythology.

The Pauline catalogue of the fruits of the Spirit ("love, joy, peace, long-suffering, kindness, goodness, faithfulness, temperance", Gal. 5. 22) shows how faith, by detaching man from the world, makes him capable of fellowship in community. Now that he is delivered from anxiety and from the frustration which comes from clinging to the tangible realities of the visible world, man is free to enjoy fellowship with others. Hence faith is described as "working through love" (Gal. 5. 6). And this means being a new creature (cf. Gal. 5. 6 with 6. 15).

B The Event of Redemption

1. Christian Self-Understanding without Christ?

We have now suggested an existentialist unmythological interpretation of the Christian understanding of Being. But is this interpretation true to the New Testament? We seem to have overlooked one important point, which is that in the New Testament faith is always *faith in Christ*. Faith, in the strict sense of the word, was only there at a certain moment in history. It had to be *revealed*; it *came* (Gal. 3. 23, 25). This might of course be taken as part of the story of man's spiritual evolution. But the New Testament means more than that. It claims that faith only became possible at a definite point in history in consequence of an *event*—viz., the event of Christ. Faith in the sense of obedient self-commitment and inward detachment from the world is only possible when it is faith in Jesus Christ.

Here indeed is the crux of the matter—have we here a remnant of mythology which still requires restatement? In fact it comes to this: can we have a Christian understanding of Being without Christ?

The reader will recall our criticism of the History of Religions school for eliminating the decisive event of Christ. Is our re-interpretation of Christianity in existentialist terms open to precisely the same objection?

It might well appear as though the event of Christ were a relic of mythology which still awaits elimination. This is a serious problem, and if Christian faith is to recover its self-assurance it must be grappled with. For it can recover its certainty only if it is prepared to think through to the bitter end the possibility of its own impossibility or superfluity.

It might well appear possible to have a Christian understanding of Being without Christ, as though what we had in the New Testament was the first discovery and the more or less clear expression, in the guise of mythology, of an understanding of Being which is at bottom man's natural understanding of his Being, as it has been given clear expression in modern existentialist philosophy. Does this mean that what existentialism has done is simply to remove the mythological disguise and to vindicate the Christian understanding of Being as it is found in the New Testament and to carry it to more logical conclusion? Is theology simply the precursor of existentialism? Is it no more than an antiquated survival and an unnecessary incubus?

Such is the impression we might derive from a consideration of the recent developments in philosophy. Might we not say that the New Testament lays bare what philosophy calls "the historicity of Being"?

Count Yorck von Wartenburg[1] wrote to Dilthey on 15 December 1892: "Dogmatics was an attempt to formulate an ontology of the higher historic life. Christian dogmatics was inevitably the antithesis of intellectualism, because Christianity is the supreme vitality."[2] Dilthey agrees: ". . . all dogmas need to be translated so as to bring out their universal validity for all human life. They are cramped by their connection with the

[1] *Briefwechsel zwischen Wilhelm Dilthey und dem Grafen Paul Yorck von Wartenburg, 1877-97.* Halle, Niemeyer, 1923.
[2] P. 154.

51

situation in the past in which they arose. Once they have been freed from this limitation they become . . . the consciousness of the supra-sensual and supra-intelligible nature of historicity pure and simple. . . . Hence the principal Christian dogmas, which include such symbols as "Son of God", "satisfaction", "sacrifice", and the like, are, in so far as they are limited to the facts of the Christian story, untenable. But once they are re-interpreted as statements of universal validity they express the highest living form of all history. They thus lose their rigid and exclusive reference to the person of Jesus, which deliberately excludes all other references."[1]

Yorck gives by way of illustration a re-interpretation of the doctrines of original sin and the atonement. He finds them intelligible in the light of what he calls the "virtual connection" which runs like a thread right through history. "Jesus is the historical demonstration of a universal truth. The child profits from the self-sacrifice of its mother. This involves a conveyance of virtue and power from one person to another, without which history is impossible. [Note the corollary—all history, not only Christian history, involves transference of power.] This is why rationalism is blind to the concept of history. And sin—not specific acts of wrong-doing, but man's sinfulness in general—is, as the religious man knows from his own experience, quite unpredictable. Is it less 'monstrous and repulsive' [as Dilthey had stigmatized the doctrine of original sin] that sickness and misery are inherited from generation to generation? These Christian symbols are drawn from the very depths of nature, for religion itself—I mean Christianity—is supernatural, not unnatural."[2]

The development of philosophy since Dilthey's day has, it would seem, amply justified these contentions. Karl Jaspers has found no difficulty in transposing Kierkegaard's interpretation of Christian Being to the sphere of philosophy. Above all, Heidegger's existentialist analysis of the ontological structure of being would seem to be no more than a secularized, philosophical version of the New Testament view of human life. For him the chief characteristic of man's Being in history is anxiety. Man exists in a permanent tension between the past and the future. At every moment he is confronted with an alternative. Either

[1] P. 158.   [2] P. 155.

he must immerse himself in the concrete world of nature, and thus inevitably lose his individuality, or he must abandon all security and commit himself unreservedly to the future, and thus alone achieve his authentic Being. Is not that exactly the New Testament understanding of human life? Some critics have objected that I am borrowing Heidegger's categories and forcing them upon the New Testament. I am afraid this only shows that they are blinding their eyes to the real problem. I mean, one should rather be startled that philosophy is saying the same thing as the New Testament and saying it quite independently.

The whole question has been posed afresh in the recent book by Wilhelm Kamlah.[1] It is true that Kamlah expressly attacks the eschatological character of the Christian understanding of Being, but that is because he misinterprets the detachment from the world which is consequent upon faith. He understands it undialectically as a simple negation of the world, and so fails to do justice to the element of "as if not" which is so characteristic of the Pauline Epistles. But the understanding of Being which Kamlah develops philosophically is manifestly a secularized version of that which we find in Christianity. For the Christian concept of faith he substitutes "self-commitment", by which he means "surrender to the universal reality", or to God as the source of all Being. Self-commitment is the antithesis of autonomy. It brings with it a revelation of the meaning of universal reality. Further, it is emancipation, bringing inward freedom through detachment from all sensual objects of desire. Kamlah himself is aware how close this is to the Christian conception of faith. He says: "The theologians have often observed the paradoxical character of this ability to trust, at least so far as the inception of faith is concerned. It has often been asked how the individual can come to believe at all if faith is the gift of God and is not to be won through human effort, and how faith can be demanded if it is outside the limit of human capacity. The question has often been left unanswered because the theologians have failed to see that this is a problem which is not peculiar to Christianity, but which belongs to the fundamental structure of our natural Being."[2]

Christian faith, properly understood, would then (on Kamlah's view), be identical with natural self-commitment. "Since it

[1] *Christentum und Selbstbehauptung*, Frankfort, 1940.   [2] P. 321.

offers the true understanding of Being, philosophy emancipates natural self-commitment and enables it to become what it was meant to be."[1] Thus it has no need of any revelation.

Christian love, through which faith operates, is open to a similar interpretation. It is equivalent to committing ourselves to our familiar surroundings. Indeed, Kamlah thinks he can correct the New Testament at this point. As he sees it, the Christian conception of love interrupts what he calls the smooth flow of history. It infringes the priority of the immediate environment in which we have been placed by history. It dissipates love by universalizing it instead of directing it to our true neighbours, those who are nigh to us. Kamlah would have us see as our neighbours those who are tied to us by the inexorable bonds of history. In this way he would emancipate the true naturalness of man.[2]

But is it really true that in the last resort the New Testament means by faith the natural disposition of man? Clearly "natural" in this context means not "empirical" but "proper to man's authentic Being". This Being has first to be set free. But according to Kamlah this does not require revelation. All that is necessary is philosophical reflection. Is faith in this sense the natural disposition of man?

Yes and no. Yes, because faith is not a mysterious supernatural quality, but the disposition of genuine humanity. Similarly, love is not the effect of mysterious supernatural power, but the "natural" disposition of man. The New Testament goes part of the way with Kamlah when it calls man-in-faith a "new creation". Its implication is that by faith man enters upon the life for which he was originally created.

The question is not whether the nature of man can be *discovered* apart from the New Testament. As a matter of fact it has not been discovered without the aid of the New Testament, for modern philosophy is indebted both to it and to Luther and to Kierkegaard. But this merely indicates the place of existentialism in the intellectual history of man, and as far as its content is concerned it owes little to its historical origin. On the contrary, the very fact that it is possible to produce a secularized version of the New Testament conception of faith

<hr />

[1] P. 326.   [2] P. 337.

proves that there is nothing mysterious or supernatural about the Christian life.

No; the question is whether the "nature" of man is realizable. Is it enough simply to show man what he ought to be? Can he achieve his authentic Being by a mere act of reflection? It is clear that philosophy, no less than theology, has always taken it for granted that man has to a greater or lesser degree erred and gone astray, or at least that he is always in danger of so doing. Even the idealists try to show us what we *really* are—namely, that we are really spirit, and that it is therefore wrong to lose ourselves in the world of things. Become what you are! For Heidegger man has lost his individuality, and therefore he invites him to recover his true selfhood. Kamlah again realizes that what he calls "genuine historical existence" may lie hidden and buried beneath the rubble of unreality, and that this is especially the case to-day when we are suffering from the after-effects of the Enlightenment. Kamlah also is aware that self-commitment is not the natural disposition of modern man, but a demand continually imposed upon him from without. There can be no emancipation without obedience.[1]

At the same time, however, these philosophers are convinced that all we need is to be told about the "nature" of man in order to realize it. "Since it is the true understanding of Being, philosophy emancipates that self-commitment which is proper to man and enables it to attain to its full stature"[2]—evidently, that means: it emancipates man for true self-commitment. Philosophy seeks to "liberate"[3] the true naturalness of man.

Is this self-confidence of the philosophers justified? Whatever the answer may be, it is at least clear that this is the point where they part company with the New Testament. For the latter affirms the total incapacity of man to release himself from his fallen state. That deliverance can come only by an act of God. The New Testament does not give us a doctrine of "nature", a doctrine of the authentic nature of man; it proclaims the event of redemption which was wrought in Christ.

That is why the New Testament says that without this saving act of God our plight is desperate, an assertion which existentialism repudiates. What lies behind this difference?

The philosophers and the New Testament agree that man can

1 P. 403.   2 P. 326.   3 P. 337.

be only what he already is. For instance, the idealists believed that the life of the spirit was possible only because they regarded man as essentially spirit. Become what you *are!* Similarly Heidegger can summon us to the resolve to exist as selves in face of death because he opens our eyes to our situation as one of ''thrownness''[1] into Nothing. Man has to undertake to be what he already is. Similarly it is reasonable for Kamlah to invite us to emancipate ourselves by an act of self-commitment, because he sees that our empirical life is already a life of self-commitment —we are already members of society, we already receive its benefits and contribute to its maintenance.

The New Testament also sees that man can be only what he already is. St Paul exhorts Christians to be holy because they have already been made holy (1 Cor. 6. 11, cp. 5. 7), and to walk in the Spirit because they are already in the spirit (Gal. 5. 25), and to mortify sin because they are already dead unto sin (Rom. 6. 11ff.); or in Johannine language, because they are not ''of the world'' (τοῦ κόσμου, John 17. 16) they can overcome the world, and because they are born of God they do not sin (1 John 3. 9). Eschatological existence is an attainable ideal because ''the fulness of time has come'' and God has sent his Son ''that he might deliver us out of this present evil world'' (Gal. 4. 4; 1. 4).

Thus the New Testament and the philosophers agree that the authentic life is possible only because in some sense it is already a present possession. But there is one difference—the New Testament speaks thus only to Christian believers, only to those who have opened their hearts to the redemptive action of God. It never speaks thus to natural man, for he does not possess life, and *his* plight is one of despair.

Why does the New Testament take this line? Because it knows that man can become only what he already is, and it sees that natural man, man apart from Christ, is not as he ought to be—he is not alive, but dead.

The point at issue is how we understand the fall. Even the philosophers are agreed about the fact of it. But they think that all man needs is to be shown his plight, and that then he will be able to escape from it. In other words, the corruption resulting

---

[1] *Geworfenheit*: see ''*Existence and Being*'' Vision Press, 1949, p. 49f. (Translator).

from the fall does not extend to the core of the human personality. The New Testament, on the other hand, regards the fall as total.

How then, if the fall be total, can man be aware of his plight? He certainly is aware of it, as the philosophers themselves testify. How can man be aware that his fall is total and that it extends to the very core of his personality? As a matter of fact, it is the other way round: it is only because man is a fallen being, only because he knows he is not what he really ought to be and what he would like to be, that he can be aware of his plight. That awareness of his authentic nature is essential to human life, and without it man would not be man. But his authentic nature is not an endowment of creation or a possession at his own disposal. The philosophers would agree thus far, for they also know that man's authentic nature has to be apprehended by a deliberate resolve. But they think that all man needs is to be told about his authentic nature. This nature is what he never realizes, but what at every moment he is capable of realizing— you can because you ought. But the philosophers are confusing a theoretical possibility with an actual one. For, as the New Testament sees it, man has lost that actual possibility, and even his awareness of his authentic manhood is perverted, as is shown by his deluded belief that it is a possession he can command at will.

Why then has the fall destroyed this actual possibility? The answer is that in his present plight every impulse of man is the impulse of a fallen being. St Paul demonstrates this in the case of the Jews. In their search for righteousness they missed the very object of their quest. They looked for justification from their own works; they wanted to have a ground for glorying before God. Here is a perfect illustration of the plight of man, of his bondage to the flesh, which the Jews were trying so frantically to escape. This bondage leads to self-glorying and self-assertion, to a desperate attempt to control our own destiny. If the authentic life of man is one of self-commitment, then that life is missed not only by the blatantly self-assertive but also by those who try to achieve self-commitment by their own efforts. They fail to see that self-commitment can be received only as a gift from God.

The glorying of the Jew over his faithfulness to the law and the glorying of the Gnostic in his wisdom are both illustrations of the dominant attitude of man, of his independence and autonomy which lead in the end to frustration. We find the same thing in idealism with its *deus in nobis*:

Lay hold on divinity; make it your own:
Down it will climb from its heavenly throne.

In Heidegger's case the perversity of such an attitude is less obvious because he does not characterize resolve as self-commitment. But it is clear that the shouldering of the accident of his destiny in the facing of death is really the same radical self-assertion on man's part. Kamlah is relatively nearer to the Christian position when he asserts that the commandment of self-commitment is capable of fulfilment because God grants an understanding of himself[1] or because "Reality" makes self-commitment possible to man by disclosing its own meaning to him,[2] or because self-commitment receives an indication of its own intelligibility from "Reality" itself.[3] But to assert the intelligibility of Reality is to my mind a counsel of despair. Is it not a desperate act of self-assertion when Kamlah says: "It is not possible to doubt altogether in the intelligibility of Reality"?[4] This surely goes to prove that the only reasonable attitude for man to adopt apart from Christ is one of despair, to despair of the possibility of his ever achieving authentic Being.

This at any rate is what the New Testament asserts. Of course it cannot prove its case any more than the philosophers can prove the intelligibility of Reality. It is a matter for decision. The New Testament addresses man as one who is through and through a self-assertive rebel who knows from bitter experience that the life he actually lives is not his authentic life, and that he is totally incapable of achieving that life by his own efforts. In short, he is a totally fallen being.

This means, in the language of the New Testament, that man is a sinner. The self-assertion of which we have spoken is identical with sin. Sin is self-assertion, self-glorying, for "No flesh should glory before God. . . . He that glorieth, let him glory in the Lord" (1 Cor. 1. 29, 31; 2 Cor. 10. 17). Is that no more than an unnecessary mythologizing of an ontological proposition? Can man as he is perceive that self-assertion involves

[1] Pp. 341, 353.   [2] P. 298.   [3] P. 330.   [4] P. 358.

guilt, and that he is personally responsible to God for it? Is sin a mythological concept or not? The answer will depend on what we make of St Paul's words to the Corinthians: "What hast thou that thou didst not receive? but if thou didst receive it, why dost thou glory, as if thou hadst not received it?" (1 Cor. 4. 7). Does this apply to all men alike, or only to Christians? This much at any rate is clear: self-assertion is guilt only if it can be understood as ingratitude. If the radical self-assertion which makes it impossible for man to achieve the authentic life of self-commitment is identical with sin, it must obviously be possible for man to understand his existence altogether as a gift of God. But it is just this radical self-assertion which makes such an understanding impossible. For self-assertion deludes man into thinking that his existence is a prize within his own grasp. How blind man is to his plight is illustrated by that pessimism which regards life as a burden thrust on man against his will, or by the way men talk about the "right to live" or by the way they expect their fair share of good fortune. Man's radical self-assertion then blinds him to the fact of sin, and this is the clearest proof that he is a fallen being. Hence it is no good telling man that he is a sinner. He will only dismiss it as mythology. But it does not follow that he is right.

To talk of sin ceases to be mere mythology when the love of God meets man as a power which embraces and sustains him even in his fallen, self-assertive state. Such a love treats man as if he were other than he is. By so doing, love frees man from himself as he is.

For as a result of his self-assertion man is a totally fallen being. He is capable of knowing that his authentic life consists in self-commitment, but is incapable of realizing it because however hard he tries he still remains what he is, self-assertive man. So in practice authentic life becomes possible only when man is delivered from himself. It is the claim of the New Testament that this is exactly what has happened. This is precisely the meaning of that which was wrought in Christ. At the very point where man can do nothing, God steps in and acts—indeed he has acted already—on man's behalf.

St Paul is endeavouring to express this when he speaks of the expiation of sin, or of "righteousness" created as a gift of God rather than as a human achievement. Through Christ, God has

reconciled the world to himself, not reckoning to it its tres-
passes (2 Cor. 5. 19). God made Christ to be sin for us, that we
through him might stand before God as righteous (2 Cor. 5. 21).
For everyone who believes, his past life is dead and done with.
He is a new creature, and as such he faces each new moment.
In short, he has become a free man.

It is quite clear from this that forgiveness of sins is not a juridical concept. It does not mean the remission of punishment.[1]
If that were so, man's plight would be as bad as ever. Rather,
forgiveness conveys freedom from sin, which hitherto had held
man in bondage. But this freedom is not a static quality: it is
freedom *to obey*. The indicative implies an imperative. Love is
the fulfilment of the law, and therefore the forgiveness of God
delivers man from himself and makes him free to devote his life
to the service of others (Rom. 13. 8–10; Gal. 5. 14).

Thus eschatological existence has become possible. God has
acted, and the world—"this world"—has come to an end.
Man himself has been made new. "If any man is in Christ, he is a new
creature: the old things are passed away; behold, they are become
new" (2 Cor. 5. 17). So much for St Paul. St John makes the
same point in his own particular language. The knowledge of
the "truth" as it is revealed in Jesus makes men free (8. 32),
free from the bondage of sin (8. 34). Jesus calls the dead to life
(5. 25) and gives sight to the blind (9. 39). The believer in
Christ is "born again" (3. 3ff.); he is given a fresh start in life.
He is no longer a worldling, for he has overcome the world
through faith (1 John 5. 4).

The event of Jesus Christ is therefore the revelation of the
love of God. It makes a man free from himself and free to be
himself, free to live a life of self-commitment in faith and love.
But faith in this sense of the word is possible only where it
takes the form of faith in the love of God. Yet such faith is still
a subtle form of self-assertion so long as the love of God is merely
a piece of wishful thinking. It is only an abstract idea so long as
God has not revealed his love. That is why faith for the Christian
means faith in Christ, for it is faith in the love of God revealed
in Christ. Only those who are loved are capable of loving.

---

[1] It is worth noting that St Paul never uses the term ἄφεσις τῶν ἁμαρτι v,
though it reappears in the deutero-Pauline literature; see e.g. Col. 1. 14;
Eph. 1. 7.

Only those who have received confidence as a gift can show confidence in others. Only those who know what self-commitment is by experience can adopt that attitude themselves. We are free to give ourselves to God because he has given up himself for us. "Herein is love, not that we loved God, but that he loved us, and sent his Son to be the propitiation for our sins" (1 John 4. 10). "We love, because he first loved us." (1 John 4. 19).

The classic statement of this self-commitment of God, which is the ground of our own self-commitment, is to be found in Rom. 8. 32: "God spared not his Son, but delivered him up for us; how shall he not also with him freely give us all things?" Compare the Johannine text: "God so loved the world, that he gave his only-begotten Son, that whosoever believeth in him should not perish, but have eternal life" (John 3. 16). There are also similar texts which speak of Jesus' giving up himself for us: ". . . who gave himself for our sins, that he might deliver us out of this present evil world" (Gal. 1. 4); "I have been crucified with Christ; yet I live; and yet no longer I, but Christ liveth in me: and the life which I live in the flesh I live in faith, the faith which is in the Son of God, who loved me and gave himself up for me" (Gal. 2. 19f.).

Here then is the crucial distinction between the New Testament and existentialism, between the Christian faith and the natural understanding of Being. The New Testament speaks and faith knows of an act of God through which man becomes capable of self-commitment, capable of faith and love, of his authentic life.

Have we carried our demythologizing far enough? Are we still left with a myth, or at least an event which bears a mythical character? It is possible, as we have seen, to restate in non-mythological terms the New Testament teaching on human existence apart from faith and in faith. But what of the point of transition between the old life and the new, authentic life? Can it be understood otherwise than as an act of God? Is faith genuine only when it is faith in the love of God revealed in Christ?

2. The Event of Jesus Christ

Anyone who asserts that to speak of an act of God at all is mythological language is bound to regard the idea of an act of

God in Christ as a myth. But let us ignore this question for a moment. Even Kamlah thinks it philosophically justifiable to use "the mythological language of an act of God" (p. 353). The issue for the moment is whether that particular event in which the New Testament sees the act of God and the revelation of his love—that is, the event of Jesus Christ—is essentially a mythical event.

(a) The Demythologizing of the Event of Jesus Christ

Now, it is beyond question that the New Testament presents the event of Jesus Christ in mythical terms. The problem is whether that is the only possible presentation. Or does the New Testament itself demand a restatement of the event of Jesus Christ in non-mythological terms? Now, it is clear from the outset that the event of Christ is of a wholly different order from the cult-myths of Greek or Hellenistic religion. Jesus Christ is certainly presented as the Son of God, a pre-existent divine being, and therefore to that extent a mythical figure. But he is also a concrete figure of history—Jesus of Nazareth. His life is more than a mythical event; it is a human life which ended in the tragedy of crucifixion. We have here a unique combination of history and myth. The New Testament claims that this Jesus of history, whose father and mother were well known to his contemporaries (John 6. 42) is at the same time the pre-existent Son of God, and side by side with the historical event of the crucifixion it sets the definitely non-historical event of the resurrection. This combination of myth and history presents a number of difficulties, as can be seen from certain inconsistencies in the New Testament material. The doctrine of Christ's pre-existence as given by St Paul and St John is difficult to reconcile with the legend of the Virgin birth in St Matthew and St Luke. On the one hand we hear that "he emptied himself, taking the form of a servant, being made in the likeness of men: and being found in fashion as a man . . ." (Phil. 2. 7), and on the other hand we have the gospel portraits of a Jesus who manifests his divinity in his miracles, omniscience, and mysterious elusiveness, and the similar description of him in Acts as "Jesus of Nazareth, a man approved of God unto you by mighty works and wonders and signs" (Acts 2. 22). On the one hand we have the resurrection as the exaltation of Jesus from the cross or grave, and on the other the legends of the empty tomb and the ascension.

We are compelled to ask whether all this mythological language is not simply an attempt to express the meaning of the historical figure of Jesus and the events of his life; in other words, significance of these as a figure and event of salvation. If that be so, we can dispense with the objective form in which they are cast.

It is easy enough to deal with the doctrine of Christ's pre-existence and the legend of the Virgin birth in this way. They are clearly attempts to explain the meaning of the Person of Jesus for faith. The facts which historical criticism can verify cannot exhaust, indeed they cannot adequately indicate, all that Jesus means to me. How he actually originated matters little, indeed we can appreciate his significance only when we cease to worry about such questions. Our interest in the events of his life, and above all in the cross, is more than an academic concern with the history of the past. We can see meaning in them only when we ask what God is trying to say to each one of us through them. Again, the figure of Jesus cannot be understood simply from his inner-worldly context. In mythological language, this means that he stems from eternity, his origin is not a human and natural one.

We shall not, however, pursue the examination of the particular incidents of his life any further. In the end the crux of the matter lies in the cross and resurrection.

(b) The Cross

Is the cross, understood as the event of redemption, exclusively mythical in character, or can it retain its value for salvation without forfeiting its character as history?

It certainly has a mythical character as far as its objective setting is concerned. The Jesus who was crucified was the pre-existent, incarnate Son of God, and as such he was without sin. He is the victim whose blood atones for our sins. He bears vicariously the sin of the world, and by enduring the punishment for sin on our behalf he delivers us from death. This mythological interpretation is a mixture of sacrificial and juridical analogies, which have ceased to be tenable for us to-day. And in any case they fail to do justice to what the New Testament is trying to say. For the most they can convey is that the cross effects the forgiveness of all the past and future sins of man, in the sense that the punishment they deserved has been remitted. But the New Testament means more than this. The cross releases men not only from the guilt, but also from the power of sin. That is why, when the author of Colossians says "He [God] . . . having forgiven us all our trespasses, having blotted out the bond written in ordinances that was against us, which was contrary to us; and he hath taken it out of the way, nailing it to the cross" he hastens to add: "having put off from himself the principalities and powers, he made a show of them openly, triumphing over them in it" (Col. 2. 13–15).

The historical event of the cross acquires cosmic dimensions. And by speaking of the Cross as a cosmic happening its significance as a historical happening is made clear in accordance with the remarkable way of thinking in which historical events and connections are presented in cosmic terms, and so its full significance is brought into sharper relief. For if we see in the cross the judgement of the world and the defeat of the rulers of this world (1 Cor. 2. 6ff.), the cross becomes the judgement of ourselves as fallen creatures enslaved to the powers of the "world".

By giving up Jesus to be crucified, God has set up the cross for us. To believe in the cross of Christ does not mean to concern·ourselves with a mythical process wrought outside of us and our world, with an objective event turned by God to our advantage, but rather to make the cross of Christ our own, to undergo crucifixion with him. The cross in its redemptive aspect is not an isolated incident which befell a mythical personage, but an event whose meaning has "cosmic" importance. Its decisive, revolutionary significance is brought out by the eschatological framework in which it is set. In other words, the cross is not just an event of the past which can be contemplated, but is the eschatological event in and beyond time, in so far as it (understood in its significance, that is, for faith) is an ever-present reality.

The cross becomes a present reality first of all in the sacraments. In baptism men and women are baptized into Christ's death (Rom. 6. 3) and crucified with him (Rom. 6. 6). At every celebration of the Lord's Supper the death of Christ is proclaimed (1 Cor. 11. 26). The communicants thereby partake of his crucified body and his blood outpoured (1 Cor. 10. 16). Again, the cross of Christ is an ever-present reality in the everyday life of the Christians. "They that are of Christ Jesus have crucified the flesh with the passions and the lusts thereof" (Gal. 5. 24). That is why St Paul can speak of "the cross of our Lord Jesus Christ, through which the world hath been crucified unto me, and I unto the world" (Gal. 6. 14). That is why he seeks to know "the fellowship of his sufferings", as one who is "conformed to his death" (Phil. 3. 10).

The crucifying of the affections and lusts includes the overcoming of our natural dread of suffering and the perfection of our detachment from the world. Hence the willing acceptance of sufferings in which death is already at work in man means: "always bearing about in our body the dying of Jesus" and "always being delivered unto death for Jesus' sake" (2 Cor. 4. 10f.).

Thus the cross and passion are ever-present realities. How little they are confined to the events of the first Good Friday is amply illustrated by the words which a disciple of St Paul puts into his master's mouth: "Now I rejoice in my sufferings for your sake, and fill up on my part that which is lacking of the afflictions of Christ in my flesh for his body's sake, which is the Church" (Col. 1. 24).

In its redemptive aspect the cross of Christ is no mere mythical event, but a historic (*geschichtlich*) fact originating in the historical (*historisch*) event which is the crucifixion of Jesus. The abiding significance of the cross is that it is the judgement of the world, the judgement and the deliverance of man. So far as this is so, Christ is crucified "for us", not in the sense of any theory of sacrifice or satisfaction. This interpretation of the cross as a permanent fact rather than a mythological event does far more justice to the redemptive significance of the event of the past than any of the traditional interpretations. In the last resort mythological language is only a medium for conveying the significance of the historical (*historisch*) event. The historical (*historisch*) event of the cross has, in the significance peculiar to it, created a new historic (*geschichtlich*) situation. The preaching of the cross as the event of redemption challenges all who hear it to appropriate this significance for themselves, to be willing to be crucified with Christ.

But, it will be asked, is this significance to be discerned in the actual event of past history? Can it, so to speak, be read off from that event? Or does the cross bear this significance because it is the cross of *Christ*? In other words, must we first be convinced of the significance of Christ and believe in him in order to discern the real meaning of the cross? If we are to perceive the real meaning of the cross, must we understand it as the cross of Jesus as a figure of past history? Must we go back to the Jesus of history?

As far as the first preachers of the gospel are concerned this will certainly be the case. For them the cross was the cross of him with whom they had lived in personal intercourse. The cross was an experience of their own lives. It presented them with a question and it disclosed to them its meaning. But for us this personal connection cannot be reproduced. For us the cross cannot disclose its own meaning: it is an event of the past. We can never recover it as an event in our own lives. All we know of it is derived from historical report. But the New Testament does not proclaim Jesus Christ in this way. The meaning of the cross is not disclosed from the life of Jesus as a figure of past history, a life which needs to be reproduced by historical research. On the contrary, Jesus is not proclaimed merely as the crucified; he is also risen from the dead. The cross and the resurrection form an inseparable unity.

(c) *The Resurrection*

But what of the resurrection? Is it not a mythical event pure and simple? Obviously it is not an event of past history with a self-evident meaning. Can the resurrection narratives and every other mention of the resurrection in the New Testament be understood simply as an attempt to convey the meaning of the cross? Does the New Testament, in asserting that Jesus is risen from the dead, mean that his death is not just an ordinary human death, but the judgement and salvation of the world, depriving death of its power? Does it not express this truth in the affirmation that the Crucified was not holden of death, but rose from the dead?

Yes indeed: the cross and the resurrection form a single, indivisible cosmic event. "He was delivered up for our trespasses, and was raised for our justification" (Rom. 4. 25). The cross is not an isolated event, as though it were the end of Jesus, which needed the resurrection subsequently to reverse it.

When he suffered death, Jesus was already the Son of God, and his death by itself was the victory over the power of death. St John brings this out most clearly by describing the passion of Jesus as the "hour" in which he is glorified, and by the double meaning he gives to the phrase "lifted up", applying it both to the cross and to Christ's exaltation into glory.

Cross and resurrection form a single, indivisible cosmic event which brings judgement to the world and opens up for men the possibility of authentic life. But if that be so, the resurrection cannot be a miraculous proof capable of demonstration and sufficient to convince the sceptic that the cross really has the cosmic and eschatological significance ascribed to it.

Yet it cannot be denied that the resurrection of Jesus is often used in the New Testament as a miraculous proof. Take for instance Acts 17. 31. Here we are actually told that God substantiated the claims of Christ by raising him from the dead. Then again the resurrection narratives: both the legend of the empty tomb and the appearances insist on the physical reality of the risen body of the Lord (see especially Luke 24. 39–43). But these are most certainly later embellishments of the primitive tradition. St Paul knows nothing about them. There is however one passage where St Paul tries to prove the miracle of the resurrection by adducing a list of eye-witnesses (1 Cor. 15. 3–8). But this is a dangerous procedure, as Karl Barth has involuntarily shown. Barth seeks to explain away the real meaning of 1 Cor. 15 by contending that the list of eye-witnesses was put in not to prove the fact of the resurrection, but to prove that the preaching of the apostle was, like the preaching of the first Christians, the preaching of Jesus as the risen Lord. The eye-witnesses therefore guarantee St Paul's preaching, not the fact of the resurrection. An historical fact which involves a resurrection from the dead is utterly inconceivable!

Yes indeed: the resurrection of Jesus cannot be a miraculous proof by which the sceptic might be compelled to believe in Christ. The difficulty is not simply the incredibility of a mythical event like the resuscitation of a dead person—for that is what the resurrection means, as is shown by the fact that the risen Lord is apprehended by the physical senses. Nor is it merely the impossibility of establishing the objective historicity of the resurrection no matter how many witnesses are cited, as though once it was established it might be believed beyond all question and faith might have its unimpeachable guarantee. No; the real difficulty is that the resurrection is itself an article of faith, and you cannot establish one article of faith by invoking another. You cannot prove the redemptive efficacy of the cross by invoking the resurrection. For the resurrection is an article of faith because it is far more than the resuscitation of a corpse—it is the eschatological event. And so it cannot be a miraculous proof. For, quite apart from its credibility, the bare miracle tells us nothing about the eschatological fact of the destruction of death. Moreover, such a miracle is not otherwise unknown to mythology.

It is however abundantly clear that the New Testament is interested in the resurrection of Christ simply and solely because it is the eschatological event *par excellence*. By it Christ abolished death and brought life and immortality to light (2 Tim. 1. 10). This explains why St Paul borrows Gnostic language to clarify the meaning of the resurrection. As in the death of Jesus all have died (2 Cor. 5. 14f.), so through his resurrection all have been raised from the dead, though naturally this event is spread over a long period of time (1 Cor. 15. 21f.). But St Paul does not only ·say: "In Christ shall all be made alive"; he can also speak of rising again with Christ in the present tense, just as he speaks of our dying with him. Through the sacrament of baptism Christians participate not only in the death of Christ but also in his resurrection. It is not simply that we *shall* walk with him in newness of life and be united with him in his resurrection (Rom. 6. 4f.); we are doing so already here and now. "Even so reckon ye yourselves to be dead indeed unto sin, but alive unto God in Jesus Christ" (Rom. 6. 11).

Once again, in everyday life the Christians participate not only in the death of Christ but also in his resurrection. In this resurrection-life they enjoy a freedom, albeit a struggling freedom, from sin (Rom. 6. 11ff.). They are able to "cast off the works of darkness", so that the approaching day when the darkness shall vanish is already experienced here and now. "Let us walk honestly as in the day" (Rom. 13. 12f.): "we are not of the night, nor of the darkness. . . . Let us, since we are of the day, be sober . . ." (1 Thess. 5. 5–8). St Paul seeks to share not only the sufferings of Christ but also "the power of his resurrection"

(Phil. 3. 10). So he bears about in his body the dying of Jesus, "that the life also of Jesus may be manifested in our body" (2 Cor. 4. 10f.). Similarly, when the Corinthians demand a proof of his apostolic authority, he solemnly warns them: "Christ is not weak, but is powerful in you: for he was crucified in weakness, yet he liveth in the power of God. For we also are weak in him, but we shall live with him through the power of God toward you" (2 Cor. 13. 3f.).

In this way the resurrection is not a mythological event adduced in order to prove the saving efficacy of the cross, but an article of faith just as much as the meaning of the cross itself. Indeed, *faith in the resurrection is really the same thing as faith in the saving efficacy of the cross*, faith in the cross as the cross of Christ. Hence you cannot first believe in Christ and then in the strength of that faith believe in the cross. To believe in Christ means to believe in the cross as the cross of Christ. The saving efficacy of the cross is not derived from the fact that it is the cross of Christ: it is the cross of Christ because it has this saving efficacy. Without that efficacy it is the tragic end of a great man.

We are back again at the old question. How do we come to believe in the cross as the cross of Christ and as the eschatological event *par excellence?* How do we come to believe in the saving efficacy of the cross?

There is only one answer. This is the way in which the cross is proclaimed. It is always proclaimed together with the resurrection. Christ meets us in the preaching as one crucified and risen. He meets us in the word of preaching and nowhere else. The faith of Easter is just this—faith in the word of preaching.

It would be wrong at this point to raise again the problem of how this preaching arose historically, as though that could vindicate its truth. That would be to tie our faith in the word of God to the results of historical research. The word of preaching confronts us as the word of God. It is not for us to question its credentials. It is we who are questioned, we who are asked whether we will believe the word or reject it. But in answering this question, in accepting the word of preaching as the word of God and the death and resurrection of Christ as the eschatological event, we are given an opportunity of understanding ourselves. Faith and unbelief are never blind, arbitrary decisions. They offer us the alternative between accepting or rejecting that which alone can illuminate our understanding of our-selves.

The real Easter faith is faith in the word of preaching which brings illumination. If the event of Easter Day is in any sense an historical event additional to the event of the cross, it is nothing else than the rise of faith in the risen Lord, since it was this faith which led to the apostolic preaching. The resurrection itself is not an event of past history. All that historical criticism can establish is the fact that the first disciples came to believe in the resurrection.. The historian can perhaps to some extent account for that faith from the personal intimacy which the disciples had enjoyed with Jesus during his earthly life, and so reduce the resurrection appearances to a series of subjective visions. But the historical problem is not of interest to Christian belief in the resurrection. For the historical event of the rise of the Easter faith means for us what it meant for the first disciples—namely, the self-attestation of the risen Lord, the act of God in which the redemptive event of the cross is completed.[1] completed.[1]

We cannot buttress our own faith in the resurrection by that of the first disciples and so eliminate the element of risk which faith in the resurrection always involves. For the first disciples' faith in the resurrection is itself part and parcel of the eschato-logical event which is the article of faith.

In other words, the apostolic preaching which originated in the event of Easter Day is itself a part of the eschatological event of redemption. The death of Christ, which is both the judgement and the salvation of the world, inaugurates the "ministry of reconciliation" or "word of reconciliation" (2 Cor. 5. 18f.). This word supplements the cross and makes its saving efficacy intelligible by demanding faith and confronting men with the question whether they are willing to understand themselves as men who are crucified and risen with Christ. Through the word of preaching the cross and the resurrection are made present: the eschatological "now" is here, and the promise of Isa. 49. 8

---

[1] This and the following paragraphs are also intended as an answer to the doubts and suspicions which Paul Althaus has raised against me in *Die Wahrheit des kirchlichen Osterglaubens*, 1941, p. 90ff. Cp. also my discussion of Emanuel Hirsch's "Die Auferstehungsgeschichten und der christliche Glaube", 1940, in *Theol. Lit.-Ztg.*, 1940, pp. 242–6.

is fulfilled: "Behold, now is the acceptable time; behold, now is the day of salvation" (2 Cor. 6. 2). That is why the apostolic preaching brings judgement. For some the apostle is "a savour from death unto death" and for others a "savour from life unto life" (2 Cor. 2. 16). St Paul is the agent through whom the resurrection life becomes effective in the faithful (2 Cor. 4. 12). The promise of Jesus in the Fourth Gospel is eminently applicable to the preaching in which he is proclaimed: "Verily I say unto you, He that heareth my words and believeth on him that sent me, hath eternal life, and cometh not unto judgement, but hath passed out of death into life. . . . The hour cometh and now is, when the dead shall hear the voice of the Son of God; and they that hear shall live" (John 5. 24f.). In the word of preaching and there alone we meet the risen Lord. "So belief cometh of hearing, and hearing by the word of Christ" (Rom. 10. 17).

Like the word itself and the apostle who proclaims it, so the Church where the preaching of the word is continued and where the believers or "saints" (i.e., those who have been transferred to eschatological existence) are gathered is part of the eschatological event. The word "Church" (ἐκκλησία) is an eschatological term, while its designation as the Body of Christ emphasizes its cosmic significance. For the Church is not just a phenomenon of secular history, it is phenomenon of significant history, in the sense that it realizes itself in history.

Conclusion

We have now outlined a programme for the demythologizing of the New Testament. Are there still any surviving traces of mythology? There certainly are for those who regard all language about an act of God or of a decisive, eschatological event as mythological. But this is not mythology in the traditional sense, not the kind of mythology which has become antiquated with the decay of the mythical world view. For the redemption of which we have spoken is not a miraculous supernatural event, but an historical event wrought out in time and space. We are convinced that this restatement does better justice to the real meaning of the New Testament and to the paradox of the kerygma. For the kerygma maintains that the eschatological emissary of God is a concrete figure of a particular historical past, that his eschatological activity was wrought out in a human fate, and that therefore it is an event whose eschatological character does not admit of a secular proof. Here we have the paradox of Phil. 2. 7: "He emptied himself"; of 2 Cor. 8. 9: ". . . though he was rich, yet for your sakes he became poor"; of Rom. 8. 3: "God, sending his Son in the likeness of sinful flesh"; of 1 Tim. 3. 16: "He was manifested in the flesh"; and above all of the classic formula of John 1. 14: "The Word became flesh."

The agent of God's presence and activity, the mediator of his reconciliation of the world unto himself, is a real figure of history. Similarly the word of God is not some mysterious oracle, but a sober, factual account of a human life, of Jesus of Nazareth, possessing saving efficacy for man. Of course the kerygma may be regarded as part of the story of man's spiritual evolution and used as a basis for a tenable *Weltanschauung*. Yet this proclamation claims to be the eschatological word of God.

The apostles who proclaim the word may be regarded merely as figures of past history, and the Church as a sociological and historical phenomenon, part of the history of man's spiritual evolution. Yet both are eschatological phenomena and eschatological events.

All these assertions are an offence (σκάνδαλον), which will not be removed by philosophical discussion, but only by faith and obedience. All these are phenomena subject to historical, sociological and psychological observation, yet for faith they are all of them eschatological phenomena. It is precisely its immunity from proof which secures the Christian proclamation against the charge of being mythological. The transcendence of God is not as in myth reduced to immanence. Instead, we have the paradox of a transcendent God present and active in history: "The Word became flesh"

Judaism and the Modern Political Myths

ERNST CASSIRER

IN ORDER to understand the campaign against Judaism launched by the leaders of the new Germany it is not enough to consider the reasons usually given. In the beginning the National-Socialist propaganda often asserted that its only aim was to break the influence of the Jews in Germany's political and cultural life. But why did this propaganda persist and why did it assume a more and more violent character after this end was attained—in a period when no Jew could any longer speak or even breathe or live in Germany? For all this we must seek a deeper reason. In this struggle there is something more than meets the eye. To be sure, personal aversions and antipathies, deeply rooted prejudices, had their share in this campaign; but they cannot account for its specific character, its brutality and ferocity. We must try to understand the phenomenon not only from its emotional but also from its intellectual side.

However we may object to the German political system, we cannot say that it ever underrated the power of "ideas" in political and social life. From the beginning the National-Socialist leaders were convinced that the victory could not be gained by mere material weapons. They knew very well that their *ideology* was the strongest and, at the same time, the most vulnerable point in their whole political system. To deny or even to doubt this ideology was to them a mortal sin. It became a *crimen laesae majestatis*—a crime of high treason against the omnipotent and infallible totalitarian state. That the Jews were guilty of this crime was obvious. They had proved it by their whole history, by their tradition, by their cultural and religious life. In the history of mankind they had been the first to deny and to challenge those very conceptions upon which the new state was built; for it was Judaism which first made the decisive step that led from a *mythical* to an *ethical* religion.

That myth is a necessary factor, a fundamental element in man's cultural life, is undeniable. It has put its stamp upon the development

73

of language, art, poetry, religion. But in all our theories of myth we used to think and to speak of it as a "primitive" activity. We looked upon it as a wild and exuberant stream springing from an unknown depth. In modern politics this stream was embanked and canalized. Myth was no longer a free and spontaneous play of imagination. It was regulated and organized; it was adjusted to political needs and used for concrete political ends. What formerly appeared to be an ungovernable unconscious process was subjected to a severe discipline. It was brought under control and trained to obedience and order. Myths were brought into being by the word of command of the political leaders. They could be made at will, becoming an artificial compound manufactured in the great laboratory of politics. The twentieth century is a technical century. It invented a new technique of myth and this invention proved to be decisive in the final victory of the National-Socialist party in Germany.

This victory was made possible because the adversaries of National Socialism never were able to understand the character and the full strength of the new weapon. In the political struggle it is always of vital importance to *know* one's adversary, to enter into his ways of acting and thinking, to understand his strength and his weakness. But the intellectual and political leaders of Weimar Germany were not prepared for this task. The political leaders were not only socialists; they were in most cases determined Marxists. They were convinced that all social and political life exclusively depends upon economic conditions. Approaching the problem from this side, they made desperate efforts to improve the economic situation of the masses and to ward off the dangers of inflation and unemployment. But in their sober, empirical, "matter of fact" way of thinking and judging they had no eyes for the explosive force of the political myths.

It is true, of course, that there was always in Germany a group of honest intellectuals and scientific men who had a strong aversion for the political ideals and slogans of National Socialism. But they too did not see the real danger; they could hardly be prevailed upon to take this danger seriously. They knew quite well that myth is a complicated and very interesting historical phenomenon, but they never thought of it as an actual power—as a power of political action. According to them myth was "primitive" thought—a mode of thought that long ago had faded away and lost its force and meaning. That was a great mistake, a capital error. When the political and intellectual leaders

74

of the German democracy began to see what was really at stake, when they began to form a clearer idea of the character of the new political myths, it was too late; the battle was in a sense decided before it had begun.

ONE of the first uses made by the new political mythology was to combat Judaism. That is by no means surprising; for Judaism had from its very beginnings attacked and rejected all those mythical elements which had hitherto pervaded and governed religious thought. The classical expression of this rejection is to be found in the words: "Thou shalt not make unto thee a graven image, nor any manner of likeness of anything that is in heaven above, or that is in the earth beneath, or that is in the water under the earth; thou shalt not bow down unto them, nor serve them." Here we have the complete break with mythical thought. For imagery is the very core of mythical thought. To deprive myth of imagery is to insure its decay.

But is not this death-blow at myth at the same time the death-blow at religion? Can religion survive myth? To answer this question it was necessary to discover a new source of religious life and religious inspiration. Ethical thought had to take precedence of mythical thought. Nobody has ever charged the Bible—the Pentateuch, the Prophetic books, the Psalms—with a lack of imagination. Herder, who in this matter was one of the best and most competent judges, who was also one of the first to feel and to analyze the specific character of great national poetry, has written a distinctive work describing and extolling *The Spirit of Hebrew Poetry* (1782-83). But in Judaism the spirit of religion is not the same as that of poetry. Just as Plato excludes poetry from his ideal state, so the Jewish prophets challenge all forms of mythical or poetical imagination. They are the first to conceive the ideal of a purely ethical religion. Poetry and myth are anthropomorphic in their very essence. But through anthropomorphism we can never find the true nature of God. Anthropomorphism leads to idolatry, not to religion. Again and again the prophets come back to this fundamental difference. Their deepest feelings and their whole religious pathos are concentrated upon and focused on this point. The nature of God is far beyond all natural and all human things; it admits of no image, no simile or likeness. All metaphorical expressions of God's essence are to be rejected. "Who hath directed the Spirit of the Lord?" asks Isaiah. "Behold the nations are as a drop of a bucket, and are counted as the small dust of the balance. . . . All nations before him are as nothing and they are counted to him less than nothing, and vanity. To whom then will ye liken God? or what likeness will ye compare unto him? The workman melteth a graven image, and the goldsmith spreadeth it over with gold, and casteth silver chains. . . . To whom then will ye liken me, or shall I be equal?" (Isaiah 40: 13 ff.). That is the end not only of anthropomorphism, but also of nationalism. The deification of nations is the same idolatry as that of natural things. All the goodliness of these things is as the flower of the field. "The grass withereth, the flower fadeth: because the spirit of the Lord bloweth upon it: surely the people is grass. The grass withereth, the flower fadeth: but the word of our God shall stand forever" (Isaiah 40: 6ff.).

THERE are, however, still other and stronger mythical elements that had to be routed out—that had to give way to the new religious ideal. Not the "ideas" or "images" are the essential elements in mythical thought. We fail to understand the full strength and significance of this thought as long as we see in myth—according to its Greek name and the etymology of the term—a mere "narrative," a recital of the memorable deeds of gods or heroes. This *epic* aspect is neither the only one nor the decisive one. Myth has a dramatic character; it expresses itself much more in actions than in mere ideas or representations.

In order to grasp its meaning we must approach it from its active side. Among all students of myth and mythology it is a generally admitted methodological maxim, that in order to understand myth we must begin with a study of *rites*. Rite is prior to myth; myth is only an interpretation of rites. "What a people *does* in relation to its gods" —says Miss Jane E. Harrison in a very interesting study on early Greek religion—"must always be one clue, and perhaps the safest, to what it thinks."* "Myth as it exists in a savage community, that is, in its living primitive form," declares B. Malinowski, "is not merely a story told but a reality lived. . . . It is not an intellectual explanation or an artistic imagery but a pragmatic charter of primitive faith and moral wisdom."** In this "pragmatic charter" the performance of certain actions, the obedience to a strict religious ritual, always plays the leading part. Even Judaism could not evade or infringe this general law

* Jane Ellen Harrison, *Prologemena to the Study of Greek Religion*, Cambridge, 1903.
** B. Malinowski, *Myth in Primitive Psychology*, London, 1926, p. 21.

of religious evolution. It is filled with all sorts of positive and negative demands; with ritual precepts and ritual taboos.

But this was only the first and preliminary step. Even here the prophets had the intellectual and moral courage to break through the fixed, traditional and inexorable order of rites and ceremonies. All this is not simply abrogated but it is eclipsed by new and higher ethical standards. In all primitive societies we find those rites that we describe as rites of "lustration." Men expiate a sin or a crime by certain purifying acts. This purification is understood in a merely physical sense. The Indians of Peru sought to purify themselves from their sins by plunging their heads in a river; they said that the river washed their sins away. But even in highly advanced stages of human culture we meet with the same conception. In Greek culture and Greek religious life this view is still prevalent; most of the Greek "kathartic" rites are of the same primitive character. "The sea washes off all the evils of men," says Euripides. This sort of "katharsis" or "purification" has nothing to do with moral standards. "We might be tempted," says Erwin Rohde, "to see in the development of Kathartic practices a fresh step in the history of Greek ethics, and to suppose that the new practices arose out of a refinement and deepening of the 'conscience' which now desired to be free from the taint of 'sin' by the help of religion. But such an interpretation (favorite as it is) is disposed of by a consideration of the real essence and meaning of the thing. In its origin and essence Katharsis had nothing whatever to do with morality or with what we should call the voice of conscience. Kathartic practices required and implied no feeling of offense, of personal guilt, of personal responsibility. The moral aspect of such cases, the guilt or innocence of the doer, is ignored or unperceived. Even in the case of premeditated murder, the remorse of the criminal or his will to amend is quite superfluous to the efficacy of purification."* Prophetic religion was the first to introduce an entirely new view; a purification that had no longer a physical but rather an ethical sense. "Your hands are full of blood," says Isaiah. "Wash you, make you clean; put away the evil of your doings from before mine eyes; cease to do evil; learn to do well; seek judgment, relieve the oppressed, judge the fatherless, plead for the widow" (Isaiah 1: 15 ff.).

The same characteristic change may be studied in the general development of the religious cult. In its beginnings no religion, no form

* E. Rohde, *Psyche*. English translation, New York, 1925, p. 294 f.

of worship, can dispense with sacrificial acts. Prayer and sacrifice are the only ways by which man can communicate with his gods. That is an elementary need and tendency of human nature which can never be completely destroyed. But the *form* of sacrifice and its meaning undergoes a slow and continuous change. In Judaism the first decisive step is the abrogation of human sacrifices. Not man, but God himself makes this step. He refuses to accept the sacrifice of Isaac and substitutes the ram, that is offered in his stead. That means an entirely new and hitherto unknown relation of man to God.

The general history of religion has shown us that the human sacrifice, in its true and original significance, is by no means purely an act of cruelty. It is regarded as the highest religious duty because it expresses, in the most striking and solemn way, the communion between God and man. In his *Lectures on the Religion of the Semites*—a standard-work in the modern history of religion—W. Robertson Smith has shown that in almost all the religions of the world, and especially in all Semitic religions, the relationship of God and man is interpreted as a form of physical kinship. "The indissoluble bond that unites man to his god," he writes, "is the same bond of blood-fellowship which in early society is the one binding link between man and man, and the one sacred principle of moral obligation." The bloody sacrifice of man is meant to confirm and to strengthen this consanguinity between the members of the tribe and their Gods.* Even in this respect the slogan of "Blood and Soil" is by no means a new device. It is only a repetition and, in a sense, a caricature of a primeval mythical conception. The blood-fellowship no longer connects man with God; it connects him with his race that has become the true and only God. Here too the religious and ethical ideals of the prophets were an incessant struggle and a fierce protest against primitive mythical motives. In this struggle not only the bloody sacrifices of men or animals are declared to be null and void. The other and milder forms of the ritual are also called into question and finally swept away. "To what purpose is the multitude of your sacrifices unto me? saith the Lord: I am full of the burnt offerings of rams, and the fat of fed beasts; and I delight not in the blood of bullocks, or of lambs, or of he goats. . . Bring no more vain oblations; incense is an abomination unto me" (Isaiah 1, 11, 13). Here the great process reaches its climax. The merely mythical creeds and purely ritual ceremonies are done away with, and only the funda-

* Cf. Robertson Smith, *op. cit.*, Edinburgh, 1889, Lectures II and V.

mental religious and ethical duties are enunciated by the great prophet.

WE ARE still, however, only in the precinct of prophetic religion. Before the new ethical and religious ideal could assume its definite shape and could have its full effect it was necessary to remove an obstacle that proved insurmountable to primitive thought and primitive social feeling. Even in the most primitive societies we find a very clear and sharp sense of moral obligation. The whole life of man is subject to inviolable rules. Every act is controlled by these social rules; every infringement is severely punished. But what is absent, or, at least, entirely undeveloped in primitive society—what is, so to speak, in an embryonic state—is the concept and ideal of *individual* moral responsibility. What matters are the consequences of an act, not its motives. These consequences are the same quite irrespective of the intention of the offender. The violation of certain taboos always brings on the gravest dangers. And this danger is conceived as a mere physical infection; it is transmissible to others in the same sense as any other physical "uncleanness" or illness; and there is no possible limit of its propagation. In this whole system there is not a shadow of individual responsibility. If a man transgresses a taboo or perpetrates a crime it is not he himself who is "marked off." His family, his friends, his whole tribe bear the same mark. Sometimes the infection attaches to the whole city in which the criminal lives. Even in highly developed cultures, as for instance in Greek culture, these conceptions are still in full sway. Revenge and punishment are also directed at the group as a whole. In the societies in which the blood-feud is regarded as one of the highest social obligations it is not necessary to take vengeance upon the murderer himself. It is enough to kill a member of his family or his tribe, for the entire family or tribe is made liable to retaliation and reprisals.

We need not say to what an extent all these conceptions that we believed to belong exclusively to the past have become a terrible reality in modern politics. Nothing is so characteristic of the German political system as the denial and complete destruction of the idea of individual responsibility. If there is any "moral" subject—the community, the nation, the race are held answerable for its actions. The acts are good or evil according as they are done by a super-race or by an inferior race.

From the beginning such a conception was impossible and inadmissible in Jewish religion. Time and again the Jewish God has

79

been charged with being a "national" God. But from its first and elementary stages Judaism conceived an ideal of monotheism that was quite incompatible with a narrow nationalism. It is true that in the development of Jewish religion the conception of individual moral responsibility was not reached all at once. It had to be prepared for slowly, for it was in strict opposition' to all the traditional social and religious conceptions.

The idea of collective guilt and collective responsibility is deeply rooted in the human mind. It has put its stamp upon the whole development of human culture. The great Greek tragedians—Aeschylus, Sophocles, Euripides—had to struggle against this idea and to remold it into a new shape. In early Judaism the same idea of a curse or punishment that is not restricted to an individual but extends to posterity is expressed in the saying that the God of Israel is a jealous God, visiting the iniquity of the fathers upon the children, and upon the third and fourth generations of them that hate Him, but showing mercy unto the thousandth generation of them that love Him and keep His commandments.

But now this rule which seemed to be fundamental and inviolable had to be overthrown in the new prophetic religion. In this respect, more than in any other, the prophets had to create a new moral and a new religious order. "For, behold," says Isaiah, "I create new heavens and a new earth: and the former shall not be remembered, nor come into mind" (Isaiah 65: 17). For this new world we are in need of a new spirit—and it is this spirit that is the very core of the prophetic vision and the prophetic promise. This new spirit no longer allows the punishment of a transgression or crime that has not been committed by the individual himself. The individual—not the family, the tribe or community—becomes the only "moral subject." "In those days they shall say no more, the fathers have eaten a sour grape, and the children's teeth are set on edge. But every one shall die for his own iniquity: every man that eateth the sour grape, his teeth shall be set on edge. Behold, the days come, saith the Lord, that I will make a new covenant with the house of Israel, and with the house of Judah: Not according to the covenant that I made with their fathers . . . But this shall be the covenant . . . I will put my law in their inward parts, and write it in their hearts" (Jeremiah 31: 29 ff.).

If we accept this pure interior religion all the former restrictions are swept away. Even the strongest social bonds lose in a sense their binding force. It is no longer blood-relationship or nationality that determines the moral will. A higher and independent ideal arises. "Behold, all souls are mine; as the soul of the father, so also the soul of the son is mine: the soul that sinneth, it shall die. But if a man be just, and do that which is lawful and right . . . he shall surely live, saith the Lord God . . . The son shall not bear the iniquity of the father, neither shall the father bear the iniquity of the son; the righteousness of the righteous shall be upon him, and the wickedness of the wicked shall be upon him" (Ezekiel 18: 4, 5, 9, 20).

YET once arrived at this point we meet with a new and great surprise. The climax of religious thought reached in the individualism of the prophets is followed by a sort of anti-climax. To individualism there is opposed another force which at first sight seems to be its very reverse. Religious thought and feeling is suddenly taking a new turn; it changes from individualism to *universalism*. Nevertheless there is no real contradiction between these two views. Far from excluding each other they complement and confirm one another; they are two different expressions of one and the same ideal. If the bond that unites man and God is no longer conceived as a physical bond, a bond of consanguinity; if religious duty does no longer consist in the performance of specific rites—it becomes clear that the new approach, the approach by man's ethical life, is open to everyone. Religion is no longer the privilege of a social class, a class of priests, nor is it the privilege of a single nation. It breaks with all traditional restrictions.

In this new prophetic religion Judaism has still to fulfill a special task; but its call is a universal one, it is not confined within the limits of the life of a single nation. "I the Lord have called thee in righteousness, and will hold thine hand, and will keep thee, and give thee for a covenant of the people, for a light of the Gentiles; To open the blind eyes, to bring out the prisoners from the prison . . ." (Isaiah 42, 6 ff.). When the remnant of Israel that has been saved will return to Jerusalem and rebuild the temple, the worship in this temple will no longer be a national worship. "At that time they shall call Jerusalem the throne of the Lord; and all the nations shall be gathered unto it, to the name of the Lord . . ." (Jeremiah 3: 17).

From this universalism there arises the ideal of perpetual peace. In its origin that is a purely religious, not a philosophical, ideal. The great philosophers of antiquity never conceived the idea of perpetual peace. It took more than two thousand years before this idea was defended and interpreted by a great philosophical thinker. At the end of the eighteenth century Kant wrote his treatise: *Vom ewigen Frieden.* Greek philosophy had eternalized war instead of peace. "War," declared Heraclitus, one of the deepest Greek thinkers, "is the father and the king of all; and some he has made gods and some men, some bondsmen and some free." War is not only a human thing; it is a divine thing, and, therefore, inevitable, inexorable, eternal.

The prophets reject this view—not because of philosophical reasons or ethical reflections but by virtue of the specific character of their religious inspiration. They are the first to envisage and describe a future state of mankind in which the nations shall beat their swords into plowshares, and their spears into pruning hooks.

That is, indeed, an "impossible" ideal; a mere "utopia." But the prophets did not fear to proclaim this utopia. "To live in the idea," says Goethe, "means to treat the impossible as if it were possible." This saying gives us the clue to the true character of prophetic religion. It was "utopian"; it was in opposition to all actual empirical facts. But it contained a great ethical and religious promise—the promise of "a new heaven and a new earth."

If we compare this conception of man's ethical, social and religious life to the "myth of the twentieth century" we feel at once the fundamental and striking difference. The prophets are inspired by the ardent wish for a perpetual peace; our modern myths tend to the perpetuation and intensification of war. The prophets dissolve the physical bond between God and man: the bond of blood-relationship. The modern myths, on the other hand, acknowledge no other duty than that which arises from the community of blood. The German leaders promised to the German people the conquest of the whole world. What the prophets promised was not the glory of the Jewish nation but its decline and fall, its deepest misery. The political myths enthrone and deify a super-race; the prophets predict an age in which all the nations shall be united under the worship of one God. There is no point of contact and no possible reconciliation between these two conceptions.

In ALL mythologies we meet with the concept of the "scapegoat." In his great compendium of mythical thought, *The Golden Bough,* I. G. Frazer has devoted a special volume to this subject. He gives us the full evidence by tracing the conception of the scapegoat through all ages and all cultures. We find this conception in primitive African and American tribes as well as in Greek culture; we find it in India and China, in Australia and Japan, in Christian Europe. It is to be found even in early Judaism. In Leviticus there is the description of the Jewish high priest, on the Day of Atonement, laying both his hands on the head of a live goat, confessing over it all the iniquities of the Children of Israel, and, having transferred the sins of the people to the beast, sending it away into the wilderness.

In their new political mythology the leaders of Germany chose the Jew as the scapegoat, upon whom the burden of all sins and all evils could be laid. We may think that in this decision they were instigated by a blind and fanatic hatred. Or we may assume that they simply followed the line of least resistance: they decided to attack a small minority unable to offer serious resistance. All this may be true—but it is only the half of the truth. What the inventors of the myth of the German super-race feared was not the physical but the moral resistance of the Jews. And they felt by no means sure that this resistance could be broken. After the expulsion and assassination of hundreds of thousands of Jews, they were not yet satisfied with their work. They were still haunted by the same fixed idea of the Jew as the evil spirit, the Devil incarnate. Mythical thought always conceives of the world as a struggle between divine and demonic powers, between light and darkness. There is always a negative and a positive pole in mythical imagination. Even in our modern political myths the process of deification had to be completed by a corresponding process, that we may describe as "devilization."

In the German pandemonium this role was assigned to the Jew. For if there was any truth in Jewish religion, in the books of the prophets, the whole myth of the twentieth century became meaningless and powerless. In spite of all its display of military power, in spite of its incomparable technique of organization and warfare, the German colossus remained, after all, a colossus with feet of clay. As soon as it was possible to doubt or to destroy its mythical foundation, its collapse was inevitable. To secure this foundation was of vital importance; and for this purpose the war against the Jews was imperative. To speak here of mere "anti-Semitism" seems to me to be a very inadequate expression of the problem. Anti-Semitism is not a new phenomenon; it had existed at all times and under all forms. But the German form

83

of persecution was something entirely new. Anti-Semitism could have led to social discrimination or to legal and political restrictions, to exceptional laws. But much more was intended here. It was a mortal combat—a life and death struggle which could only find its end in the complete extermination of the Jews.

When reading Hitler's last address marking the 11th anniversary of his National-Socialist regime, we meet with a strange phenomenon. Hitler has completely changed his tone. He is no longer promising the conquest of the world to the German race. He begins to see his defeat and he feels its consequences. But what does he say at this critical moment? Does he speak of the innumerable evils which his aggression has brought to the German people, to Europe, to the whole world? Does he think of the defeat of his armies, of the destruction of German cities? Nothing of the kind. His whole attention is still fixed on one point. He is obsessed and hypnotized by *one* thing alone. He speaks of—the Jews. If I am defeated—he says—Jewry could celebrate a second triumphant Purim festival. What worries him is not the future destiny of Germany, but the "triumph" of the Jews.

By this utterance he proves once more how little he knows of Jewish life and Jewish feeling. In our life, in the life of a modern Jew, there is no room left for any sort of joy or complacency, let alone of exultation or triumph. All this has gone forever. No Jew whatsoever can and will ever overcome the terrible ordeal of these last years. The victims of this ordeal cannot be forgotten; the wounds inflicted upon us are incurable. Yet amidst all these horrors and miseries there is, at least, one relief. We may be firmly convinced that all these sacrifices have not been made in vain. What the modern Jew had to defend in this combat was not only his physical existence or the preservation of the Jewish race. Much more was at stake. We had to represent all those ethical ideals that had been brought into being by Judaism and found their way into general human culture, into the life of all civilized nations. And here we stand on firm ground. These ideals are not destroyed and cannot be destroyed. They have stood their ground in these critical days. If Judaism has contributed to break the power of the modern political myths, it has done its duty, having once more fulfilled its historical and religious mission.

Eric Dardel

THE MYTHIC

According to the Ethnological Work of Maurice Leenhardt

We have learned by now not to see myth as simple entertainment or a
babbling. Where the nineteenth-century eye could find only an out-of-
date toy left behind by childish peoples or a cultural stage-set for leisured
social circles, the human sciences have taught us to recognise an authentic
expression of man: myth says with utmost seriousness something that is of
essential importance. What is more, it is a way of living in the world, of
orienting oneself in the midst of things, of seeking an answer in the quest
for the self. We owe this alteration of perspective to a whole group of
scholars: Cassirer, Van der Leeuw, Unger, Preuss; we owe it in a quite
special way to Maurice Leenhardt and to the original work which his
recent death left uncompleted.[1]

---

[1] In the course of a long missionary career in New Caledonia, serving the Paris Society of
Evangelical Missions (1902–26), Maurice Leenhardt became interested in the sciences of
man, sociology and ethnology. Entrusted with a scientific mission by the National Ministry
of Education, he made a research trip to Black Africa, followed, some years later, by a
scientific inquiry in Oceania, at Nouméa (1947). Called to take Marcel Mauss' place at the
École des Hautes Études, he was named to his chair in 1940. After a course in Oceanian
languages was set up at the École des Langues Orientales, he was called to ensure its instruction (1945). Death (on January 26 last) prevented him from putting a final touch, as he was
trying to do, to his scientific work, from making precise some points that seemed to him
insufficiently clear and from dispelling some misunderstandings to which studies of this type
lend themselves. Nevertheless his scholarly work as it stands is important and original.
Scattered through several journals (*Revue philosophique, Revue de Metaphysique et de Morale,
Revue d'Histoire et Philosophie réligieuses, Anthropologie,* etc.) it is especially well-represented
by some scientific publications of the Institute of Ethnology: *Notes d'Ethnologie néo-
Caledonienne,* 1930, *Documents néo-caledoniens,* 1932, *Vocabulaire et Grammaire de la Langue de
Houailou,* 1935, and by two works, which are more personal in nature, *Do Kamo* and *Arts
d'Océanie.* This body of work, although uncompleted, to which must be added two important articles in *Histoire des Réligions* (Quillet publishers), and *Histoire des Réligions* (Bloud
and Gay publishers, 1953), has contributed to the enrichment and renovation of a whole
wide sector of the science of man. It is one of those works which sustain new pioneers and
open horizons, because there was talent in Maurice Leenhardt for awakening interests and
developing vocations.

33

Like Lévy-Bruhl, to whom he often felt himself so close, Maurice Leenhardt had to make his way through pitfalls dug by the last century and its intellectual habits. When the subject of science is man himself, and when the scholar does not want to sacrifice any of his condition as a man, he must avoid the snares of language; and our language, which is so full of abstractions, begins by concealing what it is trying to show. Coming from another base than did Lévy-Bruhl, Maurice Leenhardt also had to engage in the same ceaseless struggle against language to save the experience of the 'primitive' from distorted transcription into our vocabulary of terms and notions. Man at the mythic stage sees a relation between stone and ancestor which we try to express by means of an identity: we say that for him the ancestor *is* the stone. But our verb 'to be', weakened by centuries of grammar and philosophy, absolutely lacks the living experience of the primitive who senses in the stone a mythic presence, a manifestation of the ancestor's own reality. Terms like identity, participation, consubstantiality are themselves only awkward approximations, dulled by conceptual extensions distorting the truth of the relationship. Myth, like music or poetry, requires us to be transported into the world where it has its being. It is there, for example, that the rock-ancestor identity, which is felt before it is conceived, allows its proper meaning to appear. Understanding of this order is not possible to a Western scholar unless, behind the Logos and its logical and spatial objections, something of the primitive *Mythos* survives in him. Maurice Leenhardt found this access to the mythical, not in books or theories, but in his daily experience as a missionary, hunting for a way to approach the men of Oceania and to communicate with them. That human sympathy, which enabled him to understand the primitive soul from within, gave his scientific work a very individual coloration, perhaps not so compatible with the conception of science cherished in the last century, but surely less foreign to the science of man which our own period seems to be trying to build.

In the opposite direction, Maurice Leenhardt had to protect his ethnological work against the cover-up words and the vague notions that lie in wait for the scholar off the beaten track of the natural sciences. He accordingly avoided, as much as possible, the term 'primitive', which forces on the mind an order of succession, accompanied by an order of evaluation, the 'primitive' usually being taken as anterior or inferior to the things we attribute to 'antique' or 'modern' man. The mentality imputed to the so-called primitives can be rediscovered in the heart of the Western mind;

34

inversely, the rational coexists with the mythic among less-developed peoples, to whom the term 'archaic' peoples is more appropriate.

Anxious to preserve the rights of clear language, Maurice Leenhardt rejected the overly-equivocal word 'mystic'. The Melanesian does not act under the influence of mysterious or determined forces. On the contrary, he has a clear view of the relations between the world and himself; he sees these relations through the myth as through a mirror. The fog or half-light of the mystic scarcely belong in a world where the mythic relation appears as an unveiling of the world, as a truth about being, revealing itself to man. The mythic is not a prelogical, as opposed to a logical, structure of the mind, but rather another reading of the world, a first coherence put upon things and an attitude that is complementary to logical behaviour.

I. Essence of the Mythic

On the evidence of classical mythology and the plastic commentaries on it which we have had from modern painters in search of picturesque or 'poetic' subjects, we have for a long time believed that myths were nothing but stories about gods, descents into Hell, heroic fights. Here, it was thought, was a crop of imaginary tales invented by poets, bare of anything serious or true, which our Western logic ought to look down upon as mere amusement or child's play.

But the work of ethnologists and sociologists, together with studies in 'depth psychology', have obliged us for a half-century now to revise this excessively simplified notion. They show us that myths are a language affected with seriousness, often with warmth or tenderness, corresponding to a certain picture of the world, which is perfectly valid although it obeys wholly different mental requirements than does the conduct of reason and of history. Lévy-Bruhl, in his *Primitive Mythology*, recalled the interest we moderns still take in mythic accounts, which often come down to us in the form of fairy-tales and legends, although we may have ceased to 'believe' in them. He attributed this interest to the sense of relaxed ease we feel when we plunge into this fairy-tale atmosphere where the connexions and tensions of logical relationships fade from our awareness. But the attraction exercised over us in this way by the mythical does not reduce itself to a simple mental recreation: it has deeper, positive reasons. Under the legend and the fairy-tale, there is the mythic, and the mythic includes an experience, a reaction to reality. When the 'primitive' recognises an ancestor looking at him out of the shark's or the lizard's eye, he is certainly

35

making a reference to reality, but he interprets it mythically; he expresses by this connexion, which for us lacks foundation, the impression he feels, his affective reaction to 'things'. The myth is neither 'true' nor 'false'; it is born, beyond our logic's horizon, in that 'pang' which comes upon man in the midst of things. In the myth and by means of the mythic image, there is an externalisation of the inner stirring, the emotion of man as he meets the world, his receptivity to impulses coming from 'outside', the communality of substance which welds him to the totality of beings.

If the mythic is the language of a man who feels himself thoroughly at one with the world, part of the world, form amid the forms of the universe, it is also the first rupture in his being, the first flight above, which makes the real unreal, and detaches man from his environment, and so a source of all poetry and all culture. It is not impermeable to logic, as we shall see below. But rationality is not a first-level concern for archaic thought: it occupies only a secondary place, the essential thing being to place oneself in the current of the whole world's life. As rationality assumes greater importance, the interpretation which man gives to the world may be seen to pass through three successive stages: a *mythic* stage, to which we shall confine ourselves here, an *epic* stage, and an *historic* stage. The *mythic* stage changes into the *epic* outlook when man bases his conduct and his universe on the repetition of the *model* man, on the cult of the hero: the hero being an archetype after whose qualities and gestures those of his successors are drawn, and in whom human destiny is discovered. Men, drawing back before the audacity of being themselves, have asked for a justification of their existence from the hero. Hercules, Theseus, or Hector are 'supermen', who lend authority, by their exemplary value, to the ordinary careers of simple mortals; they are the heirs of virtues and actions which transmit greatness to the daily round of commonplace life. A feeling of being strengthened with this superhuman power was necessary in order to face history . . . As Ernst Junger has commented, the epic, 'dedicated to the spirit of the tombs', made 'the introduction to history' out of this pilgrimage to the hero's graves. The historic as such does not fully emerge until men stop turning to this exemplary past, in order to dare to act for themselves, to set themselves human objectives and to adopt human means for their attainment; but above all, when their rational emancipation has set them to seeking a direction in the unfolding of events, in a word, to caring about having a History.

But even in our world, dominated by logical and historical concerns, with our explanations ruled by the principle of causality, we remain

36

sensitive to another colouring of the universe, to that actual and emotional tone which fascinates or disturbs us. The mythic even in myths would remain a closed book to us if it did not awaken some sleeping potentialities within us, an affective and imaginary predisposition always ready to react by way of myths to the world's approaches. It is well to remember once and for all that the mythic, which is closely bound up with the sphere of sentiment and of emotion, shares the universality of the emotional life which renounces reflection, and takes refuge in silence or changes under the impartial eye of the observer. There is in us that vibration of our whole being which shows itself in convictions or in beliefs, in 'verities' which we declare to be true. The romantics' myth of Nature, the myth of progress, the myth that the world is absurd—every period declares 'its' truth in this way and is warmly attached to it. Our 'truth' of the moment is often only a myth that does not know that it is one, and, as M. Jourdain put it, we make myths every day without knowing it. The myth, deep within ourselves, illumines every reality giving it direction and value. The myth is accordingly surely a universal, or fundamental, *phenomenon* which, while keeping profound motives, inexpressible emotions and feelings hidden within the secret of the individual, reveals through surface gestures, forms and words, something of that internality which, without ever growing old, lives on in man's heart century after century.

1. *The Mythic is not in the Past*

'Once upon a time', 'in the beginning', 'then' . . . ; the folk-tale takes us into the past with its first words. The myth leads back to a remote, primordial past: to events, heroes, and gods who pre-exist everything that is. The opposition between the sun and the moon derives, according to the Melanesians, from an act of unfaithfulness. Customs and rites derive from precedents that institute and justify them. The festivals which consummate group life only repeat certain sanctified rituals. It is for the present generation to actualise these precedents or archetypes in order to validate at the same moment their acts of the present time. Nothing ever begins, nothing is ever new on this horizon where the foundation of the established order also indicates, simultaneously, its origin.

An optical illusion is involved here, however, and it has been kept up in us by developed mythologies. The Melanesian myths go in quite another direction. There is nothing further removed from the historian's scrutinising of the past than the 'primitive's' attitude with respect to the

37

mythic happening. The mythic past cannot be dated, it is a past 'before time' or, better, outside of time. 'Long ago', 'one day', 'in the beginning', 'and then', all this customary vocabulary of the mythic, visibly trifles with historic time. Primordial actions are lost 'in the night of time', what happened 'once' (nobody knows when) goes on in a floating and many-layered time without temporal location. Myths of causality or origin-myths nevertheless seem to invoke, like the ancient cosmologies, some fixed periods and moments. But we must be careful in handling these elaborated 'accounts' from a later stage, where an effort at narration and explanation, on the way toward history, is foreshadowed. Maurice Leenhardt asks us to see a degeneration of the mythic in them, a rationalisation, the awakening of a still poorly emancipated historic awareness. The mythic, stripped of its power, of its perenniality, is found in them relegated to 'the beginning'.

The mythic is *present*. First, it is present in the sense that the narrator, in his account, is transported and transports the listener into the time of the happening, 'in the centre', 'down there', 'far away'. He draws the audience of the story away, but only to make them set themselves at the desired distance. The mythic actualises everything it touches: it makes the narrator an actor in his 'story', the listener a witness, the world a present without past or future. The account is made one with what it tells: it is the event itself that is being told, and, in being told, is realised. Even in the fairy-tale, the expression 'once upon a time' does not bring the past as such into the case; it evokes it, in the magical sense of the term, it calls it into being.

The mythic is even more deeply present because the original event, by repetition, is once again 'presently' produced. 'Original' means not so much 'earlier' as 'permanent'. Primordial reality lies close to present reality. Constitutive and fundamental as well as institutive and founding, it is always there, ready to be incarnated. Inversely, it does not exist by itself: to protect its power, it must be reproduced each time. The myth, in its images and narrations, transmits an experience of the perenniality of life, the return of known situations and of affective states sanctified by precedents. The old Canakas, in order to reconstitute the 'Lizard myth', express themselves in the present: they point out the hill where the lizard lives, 'waiting until the affectionate faithfulness of his loved ones returns'. Myth-time is a discontinuous time, a repeated 'now', not a duration, but an actualisation which proceeds by leaps from one 'now' to another 'now'. Van der Leeuw chose to speak of the 'eternalising' tendency of the

38

myth. It is better to content oneself, like Maurice Leenhardt, with the *perennial* character of mythic time. What we have here, in fact, is a time which has the continuity of life, and not in any sense a time which, lacking as it does any experience of death and any feeling of nothingness, could fit in with our ideas of finitude and of eternity. It is a present which sounds the affective depths of being, ignorant of the abstractions and negatives of our temporality; which awakens warmth, fear, or exaltation, and makes all nature sing in images and symbols derived from all the senses. By way of the myth, man identifies himself and his habitat with the totem, feels himself a contemporary of the totemic life and responsible for the carrying-on of existence. That is why the error *par excellence*, the major unfaithfulness, is sterility, which ruptures the chain of actualisations; or a breaking of the taboos which safeguard the correct transmission of life.

In this undifferentiated time, man may find himself in several times at once. The rock he sees *is*—now—the ancestor he sees no more; it is his 'apparition', the visible form at once hiding and revealing the invisible. The same act of awareness envelops the rock which, in its present form, remembers its old state, and the ancestor who, present in the rock, is always watching over the living. Mythic time is made up of these simultaneities, as the New Guinea myth of the man-bird shows: this man, who takes off his fungus-ridden skin to put on wings and become a bird, then slips once more into his diseased skin, moves on the affective and imaginative plane where the simultaneity of two 'moments' is translated into a rapid succession of images. By virtue of this mythic time, man feels united to all generations, to all the living: he feels himself in his grandparent as well as in his grandson, in the totemic lizard gliding across his path as well as in the ancestral tree where the past meditates on the present. Deprived of ontological ground, not knowing just 'where' his I is, the mythic man cannot distinguish what was from what will be and from what goes to make up the present. His temporality falls like petals into states, into 'nows' into which he is transported, unaware of contradictions.

The ritual must be faithful, the narration without omissions, in order that the mythic model may become a presence and a power in the person of the officiating leader or narrator. The myth is not a single story but always a *typical* story: it has an exemplary value, which, however, is concrete and alive. The totem resides in the maternal uncle, waiting for the nephew to receive its lodgment. It is present in the New Caledonian gecko lizard which assumes the colour of the twig; 'without any movement other

39

than that of his open eyes, he seems to be the living being that has one body with the forest and indicates life in the inert mass of the world'. He inhabits space and sets it in place. He is time as the power of life, as the presence which gathers all the dispersed presences in the world together. He whom the myth proclaims to be the master of the crops and of genetic life is also a revelation that lights up the world, unconscious poetry mixed with every substance and lodged in every form.

2. The Mythic is not to be confused with the Narrative
Greek, Celtic, and German mythologies are collections of accounts. Besides the *Epic* or epic account and the *Logos* or logical discourse, the myth appears as a special kind of expression. It found its form in the 'fable', an account which was without chronological localisation and was of an exemplary character. Whether it be a story of the gods or a fable, the myth necessarily seems to imply a narration, written or oral.

But among archaic peoples, the myth projects far beyond the domain of narrative and even that of language. This is true, first, because 'word' in this case goes beyond oral formulations, but also because this 'word', even enlarged to the meaning in which these peoples understand it, does not come close to covering the whole extent of the mythic.

Among the Melanesians, the decision which the father reserves to himself before a marriage request is 'word'; likewise, the avenging action which enables a man to punish an outrage inflicted on his brother by a third person; likewise, the magical operation, and likewise, thought. 'Word' is what has force, what has the solidity of a rock, what manifests being and establishes its lasting existence: tradition is the 'lasting word'; the Fame that comes down from gods and ancestors, the custom that cements society. More particularly important is the 'long-drawn-out word', otherwise the mythic account which is equivalent to the 'total life of the clan caught across the ages'. The chief's prestige is not attached to emblems or special honours, but to the fact that he is the guardian of this fundamental word: it is for him 'to recall . . . all the clan's traditions, alliances, and great hours, all the engagements, all its honour'. The chief is the word of the clan. And the word is the man: as in feudal society, it involves the whole person. The word is not a discourse, it is a force: from it issues the power to think, to act, to construct. Through it, man faces the world, exists, and knows.

Word is also what brings the world's answer back to him, what the mountain, the forest, the moon's reflection, the moving script of the sea

40

and the rustling of the leaves have to tell him. Even in our modern universe, as Jean Vogué comments, we still can feel 'the dramatic character of purple sunsets, and the serenity of the blue sky', and the poet, according to Martin Buber, still knows afresh, in the presence of the moon, 'the emotional image of the lunar fluid that flows through the body'. Here is a survival in us, as we stand before the world, of that primitive mythic where things still have the initiative, where animals and plants 'talk', where from everywhere the world's voices are heard, those calls that resound in man: diffuse presences from which come signals, orders, refusals. The mythic is that word which, from everywhere, calls men together and breaks up the darkness. It is neither allegory nor fiction, but forms and sounds, patterns and sayings which are also calls, apparitions, meanings: in short, a word.

This eternal dialogue between man and the world gives the myth as word an extreme importance and at the same time an extension which far exceeds the limits of its formulation. New Caledonian plastic art expressed this essential role in a striking way through the symbol of the protruded tongue. Whatever is most fleeting and vain in us, scattered in gossip and in official speeches, is there condensed into creative power. The Canaka carver chisels, on the door frame and on the ridge-pole of the huts, those faces of ancestors sticking out their tongues, which we might mistake for disrespectful masks. The tongue, which 'carries to the outside the traditional virtues, the manly decisions, and all the manifestations of life which the word bears in itself', becomes the symbol of wisdom, vigour, and plenitude. The word which no longer has this power is the formal word— we would say, the *logos*—in which there is a foreshadowing of abstract thought; and this, for the Oceanian, means an empty and powerless formula: for it comes out of the lips, not the deep feelings within.

The mythic, woven into this living and powerful word, clings to man. But its power is softened into an account which lacks warmth and weight, ready for mythology and literature: a decoration which the spirit has abandoned. The authentic myth keeps its vital pith in a world very different from our own, a world that has no equivalent for our verb 'to die', where our conception of life is too abstract to be grasped, but where everything that is important or affirmative, all that *is*, is alive, where there are no things, only beings participating in the same life-current—men, animals, plants or stones. The tree of life planted in the hole where the placenta is buried will live as long as the man does, and at his death, will wither. Inversely, man is hardly more than a momentary form of vegetable

41

life. It is through this other, through this co-existence with the tree, through the yam, image of his life, in a word, through the lived and projected myth, that man grasps his existence and knows himself. He sees himself only in the reflection of his being that the world gives back to him; and his life which, by itself, is not justified, finds validity only in the myth, which ties it to universal life, to all the living. It is the secret word, inscribed in sexuality, pronounced over man by ancestors and gods, *fatum*, the Latins called it: 'what has been said' about him, and what involves his existence, his destiny. But it is a word that can remain unspoken, bound to the name that is never uttered, or it can simply be read in the silent work of the carver.

The myth traces and avows the existential bond of man with his environment, with his habitat, with his clan, and the principle of his conduct. Instead of seeking, as we do, for a logical and objective relation with the world, in order to know it, break it up and master it, the 'Primitive' trusts his myths, lets himself be guided by them and sees himself by way of them. It is useless, if we want to understand his reactions and his thought, to reconstruct his myths 'scientifically' or to tell them over again in romantic attitudinising. It is better to follow the poet in his 'fantasy', then, or to listen to the musician, ask of the painter, let oneself be inspired, as they are, by those 'worlds' in their freshness and brightness. It is better above all to lend an ear to this mythic, underlying our own reason and our knowing, which the work of Jung and his school have brought to light as one of the great realities of our mental life.

The mythic is the common source of morality and of religion, of nature and of society, of the aesthetic and of exchange. It connects the individual to his clan and invests him with his social role, with his dramatic part. Yam or fish, man finds his place in the world, his ontological status, through the myth. From it comes the very strong sense of dependence which he feels with regard to the life he has received as a heritage, and of responsibility towards it. The myth controls the exchange of women by marriage among clans, in such a way as to guarantee 'the conveyance of the totemic life'. In this mythic view of things, the central place quite naturally goes to the life-myth *par excellence*, the totemic myth. The totemic lizard fertilises the crops. The path he is to follow in descending the mountain is carefully cleared. He is surrounded with respect. It is a grave error to mention him lightly; to call someone by the name of his totem is to take a liberty that hits him in his most intimate being. The totem presides over sexuality and fertility. He follows the maternal line and gives it its priority; it is he

42

whom the young girl, when she marries, brings to her new clan: a holy deposit which nephews take on from their maternal uncles and over which respect for taboos, religious fervour, exercise their care.

And now we are far from the myth-account, from the 'stories of the gods', from that colour-drained, peripheral mythic which some take to be nothing but a superstructure of society or simple-heartedness. It is in totemism, mythic time and space, the ancestral scenery, the feast where the clan is exalted, that, outside himself, the 'primitive' abides, there that he lives, from there that he will set out to discover himself when the decline of the mythic world liberates the individual. Beyond this horizon, he loses his footing in a foreign world, a world of lonely mountains, of wild expanses where the gusts of anger blow, oceanic immensities out of which the white men come ashore, those phantoms who no longer have human faces. Where the myth has nothing more to tell him, there is nothing any more, except chaos, malediction and hostility.

3. *The Mythic and the Aesthetic*
Long before it took literary form or became the 'story of the gods', the heroic adventure, and the descent into Hell, the myth found its plastic expression. The Oceanian world offers a remarkable and doubtless unique example of societies where art, far from representing a secondary activity or a trimming for life, is at the very centre of existence. The aesthetic there is not, as with us, a limited sector of activity, a luxury that is marginal to essential concerns. It is itself the aspect under which the world presents itself to man, its human face, the form given to the myth. The world, where it is first encountered by way of sensations, emotions, feelings, beliefs, manifests itself as the life of forms, in an aesthetic participation. The carved prow of a boat, some ear-rings, a diadem, everything man seems to add to the world, translate into form that wholly mythic representation and that aesthetic manner of living which dominate Oceanian society.

The aesthetic is an assent to the world: a deep accord with the natural and social environment, with the seasonal rhythm, with the aspects and changes of things; a confiding abandon to the proposals of what is felt, to everything that 'affects' and moves men, whether individually or collectively. This aesthetic attitude with respect to the world inclines man to put into his gestures and his speech, into his whole being, that form or that liking for the flourish and for elegance which often takes on the validity of custom or even of morals. It has sometimes seemed astonishing to find among these men a harmoniousness, a nobility of attitude, a 'style

43

of life' which is very far removed from the reputation for being savages which has quite thoughtlessly been given them. This aesthetic concern is shown not only in the colours, feathers, and painted designs with which the Oceanian loves to get himself up; not only in the decoration of huts, or in the arrangement of tiers and dances at the great feasts; but also in the actions of daily life and in personal behaviour. The meal where the yam, the ancestor's flesh, is consumed, takes place in silence, as becomes the celebration of a communion. The Dyaks of Borneo and the New Caledonians have been accused of crudity and grossness because the Dyak woman always walks several steps behind her husband, or because the Oceanian woman must cross four steps behind her husband if he is accompanied by other men. But to say this is to show ignorance of the fact that custom requires the Dyak to preserve his wife from snakes, scorpions and other dangers on the path, and also to forget the Oceanian woman's tact and subtlety, 'her art in intruding, bowing, standing up again, without bringing the least disturbance into the men's conversation while on the contrary having secretly charmed them'.

But the aesthetic, the expression of myth, is also a protection which makes man secure against the pressure of his environment. In the disorder and confusion of the primitive world, it is a first order put upon things. The Oceanians 'grasp the form of things before analysing things, and they have a sufficient acquaintance with them in this way . . . . Their thought is already ordered according to the aesthetic mode, long before it achieves ordering according to the logical mode.' It is perhaps not pointless to recall here that the Greek word *kosmos* and the Latin *mundus* have this aesthetic value, conjointly with their sense of 'order', of 'universe'. The first order attributed to the world was an aesthetic coherence, that arrangement which man first looked for in the aspect of things. The aesthetic slipped the screen of forms between man and things; it was a veil thrown over what was hidden in the depths and over the original chaos of which all causal myths make so much, before the *founding* and the *forming* set and ordered all things. In the shelter of this protective arranging, the 'primitive' organised his life and his society, limited but always secured by sounds, colours, and forms, by all that 'graining' which unceasingly confirmed to him the presences and the certainties by which he lived.

The world blossoms into living forms. Man himself is one of these. He is a being in a performance, he is a role, a kind of crowd-actor, on the world's scene. His gestures and his words obey tradition, express the myth, 'represent' ancestors and gods. Any personal whimsy, by breaking the

44

established aesthetic, would be gravely incorrect, involving outrage on the ancestors' honour and on the bases of society. Not ornamental or arbitrary in any way, these forms are an expression, a mythic language: the bodily array, the beautiful Maori or Guinea canoes, the tall statues on Easter Island, belong to that lexicon of forms through which the Oceanians deciphered the world's meaning. Nature, with a very sure sense of taste, is called in to join the artist in the joy of aesthetic creation: the sun gives their shine to mother-of-pearl and jade; the wind makes the feathers shake and spreads their vivid colours on the breeze; the ocean furnishes foam for the slender canoes and their chiselled prows. Working from instinct and with startling sensitivity, man brought the complicity of light and the hours into his play-acting, in order to enter into communion with the world. Songs and dances, head-dresses and ear-rings, among these people who had neither literature nor philosophy, make up the figurative vocabulary which for them took the place of ideas and of wisdom.

This symbolic activity where the symbol participates in what it represents, and joins the invisible to the visible, will develop, with the progress of logic, towards a more conscious symbolism. We can decipher without difficulty that language in which white is the colour of death, red of life, where the bird suggests the fluidity of the mythic to the imagination. When the myth has lost its force, the symbol will dry away into allegory or formalism. Allegory invaded classical mythology. Mythic images, reduced to their formal value, became themes and sayings for secularised speculation.

II. Regression of the Mythic
I. 'Birth' of the Gods

Maurice Leenhardt, in Chapter XII of *Do Kamo*, traced the process of decomposition of the myth. Nothing is more instructive as a means for understanding the specific traits of the archaic mentality compared to the mentality of advanced peoples. The myth begins to decline when the distance widens between man and the world, when things begin to separate from one another and to be situated at distinct levels.

Mythic perspective is disturbed when art, for example, evolves the third dimension. For the vision of the world which corresponds to the mythic stage spreads everything out in two dimensions. 'The myth', Maurice Leenhardt writes in *Arts de l'Océanie*, 'has no depth; it does its whole unfolding on one level.' We observe the Guinea sculptor chiselling the prow of the canoe as a crocodile with bird's feathers and a human

45

countenance. Then a being appears in whom his mythic vision finds an intelligible expression. In this way is shown 'a first discovery and taking possession of space', a sort of bodying-forth and individualisation of the object. At the same stroke the depth of space and the temporality of time are found presented. Rationality insinuates itself into the mythic mentality.

Man finds himself cut off from his environment little by little and acquires awareness of his own person. He begins to allot himself a residence in space, to measure the duration of his life, to take possession of his body. It would be impossible, certainly, to try to date these changes or to fix their causes. One can only note some steps in this penetration of the *logos* into the 'primitive' mental universe.

The myths of developed peoples have made us think that 'stories of the gods' or the deeds of heroes were indissolubly bound to myths. But that imagery which comes to us from Hesiod and Ovid only brings dead myths into the picture and can only furnish doubtful evidence. Work like that of Maurice Leenhardt does us the service of freeing us from that kind of premature conclusion. The idea of a god is not primitive; it requires an idea of the person to be evolved beforehand, and we must await a rather advanced degree of rationalisation for the person to emerge from the confusion in which it is at first submerged. The gods are only heirs: their 'stories' were shaped starting from mythic expressions formed around totems and other beings in whom the power of life declared itself. A certain hardening around the idea of power, a labour of intellection and of explanation precedes the hatching out of the divine into individual gods.

Long before the gods are clothed in a personality, it is around the life-cults, the passionate agitations, gifts and offerings into which affectivity has cast the deep intimacy of man with the world, that the myths, attuned in an aesthetic way, were formed, to regulate, in their turn, social discipline and the conduct of life. The myth pre-exists the gods, and it is in this totemic sphere that the root of mythic creation must be sought. According to Maurice Leenhardt's decisive observation, the legends of the gods and the totemic myths are often intermingled without being confused: the behaviour of archaic man proves that he always distinguishes what depends on the totem from what depends on the gods. He displays an uneasy, respectful interest with respect to totemic reality. He venerates the maternal ancestors, 'bearers of the power of life'. He strongly feels his dependence and his debt toward that life which emanates from the totem, and which the taboos envelop with sacredness. The totemic element has a strong affective tinge: piety, faithfulness, affection come from that

46

direction; man feels himself bound to it by a relation of communion, and the offering to the totem must be presented with pure hands. Condition for life's perpetuation, the totemic cult confers an extreme importance on woman and on the feminine element, which is surrounded by the extra-ordinary prestige granted to the sacred principle of life. From this come the heavy responsibilities that fall on the husband, for example, in a case where the wife dies on the point of becoming a mother, even if this death, from our point of view, is only due to natural causes. An ethical value attaches to everything that is totemic; a sort of social and moral aesthetic arises from this mythic of life, and gives those who, like the people of Dobu and of the 'Grande Terre', have kept the religious patrimony intact, an astonishing poise, a seriousness combined with ease; on the other hand, among the Trobrianders, mythic regression has brought with it the erosion of social discipline, and libertinism.

The gods took birth in a different mental region. There was once a state of things in which the god, the dead man, the aged, and even the man without rivals, remained undifferentiated. In the Houailou language, the same word *bao* designated them without distinction. Death is a passage to a new mode of existence. The same respectful idea enfolds the old man and the ancestor, the deceased and the soil to which his 'virtues' are com-municated. The earth where the ancestors are dissolved, the trees in which they survive, the winds that carry their voices, the rocks where they are watching, everything that commands strength and dignity, constitutes the divine, that divine which is scattered through the world, that invisible within the visible.

Much later the corpse will be separated from the habitat, set apart as corpse and singularised. Apart from the habitat, there will be a grave and a cemetery. The dead one will cease to be a *bao*-god in order to become a *bao*-corpse. He grows in dignity, they honour him as deceased. The world is cut up into levels of differing value, into stages. The supraterrestrial is freed from the limitations of the earthly world, at the very moment when space and time are delimited into isolated places and instants. The notion of power is emancipated from fervour and from life. The cult of deified ancestors takes precedence over the totemic taboos and observations, the masculine line over the maternal strain. The rationalisation which fixes this long maturation removes the ancestral female from the myth of life, to set her up as the goddess of fertility. The male ancestor, exalted through hero and chief, grows in power, and becomes a god. A function is assigned to him in some region of the cosmos: he is the force of the solar rays the

47

sun-god, the power of lightning, the thunder-god, the majesty of the sea, the ocean-god. Deluded in his will to power, by the desire to prolong himself and make himself big, the chief has sumptuous tombs and pyramids constructed for himself, and will mark his superiority by the quantity and cost of his offerings, by counting up the sacrifices, the bloody hecatombs which flatter his pride and assure him a vantage point with an eye to life beyond the earth. He will seek, while living, to elevate himself to divinity, to get the gods and the world into his power.

The gods will cash, little by little, the content of reality and of glory which the myths carried in themselves. They will betoken that 'other' reality, that supernatural essence, broken free of the common and day-to-day reality of simple mortals. They will be of another world, and reflective thought, 'theology', will take them in hand to define their place of being and their role. But, on the social level, grave consequences emanate from this transformation—first of all, a rupture of the equilibrium between, on the one hand, the myth oriented toward the veneration and safeguarding of life, and, on the other hand, the idea of power which exalts strength, quantity, mastery; between fervour and majesty; between the maternal-feminine and the political masculine element. The religious history of humanity is, in large part, the struggle between these two spirits and these two lineages, an antagonism intermingled with exchanges and compromises.

The drawing-back of the mythic before rationality is often accompanied by a degradation of which man himself pays the price. The ground lost by the myth is not always won by reason and freedom. All too often, magic and its formalism invade it. When the iron is defective, the African smith blames the sorcery of a woman who passed while it was being cast. This magical pre-judgment disobliges him from seeking the natural cause, a mistake in its preparation, and robs him of the desire to make corrections, a first condition of any progress. Magical rigidity brings with it stagnation or regression, and such peoples as are called primitive because their behaviour has congealed into magical mechanisms, would be better classed among the retarded, if not the degenerated. The offering falls into formalism, the sacrifice into the bloody massacres where the gods are constrained by the very quantity of the victims. Where, without the mythic horizon, men 'fervently believed . . . that the order of the world depended on the norms of their conduct', all was stiffened into a blind *fatum*, into a destiny pronounced for all eternity, in which people rested, to rid themselves of all risk and all initiative.

48

2. Mythic and Logic

The mythic does not exclude the rational, it does not precede it in time, it does not entirely disappear before its advance. It co-exists with it, and is complementary to it. The Melanesian, without abandoning any of the *no*, of the 'word' which proceeds by affective ways and derives from the myth, recognises another realm open to a certain rationality: it is that of the *sa*, of fabrication, *of technique*, where calculation and measurement enter. A logic presides, for example, over the sewing of fibre skirts, in which recourse is had to a wooden measuring stick in order to obtain fibres of equal length. This bit of stick is the object around which the idea of measure and of adjustment is formed. One might be tempted to couple this important piece of evidence with Rudolph Kassner's remark about the Greek world, where the revolution of the mind was accomplished, as he sees it, around the idea of measure, the core of all rational thought. It is a rather abbreviated logic among the Canakas, who still lack the logical materials and the considered experience which would be needed to elevate them, like the Greek world, to the idea of law and of cause; but logic it is all the same, which will gain in firmness as the native is developed. It is thus by the *intelligence of the hands* that the ascent by way of abstraction begins which will lift man to the very summits of conceptual activity.

But this is a groping progression, which a formal shell threatens to enclose at every moment. As long as the technician feels himself inspired by the original word, by revelation, he keeps the dignity and freshness of his work. But when technique is no longer understood as a gift from ancestors and gods, zeal and talent are muddied and the work degenerates. An attempt is still made to keep the form of the act and the phrase that had efficacy. But what remains is nothing but incantations and magic formulas, a technique without soul or an empty vocabulary, and nothing survives of the force that kept social organisation in balance, of the heart that used to be put into cultivating one's country. The feeling of essential intimacy is lost.

In societies where, with the advent of the Logos, nature has come out of her darkness, the myth has been driven back into the shadows. It has become suspect or it has gone underground. But even so it has not disappeared. It subsists, it subsists in the depths and continues to enliven many of the forms of our culture or to externalise many a movement of the soul. It inspires poet, novelist, and orator. It is at the bottom of certain collective sentiments which to us seem as 'natural', as 'demonstrated' as possible: national feeling, class consciousness, the republican ideal, etc. . . .

49

It sometimes assumes the face of science and the diction of reason: it is called the idea of progress, theory of evolution, or materialism. It explains the impassioned tonality which make certain 'verities' vibrate inside us, which ought to remain serene and indifferent to contradiction. The myth is what we can never 'see' in ourselves, the secret spring of our vision of the world, of our devotion, of our dearest notions. Whoever calls men to deeds of sacrifice, addresses himself, beyond all that is demonstrable and reasoned, to psychic dispositions and inner movements which can involve the individual and are of the same essence as those that take mythic form among archaic peoples.

Along the line where Lévy-Bruhl had advanced, Maurice Leenhardt completed his thinking and, on some points, went beyond him, with the freedom that direct observation could give him. Method is inseparable here from the objectives it was able to attain. Daily contact with men is the best introduction to the study of the human sciences. In any case, it is this concrete experience and this truly human comprehension that renovate our manner of understanding man in archaic civilisations and, indirectly, by comparison, permit us better to grasp certain traits of the most advanced human societies. A whole part of the human inheritance, a whole structure, as yet not well elucidated, of human reality, is thus placed within our reach; and lastly, we see more clearly into ourselves. Primitive societies are more than a geographical curiosity or a contrast to set off our own high state of culture. What we discover in them is that there may be something of the primitive and the original in the man who has always existed and who we, too, are. In breaking pathways towards this primitivity and these original things, Maurice Leenhardt wrote his name into the line of contemporary thinking, which taken together, appears as a return to the sources. Some, going back beyond the earliest philosophic speculations, ask Greek tragedy or the epic to return to us those human problems, those anxieties, those audacities, that torment of the human being as he faces the things that philosophy has rather fled from than answered. Others dig into philosophy to its very foundations, in order to find solid ground, a last basis, the root of essential questions. Tired of going along from cause to cause without ever finding the end of the chain, never surfeited by explanations which level things rather than throw light upon them, our century is turning by preference towards what is source and foundation, towards what never grows old and cannot be surmounted; and the mythic to which Maurice Leenhardt consecrated much of his research and his writing, is dominated by precisely this concern about the

50

archeus, on which everything already stands and rests, where causes are found in advance in the *raison d'être* of things. The images of fairy-tales, of fantastic narratives, of mythological figures may well seem to us to bear the marks of simplicity. But under their sometimes childish form they translate an interrogation which belongs to all the centuries, since it is man who raises these questions, man in his totality as a being at once organic, psychic, and spiritual, and he raises them in the very fact that he exists and that his life casts him into the midst of the world. At least, the mythic mentality, as Maurice Leenhardt unveiled it to us, corresponds to an attitude which is open, with respect to the world: for Oceanian man, as for ancient man, it is the universe itself that speaks of the beginnings and declares its permanence in the ephemeral, just as does the dawn of each new day, in the shrill dialogue between the real and the unreal.

Heinrich Dörrie

THE MEANING AND FUNCTION
OF MYTH
IN GREEK AND ROMAN
LITERATURE

I

During the classical period, myth and literature had a close mutual relationship. Objects of myth could only be properly expressed in high poetry—in the epic, in hymns, in tragedy. Handbooks of mythology could only have a supplementary function, perhaps to aid recollection. Such handbooks were widely available beginning in the Hellenistic period, circa 331–300 B.C. They were written on different levels and served various purposes. (See section VI below.)

The Greek mind made a careful distinction between mythology and myth—the distance between them is the same as that between history and the writing of history. The term mythology was used by the Greeks exclusively to designate factual recounting of mythological events. But myth goes further; it touches its reader or hearer closely; it has an effect, for it contains a piece of advice or more frequently a warning. Aristotle describes this effect as a "cleansing of the emotions" (pathematon katharsis, Poetics 1449 b 27). He ascribes this effect to tragedy, in his day the only form of literature that expressed myth. To have an effect of this sort was both the responsibility and the right of the poet. That is why the entire classical world was convinced that all myths had originally been announced by poets. This applies also in the historical sense. Most of the myths that continued to be effective were treated in the epic poems of the Homeric and post-Homeric period. There was no room for the idea that perhaps compilers of prosaic handbooks might have had any part in the important task of mythic creation—*mythopoeia*.

A modern analyst of the problematic nature of "myth" will do well, therefore, to remember at all times that the approach—*accessus*—to myth through handbooks is illegitimate. Such an approach has led to many erroneous concepts. Handbooks cannot help us reconstruct a definition of myth; it must be learned through the experience of poetry. It is difficult to regain this immediate experience.

The following example may enlighten us about the close relationship between high poetry and myth. With one famous exception, classical tragedy always drew on myth for its materials.[1] The poet was allowed all possible freedom to make the myth useful for contemporary questions and to apply it to them—if necessary by changing traditional details. The poet, committed to this rule for his theme, was in no way obliged to keep his distance from actuality. On the contrary, it was an aspect of his art to find and effectively apply the mirror suitable to the questions he wanted to treat.

We may imagine an analogy in the modern frame. How would it be if there had been a poetic law to the effect that a particular genre—let us say the novel—could and would only deal with materials taken from the chivalrous world surrounding King Arthur? Such a law would have established the "literary initial situation" for the shrewd knight, Don Quixote, for whom there was no other literature than that which drew its inspiration from the "myths" of the Middle Ages. The analogy we have just belabored becomes even more striking when we realize that Don Quixote allows these "myths" to determine his behavior. He sets out to realize the ideals of Christian knighthood.

This parallel is intended to clarify the following. As far as the form and content of life are concerned, the waning Middle Ages were reduced to absurdity by Miguel de Cervantes. By contrast, the validity of classical myth was much more deeply rooted. It remained unshaken by frequent, drastic alterations in social conditions. Some things changed; new demands were taken into account. But on the whole, once a period of trenchant criticism had been overcome (see section V), myth took on a lasting stature from about 400 B.C. What we have just called stature is determined only in part by the content of myth. More important, there was a consensus, never shaken, concerning the function of myth. Myth was charged with enabling statements about what is human, and especially about the deformation of what is human through longings and passion. Such a statement, supported by myth, obtains particular force and credibility because, removed from the everyday trivialities, it is raised to the sphere of what is generally accepted.

In this sense myth was universally applicable. It is true that originally it mirrored the aristocracy ethic of the Homeric period; but it had long since made itself free of this constricting connection. It must be designated as one of the great achievements of the fifth century B.C. that it brought about this universal applicability of myth. It was inevitable, though deplored by contemporaries, that this development was tied to deheroization. (The critical comparison between Aeschylus and Euripides, drawn by Aristophanes in *The Frogs*, emphasizes this difference. The fact that Euripides took steps toward deheroization was noted and judged adversely.) The heroes of the myths do not serve as ethical prototypes, to be praised or condemned. Their fate becomes exemplary less because of their actions than because of their sufferings; they serve to depict the destructive power of passion. After these radical changes, myth simply could not (and here ends the analogy introduced for clarification above) be carried *ad absurdum* to the extent that Cervantes reduced the ethic of the period preceding his to absurdity.

For myth was no longer a piece of the past; the myth was quite genuinely timeless. For centuries it did not run the risk of becoming old-fashioned; myth has never been accused of expressing yesterday's values. Myth simply could not become obsolete.

These two characteristics—universal applicability and permanent timelessness—brought about the transformation of myth to the function of a mirror. Comedy aside, we cannot name a single writer who did not make use of this mirror.[2] The impact of a work depended on the artfulness with which this mirror was employed. The cultural, intellectual, and aesthetic development that occurred in Greece can be gathered from the degree that myth was made fruitful for literature and philosophy.

If myth ever had undergone a phase when it was completely and unequivocally the expression of conscious or unconscious material, this phase was transcended in Greece. More, it is no longer evident in the period when literary tradition became established—that is, at the time of the Homeric poets. As is true for all subsequent writers, it is true for these poets that the myth does not contain its own purpose; it contains an argument, and it is told in order to bring this argument to bear. No trace leads back to a myth narrative "in itself," and it is a presumption, unsupported by any evidence, to claim what certain myths "really" mean for a time at such a distance from ours and a culture so different from ours as ancient Greece. We should quite firmly turn from the kind of interpretation of myth that was practiced until recently to the point of philistine abuse. My next few remarks may serve to illuminate the process that led to an unfortunately deeply rooted misinterpretation of the meaning of myth.

II

It would be worth special study to determine why Christianity, in spite of its frequently incisive criticism of Greek myth, was not able to shake its validity. Myth in its original rights was reestablished long before the high Italian Renaissance, with its return to ancient art forms; it was already firm during the much earlier return to Ovid (around 1300). Ovid furnished a collection of examples that were in every way on a par with those of the Old Testament. The two traditions served to confirm one another. While this connection was abandoned in Michelangelo's century—from then on the writer was forced to choose one or the other—the serious attempts to treat Biblical materials in the creation of a literature intended to demolish the domination of pagan myth failed.[3]

The literature that now clearly emerged from the clerical-sacral connection committed itself all the more firmly to myth, especially in the form given it by Ovid. A quite unusual achievement of the Renaissance and the subsequent classical period in France and Germany—one that has not been much acknowledged so far—consisted in the fact that the function of myth in the ancient sense was repeated. It was never questioned that myth contained a rich store of eternally valid experiences, safe against relativizing and not subject to the "happening." Goethe's Iphigenia no less than Euripides' use this form to express something universal, above the quotidian. Because classicism throughout Europe claimed to be the realization of the absolute and permanently valid, it could not afford to omit myth—not because of the themes it offered, but because of the immutable validity of the truths it mirrored. This unanimity in understanding myth—a common assumption among all people of culture, seldom discussed until that time—was permanently destroyed by Romanticism. It was at that time that the dissention emerged which has lasted to this day.

In 1835 Jacob Grimm published his work on German mythology. His choice of title stressed the fact that, in the author's view, German literature and usage had been built on the basis of myths just as much as were classical literature, classical art, and classical ethics. At the same time the choice of title emphasized the claim, still under dispute at the time, of German philology of being on a level with classical philology, since in both areas myth seemed to be the point of departure for all developments in art and literature. With this stress, it was completely overlooked that the Old High German stories of gods and heroes—from now on called myths— exercised a quite different function, which simply was not comparable. Thus the first step leading to today's confusion of concepts was unfortunately taken. The rich tradition of tales and legends of the early Germanic period was, sadly, not provided with an adequate catchall name (though use could have been made of derivatives of *Märe*, *Sage*, and *Kunde)*. On the contrary, the word "myth" was applied as a collective name, although "myth" applied to something quite different. (Jacob Grimm's lack of understanding went so far that he spoke of certain parts of the legends as *die Mythe*—feminine singular—a linguistic deformation that was continued for some time.)

Since scholarship was now dealing with a "German mythology" (and soon thereafter with an "Indian" and a "Finnish" one, based on the Kalevala), the concept of myth was narrowed in the sense that applied the word primarily to the archetypes of the events narrated in mythology. Examples are tales of the Great Flood, fratricide, the sacrifice of a son or daughter, a woman's leading many heroes to their death. The Brothers Grimm seem to have departed from the assumption, surely erroneous, that myth reveals native lore—more immediately understood as popular lore, the primitive, original onset of human thinking and feeling, existing before any culture. This assumption, not justified by any evidence, attained quite uncontested domination.

Instead of refining the tools used in the exploration of myth or of many myths, further blunting ensued. First, any nonhistorical tradition from any literature became designated as myth. Second, it became customary to evaluate the general validity of the "myth" in question on the basis of the facts reported in such "myths," as if the story reflected a so-called original event. We must realize that such a procedure appeared to open a road leading back to a primal period. Now it seemed to become possible to work out a kind of primal history or prehistory of human experiences, or at least of their bases—an expectation that fascinated many researchers who were more critical in other areas. Unfortunately, perhaps out of fear of jeopardizing the result that was longed for, often enough the scholars were content with insufficient analysis of superficially determined "myths." It must be remembered how readily, even frivolously, concepts of "totem" and "taboo" were identified among many cultures—and yet in the last ten years it has become highly doubtful whether the customs and concepts of North American Indians have ever been properly interpreted. It is probably that a premature joy of discovery allowed scholars to impose mistaken or at least insufficiently warranted results, on quite unrelated findings among very disparate peoples. Unfortunately, in this field premature associations and identifications prevailed. A further example will serve to illustrate these.

Around 1895 Sigmund Freud was tracing the problem of father-son conflicts. In 1896, shortly before he made his pioneering discovery, he attended a performance of Sophocles' *Oedipus Rex* in Paris. He was very much moved by the performance, as he himself noted in letters. It was his belief that the problem he was researching had been covered by a classical author who was aware of this "archetype." On the basis of his own experience, from then on Freud called the object of his investigation the "Oedipus complex." Perhaps it is a gain that this designation, which has become a label, serves to name adequately, and for many satisfactorily, this conflict of the son between father and mother. In this sense we may consider the phrase a neologism without which a new science cannot get along. But a further conclusion is entirely unwarranted—that not only the label but also the persistently postulated universal validity of the phenomenon are supported by the depth-psychological statements of classical poets. Neither Sophocles nor Seneca so much as touched upon Freud's concern in their tragedies. For the Oedipus of classical drama acts in total ignorance. He does not know that it was his father whom he killed, and he does not know that it was his mother whom he wed. Rather the myth deals with the heart-rending fate of a single individual. It never voices the idea that all sons are threatened by such a snare—that is, that all are prone to such a "complex." The classical value varies radically from Freud's. The fact that, in a mixture of guilt and innocence, Oedipus commits two terrible crimes represents such an affront to the gods that many years later they disclose and punish Oedipus' guilt. The classical writings ask only how Oedipus acts in this final phase. His efforts to resist the discovery are in vain, for the gods will exact their punishment.

It would be even more idle to refer to earlier versions of the legend, surviving only in fragments.[4] None of them ever served as an example of the "Oedipus complex." Rather they were illustrations of the fact that a human being can become unwittingly guilty; and they served to illustrate the fact that the gods meted out their punishments not according to the transgressor's intention but according to the objective severity of the guilt as pollution. Precisely because this legendary tale has a clearly visible function as exemplum, it can be stated with absolute certainty that it does not have the function Freud assigned to it. But the fact that a thoroughly modern discovery became accepted through the term Oedipus complex, as if classical myth had already contained such depth-psychological declarations—that is characteristic of the often very frivolous manner of associations indulged in all too readily by contemporary myth scholars.

It may well be that the widespread legend of the Great Flood refers back to a primal fear of flood catastrophes. It may even be that the legends of fratricide—such as Cain and Abel, Etyocles and Polynices, Romulus and Remus—and of incest among siblings testify to an original repulsion against actions that destroyed the family. (Even this statement, however, is not universally applicable. We need only recall the ancient Egyptian custom of intermarriage between brother and sister.) Legends about a father willing to sacrifice a son or daughter—Isaac, Iphigenia—are often backed by historical reminders that human sacrifice has been abolished: the gods do not want it. With every possible caution we may interpret myths as cultural-historical (but surely not psychological) documents.

The traits of Greek myth are quite different. Its essence is not at all marked by what more recent scholars understand by the word myth. For only minimally is that which makes up myth grounded in the appearance and course of the narration. Myth, after all, is much more than legend. Each myth teaches something; each myth faces its hearer with the task of making fruitful for his own situation whatever the myth demonstrates on an extraquotidian object. Myth is exemplum. And for every exemplum we must ask what purpose is served.

Though it is a step in the right direction to ask, with

Lévi-Strauss, about "structures," we must not rest there. For the structures, which are extraordinarily capable of transformation, are in the service of the function assigned to a myth. As an inviolable rule this assignment of a function happened consciously and deliberately. It makes clear the intention of a narrator, an author. This author aims at achieving a multiple purpose. Of course he wants to communicate the sequence of events, the course of the action; he may even want to use it to entertain.[5] Almost always he aims to go further, to teach, warn, admonish, advise for or against. And it is obvious that precisely this intention underlies the often cautious, often deeply radical changes the narrator or poet makes in the material. That is why from the outset myth is a cultural factor. It is a tool—for a long time even a very outstanding tool—of *paideia*. It is manipulated quite consciously, even artfully. It is very far from the unconscious.

III

The myths of the Greeks cannot be derived from a single source, either historically or functionally. It is probable that Greek myth was so rich in phenomena and variations because it mingled Hittite, Cretan, and autochthonous traditions. Though myth is maintained as a universally constant force by a tradition of secular validity, this tradition has always been able to adopt new, previously unknown elements.[6]

At the same time myth has never exerted one function only. As we shall discuss in detail below, it was an almost universal tool to explain the incomprehensible or to document a claim. That is why previous attempts to define exhaustively even only the extent of myth have remained thoroughly unsatisfactory.[7] Myths were related to the gods only in part; the relationship between myths and cults was often very slight, and often nonexistent.[8] Only for a very small number of myths—these are the myths of the *adventus* of a god—was it true that they were copied in a ritual. The principal one is the arrival of Dionysius-Bacchus, which culminated in a ritual in many places, including Athens. But the major portion by far of all myths had nothing to do with ritual.

The current but frequently insufficiently grounded concepts that tend to identify myth with the religious or sacral sphere must be thoroughly modified. Undoubtedly there are many connections between myth and religion. But it is an oversimplification to derive myth from cult or ritual or to see myth as something with religious origins, as a form that has lost the concept of faith.[9] All these attempts to define myth exhaustively, or even to justify it, have missed their mark.

Instead myth must be defined as a rich store of knowledge and experience, available to all. This store of experiences was available, as a matter of course, to answer small everyday questions and large questions, such as those concerning the world and its creation. Later the question was raised whether the mythic tales could be seen as authenticated history—a question which, after some vacillation, was answered in the negative. In the early period, which can be said to end roughly in mid-fifth century B.C., with Pindar and Aeschylus, the question of verifying the narrative presumably never arose. Only the critical thought of the waning fifth century shook the absolute certainty ("faith") that the myth encompassed valid reminiscences.[10] Subsequently, though the world of myth was not considered actual, it was still perceived as a quasi-historical area. The experiences myths contained were at a distance from everyday life, especially its trivial aspects.[11] That was why, after all, they were generally accepted in a higher sense and all the better able to be applied to questions of the present.

This continuum of mythic tradition is made clear through the literature; and ultimately we can only describe and interpret it in the light of literary evidence. But we must not forget that classical man was everywhere surrounded by visual expressions of myth. We need only recall the black- and red-figured vases, primarily of Attic origin, as well as the wall painting of Pompeii and the late-classical sarcophagi that were amply decorated with scenes from myth—not to mention the figurative decorations of the temples, most especially their tympana.

As mentioned above, myth had more than sacral aspects. Its applicability reached deep into the profane. Apparently there were no boundaries that myth could not transcend on pain of becoming blasphemous; Christianity was the first to set such limits. The objects of myth were never considered holy in a transcendental sense, so that they could only be intruded into the confusions of this world with pious awe. On the contrary, myth encompassed the full extent of the experiences in this world, often especially in harsh, in tragic situations. That is why myth was allowed to infiltrate daily life—it served as ornament and entertainment, as advice and admonition, as an aid to the imagination in difficult questions. Complicated matters could be elucidated by a mythic example; simplicities could be differentiated by mythic encoding. To this extent the presence of the mythic, not only in classical literature, but especially in the quotidian, in the rooms one lived in and the objects one used, was much more universal than, for example, the presence of the sacral in the Christianity of the high Middle Ages. Only a fraction of it was deposited in the literary realm.

IV

Frequently the Homeric poets comment on the course of actions they are narrating (the struggle for Troy, Odysseus' return) by citing examples from other myth groups. Almost regularly such examples lead to advice on the proper response to a given situation. Niobe came close to turning to stone out of grief for the death of her children; but after fasting for nine days, she began to take nourishment again (Omega 602 and 612). Therefore, Achilles advises, Priam should also partake of the meal. This may be seen as the absolute paradigm of mythic exemplum. (Schiller duplicated this theme at the end of his poem "Das Siegesfest.") The entire content of this mythological tale is not reproduced; in particular, the lesson this myth in its actual sense intends to teach is not replicated by the Homeric poet. Niobe was punished because her pride as a mother seduced her into a position of *hybris*. The tale of the cruel revenge the offended gods took is surely to be assigned to the Apollonian myths, which warned against disparaging the *maiestas* of Apollo, his sister Artemis, and their common mother, Leto. The Homeric poet, however, mentioned none of this in Omega 602–17. Only a marginal aspect is brought to bear on his subject: even Niobe, so harshly punished, finds her way back into human, commonplace life.

Here we find the point of departure of the figure of speech varied innumerable times in classical and modern literature: the mythic exemplum.

If the Homeric poems allude to extra-Trojan myths, then such knowledge is always presented as alive in the memories of preceding generations. Phoenix lived to see the dire consequences when Meleager angrily withdrew from battle, so that the city Calydon was threatened with capture and destruction (I 526–99). In his youth Nestor (A 262–72) saw the Lapithae and witnessed their ruin. Glaukus (Z 155–97) knew how his grandfather Bellerophon was driven out of Ephyra/Corinth, how he slew the chimera and thereafter found a new home in Lycia; this is given as the motive for his grandsons Sarpedon and Glaucus fighting on the side of the Trojans.

Clearly the Homeric poets are far from a systematic ordering of mythic elements. However, since later on everything was taken as authoritative if it was found in "Homer," so the subsequent literary usage of mythic elements was very strongly marked by what has just been described: the figure of speech of the mythic exemplum, and the myth as stored experience of an older and wiser generation.

V

In the seventh and eighth centuries B.C. the element of the mythic gained several additional dimensions, previously not present.

It became indispensable to the legitimation of the ruling aristocracies of the day to derive their descent from one of the dynasties named by Homer and, through these dynasties, to one of the gods or goddesses. Now genealogical myths in great number were created—surely because it was politically significant to support the right to rule by proof of divine descent.

Hesiod's didactic poem *Theogonia* was intended to do more than demonstrate the origin of the gods; rather it flowed into long catalogues of those who had had relations with gods or goddesses and thus became progenitors of famous dynasties. Others also undertook to collect such genealogical material, for its part authenticated as established memories. The poet of the *Lambda* of the *Odyssey*, the *Nekyia*, inserted into his poem a catalogue of the women who had enjoyed the affection of a god and borne him children. It had clearly become an important task of the *aoidos*, the singer, to include in his poem testimony of the divine origins of the family in whose castle he sang and from whom he received his wages. Hesiod ultimately arranged and shaped this material, which previously had surely been disordered and proliferated wildly. Only then did it become obvious how many families claimed descent from Zeus. The correctness of such a tradition was never called into question; such seemingly historical facts were received seriously and continued in the tradition. Criticism touched upon a quite different issue, which could not have been foreseen. If Zeus was the father of so many heroes—a claim, as noted, that was never doubted—then he must have seduced an equal number of women. Here we find the point of departure of the endlessly and variously used jibes that made Zeus appear as the permanent lover, the resourceful seducer. Subsequent writers never tired of inventing ever-new concurrences and ruses by which Zeus approached his love objects—as bull, as golden rain, as swan, and finally even in the guise of the husband Amphitryon.

Before this time the invention of genealogical myths had a clearly demarcated political purpose: they gave support to an aristocracy rooted in the situations described by Homer and intent on preserving it. But soon thereafter such constructions lost their purpose. However, they were by no means abandoned; rather they were elaborated on with downright relish in order to please the hearers with the amatory prowess of the father of the gods and of men.

The conservative stance adopted by Hesiod was contrasted by an awakening movement that was customarily designated by the name of Orpheus. This movement had as its aim to lead men to "salvation"—soteria—that is, to a blissful life after death. While Homeric religiosity is pronouncedly poor in eschatological motives, the question of what occurs after death takes the foreground in the Orphic movement. This leads to a different interpretation of the mythic as well. It was believed that a penalty for bad behavior and a promise of bliss for proper behavior could be read in them.[12] Accordingly, particular myths have two levels of meaning. We may disregard the profane, all too accessible, level: only the disciples of Orpheus have access to the real level, the one relevant to human salvation. Surreptitiously the comprehension of symbols becomes occult lore. The mystery of Eleusis, while not originating in Orphism in the proper sense, grew out of a comparable attitude. A single myth was made the basis of the cult through a secretly handed-down symbolic relationship. Orphism made two changes in myth: the events narrated in the myths are not located in the past but are ever present—even now the Titanic element struggles with the divine authority in each human being. Second, correct interpretation of particular myths is essential to salvation. But these two changes hardly came to expression in the literary realm. Much later, however, in the second to fifth centuries A.D., Orpheus was regarded as a key figure, as someone who had announced all theological truth and wisdom in the dawn of history, before Homer.

Now it seems at first glance as if those who wanted to view myth as the symbolic expression of basic verities or, more recently, primal experiences would find support for their conception in Orphism. There, after all, the attempt was made to penetrate through the interpretation of universally familiar mythical tales to the basic and primal truths that represent a basis common to all mankind. To document this, bold associations were often required. Because the traced analogues seemed immediately reasonable, particularly striking or accessible coincidences were taken to have been definitively proven.[13]

But the view of myth taken and understood by generalizing theology at the beginning of the twentieth century was hardly the way the classical period viewed and understood it, aside from minimal variations. Orphism offered this understanding to later generations. But the offer was refused; aside from the frequently mentioned exception of the Eleusinian mysteries, myth did not become the vehicle of a redemption lore or a religion directed to the winning of salvation.

To a much greater degree the relationship of the Greeks to myth was formed by two controversies with long-lasting consequences, which were waged in the sixth and fifth centuries B.C.

1. In an earlier phase of myth criticism, moral displeasure was dominant. It seemed unbearable that Homer and Hesiod told of gods who lied, stole, committed adultery. Homer and Hesiod could only have invented such stories because they wished to blaspheme against the gods. It seemed necessary to suppress such a tradition because it threatened the youth.[14] Subsequently Plato quite seriously adopted this line of reasoning.

2. A later phase was marked by rationalistic criticism. Now the miracles often enough reported in myths seemed factually incredible. In this phase attention was called to the absence of documentary evidence. (In defense, an argument somewhat as follows was cited. Homer and Hesiod did not really care about the surface narration. In reality the gods of myth are nature forces. All epics represent steps in the creation of the world, cosmogony, which does indeed apply to the beginnings of Hesiod's and Orpheus' theogony. Therefore the passion of Ares and Aphrodite must not be seen as a scandalous story of adultery, the poet's didactic purpose having gone far more deeply.) Because the events reported by the myths were not historical, they had to be untrue. (The defense against this argument was basically weak. It limited itself to interpreting away the miraculous elements, thus enervating the objection of incredulity.) This view of myth can be traced from the

waning fifth century B.C. to deep into Hellenism. It was subsequently given sustained support by the novellike work of Euhemerus of Messina.[15]

It is clear, then, that discussions about myth stretched very far. None of the vying tendencies gained the ascendancy: neither the tendency that called for rejecting the myths for their moral offensiveness, nor the tendency that was offended by the improbable elements. Both critical trends applied quite other criteria to myth than during the archaic period. Both together brought it about that myth was retained as an important vessel of the Greek intellect. The individual questions, even accusations, directed at the mythic tradition never seriously touched its substance. But they stimulated the search for new interpretations and new justifications.

It had, we must recall, been a long time since Greece had grown beyond the Homeric world, which was drawn in all its details in myth. The culture of the cities had long since replaced the aristocracy of the Homeric and post-Homeric world. But the new society that arose could not do without the old didactic concepts. To be sure, a very few, who were to remain outsiders, demanded that the traditional myths be abandoned. But in spite of all attacks, the mythic tradition was very firm, and what this tradition achieved could not be replaced by anything else.

Thus a downright paradoxical situation resulted which, as far as I can see, has no analogy in any other literature. Precisely in the century when myth radically fought for survival—the fifth century B.C.—the concept of myth became so rooted that it grew into a dominant continuum. This is true not only for all phases of Greek literature until the victory of Christianity, but also, and to a much greater degree, for Roman literature. Precisely in this area the Romans, who—a few tribal legends aside—had no mythological tradition of their own, adopted the Greek model in the broadest measure, with alterations and without subtractions. It was especially the adoption of mythic elements that closely connected Roman literature with Greek literature.

VI

Plato rejected the myths insofar as they were immoral, and to Aristotle *mythodes* stood for whatever was unproven and unscientific. With these two notable exceptions, from about 400 B.C. to the threshold of the Middle Ages, the following concept of the nature of myth prevailed. What was voiced in myth was not history but was supratemporal; myth encompassed a world of examples. Looked at in this way, mythology was only in small part the myths of the gods. Though everyone knew the facts that have been reported from time immemorial, they hardly mattered in the literary treatment. For interest turned decidedly on the human beings who acted and suffered in the myths. This recognition decisively abandoned a path delineated by Pindar and Aeschylus: the human beings of mythology were by no means heroes of moral decision; rather the figures of mythology were subjected to a lasting deheroization. All the actors were subject to instinct, even impulsiveness. For the passions were seen as irresistible forces.[16] Eros especially was such a despotic ruler that all humans—those of the myth and those of the present day—were subject to his rule. Thus, from Euripides to Ovid, mythology grew into an abundant collection of examples of "human nature."

But this human nature was not seen in the sense of modern humanity; only rarely did heroic decision triumph over instinct and passion. Stimulating examples of this dynamic were furnished by history rather than myth, such as Leonidas' heroic decision at Thermopylae or the assassination of the tyrant by Harmodius and Aristogiton. The conflict between duty and inclination was, characteristically, not a theme in classical literature to the extent that it was devoted to mythology.[17] Rather, the proper subject was the deformation of a personality that was originally great, unable to release himself from the web of its passion—this was as true for Hippolytus as it was for Phaedra, for Medea as well as for Oedipus; it was true not only for familiar figures from tragedy, but also for the characters of the Hellenistic epyllion as well as the passion-plagued figures in Ovid.

The deceptive term "tragedy of inevitability" applied only in the following clearly demarcated sense: myth teaches us the ineluctability of the affects, most particularly love. Hellenistic and Roman literature were to compete in mirroring ever-new variations of erotic *furor* in mythic events. What was fateful was the inescapability of the entanglement, because it expressed a condition that applied to all men.

The literary form of mythology since Euripides was not exemplary in the sense that heroic actors behaved properly, thus offering models.[18] Rather literature oriented to myth depicted and taught through faulty behavior, through the inevitable entanglements. The one exception to this rule was Hercules, who opted for the narrow, steep road and was frequently praised as an example of the philosophically correct decision. This attitude was held by Prodicus of Ceos and subsequently by the Cynics.

This variation introduced by Euripides allowed mythology to place a contemporary image of man in the mythic frame. It is not, therefore, saying too much to claim that mythic tale (in epic) and the unfolding plot in the mythic frame (in tragedy) properly became the means of representing mankind. In this area we encounter important statements about classical humanity.

An example may serve to prove the point. Quite intentionally Apollonius of Rhodes (circa 250 B.C.) does not depict the protagonist of his epic, Jason, as a cheerful go-getter; he is shown as a basic loner, who lives for a great task. He does not command superhuman powers but is aware of his responsibility to use the means at his disposal—especially the ship *Argo* and his twelve companions—meaningfully and without running unnecessary risks. This awareness brings him into conflict with his companions at times.[19] This depiction by no means established a model. Rather it served to prove that the uncommon dangers of a long journey to a foreign land can only be mastered when a nature such as Jason is shown as possessing guides the journey of the *Argo*.

Earlier it might have seemed that the epic had been condemned to die out. The fact that mythology overcame the fifth-century crisis that threatened its existence had serious significance for the survival of the epic. The very same mythology, filled with new meaning, once more furnished the material for epic poetry. Although already pronounced dead by Callimachus, it gained new life, for the old reciprocal relation between myth and epic was reestablished. It was precisely for this reason that Virgil, in an epic, was able to express what he wished to make vivid to the Romans of his time: *arma virumque*. In order to present the humanity of Aeneas, he frequently referred back to the model supplied by Apollonius of Rhodes.

Along with the total material of mythology, Rome also adopted the concept just defined. Many epics and many more tragedies were composed in Rome.[20] One thing, however, mythology was not able to achieve; ideal figures, compelling models were not within its vocabulary. In this regard Rome kept strictly to the rules; the historical exemplum was created. The history of Rome was turned into a kind of hall of fame, where such figures as Regulus, Cincinnatus, and Cato were worshiped. The Greek myths had little of this; the great poets no more than the nonliterary or semiliterary tradition ever praised their heroes or raised them to the rank of the exemplary—with the exception of Hercules, cited above. The Homeric Achilles may have been the strongest man in Troy, but he was anything but a model retainer. His wrath endangered the common enterprise. That is why the hero of the Iliad cannot be compared with Virgil's hero, with Aeneas. In reality Aeneas stepped outside the myth; he initiated the line of the great historical exempla. To this extent Virgil suspended the separation between myth and history, which was usually thoroughly observed, in the service of his hero.

When shaping mythic themes, the poets, like all creative artists, were only loosely limited by the framework of the action. Of course the principal facts could not be ignored; but in the actual elaboration, the poet was generally free. Most particularly, the poet was granted the liberty of stressing the motives of the protagonists in such a way as to make them correspond to his poetic intention. Additions and alterations were in large measure seen as permissible. In one of the most telling examples of such alterations, Jason's infidelity to Medea and Medea's revenge on her rival are traditional elements; but Medea's killing of her own children in order to hurt Jason is Euripides' addition.

To the same extent the poet was not obligated to adopt rigidly the versions of a legend as they were offered by an authority, such as Homer. In this area there was ample room for partial myth criticism—that is, for correcting details which in the new version become inessential. A considerable number of presumptions could be altered, with the undisputed claim of presenting them properly—that is, tailored to the inherent purpose of the myth. The often-cited principle of "nothing without proof"—amartyron ouden—applies only to names and events,[21] not to the interpretation of a myth.

In this sense, a poet eager and able to make use of them had almost unrestricted access to the nearly inexhausible supply of traditional materials. In the Hellenic period a number of handbooks came into being that furnished this material. Some of them were designed to offer their subjects to future poets; others were dedicated to ordering the whole area, preferably along genealogical lines; still others furnished collections on a particular theme, such as tales of metamorphosis. Finally, there were books that correspond to our tales of the great operas, meant to educate their readers about mythic materials they might encounter in reading or in the theater—such as the *fabulae* of Hyginus.

Certainly attempts were made to raise control over this material to a technical skill, turning mythology to an end in itself, used for its own sake; but such attempts were soon abandoned.[22] A poet— we may point to Ovid as an example—had to be able to estimate how much of the detail of the myth and how much subtlety he could expect his readers to absorb. But these are reflections that must be weighed before employing any genre; excess and banality must always be avoided.

VII

Classical literature has always claimed to transcend its own day. Homer, who held undisputed sway for more than a millennium, is the chief example. Many authors hoped for a similar secular fame, especially should they succeed in outdoing Homer; commitment to mythology also meant competition with Homer. The modern postulate that a poet must work within his own day—that is, observe the laws of realism—would in the classical period have been considered valid for only a few genres, such as satire or *mimus*.[23] For the condition, actually considered to have priority, that the poet must have an ulterior, moral purpose was, in the classical view, more easily met if the poet was not restricted to the everyday and trivial. The inexhaustible means that allowed him to preserve distance and still remain factual were the matter of mythology.

The high poetry of the Greeks and Romans, of the Middle Ages, and of all contemporary classical revivals avoids two devices as being quite simply antipoetic: reference to the present, and approximations of the trivial. In this respect classical literature and the material considered to be literature today were diametrically opposed. Nevertheless, the central theme of classical literature was man.

The irreconcilable condition thus created could be resolved only with the help of mythology. And because the incompatibility had to be reconciled, myth was indispensable.

The listening and reading audience was disposed along the same lines. Each poet could assume that the basic lines of mythological action were well known; anyone rash enough to confuse the wooden horse outside the gates of Troy with the wooden bull of Daedalus marked himself as boorish—like Trimalchio in Petronius' Satyricon (52:2). It is quite certain that the universal applicability of mythology was a given only so long as familiarity with mythology was an unshakable part of the education of the reading public. This was precisely the reason why an extensive mythologi-cal-mythographical literature arose and became current. Anyone who feared that, like Trimalchio, he would leave himself open to embarrassment could make use of it to increase his knowledge-ability. But this familiarity was never in question during the classical period.[24]

The poet who dealt with the material offered by mythology did not, like a modern writer, worry about suspense. In isolated episodes he might be eager to supply suspenseful narration, a task that in tragedy was often assigned to the messenger's report. With this technique the poet not only related what could not be shown on the stage but also introduced suspense. Yet on the whole the poet was not interested in suspense and was free to concentrate on the essentials. He could and should emend the tradition, the course of events known to all, transform them so that the specifi-cally human quality of the protagonists was fully stressed. For an educated public felt sufficient suspense in following, not the course of the action, but the modifications introduced by the individual poet.

For all these reasons myth is an element indispensable to classical poetry. The tie to mythology granted a great deal of freedom to the classical poet—the freedom of removing himself from the present,[25] the freedom to depict mankind far from triviality and a workaday existence. These freedoms, it was felt, assured him of penetrating to the essentials. The frame offered by myth was elastic enough not to cramp the freedom of the chosen material. We recall the richness of the mythic material treated by Ovid.

For these reasons classical poetry and classical myth determine each other. This reciprocal relationship raises both to cultural factors of high intensity and binding force. There is no doubt that, as a consequence, classical poetry was something unique and became the model for contemporary literature during significant epochs because new literature was always able to base itself on myth as something ever present. Such a premise applies to no modern literatures.

Only classical poetry was able always to look up to the world of mythology. Above we have shown why this reference did not contain within itself either the risk of falling prey to schematization nor the danger of becoming unrealistic. Such perils existed only for those poets who were not up to their poetic task.

Mythology was a world in which simple laws,[26] and especially simple human relations in hate and love, fear and bewilderment,[27] reigned. The world of mythology was neither a counterworld nor was it the ideal world. But for the classical poets it was, to a high degree, the *proper* world, because it allowed the presentation and interpretation of man in his proper shape. We could even designate the world of mythology as the properly epic and tragic world.

Translated by Ruth Hein

Notes

1. The exception was *The Persians* by Aeschylus, which deals with an event from the recent past—the defeat of Xerxes in 480 B.C. This was seen as an event of such consequence that it was equated in worth with myth. Thus even Xerxes gains something of the stature of the defeated hero of tragedy, for all the glory of Athens is set in opposition.
   In Rome, Naevius created a dramatic category, the so-called *praetexta*, in which the action was carried by outstanding Romans. The label "historical tragedy" is a modern one; in the classical view, such a play simply was not a tragedy.
2. Even comedy was, at the outset, a comedy of folk tales or a travesty of myth. At all times it was capable of returning to this origin, as often happened as late as the midfourth century. We need only recall the theme of Amphitryon, which entered world literature.
3. The *Heroides Sacrae* are an instructive example. These tales competed with Ovid, who had allowed heroines, in their distress, to write to the faithless lover. This overly pagan insertion was in part corrected, in part surpassed. Heroines of the Old Testament or of pagan legend are accountable for their confession of faith, which generally leads to martyrdom.
4. One such version is recounted in a brief summary in the *Nekyia*, gamma 271–80. According to it, the gods immediately made the desecration known. Epikaste, Oedipus' mother and wife, cursed her son and hung herself. By adding the circumstance that the discovery occurs only much later, Sophocles altered the legend. According to Homer and others, the mother's curse is the cause of pain and disaster; Oedipus nevertheless continues to rule over Thebes for many years. The curse punishes but does not destroy him.
5. This is indeed a primal function of the telling of myths, as is evidenced by the song of Demodocus (Theta 266–368). The guest, who is still not recognized, should be entertained; the singer is prepared even for such a function; he sings the cheerfully frivolous song of Ares and Aphrodite.
6. One example is Pygmalion. I have researched the manifold variations of the influence through time of this myth in *Pygmalion. Ein Impuls Ovids und*

seine Wirkungen bis in die Gegenwart, Rheinisch-Westfälische Akademie der Wissenschaften, Lectures G 195 (with summaries in English and French), (1974).

7. In a sense of irony, G.S. Kirk *(Myth: Its Meaning and Functions in Ancient and Other Cultures,* Cambridge, Eng., and Berkeley, 1970, pp. 242–43) cites the attempt at a definition by H. J. Rose in *A Handbook of Greek Mythology,* 5th ed. (London, 1953), p. 14. Even though Rose's formulation—"Greek myths . . . reflect the national character"—is open to attack, on the whole Rose is more correct than Kirk in stressing the peculiarity of Greek myths as compared to all other pseudomyths. For it is Greek myth that became a cultural factor.

8. Only one myth represents an exception to this statement—the Eleusinian myth of the disappearance of Persephone, her reappearance, and the spread of agriculture. In this case a symbolic relationship such as was postulated for all myths was applied to the search, the discovery, and the mission. For further discussion, see my essay "Philosophie und Mysterium. Zur Legitimation des Sprechens auf zwei Ebenen durch Platon," in *Verbum et Signum:* Festschrift für F. Ohly (Munich, 1975), no. 2, pp. 9–24.

9. This is the formulation considered fundamentally valid by U. von Wilamowitz *(Der Glaube der Hellenen,* Berlin, 1932, 1:1–5).

10. Not only von Wilamowitz but also the majority of his contemporaries had great difficulty in forming abstractions from the concept of "religious certainty." It had been felt so intensely—its converse being doubt—that it was considered as an absolute, applicable also to pre-Christian religiosity.

11. Of course it was quite possible, for a joke, to translate mythic themes into the trivial environment. Examples of this are frequently offered by the Old Comedy in Syracuse and Athens and later the mockery of the Cynics, adopted more than once by Lucian but also by Seneca in the *apocolocynthosis.* It was possible; but it remained peripheral.

12. Most particularly, the punishment of the forty-nine Danaides who slaughtered their husbands during their wedding night was seen as a warning example for all who missed the purpose—*telos*—of their life; they were condemned to purposeless activity for the rest of their lives. Just as these young women culpably missed their *telos* in marriage, so anyone becomes culpable who misses the dedication of Orphism.

13. A favorite device was to combine linguistic associations—so-called etymologies—with the associations furnished by the myth. The standard contemporary interpretation of myth, which proceeds almost entirely by association, has much in common with Orphic interpretation. I assume the missing link to be the religious speculations of the late Romantic period—especially those of F. Creuzer, J. Görres, and J.J. Bachofens, which claimed to be able to show evidence of a mystical-mythic religious primal awareness among the people of antiquity. More narrowly specialized scholars were soon in a position to overcome this attitude, especially thanks to A. Lobeck, *Aglaophamus* (Königsberg, 1829), even though Nietzsche and H. Usener had affinities with the trend just described. While criticism of late Romantic interpretations was extremely severe among specialized scholars, to this day such criticism has not sufficiently prevailed in those areas in which more than one area of scholarship connect (ethnology, religious studies, psychology). In these fields it is still the rule that whatever pleases is allowed.

14. Conversely, the tradition was excepted insofar as it covered interpretation of the names of the gods. There was a wealth of speculation concerning the etymology of the divine nomenclature—that is, attempts were made to penetrate to the proper and true meaning of the names of the gods by linguistic associations. Precisely in the case of a god, pure nature must be reflected in the name. This was an aspect of ancient theology that was long seriously studied.
15. Euhemerus of Messina was employed from 311 to 298 by King Cassadrus, one of Alexander's successors. He gave a kind of historical foundation to the cult of the ruler that was newly emerging: even Uranus, Cronos, and Zeus had been humans, though they had understood how to become recognized as gods.
16. Here there is a close connection between tragedy, which presents the passions, and the Stoic teaching of the affects. Chrysippus made a point of collecting statements by Euripides that pertained to the topic central to his doctrine; ultimately he included all of *Medea* by Euripides in his collection of examples. Diogenes Lartius, 7, 180.
17. This conflict is embedded in book 4 of Virgil's *Aenead*. Aeneas' attraction to Dido is in conflict with the mission *fate* has set for him. Without putting up much of a fight, Aeneas obeys the command of the *fatum*. This is not a dramatic conflict in the nineteenth-century sense.
18. Herein lies the reason why nineteenth-century classicism could not form a relationship to Euripides and his many successors. To the extent that they were seen from the viewpoint of the classicists, Aeschylus and Sophocles were also understood unilaterally, at heart. Classicism, with its didactic orientation, was prevented from gaining a broader basis.
19. Conclusive arguments for this view are given in Hermann Fränkel, "Ein Don Quijote unter den Argonauten des Apollonios," *Museum Helveticum* 17 (1960): 1–20.
20. One single epic had a historical subject, unlike all the others, which treated mythical ones. This was Lucan's epic treatment of the civil war. The actors in this epic, then, are not mythic heroes. It was long considered a scholarly crux why Lucan had forsworn the opportunity of allowing the gods to have some effect on the actions he describes, as was done in epics before and after his time. For this is an element in the mythic frame: in suprahistorical times the gods are present in men. These coordinates of myth could not be applied to an action occuring in real time, such as the civil war. Surely the barely twenty-five-year-old Lucan understood this impossibility.
21. Callimachus, 612 Pfeiffer.
22. On the one hand it was tempting to search out far-fetched tales and to be the first to give them poetic treatment; this was the area in which Callimachus became pre-eminent. On the other hand, the temptation existed to confront the readers with riddles by offering mythological material in artful encoding. One example of this is Lycophron's Alexandra (the name is intended for Cassandra; her brother is Paris, who is also called Alexander). Aside from a few efforts along this line, it never happened that mythology degenerated into a kind of virtuosity, thus becoming an end in itself.
23. Even comedy does not apply in this case. Though in Aristophanes' time it was directed solely to reality, Menander and his period turned it toward universal validity. The center of the action is occupied, not by mythic figures, but by

clearly characterized personalities: the miser, the misanthrope—*dyskolos*—
the boastful soldier, the cunning slave, the deceived deceiver.

24. It would have been unthinkable to represent a plot taken from current events
    under a title borrowed from mythology, as is done in George Bernard Shaw's
    Pygmalion, Jean Anouilh's *Antigone,* or the film *Orfeo Negro.* During the
    nineteenth century it became customary to indicate the distance from the
    classics by the adjective "new"; thus Karl Immermann's *Der Neue
    Pygmalion*—a form of the title that can without a doubt be traced back to
    Jean-Jacques Rousseau's *La nouvelle Héloïse.* Our contemporary custom
    shows that the awareness of myth is waning among both authors and their
    audience. What remains is a generally inappropriate ceremonial use—for ex-
    ample, the Oedipus complex, discussed in section II.

25. The Augustan poets almost literally fought for this freedom. For Augustus
    urged them to treat his achievements in epic form. Had this come about, all of
    the freedoms defined above would have been abrogated.

26. Basically, these were still the conventions of Homeric poetry, in which gods
    acted out of human motives. The discussion on this point has ceased to exist
    since the third century B.C. The acceptance of myth brought with it its special
    conditions and laws.

27. I use the term "bewilderment" to translate the highly controversial concept of
    eleos.

Mircea Eliade

THE PRESTIGE OF THE

COSMOGONIC MYTH

A myth relates a sacred story, that is to say, it recounts a primordial event that occurred at the beginning of time. But to tell a sacred story is equivalent to revealing a mystery, because the characters in a myth are not human beings. They are either gods or civilizing heroes, and therefore their *gesta* constitute mysteries: man would not know these tales if they were not revealed to him. Consequently, a myth is a story of what happened—what the gods and supernatural beings did—at the beginning of time. "To recount" a myth is to proclaim what occurred then. Once "told," in other words, once revealed, the myth becomes the apodictic truth: it establishes truth. "It is so because it is said to be so," the Netsilik Eskimos declared in order to justify the validity of their sacred history and their religious traditions. The myth proclaims the advent of a new cosmic situation or narrates a primordial event, and so it is always the story of a "creation"; it tells how something has been effectuated, has begun to be. That is why the myth is interdependent with ontology; it deals solely with realities, with what really happened, with what was clearly manifest.

We are speaking, to be sure, of sacred realities because, in archaic societies, it is the sacred that is pre-eminently the real. Whatever belongs to the realm of the profane does not participate in being, precisely because the

Translated by Elaine P. Halperin.

I

profane was not ontologically founded by the myth; it has no instructive model. No god, no civilizing hero, ever revealed a profane act. Everything that the gods or the ancestors did, and consequently everything that the myths recount about their creative activity, is part of the realm of the sacred and therefore participates in being. On the other hand, what men do on their own initiative, without a mythical model, belongs to the realm of the profane; therefore it is, in the end, a vain and illusory activity.

Essentially, it is this aspect of the myth that should be stressed: the myth reveals absolute holiness because it recounts the creative activity of divine beings and discloses the sanctified nature of their works. In other words, the myth describes the varied and sometimes dramatic irruption of the sacred into the world. For this reason many primitive peoples do not recount myths indiscriminately at any time or place but solely during those seasons of the year that are richest in ritual (autumn, winter) or during an interval between religious ceremonies; in a word, during a lapse of sacred time.[1] It is the irruption of the sacred into the world—an irruption recounted by myth—which really establishes the world. Each myth tells how a reality came into being, whether it be a total reality like the cosmos or merely a fragment: an island, a species of vegetable, a human institution. In telling *how* things came to exist an explanation is also given, and, indirectly, another question is answered: *why* they came to exist. The "why" always overlaps with the "how." And this is true for the simple reason that by telling *how* a thing is born one reveals a manifestation of the sacred, the ultimate cause of any real existence.

Everything that has been created occurred at the beginning of time: *in principio*. For all creation, all life, begins in time; before a single thing existed, its own time could not exist. There was no cosmic time before the cosmos came into existence. Before a certain vegetable species was created, time, which causes it to grow, bear fruit, and perish, did not exist. That is why all creation took place at the beginning of time. Time sprang up with the first appearance of a new category of existents.

On the other hand, every creation, being a divine act, also represents an irruption of creative energy into the world. Every creation springs from a plenitude. The gods create out of excessive power, out of an overflow of energy. Creation is the result of an ontological superabundance. That is why the myth, which recounts this sacred *ontophanie*, this triumphant manifestation of the fulness of being, became the exemplary model

1. R. Petazzoni, "The Truth of Myth," *Essays on the History of Religions* (Leyden, 1954). pp. 11–23, esp. pp. 13 ff.

2

for all human activities. For it alone reveals the real, the superabundant, the efficacious. "We must do as the Gods did in the beginning," an Indian text asserts (*Shatapatha Brâhmana*, VII, 2, I, 4). "So did the Gods, and so do men," *Taittiriya Br.* (I, 5, 9, 4) adds. The dominant function of the myth is therefore to fix the models for all the rites and significant human activities—subsistence or marriage as well as work, education, art, or knowledge. In conducting himself as a fully responsible human being, man imitates the gods' exemplary gestures, copies their acts, be it a simple physiological function such as eating or a social, economic, cultural, or military activity. This faithful imitation of divine models has a twofold consequence: on the one hand, by imitating the gods, man remains within the sacred and therefore within the confines of reality; on the other, the world is sanctified by the uninterrupted reactualization of divine, exemplary gestures. The religious conduct of man contributes to the maintenance of the world's holiness.

It is rather interesting to note that religious man assumes a humanity that possesses a transhuman, transcendental model. He sees himself as truly man solely to the extent that he imitates the gods, the civilizing heroes of the mythical ancestors. This means that religious man wills himself to be different from what he happens to be at the level of his secular experience. Religious man is not given; he creates himself by drawing close to divine models. As we have already stated, these models are preserved by myths, by the story of divine *gesta*. Therefore the man who belongs to traditional societies, like modern man, believes himself to be created by history; but the only history that interests him is sacred history, revealed by myths—the history of the gods. Yet modern man wants to be constituted solely by human history, hence precisely by that sum of acts which, for pre-modern man, is of no interest, since it lacks divine models. What we wish to emphasize is that, from the start, religious man fixes the model he wishes to attain on a transhuman level—the level revealed by myths. A man becomes truly a man solely by conforming to the teachings of the myths, that is to say, by imitating the gods.

At this point let us illustrate these preliminary remarks on the structure and function of myths by a few examples concerned with sacred time and space. We chose sacred time and space because the behavior of religious man in regard to them represents the best illustration of the essential role played by the myth. In the eyes of religious man, space is not homogeneous: it exhibits fissures; that is to say, portions of space exist that are qualitatively different from others. There is a sacred and therefore "strong,"

3

significant space, and there are others, non-sacred spaces, which consequently lack structure and consistency—in a word, which are amorphous. Furthermore, this spatial non-homogeneity manifests itself to religious man by means of the experience of an antithesis between sacred space—the only one which is real, which truly exists—and all the rest, the shapeless expanse that surrounds him.

We must immediately add that the religious experience of the non-homogeneity of space constitutes a primordial one, homologous with a "founding of the world." This is not a matter of theoretical speculation but of a primary religious experience which precedes any reflection about the world. The world can be constituted, thanks to the fissure affecting space, because it is this fissure which marks the "fixed point," the central axis of all future orientation. Whenever the sacred manifests itself in any hierophancy, there is not only a split in the homogeneity of space but also a revelation of absolute reality which is in direct contrast to the non-reality of the vast, surrounding expanse. The manifestation of the sacred establishes the world ontologically. In the homogeneous and infinite expanse, where no guidepost is possible and therefore no orientation can be effected, hierophancy reveals an absolute "fixed point," a "center."

We can see the extent to which the discovery, or, one might say, the revelation, of sacred space holds an existential value for religious man; for nothing can begin, nothing can be done, without a prior revelation, and any orientation implies the existence of a fixed point. This is the reason why religious man has always endeavored to establish himself within the "center of the world." In order to live in the world, one must found it, and no world can be born in the "chaos" of homogeneity and in the relativity of secular space. The discovery of projection of a fixed point—the "center"—is equivalent to the creation of the world. We hasten to recall examples that illustrate in the clearest fashion the cosmological value of the ritual orientation and the construction of sacred space.

Any religion suffices to demonstrate the non-homogeneity of space as it is experienced by religious man. Let us select an example that is meaningful to everyone: a church in a modern city. In the eyes of the faithful this church participates in space other than that of the street where it happens to be. The door that leads to the inside of the church signifies, in actuality, a solution of continuity. At the same time the threshold that separates the two spaces indicates the distance between two worlds of being—secular and religious. This threshold is both the boundary that separates and contrasts these two worlds and the paradoxical place in

4

which these worlds communicate, where the transition from the profane to the sacred can be effected.

From what we have just said one can understand why the church participates in space that is entirely different from that of the human agglomerations which surround it. Within the sacred inclosure the profane world is transcended. At more archaic levels of culture this possibility of transcendance is expressed by diverse images of an opening:[2] there, within the sacred walls, communication with the gods has become possible; consequently, there must be a "door" up above through which the gods can descend to the earth and man, symbolically, can rise to the heavens. And, indeed, this was the case for many religions; the temple, properly speaking, represents an "opening" toward the heavens and insures communication between the world and the gods.

Any sacred space implies hierophancy, an irruption of the sacred, the result of which is to detach territory in the surrounding cosmic environment and to render it qualitatively different. If no theophany, no sign of any kind, sanctified a place, then man consecrated it. For, as we have seen, the sacred is pre-eminently the real—at once power, efficiency, source of life, and fertility. Religious man's desire to live within the sacred is equivalent, in fact, to his desire to be fixed within objective reality, to live in a real and effective world and not in an illusion. This behavior is confirmed on every level of life, but it is principally evident in religious man's desire to live uniquely in a sanctified world, that is to say, in a sacred space. This is why techniques of orientation have been elaborated; these are, properly speaking, techniques concerned with constructions of sacred space. But it would be wrong to believe that this refers to a human endeavor, that man is able to consecrate a space by his own effort. Actually, the ritual by which he constructs a sacred space is adequate only to the extent that he reproduces the work of the gods. And, as we have seen, it is myth that reveals the history of divine works to him, offering him a model he can imitate.

To attain a fuller understanding of the need to construct sacred space ritually, one must take into account the conception that primitive and traditional societies held of the world. A man from such a society believes that an antithesis exists between the territory which he and his people inhabit and the unknown and undetermined space that surrounds him. The former is the world, the cosmos; the latter is no longer a cosmos but

2. A few examples are to be found in my study, "Centre du monde, temple, maison," *Le Symbolisme cosmique des monuments religieux* (Rome, 1957), pp. 57–82, esp. pp. 72 ff.

5

a kind of "other world," an alien, chaotic space inhabited by larvae, demons, "foreigners" (and associated, moreover, with demons and the souls of the dead). At first glance this split in space seems to be due to the contrast between an inhabited and organized territory, therefore "cosmicized," and the unknown space that extends beyond its frontiers; we have "cosmos," on the one hand, and "chaos," on the other. But we will see that, while an inhabited territory is a "cosmos," this is precisely because it has been previously consecrated, because in one way or another it is the work of the gods or is in communication with the world of the gods.

All this emerges very plainly from the Vedic ritual concerning the occupation of a territory: possession becomes legally valid by virtue of the erection of an altar of fire dedicated to Agni. Because of this altar Agni is present, and communication with the world of the gods is assured. But the significance of the ritual is more complex; if all its articulations are taken into consideration, we see why the consecration of a territory is equivalent to its "cosmicization." Actually, the erection of an altar to Agni is nothing but a reproduction of creation on a microcosmic scale. The water with which the clay is mixed is associated with primordial water; the clay used for the base of the altar symbolizes the earth; the lateral walls represent the atmosphere; etc. Consequently, the erection of an altar of fire—which alone warrants the occupation of a territory—is equivalent to the cosmogony.[3]

An unknown, foreign, unoccupied territory nonetheless participates in the fluid and larva-like modality of chaos. In occupying it, man transforms it into cosmos by a ritual repetition of the cosmogony. What is to be "our world" must be "created" beforehand, and any creation possesses a mythical model: the gods' creation of the universe. When the Scandinavian colonists took possession of Iceland and cleared it, they did not look upon this enterprise either as an original endeavor or as a human and secular accomplishment. In their eyes this labor was but the repetition of a primordial act: the transformation of chaos into cosmos by the divine act of creation. Consequently, everything that is not "our world" is not yet a "world," and a territory becomes "ours" only by creating it anew—in other words, by consecrating it.

In this instance one realizes the major role played by the cosmogonic myth. For it is this myth that reveals how the world was first created. Men

3. Cf. the texts cited in my *Le Mythe de l'éternel retour* (Paris: Gallimard, 1949), pp. 112 ff.; English trans., *The Myth of the Eternal Return* (London: Routledge & K. Paul, 1955).

6

have but to imitate this instructive gesture of the gods. The following example illustrates what we have just said. According to a myth of the Achilpa, an Australian tribe, in the beginning the Holy Being, Numbakula, "cosmicized" their future territory, created their ancestor, and established their institutions. Numbakula fashioned a sacred stake from the trunk of a gum tree and, having first anointed it with blood, climbed it and disappeared into the heavens. This stake represents a cosmic axis, for the territory surrounding it became inhabitable and consequently transformed into a "world." For this reason the ritual role of the sacred stake is a considerable one; the Achilpa take it with them during their peregrinations, and they decide which direction to take according to the way the stake inclines. This allows the Achilpa, despite continuous travels, always to find themselves in "their world" and also to remain in communication with the heavens, where Numbakula had disappeared. If the stake is broken, catastrophe ensues; in a way, it is the "end of the world"—regression into chaos. Spencer and Gillen relate a legend in which the sacred stake was once broken and the entire tribe fell prey to anguish; its members wandered aimlessly for a while and finally sat on the ground and allowed themselves to die.[4]

This example is an admirable illustration of both the cosmological function of the ritual stake and its soteriological role; for, on the one hand, the ritual stake is a reproduction of the one employed by Numbakula to "cosmicize" the world and, on the other, the Achilpa believe that through it they can communicate with the celestial domain. And so human existence is made possible by this permanent communication with the heavens. The Achilpa's "world" becomes truly their world only to the extent that it reproduces the cosmos as organized and sanctified by Numbakula. One cannot live without a vertical axis that permits an opening into the transcendent and, at the same time, makes orientation possible; in other words, one cannot live in chaos. Once contact with the transcendent is broken and the orientation is disrupted, it is no longer possible to live in the world, and so the Achilpa allow themselves to die.

The ritual stake of the Achilpa "supports" their world and assures communication with the heavens. We have here the prototype of a cosmological image that was very widespread: that of the *axis mundi*, the cosmic axis that supports the heavens and simultaneously paves the way to the

4. Sir B. Spencer and F. J. Gillen, *The Arunta* (London: Macmillan & Co., 1927), I, 374. 386; cf. also E. de Martino, "Angoscia territoriale et riscatto culturale nel mito Achilpa delle origini," *Studi e materiali di storia della religioni*, XXIII (1951–52), 51–66.

world of the gods. We cannot detail here the innumerable images of the cosmic axis. It will suffice to state that all myths which stress the Tree of the World, the Cosmic Mountains, pillars, stone columns, or ladders that link the earth with the heavens, express this fundamental idea: that a "center of the world" exists thanks to which communication with the heavens can be accomplished and around which the totality of the habitable world extends. The "center" is the place where a split in the ontological level was effectuated, where space becomes sacred, therefore pre-eminently real. This also means that the universe is created from its center and extends from a central point that is like its "navel." Thus, according to the *Rig Veda* (X, 149), the universe is born and evolves; it starts from a nucleus, from a central point. Jewish tradition is even more explicit: "His Holiness created the world like an embryo. Just as the embryo grows from the navel, so God began to create the world. Starting with the navel, it spread out thence in all directions."[5]

The occupation of an unknown or foreign territory, the establishment of a village, the construction of a sanctuary or merely of a house, constitute so many symbolical repetitions of the cosmogony. Just as the visible universe develops from a center and spreads in four directions, just so does the village grow around a crossroads. In Bali as well as in certain regions of Asia, when a new village is first under construction, an effort is made to find a natural crossroads where two perpendicular roads intersect. The division of the village into four sectors corresponds to the division of the universe into four horizons. Often an empty place is left in the middle of the village; there, a little later, the cultural house will be built, the roof of which will symbolically represent the heavens (in some cases the heavens are indicated by the top of a tree or by the image of a mountain).[6] At the other end of the village one will find the world of the dead, symbolized by certain animals (snakes, crocodiles, etc.) or by ideograms depicting darkness.[7] The cosmic symbolism of the village is repeated in the structure of the sanctuary or the cultural house. At Waropen, in New Guinea, the "house for men" is placed in the middle of the village. Its roof represents the celestial archway, and the four walls correspond to the four directions of space.

5. Rabbinical text cited in *Le Mythe de l'éternel retour*, p. 36.

6. C. Tg. Bertling, *Vierzahl, Kreuz und Mandal in Asien* (Amsterdam, 1954), p. 11.

7. This iconographic complex is to be found in China, India, Indonesia, and New Guinea (cf. Bertling, *op. cit.*, p. 8).

8

One is scarcely surprised to encounter analogous conceptions in ancient Italy and among the ancient Germans. We are, after all, dealing with an archaic and very widespread notion: the city is an *imago mundi;* consequently, its construction imitates cosmogony. The Roman *mundus* was a circular ditch, divided into four parts. It was both an image of the cosmos and an exemplary model of the human habitat. It has been correctly suggested that the *Roma quadrata* must be conceived not as having the shape of a square but as being divided into four parts.[8] The *mundus* was obviously associated with the *omphalos,* the earth's umbilicus: the city was situated in the middle of the *orbis terrarum.* It has been demonstrated that the same ideas explain the structure of Germanic villages and cities.[9] In extremely diverse cultural contexts we always find the same cosmological pattern and the same ritual scenario: settling down in a territory is equivalent to founding the world. In other words, man progressively occupies increasingly vast areas of the planet and "cosmicizes" them in accordance with the model revealed by the cosmogonical myth. Thanks to this myth, man also becomes a creator. At first glimpse all he seems to do is to repeat indefinitely the same archetypal gesture. In reality, however, he conquers the world, organizes it, and transforms the natural landscape into a cultural environment. Herein resides the great secret of myths: they incite man to create. They continuously open up new perspectives for his creative genius, although superficially they seem to paralyze human initiative because they appear to be intangible models.

In all traditional societies, to "cosmicize" a space is equivalent to consecrating it, because the cosmos, being a divine work, is sacred by virtue of its very structure. To live in a cosmos is, above all, to live in a sanctified space, one that offers the possibility of communication with the gods. We have seen that the Achilpa's sacred stake symbolizes both an opening toward the transcendent and communication with the heavens where Numbakula had disappeared. Hence the "cosmicization," therefore the consecration, of space by some kind of ritual technique of orientation is also repeated when a house is being built. One perceives this "cosmicization" in the very structure of the home. Among a good many archaic peoples, particularly among hunters and seminomadic shepherds, the home possesses a symbolism that transforms it into an *imago mundi.* Among the nomads the stake that supports their tent is associated with the cosmic axis; for sedentary peoples a central pillar or the hole for smoke evacua-

8. Cf. Werner Müller, *Kreis und Kreuz* (Berlin, 1938), pp. 60 ff.

9. *Ibid.,* pp. 65 ff.

9

tion[10] plays the same role. All this represents the symbolism of the "center of the world"; having examined it in several prior works, we shall not come back to it.[11] And so we conclude: just as occupied territory, the city or village, reproduces the universe, so does the home also become an *imago mundi* because of the ritual orientation and the symbolism of the center.

In summary we might say that traditional societies want to live continuously in a sacred space and that it is myth which teaches them how they must build this sacred space: by imitating the work of the gods—cosmogony. Therefore the myth forces religious man to become responsible for the creation of the world in which he has chosen to live. To settle down in a land, to build a village, calls for a vital decision, an existential choice. For tragic, bloody cosmogonies also exist, and, as the imitator of divine gestures, man is compelled to repeat these gestures. The bloody sacrifices on the occasion of building a city or a house are explicable in terms of the need to imitate the primordial sacrifice by virtue of which the gods created the cosmos.

Since "our world" is a cosmos, any external attack threatens to transform it into chaos. And since "our world" was founded by imitating the exemplary work of the gods—cosmogony—those enemies who attack it are associated with the enemies of the gods, the demons and especially the archdemon, the primordial dragon that was conquered by the gods in the beginning of time. An attack against "our world" can be likened to the revenge of the mythical dragon that rebels against the work of the gods, against the cosmos, attempting to reduce it to nothingness. The enemies are ranked with the powers of chaos. Any destruction of a city is equivalent to a regression to chaos. Any victory against the attacker repeats the gods' exemplary victory over the dragon (that is, over chaos). The dragon is the exemplary figure of the sea monster, of the primordial serpent, a symbol of the cosmic waters, of darkness, of night and death—in short, of the amorphous, the potential—everything that has no "form." The gods had to conquer and destroy the dragon so that the cosmos could be created. It was with the body of Tiamat, the sea monster, that Marduk fashioned the world. Just as the gods' triumph over the forces of darkness, of death and chaos is repeated each time the city is victorious over its invaders, so must the gods' victory over the dragon be repeated symbolically each year; for each year the world must be re-created.

10. Cf. my *Le Chamanisme* (Paris: Payot, 1951), pp. 235 ff.

11. Cf. *Le Mythe de l'éternel retour*, pp. 30 ff.; *Images et symboles* (Paris: Gallimard, 1952), pp. 33 ff.; and "Centre du monde, temple, maison," *op. cit., passim.*

10

And so we see that the principal function of the cosmogonic myth is to serve as an exemplary model for the periodic regeneration of time. Each new year is a resumption of time from its beginning, that is to say, a repetition of the cosmogony. A great many of the New Year's rituals can be explained as an attempt to revive primordial time, "pure" time, the time of the creation. The ritual struggle between two groups of contestants, the return of the dead, the saturnalia and orgies—all these are elements which signify that, at the end of this year and while we await the new one, the mythical advent representing the transition from chaos to cosmogony is being repeated. The Babylonian New Year's ceremony, the akîtu, is fairly conclusive. During this ceremony, Enuma elish, the "Poem of the Creation," was recited. This ritual recitation revivified the struggle between Marduk and the sea monster, Tiamat, which took place at the beginning of time. This struggle was re-enacted by two groups of contestants. The mythical event became actual. "May he continue to vanquish Tiamat and abbreviate its days!" the person officiating would exclaim. The struggle, Marduk's victory, and the creation of the world were taking place at that very instant, hic et nunc.[12]

Why did men from traditional societies feel the need to relive the cosmogony annually? In order to regenerate the world by reintegrating original sacred time, the time when the creation of the world occurred. On the Iranian New Year's Day, called the Nauroz, the king would proclaim: "Here is a new day of a new month of a new year; we must renew what time has worn out!" Time had worn out human beings, society, the cosmos; and this destructive time was profane time, duration—to be exact, history. For time, like space, is not homogeneous; there is a sacred time, eternally present because it is eternally repeatable, and profane time, the irreversible duration which implacably leads to death. And just as religious man wishes to live continuously in a sacred space, where the possibility of communication with the divine world exists, so does he attempt to escape from the confines of profane time and to rediscover sacred time.

In all the pre-Judaic religions sacred time was the time of the myth, primordial time, in which the exemplary acts of the gods were accomplished. But in reactualizing primordial time, that profane time which was already past, the time that contains death in its own duration, was suppressed. All the individual and collective purifications that took place on the occasion of the new year came after the abolition of time gone by and, consequently, after the abolition of all that time had worn out. Time was

12. Cf. Le Mythe de l'éternel retour, pp. 89 ff.

reborn "pure," just as it was in the beginning, from the very fact that at each new year the world was created anew. By reiterating the cosmogony, primordial sacred time was restored. The re-creation of the cosmos implied the regeneration of time. The interdependence of the cosmos and cosmic time was so thoroughly perceived by pre-modern man that in many languages the term designating the "world" is employed to mean the "year." For example, certain North American tribes say "the world is past," or "the earth is past," to mean that "a year has passed."[13]

By examining the cosmological symbolism of the temples, we gain a better understanding of this close kinship between space and sacred time. Since it is an *imago mundi*, a cosmos in miniature, the temple also represents the cosmic, temporal rhythms. The Vedic altar was not merely the cosmos; it was also the year—that is to say, cyclical time. Besides its cosmological symbolism, the Temple of Jerusalem also possessed a temporal symbolism: the twelve loaves of bread that were placed on the table were the twelve months, and the candelabra with seventy branches represented the Decans. In the Greco-Latin domain, H. Usener showed his thorough understanding of the etymological kinship between *templum* and *tempus*. We find an analogous symbolism on archaic levels of culture. The Dakota Indians affirm that the year is a circle around their sacred hut, which represents the world.[14] The profound reason for all these symbols is clear: the temple is the image of the sanctified world. The holiness of the temple sanctifies both the cosmos and cosmic time. Therefore, the temple represents the original state of the world: the pure world that was not worn out by time or sullied by an invasion of the profane. This is the very image of the world as it was before history, at the very moment when it emerged from the hands of the Creator.

It is fitting to note that, by periodically repeating the cosmogony and by annually regenerating time, religious man is attempting to recover the original purity and holiness of the world as still preserved symbolically in the temple. In other words, religious man wants to live in a cosmos that is similar in holiness to that of the temple. The cosmogonic myth reveals to him how to rediscover this primordial holiness of the world. Therefore, thanks to the cosmogonic myth, religious man from the pre- and extra-Mosaic societies attempts to live in continuous imitation of the gods. It is this myth that teaches him how to found a humanity beyond man's

13. A. L. Kroeber, *Handbook of the Indians of California* (Washington, D.C.: Government Printing Office, 1925), pp. 177, 498.

14. Werner Müller, *Die blaue Hutte* (Wiesbaden: F. Steiner, 1954), p. 133.

12

immediate, profane experience—a humanity that finds its model in the transcendental world of the Gods.

All creations—divine or human—are definitively dependent upon this model which constitutes the cosmogony. To create is, after all, to remake the world—whether the "world" happens to be a modest cabin, a humble tool, or a poem. The repetition of the cosmogony, whether periodic or not, is not an absurd and childish superstition of a humanity squatting in the darkness of primordial stupidity. In deciding to imitate the gods and to repeat their creative acts, primitive man had already taken upon himself that which, later, was revealed to us, the moderns—the very destiny of man. By this I mean the creation of the world we live in, the creation of the universe in which one wishes to live.

CHAPTER I

MYTH AND REALITY

IF WE look for "speculative thought" in the documents of the ancients, we shall be forced to admit that there is very little indeed in our written records which deserves the name of "thought" in the strict sense of that term. There are very few passages which show the discipline, the cogency of reasoning, which we associate with thinking. The thought of the ancient Near East appears wrapped in imagination. We consider it tainted with fantasy. But the ancients would not have admitted that anything could be abstracted from the concrete imaginative forms which they left us.

We should remember that even for us speculative thought is less rigidly disciplined than any other form. Speculation—as the etymology of the word shows—is an intuitive, an almost visionary, mode of apprehension. This does not mean, of course, that it is mere irresponsible meandering of the mind, which ignores reality or seeks to escape from its problems. Speculative thought transcends experience, but only because it attempts to explain, to unify, to order experience. It achieves this end by means of hypotheses. If we use the word in its original sense, then we may say that speculative thought attempts to *underpin* the chaos of experience so that it may reveal the features of a structure—order, coherence, and meaning.

Speculative thought is therefore distinct from mere idle speculation in that it never breaks entirely away from experience. It may be "once removed" from the problems of experience, but it is connected with them in that it tries to explain them.

In our own time speculative thought finds its scope more severely limited than it has been at any other period. For we possess in science another instrument for the interpretation of experience, one that has achieved marvels and retains its full fascination. We do not allow speculative thought, under any circumstances, to en-

143

croach upon the sacred precincts of science. It must not trespass on the realm of verifiable fact; and it must never pretend to a dignity higher than that of working hypotheses, even in the fields in which it is permitted some scope.

Where, then, is speculative thought allowed to range today? Its main concern is with man—his nature and his problems, his values and his destiny. For man does not quite succeed in becoming a scientific object to himself. His need of transcending chaotic experience and conflicting facts leads him to seek a metaphysical hypothesis that may clarify his urgent problems. On the subject of his "self" man will, most obstinately, speculate—even today.

When we turn to the ancient Near East in search of similar efforts, two correlated facts become apparent. In the first place, we find that speculation found unlimited possibilities for development; it was not restricted by a scientific (that is, a disciplined) search for truth. In the second place, we notice that the realm of nature and the realm of man were not distinguished.

The ancients, like the modern savages, saw man always as part of society, and society as imbedded in nature and dependent upon cosmic forces. For them nature and man did not stand in opposition and did not, therefore, have to be apprehended by different modes of cognition. We shall see, in fact, in the course of this book, that natural phenomena were regularly conceived in terms of human experience and that human experience was conceived in terms of cosmic events. We touch here upon a distinction between the ancients and us which is of the utmost significance for our inquiry.

The fundamental difference between the attitudes of modern and ancient man as regards the surrounding world is this: for modern, scientific man the phenomenal world is primarily an "It"; for ancient—and also for primitive—man it is a "Thou."

This formulation goes far beyond the usual "animistic" or "personalistic" interpretations. It shows up, in fact, the inadequacies of these commonly accepted theories. For a relation between "I" and "Thou" is absolutely *sui generis*. We can best explain its unique quality by comparing it with two other modes of cognition: the relation between subject and object and the relation that exists when I "understand" another living being.

The correlation "subject-object" is, of course, the basis of all scientific thinking; it alone makes scientific knowledge possible. The second mode of cognition is the curiously direct knowledge which we gain when we "understand" a creature confronting us— its fear, let us say, or its anger. This, by the way, is a form of knowledge which we have the honor of sharing with the animals.

The differences between an I-and-Thou relationship and these two other relationships are as follows: In determining the identity of an object, a person is active. In "understanding" a fellow-creature, on the other hand, a man or an animal is essentially passive, whatever his subsequent action may turn out to be. For at first he receives an impression. This type of knowledge is therefore direct, emotional, and inarticulate. Intellectual knowledge, on the contrary, is emotionally indifferent and articulate.

Now the knowledge which "I" has of "Thou" hovers between the active judgment and the passive "undergoing of an impression"; between the intellectual and the emotional, the articulate and the inarticulate. "Thou" may be problematic, yet "Thou" is somewhat transparent. "Thou" is a live presence, whose qualities and potentialities can be made somewhat articulate—not as a result of active inquiry but because "Thou," as a presence, reveals itself.

There is yet another important difference. An object, an "It," can always be scientifically related to other objects and appear as part of a group or a series. In this manner science insists on seeing "It"; hence, science is able to comprehend objects and events as ruled by universal laws which make their behavior under given circumstances predictable. "Thou," on the other hand, is unique. "Thou" has the unprecedented, unparalleled, and unpredictable character of an individual, a presence known only in so far as it reveals itself. "Thou," moreover, is not merely contemplated or understood but is experienced emotionally in a dynamic reciprocal relationship. For these reasons there is justification for the aphorism of Crawley: "Primitive man has only one mode of thought, one mode of expression, one part of speech—the personal." This does not mean (as is so often thought) that primitive man, in order to explain natural phenomena, imparts human characteristics to an inanimate world. Primitive man simply does not know an inanimate world. For this very reason he does not "personify" inanimate phenomena nor does he fill an empty world with the ghosts of the dead, as "animism" would have us believe.

The world appears to primitive man neither inanimate nor empty but redundant with life; and life has individuality, in man and beast and plant, and in every phenomenon which confronts man— the thunderclap, the sudden shadow, the eerie and unknown clearing in the wood, the stone which suddenly hurts him when he stumbles while on a hunting trip. Any phenomenon may at any time face him, not as "It," but as "Thou." In this confrontation, "Thou" reveals its individuality, its qualities, its will. "Thou" is not contemplated with intellectual detachment; it is experienced as life confronting life, involving every faculty of man in a reciprocal relationship. Thoughts, no less than acts and feelings, are subordinated to this experience.

We are here concerned particularly with thought. It is likely that the ancients recognized certain intellectual problems and asked for the "why" and "how," the "where from" and "where to." Even so, we cannot expect in the ancient Near Eastern documents to find speculation in the predominantly intellectual form with which we are familiar and which presupposes strictly logical procedure even while attempting to transcend it. We have seen that in the ancient Near East, as in present-day primitive society, thought does not operate autonomously. The whole man confronts a living "Thou" in nature; and the whole man—emotional and imaginative as well as intellectual—gives expression to the experience. All experience of "Thou" is highly individual; and early man does, in fact, view happenings as individual events. An account of such events and also their explanation can be conceived only as action and necessarily take the form of a story. In other words, the ancients told myths instead of presenting an analysis or conclusions. We would explain, for instance, that certain atmospheric changes broke a drought and brought about rain. The Babylonians observed the same facts but experienced them as the intervention of the gigantic bird Imdugud which came to their rescue. It covered the sky with the black storm clouds of its wings and devoured the Bull of Heaven, whose hot breath had scorched the crops.

146

In telling such a myth, the ancients did not intend to provide entertainment. Neither did they seek, in a detached way and without ulterior motives, for intelligible explanations of the natural phenomena. They were recounting events in which they were involved to the extent of their very existence. They experienced, directly, a conflict of powers, one hostile to the harvest upon which they depended, the other frightening but beneficial: the thunderstorm reprieved them in the nick of time by defeating and utterly destroying the drought. The images had already become traditional at the time when we meet them in art and literature, but originally they must have been seen in the revelation which the experience entailed. They are products of imagination, but they are not mere fantasy. It is essential that true myth be distinguished from legend, saga, fable, and fairy tale. All these may retain elements of the myth. And it may also happen that a baroque or frivolous imagination elaborates myths until they become mere stories. But true myth presents its images and its imaginary actors, not with the playfulness of fantasy, but with a compelling authority. It perpetuates the revelation of a "Thou."

The imagery of myth is therefore by no means allegory. It is nothing less than a carefully chosen cloak for abstract thought. The imagery is inseparable from the thought. It represents the form in which the experience has become conscious.

Myth, then, is to be taken seriously, because it reveals a significant, if unverifiable, truth—we might say a metaphysical truth. But myth has not the universality and the lucidity of theoretical statement. It is concrete, though it claims to be inassailable in its validity. It claims recognition by the faithful; it does not pretend to justification before the critical

The irrational aspect of myth becomes especially clear when we remember that the ancients were not content merely to recount their myths as stories conveying information. They dramatized them, acknowledging in them a special virtue which could be activated by recital.

Of the dramatization of myth, Holy Communion is a well-known example. Another example is found in Babylonia. During each New Year's festival the Babylonians re-enacted the victory which Marduk had won over the powers of chaos on the first New

Year's Day, when the world was created. At the annual festival the Epic of Creation was recited. It is clear that the Babylonians did not regard their story of creation as we might accept the theory of Laplace, for instance, as an intellectually satisfying account of how the world came to be as it is. Ancient man had not thought out an answer; an answer had been revealed to him in a reciprocal relationship with nature. If a question had been answered, man shared that answer with the "Thou" which had revealed itself. Hence, it seemed wise that man, each year, at the critical turn of the seasons, should proclaim the knowledge which he shared with the powers, in order to involve them once more in its potent truth.

We may, then, summarize the complex character of myth in the following words: Myth is a form of poetry which transcends poetry in that it proclaims a truth; a form of reasoning which transcends reasoning in that it wants to bring about the truth it proclaims; a form of action, of ritual behavior, which does not find its fulfilment in the act but must proclaim and elaborate a poetic form of truth.

It will now be clear why we said at the beginning of this chapter that our search for speculative thought in the ancient Near East might lead to negative results. The detachment of intellectual inquiry is wanting throughout. And yet, within the framework of mythopoeic thought, speculation may set in. Even early man, entangled in the immediacy of his perceptions, recognized the existence of certain problems which transcend the phenomena. He recognized the problem of origin and the problem of *telos*, of the aim and purpose of being. He recognized the invisible order of justice maintained by his customs, mores, institutions; and he connected this invisible order with the visible order, with its succession of days and nights, seasons and years, obviously maintained by the sun. Early man even pondered the hierarchy of the different powers which he recognized in nature. In the Memphite Theology, which will be discussed in chapter ii, the Egyptians, at one point, reduced the multiplicity of the divine to a truly monotheistic conception and spiritualized the concept of creation. Nevertheless, they spoke the language of myth. The teachings of such documents can be termed "speculative" in recognition of their intention, if not of their performance.

To give an example, let us anticipate our colleagues and consider various possible answers to the question of how the world came into being. Some modern primitives, the Shilluk, in many respects related to the ancient Egyptians, give the following answer to this question: "In the beginning was Ju-ok the Great Creator, and he created a great white cow who came up out of the Nile and was called Deung Adok. The white cow gave birth to a man-child whom she nursed and named Kola."[1] Of such a story (and there are many of this type) we can say that apparently any form which relates the coming into being as a concretely imagined event satisfies the inquirer. There is no shadow of speculative thought here. Instead there is immediacy of vision—concrete, unquestioned, inconsequential.

We move one step farther if the creation is imagined, not in a purely fantastic manner, but by analogy with human conditions. Creation is then conceived as birth; and the simplest form is the postulate of a primeval couple as the parents of all that exists. It seems that for the Egyptians, as for the Greeks and the Maoris, Earth and Sky were the primeval pair.

The next step, this time one which leads in the direction of speculative thought, is taken when creation is conceived as the action of one of the parents. It may be conceived of as birth by a Great Mother, either a goddess, as in Greece, or a demon, as in Babylonia. Alternatively it is possible to conceive creation as the act of a male. In Egypt, for instance, the god Atum arose unaided from the primeval waters and started the creation of cosmos out of chaos by begetting on himself the first pair of gods.

In all these creation stories we remain in the realm of myth, even though an element of speculation can be discerned. But we move into the sphere of speculative thought—albeit mythopoeic speculative thought—when it is said that Atum was the Creator; that his eldest children were Shū and Tefnūt, Air and Moisture; that their children were Geb and Nūt, Earth and Sky; and their children, again, the four gods of the Osiris cycle through whom (since Osiris was the dead king as well as god) society is related to the cosmic powers. In this story of creation we find a definite cosmological system as the outcome of speculation.

Nor does this remain an isolated instance in Egypt. Even chaos itself became a subject of speculation. It was said that the primeval waters were inhabited by eight weird creatures, four frogs and four snakes, male and female, who brought forth Atum the sun-god and creator. This group of eight, this Ogdoad, was part, not of the created order, but of chaos itself, as the names show. The first pair was Nūn and Naunet, primeval, formless Ocean and primeval Matter; the second pair was Hūh and Hauhet, the Illimitable and the Boundless. Then came Kūk and Kauket, Darkness and Obscurity; and, finally, Amon and Amaunet, the Hidden and Concealed ones—probably the wind. For the wind "bloweth where it listeth and thou hearest the sound thereof but canst not tell whence it cometh and whither it goeth" (John 3 : 8). Here, surely, is speculative thought in mythological guise.

We also find speculative thought in Babylonia, where chaos is conceived, not as a friendly and co-operative Ogdoad which brings forth the creator, Sun, but as the enemy of life and order. After Ti'amat, the Great Mother, had given birth to countless beings, including the gods, the latter, under the guidance of Marduk, fought a critical battle in which she was overcome and destroyed. And out of her the existing universe was constructed. The Babylonian placed that conflict at the basis of existence.

Throughout the ancient Near East, then, we find speculative thought in the form of myth. We have seen how the attitude of early man toward the phenomena explains his mythopoeic form of thought. But, in order to understand its peculiarities more fully, we should consider the form it takes in somewhat greater detail.

THE LOGIC OF MYTHOPOEIC THOUGHT

We have hitherto been at pains to show that for primitive man thoughts are not autonomous, that they remain involved in the curious attitude toward the phenomenal world which we have called a confrontation of life with life. Indeed, we shall find that our categories of intellectual judgment often do not apply to the complexes of cerebration and volition which constitute mythopoeic thought.

And yet the word "logic" as used above is justified. The ancients expressed their "emotional thought" (as we might call it) in terms of cause and effect; they explained phenomena in terms of time and space and number. The form of their reasoning is far less alien to ours than is often believed. They could reason logically; but they did not often care to do it. For the detachment which a purely intellectual attitude implies is hardly compatible with their most significant experience of reality. Scholars who have proved at length that primitive man has a "prelogical" mode of thinking are likely to refer to magic or religious practice, thus forgetting that they apply the Kantian categories, not to pure reasoning, but to highly emotional acts.

We shall find that if we attempt to define the structure of mytho-poeic thought and compare it with that of modern (that is, scientific) thought, the differences will prove to be due rather to emotional attitude and intention than to a so-called prelogical mentality. The basic distinction of modern thought is that between *subjective* and *objective*. On this distinction scientific thought has based a critical and analytical procedure by which it progressively reduces the individual phenomena to typical events subject to universal laws. Thus it creates an increasingly wide gulf between our perception of the phenomena and the conceptions by which we make them comprehensible. We see the sun rise and set, but we think of the earth as moving round the sun. We see colors, but we describe them as wave-lengths. We dream of a dead relative, but we think of that distinct vision as a product of our own subconscious minds. Even if we individually are unable to prove these almost unbelievable scientific views to be true, we accept them, because we know that they can be proved to possess a greater degree of objectivity than our sense-impressions. In the immediacy of primitive experience, however, there is no room for such a critical resolution of perceptions. Primitive man cannot withdraw from the presence of the phenomena because they reveal themselves to him in the manner we have described. Hence the distinction between subjective and objective knowledge is meaningless to him.

Meaningless, also, is our contrast between reality and appearance. Whatever is capable of affecting mind, feeling, or will has thereby established its undoubted reality. There is, for instance, no reason why dreams should be considered less real than impressions received while one is awake. On the contrary, dreams often affect one so much more than the humdrum events of daily life that they appear to be more, and not less, significant than the usual perceptions. The Babylonians, like the Greeks, sought divine guidance by passing the night in a sacred place hoping for a revelation in dreams. And pharaohs, too, have recorded that dreams induced them to undertake certain works. Hallucinations, too, are real. We find in the official annals of Assarhaddon of Assyria[2] a record of fabulous monsters—two-headed serpents and green, winged creatures—which the exhausted troops had seen in the most trying section of their march, the arid Sinai Desert. We may recall that the Greeks saw the Spirit of the Plain of Marathon arisen in the fateful battle against the Persians. As to monsters, the Egyptians of the Middle Kingdom, as much horrified by the desert as are their modern descendants, depicted dragons, griffins, and chimeras among gazelles, foxes, and other desert game, on a footing of perfect equality.

Just as there was no sharp distinction among dreams, hallucinations, and ordinary vision, there was no sharp separation between the living and the dead. The survival of the dead and their continued relationship with man were assumed as a matter of course, for the dead were involved in the indubitable reality of man's own anguish, expectation, or resentment. "To be effective" to the mythopoeic mind means the same as "to be."

Symbols are treated in the same way. The primitive uses symbols as much as we do; but he can no more conceive them as signifying, yet separate from, the gods or powers than he can consider a relationship established in his mind—such as resemblance—as connecting, and yet separate from, the objects compared. Hence there is coalescence of the symbol and what it signifies, as there is coalescence of two objects compared so that one may stand for the other.

In a similar manner we can explain the curious figure of thought *pars pro toto*, "a part can stand for the whole"; a name, a lock of hair, or a shadow can stand for the man because at any moment the lock of hair or shadow may be felt by the primitive to be pregnant with the full significance of the man. It may confront him with a "Thou" which bears the physiognomy of its owner.

An example of the coalescence of a symbol and the thing it stands for is the treating of a person's name as an essential part of him— as if it were, in a way, identical with him. We have a number of pottery bowls which Egyptian kings of the Middle Kingdom had inscribed with the names of hostile tribes in Palestine, Libya, and Nubia; the names of their rulers; and the names of certain rebellious Egyptians. These bowls were solemnly smashed at a ritual, possibly at the funeral of the king's predecessor; and the object of this ritual was explicitly stated. It was that all these enemies, obviously out of the pharaoh's reach, should die. But if we call the ritual act of the breaking of the bowls symbolical, we miss the point. The Egyptians felt that *real* harm was done to the enemies by the destruction of their names. The occasion was even used to cast a propitious spell of wider scope. After the names of the hostile men, who were enumerated "that they should die," were added such phrases as: "all detrimental thought, all detrimental talk, all detrimental dreams, all detrimental plans, all detrimental strife," etc. Mentioning these things on the bowls to be smashed diminished their actual power to hurt the king or lessen his authority.

For us there is an essential difference between an act and a ritual or symbolical performance. But this distinction was meaningless to the ancients. Gudea, a Mesopotamian ruler, describing the founding of a temple, mentions in one breath that he molded a brick in clay, purified the site with fire, and consecrated the platform with oil. When the Egyptians claim that Osiris, and the Babylonians that Oannes, gave them the elements of their culture, they include among those elements the crafts and agriculture as well as ritual usages. These two groups of activities possess the same degree of reality. It would be meaningless to ask a Babylonian whether the success of the harvest depended on the skill of the farmers or on the correct performance of the New Year's festival. Both were essential to success.

Just as the imaginary is acknowledged as existing in reality, so concepts are likely to be substantialized. A man who has courage or eloquence possesses these qualities almost as substances of which he can be robbed or which he can share with others. The concept of "justice" or "equity" is in Egypt called *ma'at*. The king's mouth is the temple of *ma'at*. *Ma'at* is personified as a goddess; but at the same time it is said that the gods "live by *ma'at*." This concept is represented quite concretely: in the daily ritual the gods are offered a figure of the goddess, together with the other material offerings, food and drink, for their sustenance. Here we meet the paradox of mythopoeic thought. Though it does not know dead matter and confronts a world animated from end to end, it is unable to leave the scope of the concrete and renders its own concepts as realities existing per se.

An excellent example of this tendency toward concreteness is the primitive conception of death. Death is not, as for us, an event —the act or fact of dying, as Webster has it. It is somehow a substantial reality. Thus we read in the Egyptian Pyramid Texts a description of the beginning of things which runs as follows:

> When heaven had not yet come into existence,
> When men had not yet come into existence,
> When gods had not yet been born,
> When death had not yet come into existence. . . . .[3]

In exactly the same terms the cupbearer Siduri pities Gilgamesh in the Epic:

> Gilgamesh, whither are you wandering?
> Life, which you look for, you will never find.
> For when the gods created men, they let
> death be his share, and life
> withheld in their own hands.

Note, in the first place, that life is opposed to death, thus accentuating the fact that life in itself is considered endless. Only the intervention of another phenomenon, death, makes an end to it. In the second place, we should note the concrete character attributed to life in the statement that the gods withheld life in their hands. In case one is inclined to see in this phrase a figure of speech, it is well to remember that Gilgamesh and, in another myth, Adapa are given a chance to gain eternal life simply by eating life as a substance. Gilgamesh is shown the "plant of life," but a ser-

pent robs him of it. Adapa is offered bread and water of life when
he enters heaven, but he refuses it on the instruction of the wily
god Enki. In both cases the assimilation of a concrete substance
would have made the difference between death and immortality.

We are touching here on the category of *causality*, which is as
important for modern thought as the distinction between the subjective and the objective. If science, as we have said before, reduces the chaos of perceptions to an order in which typical events
take place according to universal laws, the instrument of this conversion from chaos to order is the postulate of causality. Primitive
thought naturally recognized the relationship of cause and effect,
but it cannot recognize our view of an impersonal, mechanical, and
lawlike functioning of causality. For we have moved far from the
world of immediate experience in our search for true causes, that
is, causes which will always produce the same effect under the
same conditions. We must remember that Newton discovered the
concept of gravitation and also its laws by taking into account three
groups of phenomena which are entirely unrelated to the merely
perceptive observer: freely falling objects, the movements of the
planets, and the alternation of the tides. Now the primitive mind
cannot withdraw to that extent from perceptual reality. Moreover,
it would not be satisfied by our ideas. It looks, not for the "how,"
but for the "who," when it looks for a cause. Since the phenomenal
world is a "Thou" confronting early man, he does not expect to
find an impersonal law regulating a process. He looks for a pur-
poseful will committing an act. If the rivers refuse to rise, it is not
suggested that the lack of rainfall on distant mountains adequately
explains the calamity. When the river does not rise, it has *refused*
to rise. The river, or the gods, must be angry with the people who
depend on the inundation. At best the river or the gods intend to
convey something to the people. Some action, then, is called for.
We know that, when the Tigris did not rise, Gudea the king went
to sleep in the temple in order to be instructed in a dream as to the
meaning of the drought. In Egypt, where annual records of the
heights of the Nile flood were kept from the earliest historical
times, the pharaoh nevertheless made gifts to the Nile every year
about the time when it was due to rise. To these sacrifices, which

were thrown into the river, a document was added. It stated, in the form of either an order or a contract, the Nile's obligations.

Our view of causality, then, would not satisfy primitive man because of the impersonal character of its explanations. It would not satisfy him, moreover, because of its generality. We understand phenomena, not by what makes them peculiar, but by what makes them manifestations of general laws. But a general law cannot do justice to the individual character of each event. And the individual character of the event is precisely what early man experiences most strongly. We may explain that certain physiological processes cause a man's death. Primitive man asks: Why should *this* man die *thus* at *this* moment? We can only say that, given these conditions, death will always occur. He wants to find a cause as specific and individual as the event which it must explain. The event is not analyzed intellectually; it is experienced in its complexity and individuality, and these are matched by equally individual causes. Death is *willed*. The question, then, turns once more from the "why" to the "who," not to the "how."

This explanation of death as willed differs from that given a moment ago, when it was viewed as almost substantialized and especially created. We meet here for the first time in these chapters a curious multiplicity of approaches to problems which is characteristic for the mythopoeic mind. In the Gilgamesh Epic death was specific and concrete; it was allotted to mankind. Its antidote, eternal life, was equally substantial: it could be assimilated by means of the plant of life. Now we have found the view that death is caused by volition. The two interpretations are not mutually exclusive, but they are nevertheless not so consistent with each other as we would desire. Primitive man, however, would not consider our objections valid. Since he does not isolate an event from its attending circumstances, he does not look for one single explanation which must hold good under all conditions. Death, considered with some detachment as a state of being, is viewed as a substance inherent in all who are dead or about to die. But death considered emotionally is the act of hostile will.

The same dualism occurs in the interpretation of illness or sin. When the scapegoat is driven into the desert, laden with the sins of the community, it is evident that these sins are conceived as having substance. Early medical texts explain a fever as due to "hot" matter's having entered a man's body. Mythopoeic thought substantializes a quality and posits some of its occurrences as causes, others as effects. But the heat that caused the fever may also have been "willed" upon the man by hostile magic or may have entered his body as an evil spirit.

Evil spirits are often no more than the evil itself conceived as substantial and equipped with will-power. In a vague way they may be specified a little further as "spirits of the dead," but often this explanation appears as a gratuitous elaboration of the original view, which is no more than the incipient personification of the evil. This process of personification may, of course, be carried much further when the evil in question becomes a focus of attention and stimulates the imagination. Then we get demons with pronounced individuality like Lamashtu in Babylonia. The gods also come into being in this manner.

We may even go further and say that the gods as personifications of power among other things fulfil early man's need for causes to explain the phenomenal world. Sometimes this aspect of their origin can still be recognized in the complex deities of later times. There is, for instance, excellent evidence that the great goddess Isis was, originally, the deified throne. We know that among modern Africans closely related to the ancient Egyptians the enthroning of the new ruler is the central act of the ritual of the succession. The throne is a fetish charged with the mysterious power of kingship. The prince who takes his seat upon it arises a king. Hence the throne is called the "mother" of the king. Here personification found a starting-point; a channel for emotions was prepared which, in its turn, led to an elaboration of myth. In this way Isis "the throne which made the king" became "the Great Mother," devoted to her son Horus, faithful through all suffering to her husband Osiris—a figure with a powerful appeal to men even outside Egypt and, after Egypt's decline, throughout the Roman Empire.

The process of personification, however, only affects man's attitude to a limited extent. Like Isis, the sky-goddess Nūt was considered to be a loving mother-goddess; but the Egyptians of the New Kingdom arranged for their ascent to heaven without reference to her will or acts. They painted a life-sized figure of the goddess inside their coffins; the dead body was laid in her arms; and the dead man's ascent to heaven was assured. For resemblance was a sharing of essentials, and Nūt's image coalesced with its prototype. The dead man in his coffin rested already in heaven.

In every case where we would see no more than associations of thought, the mythopoeic mind finds a causal connection. Every resemblance, every contact in space or time, establishes a connection between two objects or events which makes it possible to see in the one the cause of changes observed in the other. We must remember that mythopoeic thought does not require its explanation to represent a continuous process. It accepts an initial situation and a final situation connected by no more than the conviction that the one came forth from the other. So we find, for instance, that the ancient Egyptians as well as the modern Maori explain the present relation between heaven and earth in the following manner. Heaven was originally lying upon earth; but the two were separated, and the sky was lifted up to its present position. In New Zealand this was done by their son; in Egypt it was done by the god of the air, Shū, who is now between earth and sky. And heaven is depicted as a woman bending over the earth with outstretched arms while the god Shū supports her.

Changes can be explained very simply as two different states, one of which is said to come forth from the other without any insistence on an intelligible process—in other words, as a transformation, a metamorphosis. We find that, time and again, this device is used to account for changes and that no further explanation is then required. One myth explains why the sun, which counted as the first king of Egypt, should now be in the sky. It recounts that the sun-god Rē became tired of humanity, so he seated himself upon the sky-goddess Nūt, who changed herself into a huge cow standing four square over the earth. Since then the sun has been in the sky.

The charming inconsequentiality of this story hardly allows us to take it seriously. But we are altogether inclined to take explanations more seriously than the facts they explain. Not so primitive man. He knew that the sun-god once ruled Egypt; he also knew that the sun was now in the sky. In the first account of the relation between sky and earth he explained how Shū, the air, came to be between sky and earth; in the last account he explained how the sun got to the sky and, moreover, introduced the well-known concept of the sky as a cow. All this gave him the satisfaction of feeling that images and known facts fell into place. That, after all, is what an explanation should achieve (cf. p. 16).

The image of Rē seated on the cow of heaven, besides illustrating a nonspeculative type of causal explanation which satisfies the mythopoeic mind, illustrates a tendency of the ancients which we have discussed before. We have seen that they are likely to present various descriptions of identical phenomena side by side even though they are mutually exclusive. We have seen how Shū lifted the sky-goddess Nūt from the earth. In a second story Nūt rises by herself in the shape of a cow. This image of the sky-goddess is very common, especially when the accent lies on her aspect as mother-goddess. She is the mother of Osiris and, hence, of all the dead; but she is also the mother who gives birth each evening to the stars, each morning to the sun. When ancient Egyptian thought turned to procreation, it expressed itself in images derived from cattle. In the myth of sun and sky the image of the sky-cow does not appear with its original connotation; the image of Nūt as a cow evoked the picture of the huge animal rising and lifting the sun to heaven. When the bearing of the sun by Nūt was the center of attention, the sun was called the "calf of gold" or "the bull." But it was, of course, possible to consider the sky, not predominantly in its relation to heavenly bodies or to the dead who are reborn there, but as a self-contained cosmic phenomenon. In that case Nūt was described as a descendent of the creator Atum through his children, Shū and Tefnūt, Air and Moisture. And she was, furthermore, wedded to the earth. If viewed in this manner, Nūt was imagined in human form.

We see, again, that the ancients' conception of a phenomenon differed according to their approach to it. Modern scholars have reproached the Egyptians for their apparent inconsistencies and have doubted their ability to think clearly. Such an attitude is sheer presumption. Once one recognizes the processes of ancient thought, their justification is apparent. After all, religious values are not reducible to rationalistic formulas. Natural phenomena, whether or not they were personified and became gods, confronted ancient man with a living presence, a significant "Thou," which, again, exceeded the scope of conceptual definition. In such cases our flexible thought and language qualify and modify certain concepts so thoroughly as to make them suitable to carry our burden of expression and significance. The mythopoeic mind, tending toward the concrete, expressed the irrational, not in our manner, but by admitting the validity of several avenues of approach at one and the same time. The Babylonians, for instance, worshiped the generative force in nature in several forms: its manifestation in the beneficial rains and thunderstorms was visualized as a lion-headed bird. Seen in the fertility of the earth, it became a snake. Yet in statues, prayers, and cult acts it was represented as a god in human shape. The Egyptians in the earliest times recognized Horus, a god of heaven, as their main deity. He was imagined as a gigantic falcon hovering over the earth with outstretched wings, the colored clouds of sunset and sunrise being his speckled breast and the sun and moon his eyes. Yet this god could also be viewed as a sun-god, since the sun, the most powerful thing in the sky, was naturally considered a manifestation of the god and thus confronted man with the same divine presence which he adored in the falcon spreading its wings over the earth. We should not doubt that mythopoeic thought fully recognizes the unity of each phenomenon which it conceives under so many different guises; the many-sidedness of its images serves to do justice to the complexity of the phenomena. But the procedure of the mythopoeic mind in expressing a phenomenon by manifold images corresponding to unconnected avenues of approach clearly leads away from, rather than toward, our postulate of causality which seeks to discover identical causes for identical effects throughout the phenomenal world.

We observe a similar contrast when we turn from the category of *causality* to that of *space*. Just as modern thought seeks to establish causes as abstract functional relations between phenomena, so it views space as a mere system of relations and functions. Space is postulated by us to be infinite, continuous, and homogeneous—attributes which mere sensual perception does not reveal. But primitive thought cannot abstract a concept "space" from its experience

of space. And this experience consists in what we would call quali-
fying associations. The spatial concepts of the primitive are concrete orientations; they refer to localities which have an emotional
color; they may be familiar or alien, hostile or friendly. Beyond
the scope of mere individual experience the community is aware
of certain cosmic events which invest regions of space with a particular significance. Day and night give to east and west a correlation with life and death. Speculative thought may easily develop in
connection with such regions as are outside direct experiences, for
instance, the heavens or the nether world. Mesopotamian astrology
evolved a very extensive system of correlations between heavenly
bodies and events in the sky and earthly localities. Thus mythopoeic thought may succeed no less than modern thought in establishing a co-ordinated spatial system; but the system is determined,
not by objective measurements, but by an emotional recognition
of values. The extent to which this procedure determines the primitive view of space can best be illustrated by an example which will
be met again in subsequent chapters as a remarkable instance of
ancient speculation.

In Egypt the creator was said to have emerged from the waters
of chaos and to have made a mound of dry land upon which he
could stand. This primeval hill, from which the creation took its
beginning, was traditionally located in the sun temple at Heliopo-
lis, the sun-god being in Egypt most commonly viewed as the creator. However, the Holy of Holies of each temple was equally sacred; each deity was—by the very fact that he was recognized as
divine—a source of creative power. Hence each Holy of Holies
throughout the land could be identified with the primeval hill.
Thus it is said of the temple of Philae, which was founded in the
fourth century b.c.: "This [temple] came into being when nothing
at all had yet come into being and the earth was still lying in darkness and obscurity." The same claim was made for other temples.
The names of the great shrines at Memphis, Thebes, and Her-
monthis explicitly stated that they were the "divine emerging
primeval island" or used similar expressions. Each sanctuary possessed the essential quality of original holiness; for, when a new
temple was founded, it was assumed that the potential sacredness
of the site became manifest. The equation with the primeval hill

received architectural expression also. One mounted a few steps or followed a ramp at every entrance from court or hall to the Holy of Holies, which was thus situated at a level noticeably higher than the entrance.

But this coalescence of temples with the primeval hill does not give us the full measure of the significance which the sacred locality had assumed for the ancient Egyptians. The royal tombs were also made to coincide with it. The dead, and, above all, the king, were reborn in the hereafter. No place was more propitious, no site promised greater chances for a victorious passage through the crisis of death, than the primeval hill, the center of creative forces where the ordered life of the universe had begun. Hence the royal tomb was given the shape of a pyramid which is the Heliopolitan stylization of the primeval hill.

To us this view is entirely unacceptable. In our continuous, homogeneous space the place of each locality is unambiguously fixed. We would insist that there must have been one single place where the first mound of dry land actually emerged from the chaotic waters. But the Egyptian would have considered such objections mere quibbles. Since the temples and the royal tombs were as sacred as the primeval hill and showed architectural forms which resembled the hill, they shared essentials. And it would be fatuous to argue whether one of these monuments could be called the primeval hill with more justification than the others.

Similarly, the waters of chaos from which all life emerged were considered to be present in several places, sometimes playing their part in the economy of the country, sometimes necessary to round out the Egyptian image of the universe. The waters of chaos were supposed to subsist in the form of the ocean surrounding the earth, which had emerged from them and now floated upon them. Hence these waters were also present in the subsoil water. In the cenotaph of Seti I at Abydos the coffin was placed upon an island with a double stair imitating the hieroglyph for the primeval hill; this island was surrounded by a channel filled always with subsoil water. Thus the dead king was buried and thought to rise again in the locality of creation. But the waters of chaos, the Nūn, were also the waters of the nether world, which the sun and the dead have to cross. On the other hand, the primeval waters had once contained all the potentialities of life; and they were, therefore, also the waters of the annual inundation of the Nile which renews and revives the fertility of the fields.

The mythopoeic conception of *time* is, like that of space, qualitative and concrete, not quantitative and abstract. Mythopoeic thought does not know time as a uniform duration or as a succession of qualitatively indifferent moments. The concept of time as it is used in our mathematics and physics is as unknown to early man as that which forms the framework of our history. Early man does not abstract a concept of time from the experience of time.

It has been pointed out, for example, by Cassirer, that the time experience is both rich and subtle, even for quite primitive people. Time is experienced in the periodicity and rhythm of man's own life as well as in the life of nature. Each phase of man's life—childhood, adolescence, maturity, old age—is a time with peculiar qualities. The transition from one phase to another is a crisis in which man is assisted by the community's uniting in the rituals appropriate to birth, puberty, marriage, or death. Cassirer has called the peculiar view of time as a sequence of essentially different phases of life "biological time." And the manifestation of time in nature, the succession of the seasons, and the movements of the heavenly bodies were conceived quite early as the signs of a life-process similar, and related, to that of man. Even so, they are not viewed as "natural" processes in our sense. When there is change, there is a cause; and a cause, as we have seen, is a will. In Genesis, for instance, we read that God made a covenant with the living creatures, promising not only that the flood would not recur but also that "while the earth remaineth, seedtime and harvest, cold and heat, summer and winter, day and night shall not cease" (Gen. 8:22). The order of time and the order of the life of nature (which are one) are freely granted by the God of the Old Testament in the fulness of his power; and when considered in their totality, as an established order, they are elsewhere, too, thought to be founded upon the willed order of creation.

But another approach is also possible, an approach not toward the sequence of phases as a whole but toward the actual transition from one phase to another—the actual succession of phases. The varying length of the night, the ever changing spectacles of sunrise and sunset, and the equinoctial storms do not suggest an automatic smooth alternation between the "elements" of mythopoeic time. They suggest a conflict, and this suggestion is strengthened by the anxiety of man himself, who is wholly dependent upon weather and seasonal changes. Wensinck has called this the "dramatic conception of nature." Each morning the sun defeats darkness and chaos, as he did on the day of creation and does, every year, on New Year's Day. These three moments coalesce; they are felt to be essentially the same. Each sunrise, and each New Year's Day, repeats the first sunrise on the day of creation; and for the mythopoeic mind each repetition coalesces with—is practically identical with—the original event.

We have here, in the category of time, a parallel to the phenomenon which we recognized in the category of space when we learned that certain archetypal localities, like the primeval hill, were thought to exist on several sites throughout the land because these sites shared with their prototype some of its overwhelmingly important aspects. This phenomenon we called coalescence in space. An example of coalescence in time is an Egyptian verse which curses the enemies of the pharaoh. It must be remembered that the sun-god Rē had been the first ruler of Egypt and that the pharaoh was, to the extent that he ruled, an image of Rē. The verse says of the enemies of the king: "They shall be like the snake Apōphis on New Year's morning."[4] The snake Apophis is the hostile darkness which the sun defeats every night on his journey through the nether world from the place of sunset in the west to the place of sunrise in the east. But why should the enemies be like Apophis on New Year's morning? Because the notions of creation, daily sunrise, and the beginning of the new annual cycle coalesce and culminate in the festivities of the New Year. Hence the New Year is invoked, that is, conjured up, to intensify the curse.

Now, this "dramatic conception of nature which sees everywhere a strife between divine and demoniac, cosmic and chaotic powers" (Wensinck), does not leave man a mere spectator. He is too much involved in, his welfare depends too completely upon, the victory of the beneficial powers for him not to feel the need to participate on their side. Thus we find, in Egypt and Babylonia, that man—that is, man in society—accompanies the principal changes in nature with appropriate rituals. Both in Egypt and in Babylonia the New Year, for instance, was an occasion of elaborate celebrations in which the battles of the gods were mimed or in which mock-battles were fought.

We must remember again that such rituals are not merely symbolical; they are part and parcel of the cosmic events; they are man's share in these events. In Babylonia, from the third millennium down to Hellenistic times, we find a New Year's festival which lasted several days. During the celebration the story of creation was recited and a mock-battle was fought in which the king impersonated the victorious god. In Egypt we know mock-battles in several festivals which are concerned with the defeat of death and rebirth or resurrection: one took place at Abydos, during the annual Great Procession of Osiris; one took place on New Year's Eve, at the erection of the Djed pillar; one was fought, at least in the time of Herodotus, at Papremis in the Delta. In these festivals man participated in the life of nature.

Man also arranged his own life, or at least the life of the society to which he belonged, in such a manner that a harmony with nature, a co-ordination of natural and social forces, gave added impetus to his undertakings and increased his chances for success. The whole "science" of omens aims, of course, at this result. But there are also definite instances which illustrate the need of early man to act in unison with nature. In both Egypt and Babylon a king's coronation was postponed until a new beginning in the cycle of nature provided a propitious starting-point for the new reign. In Egypt the time might be in the early summer, when the Nile began to rise, or in the autumn, when the inundation receded and the fertilized fields were ready to receive the seed. In Babylonia the king began his reign on New Year's Day; and the inauguration of a new temple was celebrated only at that time.

This deliberate co-ordination of cosmic and social events shows most clearly that time to early man did not mean a neutral and abstract frame of reference but rather a succession of recurring phases, each charged with a peculiar value and significance. Again, as in dealing with space, we find that there are certain "regions" of time which are withdrawn from direct experience and greatly stimulate speculative thought. They are the distant past and the future. Either of these may become normative and absolute; each then falls beyond the range of time altogether. The absolute past does not recede, nor do we approach the absolute future gradually. The "Kingdom of God" may at any time break into our present. For the Jews the future is normative. For the Egyptians, on the other hand, the past was normative; and no pharaoh could hope to achieve more than the establishment of the conditions "as they were in the time of Rē, in the beginning."

But here we are touching on material which will be discussed in subsequent chapters. We have attempted to demonstrate how the "logic," the peculiar structure, of mythopoeic thought can be derived from the fact that the intellect does not operate autonomously because it can never do justice to the basic experience of early man, that of confrontation with a significant "Thou." Hence when early man is faced by an intellectual problem within the many-sided complexities of life, emotional and volitional factors are never debarred; and the conclusions reached are not critical judgments but complex images.

Nor can the spheres which these images refer to be neatly kept apart. We have intended in this book to deal successively with speculative thought concerning (1) the nature of the universe; (2) the function of the state; and (3) the values of life. But the reader will have grasped that this, our mild attempt to distinguish the spheres of metaphysics, politics, and ethics, is doomed to remain a convenience without any deep significance. For the life of man and the function of the state are for mythopoeic thought imbedded in nature, and the natural processes are affected by the acts of man no less than man's life depends on his harmonious integration with nature. The experiencing of this unity with the utmost intensity was the greatest good ancient oriental religion could bestow. To conceive this integration in the form of intuitive imagery was the aim of the speculative thought of the ancient Near East.

NOTES

1. Seligmann, in *Fourth Report of the Wellcome Tropical Research Laboratories at the Gordon Memorial College, Khartoum* (London, 1911), Vol. B: *General Science*, p. 219.
2. D. D. Luckenbill, *Ancient Records of Assyria and Babylonia*, Vol. II, par. 558.

3. Sethe, *Die altaegyptischen Pyramidentexte nach den Papierabdrücken und Photographien des Berliner Museums* (Leipzig, 1908), par. 1466.

4. Adolph Erman, *Aegypten und aegyptisches Leben im Altertum*, ed. Hermann Ranke (Tübingen, 1923), p. 170.

SUGGESTED READINGS

CASSIRER, ERNST. *Philosophie der symbolischen Formen II: Das mythische Denken*. Berlin, 1925.

LEEUW, G. VAN DER. *Religion in Essence and Manifestation: A Study in Phenomenology*. New York, 1938.

LEVY-BRÜHL, L. *How Natives Think*. New York, 1926.

OTTO, RUDOLF. *The Idea of the Holy: An Inquiry into the Non-rational Factor in the Idea of the Divine and Its Relation to the Rational*. London, 1943.

RADIN, PAUL. *Primitive Man as Philosopher*. New York, 1927.

REVIEW

MYTHIC THOUGHT IN THE ANCIENT NEAR EAST

By Theodor H. Gaster

*Before Philosophy** is an attempt by certain members of the Oriental Institute in Chicago to recover and expound " the view which the ancient peoples of Egypt and Mesopotamia took of the world in which they lived."

The exposition is geared to a particular thesis, formulated by Professor and Mrs. Henri Frankfort in an introductory chapter. Like primitive peoples in general, we are told, the ancient Egyptians and Mesopotamians did not so much speculate about the world around them as feel its impact in a series of personal relationships. Nature was to them a *thou* rather than an *it*—the other party to an encounter rather than an entity to be examined from without. Hence they thought of its phenomena mythopoeically rather than intellectually—not as they might be in and of themselves but rather as they manifested themselves in direct contact. A storm, for example, was not a meteorological condition to be analyzed and explained by objective science, but a terrifying (or at least awesome) *encounter*, and might therefore be represented as a monstrous bird flapping its giant wings. Moreover, since the same object could confront a man in a number of different circumstances and strike him with varying impacts, nothing possessed for him a single intrinsic character; it might assume a new " identity " from moment to moment.

Against this background of mythopoeic thought, it is argued, the perennial problems of human existence—the problem of man in nature, of fate and of death—were seen in a light different from our own, obsessed as we are by the intellectual and speculative approach which was subsequently introduced by the Greeks. Accordingly, in terms of the history of ideas, the *Weltanschauung* of the ancient Near East—and, for that matter, of primitive man everywhere—remains perforce a closed book unless and until its distinctive underlying mentality is apprehended.

The basic fault of this thesis is that it simply fails to understand the nature of *poetry*, which is what—without knowing it—it is really discussing. The human mind, as Cassirer pointed out, works affectively as well as intellectually. In the one case, it expresses itself in art and poetry; in the other, in science and speculative thought. But this does not mean that either precedes the other, or that one can simply turn the a-logical into the pre-logical and assert blithely that, before the Greeks came along, this was the only way in which all men thought at all times everywhere. Yet that is precisely what Frankfort and his colleagues suggest. They have taken a

* BEFORE PHILOSOPHY: The Intellectual Adventure of Ancient Man. An Essay on Speculative Thought in the Ancient Near East. By H. and H. A. Frankfort, John A. Wilson, and Thorkild Jacobsen. Pelican Books, 1949, Pp. 275.

body of poetic and artistic texts—myths and tales—and proceeded to argue that the poetic and artistic mentality which underlies them is representative of ancient and primitive thought in general. This is like saying that every nineteenth-century Englishman necessarily conceived of a Grecian urn as a still unravished bride of quietness or that he could not think of spring except as a hound on winter's traces.

Then, too, this thesis fails to bear in mind that mythopoeia is a matter not only of conception but also of expression, and that it is often a mere stylistic device, a technique of articulation, a deliberate and conscious artifice. In other words, a crucial distinction has to be made between what Cassirer has called conscious " transposition and substitution " on the one hand and " genuine radical metaphor " on the other. When, for example, we read in a Babylonian text that salt is invoked to " break my enchantment, loose my spell," etc., we have no right to infer—as do Frankfort and his collaborators—that to the Mesopotamian mind salt was *necessarily* conceived not as a mere inanimate substance but as " a fellow-creature with special powers." This is to confuse poetic personification with conceptual animism, an *ad hoc* stylist metaphor with radical mythopoeia. One recalls, for instance, the story in Plutarch (*De coh. ira*, 5, p. 455) that Xerxes once addressed a personal letter to Mount Atlas, or that in Herodotus (vi 35) relating that Xerxes once threatened the Hellespont with branding and scourging. Does this imply that everyone in either epoch necessarily regarded a mountain or a sea as animate?

A further objection to the basic premise of this volume is that while it lays great emphasis on the influence of geography and climate upon *Weltanschauung*—an insistence anticipated long since by Herodotus (x 22), Hippocrates (v, 200–21 Adams), Aristotle (*Pol.* vii 7) and others—it fails altogether to take into account the fact that many of the concepts which are cited as typically Mesopotamian or Egyptian are commonplace elsewhere. Thus, the notion that the first man was moulded out of clay appears also in Classical myth (e.g., Aristophanes, *Birds* 686; Horace, *Odes I*, xvi 13–15) and was likewise taught by Parmenides. It is equally common in primitive creation stories (see Stith Thompson, *Motif-Index of Folk Literature*, A 1241). Similarly, as the late Maurice Canney has shown, the notion of the primordial hill or mound is by no means confined to Egypt, but is widespread among primitive peoples in several parts of the world. Or take the idea, developed in the Sumerian myth of Enki and Ninmah, that deformed persons are the product of an attempt on the part of some playful god or malevolent marplot to imitate the work of the creator; this too has analogies in other cultures (compare Stith Thompson, *op. cit.*, A 1335.2).

Nor is it necessary to assume that a myth which describes the distribution of departmental duties among various gods and goddesses was deliberately designed to build up the picture of the universe as a cosmic state administered on the lines of conventional Mesopotamian society; for the basic concept of a distribution of functions underlies rather than issues out of the organization of society and may therefore have been attributed automatically to the divine realm without having to have been projected from a human model.

Again, what are here termed " myths of evaluation "—that is, stories designed to demonstrate the superiority in the social structure of the farmer to the shepherd or of one metal to another, are by no means the product of an exclusive Mesopotamian mentality. The *débat* is a recognized genre of folk-literature everywhere.

The introductory chapter is followed by more detailed essays, from the expert pens of J. A. Wilson and Thorkild Jacobsen respectively, on the cultures of Egypt and Mesopotamia. It cannot be said, however, that either exposition really supports the basic thesis of the volume. Wilson, for his part, seems on the whole to pursue an independent course, and only in a few perfunctory asides does he make a courteous bow in the direction of the mythopoeic hypothesis. Jacobsen, on the other hand, goes to the opposite extreme and tries hard to meet the requirements of his assignment by reading mythopoeic mentality into the texts rather than out of them. Moreover, he tends more than once to compromise his argument by evident confusion of thought.

Character, for instance, *is constantly confused with personality*, as when we are told (p. 143) that because flint always and everywhere shows a tendency to flake under the craftsman's tool, to the average Sumerian who observed this fact, "a particular lump of flint had a clearly recognizable personality and will." Clearly and recognizably, it had nothing of the kind; all it had was a characteristic. To assume that this was regarded as evidence of volition and that the Sumerian therefore envisaged the phenomenon mythopoeically rather than intellectually is simply to beg the question; it is a glaring example of *petitio principii*.

Comparison is confused with identification. Thus, in a certain Accadian text, a man who proclaims his immunity to witchcraft declares: " I am heaven, you cannot touch me; I am earth, you cannot bewitch me." " His attention," says Jacobsen (p. 145), " is centered on a single quality of Heaven and Earth [note the gratuitous and tendencious capitals! T.H.G.], their sacred inviolability. When he has made himself identical with them, this quality will flow into him and merge with his being." But is such a conscious conceptual process really involved? Surely, all that the speaker is really doing is to indulge in the figure known to grammarians, on the verbal level, as *comparatio compendaria*. He is not conceptually identifying himself with heaven and earth, since no real absorption of qualities is involved; he is saying merely that, of the moment, he is in one respect in the same position as are they: " I am of this moment as good as heaven and earth." After all, if an overburdened office-worker observes that " I am the pack-horse around here," he is not actually identifying himself with that beast; all he is saying, by *comparatio compendaria*, is that he is in the same position, as good as, a pack-horse!

Function is confused with volition. An incantation accompanying the familiar act of *envoûtement*, in which images of an enemy are burned in order to work witchcraft upon him, invokes the fire to " judge . . . my cause, hand down the verdict." " The fire," says Jacobsen (p. 147), " has a will of its own; it will burn the images . . . only if it so chooses. And in deciding whether to burn the images or not, the fire becomes a judge between the man and his enemies. . . . The power which is in fire has taken definite form, has been interpreted in social terms; it is a judge." It is not; it merely produces the same effect or end-result as does a judge passing sentence. The appeal is not to will, but to action or function, i.e., " Be effective in discomfiting my enemies in the same way as would a judge who condemned them." To assume that the speaker was thinking " mythopoeically " and therefore attributing personality and volition to the fire is, once again, a case of *petitio principii.*

Dual identity is confused with deliberate identification. In certain cultic ceremonies (e.g., in the rite of the " sacred marriage ") the Babylonian king was represented as being the god Tammuz. What this implies, says Jacobsen (p. 215), is that " by being like, by enacting the rôle of, a force in nature, a god, man could in the cult enter into and clothe himself with the identity of these powers, with the identity of the gods, and thus his own actions, when thus identified, cause the powers involved to act as he would have them act." But *did* the king really " enter into " the identity of the god? Would it not be truer to say that king and god were parallel manifestations of the same being in its punctual and durative aspect respectively, so that the king always was a god, and what was involved in the rites under discussion was merely a dramatization of that fact rather than the assumption of a new identity? *

Failure to reckon with the fact that primitive thought is supremely conscious of the parallelism between the punctual and the durative, the real and the ideal, also leads Jacobsen to the dubious idea that the ancient Mesopotamian transferred to the cosmos the pattern of his own state, mentally projecting upon it his own social order. That the world of nature and of the gods was indeed pictured as a kind of double of earthly life can scarcely be doubted, but does this imply a conscious mythopoeic transference to that realm of the patterns of human society? Surely it may be argued just as well that the relationship between the cosmos and the immediate state, or between the world of gods and that of men, consisted in the fact that they were regarded as parallel manifestations of the same natural order on the durative and punctual plains respectively? In that case, it would be just as true to say that earth " reproduced " heaven as that heaven " reproduced " earth. In point of fact, neither would have " reproduced " the other; they would have been simply the " long-shot " and " close-up " view of the same thing.

To sum up: *Before Philosophy* is certainly a provocative and stimulating work. It provides eloquent testimony to the genius of the late Henri

---

* On this point, see more fully the reviewer's observations in *The Review of Religion,* IX (1945), 267ff. and in *Numen,* I (1954), 188–90.

Frankfort for opening windows in stuffy places and for introducing new perspectives into established scholarly disciplines sorely in need of them. It is also extremely useful for its excellent surveys of Egyptian and early Mesopotamian myth by two of the foremost masters of those subjects. Unhappily, however, its merits have been compromised by the fact that the exposition has been harnessed to an altogether untenable preconception.

Columbia University.

BOOKS RECEIVED

THE HERITAGE OF THE PAST: From the Earliest Times to the Close of the Middle Ages. By Stewart C. Easton. New York: Rinehart & Co., 1955. Pp. 795. $6.—A well written introduction to the cultural history of mankind from the Neanderthal Man to the emergence of the European states and nationalism. Excellent illustrations.

THE MYTH OF THE ETERNAL RETURN. By Mircea Eliade. Translated from the French by Willard R. Trask. New York: Pantheon, 1955. Bollingen Series, no. 46. Pp. 195. $2.75.—Ontological ideas of archaic man in his myths and symbols of history as repetitive.

CONTRIBUTO ALLA STORIA DEGLI STUDI CLASSICI. Per Arnaldo Momigliano. Roma: Edizione di Storia e Letteratura, 1955. Pp. 418.—Collected essays on the history of classical studies from the author's articles in English and Italian periodicals.

ARISTOTELES POLÍTICA. Edición Bilingüe y Traducción por Julian Marias y Maria Araujos. Introducción y Notas de Julian Marias. Madrid: Instituto de Estudios Politicos, 1951. Pp. lxxii, 281 (Greek text and Spanish translation on pages facing each other with duplicate page numbers). 150 pesetas.—Greek text is that of W. L. Newman's *The Politics of Aristotle* (4 vols., Oxford, 1887–1902).

ASTROLOGY IN ROMAN LAW AND POLITICS. By Frederick H. Cramer. Philadelphia: American Philosophical Society, 1954. Pp. 291. $5.—The impact of fatalistic astrology on Roman political and military leaders, from the hellenistic era to 235 A.D. " Scientific " astrology as a form of Stoic rationalism.

THE MATERIAL LOGIC OF JOHN OF ST. THOMAS: Basic Treatises. Translated by Yves R. Simon, John J. Glanville, G. D. Hollenhorst. With a Preface by Jacques Maritain. University of Chicago Press, 1955. Pp. xxiv, 638. $10.—A Thomistic commentator's exposition of Aristotle's logic and theory of knowledge.

THOMAS OF BRADWARDINE HIS TRACTATUS DE PROPORTIONIBUS: Its Significance for the Development of Mathematical Physics. Edited and translated by H. Lamar Crosby, Jr. Madison: University of Wisconsin Press, 1955. Pp. 203. $3.50.—An important source of pre-Galilean mechanics in the 14th-century school of Oxford; Bradwardine's *Treatise on Proportions* was widely read at Paris and other scholastic centers of Europe during the next century.

SUMERIAN MYTHOLOGY: A REVIEW ARTICLE[1]

THORKILD JACOBSEN

THE study of ancient Mesopotamian civilization may be said to have reached the threshold of a new epoch. For only now does the vast and profoundly important early Sumerian literature begin to be accessible in a real sense. It is not that the task of publishing the thousands of fragments of clay tablets upon which this literature was inscribed has only now begun. Rather the major part, and in many respects the heavier end, of that task was accomplished in long years of valiant work by many devoted scholars. If any single name should be mentioned, it would perhaps be that of Edward Chiera, whose contribution—judged on the double standard of quality and quantity combined—is outstanding.[2] Chiera also accomplished the first and most difficult part of the task of distinguishing the various compositions involved and of assigning the relevant fragments to them so that now, when the style and subject matter of the major literary compositions are known, the placing of new fragments—even small ones—has become incomparably easier.[3]

With all this work done, however, the compositions remained fragmentary. For most of them the statement was true—

and for many of them it still holds—that "the story seemed to make no connected sense; and what could be made out, seemed to lack intelligent motivation" (Dr. Kramer, with reference to the myth of Inanna and Enki).[4] Hence many more of the fragments lying unpublished in the museums of Istanbul and Philadelphia had to be made available, for each such fragment now promised unusual returns: a few lines, unimportant in themselves, might furnish the link between large but separately unintelligible sections of a story and thus for the first time make that story understandable. It is greatly to Dr. Kramer's credit that he clearly realized the import of this situation and that he energetically bent his efforts toward publishing and placing more texts. In Istanbul he collated earlier publications and copied 170 hitherto unpublished fragments;[5] some 675 further fragments in the University Museum in Philadelphia are being prepared for publication by him. When these texts have been made available, Dr. Kramer will have lastingly inscribed his name in the annals of Sumerology, and Sumerology itself can enter upon a new era—an era of interpreting and evaluating Sumerian literature.

Dr. Kramer plans to publish the results of his researches in a series of seven volumes, of which the book here reviewed represents the first. Volumes II–VI will be devoted primarily to source material; they will give the text of the Sumerian compositions in transliteration accompanied by translation and notes. Hitherto

---

[1] S. N. Kramer, *Sumerian Mythology: A Study of Spiritual and Literary Achievement in the Third Millennium B.C.* (Philadelphia, 1944).

[2] In painstaking exactitude of copies, translations, and interpretation, nobody surpasses Poebel, but he has published relatively little in this field. Radau's copies and translations are very commendable, his interpretations less so. De Genouillac and Langdon will be gratefully remembered by workers in this field chiefly for the large volume of materials which these two scholars made available.

[3] We have in mind especially the results embodied in the introduction to *SRT, SEM, STVC,* and in the article *JAOS,* 54 (1934), 407–20. Dr. Kramer, who edited all but the first of these after Dr. Chiera's death, deserves great credit for having made these important studies of Chiera available.

[4] *Op. cit.,* p. 65.

[5] S. N. Kramer, "Sumerian Literary Texts from Nippur in the Museum of the Ancient Orient at Istanbul." *AASOR,* Vol. XXIII (New Haven, 1944). We abbreviate it as *SLiT.*

unpublished documents utilized to establish the text will be added in autograph copy. Each volume will deal with one literary genre: epics, myths, hymns, lamentations, and wisdom texts. A concluding volume will endeavor to sketch the religious and spiritual concepts of the Sumerians as revealed in the previously published materials.

This plan seems excellently conceived. One might—considering the difficulties still attending the translation of Sumerian—have preferred that translations and notes should be published separately from transliterations and copies, but the point is not very important. The main thing is that the texts now unpublished or scattered in fragments in a variety of publications will be brought together in orderly, practical, and convenient fashion so that they will be readily available for study.

The first volume of the series is intended as introductory. It is meant, the author states, to give "a detailed description of our sources together with a brief outline of the more significant mythological concepts of the Sumerians as evident from their epics and myths" (p. ix). After the first chapter, which traces the decipherment of cuneiform and the history of Sumerology (pp. 1-25), follows a discussion of "The Scope and Significance of Sumerian Mythology" (pp. 26-29). Then comes the actual substance of the book, which retells the more important Sumerian myths under the headings "Myths of Origins" (pp. 30-75), "Myths of Kur" (pp. 76-96), and "Miscellaneous Myths" (pp. 97-103). Interspersed among the stories are sections endeavoring to reconstruct and interpret in more systematic fashion the Sumerian cosmogonic concepts as a whole. The book is profusely illustrated with excellent photographs of ancient Mesopotamian seal impressions, tablets, and copies of tablets. The latter—uniting in one place copies which Kramer

had previously published in various journals, and adding a few unpublished ones—constitute a most welcome feature. Very useful also are the notes in which Kramer lists the fragments utilized for reconstructing the text of each myth treated. A number of misprints in figures and abbreviations will, we understand, be corrected by the author elsewhere. The completeness with which the material has been utilized and the various fragments assigned to their proper places is admirable. We have noted only one omission: the bilingual fragment *OECT*, VI, Pl. XVI, K. 2168, contains on the obverse the beginning of the myth which Dr. Kramer calls "The Creation of Man" and on the reverse a few lines dealing with the creatures formed by Ninmah.

Although the introductory chapters of Dr. Kramer's book—sketching the history of Sumerology in a somewhat personal perspective and outlining the older history of Mesopotamia strictly in racial terms—contain much which would normally have invited comment, all such points are necessarily overshadowed by the immediate importance of the chief subject matter of the book. Has the author been able—as he is himself firmly convinced that he has—to "reconstruct and translate in a scientific and trustworthy manner the extant Sumerian literary compositions" (p. xi)? This issue is crucial and must take the central place in any review. We shall therefore proceed directly to a discussion of the statement of Sumerian mythological concepts given by Dr. Kramer, considering first the translations upon which that statement is based, then both specific and general questions of interpretation.

It is perhaps hardly necessary to mention that two different translators will occasionally arrive at somewhat different results; for all translating involves a choice between possibilities and allows the personal factor a certain amount of play. A reviewer thus has the advantage of being able to state alternatives whenever they seem to him to merit attention.

I. TRANSLATIONS

In trying to form an opinion about translations such as those offered in Dr. Kramer's book, one will consider—but will not attach undue importance to—instances of mere inexactitude. Lack of precision is unfortunate but rarely really serious even if, as here, instances of it occur in disporportionate numbers. A few examples chosen at random will show what we have in mind:

A b - s í n is "furrow" (see Landsberger, *ana ittišu*, p. 158) and not "crops" (p. 54 and *passim*). When the god Enki had put the plow in order, he did not roar at the crops (p. 61) but "opened the mouth of the furrow," that is, "opened up a furrow" (on the use of the locative construction here, cf. Poebel, *AOF*, IX [1933/34], 254–55).

The correct rendering of the city name mentioned on page 100 is Aktab, not Shittab (see Poebel, *JAOS*, 57 [1937], 359 ff.).

B á r a , borrowed by Akkadian as *parakku*, means "throne dais" (see Schott, *ZAnF*, VI [1931], 19 ff.; Landsberger, *ibid.*, VII [1933], 292 ff.), not "shrine" (p. 59 *passim*).

G e - g u n₄ - n a is not "grove" (p. 60) but a special kind of dwelling, or room in a dwelling, serving approximately as audience hall and dining-hall combined (for the former use see especially the Eshtar hymn, *RA*, XXII [1925], 170–71, rev. 5–8).

Ḫ i - LI g ù r - r u , said of a young woman, is not "bountiful" (p. 54) but "(physically) attractive." The meanings of ḫ i - LI shade off from that of "sex appeal" (compare Thureau-Dangin in *RA*, XI [1914], 153).

K ù - g á l [6] is not "knower" (pp. 51 and 61) but "inspector of canals." It was borrowed by Akkadian as *gugallu* and meant originally "one who stocks (ponds and rivers) with fish," k u₆ - g á l . (Cf. Thureau-Dangin, *RA*, XXXIII [1936], 111, and Meissner, *MAOG*, XIII, No. 2, pp. 8–9. Meissner's meaning 2 belongs closely with 3 and here may belong also *gugallu* as an epithet of Adad. See also Gudea, Cyl. B xiv.26.)

M á and m á - g u r₈ , the terms by which Nanna's vessel is designated, do not mean "gufa" (pp. 41 and 48) but "boat" and "barge." One cannot travel upstream in a gufa; Nanna travels from Ur to Nippur in the story dealt with on pages 47–49.

M a š k i m is not "ambusher" (p. 35) but—rather differently—the legally empowered agent of a court or of a high judicial or executive official (see, e.g., Landsberger, *ZAnF*, IV [1929], 276). The best English rendering (suggested to me by Dr. A. Heidel) would appear to be "deputy."

The canal of primeval Nippur is said to have been "sparkling" (m u l ; the Akkadian translation has *muttanbiṭum*), not merely "pure" (p. 43), and Karusar was not "its quay where the boats stand" (p. 43) but "its quay where the boats moor" for ú s means "to lie up against" and is —like its Akkadian counterpart *emēdu*— the usual term for "to moor." The Akkadian translation of the story renders the whole phrase as *maklútum*, "harbor quay."

The author not infrequently omits— without informing the reader—lines or parts of lines in connected translation. Thus on page 51, after the sentence "Emesh bent the knees before Enten," the phrase "making supplication to him" has been omitted. On page 54, after the description of Ashnan, "Grain," as "a maid

[6] Or do the texts in question actually have k u₆ - g á l ? We would not so expect.

kindly and bountiful is she," the line "lifting (her) head in trusting fashion from her field" has been omitted. On page 68, after "Falsely has he uttered the name of his power, the name of the Abzu," the line "guilefully has he sent thee as messenger to me" is missing. On page 98, after "Ziusudra opened *a window* of the huge boat," a line voicing his thoughts in so doing: "I shall let the light of the hero Utu (i.e., of the sun) enter into the interior of the huge boat," has fallen out. On page 102, after the line "The farmer more than I, the farmer more than I, the farmer what has he more than I?" two further lines, virtually repeating the previous sentence, but mentioning the farmer Enkimdu by name and epithet, have been omitted. While nothing much is lost by the last-mentioned omission one rather regrets that Dr. Kramer begins translating the myth of Enki and Ninhursaga with its fifth and not with its first line (p. 55) since the omitted section is important for the setting of the story:

When you were dividing the virgin earth (with your fellow gods), you!
The land of Tilmun was a region pure,
When you were dividing the pure earth (with your fellow gods), you!
The land of Tilmun was a region pure.[7]

[7] We restore the text (Langdon, *Le Poème sumérien du Paradis, du Déluge* ... [Paris, 1919], Planche I, 1–4) as follows:

[k i s i k i l]-à m e - n e - b a - à m me - e n - z é - e n
[k u r] ᵗTilmun¹ ki k û - g a - à m
[k i k û]-g a e - n e - b a - à m me - e n - z é - e n
ᵗk u r Tilmun¹ ki k û - g a - à m

and derive e - n e - b a - à m from b a , Akkadian *zâzu*, "to divide," "to receive as one's portion in the division into severalty of property held in common." The form offers a welcome example of the second person plural preterite active of the a - theme of the Sumerian verb. The mark of this theme, the prefix a - (contracted with following e in the second person singular and plural preterite active), has hitherto been considered a mere phonetic or dialectal variant of the prefix e - / i -, and the difference in meaning of the two prefixes has been largely overlooked. This difference may be defined—provisionally—as similar to the difference in tempo between aorist (e - / i -) and imperfect (a -) as described by Jespersen, *Philosophy of Grammar,* p. 276: "The Aorist carries the narrative on, it tells us what happened next, while

The reference is to the beginning of time when the world and its various cities and city-states were apportioned among the appropriate gods, and Enki and Ninhursaga received Tilmun as their share. The two deities are here in the opening lines of the myth addressed directly in the second person; then the storyteller lapses into ordinary narrative style.[8]

the Imperfect lingers over the conditions as they were at that time and expatiates on them with more or less of prolixity." The lingering force of the a - theme occasions a significant shift of tenses in Akkadian renderings of its forms: Sumerian "present" and "preterite" active are both rendered as "present" (i.e., fientic durative?) in Akkadian, while Sumerian "present" and "preterite" passive are rendered, respectively, by present IV.1 and permansive I.1 in Akkadian. We hope to treat of the a - prefix in wider context elsewhere and refer for the time being to Poebel, *PBS,* VI, 115 (preterite active), and *AJSL,* L (January, 1934), 147 (passive) for its morphology; Poebel's term for the preterite active, "active permansive," shows that he recognized the basic meaning of the theme quite clearly at the time. The enclitic - à m at the end of the form serves here to mark circumstance of time—a frequent usage. [After the above was written, Dr. Kramer's study, *BASOR,* "Supplementary Studies No. 1," has become available. The transliteration and photograph there published favor a restoration [k i k û - g] a "The pure earth" in line 1.]

[8] The introductions to Sumerian tales bid for the listener's attention and therefore make use of a great variety of stylistic devices. This does not always stand out in Dr. Kramer's renderings. The story of Martu's marriage, for instance, purports to be an account given by a hoary old tree which had lived in primeval times and could therefore tell what had then happened. It begins (*SEM* 58, 1–9; Dr. Kramer deals with it on p. 100 of his book):

"When Ninab was (but) Aktab was not (yet),
When the pure crown was (but) the pure tiara was not,
When the pure herb was (but) the pure cedar was not,
When the pure salt was (but) the pure potash was not,
When cohabiting and conception were,
When pregnancy and birthgiving were,
I, the . . . . of the pure Cedar, was; I, the forebear of the *mesu*(?)-tree,
I, the parent of the White Cedar, the kinsman of the Hashuru-tree, was.
In those days . . . . etc. . . . ."

We restore lines 5–6 as follows: g i š - d uₙ - d uₙ - ᵗga¹ š [à - g a š u - t i - a] l - m e - a š à -ᵗt û¹ - š à - t û - m a ᵗt u - d a¹ l - m e - a . Note that, syntactically, l - m e - a and n u - m e - a can be used with participial force: "being," "not being"; "when . . . . was," "when . . . . was not." For an especially clear instance see *SRT,* Nos. 6 and 7, 1. 94.

Another interesting example is the introduction to

Lack of precision in renderings and translations and unadvertised omission of phrases or whole lines, such as have been exemplified above, undoubtedly constitute blemishes but hardly more.

Often the translation chosen is critical to our understanding of a story, and the alteration of a single word in the translation will bring that part of the story into a more intelligible context. We shall consider here only three such cases.

1. Recounting the myth which he has

_____

the myth of Enlil and Ninlil (dealt with by Dr. Kramer on p. 43):

    Dur-an-ki uru na-nam àm-
        dúr-ru-dè-en-dè-en
    Nipru^{ki} uru na-nam àm-dúr-
        ru-dè-en-dè-en
    Dur-^{giš}gišimmar uru na-nam
        àm-dúr-ru-dè-en-dè-en
    íd sal-la íd kù-bi(!?) na-nam

"In Duranki, in that very city we are living.
In Nippur, in that very city we are living.
In Durgišimmar, in that very city we are
    living.
None but the Idsalla was its pure river. . . . ."

The narrator is telling his listeners that the scene of the ancient tale which he is going to narrate is none other than their own town of Nippur, thus bidding fair to interest them.

The word na-nam does not mean "behold." as Dr. Kramer translates it but has identifying and restrictive force: "It is/was . . . . and none other" (or: ". . . . and no more"; or: ". . . . and no less"); it is therefore often rendered in Akkadian by -ma. In the sentences under discussion it seems to be used parenthetically: "Duranki—it and no other was the city (in question)—we inhabit." i.e., "We are living in that very city, (in) Duranki." The text Barton, MBI 4, varies from the one quoted above (Pinches, JRAS, 1919, p. 190) by seemingly reading [u r u^{ki} n]a-n am instead of Dur-an-ki (thus apparently also the catalogue published by Dr. Kramer in BASOR, No. 88, pp. 10–19, ll.5), by adding the determinative ki after uru, and by introducing the verbal form with the dative na- (see n. 12 below): na-an-dúr-ru-dè-en-d'e-en. This dative seems to have reference to Enlil, and its force is best rendered by a possessive pronoun: "In his very city, in his very city we are living." The Akkadian translator (JRAS, 1919, p. 190)—perhaps not a Nippurian—dissociates himself from the Sumerian narrator and his public, reporting rather than translating the meaning of these lines. He has: ina II (i.e., Dur-an-ki) áli-šu-nu šu-nu ú-ši-ba, "They (i.e., the Sumerian narrator and his audience) dwelt in their (i.e., Enlil and Ninlil's?) city Duranki." In the third line we read Dur-^{giš}gišimmar, following Pinches (op. cit.) and Van der Meer (Iraq, IV [1937], 144 ff., No. 88 1) rather than Langdon (RA, XIX [1922], 68, n. 7). The reasons underlying Dr. Kramer's rendering "the 'kindly wall' " are not clear to us.

renamed "The Feats and Exploits of Ninurta," Dr. Kramer writes:

Hearing of her son's great and heroic deeds, his mother Ninmah—also known as Ninhursag and Nintu, and more originally perhaps as Ki, the mother earth—is taken with love for him; she becomes so restless that he is unable to sleep in her bedchamber [p. 81].

The Sumerian word a r ḫ u š, which underlies Dr. Kramer's paraphrase "is taken with love for him," corresponds to Akkadian rêmu (root r-ḫ-m), "pity," "compassion," but not to râmu (root r-ʾ-m), "love," which is k i - á g (a) in Sumerian. That rêmu and râmu, treated as one in Delitzsch's Handwörterbuch, are distinct in both form and meaning was shown long since by Barth (ZA, XXII [1909], 1–5).

The mother's pity and compassion for her son, who is far from home, alone in a foreign country, cannot take on the overtones of a love affair without serious detriment to our understanding of the myth.

2. In the myth of Enlil and Ninlil, Enlil is outlawed by the assembly of the gods in Nippur for having raped young Ninlil. Banished by the gods of the world above, Enlil can turn only to the one other great realm of the Mesopotamian universe, that of the nether world, and so—headed for those dark regions—he leaves Nippur.[9] In

⁹ The relevant section reads:

    ᵈEn-líl Ki-ûr¹ im-ma-ni-in-ᴅᴜ-ᴅᴜ
    ᵈEn-líl Ki-ûr¹ dib-dib²-da-ni
    dingir gal-gal ninnu-ne-ne
    dingir nam-tar-ra imin-na-
        ne-ne
    ᵈEn-líl Ki-ûr-ra [im-ma-ni¹-
        dab-bé-ne]⁴
    ᵈEn-líl ú-zug⁴-e⁴ [uru-ta ba-
        ʼr a-è]⁴
    ᵈNu-nam-nir ú-zug⁴-e⁴ uru-ta
        ba-ra-ʼè¹
    ᵗ⁴En-líl níg-nam-ma² nam² mu-
        un-tar-ra-šè
    ᵗ⁴Nu-nam-nir¹⁰ nam-šè nam² mu-
        un-tar-ra-šè
    ᵈEn-líl í-du . . . . etc. . . . .

The text is based on Barton, MBI, 4.ii.11–13, for its first three lines; from then onward on Pinches, JRAS, 1919, pp. 190–91. Variants are: ¹SEM 77: +-r a. ²SEM 77: +-b é-. ³SEM 77: +-i n-. ⁴Thus MBI 4.

Dr. Kramer's rendering (pp. 43–47) all reference to the arrest of Enlil and to the verdict banishing him has been omitted. Enlil's journey to the underworld, accordingly, appears devoid of motivation.

When Enlil leaves Nippur, Ninlil, who is pregnant with his child, decides to follow. On her way she comes first to the city gate; she tells the gatekeeper that she is his queen and that she carries his king

Enlil's child under her heart. The gatekeeper, who is actually Enlil himself in disguise, answers her—according to Dr. Kramer's translation (p. 45)—as follows:

The "water" of my king, let it go toward heaven, let it go toward earth,
Let my "water," like the "water" of my king, go toward earth.

Thereupon Enlil, in his guise of gatekeeper, unites with Ninlil, engendering the deity Ninazu.[10]

It is not clear to us how Dr. Kramer arrived at the above translation and what meaning he would assign to such a speech in this context. To us it appears to obscure the story. In the Sumerian the lines in question read:

a l u g a l - m u a n - š è ḫ é - d u a - m u
k i - š è ḫ é - d u
a - m u a l u g a l - m u - g eₜₛ k i - š è ḫ é -
i m - m a - d u

Let my precious scion of the king go to heaven, let *my* scion go to the earth,
Let *my* scion in place of my precious scion of the king go to the earth.[11]

---

[1] *MBI* 4: ᴋᴀ +ꜱᴀʀ. [2] *MBI* 4 and *SEM* 77: - g e. [7] *MBI* 4: omits this line. [8] *SEM* 77: - š ê. [9] *SEM* 77: omitted. [10] *SEM* 77: + n í g -.

"Enlil came walking into Kiur
And while Enlil was passing through Kiur
The fifty senior gods
And the seven gods who determine destinies
Had Enlil arrested in Kiur:
"This sex-criminal Enlil will leave the town!
This sex-criminal Nunamnir will leave the town!"
Enlil, in accordance with that which had been decided as destiny,
Nunamnir, in accordance with that which had been decided as destiny,
Enlil (did) go (away) . . . . etc. . . . ."

The Akkadian translation reads, beginning with the fifth line:

ᴍɪɴ (i.e., ᵈ*En-lil*) *i-na* ᴍɪɴ (i.e., *Ki-ùr-ra*) *ú-šd-ḫa-zu-ú*
ᴍɪɴ (i.e., ᵈ*En-lil*) *mu-su-uk-kum i-na a-li li-ṣi*
ᴍɪɴ (i.e., ᵈ*Nu-nam-nir*) *mu-su-uk-kum i-na a-li li-ṣi*
ᴍɪɴ (i.e., ᵈ*En-lil*) *a-na šim-ti šd ta-ši-mu*
ᴍɪɴ (i.e., ᵈ*Nu-nam-nir*) *a-na šim-ti šd ta-ši-mu*
ᴍɪɴ (i.e., ᵈ*En-lil*) *il-la-ak* . . . . etc. . . . .

The word û - z u g (borrowed by Akkadian as (*m*)*usukku*, fem. (*m*)*usukkatu*), denotes a person who is sexually unclean, who is dangerous to the community because he is under a sexual taboo. This term may be used of a menstruating woman or—as here—of a person who has committed a sex crime, rape. The - e which follows the word we interpret as the demonstrative - e , "this" (see Poebel, *GSG*, §§ 223–26). Related to the latter is probably a "vocative" - e which occasionally occurs. Examples in IV R, Pl. 9, obv. 5: aja-ᵈN a n n a - u m u n - a n - g a l - e n i r - g á l d i m - m e - e r - e - n e / a-bu ᵈ*Na-an-nar be-lum* ᵈ*A-num rabu-u e-til-li ilt*ᵐᵉ⁻ᵉš, "O father Nanna, lord, great Anu, respected one among the gods"; the first line of Lugal-e: l u g a l - e uₜ m e - l á m - b i n i r - g á l , "O king, storm whose sheen inspires respect"; and Exaltation of Inanna (*RA*, XI [1914], 144, obv. 5): l u g a l d i m - m e - e r - e - n e - k eₜ, "O king of the gods!" Cf. also Frank, *ZAnF*, VII (1933), 195, obv. 9 and 2; S. A. Smith, *Miscellaneous Assyrian Texts*, Pl. 24, ll. 18 and 22, etc. For the semantic range involved, cf. the similar use of Egyptian *pw*, "this," in vocatives. See Gardiner, *Egyptian Grammar* , § 112.

[10] The Sumerians, it would appear, considered it possible for a woman to continue to conceive though already pregnant.

[11] The words a l u g a l - m u (representing a l u g a l (- a k) - m u) appear to contain an intentional ambiguity which is not easily rendered in English. The words may—and thus Ninlil is meant to interpret them—be understood to contain the possessive suffix first person singular in its caritative meaning: "my (beloved) seed (i.e., offspring) of the king," i.e., "my (dear) prince." They may also, however, be understood as containing a genitive of characteristic followed by the possessive suffix first person singular in its possessive meaning "my 'king's seed,'" i.e., "my royal offspring, engendered by me, a king, and thus of royal essence." With this genitive of characteristic compare the similar genitive in a n u n - a k - e n e, "the athelings," literally: the "magnate's seed", describing the gods as those of noble lineage. In their first sense these words could be fittingly spoken by a gatekeeper, a servant of Enlil; in the second sense they fit Enlil in his true identity.

On the use of - g eₜ (< g i m i n ; see Poebel, *MVAG*, 1921.1, p. 15) in the sense of "as equivalent of," compare *PBS*, VIII.2, No. 162, m u n u s š u - g i m u n u s k a š - š i - t u m 5 g í n - g u š k i n - g i m i - n a m , "One old woman, a Kassite, being the equivalent of 5 shekels gold"; and see also Lugal-e Tablet X.1 ff., where - g eₜ (translated *ki-i*) in Ninurta's verdicts serves to connect crime with punishment: "in recompense, retribution, for (that)."

This gives very good sense. When Enlil was banished, Ninlil faced a deep inner conflict. She was his, the mother of his child; she could not do otherwise than follow him wherever he might go. But, in so doing, she would take with her to live forever in the gloom of the underworld her unborn child, Sîn. In this her royal child and its fate centers all she most dearly values, all she lives for. She must therefore necessarily fall an easy prey when the gatekeeper—playing on her deepest fears in professed anxiety for the future fate of Sîn—holds out to her the possibility of saving him for the world of light: she willingly unites with the gatekeeper to conceive another—not royal—child, who may take Sîn's place in the underworld.

All this is essential for understanding the tale and is necessarily lost if the passages here discussed are omitted or inexactly rendered. Lost, too, is the further point that in due time Enlil's word—as must a god's word—comes true: Sîn, the bright moon-god, belongs to the world above while Ninazu belongs to the world below. Lost, finally, are the possible overtones: the constant fight of light and darkness in the waxing and waning moon as parallel to the fight of light and darkness over him before he was yet born.

3. As a last example may serve Dr. Kramer's rendering of the beginning of the myth of the pickax (pp. 51–53). Dr. Kramer is not altogether satisfied with his version, fears that it may seem "sodden, stilted, and obscure" (p. 51), but defends it on the ground that "the background and situation which these words and phrases imply and assume, still elude us; and it is this background and situation, part and parcel of the Sumerian mythological and religious pattern and well known to the Sumerian poet and his 'reader,' which are so vital to a full understanding of the text" (p. 52). The translation reads:

The lord, that which is appropriate verily he caused to appear,
The lord whose decisions are unalterable,
Enlil, who brings up the seed of the land from the earth,
Took care to move away heaven from earth,
Took care to move away earth from heaven.
In order to make grow the creature which came forth,
In the "bond of heaven and earth" (Nippur) he stretched out the . . . .

He brought the pickax into existence, the "day" came forth,
He *introduced labor*, decreed the fate,
Upon the pickax and basket he directs the "power."
Enlil made his pickax exalted,
His pickax of gold, whose head is of lapis lazuli,
The pickax of his house, of . . . . silver and gold,
His pickax whose . . . . is of lapis lazuli,
Whose *tooth* is a one-horned ox ascending a large wall.

The lord called up the pickax, decrees its fate,
He set the *kindu*, the holy crown, upon his head,
The head of man he placed in the mould,
Before Enlil *he* (man?) *covers* his land,
Upon his black-headed people he looked steadfastly.
The Anunnaki who stood about him,
He placed *it* (the pickax?) as a gift in their hands,
They soothe Enlil with prayer,
They give the pickax to the black-headed people to hold.

Checking through this translation to see what causes the impression of which Dr. Kramer speaks, one's attention is drawn to the last of the three sections. Here, after the second line, Dr. Kramer has followed a version which omits a line of the original.

This omitted line and the lines following it read in Sumerian:

u z u - è ᵍⁱˢa l - a - [n i   m i - n] i - i n - d ù
s a g   n a m - l ú - u l ú   ù - š u b - b a   m i -
n i - g á l
ᵈE n - l í l - š è   k a l a m - m a - n i   k i   m u -
u n - š i - i n - d a r ⟨- r e⟩
s a g - g i₄ - g a - n i - š è   i g i - z i   n a m -
m i - i n - b a r¹²

(And) drove his pickax into the u z u - è .⁻

In the hole (which he thus made) was the vanguard of mankind,

(And) while (the people of) his land were breaking up through the ground (like plants) toward Enlil

He eyed his black-headed ones in steadfast fashion.

---

¹² The text is based on *SRT* 19, *SEM* 34, *PBS*, X.2, p. 16, *SK* 207, and *TRS* 72 as follows: *First line*. Restored on the basis of *SRT* 19: u z u - è ᵍⁱˢa l - a - [n i . . . . .] and *SEM* 34: [. . . m i - n] i - i n - d ù . *TRS* gives [u z] u - m ù - a ᵍⁱˢ(! ?)ₐl(! ?) (read thus for ꜱᴀɢ-ɴᴜ) g á - g á - d è , "When the pickax was being applied in Uzumua"; *SK* 207 retains [. . .] ᵍⁱˢₐl [. . .] ; *PBS*, X.2, p. 16 (perhaps only Langdon's copy?) omits the line. *Second line*. Preserved in part by *PBS*, X.2, p. 16, and *SEM* 34, fully by *TRS* 72. *SEM* 34 has -g á l , "was," *TRS* 72 -g a r , "was situated," as the last sign; the last mentioned text also writes the determinative ɢɪˢ before ù - š u b - b a . *Third line*. Preserved in full by *PBS*, X.2, p. 16, and *TRS* 72 (read k a l a m - m a - n i(! ?) k i m u - u n(! ?) - š i(! ?) - i n - d a r - r e), in part by *SEM* 34 and *SK* 207. The latter reads [k a l a] m - m a - n a k i ᴋᴜ m u - u n - d a r - ˹a˺ . We consider the present form of the verb—as given in *TRS* 72—the better text. It should be noted that the present tense is often used in Sumerian—as it is in Akkadian—to express attendant circumstance. It is then to be rendered by a participle or a durative past (". . . . ing" or "was . . . . ing") in English. Cf. *PBS*, X.2, p. 14, rev. 8 ff.: ᵈE n - l í l l u g a l k u r - k u r - r a - k e₄ i g i - z i - t i - l a s a g - k i - z a l a g - g a - n i m u - u n - š i - i n - b a r ᵈI š - m e - ᵈD a - g á n - n a n a m m u - n i - i b - t a r - r e . . . . ᵈE n - l í l - l e n a m - š è m u - n i - i n - t a r , "Enlil, the king of all countries, looked with a true eye of life and with a clear brow at him. Determining destiny for Ishme-Dagān . . . . such and such things . . . . did Enlil determine for him as (his) destiny." Cf. also *HiA V*. 6, 12, u₄ - b a ᵈE n - k i - k e₄ ᵈE n - l í l - r a g ù m u - u n - n a - d é - e , "At that time Enki was saying to Enlil," where u₄ - b a clearly shows that no "present" or "future" tense (in the strict sense of that term) is intended. The usage is parallel to Akkadian usage, e.g., in *A pâ-šu ipuš-ma iqabbi izakkara ana B*, "A opened (lit.: 'worked') his mouth saying (the reference is primarily to articulate sound), saying (more precisely 'calling to mind,' 'calling up images, concepts'; the reference is primarily to meaning) to B." As for the meaning of k i . . . . d a r , cf. d a r , *litû*, "to cleave," "to split," Deimel, *ŠL*, 114.9; and k i - i n - d a r , *nigi₄₄u*, "crack (in the earth)," *ibid.*, 461.101. We know of no such meaning as "to clothe" for k i . . . . d a r . *Fourth line*. *SEM* 34 reads m u - š i - for n a m - m i - ; *TRS* 72 seems to read the verb as m u - u n - p à , but de Genouillac's copy may be doubted (m u - u n - š i - b a r(! ?)) . *SK* 207 omits the line.

The verbal form n a m - m i - i n - b a r shows the dative prefix n a - (or rather the datival verbal element (-) n a - in initial position?): "toward his black-headed ones the eye was opened in trusty fashion for him." The datival force of this relatively frequent "prefix" (see already above, n. 8) may be demonstrated most clearly, perhaps, by a comparison of two variant forms of Eannatum's name quoted in the "Stele of the Vultures." In obv. v. 20 ff., the author of that inscription tells about the name which Ningirsu gave Eannatum as follows: É - a n - n a - t û á(! ?) - t u k u - e k u r - a d u₁₇ - é š n a - e É - a n - n a - t û - r a m u ᵈI n a n n a - k e₄ e - n i - s a₄ - a - n i   É - a n - n a - ᵈI n a n n a - i b - g a l - k a - k a - a - t û m u m [u] - n i - [s a₄], "He (i.e., Ningirsu) named Eannatum—(this being) his name (by) which Inanna had named him: 'The one worthy of the Eanna of Inanna of Ibgal'—(by) the (new and longer) name: É - a n - n a - t û - á - t u k u - e - k u r - a - d u₁₇ - é š - n a - e (i.e., 'Eannatum, the possessor of strength, will sound for him [i.e., for Ningirsu] the battle cry in the enemy land')." Shortly afterward the author of the "Stele of the Vultures" again refers to this new name (vi.1 ff.), but now he quotes Ningirsu's actual words in naming Eannatum. Here n a -, "for him," is replaced with m á -, "for me": á - t u k u - e m u - p à - d a ᵈN i n - g í r - s û - k a - k e₄ É - a n - n a - t û - m e k u r - a d u₁₇ - é š m [á - e] n í g - u l - l í - a - d [a] g ù n a m - m i - d é , "The possessor of strength, the one made known by name by (me) Ningirsu, Eannatum, will sound for me the battle cry in the enemy land' he called out unto him alongside the original one (i.e. the original name, É - a n - n a - t û)."

Further instances of (-) n a - used initially are the well known: *X*. n a - e - a , "what X. is saying unto him," in the introduction to letters; the introductory line of Inanna's Descent (we quote l. 3), ᵈI n a n n a a n - g a l - t a k i - g a l - š è g e š t u - g a - n i n a - a n - g [u b] , "(As for) Inanna her mind was turned (lit.: 'was set') for her away from the great(er) heaven and toward the great(er) earth." Cf. also Elevation of Inanna (*RA*, XI [1914], 144–45, l. 13): A n - n a - r a i(n i m) - b a l a b a r - z é - e b - b a - k e₄ ḫ û l - l e - e š n a m - m i - i n - g a r , *ana ᵈA-nu na-pa-le-e ṭu-ub ka-bat-ti ḫa-diš iš-ša-kin-šum-ma*, "For Anu was joyfully established rejoinder of good(ness of) liver," i.e., "A pleasant answer joyfully suggested itself to Anu"; and Gudea, St. B, vii.4: n a - m u - d û , "He built it for him." (The existence of a datival prefix n a - has often been assumed. For recent views of this n a - and its meaning see Falkenstein, *ZAnF*, XI [1939], 183, and literature there quoted. The passage on which Falkenstein

The u z u - è , literally the "flesh producer," into which Enlil drove his newly fashioned pickax, is called U z u - m ú - a , the "(place where) flesh sprouted forth," in one of the variants of our text, and as such we know it well.[13] It is a frequently mentioned sacred spot in Nippur, and our text shows with all desirable clarity the reason for its sacred character: here in primeval times the earth produced mankind; for the first men grew up from the earth like plants according to a tradition vouched for also in the introductory lines of the myth of Enki and E-engurra:

a - r i - a n a m - b a - t a r - r a - b a
m u ḫ é - g á l a n a ù - t u - d a
u k ù - e ú - š i m - g e₁₈ ki i n - d a r - a - b a

When destinies had been determined for (all) engendered things,
When in the year (known as) "Abundance, born in heaven, ..."

<hr />

comments contains, in our opinion, the n a - of negated wish.)

Just as a dative element (-) n a - is found both initially and medially (as "prefix" and as "infix") in the Sumerian finite verb, so corresponds apparently the element (-) b a - , "for it," which occurs as infix in Urukagina Oval Plaque (cf. ii.7, n u - n a - s l - m u , "He was not giving unto him," i.e., unto the royal archer, with ii.9, n u - b a - s l - m u , "He was not giving unto it," i.e., unto the archer's donkey; cf. also Eannatum, Mortar iv.8), to the better-known "prefix" b a - (on its use with nonpersonals see Falkenstein, OLZ, 1933, Sp. 303-4). Similarly, the "prefix" bé - / b í - , "at it," "on it," has a corresponding "infix" - b eₓ - (cf. Poebel, AS, No. 2, pp. 16-19; we would prefer to assume that the meaning "with them" derives from a locative "at it/them"). We hope to return elsewhere to these correspondences, to the question of difference of grammatical function in different position, and to their general implications for the structure of the Sumerian verb.

[13] Uzumua is mentioned also in KAR 4, obv. 24, and in CT, XV, 31, 4 ff. Dr. Geers calls my attention to Van der Meer, "Tablets of the ḪAR-RA = ḪUBULLU Series . . . . ," Iraq, VI (1939), 144 ff., No. 88, i.15, where it is explained as (a part of, or a term for) Nippur. See also Heidel, Babylonian Genesis, p. 57, n. 40, and literature there cited. We assume u z u - m ú - a to have been abbreviated from a longer form: k i - u z u - m ú - a , "the place where flesh sprouted forth" (on construction cf. GSG, § 718), but other etymologies seem possible and may prove preferable.

The people had broken through the ground like grass (lit.: plants and herbs).[14]

The meaning of Enlil's action thus becomes clear: with his pickax he breaks the hard top crust of the earth which has thus far prevented the first men, developed below, from sprouting forth just as such a crust will often prevent germinating plants from breaking through. At Enlil's blow man becomes visible in the ù - š u b , i.e., in the hole left by the clod which Enlil's blow has broken loose;[15] and, as man after man shoots forth from the earth, Enlil contemplates his new creatures with approval.

Once this passage has been clarified, the structure of the story as a whole begins to stand out. After Enlil had separated Heaven and Earth, he bound up the wound occasioned to Earth when the "bond of Heaven and Earth" which had united her with Heaven was severed:

u z u - è s a g m ú - m ú - d è
d u r - a n - k i - k a   b ú r u   n a m - m i - i n - l á

(And) bound up for her (i.e., for Earth) the gash[16] in the "bond of Heaven and Earth"

[14] Dr. Kramer, who treats of this passage on p. 62 of his book, translates:

"After the water of creation had been decreed.
After the name ḫegal (abundance), born in heaven,
Like plant and herb had clothed the land, ..."

But a - r i - a —which we have rendered "(all) engendered things"—means actually "seed," "offspring" (lit.: "ejaculated semen virile"). Akkadian riḫūtu, not "the waters of creation"; nor does n a m . . . . t a r have the connotation of "decreed" as here used. It means to decree a "fate," the form or modus under which something is to exist, not to call that something into existence. On k i . . . . d a r see n. 12 above.

[15] On the meaning of ù - š u b , or rather of its Akkadian counterpart nalbantu, see von Soden, ZAnF, XI (1939), 64, n. 3. Von Soden shows that nalbantu denotes a cavity shaped like an inverted truncated pyramid of square ground plan. He translates it "Ziegelgrube." In our passage—as indicated above—the word apparently refers to the hole left by the clod broken off by Enlil's pickax.

[16] On b ú r u (presumably < b u r a with a > u after r ; cf. Poebel, GSG, §§ 723 and 470, also JAOS, 57 [1937], 51 ff.), "fissure," "gash," cf. my remarks in OIP, XLIII, 170-71, No. 42, n. †.

So that the "flesh producer" might grow the vanguard (of mankind).

The place of this wound, and of the severed bond, was in Nippur, the sacred area D u r - a n - k i , for D u r - a n - k i means "the bond of Heaven and Earth." In D u r - a n - k i was located U z u - m ú - a , which, after the wound had been closed, grew the first men.

We may thus offer the following translation which, though we consider the main lines certain, is still open to much improvement in detail:

The lord did verily[17] produce the normal order,
The lord whose decisions cannot be altered,
Enlil, did verily speed to remove Heaven from Earth
So that the seed (from which grew) the nation could sprout (up) from the field;

---

[17] The element n a n g a - , n a m g a - (on n > m before g see Poebel, GSG, § 63), which introduces the finite verb of this and several of the following lines, is an element of relatively frequent occurrence. (Note apart from this passage PBS, X.2, p. 6, rev. i.18–19; BE, XXIX.1, No. 2.34 [cf. p. 70]; Lugalbanda epic, 167–69; TRS 12, 104–6; SRT 3, iii.18; SRT 6.81–82; vase inscription of Enshakushanna, RA, XIV [1917], 152, and TRS 50, 57–58. The latter passage is not clear.) Its place in the verbal chain—always at the beginning before the prefix—classes it with the modal elements such as optative b é - / b a - , cohortative g a - , negative n u - , negating wish n a - , etc. The force of the mode marked by n a n g a - , n a m g a - is suggested by the Metropolitan Syllabary (Langdon, JSOR, I [1917], 22–23, obv. i.12–15), which translates n a m - g a - as tu-ia-ma, mi-in-di, ap-pu-na, and pi-qd-at, and by BE, XXXI, No. 46, i.2 (cf. Kramer, JAOS, 60 [1940], 251), which translates ra(?)-i-ma. Basic in these words is an appeal to the listener's own judgment and experience; they present a fact or conjecture as "evident," "obvious," as a necessary inference from the premises, but they tend to shade off into the more general, affirmative meaning "surely," "verily." (Cf. the translation of these words suggested by Landsberger, ZAnF, IX [1936], 73, and by Thureau-Dangin, RA, XXX [1933], 30, and Analecta orientalia, XII, 308. Ra-i-ma may be considered permansive I₁ of a root r-ʾ-i, "it is seen" [cf. رأى]. followed by -ma: "it is seen that," "it is evident that" > "surely," "verily"; cf. the material on raʾi collected by Ungnad in ZAnF, iv [1929], 71. We may therefore tentatively define the mood marked by n a n g a - as an inferentative-affirmative mood. Its force may be rendered approximately by "obviously" and by "verily."

Did verily speed to bring the Earth out from (under) Heaven (as a) separate (entity)
(And) bound up for her (i.e., for Earth) the gash in the "bond of Heaven and Earth"
So that the "flesh producer" could grow the vanguard (of mankind).

He caused the pickax to be, (when) daylight was shining forth,
He organized the tasks, the pickman's way of life,
(And) stretching out (his) arm straight toward the pickax and the basket
Enlil sang the praises of his pickax.
His pickax was of gold, its head(?) of lapis lazuli,
His (well) trussed[18] pickax was of gold and mesu silver,
His pickax was . . . .
Its point was valiant, a lone bastion projecting from a great wall.[19]
The lord . . . ed the pickax, giving it its qualities
. . . . , the pure crown he placed upon (his) head
(And) drove his pickax into the "flesh producer."
In the hole (which he thus made) was the vanguard of mankind
(And) while (the people of) his land were breaking through the ground toward Enlil
He eyed his black-headed ones in steadfast fashion.
The Anunnaki (gods) stepped up to him,
Laid their hands upon their noses (in greeting),
Soothing Enlil's heart with prayers,
Black-headed (people) they were requesting(?) of him.

---

[18] Very doubtful. We tentatively restore ᵍⁱˢal-ʾsa(!?)-lá(!?)ʾ-a-ni. Dr. Kramer seems to read ᵍⁱˢal-6 (or gá)-a-ni, but "the pickax of his house" would be ᵍⁱˢal-6-(or gá)-a-na.

[19] Our rendering of s i as "bastion" is based on s i - b à d (. a k) , sittu, "bastion." The comparison seems to be with bastions of a very long and narrow type such as found, e.g., in Agrab (OIP, LVIII, 221, Fig. 170). TCL 72 has û - t u - d a , "born of," instead of è - a , "projecting from." This variant would appear to render Dr. Kramer's interpretation of the line less likely.

Having thus considered specimens of the translations offered in the book under review, we turn next to questions of interpretation, to deal first with certain specific interpretational concepts presented in it.

II. SPECIFIC INTERPRETATIONAL CONCEPTS

A. THE CREATION OF THE UNIVERSE

Dr. Kramer bases his statement of Sumerian cosmogonic concepts on a passage in the introduction to the tale of "Gilgamesh, Enkidu, and the Nether World," which he translates (p. 37):

After heaven had been moved away from earth,
After earth had been separated from heaven,
After the name of man had been fixed;

After An had carried off heaven,
After Enlil had carried off earth, ...

This translation is substantially correct, as is the subsequent interpretation:

Heaven and earth, originally united, were separated and moved away from each other, and thereupon the creation of man was ordained. An, the heaven-god, then carried off heaven, while Enlil, the air-god, carried off earth [p. 38].

Having established these facts, Dr. Kramer proceeds to ask three major questions: (1) Were heaven and earth conceived as created, and if so, by whom? (2) What was the shape of heaven and earth as conceived by the Sumerians? (3) Who separated heaven from earth? We shall consider his answers one by one.

1. *Before heaven and earth.*—Dr. Kramer finds the answer to his first question in the text *TRS* 10, an early version of the great catalogue of divine names known as A n *Anum*, which lists the divine name ᵈA m a - ù - t u - a n - k i , "The mother who gave birth to heaven and earth," as an epithet of the goddess Nammu. He writes:

In a tablet which gives a list of the Sumerian gods, the goddess Nammu, written with the ideogram for "sea," is described as "the mother, who gave birth to heaven and earth." Heaven and earth were therefore conceived by the Sumerians as the created products of the primeval sea [p. 39].

By giving this, and only this, answer to his first question, Dr. Kramer creates the impression that Sumerian cosmogonic concepts were all smoothly integrated—that the Sumerians had a single answer to questions concerning ultimate beginnings. Such, however, was not the case. The very same text from which Dr. Kramer derives his evidence on Nammu contains two other, different, traditions concerning world origins, one of which—since it is placed at the very beginning of the text— may even be surmised to have been considered the most important of the three. These two traditions, the "Genealogy of Anu" and the "Genealogy of Enlil," are both well deserving of attention.

The "Genealogy of Anu" carries the parentage of heaven deified back through A n - š á r - g a l , "The greater horizon" —apparently the horizon where the greater heaven and the greater earth were thought to meet—to a divine entity E n - u r u - u l l a , "The lord of the primeval city." Since this deity is known from other sources to be located in the nether world, we may assume that "the primeval city" is the city of the dead, the "great dwelling." Death, it would appear, was and ruled before life and all that is came into being—that is, all life originated in (or emanated from) death, lifelessness. The other tradition, the one which in *TRS* 10 is placed at the beginning, but which in later versions of the list appears as the genealogy of Enlil, traces cosmic origins back through fifteen divine pairs. Among these are the powers manifest in Earth viewed in their male and female aspects as ᵈE n - k i , "The earth lord," and ᵈN i n - k i , "The earth lady," and the powers manifest in Heaven represented by ᵈE n - a n - n a and ᵈN i n - a n - n a , "The sky lord" and "The sky lady." At the beginning of the genealogy, before everything else, stands the active principle of the world itself, its *modus operandi*,[20] personified as ᵈE n - m e - š á r - r a , "Lord (e n) *modus operandi* (m e) of the universe (š a r r - a (k)) " and ᵈN i n - m e - š á r - r a , "Lady *modus operandi* of the universe." And from them issued life: "Lord days of life" and "Lady days of life." These highly interesting speculations concerning world origins cannot well be ignored in a statement of Sumerian cosmogonic concepts.

Returning to Dr. Kramer's treatment of the speculations centering in the goddess Nammu, it must be pointed out that the sign with which her name is written does not—as Dr. Kramer avers—mean "sea." "Sea" is a - a b b a (k) in Sumerian; the sign with which Nammu's name is written denotes—if read e n g u r —primarily the body of sweet water which the Mesopotamians believed lay below the earth, feeding rivers and wells but best observable in the watery deep of the marshes. Nammu is therefore the "watery deep" of the Mesopotamian marshes extending below the surface of the earth as

[20] The Sumerian word m e , here rendered as "modus operandi," means approximately "set, normative pattern (of behavior)," "norm." Etymologically it may be considered as the noun ("being" = manner of being) which corresponds to the verb m e , "to be." It is used characteristically of the totality of functions pertaining to an office or a profession (cf., e.g., Gudea, Cyl. B, vi.23, vii.11, 23, etc.), of rites, and of mores (cf., e.g., Kramer, *AS*, No. 12, p. 24, l. 70; *PBS*, X.2, p. 1, obv. iii.12–13; see n. 23 below). Instructive also is m e - t e , "approaching the norm" = "proper," "fitting" (Akkadian (w)*asmu*). Landsberger, to whom the clarification of this term is largely due, translates "Göttliche Ordnungen von ewiger, unveränderlicher Geltung" (*Islamica*, II [1927], 369). In his earlier detailed study of the word (*AOF*, II [1924], 66) he proposed " 'specifisch göttliche Gewalt (Funktion)' oder 'heilige Macht' "

the water-bearing strata. She is not the sea.[21]

[21] The Yale Syllabary (*YOS*, I, Pl. 53.57–60) and the duplicate text *CT*, XXXV, 1, 1.46–49, list four meanings of the sign with their reading. The meanings seem to be arranged in pairs comprising first a name of an entity, then the name of the deity of that entity:

i	ENGUR	na-a-ru	"river"
i - i d	ENGUR	ᵈÍd	"the god (of the river) Id"
e n - g u r	ENGUR	ap-su-u	"the *apsú*"
n a m - m u	ENGUR	ᵈNammu	"the goddess (of the *apsú*) Nammu"

A further reading—originally perhaps pertaining to a separate sign which in time became merged with ENGUR—is g i - l u - g u (Meissner has suggested the emendation z i(!) - k u(!) - u m(!), "heaven," Akkadian *šamú* [see *SAI*, 7737 and Deimel, *ŠL*, 484.8]). As translation of e n g u r occurs also *engurru* which is merely the Sumerian word itself in Akkadian garb (see Deimel, *ŠL*, 484.2).

The reading with which we are here concerned is e n g u r , translated as *apsú*, and forming a pair with the divine name Nammu. There can be little doubt about its basic meaning. Its Akkadian counterpart, *apsú*, denotes the sweet waters of the underground water-bearing strata of Mesopotamia, waters which may be reached when one digs down deep to lay the foundations of a temple, but which also appear in pools and marshes where the surface of the plain naturally dips down below the water table (see the current dictionaries *sub voce* and Jensen, *RLA*, I. 122–23).

As *apsú* is used in Akkadian so is e n g u r and its approximate synonym a b z u ((from this word derives Akkadian *apsú*) in Sumerian. Gudea tells us that the subterranean *temennu* (lit.: "*temennu* of the a b z u") of the temple Eninnu in Lagash "consults together" with Enki down in "the house of the e n g u r" (é - a n - g u r₄ - r a - k a , Cyl. A, xxii. 11–13; cf. *JNES*, II [1943], 118). Here, accordingly, the e n g u r is deep down in the ground. Ur-Nanshe, on the other hand, invokes the reeds of the marshes as "reed-of-the-canebrake of the e n g u r" (g i . g i š . g i e n g u r (.r a) , Diorite plaque i.2; cf. *JNES*, II [1943], 118) and states that its root is in one place with Enki. Here, accordingly, the e n g u r is the subterranean waters as they come to the surface in the marshes.

Although the notion underlying the words e n g u r , a b z u , and *apsú* is thus in itself clear and well defined, one might, of course, raise the question whether occasionally one or the other of these terms might not have been used more loosely to include also the other large body of terrestrial water, the sea. On the whole, we believe, the answer must be in the negative.

The Akkadians—as shown by *Enūma eliš*—distinguished quite clearly *Apsú*, conceived as male, from his spouse *Ti'āmat*, the sea, conceived as female. Nor are e n g u r or a b z u ever translated as *tāmtu*, "sea," in Akkadian; this translation pertains to a b and a - a b - b a . But also the Sumerians treat e n g u r and a b z u as distinct in meaning from a - a b - b a , "the sea." We need quote only

The point just made is not unimportant, for it places the ideas with which we are here concerned in a particular group of Mesopotamian cosmogonic speculations. That group envisages the origin of the world along lines suggested by the manner of formation of alluvial Mesopotamia itself: through continual deposits

of silt in the riverain marshes. Nammu, the deep which deposits the silt, is to this day "giving birth" to earth in Mesopotamia. By identifying Nammu with the sea, Dr. Kramer must necessarily lose sight of the basic meaning of the speculations of which he treats. Accordingly, later on (p. 75), he is at a loss to explain why the particular combination Nammu-Ninmah-Enki should be involved in the creation of man. The answer is not difficult. In the text to which Dr. Kramer has reference man was made—as one would make a clay figurine—from "the clay above the *apsû.*" This clay typifies the silt which the watery deep of the marshes (Nammu) deposits on the shore (Ninmah), and correspondingly Ninmah (Kramer rightly identifies her with Ki, "The firm ground") is in the myth to "stand above" Nammu to receive the child—the silt—when Nammu gives birth to it. The deposited clay owes its plasticity, its ability to receive form, to its content of water. This explains the presence of Enki, who represents the

---

the passage which describes Enki's departure for Nippur in the myth of Enki and É-engurra (Dr. Kramer's translation may be found on p. 63 of his book):

dEn-ki zi-ga-na (var. -ni) k u₄
   i-zi (var. izi) šu na-zi
a b . z u - e (var. -a) u₄ - e à m (var.
   n a m) - m a - g u b (var. l á - a)
e n g u r - r a ḫ úl-l a m u - n i - i b (var.
   - i b) - t û m
a - a b - b a - k a (var. -a , - g e₁₅) n í
   m u - u n (var. om.) - d a - g á l
íd - m a ḫ - e (var. - g e₁₅) s u - z i m u -
   u n (var. om.) - d a (var. + - a n) - r i
íd - B u r a n u n - n a(!) l u (var. t u₁₅ - u l û)
   s û r m u - u n - d a - a n - z i

"When Enki rose the fishes rose, raised (their)
   hands (in prayer) to him—
He stood, a marvel unto the *Apsû.*
Brought joy to the E n g u r .
To the Sea (it seemed that) awe was upon him,
To the Great River (it seemed that) terror
   hovered around him,
While at the same time the Southwind stirred
   the depths of the Euphrates."

The variants affecting the sense are: "He floated" or "hung suspended" instead of "He stood" in the second line; "Awe was upon him as (it is upon) the sea" and "Terror hovered around him as (it hovers around) the great river" in the fourth and fifth lines. Besides the translation of ll. 2–6 given above, one might also consider: "He stepped—a marvel to behold—up to the *apsû,* was carried in joy into the e n g u r . In the sea awe was upon him, on the great river terror hovered around him, in the Euphrates the southwind stirred the depths when he arrived thither (lit.: 'with him')." On any translation the e n g u r and the "sea" (a - a b - b a) are different entities. Another passage which shows the two words to represent distinct entities is *A O,* 4331 + 4335, iv, 1–2; *NFT,* p. 206; Poebel, *ZAnF,* III (1927), 162.

In favor of a less strict usage we could at best quote passages like *TC,* VI, 47, l. 2, which points up a resemblance between Ea and Ereshkigal as follows: a-me dÉ-a ki-i ᶠapˡ-su-ú ap-su-ú tam-tim tam-tim dEreš-ki-gal, "Ea resembles the *apsû,* the *apsû* the sea, the sea Ereshkigal." However, as anyone conversant with theological texts of the type of *TC,* VI, 47, will know, such associations are important rather for what they tell about Mesopotamian speculative thought than as precise contributions to lexicography.

Little is gained also from V R, Pl. 51, iii.77–78: dNammu nin ab-gal-l [a . . .], dMIN be-el-tu íd ina tam-tim [. . .], for the lacuna in the text leaves

the exact relations between Nammu and the sea or lake undetermined: "Nammu, the lady who in(to)/from the/a great sea/lake [. . .]." That etymologically the term a b z u and the terms for sea, a b and a - a b b a (k), may be related, and that correspondingly in a remote past the Sumerians may have distinguished the bodies of water involved less sharply, is possible (a suggestion to that effect has been made by Poebel; see *Z AnF,* III [1927], 258, and *apud* Jensen, *RLA,* I, 122) but is not, of course, immediately relevant to the usage of historical times.

Under these circumstances the likelihood that in historical times e n g u r , a b z u , and *apsû* were used—even occasionally—to include also the sea appears rather problematical. To set aside their clear and well-established meaning "sweet waters of the subsoil and of pools and marshes" and to assume instead this questionable meaning "sea" to be their primary and basic connotation seems decidedly unadvisable, the more so since the deities connected with the e n g u r and the a b z u / *apsû,* Nammu and Enki, played a very prominent role in Mesopotamian religious thought, as did the sweet waters of the subsoil, of rivers, wells, canals, and of the marshes, in the life and outlook of the Mesopotamian himself. The sea, on the other hand, was an almost negligible factor in his life. It would be very strange indeed if he had chosen it and the divine powers manifest in it as his most popular object of worship.

sweet waters and who himself issued from Nammu. Just as the deep which deposits the clay, the firm ground which receives it, and the water which gives it plasticity are all involved in the making of a clay figurine, so were these forces involved in the making of man, a process which the myth sees as entirely analogous.

2. *The shape of heaven and earth.*—The second of Dr. Kramer's three questions has reference to the shape of heaven and earth: "What was the shape of heaven and earth as conceived by the Sumerians?" He finds the answer in two lines from the myth of Lahar and Ashnan on which he comments as follows (p. 39):

The myth "Cattle and Grain" . . . . , which describes the birth in heaven of the spirits of cattle and grain, who were then sent down to earth to bring prosperity to mankind, begins with the following two lines:

After on the mountain of heaven and earth, An had caused the Anunnaki (his followers) to be born, ...

It is not unreasonable to assume, therefore, that heaven and earth united were conceived as a mountain whose base was the bottom of the earth and whose peak was the top of the heaven.

What Dr. Kramer here proposes is a Sumerian *Weltberg*. His argument rests, as will be seen, on a tacit assumption that the genitive in the Sumerian phrase ḫur-sag an-ki-bi-da-ke₄, "on the mountain of heaven and earth," can represent, and can represent only, an appositive genitive with identifying force: "the mountain of (= which is) heaven and earth." Such an assumption, however, is not admissible a priori. In the first place, the proposition that Sumerian possessed the appositive genitive is open to the gravest doubts. Nobody has yet demonstrated—or, as far as we know, even suggested—that this was the case. Sec-

ond, one would hesitate—even if it could be shown that Sumerian possessed such a genitive—to interpret the particular genitive in ḫur-sag an-ki-bi-da-ke₄ as other than a normal "possessive" genitive (range of meaning approximately: in the sphere of), for the "possessive" genitive fits the context perfectly. The Sumerian word ḫursag usually has reference to the range of mountains bordering the Mesopotamian plain on the east. As seen on the eastern horizon, its shining peaks towering from earth up into heaven, the ḫursag appears indeed to belong equally to both of these cosmic entities, and the epithet here applied to it, "of both heaven and earth," is therefore as forceful as it is apt.

The interpretation of the phrase here given was seen and clearly set forth already by Chiera in *SRT*, page 27, note 2. Chiera also noted (*ibid.*, p. 29, n. 3) that the scene of events as indicated in the introductory lines of the myth (the ḫursag on the eastern horizon) is in full agreement with the later statement that Lahar and Ashnan came into being in Du₆-kù, "the holy mound," for Du₆-kù was located by the Sumerians in the mountains on the eastern horizon where the sun rises.[22] Indeed, it was probably the luxuriant vegetation, the wondrously fresh green pastures of the foothills, contrasting so markedly with the barren Mesopotamian plain, that led the Sumerians to seek the origin and home of Lahar, the power manifesting itself in the thriving flocks, in the faraway green hills.

We must thus conclude that there is in these lines no evidence for a Sumerian *Weltberg*.

3. *The separation of heaven and earth.*—Dr. Kramer's answer to his third question is correct. It was Enlil who separated heaven and earth.

[22] See V R, Pl. 50, l. 5. Cf. Jensen, *RLA*, I, 122.

B. THE ORGANIZATION OF THE UNIVERSE

On pages 41–75 Dr. Kramer deals with the organization of the universe, dividing the subject into the organization of heaven and the organization of earth; the latter, which subsumes the creation of man, we shall treat separately.

The section on the organization of heaven occupies only one of the thirty-four pages and is based largely on scattered phrases culled from a variety of literary texts. Important relevant myths are the "Myth of the Elevation of Inanna" (*RA*, XI [1914], 144–45; cf. also *RA*, XII [1915], 74–75), especially lines 24 ff., and the "Eclipse Myth" (*CT*, XVI, 19). Both of these sources are ignored as, indeed, are most of the very large and very important Sumerian mythological materials which happen to have come down to us in late copies only. The reasons for the omission of this material, seemingly deliberate, are not clearly stated anywhere in the book.

Since we are discussing the organization of heaven, we would call attention to a passage on page 74:

Enlil, the air-god, now found himself living in utter darkness, with the sky, which may have been conceived by the Sumerians as made of pitch-dark lapis lazuli, forming the ceiling and walls of his house, and the surface of the earth, its floor. He therefore begot the moon-god *Nanna* to brighten the darkness of his house.

For the sake of clarity it should be said that this passage is not, to our knowledge, a paraphrase of any extant Sumerian myth. The conception of the universe as a dark house, and of the moon-god as a lamp begot to light it, is rather the author's own vivid synthesis, a suggestion as to what the Sumerians *may* have thought.

The organization of the earth Dr. Kramer presents by retelling nine differ-

ent Sumerian myths. Some of these, such as "Enlil and Ninlil" and "Enki and Ninhursaga," are concerned primarily with origins (the former also with status: chthonic or celestial), while others, such as "The Myth of the Pickax," "Lahar and Ashnan," and "Emesh and Enten," deal with both origin and relative value. Only "Enki and Shumer" and in a sense "Inanna and Enki" deal primarily with organization—the latter in so far as it seeks to explain the scope of Inanna's powers. The myth of "Enki and Eridu," giving the building history of Enki's temple, stands somewhat apart. So, too, does "The Journey of Nanna," which seems concerned primarily with the prosperity of Ur.

We have commented on sections of two of these myths above ("Enlil and Ninlil" and "The Myth of the Pickax") and—since considerations of space prohibit detailed discussion—here add only a few remarks on the others.

The statement on page 53 ("Lahar and Ashnan"), "But the Anunnaki were unable to make effective use of the products of these deities; it was to remedy this situation that man was created," seems to rest on the lines translated: "The Anunnaki of the Dulkug eat, but remain unsated; in their pure sheepfolds milk, ... , and good things, the Anunnaki of the Dulkug drink, but remain unsated" (p. 73). These lines, however, merely express the fact that the Anunnaki so liked the good products of Ashnan and Lahar (primarily bread and milk) that they never tired of eating and drinking them. This is the sense in which negated forms of *šebû*—to which s i corresponds in the meaning "to satiate"—are used elsewhere in Mesopotamian literature (see, e.g., Delitzsch, *HW*, pp. 636–37). We should accordingly translate "unsatiably" and not "but remained unsated." The meaning of the third section of the passage of Lahar and Ashnan translated on pages 72–73 and—much more serious—the greater part of the myth of Enki and Ninhursaga is fatally obscured through the erroneous interpretation of Uttu as "goddess of plants" instead of as goddess of "weaving" and/or "washing" clothes. The latter interpretation—and the only one which fits the myths—has been conclusively established by Scheil (see, e.g., Langdon, *Le Poème sumérien* ... , pp. 152 ff., where the relevant syllabary passages are quoted). In the myth of Enki and Shumer the latter (as the principality centering around Nippur) stands on a line with the principality of Ur (not in the relation of country and capital) and with that of Meluhha. The blessing on Shumer, mentioning its "matrix" which gives birth to kings and *enu*'s, has been largely misunderstood in the translation on page 59.[23]

C. THE CREATION OF MAN

The tradition according to which man sprouted, as though he were a plant, from the soil of Uzumua has been discussed

[21] Enki touches first on Shumer's cultural leadership: it sets the norms, the standards of right behavior. U t u - è - t a u t u - š ú - u š u k ù - e m e s ì - m u cannot—for reasons of grammar—mean "the people from sunrise to sunset obedient to the divine decrees" but must be rendered: "(Thou Shumer) who dost set (lit.: 'give') norms for the people from sunrise to sunset," i.e., from the farthest east to the farthest west. He then mentions Shumer's powers as "kingmaker": it has authority to confer the high offices of "king" and "*enu*." The relevant lines—which belong closely together—have been separated by Dr. Kramer and distributed to two of the sections into which he divides the text. They read:

u m u nₐ - z i - k i - d i n g i r - ù - t u - z a
a n - g eₙ š u n u - t e - g á
l u g a l ù - t u s u ḫ - z i - k é s - d i
e n ù - t u s a g m e n g á - g á

"Thy true matrix, the place which gives birth to gods, is untouchable like heaven.
It gives birth to kings, ties(?) rightly the pectoral(?),
It gives birth to *enu*'s, sets the crown on(?) (their) heads."

The crown and pectoral(?) are symbols of office; the phrase "which gives birth to gods" may have reference to deified rulers.

above.[24] The tradition which Dr. Kramer treats (pp. 68–72) assumes that man was formed from clay much as a figurine is made. Unfortunately, the section dealing with the actual birth of "the clay above the *apsû*" and the fashioning of man from it is lost in a lacuna of the text. The following sections deal not with man as such but rather with certain freak types of human existence (e.g., the eunuch, the barren woman) and unfortunate general forms of human life such as that of the old man suffering under the debilities of extreme age (typified in Enki's creature U₄ - m u - u l , "My day is ancient"). The origin of these forms of human existence is traced to a mischievous contest between Enki and Ninmah when these gods were in their cups. One was to make freaks, the other was to cope with the freak, find a way to integrate it with the world order, a way in which it might gain a living. The meaning of this part of the myth seems to have escaped Dr. Kramer.

D. MYTHS OF KUR

A special section of Dr. Kramer's book, pages 76–96, is devoted to myths about a monster called Kur. He writes:

Kur thus cosmically conceived is the empty space between the earth's crust and the primeval sea. Moreover, it is not improbable that the monstrous creature that lived at the bottom of the "great below" immediately over the primeval waters is also called Kur; if so, this monster Kur would correspond to a certain extent to the Babylonian Tiamat. In three of our "Myths of Kur," it is one or the other of these cosmic aspects of the word *kur* which is involved [p. 76].

[24] Another form of the tradition is preserved in *KAR* 4. This text also mentions the separation of heaven and earth: uₐ a n k i - t a t a b - g e - n a - b a d - a - t a b à - a - [b a] , "When heaven from earth—from the far removed trusty twin—had been parted," and proceeds to tell of a divine decision to create man in Uzumua (obv. 24–25). But the decision is taken at an assembly of all the gods, and man is to be fashioned from the blood of the two Lamga gods who are to be slain for that purpose.

Since the monster Kur is a new concept in Sumerian mythology—except for occasional references to it in earlier writings of Dr. Kramer—it will be worth while to consider briefly the material adduced for it.

1. *First myth of Kur.*—The first "myth" quoted under the heading "The Destruction of Kur: The Slaying of the Dragon" (p. 76) appears—we can think of no other way of describing it—to have been derived by means of a series of conjectures from a misunderstood passage in the introduction to the tale of "Gilgamesh, Enkidu, and the Nether World." We may illustrate by quoting Dr. Kramer's own outline of the story, printing in italics the words which connect one such conjecture with the next:

After heaven and earth had been separated, An, the heaven-god, carried off the heaven, while Enlil, the air-god, carried off the earth. It was then that the foul deed was committed. The goddess Ereshkigal was carried off violently into the nether world, *perhaps* by Kur itself. Thereupon Enki, the water-god, whose Sumerian origin is uncertain, but who toward the end of the third millennium B.C. gradually became one of the most important deities of the Sumerian pantheon, set out in a boat, *in all probability* to attack Kur and avenge the abduction of the goddess Ereshkigal. Kur fought back savagely with all kinds of stones, large and small. Moreover it attacked Enki's boat, front and rear, with the primeval waters which it *no doubt* controlled. Here our brief prologue passage ends, since the author of "Gilgamesh, Enkidu, and the Nether World" is not interested in the dragon story primarily but is anxious to proceed with the Gilgamesh tale. And so we are left in the dark as to the outcome of the battle. *There is little doubt,* however, that Enki was victorious. Indeed it is *not at all unlikely* that the myth was evolved in large part for the purpose of explaining why, in historical times, Enki, like the Greek Poseidon, was conceived as a sea-god; why he is described as "lord of the abyss"; and

why his temple in Eridu was designated as the "sea-house" [p. 79].

Since the whole story is built around the assumption that Ereshkigal in the beginning of time was abducted violently to the nether world, we may begin our comments with the three lines on which that assumption rests. They read:

u₄ An-né an ba-an-túm-a-ba
ᵈEn-líl-le ki ba-an-túm-a-ba
ᵈEreš-ki-gal-la-ra (var. om. -ra)
  kur-ra sag-rig₇-ga-šè im-ma-
  ab-rig₇-ga-a-ba

These lines are translated by Dr. Kramer on page 37 as follows:

After An had carried off heaven,
After Enlil had carried off earth,
After Ereshkigal had been carried off into Kur
  as its prize.

In his comments on the text on page 38 he explains that "the goddess Ereshkigal, the counterpart of the Greek Persephone, whom we know as queen of the nether world, but who originally was probably a sky-goddess, was carried off into the nether world, perhaps by Kur." Actually, however, the verb-phrase s a g - r i g₇ - g a - š è . . . . r i g₇ does not mean, as Dr. Kramer translates it, "to carry off as a prize," but literally "to present as a presented present." It is a somewhat overloaded variant of the phrase s a g - š è . . . . r i g₇ , "to present as a present," used typically of (1) votive offerings (including persons: votaries) presented to a deity and (2) the dowry given to a woman at her marriage. Ereshkigal, whom Dr. Kramer assumes to be the subject of the passive form of the verb, is actually the dative object, as shown by the dative suffix - r a which follows her name in the text given on Plate VIII. We must accordingly translate quite differently:

After An had carried off heaven,
After Enlil had carried off the earth,

(And) after it (the earth) had been presented as dowry to Ereshkigal in the nether world (var.: to Ereshkigal and the nether world).

For the concept that the earth (k i) belongs to Ereshkigal we might perhaps be justified in quoting her Akkadian epithet *šarrat erṣetim*, "Queen of the earth." It seems quite likely that "the earth" (k i) should have been considered somehow to be associated with or to have belonged originally to the "great(er) earth" (k i - g a l), Dr. Kramer's "great below," of which Ereshkigal's name (e r e š - k i - g a l - l a) indicates her to be ruler. There is thus in the lines quoted no support whatever for the assumption that a "foul deed" (p. 79), an abduction of Ereshkigal, was ever committed. Nor is there any evidence for the related suggestion that Ereshkigal "originally was probably a sky-goddess" (p. 38). Nor can Enki's boat ride, referred to in the following lines, now be plausibly explained as an expedition undertaken to avenge that abduction. For the time being we must content ourselves with the fact that we do not yet know the myth to which it has reference.[25] In passing, it may be noted that Enki's name is perfectly good Sumerian and means "The lord of the earth" (more originally, perhaps, "Lord Earth"). It happens to be one of the first Sumerian divine names attested, occurring already on tablets from Jemdet Naṣr.[26] The name also appears, immediately following that of Enlil, at the head of our oldest Sumerian lists of gods, those from Fara.[27]

[25] One might guess—but it could be no more than a guess—that the myth aimed at explaining how Enki, the sweet waters in the ground, came to occupy his present position (see n. 28 below) separating the earth above (k i) from the underworld (k i - g a l, "the great(er) earth") below. It is only fitting, before leaving the passage with which we have been dealing, to call attention to Dr. Kramer's earlier—and far more cautious—treatment of it in *AS* No. 10, pp. 3 and 34 ff.

[26] Langdon, *OECT*, VII, No. 99.

[27] Deimel, *Schultexte aus Fara* (Leipzig, 1923), Nos. 1.1.4, 5.1.2, etc.

The suggestion that Enki's "Sumerian origin is uncertain" seems therefore particularly unfortunate. So also is the characterization of Enki as a sea-god and the comparison with the utterly different Greek Poseidon. Enki was primarily god of the sweet waters, of wells and canals, and of the *apsû*. His connections with the salt water, the sea (a - a b b a (k)), are at best peripheral, the sea playing a very small role in the life of the Sumerians, a very large one in that of the Greeks.[28]

[28] The assumed connection of Enki with the sea and the translation of the name of his temple in Eridu, É - e n g u r a (k), as "sea-house" (p. 79 *passim*) are largely based on the belief that a b z u and e n g u r denote "sea," which we have discussed in n. 21 above. Concerning É - e n g u r a (k) in Eridu it should be noted that the "sea" on which Eridu was situated was in reality an inland lake, as shown by R. Campbell Thompson's finds of fresh water shells on the site (*Archaeologia*, LXX [1920], 124–25). Both Akkadian *tâmtu* and Sumerian a - a b b a (k) could be used for "lake" as well as for "sea" (cf. Jensen, *RLA*, I, 123; Unger, *ibid.*, 404–5). The flora and fauna of its immediate surroundings (Myth of Enki and Eridu, ll. 75 ff.: reed thickets, fruit-bearing orchards, birds, and fishes; cf. Kramer, p. 63) are those of a fresh-water lake, not of the sea. The e n g u r, from which the temple is named, is therefore the water-bearing strata at the lake bottom from which water seeps into the lake from the surrounding soil and, cosmically conceived, the "house of the e n g u r" stretches underground with the water table to Lagash where the substructure of É - n i n n u reaches down into it (see n. 21 above). Thus we also understand the description in the legend of the Kishkanû (*CT*, XVI, 46–47, 187–92): Enki, the god of the sweet waters in the earth, lies in the chambers of Nammu, goddess of the water-bearing strata; these chambers are down in the earth just above the "surface of the underworld" (ḫ i LIB written ICI-KUR(.r a), i.e., "surface of the underworld"; see Deimel, *ŠL*, 449.174).

⁴E n - k i - k eₐ (var. + k i -) d u - d u - a - t a Eridu^kⁱ - g a ḫ é - g á l s i - g a - à m
ša ⁴É-a (var. ⁴ᴮᴱ) tal-lak-ta-šu ina E-ri-du (var. Eri-duₐₐ) ḫé-gál ma-la-a-ti
k i - d ú r - a - n a k i ḫ i LIB - à m
šu-bat-su a-šar ir-ṣi-tim-ma
k i - n á - a i t i m ⁴N a m m u - à m
ki-iṣ-ṣu-šu (var. -šú) ma-aṣa-lu (var. -al-la(?)) šd ⁴ᴹᴵᴺ

"The haunts of Enki in Eridu are full of bounty. Where he sits is the surface of the underworld, Where he lies is the chamber of Nammu."

Literally translated, the last lines read: In his place where he is sitting is the place (of the) surface of the underworld, in the place where (he is) lying is the (bed)chamber (of) Nammu (the Akkadian version seems to reverse "place where (he is) lying" and "chamber").

2. *Second myth of Kur.*—The second myth quoted under the heading "The Destruction of Kur: The Slaying of the Dragon" is the well-known l u g a l - e u₄ m e - l á m - b i n i r - g á l. Dr. Kramer retells the first part of this myth—the only part here relevant—as follows:

After a hymnal introduction the story begins with an address to Ninurta by Sharur, his personified weapon. For some reason not stated in the text as yet available, Sharur has set its mind against Kur. In its speech, therefore, which is full of phrases extolling the heroic qualities and deeds of Ninurta, it urges Ninurta to attack and destroy Kur. Ninurta sets out to do as bidden. At first, however, he seems to have met more than his match and he "flees like a bird." Once again, however, Sharur addresses him with reassuring and encouraging words. Ninurta now attacks Kur fiercely with all the weapons at his command, and Kur is completely destroyed [p. 80].

This interpretation differs most strikingly from those given by earlier scholars who have worked on the myth in that it treats the word k u r , "the mountains," "the enemy land," as if it were a proper name, the name of Ninurta's antagonist. This antagonist, Kur, is supposed to have been a "large serpent which lived in the bottom of the 'great below' where the latter came in contact with the primeval waters" (p. 78).

The texts concerned—as far as known to the reviewer—contain no evidence whatsoever that might support these assumptions. On the contrary the Akkadian translation of l u g a l - e ú₄ m e - l á m - b i n i r - g á l with unfailing consistency treats the word k u r as a geographical term, translating it by *šadê*, "the mountains." Never once does the translator take this word over untranslated as is his custom with proper names. Thus the line from which Dr. Kramer con-

cludes that "Sharur has set its mind against Kur" reads:

u₄ - b i - a   e n - n a (var. om.)   ᵍⁱˢt u k u l - a - n i k u r - r a g e š t u m i - n i - i [n - g á l]

i-nu-šú šá be-li kak-ka-šú ina šadi-i uz-na-a-šú ba-[šá-a][29]

In those days was the attention (lit.: the ear) of the weapon of the lord (directed) toward the mountains.

This means that Sharur, Ninurta's weapon personified, elsewhere called his "general," kept an eye on the mountains, that unruly region on the borders of the Mesopotamian plain whence danger of attack ever threatened. The phrase g e š t u . . . . g á l which must be restored in our line means "to direct one's attention toward," literally "(one's) ears being (toward)." It does not have the connotation "to set one's mind against." K u r is here as elsewhere translated by *šadê*, "the mountains," quite differently from the way in which the real name of Ninurta's opponent, Asag (Á - s à g) , is treated. This name is not translated but is correctly taken over into Akkadian as *Asakku*. Asag, who is not mentioned by Dr. Kramer at all, is the enemy against whom Sharur warns. He has been begotten on Ki, the Earth, by the god of heaven, Anu, has been chosen king by the plants, and his warriors, various stones, raid the cities. Sharur calls upon Ninurta to protect the country against Asag and Ninurta defeats him. That Asag, and not a nonexistent being Kur, is Ninurta's antagonist has never been doubted by earlier translators. It is, besides, clearly stated in other literary texts.[30] Since there is thus no evidence

[29] Haupt, *ASKT*, No. 10, p. 80, ll. 25–26; J. 5326 (Geller, *AOTU*, I.4, p. 279); and Kramer, *SLiT* 6 rev. The reading e n - n a of *SLiT* 6 is preferable to e n given by *ASKT* 10 (and by J. 5326?). The damaged signs at the end of l. 25 in *ASKT* 10 are undoubtedly to be read with J. as g e š t u m i(! ?) - n i - i [n - . . .] The first sign of ba-[šá-a] is preserved in J. alone.

[30] On *Asakku* see, e.g., Ebeling, *RLA*, II, 108–9.

for the existence of a personage Kur in Sumerian mythology, we need not discuss the question of his supposed outward form. As for Asag, we can offer no opinion; the myth seems to treat of him in human terms but gives no definite clue to his shape. Nor need we deal in detail with the meaning of the section which describes the conditions remedied by Ninurta after he had vanquished Asag. We shall state only that we believe Asag, "The Crippler,"[31] to typify the frigid cold of winter, Ninurta the forces of spring. Their battle which takes place over the mountains can be heard in the roar of the thunderstorms which herald the Mesopotamian spring. Before Asag was vanquished, the subterranean waters used to go up into the far mountains where they froze, but Ninurta built the ḫursag, the near ranges, to prevent the waters from so doing and led them into the Tigris. This seems to have reference to that melting of the snows on the high mountains in spring which causes the yearly flood. Altogether the myth of Ninurta and Asag appears to be a nature myth telling of the yearly battle of spring and winter

3. *Third and fourth myths of Kur.*—Two more myths are listed as myths of Kur: "Inanna and Ebih" and "The Descent of Inanna." Since the word k u r as used in these myths is not claimed by Dr. Kramer to refer to a personal being, monstrous or otherwise, we need not discuss these two myths in detail. We may therefore conclude our comments on the chapter "Myths of Kur" with the statement that—as far as we can see—evidence for the existence of such a being is still lacking.[32]

[31] Á-sàg, literally "the one who smites the arm," corresponds to Akkadian *kamû*, "the one who binds," "the one who lames" (cf. Deimel, *ŠL*, 334.104).

[32] In view of the intrinsic interest of the subject, a few words may be said of "biblical parallels." As some relationship—indirect—may reasonably be assumed

It remains to consider Dr. Kramer's interpretation of his material in the wider

to exist between the Sumerian and the biblical deluge stories (p. 97), so one would not a priori reject the possibility that Sumerian dragons—though not Kur—may be remote cousins, less likely ancestors, of Leviathan and similar monsters of a later day (pp. 13 and 76 ff.). Much painstaking work must yet be done, however, before the Mesopotamian concepts are so far clarified that the problem can be at all fruitfully attacked or even formulated. Generalities such as the mere belief in "a" dragon and "a" dragon-slayer mean practically nothing, for in all questions of cultural influence it is not the abstract and the simple but the particular and the complex which furnish reliable evidence.

This must be kept clearly in mind when one evaluates the implications of even such attractive suggestions as that the Sumerian lamentations are forerunners (p. 14) of the "Book of Lamentations." (Forerunners in the sense of compositions of an earlier age treating of similar subjects? Yes, certainly. Forerunners in the sense that the "Book of Lamentations" stands in a Sumerian literary tradition from which it derives literary patterns and phraseology? Surely not until it has been shown that the extant similarities go beyond what similar subject matter and similar situations will naturally suggest to any good poet.) It is far more imperative with remarks such as that on p. 82 that the passage giving Ninurta's verdicts on the stones "in style and tone, *not in content*, is very reminiscent of the blessing and cursing of Jacob's sons in the forty-ninth chapter of Genesis." Here the reader who is intent on "parallels" must make clear to himself that the similarities pointed to are on such a high level of abstraction that they can have no bearing on questions of cultural (stylistic) influence: they will hold equally with any series of motivated blessings, curses, or verdicts in any literature anywhere at any time. Similarly with the "Cain-Abel motif" (in Pan-Babylonistic parlance this used to mean "*Brudermord*") which is mentioned whenever a Sumerian myth treats of the rivalry between shepherd and farmer (pp. 49, 53, 101). Here again the reader should note that Dr. Kramer does not speak in terms of cultural influence. The contrast and rivalry of two ways of life, of the desert and the sown, goes through all Near Eastern history: it is of a nature to seek literary expression spontaneously, independently at varying times and places. That the Hebrew and the Sumerian stories have as their theme this ever present social and economic contrast is not significant; what *is* significant is rather the utter difference of treatment and of underlying emotional attitude in the two cases. The shepherd-farmer problem and its literary formulation must be different in a near-tribal community from what it is in a highly integrated state. It is not likely that any of the Sumerian stories ever influenced that of Cain and Abel; that we are, in any sense, dealing with the borrowing of a literary motif.

Indeed, the great problem which the Sumerian material raises is not a comparative problem; it is rather to understand, first and foremost, that literature in its own Sumerian setting—to interpret it as the expression of Sumerian culture itself. When that has been done, and only then, will it be possible to

and more significant sense of the word: his evaluation of the Sumerian myths as a

make valid comparisons and to test Dr. Kramer's extremely bold dictum concerning the Sumerian compositions that "the form and contents of the Hebrew literary creations and to a certain extent even those of the ancient Greeks were profoundly influenced by them" (p. viii).

For the time being side glances seem more likely to distract. Thus we would suggest that the text which serves as frontispiece and which is said to describe the state of man "before the 'confusion of tongues' " and to be "very reminiscent of Genesis XI:1," would have been differently interpreted by Dr. Kramer if he had sought Mesopotamian rather than biblical parallels for its phraseology. The passage which interests us reads:

"In those days the land Shubur (East), the place of plenty, of righteous decrees,
Harmony-tongued Sumer (South), the great land of the 'decrees of princeship,'
Uri (North), the land having all that is *needful*,
The land Martu (West), resting in security,
The whole universe, the people *in unison*
To Enlil in one tongue *gave praise*."

A key term of this passage, e m e - ḫ a - m u n , which Dr. Kramer translates "*harmony-tongued*," occurs also in an address to the divine judge Utu in V R, Pl. 50, l.69–70 (cf. IV R, Pl. 19.2, 45–46):

e m e - ḫ a - m u n   m u - a š - g e₁₁   s i   b a - n i - í b - s á - e
li-id-an mit-ḫur-ti (li-ša-in šu-[me tuš-te]-šir

"Mutually opposed testimonies thou dost straighten out as (were they but) one single statement."

The reference is to the judge's task of finding the facts of a case. In the phrase *lišān mitḫurti (lišān*, sg. with collective force [see Delitzsch, *HW*, p. 386], is in the construct state before the genitive of characteristic *mitḫurti* [Inf. I.2 of *m-ḫ-r*; the *-t-* has reciprocal force]), the word *mitḫurtu* is used in its original meaning of "being mutually opposed" and not in its derived meaning of "matching one another," "corresponding to one another" (this latter shade predominates in the related adjective-adverb *mitḫāru* and *mitḫāriš*), as may be seen from its Sumerian counterpart ḫ a - m u n which denotes "conflicting," "mutually opposed" (cf. r i - ḫ a - m u n , "whirlwind" [Akkadian *ašamšutu*, Deimel, *ŠL*, 86.103], literally "(a) mutually opposed blowing" [cf. r i , translated as *šiq idri, ibid.*, 86.16], a clashing of two winds blowing in opposite directions).

On this basis, then, e m e - ḫ a - m u n in the passage under consideration would seem to mean not "harmony-tongued" but "(of) mutually opposed tongues" in the sense of "comprising people of widely different opinions." In corresponding sense, as equivalent to "expression of opinion," one will naturally interpret "tongue" also in the last line of the passage and translate: "to Enlil *with* one tongue gave praise." The line then expresses that on one thing the motley of countries and people mentioned could all agree: praise to Enlil. It is unity of mind, not unity of language, with which the ancient poet is concerned.

literary and as an intellecual achievement. Dr. Kramer is the first to undertake such an evaluation. He has endeavored to bring system and order into his materials, to understand—as he sees them—their underlying pattern of thought. The reviewer notices that the resultant synthesis differs not inconsiderably from the one to which his own research has led him and which he has recently had opportunity to clarify to himself in a few lectures soon to be published. Such difference, however—at the present stage of our knowledge—is not seriously disturbing. We are as yet in the earliest and most tentative stages of penetrating the inner structural coherence of these Sumerian materials, of clarifying the cultural system in which they are imbedded and from which alone they derive their intellectual and emotional meaning. The task is exceedingly difficult and most delicate. But each individual approach will contribute, will explore new possibilities. Differences of interpretation at this stage are therefore to be expected and even welcomed. For it is precisely in attention to and discussion of differences that we may hope to progress toward a truer insight.

It seems useful therefore to express clearly those divergencies of interpretation which seem to be of greatest significance in our various attempts to achieve a consistent picture.

III. GENERAL INTERPRETATIONAL APPROACH

Good interpretation undoubtedly has its mainspring in sincere love of that which is to be interpreted. But such love, if it is to lead to understanding, must be in a very special sense unselfish, neither closing its eyes in blind admiration nor impetuously trying to make over what it loves to suit its own desires. It must be the tempered passion of one who loves wisely.

These maxims, trite but true, are not always, it would seem, strictly observed in the book under discussion. Thus many of the aesthetic value judgments scattered through its pages seem overly enthusiastic and may thereby defeat their purpose, setting the reader against the Sumerian tale rather than leading him on to appreciation.

The myth of Enlil and Ninlil as given in the book tells how Ninlil's mother deliberately makes her daughter expose herself so that she may be raped by Enlil, how Enlil abandons her as soon as he has raped her, how she follows him and is seduced three times in succession by men whom she meets on the road—all of them, as it turns out, Enlil in disguise. The story is presented to the reader as "this delightful myth" (p. 43).

The story of Inanna and Enki tells how Enki while drunk presented to Inanna a great many powers, how Inanna made off with these powers in her boat, and how Enki, when he became sober, tried to stop the boat and take back his gift. The tale is introduced to the reader as "this magnificent myth with its particularly charming story" (p. 64).

Little is gained by such appreciation *quand même*.

As for the first story, Dr. Kramer was in a difficult position, since the motivations and meaning of the events in the story seem to have largely escaped him. Thus the story becomes merely brutal, losing the strange undertone of inevitability which it has when the psychology of its characters and the moral norms governing their actions are understood. Even so, however, an adjective like "wild" or even "brutal" would have done better to prepare the reader than does the incongruous "delightful."

As for the second story, Dr. Kramer understood the essentials of the tale correctly, but "magnificent" is out of tune. Here it might have been stressed that this story is one in a much lighter vein. The conflict is not serious, for, since Inanna is Enki's favorite daughter, he cannot lose much to her. Whatever he gives her stays—so to speak—in the family. Thus the listener is free to enjoy the unwonted spectacle of Enki, the most clever and crafty of all the gods, caught in a dilemma of his own making, a dilemma of which his quick-witted daughter is not slow to take advantage. It may be added that the prize for which they play is nothing as ponderous as "the basis of the culture pattern of Sumerian civilization" (p. 66) but merely a motley of powers and activities with which the many-sided Inanna was thought to have connection.

As overenthusiasm is unfavorable to understanding, so also is too harsh censure. In the myth of Enki and Ninhursaga the latter gives birth to various deities, each to heal a part of Enki's aching body. In each case the name of the healing deity is compounded with the Sumerian word for the relevant part of the body. This draws the following salvo:

> Moreover, the superficiality and barren artificiality of the concepts implied in this closing passage of our myth, although not apparent from the English translation, are brought out quite clearly by the Sumerian original. For the fact is that the actual relationship between each of the "healing" deities and the sickness which it is supposed to cure, is verbal and nominal only; . . . . [p. 59].

It would undoubtedly have helped the reader more toward appreciating the ancient tale if—instead of chiding the Sumerians for not being more modern in their thinking—the author had explained why they thought as they did. The conviction that a name somehow partakes of the reality of that which it denotes is a prominent feature of Sumerian, as of most other, mythopoeic thought. It has its basis in the fact that this form of thought does not recognize different levels of reality.

By closing one's heart against such ways of thought, one bars one's self from deeper understanding of the ancient mind and of ancient poetry. Thus Dr. Kramer —averse to mere "verbal" and "nominal" relationships—must fail to appreciate the rather fine piece of narration which the beginning of this self-same myth constitutes. The narrator of the myth—since a name partakes of the reality of what it means—refers to the deity Ninhursaga under her several names according as the essence of these names is manifest in or foreshadows Ninhursaga's role in the stream of events narrated. She is N i n - s i k i l - l a , "The pure (i.e., virgin) lady," before Enki unites with her. In the section telling of Enki's advances to her she is N i n - t u   a m a   k a l a m m a , "The lady who gives birth, the mother of the land," the name bringing into focus the possibility latent in her, a possibility which begins to be realized with the event here related. When Ninhursaga finally accepts Enki, she is D a m - g a l - n u n - n a , "The great spouse of the prince (i.e., of Enki)." And when—as the fertile soil— she conceives and gives birth to vegetation she is N i n - ḫ u r - s a g - g á , "The lady of the mountain," for on the lush green mountain slopes in the east the earth manifests its powers to produce the luxuriant vegetation of spring as it does nowhere else.

The student of ancient mythology dares not cling to his own criteria for what constitutes logical thinking so pertinaciously that these criteria become barriers preventing him from entering sympathetically into other, earlier modes of thought. So too must he ever be on guard against reading into the ancient words his own con-

cepts, born, formed, and determined in a world of scientific outlook and experimental technique.

To a modern scientifically trained mind the concept "fire" can mean: "oxidation, the oxygen of the atmosphere combining with the substance burnt." But something entirely different filled the mind of the ancient Mesopotamian when he consigned images of his enemies to the fire and addressed it as follows: "Scorching God Fire, warlike son of Heaven, thou, the fiercest of thy brethren, who like Moon and Sun decidest lawsuits, judge thou my case, hand down the verdict. Burn, O God Fire, the man and woman who bewitched me."[33] Concepts are not necessarily identical because their referent is the same. The words "God Fire," "fire," "combustion," "oxidation," may all refer to one objective reality, yet each symbolizes a different concept entirely. Were we—in the above prayer—to progress gradually through such stages as "God Fire," "fire," and "combustion," to "oxidation," we would remove with each "translation" one step further from understanding what filled the ancient speaker, until with "oxidation" all bridges had been cast off. The concept "oxidation," the total mental reaction which this word symbolizes, could not possibly have been entertained by him.

For the Mesopotamians, as for us, things are what we make them, that is to say, what our concepts of them are. And one cannot add to, or subtract from, or make substitutions for, a concept without emerging with a new and different concept.

We are stating these rather obvious facts in order to make clear why we are reluctant to follow Dr. Kramer in his efforts to express Sumerian mythology "rational-

[33] *Maqlû*, II, 104–8. Cf. G. Meier, *Die Assyrische Beschwörungssammlung Maqlû* (Berlin, 1937), pp. 16–17.

ly.' These efforts amount exactly—it seems to us—to substituting concepts such as "combustion" and "oxidation" for concepts like "God Fire"—under the impression that one is still rendering Sumerian thought.

Dr. Kramer states his method on page 73. Speaking of Sumerian cosmogony, he rejoices that "when these concepts are analyzed; when the theological cloak and polytheistic trappings are removed . . . ., the Sumerian creation concepts indicate a keenly observing mentality . . . . etc." He seems quite unaware that what he is here removing is not a "cloak," not "trappings," but the very categories constitutive of Sumerian thought, its whole conceptual apparatus. When that has been removed, there can be nothing left. Those and none other were the terms in which the Sumerians could and did think. Without them there is no Sumerian thought.

A few of the results of this method may be considered in more detail. We quote:

Heaven and earth were conceived as *solid* elements. Between them, however, and *from them*, came the gaseous element *air*, whose main characteristic is that of expansion. Heaven and earth were thus separated by the expanding element *air* [p. 73; italics are Dr. Kramer's].

For the god Enlil (i.e., the storm viewed as, and reacted to as, a personal being with divine powers: "Lord Storm") has been substituted the modern scientific concept "the gaseous element *air*, whose main characteristic is that of expansion." With the term "air" instead of "storm," "wind," we are already on dangerous ground. There is, as far as we know, no term for "air at rest" in either Sumerian or Akkadian: all those we have denote "air in motion," i.e., they symbolize concepts limited approximately as are those suggested by our words "wind" and "storm," and only thus may they be ren-

dered. Constitutive for the further term "gaseous element" is the notion that there are various substances which have the same form as air. This was realized in Europe as late as the eighteenth century; up to that time it had been supposed that air is one homogeneous substance. That the main characteristic of air is that of expansion (Dr. Kramer has in mind, as the context shows, its ability to exert outward pressure) may—at least in a modified form—seem true to the physicist, but we doubt very much whether this is the characterization the man in the street would give; and we cannot imagine how the Sumerians without experiments would hit upon the notion that heated air expands more than does a comparable volume of solids or fluids heated to the same temperature. With the terms "solid," "gaseous," "element," the constitutive notion of a tripartite scheme of possible forms under which matter can exist (as solids, liquids, or gases) has been introduced and imputed to the Sumerians—if we understand Dr. Kramer's text correctly, consciously so. It seems unnecessary to go on demonstrating how utterly divorced these notions are from the Sumerian concept of a "Lord Storm," the essentials of which they are supposed to render. In the first paragraph on page 74 the reader may find language implying that the Sumerians were aware of a relation between density and gravitational pull: "Air, being lighter and far less dense than either heaven or earth, succeeded in producing the *moon*." He may then check with pages 43–47 to see how far the concepts involved are truly the same. The immediately following lines of the paragraph read like the Nebular Hypothesis of Laplace seen through a glass darkly.

But this must suffice. We hope that we have expressed ourselves clearly so that if we end up on a positive note by suggesting that Enlil, "Lord Storm," may have been imagined to have separated heaven and earth in somewhat the manner in which strong wind may momentarily blow under and lift a tent cloth or a large heavy sheet lying on the ground, neither the reader nor Dr. Kramer will conclude that this is "the same thing" that he has been saying all along. Differences of two worlds and of four millennia may not be ignored.

We have come to the end of our review and may sum up. We have found in Dr. Kramer's book much which calls for unqualified praise, especially in matters relating to the establishing of the text of the Sumerian compositions, which is a task of prime importance.

We have also found points on which we tend to differ with the author, almost exclusively, we may stress, in matters relating to translation and interpretation. The fact that such differences exist in no way lessens our appreciation of the other wholly excellent aspects of the author's work and our clear recognition of the urgency, value, and extreme importance of the larger project of which the book under review forms a part. The central task of that project—the establishing of the text of the Sumerian literary compositions, the finding, placing, copying, and publication of new fragments—can be satisfactorily accomplished even though the meaning of the text may not always be fully understood. And that task, we repeat, is without question the most urgent of all those which confront Sumerologists today. Here Dr. Kramer has demonstrated his industry and ability so convincingly that in our considered opinion no other scholar would be as competent as he to carry this important work to a speedy and satisfactory conclusion.

ORIENTAL INSTITUTE
UNIVERSITY OF CHICAGO

GREEK MYTHOLOGY: SOME NEW PERSPECTIVES

A NEW approach to the ancient world is only too often a wrong approach, unless it is based on some concrete discovery. But I think it fair to talk of new *perspectives*, at least, in the study of Greek mythology. Certainly the old and familiar ones are no longer adequate. Indeed it is surprising, in the light of fresh intuitions about society, literacy, the pre-Homeric world, and relations with the ancient Near East, that myth—one of the most pervasive aspects of Greek culture—has been left in its old and rather cobwebby pigeon-hole. Rose's simple paraphrases are accepted as adequate for students; Nilsson's sparse pages in his history of religion are rightly respected, though some of them are too simple; the Murray-Cook-Harrison-Cornford reconstruction of religion, ritual and myth is regarded as a little excessive, but perhaps not too far out; Kerényi and Eliade are roughly tolerated, if not widely read by Classicists, and their books are ordered in profusion for the library; the psychological side is adequately taken care of, or so it is supposed, by what is left from Freud and Jung, with Cassirer as sufficient authority for the sources of mythical imagination.

Many of these critics had their moments of brilliant insight, but most were misleading in their theories taken as a whole. We can now accept that many myths have ritual counterparts, and some have ritual origins, without having to adopt Cornford's belief, developed after Harrison, Frazer and Robertson Smith, that all myths are such.[1] Jane Harrison's Eniautos-Daimon is now known to be an aberration, and in spite of the brilliant texture of her *Themis* little that is original in it can also be said to be correct. Malinowski's division of myths based on Trobriand categories is useful up to a point, but it conceals too many real distinctions and wrongly denies the possibility of a reflective undertone. Eliade's catch-phrase *in illo tempore* summarises one aspect of many myths, not the central aspect of all. Kerényi's works, when they are not simply re-tellings of tales, are replete with Jungian archetypes, a questionable dogma; and Cassirer's theory of myth as a symbolic form effectively reduces it to a mere segment of religion.[2]

This is indeed one of the crucial problems: the relation of myths to religion. Needless to say, the relation is a complex one. That myths are either identical with or a part of religion was widely assumed in the last century, mainly because many Greek myths are concerned with the birth and development of deities. Greek myths, as we shall see, are not typical. Yet there *is* an important overlap between myths and religion, and determining its extent is one of the hardest parts of understanding myths in general. One is not helped by the anthropological practice of envisaging all myths as *sacred* tales—a definition that has become especially confusing because of ambiguities in the meaning of 'sacred'. The movement known as 'functionalism', associated with Malinowski and Radcliffe-Brown, treated any machinery for maintaining the social structure as sacred.[3] Myths were obviously part of that machinery, in certain of their uses, and therefore were sacred even when they did not focus on gods or spirits. A different application of the term is seen in Eliade; myths are concerned with the creative past and revive some of its power, and so they are sacred.[4] But a word that combines the complexities of 'sacer' with the sentiments of Victorian Christianity is unsuitable for either of these functions, even when they are not exaggerated.

---

[1] Cornford's views are most clearly exemplified in 'A ritual basis for Hesiod's Theogony' in *The Unwritten Philosophy* (Cambridge, 1950) 95 ff.

[2] B. Malinowski: see especially *Myth in Primitive Psychology* (1926), reprinted in R. Redfield (ed.), *Magic, Science and Religion* (Boston, 1948, paperback ed. Doubleday-Anchor no. A 23); M. Eliade: see e.g. *The Myth of the Eternal Return* (London, 1954);

E. Cassirer: see *The Philosophy of Symbolic Forms* vol. ii (New Haven, 1957).

[3] A. R. Radcliffe-Brown, e.g. *Structure and Function in Primitive Society* (London, 1952) 178 ff., and cf. *The Andaman Islanders* (Cambridge, 1922) ch. 6, esp. 397 ff.

[4] Cf. e.g. *Patterns in Comparative Religion* (London, 1958) ch. 1.

'Supernatural' is another term that has been complicated by Christianity and is still widely employed by anthropologists. Not all that is supernatural is caused by gods. Myths can be both sacred and supernatural, but one needs to say precisely what this implies in relation to religious belief and practice. Many, probably most, myths are 'about' gods in one way or another, since they tend to emanate from societies deeply involved with polytheism; but it is no less true that many myths are not essentially concerned with gods, but rather with human types acting in a world that may be supernatural but is not religious. It is unreasonable to exclude all non-sacred tales, in the obvious sense, from the study of myths; and the old idea (perpetuated by C. Robert, Kerényi and many others) that Greek mythology consists only of tales about the gods—the rest being heroic saga or Panhellenic legend—should be abandoned.

It should be abandoned not least because it disguises a fundamental part of any reasonable definition of myths: that they are stories, and traditional ones at that. Heroic tales in Greece were traditional no less than divine ones, and they can tell us something about the genre as a whole.[5]

It takes special qualities to make a tale survive from generation to generation—to make it traditional, in fact. Such qualities are various. They may be mainly narrative and dramatic, and in that case we have the kind of myth that is often called folktale. Sometimes they are more obviously practical in their effect, for example in reminding people of social rules and tribal traditions or in supporting institutions like marriage or kingship. These are what Malinowski called charter myths. Sometimes a tale is remembered because it is connected with a god or cult and is reinforced by religion. Often its traditional quality depends rather on aetiology in its deeper sense, on the ability to explain something, to offer an acceptable context for a reality that is worrying or puzzling—the fact of death, for instance, or irritating restrictions on the desire for women or property. And at other times a tale seems to have permanent appeal because of a more indefinable effect, because it embodies some powerful, mysterious and liberating subject or symbol. These are the main ways in which a tale may establish a hold on a group or community. But the analysis is obviously schematic, and in practice a tale will tend to possess more than one of these special qualities, which are not mutually exclusive. A charter myth often turns out to be aetiological in some degree; what is primarily seen as a folktale may also have charter aspects; a myth closely associated with religion often tends to be speculative or explanatory as well. Moreover a tale's emphasis can alter from generation to generation in response to changing social pressures and preoccupations. Boas and Benedict used to stress the movement from folktale to sacred myth and vice versa; that is true, but only part of the truth.[6] Any traditional tale, sacred or not, can take on different emphases, and it does so because the telling of tales is, in many non-literate societies, a primary mode of communication and discourse and an important factor for stability or, if necessary, for change.

One request, therefore, to be made of anthropologists is that they should devote special attention to myths as tales; that they should study all tales, not just sacred ones, in an effort to understand the criteria and changing tendencies of different kinds of oral tradition. Some anthropologists—and especially those who have worked in Africa, like Goody, Lienhardt and Evans-Pritchard—are aware of this. To others, Classical studies can offer

[5] It may be that 'traditional tale' is as far as one can reasonably go in defining the common quality of everything that tends to be classified as a myth (excluding specialised applications like 'falsehood'). Not all traditional tales, of course, are myths, even in this broad sense; for example tales that are clearly historical in essence may become traditional and yet have none of the other qualities that belong to one or another type of myths. The problem of definition (which also includes the question of the relation of myths to folktales) is an awkward one; it is necessary to remain aware of it, yet it is also legitimate to by-pass it to some extent, at least until the special properties of commonly accepted instances have been further explored.

[6] F. Boas, *Tsimshian Mythology* (Washington, D.C., 1916) 879 ff.; R. Benedict, *Encyclopaedia of the Social Sciences* xi (1933) 179.

some small help; for Milman Parry's examination of one product of a predominantly oral culture, namely the Serbocroation epic, has led to a moderately sophisticated discussion among Homerists of types of variation in oral traditions.[7] There has been relatively less discussion among anthropologists of such general but important questions as this, mainly because of the unavoidable fragmentation of field studies and the reluctance of the individual observer to surrender the exemplary qualities of his own special area. Yet some agreement on the common tendencies of oral traditions is specially needed at the present time, when the last traditional groups are being sucked into the odorous swamp of modern literacy. Only so can the obvious distinctions be recognised; for example between the kind of literacy created by the irruption of the Bible and the kind created by the irruption of an oil company, or between both of these and the kind produced in ancient Greece by the sudden introduction of a viable writing system into an otherwise advanced society.

Discussion of the nature of myths has been left for so long to anthropologists, psychologists and students of religion that observations from the direction of Classical studies are apt to be regarded as irrelevant or even impudent. Anthropologists have made such wonderful progress in so many directions that they feel little inclination to question Malinowski's doctrine that the only person qualified to understand the nature of myths is the one who 'has the mythmaker at his elbow'. Yet we are in a position to emphasise one thing at least: that there are many different kinds of myth, that myths have different functions and, presumably, different origins, and that monolithic theories of myth are out-of-date. We can do so because of our distance from the diversity of types in modern tribal cultures; and because neither Greek myths nor other ancient ones respond to any unitary theory. The myth-and-ritual school, admittedly, drew comfort from the support of Cornford and others for the old idea that all myths are derived from rituals; but many serious students of ancient myths would now deny them that comfort.[8] And one has only to look at the other general theories—that all myths are allegories of nature, or explanations of some kind, or not explanations but charters, or reflexions of unconscious desires or fears, or expressions of symbols or structures in the collective mind—to see that none of them can possibly account for most, let alone all, of the obvious claimants to the title of 'myth'.

A slight but necessary shift of perspective suggests, indeed, that Greek myths do not fit easily into *any* account of the nature and functions of myths in general. I do not know quite what most Classical scholars and teachers feel about this. Do they persist in regarding Greek mythology as the pattern and exemplar against which all other myths should be judged? That, of course, is the traditional attitude, and it derives from the Renaissance itself, when Greek myths were virtually the only ones known and when they became, with the Bible, a primary source for literature and art. Later, when other European traditional tales were noticed, they tended to be given different names (like 'folktales') if they failed to fit into the aristocratic pattern of Greek myths. The myths of savage societies avoided that fate, and a few surprising thematic resemblances—like the primeval separation of earth and sky—perpetuated the idea of Greek myths as somehow still archetypal. Something of this attitude still maintains itself among anthropologists, who, though no longer trained in the Classics, tend to be as happy as Frazer or Robertson Smith was to cite a Classical parallel, real or imaginary. Even Lévi-Strauss, who admits to knowing very little about Greek mythology, hit upon the Oedipus tale as object of a notorious demonstration of his method, and recently Edmund Leach has chosen to elucidate Lévi-Strauss's theory of myth by applying it, not too fruitfully, to further Greek examples.[9] On the contrary, now that a

[7] Cf. *The Making of Homeric Verse* (Oxford, 1971), ed. Adam Parry, lii ff.; and as one specific instance of such discussion see A. Parry, *Yale Classical Studies* xx (1966) 177 ff., and G. S. Kirk, *Proceedings of the Cambridge Philological Society* n.s. xvi (1970) 48 ff.

[8] E.g. Joseph Fontenrose, *The Ritual Theory of Myth* (Berkeley, 1966).

[9] C. Lévi-Strauss, *Structural Anthropology* (London, 1963) 213 ff.; E. R. Leach, *Lévi-Strauss* (London, Fontana Books, 1970) 68 ff.

mass of information is available about myths of other cultures, living and dead, it can be seen that Greek mythology, far from being typical, is exceptional in several important respects. In some ways it is richer than most other sets of myths, but in others, as we shall see, it is poorer. At any rate we must be careful in using Greek myths for the elucidation of non-Greek ones, and conversely the manifold comparative material from other cultures is not always so cogent for Greek myths as Jane Harrison and her brilliant friends used to think.

What then *are* the special characteristics of Greek mythology? Certain things go without saying: its breadth and complexity, its relative freedom from physiological pre-occupation. Yet Nordic myths, for instance, provide some parallel here, and the special properties I have in mind are rather these: the thematic limitations of Greek divine myths; the number, superficial variety and conventionalised plots of the heroic ones; and in general the lack of fantastic and imaginative themes in comparison with many other cultures. Some at least of these qualities are the result of one central condition—that Greek mythology as we know it is a *literate* mythology, one based on genuinely traditional tales (no doubt), but one that was elaborated and adjusted for several generations in accordance with developed literary criteria.

That is an important point, and I develop it further. Literacy makes an enormous difference to a mythical tradition. In Greece the content of oral myths was retained as the basic plot-element of literature, but new kinds of elaboration and variation changed the underlying emphases. One important new factor is the individual author aware of his own artistic entity, the poet no longer content to act as a link in a traditional chain. Archilochus in the mid-seventh century is typical: he accepts much of the language and some of the situations of the oral epic tradition, but drastically alters the ethos. Pindar not only extrudes certain crude elements of the traditional tales, but deliberately idealises the quality of *arete*, aristocratic virtuosity and privilege, in the mythical heroes. The tragedians freely adjust their mythical plots to illuminate political and social problems of their own day, as Aeschylus does with Zeus and Prometheus, and Sophocles with Antigone and Philoctetes. In one way these reflective and analytical poets were following a genuinely traditional practice of constantly elaborating the old myths, of bringing them up to date. In another they departed radically from the social continuity of the process by recording their own individual reactions rather than those of the community as a whole.

Greek mythology as we know it depends on writers like these. The poets of the Classical age were ultimately the main source—apart from Homer and Hesiod—for the later mytho-graphers who supply many of the details to be found in modern handbooks and encyclo-paedias. But there were other agents of distortion, too: antiquarians and genealogists in the logographical tradition, philosophical allegorisers, learned Alexandrian poets like Callimachus. Yet suppose the Hellenistic and Greco-Roman versions *did* become rather different from their oral prototypes; what about Homer and Hesiod? They, surely, stood at the very beginning of the literate era, and their information (whatever their precise mode of composition) was derived more or less directly from the oral tradition; therefore the myths they record ought to reflect the true tone of Greek mythology before it became adulterated by literate elaboration. There are two drawbacks to this commendable observation. First, the mythical range of Homer and Hesiod is fairly limited, especially in relation to the heroic myths (by which I mean those about Heracles, Perseus and so on as opposed to the quasi-legendary figures of Achilles, Agamemnon and the rest). Second, Hesiod almost certainly added a measure of order to the process of theogony; and passages in Homer too show that the nature of Zeus's power and his relation to older forces like the Giants and Titans were already under interpretation in the pre-Homeric epic tradition. To put it in another way, that tradition was already so highly developed in a literary sense that, although not technically literate, it had already acquired some of the destructive qualities associated with literacy; and something similar is probably true of the theogonical tradition brought to a head by Hesiod.   Here we confront an odd thing about the Greeks: that they lived for hundreds of years in an international *milieu* that was extensively literate, and yet themselves remained illiterate (except for the limited and peculiar span of Linear B) till the ninth or eighth century B.C.   By then they were already advanced in ideas, social structure and the techniques of warfare, art and building; also in a highly organised poetical tradition.   The functional emphases of myths must have suffered severe erosion even before the onset of literacy.   We must not make the mistake of counting pre-Homeric Greece, just because it was illiterate, as in other ways comparable with those societies—mostly 'savage' ones studied by anthropologists—in which myths are integral.   We must be careful, too, not to classify modes of thinking as revealed in Homer as necessarily irrational or 'mythopoeic', to use a dubious term.   If we incline to believe that many Greek myths must at some time have been organically connected, like those of so many other societies, with the problems and paradoxes of social and personal life, then the stage at which they were so did not lie in the centuries immediately before Hesiod and Homer, or even in those of the Achaean kingdoms.   It lay far back in the mists of pre-history, and its *locus* was Asia as much as the Greek peninsula itself.

I have suggested that Greek mythology, partly as a consequence of these effects of literacy, is unusual in three respects: the thematic restrictions of the divine myths, the elaborate but conventionalised heroic myths, and the shortage of fantasy and imagination by comparison with many other mythologies.   Those who regard Classical mythology as supreme will feel that each of these assertions needs defending.

Consider the divine myths first.   Much of the divine action of the *Iliad* and *Odyssey* must be excluded—for example, the developed conversations on Olympus and many of the divine interventions on the battlefield.   These are the special contribution of literary artists; they became part of Classical mythology, if you like, and they elaborated earlier motifs, but in their developed forms they are unlikely to be typical of the ancient heritage of traditional oral tales.   What remains of that heritage in its divine aspects?   What is known from the rest of Homer and from other Greek literature, which constantly alludes to the Olympian deities and their acts?   Surprisingly little beyond the birth of each god and the acquisition of his or her special functions.   It is the mythical cosmogony and theogony that is the richest part of Greek divine mythology (and it is not my fault if most of it is derived from Asiatic myths like the Babylonian *Enuma Elish* and the Hurrian succession-myth about Kumarbi).   Kronos's castration of Ouranos and his swallowing of his own children is powerful mythical material, obviously ancient and truly imaginative.   Subsequent proliferation is less so; it is more conventional and repetitive, and once the Titans are out of the way the mythical process of theogony begins to flag.   The element of *story* diminishes. Zeus gets various wives and mistresses, divine or human; some of these episodes are dramatic enough (his transformation into the shower of gold to penetrate Danae, his anticipation of Amphitryo in the bosom of Alcmena), but others are sketchy, allegorical or excessively abstract (his swallowing of Metis and consequent birth of Athena from his head).   *Gamos* and transformation; they are motifs full of liveliness and a kind of imagination, but even so Zeus does not have much in the way of a personal mythical history—less, at any rate, than one is accustomed to think.   Most of the other gods and goddesses are no solider in this respect.   What does Hermes do apart from being a miraculous, resourceful and mischievous baby, one who invents the lyre and steals Apollo's cattle (by a common folktale motif) before being made into herald and *psuchopompos*?   It is true that he appears incidentally in many other tales, most of them heroic ones, and he acquired an important cult; but in his own right as an anthropomorphic *persona* he has few traditional actions to boast of.   Athena is similar; her myths (aside from her birth) almost all concern her cult and her functions as palace- and city-goddess.   Apollo is born in Delos, and we possess a long account of how this took place.   But essentially the myth as we know it is a learned aetiological response to a paradox—how is it that a dry little island like Delos is one of his two main cult-places? The other part of the surviving *Hymn* describes how he overcame the dragon Pytho at Delphi and then brought the Cretan sailors to be his priests; but again this is an almost scholarly exercise, probably no earlier in ultimate origin than the tenth or ninth century B.C., on certain details of his actual worship. Aphrodite, too, does little of a specific kind after her remarkable birth. Her embroilment with Ares is sophisticated and relatively late, and the affairs with Adonis and Anchises and the contest judged by Paris probably derive from Asiatic prototypes. Poseidon has the building of the walls of Troy to his credit and competes with Athena at Athens; both are local myths, perhaps of the late second millennium, but in his more general functions as god of horses, water and earthquakes he receives rather little in the way of narrative and dramatic development. I am thinking, as a possible standard of comparison, of the Nordic gods of Asgard and of the Mesopotamian gods, Enlil, Enki and Inanna and their Akkadian equivalents. How much richer were those non-Greek gods in tales, not only of birth and development and the acquisition of cult and function, but also of dramatic and creative actions towards each other and mankind! If divine myths were systematically reduced to separate motifs of the Stith Thompson type, I suspect that the Greek gods and goddesses would account for a markedly smaller number than their Nordic and Mesopotamian counterparts, in spite of the fragmentary evidence for the latter; or than the active and varied gods and culture-heroes of many savage societies.

Some of the reasons for the thematic limitations of these divine myths can be conjectured —if one is prepared to abandon the idea that all Greek myths are perfect of their kind. Simple bowdlerisation and rationalisation are relatively unimportant, and the Ouranos-Kronos myth shows that the Greeks were prepared to retain tales that were strange and apparently immoral. A more significant cause is the unusually diverse origin of the Greek gods and goddesses as compared, once again, with the Nordic deities or the city-gods of ancient Mesopotamia. Zeus is an Indo-European sky-god and patriarch, Athena a Minoan/Mycenaean house- and palace-goddess, Hera a local Argive mother-wife fertility type, Apollo a distinctively Asiatic newcomer, Artemis part Asiatic mother, part mistress of animals, Aphrodite an Ishtar-like sex-queen, Hephaestus a Lemnian and Asiatic craftsman-god—and so on. Now when deities are borrowed or transported from abroad it is their general powers and functions, not their specific associations and incidental biography, that survive the move. Conversely, autochthonous deities like Hera tend to lose their local folklore in the process of syncretism and expansion. That is one important reason for a limitation of mythical incident. Another is that the Mesopotamian gods and their other Asiatic offshoots, from which so much of the Greek pantheon seems to be derived, were not ideally suited to Greek needs. Some were etymological in inspiration; most of their mythical actions were performed before men were even created; as city-gods they were largely irrelevant to Greek requirements; and even in their nature-functions they reflected conditions that were simply extraneous in Greek terms. The Greeks did not have to bother much about floods or droughts, and that is why certain Mesopotamian obsessions like the great flood and the destruction of mankind, when they appear in Greek form, seem half-hearted and badly integrated into the total mythological context.[10] The 'plan of Zeus' at the beginning of the *Iliad* was probably in origin a reflexion of the Mesopotamian or Egyptian gods' recurrent itch to destroy mankind; the *Cypria* preserved the idea, but in the *Iliad* this un-Hellenic conception is in process of being watered down into Zeus's more limited intention of gratifying Thetis by avenging Achilles.[11]

---

[10] Great flood: cf. *ANET²* (=*Ancient Near Eastern Texts*, ed. J. B. Pritchard, 2nd ed., Princeton, 1955) 42–4 (Sumerian); *ibid.* 93–5, also W. G. Lambert and A. R. Millard, *Atra-hasīs* (Oxford, 1969) 67 ff. (Akkadian). In Greek contexts the flood is variously associated with Ogygus, Deucalion, Lycaon.

[11] *Iliad* i 5; on the *Dios boule* cf. schol. A Vind 61 and *fr.* 1 of the *Cypria*, most conveniently in Homer, OCT vol. v, pp. 117 f.

D

Two members of the Greek pantheon form an exception to the paucity of divine incident beyond birth and development. I refer of course to Demeter and Dionysus. Demeter is part-subject of the remarkable and widespread myth about the rape of Kore, her mother's search for her through the world, the infertility that resulted, and the foundation of the cult at Eleusis. Dionysus is the subject of unusual tales of resistance and madness, of drunkenness, hysterical mountain dances, and the *sparagmos* or tearing apart either of the god himself, or of a votary, or of a wild animal. Both of them—and this is the significant fact—are fertility deities, and both sets of myths have strong foreign connexions. The disappearing fertility-god theme is clearly Mesopotamian; Dionysus is Phrygian or Thracian. But the Kore-tale was saved by being grafted on to a local fertility-cult at Eleusis at some time in the Bronze Age; and Dionysus fitted so neatly into the place of local tree- and vegetation-daemons that he succeeded in keeping some of his alien biography as well as absorbing certain local folktale-incidents.

In general, however, the divine myths are thematically somewhat jejune, and I have suggested some historical reasons for this being so. The heroic myths present different problems. My own rather Farnellian view of the heroes (and again I do not mean the historicising warriors of Homer, but figures like Heracles, Perseus and Jason) is that they are diverse in type and origin.[12] Some were shaped after the model of imprecisely-remembered Bronze-Age princes, who then acted as magnet for folktale themes of success and danger. Some were almost anonymous figures of local cult, based occasionally on a surviving Mycenaean tomb. Others were hypostatised folktale heroes; a few were functional daemons, recipients of cult like Asclepius the embodiment of healing. Most of the myths that surround these diverse figures are primarily of folktale type, compounded of a limited set of common themes concerning tests and quests, superhuman adventures, acts of exemplary ingenuity, pollution and hardship, quarrelling kinsfolk and offended deities. A few brilliant incidents stand out, but in general there is little that is either unexpected or profoundly imaginative. The specific emotions aroused are predominantly those of simple excitement, satisfaction at the triumph of the underdog, or other kinds of wish-fulfilment. Social preoccupations are hardly visible; religious and ritual connexions, though commoner than appear on the surface, are not strongly marked and are quite often the result of secondary and learned aetiology.

If that is so, how is it that the heroic myths—all of them, not only the special ones like Oedipus or Theseus and the Minotaur—make such a deep impression on us? I suggest it is because of their careful complexity, their rich and realistic elaboration of place and personnel. This is a complete and vital world, remote enough to be romantic and intriguing yet sufficiently detailed to be sympathetic and alive—and that was so for Greeks of the Classical age as much as for ourselves. It was this kind of quality, rather than a wide range of substantially different incident, that made the strongest appeal. The quality is reinforced, admittedly, by a few themes of unusual power and imagination; but they *are* few (as I shall attempt to confirm shortly), even by comparison with other sets of myths and other cultures. Which leads to the third and most paradoxical property that I assigned to Greek myths—their deficiency, apart from a few striking instances, in fantasy and imagination.

Let me begin by reminding you of certain qualities of various non-Greek myths.[13] In an

[12] Cf. L. R. Farnell, *Greek Hero Cults and Ideas of Immortality* (Oxford, 1921) esp. pp. 19 ff.

[13] Brief references for what follows in the main text: Shukallituda, cf. S. N. Kramer, *Mythologies of the Ancient World* (Garden City, N.Y., 1961; Doubleday Anchor no. A 229) 117 f.; Geriguiaguiatugo, C. Lévi-Strauss, *Le Cru et le cuit* (Paris, 1964) 43 ff., cf. G. S. Kirk, *Myth, its Meaning and Functions* (Cambridge and Berkeley, 1970) 64 f.; Winnebago trickster, cf. P. Radin, *The Trickster* (London, 1956) 38 f.; Egyptians: cf. J. A. Wilson in Frankfort, Frankfort, Wilson and Jacobsen, *Before Philosophy* (Penguin Books, 1949) 54–6; Kumarbi, *ANET*² (cf. n. 10 above), 120 f., cf. Kirk, *Myth* (above) 214–19; Loki, cf. E. O. G. Turville-Petrie, *Myth and Religion of the North* (London, 1964) ch. 5; Zuni, cf. R. Benedict, *Zuni Mythology* (New York, 1935) *passim*; Pitjandjara, cf. C. P. Mountford, *Ayers Rock* (Sydney, 1965) *passim*.

ancient Sumerian tale the gardener-god Shukallituda plants a special tree to shade his garden; Inanna the queen of heaven lies down under it and falls asleep, and he rapes her. But why did she go to sleep under this tree, so far from her usual haunts, and why did the pious gardener run amok? One kind of answer is that this is not the sort of question that myths envisage or care about. Why are Adam and Eve in the Garden of Eden, and what is the Tree of Knowledge doing there? An equally silly question, you may say, as might the story-teller himself. Why does young Geriguiaguiatugo in a Bororo myth have a grandmother who tries to kill him, and then with her waste gases instead of in a more straightforward manner? The analytical answer stresses that this is a variant on the theme of excrement and its symbolic relation to nature and culture; but in dramatic terms the strangeness does not matter, in fact the stranger the better. Why does Trickster in the Winnebago cycle have a male member so long that he has to carry it in a box slung over his shoulder, and why do bits of it turn into plants when they are bitten off by a chipmunk? We can answer if we choose in terms of superficial aetiology or wish-fulfilment; but in narrative terms this kind of fantastic exaggeration and inconsequence needs no explanation— it gives the tale a kind of extra dimension and even a bizarre charm. Why did the ancient Egyptians swallow the odd and inconsequential idea that the sky is held up on posts or rather, if you prefer, by the legs of a celestial cow? Because the reason must be something like that, and in any case that is how a tale should be—surprising and fantastic. Is it not absurd that the male Hurrian god Kumarbi becomes pregnant with the weather-god and actually discusses with him the difficult problem of precisely how he is to be born? It is absurd by the standards of logic and obstetrics, but that is not what myths are primarily about. Why is the Norse trickster Loki a homosexual, and what has this to do with his odd combination of creativity and malice? Nothing at all, by ordinary standards; but myths are not interested in the ordinary. Why in the Zuni emergence-myth should the War Twins descend through a lake into a world within the earth, and lead therefrom a few insubstantial creatures who become our ancestors? That is a fantastic idea, largely remote from real life: a typically mythical idea. Why did the Pitjandjara aborigines determine the relations of their mythical ancestors by the positioning of vaguely animal-like crevices on the great monolith of Ayers Rock? Not because they were savage or stupid, but because mythical truth, the truth of the Dreamtime, reveals itself like that, by almost random association.

It is plain that the same kind of question and answer could not often be applied to Greek myths as we know them. What it reveals is mainly the kind of fantasy that depends on inconsequence. I shall return to this at the end, and for the moment merely remark that the orderly complexity of Greek heroic myths, in particular, is quite the opposite of inconsequentiality; and therefore that in this respect Greek mythology is unusual.

From this kind of inconsequential fantasy I want to distinguish a more positive kind of imaginative fantasy. There is a kind of imagination that does not depend on unusual combinations, unexpected juxtapositions or simple exaggerations, but rather on concepts or images that are in themselves poetical and suggestive. The idea of a Tree of Knowledge, or of a luscious fruit or delicious fountain that must nevertheless be avoided by men, is evocative in this sense; so is that of a ghost-world under the earth. Greek myths are not strikingly fertile in this kind of imaginative theme—but are more so, perhaps, than in inconsequential fantasy. Let us survey the evidence more systematically.

The greatest imaginative concentration in Greek mythical sources is found in parts of Hesiod. In the birth and development of the gods, as distinct from their later activities, there is no lack either of fantasy or of thematic variety. The idea of the sky as father refusing to separate from the earth as mother, his castration by the infant Kronos from within the womb, and the structurally similar motif of Kronos in turn preventing the growth of his children by swallowing them as they are born from Rhea, are striking enough.

They are, however, and I repeat, substantially Mesopotamian in derivation. Subsequent details of cosmogony and theogony—the establishment of weather-god Zeus's rule, the assignment of parts of the cosmos to different deities, the fight against a monstrous progeny of the displaced older gods—likewise reproduce, but in a more attenuated form, some widely diffused Asiatic themes.[14] Zeus is less picturesque as a champion than Marduk in the Babylonian Creation Epic; the Titans seem a colourless collection after Kingu and the unpleasant Tiamat; Typhoeus is a feeble substitute for the sinister stone giant Ullikummi in the Hurrian succession-myth. Hesiod does his best with snake-women and hundred-handed giants, and the result is not negligible.[15] Even so, the exceptional power and purity of some of the great Mesopotamian imaginative prototypes have been diminished. Equally the Greek conception of Hades, the dark kingdom under the earth where Zeus's brother rules over the insubstantial dead, powerful though it is, seems less so when we compare it with the model from which it is surely derived, the Mesopotamian 'House of Dust'. Not even Homer's elaborate underworld-scenes in the eleventh and twenty-third Odyssey, still less the learned variations on the depth and darkness of Tartarus in Hesiod's Theogony, can rival the force and terror conveyed by a few Sumerian and Akkadian tablets—the record of Inanna's descent through the seven gates of Hell, at each of which she is further stripped until she is hauled naked before her pitiless sister Ereshkigal, queen of the dead, to be instantly killed and hung on a hook; or the obstinate and fatal quest of Enkidu for King Gilgamesh's pukku and mikku that have fallen through a hole into the world below.[16]

The Golden Age comes to an end and Prometheus becomes involved in a long quarrel with Zeus. Here Greek myth goes beyond Asiatic themes—although they are still present. The trick over the sacrifices seems to develop a detail of the Akkadian tale of Adapa, and the creation of woman is familiar through the ancient Near East.[17] Yet the idea of a mediator between men and gods, as Prometheus became, is foreign to the Asiatic conception of men as slaves of the gods, and a far cry, even, from the role of the king as high priest and divine representative on earth. The combination in the Pandora-episode of folktale themes about the origin of evils with those about the social drawbacks of the female sex could be Greek in inspiration. Hesiod continues with the tale of the five races or generations of mankind; it contains, as well as some obvious expansions, remarkable flashes of genuinely mythical imagination—the impious retarded boobies of the silver race, the ghastly grey-headed babies of the iron.[18] The metallic schema may be Iranian, but certain of the undeniably fantastic details are probably Greek. With the Golden Age itself the Greeks did no less well. Again it is based on an Asiatic conception and reflects the world of the Mesopotamian gods before men were created, tempered perhaps by the Egyptian idea of a blessed land of the semi-divine dead; but in the Hesiodic and Pindaric vision of a land without toil, a land of golden flowers where the sons of gods dwell, it takes on new power and meaning.

Theogony and the early history of men give rise, then, to a number of fantastic themes; and the fantasy is not primarily of the inconsequential kind. Many of these ideas are Asiatic in derivation, some have been attenuated, but the notable thing is that the Greeks did not subject all of this material to wholesale purification. Their careful retention and evident enjoyment of the tales of Kronos castrating his father and Aphrodite's birth from the discarded member (although a nicer version of her birth admittedly made some headway) stand in contrast with the taste that deprived most of the heroic myths of what H. J. Rose

[14] Cf. P. Walcot, Hesiod and the Near East (Cardiff, 1966) chs. i and ii.

[15] Hesiod, Theogony 295 ff. (Echidna), cf. 821 ff. (Typhoeus); 665 ff. (Titans and 100-handed giants).

[16] Inanna's descent: ANET², 52–7; Enkidu: ibid., 97–9 (i.e. Epic of Gilgamesh, tablet XII).

[17] Adapa: ANET², 101–3; cf. Kirk, Myth, 122–5, 130 f.

[18] Hesiod, Works and Days 131 f. (silver race), 181 (grey-headed babies).

described as 'horrible features'.[19] This is a puzzle in itself. Why did the Greeks elevate (or reduce) so many of their traditional themes to the moral level of a parish magazine, leaving only the theogony with the uninhibited vigour of myths in other cultures? Was it because they were puritanical and prudish? Surely not; no one who knows the literature of the Classical age can call them that—no one who recalls that at almost every corner one came across a stone pillar from which protruded an erect male member, that enormous models of the same organ were prominent in several of the festivals of the sacral year, and that the handling of imitation female genitalia was a common religious act. Ritual matings in the so-called Hieros Gamos may have been too much emphasised by our enthusiastic predecessors, but there can be no doubt that from a tender age the ancient Greeks, girls as well as boys, were confronted with sex in forms that would have been regarded as acceptable even today. Perhaps the answer is this: that the Greeks were prepared to tolerate almost anything in a religious context, especially since so much of their religion was connected with fertility in one or other of its aspects; but did not feel that sex belonged in literature. Heraclitus, after all, thought that songs about phalluses were acceptable only in a religious procession.[20] A roughly converse inconsistency affected the Zuni and Hopi Indians of the Pueblo culture, who were agreeably uninhibited in their ordinary social relations but so respectable in ritual matters that they obstinately denied any sexual connotation in their annual hoop-and-stick races.[21] Apart from this possibility, the admiring conception of the Heroic Age itself was hostile to physiological myths. Excrement was ruled right out, and only Heracles of the major figures was periodically credited with behaviour that would once have raised an eyebrow in Surbiton.

The lack of inconsequential fantasy in the heroic myths is hardly surprising, because they depend so heavily on the weaving together of folktale themes—as well as on the agglomeration of different regional tales. Folktales tend to be naturalistic in colouring; they may include supernatural or magical elements, but their basic social situations are only slightly different from those of real life. That, in a way, is the point of this kind of tale. The concentration of themes produces a sequence of actions that becomes improbable in the end, but this is something different from the startling and even traumatic juxtapositions that we know from other mythologies. The myth of Athamas is a typical Greek instance. It begins with an element of the supernatural in that his first wife was Nephele, originally a cloud-woman designed by Zeus to punish Ixion. Ino, who replaced her, resorted to a complex stratagem in order to destroy her step-children: she persuaded the women of Boeotia to roast the seed-corn, the crops failed, the Delphic oracle was duly consulted, and Ino managed to tamper with its response. Athamas was consequently on the point of sacrificing his son Phrixus when a prodigious ram bore the boy away, with his sister, to Colchis. Little Helle fell off and gave her name to the Hellespont, and the ram provided the golden fleece that became the object of the Argonauts' quest. Meanwhile Athamas was driven stark mad by Hera and shot one of his sons by Ino, mistaking him for a stag. Ino seized the other and leapt into the sea, where she turned into the sea-goddess Leucothea: again a touch of the supernatural, as indeed is the ram. The story is actually more complicated than that, and was so already by the time Sophocles wrote a tragedy about it. But the point is that it is based on a sequence of common folktale themes—jealousy of a rival, hatred of step-children (or step-mother), ingenious means of causing a disaster (or arranging a murder), misusing an oracle, being forced to sacrifice one's own child, miraculous rescues, aetiological explanations of odd place-names, quests, being driven mad as a punishment for offending a deity,

[19] H. J. Rose, *A Handbook of Greek Mythology* (London, 1953) 14.

[20] Heraclitus *fr.* 15 Diels-Kranz (*cf.* Kirk-Raven, *The Presocratic Philosophers* [Cambridge, 1963 etc.] 211 f.): 'If it were not for Dionysus that they made the procession and sang the hymn to the shameful parts, the deed would be most shameless . . .'.

[21] R. Benedict, *Patterns of Culture* (Boston, 1934 etc.) 123-6.

killing a loved one by mistake, and so on. Most of these themes are piquant extensions of possible situations, and it is their concentration upon one set of people, together with occasional supernatural details, that makes the whole tale implausible in realistic terms. The total effect is not one of fantasy either in the traumatically inconsequential or in the deeply imaginative sense.

Imagination in this second sense, the kind that depends on an evocative subject or symbol, occurs sporadically in the heroic myths. The labyrinth is a case in point, and it does not matter if the idea of the monstrous creature at the heart of the maze is partly determined by Minoan bull-jumping on the one hand, the intricate plan of Cretan palaces on the other. The important thing is that the Greeks developed this mythical idea in a form that allows little improvement. It was left for others to elicit all the symbolic implications, as it was with the tale of Oedipus, but the basic narrative was complete. Medusa was a similarly potent concept. The idea is not the private property of the Greeks, but their version of it was uniquely spare and pure in itself, and was moreover associated with other Perseus themes that made a satisfyingly complex tale. Pegasus and Bellerophon are based no doubt partly on the Akkadian tale of Etana and the eagle,[22] but the whole Bellerophon cycle, so far as we can guess from tantalising fragments, developed an imaginative force of its own. The idea of the Centaurs is another powerful one, perhaps more exclusively a Greek invention. No Mediterranean myth about semi-tame horses is likely to be much earlier than around 1700 B.C., when the domesticated horse was introduced into the eastern Mediterranean world; but man-horses do not appear alongside the bull-men and other mixed types on Mesopotamian cylinder-seals, and may therefore be a Greek invention. The Centaurs are prominent in Greek heroic myths; they are no anonymous group like the Satyrs—on the contrary Cheiron is a key figure in heroic education and has several important myths of his own, and Nessus and Pholus, too, are quite strongly individualised. Perhaps it is only when the horse-man concept is set beside that of the Cyclopes, another equivocal clan half barbarous and half divine, that its most imaginative implications for the relation of culture and nature can be properly appreciated.[23]

Then there are the recurrent themes of old age and the distinction between mortality and immortality—Peleus and Tithonus crumbling into senility while their divine brides remain irritatingly young, or the monstrous grey-haired girls, the Graeae themselves. Change of sex is not a common theme and has little to do with folktale, but it receives powerful expression in the myth of Caenis who became Caeneus in revulsion from Poseidon's love, and then set up his (possibly phallic) spear to be worshipped in the market-place—Caeneus who could not be wounded, but had to be bludgeoned into the earth by Centaurs after the riotous Lapith wedding-feast. And to particular imaginative acts or subjects there must be added the general aura of fantasy conferred by the close connexion between heroes and the gods themselves. The heroes behave for the most part like extraordinary humans; only Heracles can begin to emulate the Amerindian Coyote or African Spider as a culture-hero; but even Perseus and Jason, Oedipus and Theseus, draw imaginative force from the environment in which they move, an environment partly Mycenaean but partly that of the Golden Age.

That Greek myths contain moments of brilliant imagination cannot be denied; the significant fact is that the moments are few in relation to the number of mythical characters and the complexity of the whole system. This kind of imagination is not common among the Greeks as we know them; but it never, fortunately, quite disappeared. There were a few remarkable outbreaks even after the oral period and outside the direct mythical tradition. Conspicuous instances are Pherecydes of Syros and the great Aristophanes. Pherecydes' cosmogony owes something to the Hesiodic tradition, and the five (or seven) recesses in

[22] Etana: *ANET*², 114–18. [23] *Cf.* Kirk, *Myth* 152 ff., esp. 170 f.; P. Vidal-Naquet, *Annales* v (1970) 1285–7.

which fertile seed is placed may be oriental in inspiration; but the wedding of Zas and Chthonie, at which Zas weaves a cloth depicting sea and the surface of the earth and gives it to his chthonic bride, and the spreading of the cloth over a winged oak representing the earth's substructure, are a genuinely imaginative mythical conception, one that shines out from the exiguous fragments we possess.[24] As for Aristophanes, in him both kinds of fantasy—inconsequence and brilliantly positive imagination—find a new form. Sometimes he brings old themes to life—the dung-beetle is Pegasus—but the city of birds and Dicaeopolis's separate peace, to look no further, are new and striking inventions.

The Greek mythical tradition, then, has its moments of luminous fantasy; but many of them are foreign in inspiration, and its strongest qualities remain those of narrative ingenuity rather than of poetic insight. I may not have entirely convinced you of this; but the slight role of inconsequentiality, in comparison with most other mythologies, is surely hard to deny. Usually, when it is noticed at all, it is regarded as a matter for congratulation, a commendable by-product of Greek rationality; and I want to end by emphasising how misleading such an assessment might be. Aristophanes should remind us that inconsequentiality is not necessarily a negative quality. Foreign myths are not inconsequential just because they have been made up by poor ignorant savages wandering round in a sort of Lévy-Bruhlian daze. Inconsequence is not just a nasty accident of primitivism; it is a valid facet of the mythical imagination, one of the ways in which traditional tales fulfil some of their most crucial sociological and psychological functions. The displacement of ordinary events, the reversal of normal roles and expectations, are common to myths and to dreams. In each the immediate cause of the displacement may be fortuitous—a heavy supper, or the juxta-position of disparate themes in a loose oral tradition. There may also be artistic reasons for inconsequence; many audiences like unexpectedness in their stories, and in an oral society fantasy can become an independent literary category. But displacement in myths is more than just a matter of style, taste or accident. It accords with certain features of ritual, like the reversal of roles and sexes on special occasions. The ritual rejection of normal life is deliberate, and its purpose is agreed to be the establishment of a potent non-secular interlude, as in rites of passage, or to confirm the connexion of society with a sacred and abnormal past. We may reasonably suppose that fantastic myths do something analogous. For the liberating effect of myths is not caused just by a mysterious and evocative subject or symbol; it can be the result of restructuring experience in an apparently random or secret way. There is something indefinably powerful, almost holy, in this kind of fantasy. It is absorbing not only because of its supernatural or dreamlike connexions, but also because it enables one to see life quite differently, to sense strange archaic possibilities behind the façade of existence. That is a perspective, an approach, that deserves the most careful investigation, and might enable us to give some answer, at least, to questions like these: For how long had the Greeks managed to live without this kind of fantasy, or with so little of it? And how was their peculiar creativity affected by what looks, from a certain point of view, like a kind of emotional and even intellectual deprivation?[25]

G. S. Kirk.

The University of Bristol

---

[24] The possibility that the oak and cloth are also oriental in derivation is re-raised by M. L. West, *Early Greek Philosophy and the Orient* (Oxford, 1971) 52–60; his arguments at this point are far from decisive.

[25] This article is a substantially unchanged version of a talk given to the Triennial Conference of Classical Societies in Cambridge in July 1971.

H. and H. A. Frankfort, John A. Wilson, Thorkild Jacobsen, William A. Irwin. The
Intellectual Adventure of Ancient Man: An Essay on Speculative Thought in the Ancient
Near East. The University of Chicago Press, Chicago, 1946. VI, 4C1 pp.

As the subtitle indicates, this book represents an attempt to describe, analyze,
and evaluate some of the more significant aspects of speculative thought in the ancient
Near East. The sources utilized consist almost entirely of the literary remains of three
Near Eastern peoples: the Egyptians, the Mesopotamians (Sumerians and Accadians), and
the Hebrews. The volume is therefore divided into three major divisions entitled "Egypt",
"Mesopotamia", and "The Hebrews." The speculative thought of the ancient Egyptians, that
is, roughly speaking, their metaphysics, politics, and ethics, are described and
analyzed by John Wilson under the rubrics "The Nature of the Universe," "The Function of
the State," and "The Values of Life;" that of the Mesopotamians is treated by Thorkild
Jacobsen under the headings "The Cosmos as a State," "The Function of the State," and
"The Good Life;" that of the ancient Hebrews is discussed by William A. Irwin in chapters
entitled "God," "Man," "Man in the World," and "Nation, Society, and Politics," Preceding
these three main divisions is a theme-setting introductory chapter by H. and H. A.
Frankfort, entitled "Myth and Reality;" it analyzes the psychological characteristics
which distinguish ancient Near Eastern thought with particular stress on its supposedly
irrational approach and mythopoeic logic. Finally the same authors conclude the book with
a chapter entitled "The Emancipation of Thought from Myth," which begins with a brief
comparative survey of Egyptian, Mesopotamian, and Hebrew speculative thought, and concludes with a sketch of the doctrines of the early Greek philosophers from Thales to
Parmenides, who, according to the authors, destroyed the last hold of myth on thought.

As is obvious from the preceding outline of its contents, the volume undertakes to
present a far-reaching and many-sided synthesis of the intellectual and spiritual
concepts prevailing during a long and productive period in the history of civilization,
and the authors are to be congratulated on their courage and optimism as well as on their
significant achievement. Near East scholars are only too well aware how complex,
difficult, and at times truly heart-rending a task it is to dig out, piece together, and
formulate the philosophic and religious concepts of the ancients from their varied,

fragmentary, and not too lucid literary remains. Not only the educated layman, therefore, but the Near East specialist as well is deeply indebted to the authors for their clearly worded and highly stimulating efforts on a subject so elusive and yet so attractive as ancient man's speculative thought.

Now while on the whole the book represents a noteworthy and valuable contribution to the history of man's spiritual development, it must not be inferred that all (or even most) of its conclusions and generalizations are to be taken as valid and final. Indeed it is good to note that the authors themselves are not unaware of the subjective and one-sided character of some of their interpretations and hypotheses and forewarn the reader to a certain extent. The basic difficulty lies of course with the present status of our source material. If we take Mesopotamia as an example -- and it is only of the Mesopotamian material that the reviewer is qualified to speak -- we find in the first place that the texts utilized spread over a period of some two thousand years, from the third to the first millennium B.C. Throughout this long period, the land witnessed numerous ethnic and political upheavals; the very language changed from Sumerian to Akkadian. Under such circumstances it is obviously no simple task to extract the typical Mesopotamian mind and to abstract its underlying philosophic and religious concepts. In addition to this fundamental difficulty, there is the matter of the fragmentary and obscure character of many of the literary texts. In particular the Sumerian literary composition -- and these are far more numerous and on the whole more significant for the problem than those written in Akkadian -- are only now in the process of being translated and interpreted by a mere handful of scholars, and only with a fair degree of success. As matters now stand there is considerable room for differences of opinion on the actual translation of some of this material, not to speak of its more general interpretation within the framework of Mesopotamian thought. It is some of these differences of opinions which are presented in the pages to follow.

To begin with the introductory chapter "Myth and Reality," it is of the utmost importance to note that it contains a number of statements with regard to the characteristic features of the mind of Near Eastern man, whose validity is more than doubtful, at least as far as Mesopotamia is concerned. It is the underlying conviction of the authors of this chapter -- and fortunately it is this conviction which serves as the unifying theme for the several divisions of the book -- that the ancients were unable to think reflectively; that they lacked the detachment of intellectual inquiry; that their thought was *of necessity* "wrapped in imagination;" that the cosmos always appeared to them as a

"Thou" experienced emotionally in a dynamic reciprocal relationship and that, like primitive man, therefore, they simply did not know an inanimate world; that in the ancient Near East, as in present day primitive society, thought did not operate autonomously, but the whole man confronted a living "Thou" in nature, and that all experience of this "Thou" could be conceived only as action and thus necessarily takes the form of a story; that therefore the ancients could only tell myths and were presumably unable to present analyses or conclusions. In order to illustrate the inability of the ancient Mesopotamian to think of natural events other than in a mythopoeic framework, the authors give the following example: "We would explain, for instance, that certain atmospheric changes broke a drought and brought about rain. The Babylonian observed the same facts but experienced them as the intervention of the gigantic bird Imdugud which came to their rescue. It covered the sky with the black storm clouds of its wings and devoured the Bull of Heaven, whose hot breath had scorched the crops."

Now at least as far as Mesopotamia is concerned, this psychological analysis of the mind of ancient Near Eastern man is without basis in fact. In the case of the Sumerians, for example, there is good evidence to show that they had a group of thinkers who were quite capable of viewing nature with a detached and reflective mind;[1] that they were quite aware that nature was inanimate as well as animate and that they actually made this distinction in word as well as thought;[2] that within the narrow range of their limited and superficial data they succeeded in working out a systematic metaphysics and theology which became more or less paradigmatic for large parts of the Near East, and that this was probably due to no small extent to their rational approach and relatively consistent logic. Finally, to take the example cited by the authors, it is most unlikely that even the average Mesopotamian, not to speak of his more reflective brother, would say of the

1. Cf. e.g. the Sumerian passage quoted in *SM* 113 note 37 where the *an* and *ki* of the first two lines cannot possibly be rendered other than "heaven" and "earth" in the sense of *physical* realms and not as living entities; for additional proof cf. line 4 of the same passage.
2. Thus the Sumerian phrase for living creature is usually *níg-zi-gál*, Akkadian *šiknat napištim*, "that which has breath," in short, our very word "animate." This expression, be it noted, is used only of men and animals, and never of such natural phenomena as plants and trees, stones and metal, rivers and fields, Obviously, therefore, there were Sumerian thinkers who actually divided nature into animate and inanimate, the distinguishing criterion being the capacity to breathe. To be sure, for the purpose of myth and fable, prayer and ritual, some one or another inanimate object might be treated *as if* it were animate; indeed to a certain extent this happens in our own day and age. But that is by no means the same as saying that the Mesopotamian mind was unable to conceive nature and the cosmos except as a living "Thou".

drought-breaking rain that it was the Imdugud bird who devoured the Bull of Heaven; like the average man today he would probably say that it was the clouds[3] which brought the refreshing rain.[4]

What has misled the authors into a mistaken notion of the basic characteristics of speculative thought in the ancient Near East is the essentially mythopoeic nature of their source material. For, again restricting ourselves to Mesopotamia, it is quite true that relatively little detached speculative thought on nature and the cosmos is to be found in the extant literary material, since by far the larger part consists of myths and epic tales, hymns and lamentations, that is, literary genres which utilize a highly mythopoeic approach and technique. But this fact hardly justifies the conclusion that the early Mesopotamian thinkers were incapable of rational and detached thought in regard to nature in the universe, or that they failed to develop a systematic metaphysics and theology; indeed, our literary sources, in spite of their essentially mythopoeic character, presuppose the existence of such systems and reflect them at every turn. All that one is justified in concluding from the one-sided character of our Mesopotamian literary material is that the early Mesopotamian scribes and men of letters had failed to develop a *written* literary genre to serve as an adequate vehicle for the expression of their metaphysics and theology. Just so, to take an analagous situation, the early Mesopotamain scribes failed to develop an adequate historical literary genre, in spite of the fact that there is every evidence to show that at least in the second half of the third millennium B. C. some of them had a fairly reliable knowledge of the more important political events of their own generation and to a certain extent even of those which had taken place in earlier times.[5]

3. Unfortunately both the meaning and reading of IM-*dirig*, the Sumerian compound word for "cloud," are still uncertain, and so the primary notion behind the word still escapes us.
4. It is to be noted that at least as far as the reviewer's acquaintance with the Sumerian sources is concerned, there is no literary evidence to indicate the existence of the mythopoeic notion that the "Imdugud" bird, representing the black storm, devoured the Bull of Heaven, representing the scorching drought; note, too, that the reading of the word written   IM-DUGUD is still uncertain; cf. Thureau-Dangin, *RA* 24:199ff. and Witzel *ZA* 40:95.
5. Nor is there reason to believe that future excavations will bring to light texts inscribed with the Sumerian metaphysical and philosophical speculations. For in spite of the fact that the material at our disposal contains but a small fraction of the Sumerian literary remains, it does represent a fair cross-section of Sumerian literature as a whole. And while we do find among them a well developed "wisdom" genre, it is "practical" rather than "theoretical" in character, that is, it consists of compositions devoted to proverbs, fables, and sundry didactic purposes, but does not include any devoted to arguments and discussions concerning the nature of the cosmos

If we now take several of the more significant cosmogonic concepts of the Sumerians as revealed in their mythopoeic literature at our disposal, it will become quite clear that these could only have resulted from a detached intellectual speculation on the nature of the cosmos whose conponent realms were viewed as inanimate physical entities and not as living "Thou's". Thus we find that the Sumerian thinkers assumed that before the universe came into being there existed nothing but water, that is, they postulated the existence of a primeval sea;[6] that out of this primeval sea there somehow came into

and its method of operation. To judge from the present evidence, the best that we may hope for in this direction is to recover at least some of the more significant Sumerian metaphysical and theological *conclusions* (conclusions, be it noted, but not proofs and arguments) in the *introductory* lines to some of the myths and epic tales. Unfortunately the relevant passages available to date are relatively few, and even the contents of these few are not infrequently either fragmentary or obscure.

6. In *JNES* 5: 139 f. it is argued that the sign *ENGUR*, the sign with which is written the name of the goddess Nammu, "the mother who gave birth to heaven and earth", when read *engur*, does not mean "sea" but rather "the sweet waters of the subsoil and of pools and marshes"; hence the conclusion that the Sumerians conceived the universe as coming into being in the midst of the primeval sea is unjustified. The reader will note, however, that it is admitted there that to judge from the etymology of the words *abzu* and *a-ab-ba* "in a remote past the Sumerians may have distinguished the bodies of water involved less sharply". In other words, at some "remote" time *abzu* and *a-ab-ba* could be used more or less interchangeably, and since *abzu* and *engur* are "approximately synonymous", it is obvious that *engur*, too, could be used more or less interchangeably with *a-ab-ba* in the "remote past". But there is reasonably conclusive evidence that even in later and historical times the words *engur*, *abzu*, and *a-ab-ba* could at times be used interchangeably. Thus we find certain water monsters described as *la-ḫa-ma-engur-ra ninnu-bi*, "the fifty laḫama of the Engur", in *PBS* V 25 ii 29 and *PBS* X 2 No. 1 iii 6; in both cases they are mentioned in connection with Enki. Now the monster of the *engur* called *la-ḫa-ma*, it seems reasonable to assume, is certainly identical on the one hand with the monster described as *laḫmi A-AB-BA šut ᵈEa* (*CT* 17:42,25) and with a *laḫmu* monster described as *šut tamtim ša malû puluḫta* (Gray, Šamaš 20 iv 3) and with the *laḫamu*-monster who accompanied Tiamat in battle gainst Marduk; on the other hand it is identical with the *la-ḫa-ma-abzu* of *Gudea Cyl.* I 24:27. Note finally that in note 21 of *JNES* 5:139 f., in the case of the six-line passage cited on p. 140, it seems to be argued that *a-ab-ba* and *engur* must stand for different entities since they are mentioned in different (though parallel)lines, while on the other hand, *engur* and *abzu* are "approximately synonymous" even though these, too, are mentioned in different parallel lines. In short, as far as our available data goes, there is no evidence to indicate, that the Sumerians, like the Akkadians who composed the *Enuma eliš* epic, divided the sea into a male principle "sweet water" (*abzu* or *engur*) and female principle "bitter water" (*a-ab-ba*); the sea was conceived as a single body of water completely surrounding the universe, above, below, and on all sides, and the terms *a-ab-ba*, *engur*, and *abzu* are all more or less synonymous, with *a-ab-ba* used primarily for the sea as a geographically conceived body of water, (cf. also note 16). Just how the Sumerians explained the existence of "fresh water" as opposed to "bitter water" is not clear, but cf. perhaps *SS* 1:12, 43ff. where the sweet water is said to come from a *KI-a-ki-a- DU.DU;* perhaps, too, there is some significance to the fact that it is the sun-god Utu who is ordered by Enki to bring up the sweet water from the earth.

being the universe consisting of heaven superimposed over earth and in contact with it, and that later heaven was separated from earth by the atmosphere. [7] Now how could the ancient Sumerian thinkers come to the conclusion that first there was the sea and that the universe came into being within it, if not by realizing on the intellectual and rational level that the universe was surrounded by water on all sides, that is, that there was water above the heavens and below the earth as well as all around it? [8] Similarly why did they pick on the atmosphere as the realm separating heaven from earth, if it were not one again for the realization on the rational level that the atmosphere is actually situated between heaven and earth and that, moreover, unlike these two solid bodies, it consists of a substance which could expand and thus separate two touching surfaces. [9]

Similarly if we turn to the fundamental theological concepts of the Sumerians, concepts which may be said to formulate the creed and faith, the dogma and doctrine of large parts of the ancient Near East, we find that these, too, originated and developed on the intellectual plane; they were worked out quite logically and rationally on the analogy of man and his institutions. From as far back as we have written records to the very end of the Mesopotamian civilization, the fundamental metaphysical concept of the theologians, the concept that was central and axiomatic to all their religious speculations, was the assumed existence of a pantheon consisting of a group of living beings, man-like in form, but superhuman and immortal, who though invisible to mortal eye, guide and control the cosmos in accordance with well laid plans and duly prescribed laws. Be it the great cosmic realms heaven and earth, sea and atmosphere, be it the major astral bodies sun, moon, and planet, be it such atmospheric forces as wind, storm and tempest, or finally, to take the earth, be it such natural phenomena as river, mountain, and plain, or such cultural phenomena as city and state, dyke and ditch, field and farm, or even such implements as the pickaxe, brickmold, and plow -- each of these was deemed to be under the charge of one or another anthropomorphic but superhuman being who guided its activities in accordance with established rules and regulations.

Now how did the ancient Sumerian thinker come upon this notion of an anthropomor-

7. Cf. *SM* 37 ff.
8. He thus explained the existence of rain, of wells, pools, and rivers, and of the *a-ab-ba-sig* and the *a-ab-ba-igi-nim* "the lower sea" and "the upper sea", which between them surrounded the earth on all sides.
9. As seen, for example, by any observing Sumerian when blowing up a leather bottle, or in the expansion of the chest upon taking a deep breath of air.

rhic but superhuman pantheon in control of the cosmos and its diverse entities and
rhenomena? Surely not by noting any physical resemblance between these latter and human
beings; presumably no one will argue that the Mesopotamian, in looking up at the sky
found it to resemble a huge man with a beard, or that in looking down to the earth, saw
a huge woman with bulging breasts. Nor is there any reason to believe that the Sumerian
thinkers conceived such entities as the sky, earth, sun, moon, river, pickaxe, etc., as
"somehow alive" with "wills of their own;"[10] all the available evidence clearly indicates
that it was not the sky that was thought of as alive, but the human-like being in charge
of the sky; it was not the earth that was thought to be alive, but the human-like being
in charge of the earth; it was not the Tigris and Euphrates Rivers that were alive, but
the human-like being in charge of these rivers that was alive, etc. etc. And since it is
obvious that the Mesopotamian theologian could not possibly have seen these human-like
beings with his own eyes, we must conclude that he in some way *inferred* their existence;
in other words his reason told him that these beings existed even though he was unable
to see them. Nor is the basis for this inference hard to fathom; the ancient thinker
reasoned quite naturally and logically from the known to the unknown. Taking his cue
from human society as he knew it, he noted that all lands and cities, all palaces and
temples, all fields and farms, in short all imaginable institutions and enterprises are
tended and supervised, guided and controlled by living human beings; without them, lands
and cities become desolate, temples and palaces crumble, field and farm turn to desert
and wilderness. Surely therefore the cosmos and all its manifold phenomena must also be
tended and supervised, guided and controlled, by living beings in human form. However,
the cosmos being far larger than the sum total of human habitations, and its organization being far more complex, these living beings must obviously be far larger and
stronger than ordinary humans.[11] Above all they must be immortal; otherwise the cosmos
would turn to chaos upon their death, and the world would come to an end, alternatives
which for obvious reasons did not recommend themselves to the Sumerian metaphysician. It
was each of these invisible, anthropomorphic, but at the same time superhuman and

10. Cf. Jacobsen on p. 130 of the book under review.
11. In the available literature we have practically no texts revealing the theological
    speculations concerning the size and strength of the deities in relation to man.
    But that such speculation was current among the Mesopotamians is obvious from the
    "birth of a deity" passages in the myth "Enki and Ninḫursag," where it is stated
    that the goddesses needed only nine days of pregnancy instead of nine months, and
    that moreover they gave birth without pain (cf. *SS* 1:12, 77 ff.).

immortal beings which the Sumerian designated by the word *dingir*, which the Akkadians rendered as *ilu*, and which we translate by the word "god."[12]

Moreover, just as the doctrine of the existence of a pantheon developed from what may be termed a common-sense approach to the question "How is the cosmos run?", so, too, did the notions concerning its organization. In the first place it seemed reasonable to the Sumerian theologian to assume that the deities constituting the pantheon were not all of the same importance, or of equal rank. The god in charge of the pickaxe and brickmold could hardly be expected to compare with the deity in charge of the sun, nor could the deity in charge of dykes and ditches be expected to equal in rank the god in charge of the earth as a whole. Then, too, it seems not unreasonable to assume, on analogy with the political organization of the human state, that at the head of the pantheon was a deity who was recognized by all the others as their king and ruler. And so we find the Sumerian pantheon conceived as functioning as an assembly with a king at its head, the most important groups in this assembly being the seven gods who "decree the fates" and the fifty deities known as "the great gods."[13] But the most significant division set up by the Sumerian theologians within their pantheon is that between creative and non-creative deities, a notion arrived at quite rationally as a result of their cosmogonic concepts. For according to these concepts, the basic components of the cosmos are heaven and earth, sea and atmosphere: every other cosmic entity and phenomenon can exist only within one or another of these realms. Hence it was reasonable to infer that the deities in control of heaven and earth, sea and air, were the creating gods; that is, it was one or another of these four gods who created every other cosmic entity in accordance with plans which originated with them. Consequently the heaven-god Anu, the air-god Enlil, the water-god Enki, and the earth-goddess Ninhursag (under the assumption that she represents a goddess once known as Ki), were treated as the four leading deities of the Sumerian pantheon, and are frequently grouped together as a quartette of deities in a class by themselves.[14]

12. Unfortunately the etymology of *dingir* (or better, *digir*) is still obscure (note that the final syllable *gir* may be the same as the final *gir* of *kengir* "Sumer"), otherwise we might at least have one of the primary notions behind the Sumerian concept of the nature of "godhood" just as for example the word *lugal* (literally "great man") furnishes an inkling of one of the notions originally associated with kingship.
13. Cf. Jacobsen's excellent in discussion in *JNES* 2:167 ff.
14. Cf. *PBS* IV 1:24 ff. When it comes to the creation technique attributed to these deities, it is to be noted that once again the Sumerian theologians developed a

Finally, the Sumerian theologian, again no doubt taking his cue from the human world about him, adduced a significant metaphysical inference in answer to the problem as to what keeps the cosmic entities and phenomena, once created, operating continuously and harmoniously, without conflict and confusion; this is the concept designated by the Sumerian word *me* whose exact rendering is still not quite certain. To judge from the various contexts, it would seem to denote a set of rules and regulations assigned to each cosmic entity and phenomenon for the very purpose of keeping it operating forever in accordance with the plans laid down by the creating deities.[15]

The preceding paragraphs, it is hoped, will have brought out clearly the essentially rational character of the Sumerian speculative thought devoted to cosmology and theology. At least this particular ancient man, the early Sumerian metaphysician, must have arrived at his answers to the various cosmological and metaphysical problems confronting him, not through revelation "in a reciprocal relationship with nature", but by thinking them out rationally to his intellectual satisfaction. The existence of an invisible, and anthropomorphic but superhuman pantheon organized as a hierarchy topped by four deities who ruled the four realms of the cosmos and who planned the creation of all other cosmic entities and phenomena within them, and prescribed the rules governing their continuous and harmonious functioning-- all this was accepted as axiomatic by the Sumerian philosophers who postulated it as a logical inference based on their experience with the civilized human world about them.[16] Indeed it is not unreasonable to assume that

14 doctrine which became dogma throughout the Near East, that is, the doctrine of the creative power of the divine word. According to this doctrine, all that the creating deity had to do was to lay his plans, utter the word, and it came to be (cf. e.g. such lines as *mu-nam-lú-lu₆ ba-gar-ra-a-ba* in *SM* 113; the phrase *ì-šag₅-hé-àm-ba* in *AS* 12:32, 151, 161; cf. also *SS* 1:8, note 28b; it is to be noted of course that at least the mythographers are by no means consistent in this matter, and at times make the gods perform some physical activity when doing their creating; cf. e.g. "The Creation of Man" in *SM* 68 ff.). The notion of the creative power of the divine word, too, is a rational inference; it arose in the mind of the Sumerian theologian in all probability as a result of his observation of the powers of a human king; that is, he reasoned, if the latter could achieve so much of what he wanted merely by the word of his mouth, how much more so the immortal and superhuman creating deities in charge of the major realms of the universe.

15. Cf. now *JNES* 5:139, note 20.

16. To be sure, the metaphysical and theological postulates outlined above represent what may be described as only the central core of their speculations, and that, no doubt, in a highly oversimplified form. Actually these early thinkers who laid down the major lines of the Sumerian theological system, and particularly their later and less creative colleagues, must have evolved many another theological notion in a futile attempt to resolve the inconsistencies and contradictions inherent in a polytheistic system of religion. Moreover, the early Sumerian thinkers must have

it was to no small extent precisely because they carried high intellectual conviction
that the theological concepts involved in this postulate became the fundamental world
view of the early Mesopotamian, his faith and his creed. For while we have no way
knowing the fundamental cosmological and theological notions that had preceded them in
Mesopotamia, or how close was the resemblance between them, we may well assume that
these earlier concepts, whatever their character, had long passed their creative stage.
The intellectual superiority of the teachings developed and propagated by the Sumerian

16 tried to reconcile at least some of the religious ideas of their predecessors with
   their own, especially if these were imbedded in ritual practices tending to defy any
   revolutionary change. Particularly in the matter of the births of the deities and
   their family interrelationships, the theological systematizer must have run into all
   sorts of problems and complexities which he no doubt tried to reconcile and explain
   away in one fashion ot another. But it must be stressed that our present sources
   unfortunately fail to furnish a clear idea of the speculations underlying these
   attempts. For the fact is that our basic sources, that is, the myths, hymns, and god-
   lists, contain genealogical statements which are extremely brief and laconic, and
   which therefore shed little light on the speculations behind them. Moreover they
   nearly all stem from a relatively late date when theological speculation had been
   rife for centuries, and after Sumer had undergone a number of political changes
   which left their deep, if largely unrecognizable imprint on these divine genealogies.
   Thus, for example, the goddess Nammu is stated to be "the mother who gave birth to
   heaven and earth" (cf. *SM* 39); Nammu was thus presumably the mother of the heaven-
   god Anu and the earth-goddess Ki. But in the god lists she seems to be treated as
   one of the deities in the circle of Anu (cf. *TRS* 10:29-37 and *CT* 24:122 ff. = *ibid,*
   20: 15ff.); it is not clear just what the relationship is, but it certainly does not
   seem to that of a mother. Moreover, going on assumption that reason demanded the
   existence of a father as well as mother for the birth of offspring (and the fact
   that such words for sea as *a-ab-ba*, *abzu* and *ab* all contain the element *ab* "father"
   indicates clearly that there was a god as well as a goddess of the primeval sea), who
   was the deity? To be sure Enlil is given the name, or better the epithet, *ab* in the
   god-lists (cf. e.g. *TRS* 10:41; *CT* 24:22, 98), but it seems hardly likely that
   Enlil, who at least in historical times has nothing to do with the sea, is to be
   identified with the *ab* in *a-ab-ba* and *ab-zu;* note too, if that should be the case
   it would be necessary to assume that Enlil was conceived by the theologians as the
   father of Anu and Ki. In historical times, it was of course Enki who was conceived
   as the lord of.the sea; cf. particularly the passage cited in *JNES* 5:140 which indicates clearly that he was the ruler of the *abzu*, *engur*, *a-ab-ba* as well as the *íd-
   mah* and the *buranun*. In the god-lists and in the myths, however, he is stated to be
   the son of Nammu, not the husband. What moreover is intended with the well-known
   genealogies of Anu and Enlil in which Nammu and her consort do not seem to be
   mentioned at all (cf. now *JNES* 5:138-9)? Similarly it seems reasonable to conclude
   that the goddess Ki "earth" was identical with Ninhursag of the historical periods.
   But if that is the case she might be expected to have been the mother of Enlil and
   the husband of Anu since Anu was probably conceived as his (i.e. Enlil's) father
   (cf. the often quoted *SAK* 154:3, 16). And yet this is hardly borne out by our texts,
   which regularly designate her husband as Šulpae. On the other hand, in the case of
   many deities, their parentage seems well established in historical times. Thus Nergal,
   Ninurta, and Nanna are everywhere conceived as the sons of Enlil; Utu and Inanna are
   the children of Nanna and Ningal; Iškur, Martu, and Bau (the readings Babu and Baba
   may be   phonetic variants only) are everywhere stated to be the children of Anu,
   etc. etc.

thinkers was therefore all the more apparent, and their wholehearted acceptance by the
ruling caste was more or less inevitable, particularly since it is not unlikely that
these Sumerian thinkers were at the same time temple and court officials of high influence. Just so for example, the acceptance of the monotheistic teachings developed and
propagated by the Hebrew thinkers of a much later day was due to no small extent to their
intellectual superiority over the earlier polytheistic notions which had long lost their
creative vigor.

Now there can be little doubt that the early Sumerian thinkers responsible for the
basic metaphysical and theological concepts prevailing in Mesopotamia during the third
millennium B.C. had evolved and formulated them only after considerable discussion and
debate among themselves. Moreover, since they were convinced that they were in possession of profound cosmic truths of utmost importance to their own conduct and that of
their fellow beings, they no doubt propagated them zealously and fervently by word of
mouth in order to have them accepted as the official and universal faith of the land;
they must therefore have formulated and utilized many an argument and proof for their
support. But, as already pointed out, there is little likelihood that we will ever recover the contents of these arguments and discussions, since the Sumerian scribes and
men of letters failed to develop a written literary genre to serve as a vehicle for
their expression and conservation. All that we can hope is to dig out and piece
together a few of the *conclusions*-- not the reasons and arguments supporting them--
from the Sumerian texts of a much later day, particularly from their myths, a literary
genre popular with the Sumerian scribes functioning in the Edubba. But in doing so, it
is all-important to bear in mind that the Mesopotamian *mythographers* were *not* primarily
philosophers and theologians interested in speculative thought, but rather scribes and
poets whose main concern was the glorification and exaltation of the gods and their
deeds. [17] Unlike the former these mythographers were not interested in discovering new
cosmological and theological truths; they accepted the current theological notions and
practices without any real insight into their origin and growth.

17 The forerunners and prototypes of the Sumerian mythographers are not to be sought
among the early thinkers and philosophers, that group of influential palace and
temple officials who probably evolved the basic lines of Sumerian metaphysics and
theology, but rather among the poets and minstrels who from earliest days had composed and recited oral lays in honor of the heroes, and probably also of the gods,
in order to entertain their lordly and courtly audience; cf. *PAPS* 90:120 ff.

Their aim was to compose a narrative poem in which they attempted to explain the origin and being of one or another of these notions and practices in a manner that would prove to be appealing, inspiring, and entertaining. That is, they were not concerned with proofs and arguments which appeal to the intellect; their first interest was in telling a story or in describing an event which would appeal primarily to the emotions.[18] They therefore did not resort to logic and reason as their literary tools, but to imagination and fantasy. Consequently, in telling their story or in describing the particular event, these poets did not hesitate to invent motives and incidents patterned on human action which could not possibly have any basis in reasonable speculative thought, nor did they hesitate to adopt legendary and folkloristic motifs that had nothing to do with rational cosmological inquiry and inference.[19] To assume that these Mesopotamian *myths* are representative of the *speculative thought* of the early philosophers and theologians who developed the basic lines of Sumerian cosmology and theology, is as fallacious as it would be to assume that the myths and legends collected in the Haggadic portions of the Talmud and in the Midrashim are representative of the early Hebrew thinkers who evolved and taught the concept of monotheism.[20]

Turning now to Jacobsen's most important chapter on Mesopotamian speculative thought, "The Cosmos as a State", one cannot but admire and applaud the care and thoughtfulness with which it is written, the logic of its organization, the devotion to minute detail, the lucidity of its statements and summations. Indeed all who have

18 That the scribes themselves were conscious of this, their main aim, is indicated by the fact that the myths regularly end with the word *ža-sal* immediately preceded by the name of the deity who is the main protagonist of the myth. This is exactly the the same phrase that regularly comes at the end of the epic tales, indicating clearly that the underlying attitude on the part of the scribes and poets was the same for myth and epic. Similarly, royal songs of praise were regularly composed in the *é-dub-ba*, cf. especially *TRS* CLV v 27 ff.

19 In *SS* 1:7 I was wrong in stating that "by and large the poet is translating into mythological language the results of his contemplation and speculation on certain natural phenomena involved in the agricultural life about him;" cf. the sentence preceding this quotation where the word "some" might better have read "most."

20 On page 8 of the book under review, the character of myth is summarized as follows: "Myth is a form of poetry which transcends poetry in that it proclaims a truth; a form of reasoning which transcends reasoning in that it wants to bring about the truth it proclaims; a form of action, of ritual behaviour, which does not find its fulfilment in the act but must proclaim and elaborate a poetic form of truth." If the authors intend this definition of myth to be taken seriously -- and they have of course every right to define the term in their own way -- not a single one of the Sumerian myths should have been included in the book, since they hardly qualify on any of the three counts Particularly there is not the slightest evidence whatever that the Sumerian myth, as we have it, was "a form of action"; it was nothing more than a literary genre developed by the scribe in his *é-dub-ba*, comparable to the epic tale and the "wisdom" literature (cf. also *JCS* 1:6, note 3d).

followed Jacobsen's contributions in the past decade, particularly those in the
Sumerian field, have learned to recognize and appreciate their fundamental importance
and significance. It is particularly obvious from his published work that he has devoted
much time and thought to the Sumerian literary material; his relevant studies will take
their place among the most original and stimulating in the field.[21] In spite of all
this, however, I regret to say that I find myself in disagreement with most of his
generalizations and conclusions on Mesopotamian speculative thought as stated in this
chapter. For they are grounded on two major fallacies: (1) he attributes to the early
Sumerian thinkers a psychological attitude towards the phenomena of nature which they
never had, and (2) by failing to realize the true character of the purpose and techniques of the mythographers he reads into their works cosmological speculations of a
rational and logical character which they never intended. To follow the argument more
clearly let us analyze this chapter section by section, omitting only the first, on the
influence of environment in Egypt and Mesopotamia, which is primarily introductory and
summary in character.

In the second section, "Date of the Mesopotamian View of the World", we find the
rather startling statement that with the advent of the Proto-literate period,
Mesopotamian civilization crystallized, "as it were, overnight." Thus, it is stated,
"the fundamental pattern, the controlling framework within which Mesopotamia is to live
its life, formulate its deepest questions, evaluate itself and evaluate the universe,
for ages to come,.flashes into being, complete in all its main features" (p. 128). Now
this hypothesis of the overnight crystallization of Mesopotamian civilization -- and it
is to be borne constantly in mind that all statements concerning prehistoric Mesopotamia,
including the one presented in the lines that follow, can, in the nature of things, be
nothing other than hypothetical inferences and theories -- seems to be neither readily
justifiable not highly illuminating. An hypothesis which seems to conform more to the
evidence on hand and which promises a more productive approach to the problems involved,

21 Cf. particularly his review article of *SM* in *JNES* 5:128-152 where he takes issue --
and in more than one instance quite rightly -- with a number of its translations and
conclusions. However, except for several examples pertinent to this review, it is
preferable to leave the detailed discussions to the time when the scientific editions
of the relevant poems will be made available in order that the reader might be able
to follow the arguments with the full extant text before him. But this is a good
opportunity to mention one major correction made by Jacobsen. In sketching the contents of the poem *lugal-e-u₄-me-lám-bi-nir-gál* I was quite wrong in assuming that
Ninurta's struggle was against Kur (that is, *kur* personified) as a whole, rather
than against the Asakku who was one of the fierce demons who dwelt in the *kur.*

is the following. The crystallization of Mesopotamian civilization as known in early
historic days, that civilization in which, to judge from linguistic testimony, the
Sumerians played a predominant role, began to take place in the course of the Proto-
literate period as the result of a long era of cultural cross-fertilization involving
at least three ethnic groups. Thus, long before the Sumerians arrived on the scene,
life in Lower Mesopotamia began as a peasant-village culture introduced by a still un-
identifiable ethnic group that was probably neither Semitic nor Sumerian in origin.
Following a period of infiltration and invasion by the Semites from the west, this
peasant-village culture developed over the centuries into a high urban civilization
which, on the political level, reached at times empire proportions. The political sway
of this predominantly Semitic Mesopotamian empire was brought to an end by the primitive
Sumerian hordes after a protracted military struggle which ended in the invasion of
Lower Mesopotamia by the Sumerian conquerors. As a result of this invasion and.conquest,
Lower Mesopotamia suffered a period of stagnation and regression culminating in the
relatively barbaric and immature Heroic Age.[22] It is the period following on the Sumerian
Heroic Age which witnessed a rather unusually fruitful cultural fusion between the
barbaric Sumerian conquerors and the originally far more civilized native population.
Particularly this was the period that probably witnessed the invention of the Sumerian
system of writing, and produced a group of administrators and intellectuals in the
temples and palaces, under whose productive leadership the later historic Mesopotamian
civilization, with its predominantly Sumerian stamp, began to crystallize.[23]

Turning to the next section in the chapter, "The Mesopotamian Attitude Toward the
Phenomena of Nature," it is to be noted that its fundamental conclusion is largely
unfounded and invalid; it was arrived at by ascribing to speculative thought the views
and notions characteristic of magic and myth. Thus we find there such statements as
"any phenomenon which the Mesopotamian met in the world around him was thus alive, had
its own personality and will, its distinct self," or that the Mesopotamian actually
spoke "of stones and stars, winds and waters, as citizens and as members of legislative
assemblies." Now whatever their validity for the incantation priest and mythographer,
there is not the slightest evidence that such views were held by the early Sumerian

22 This is the period of Enmerkar-Lugalbanda-Gilgameš whose political organization is
   characterized by Jacobsen as "primitive democracy", cf. especially *JNES* 2:165ff. and
   p. 172.
23 The hypothesis outlined above, together with the evidence on which it is based, is
   developed in detail in a study to appear in the near future in the *AJA*.

thinkers who believed in the existence of an invisible, anthropomorphic pantheon in
control of the cosmos and all its varied phenomena. These men did not confuse the animate
with the inanimate; they certainly looked upon air and water, reed and tree, metal and
stone, as lifeless objects without personality and without will. Similarly, the four
realms which made up the Sumerian cosmos, heaven and earth, sea and atmosphere, were not
conceived by the Sumerian metaphysicians as animate; there were animate beings in them,
such as deities, men, animals, but the physical realms themselves were not thought of as
having life, will, or personality.[24] Indeed it is no doubt just because the cosmos was,
as far as they could see, predominantly inanimate, without will and intelligence, that
these early thinkers found themselves confronted with their basic problem, that is, how
could the lifeless, unintelligent entities which comprise the cosmos function consistently and harmoniously, day after day, year after year, generation after generation; surely,
they inferred, they must be watched over and controlled by powerful living creatures
filled with profound wisdom and understanding. In short the very idea of the existence
of a pantheon such as that described in the preceding pages would never have come to the
Mesopotamian thinker had he not made the distinction between animate and inanimate.

     In the following sections of the chapter, devoted to a discussion of the structure of
the cosmic state, and to its leaders, we unfortunately find repeated again and again
the same unfounded generalizations concerning the animate character of all cosmic
entities and phenomena. But, in addition, these pages reveal a number of misconceptions
with regard to the leading Sumerian deities based largely on some rather extraordinary
and, at least to my mind, far-fetched psychological analyses of a purely subjective
character.[25] Thus, after considerable speculation on how the sky affects man when "in a
singularly receptive mood," it is concluded that the Mesopotamians took Anu to represent
"majesty and absolute authority," while Enlil, on the other hand, is interpreted as the
god of storm, and so is said to represent force. Thus, the argument continues, while Anu
runs the universe by authority alone, authority which is freely and voluntarily accepted,
it is Enlil who takes the stage when force enters the picture. In other words we are

---

24 Note that even Jacobsen admits that the sky could be conceived apart from the deity
   and that then "it receded into the category of things and became a mere abode for
   the god" (p. 138).
25 Cf. e.g. the following statement in connection with the assumed effect of the majesty
   of the sky on man: "Beyond all, however, the experience of majesty is the experience
   of power, of power bordering on the tremendous, but power at rest, not consciously
   imposing its will. The power behind majesty is so great that it need not exert itself.
   Without any effort on its part it commands allegiance by its very presence; the on-
   looker obeys freely, through a categorical imperative rising from the depths of his
   his own soul" (p. 138).

evidently to assume that the Sumerian pantheon was conceived as ruled at the same time
by two supreme deities whose powers complemented one other: by Anu, who exercised
authority without force, and by Enlil, who supplied the force when necessary. Now this
theory of a division of power between Anu and Enlil hardly conforms to the available
evidence. In the first place, as will soon become evident, Enlil is not the god of the
storm at all; hence his function in the universe is not to be understood primarily in
terms of violence and force. Moreover, if we go back to the earliest historical period,
that is approximately the middle of the third millennium B.C., it is generally agreed
that it was Enlil alone who was then conceived as the supreme ruler of the universe,
supreme, that is, from the point of view of authority as well as force. To be sure --
and this is what may have influenced Jacobsen's conclusions -- in the Sumerian texts we
do frequently find the two deities coupled together in the order Anu, Enlil. But this
is probably due to the fact that at one time, in prehistoric days, it was Anu who was
conceived as the supreme ruler of the universe, and it was perhaps as a result of some
important but still unknown political event that this supremecy was turned over to
Enlil, just as in a much later day it was transferred from Enlil to Marduk.[26] In any
case, whoever it was that was conceived as the supreme deity in a given period, he was
thought of as supreme in force as well as authority.

Returning to the god Enlil, it is most unfortunate that Jacobsen continues the
misconceptions in the interpretation of his name and character which have long tended to
dominate cuneiform literature.[27] Actually Enlil was conceived in historical times not
only as the supreme ruler of the pantheon, but as a most beneficent deity who was
responsible for much of the planning and creating of the most productive features of the
cosmos.[28] What has misled some scholars into assuming that he was primarily a god of
violence and destruction is, in the first place, a mistranslation of the word *lil* as
"storm"; actually it is to be rendered as "wind," "air," "spirit," and thus has to a certain
extent the same semantic range as the Hebrew *ruach*.[29] Secondly, because it so happened
that among the earliest Sumerian compositions published there was to be found an unusually large proportion of lamentations, particularly of the "enem" type,[30] scholars
tended to conclude that Enlil was by nature violent and destructive, and that his "word"

26 Cf. especially *PBS* X 4:36ff.
27 Cf. e.g. Nötscher in *RLA* II 384-5; Dhorme, *Les Religions de Babylonie et d'Assyrie* 27.
28 Cf. *SM* 42; *RLA* II 385.
29 Cf. Landsberger as quoted by Falkenstein in *ZA* 45:28.
30. In addition to the bilinguals in *SBH*, cf. particularly *VS* II and X and *CT* 15.

was always evil. What they seemed to fail to realize was that it is only in *lamentations* that Enlil is so pictured, and for obvious reasons. For the destruction which gave rise to the lamentation was due to the desision of the gods, and since Enlil was the supreme deity who had the final say in this decision, it was he who had the unhappy duty of carrying out the decreed destruction.[31] If on the other hand we take the hymns and the myths, we find that Enlil is glorified as a friendly and fatherly deity who watches over that safety and well-being of Sumer in particular, and who brings destruction to its enemies.[32]

As for the sections devoted to the deities Ninḫursag and Enki, these, too, contain a number of highly speculative and largely subjective analyses and assumptions with regard to the Mesopotamian mind which, according to the author, gained its understanding of the earth "in direct experience of it as inner will and direction." Moreover, in the case of Enki, there are a number of problems crucial to any attempt to get at the origin of the god and his name which seem to be ignored altogether. Thus unlike *an* and *en-líl*, the name *en-ki* is a genitive complex[33] and may therefore actually be an epithet which was substituted for the real name of the deity, just as for instance the epithet *(n)in-an-na* was substituted for the Semitic name Ištar, and the epithet *nin-ḫur-sag-gá* may have been substituted for a more original name Ki. Secondly, why should a deity who is

---

31 Note particularly that Jacobsen, too, uses the lamentation as his basic source for the conclusion that Enlil is a wild and raging deity; actually the texts cited on p. 141ff. only say that Enlil called such violent forces as the storm and evil wind, the tempest and fire, as agents to carry out the destruction decreed by the gods, and nowhere in the texts is Enlil identified with any of these forces. Note, too, that the last citation from *SBH* on p. 144 which is claimed to reveal Enlil's rage as "almost pathological, an inner turmoil of the soul which renders him insensate, inaccessible to all appeals", might well be taken by those less prejudiced against Enlil to indicate just the opposite, that is, that he is really a "softy" at heart. For he has to close his heart and seal his ears in order to avoid the pleas and prayers directed to him since otherwise he might be moved to pity and thus find it impossible to carry out his repugnant but obligatory task.

32 There are two additional sources of error which have misled scholars in the interpretation of the character of Enlil: (1) the phrase *lugal-a-ma-ru-ᵈen-líl-lá* (Gudea Cyl. A 12:2 and 23:14) was taken to refer to Enlil (cf. Paffrath, *Götterlehre* 116; Dhorme, *op. cit.* 27) when it actually refers to Ningirsu; and (2) the composition published in *CT* 15:11-12 has been taken by some scholars to be an Enlil hymn because of its colophon, although nearly every line of its contents indicates clearly that it is a Ninurta hymn (cf. Zimmern in *VS* II p. VIII; Nötscher in *RLA* II 384; note, too, Meissner's statement in *Bab. und Assyrien* 155). As for the colophon which reads *ir-šèm-na-ᵈen-líl-lá-kam*, either the name Enlil is a scribal oversight for Ninurta, or perhaps it was chosen because Ninurta belongs to the Enlil circle of deities, although to date I know no other example in Sumerian literature which indicates such a scribal practice.

33 Cf. the innumerable examples of the subject form *en-ki-ke₄*.

primarily conceived as a water-god be given the name *en-ki*, which, at least on the
surface, certainly can only mean "lord of the earth" and not "lord of the waters"?[34]
This title "lord of the earth" seems to indicate that he was impinging to some extent on
the authority of Enlil who "had carried off the earth" after its separation from
heaven.[35] Finally there is the fact that, unlike Anu and Enlil, Enki, at least toward the
very end of the third millenium, has a Semitic name, that is, Ea.[36] Just what all these
facts add up to is by no means easy to fathom; perhaps they point to the possibility
that the water-god Ea-Enki was originally a Semitic deity who at a very early period was
adopted and fitted into the Sumerian pantheon under the name *en-ki*, as a result of the
growing political importance of his worshippers.

Turning finally to the section in the chapter dealing with the Sumerian myths
selected by the author to illustrate the Mesopotamian world view, it is all-important
that the reader bear in mind this rather unusual anomaly, that while on the whole the
translations of the cited passages show great care in linguistic detail and keen insight
into the meaning of the text -- in not a few cases, as I shall have occasion to point
out here and in future studies, Jacobsen has penetrated the meaning of the original
where I have failed to do so -- the accompanying analyses of the contents of the myth as
a whole, on the other hand, are highly speculative and far from trustworthy; they
attempt to read into the myths cosmological notions and psychological motives which
their authors never intended.[37] In the following paragraphs, therefore, it is only the
actual translations of the cited passages which will be analyzed, particularly where a
difference of opinion in regard to the meaning of the text is crucial to the meaning
of the understanding of the myth as a whole.

First, then, the myth of Enlil and Ninlil, which tells of the begetting of Nanna
and his three underworld brothers. The major point of difference between the version of
the myth presented here and that outlined in *SM* 43 ff., consists of the introduction of

34 On the character of Enki as the lord of all bodies of water, salt and fresh, cf. notes
6 and 16. But even if Enki should be considered as god of the sweet waters only, there
is still reason to call him "lord of the earth;" a title such as *en-abzu* or *en-engur-
ra* would seem more appropriate on the view that *engur* and *abzu* stand only for the
sweet waters.
35 Cf. *IS* 10:3, 11. Note, too, that the text published in *JAOS* 63:191 ff. seems to indicate a conflict between Enlil and Enki, and one in whch the latter seems to have
been victorious to a certain extent.
36 Cf *RLA* II 375. That Ea is a Semitic word seems to be proved by the fact that in proper
names it is combined regularly with Semitic elements only.
37 Cf. particularly pp. 155-9 and p. 168 of the book under review; for the basic mis-
conception of the nature of the Sumerian myths, cf. p.   ff. of this review.

the motif of the rape of Ninlil by Enlil, and the consequent arrest of the latter and his banishment to the nether world. Now the passage describing the seizure of Enlil by the gods and his banishment offers but little difficulty, although, as far as I know, Jacobsen is the first to have gathered its real meaning and import.[38] On the other hand, the motive for the seizure and banishment of Enlil, which Jacobsen concludes to be the rape of Ninlil, is, unless I am very much mistaken, based on an erroneous translation of the relevant lines; it renders as negatives two verbal forms which should be rendered as positives, and interprets one of the crucial lines as an exclamatory question implying a negative answer, when it is actually a straight declarative sentence. In short, as the translation in SM 44 indicates, not only is there no question of Ninlil's being raped by Enlil, on the contrary, at the instigation of her mother, Ninlil sets the trap and gets her man.[39]

38 Jacobsen's transliteration and translation of the passage will be found in *JNES* 5:132-3, note 9. It is to be noted, however, that the translation of the verb *ba-ra-è* in lines 6 and 7 of the passage as "will leave" is unjustified since it should then read *ba-ra-è-dè;* the rendering of *ba-ra-è* is "he left." These two lines, therefore, are not part of a direct discourse attributed to the gods, as indeed is also indicated to a certain extent by the fact that there is no statement in the text designating these two lines as the words of the deities.

39 The passage reads as follows (cf. *BBI* pl. VIII 13ff. and particularly the photograph on pl. XXXII of the same work or on pl. XI of *SM*; the first four lines are duplicated in *JRAS* 62:190, 13 ff., the several variants involved are not pertinent to the present discussion):

u_4 *-ba ki-siki̯l ama-ugu-na ša na mu-un-ri-ri*
^{d}*nin-lɪ̯l-li* ^{d}*nun-bar-še-gu-nu ša na mu-un-ri-ri*
i̯d-kug-ga nunuz-e i̯d-kug-ga-àm a nam-mi-tu$_5$*-tu*$_5$
^{d}*nin-lɪ̯l-li gù-id-nun-bi-ir-ka nam-mu-ni-du̯-dè*
.i-bi̯-kug-ga-àm ù-mu-un-e i-bi̯-kug-ga-àm .i-bi̯ ba-ši-bar-ri
kur-gal-a-a-^{d}*mu-ul-lɪ̯l i-bi̯-kug-ga-àm i-bi̯ ba-ši-bar-ri*
sipad-na-NE-nam-tar-tar-ri i-bi̯-kug-ga-àm :i-bi̯ ba-ši-bar-ri
a-da-lam mu-bi àm-i-i te àm-mi-su-ub-bi
šà-ḫùl-a ḫi-li šà-g̯i-si a-na-àm mu-un-di-ni-ib-kɪ̯d-kɪ̯d
....[na]mu-un-ni-in-ri-ga mu-uš-túg ŠI mu-na-si-èm
[i̯d-kug]-ga-àm munus-e i̯d-kug-ga-àm .im-ma-ni-tu$_5$*-tu*$_5$
[^{d}*nin-lɪ̯l]-li gù-id-gù-nun-bi-ir-ka .i-im-du-dè*
[.igi-kug-g]a-àm lugal-e igi-kug-ga-àm igi .im-ma-ši-in-bar
[kur-gal]-a-a-^{d}*en-lɪ̯l .igi-kug-ga-àm igi .im-ma-ši-in-bar*
[sipad-na-NE]-nam-tar-tar-ri .igi-kug-ga-àm igi-im-ma-ši-in-bar

A comparison of the translation in SM 44 with that on pp. 152-3 of the book under review shows that the most crucial differences involve the rendering of the verbal forms *nam-mi-tu*$_5$*-tu*$_5$ and *nam-mu-ni-du-dè* in the third and fourth lines of the passage, which because of the ambiguous *nam-* may be taken either as negatives or positives, depending on the context (cf. now Falkenstein, *ZA* 47.181 ff.; for the translation of the first lines of our passage, cf. Falkenstein, *ZA* 47.194 ff. and *ZA* 48.118 ff., and note that in the case of the verb *na—ri*, Falkenstein has mistaken *na* for a thematic particle). SM 44 takes these two verbal forms as positives (thus "wash thyself" and "walk" for Jacobsen's "do not bathe" and "do not climb") since the tenth line of the passage, if rendered as a usual declarative sentence reads "... unto the

The second myth treated in this section is the "Tilmun" poem involving primarily the deities Enki and Ninḫursag. The reader is now in a position to follow the text with transliteration, translation, and commentary in *SS* No. 1; whatever differences in translation and interpretation are found in the work under review will have to await Jacobsen's future linguistic documentation.[40]

39 proferred instructions she at the same time gave heed" (for *ŠI* with the meaning "at the same time," cf. *GSG* 406 and *AS* 10:18, note 49); the "at the same time" probably refers to Ninlil's action as described in the preceding line 9 of the passage whose meaning is obscure, and whose word division is largely a matter of guesswork and may turn out to be quite incorrect, but whose initial words *šà-ḫúl-a* "joyous heart" (or perhaps "with joyous heart") tend to indicate that Ninlil was only too happy to carry out her mother's instructions. Jacobsen, however, having concluded that the motive for the seizure of Enlil by the gods is rape, renders the lines as an exclamatory question implying a negative answer, a translation that, as far as I am aware, is unparalleled and unjustified.

Several other points to be noted are (1) the rendering "climb" for the verbal forms in lines 4 and 12 of the passage seems to be based on the reading *gub* of the sign *DU*, a reading which seems unlikely since the verbal form would then have ended in *-gub-bu-dè* rather than *- DU-dè;* (2) the translation "he will embrace thee" for *mu-bí àm-i-i* (line 8 of the passage) must be a guess based on the context; as far as I am aware there is no lexicographical evidence to support it; (3) Jacobsen's rendering "woman" for the *nunuz-e* of line 3 of the passage is of course preferable to "maid"; note the interesting fact that the Emesal writes *nunuz* for the Eme-KU *munus;* (4) the translation "forthwith" for *adalam* in line 8 of the passage is quite justified fied; it was an error to omit it in *SM*. As for the positive statement that follows the translation on p. 153, that "Enlil sees Ninlil, tries to seduce her, and when she refuses, takes her by force," it is to be carefully noted that except for Enlil's catching sight of Ninlil, the evidence for this statement is far from assured; it seems to be based on *BBI* 4 i 28-9 which may perhaps be restored to read: [*lugal-e* NE]*-bí-e inim mu-na-ab-bi nu-da-ra-ši-ib-še-gi* [*d en-líl*]*-li* NE*-bí-e inim mu-na-ab-bi nu-un-da-ra-ši-ib-še-gi* "[the king] .... says a word to her (but) she is unwilling, [Enlil] ....' says a word to her (but) she is unwilling" (for the *-da-ra-* cf. *AS* 12:79 comment to line 85). From there on, as can be seen from the photograph of the tablet, the text is destroyed either wholly or in part for about fifteen lines, and there is nothing to indicate that Enlil attacked Ninlil and raped her.

Finally in the case of the passage translated on p. 154 (beginning with the lines "Enlil calls unto the gatekeeper") it will be noted that its first line corresponds to line 5 of the first-cited passage in *SM* 45, that they then correspond except for relatively minor deviations in the renderings for the next five lines, but that from there on they diverge almost entirely. This is due to the fact that Jacobsen follows here the text of the bilingual published in *JRAS* 62:191, 16-end while the translation in *SM* follows *BBI* 4 ii 26 ff. and several unpublished duplicates (cf. *SM* 114, note 48 where *SEM* 76 is to be added). Moreover, it is to be noted that the bilingual shows a confused text at this point, since lines 17-18 of its reverse are written in the Emesal, although according to line 16 it is Enlil, not Ninlil, who is speaking. Also to be noted is the fact that the renderings "Thou shalt, O man, not embrace, thou shalt, O man, not kiss" (for *JRAS* 62:191,21) and "Has Enlil shown favor" (for *ibid.*, line 23) are hardly justified by the text, and are no doubt based on the context.

40 For an attempt to justify the translation of the first four lines of the myth, cf. *JNES* 5:131, note 7; it seems to me to fail for the following reasons: (1) According to this translation (cf. especially the statement at the very end of the note which

Following a brief sketch of the myth devoted to Enki and the organization of the universe, which in the main agrees with the outline of the myth to be found in *SM* 62 ff., the chapter continues with the myth devoted to the creation of man, in which Enki and Ninmaḫ are the major protagonists. As the reader will note, the version given in this chapter and that to be found in *SM* agree closely up to the point where Enki starts the creating; from there on the divergence between the two versions is quite considerable. But since, in spite of a renewed and careful study of the available text of the myth, I am still unable to find little to justify Jacobsen's statements with regard to the second half of the myth, it will be wiser to await his detailed linguistic analysis before reaching a definite conclusion.[41]

The last Sumerian myth[42] treated in this chapter concerns the wooing of Inanna by the shepherd-god Dumuzi; its contents are outlined in *SM* 101-3. A comparison of the two versions reveals once again that while there is considerable agreement with regard to the earlier portions of the myth, they differ radically in the interpretation of the contents of the latter half of the myth. A renewed study of the text shows that while

40 refers to the publication of *SS* 1; it indicates that the translation for the first and third lines should be identical, since even in the first line the adjective following *ki* is *kug*, not *sikil*) lines 1 and 2 are identical in reading with lines 3 and 4; in view of what is known of Sumerian poetry, it is much more likely that line 1 begins with a word of general meaning such as *ki* "place" while line 3 begins with a word which actually names the place intended (note, too, that the break at the beginning of lines 2 and 4 seems to be too large for the restoration of the sign KUR alone, unless it be assumed that these lines are indented, in which case they should of course not be numbered separately). (2) Jacobsen's translation of the second half of lines 1 and 3 has a forced ring which is difficult to pin down; particularly it seems rather unlikely that the *-ba-* is here used with the meaning "divide". Finally, there is one other point worth mentioning in connection with this myth: Jacobsen was quite right in pointing out in *JNES* 5:143 that I omitted a reference to Scheil in which it is shown that the goddess Uttu had something to do with clothing rather than plants. However it is difficult to see how this justifies the statement there made that "the greater part of the myth of Enki and Ninḫursagga(sic!) is fatally obscured"; indeed the outline of the story of the myth in the book under review agrees to a very large extent with that in *SM* and in *SS* 1.

41 Particularly doubtful is the correctness of the statement that Enki fashioned *two* creatures; the relevant text seems to have room for the creation of only one creature. Far from certain, too, is the assumption that the phrase *u_d-mu-ul* represents the name given by Enki to the creature he created, and quite doubtful, too, of course is its assumed meaning "my day is remote," and the resulting conclusion that it was he who "brought into the world sickness and all other miseries attendant upon old age." In fact, the reader will do well to note that, for the present at least, the final part of the myth is still basically and tantalizingly unintelligible.

42 The chapter does not end, however, with this Sumerian myth; it concludes with a detailed analysis of the Akkadian poem *Enuma eLish*. In the case of this myth, too, an excellent translation is marred by unjustifiable interpretations attributing to the authors of the myth theological and cosmological speculations which they never intended.

Jacobsen has seen penetratingly in several places where I failed to see, particularly in the first half of the text, he has seriously misinterpreted the latter half. However, as will soon become apparent, even the *SM* version of this part of the myth now needs considerable revision. Fortunately the major part of the text of the myth is extant and available in published form, and the following transliteration and translation should make it possible for the cuneiformist to make his own decision in the crucial cases.[43]

Transliteration

1. *lú-ki-sikil túr* ....   2. *ki-sikil-^dinanna amaš* ....
3. *ab-sín-na-GAM-GAM_e(?)* ....   4. *^dinanna ..-e-RI-LU-LU* ....
5. *túg(?)* ....   6. *in-nín* ....
7. *...-DU nu-me-en NE* ....   8. *....-ta AN AN* ....
9. *.... dam-si̯pad-da* ....
10. *šeš-a-ni ur-sag-šul-^dutu*
11. *kug-^dinanna-[ra] gù mu-un-na-dé-e*
12. *nín-mu ḫé-tuku-tuku su₈-ba-dè*
13. *ki-sikil-^dinanna za-e a-na-aš nu-ub-še-gi-en*
14. *iá-ni dùg-ga-àm ga(!)-ni dùg-ga-àm*[44]
15. *lú-su₈-ba níg-šu-dug₄-ga-ni za lag-za lag-ga-àm*[45]
16. *^dinanna ḫé*[46]*tuku-tuku ^dtu-mu-zi-[dè]*[47]
17. *[u]nu-lú-šuba-lú za-e a-na-[aš] nu-ub-še-gi-en*[48]
18. *iá-ni dùg-ga mu-un-da-kú-e*
19. *an-dùl-e-lugal-la*[49] *za-e a-na-aš nu-ub-še-gi-en*
20. *[me(?)-e(?)] su₈-ba-dè*[50] *ba-ra-mu-tuku-tuku-un*[51]

43. The poem is reconstructed from the following texts: 1-end = A (*SRT* 3) obv. and rev.; 10-26 = B (*SEM* 92) obv; 34(?)-39(?) = C (*SEM* 93) obv.; 46-56 = C rev.; 60-74(?) = B rev.
44 In B the line seems to read *[.iá-dùg-ga-k]e₄ ga-dùg-ga-ke₄.*
45 In B the second part of the line probably reads *níg-šu-dug₄-ga-za lag-za lag-ga-[ke₄].*
46 B inserts *-e-* after *ḫé-.*
47 B has the expected Eme-KU form *^ddumu-zi.*
48 B inserts two lines between lines 17 and 18, which read: *.iá-dùg-ga-àm ga-[dùg-ga-àm] [lú]-su₈-ba níg-šu-dug₄-ga za lag-za lag-[ga-àm].* For the writing *su₈-ba*, cf. note 76.
49 B seems to have *-e* for *-la.*
50 In B an illegible gloss follows *-dè.*
51 B probably inserts *-un-* after *ba-ra-mu-.*

21. [túg(?)]-gibil-la-na⁵² ba-ra-mi-ni-ga-ga-an⁵³

22. ....-mu-dè⁵⁴ DI ba-ra-mu-e-en

23. k[i-s]ikil-mèn me-e mu-un-kàr-e⁵⁵ dè-mu-tuku-tuku-un⁵⁶

24. mu-un-kàr-gu-gùn-gùn-a-da⁵⁷

25. mu-un-kar-še-gùn-gùn-a-da

26. .... gú ....

(Approximately 7 lines destroyed.)

34. me[-e] ....

35. inim(?)-bi ....

36. sipad-ra ....

37. lugal-[e-pa₅-apin] ....

38. su₈-ba-ᵈtu-mu-s[i] ....

39. ... dug₄-gi-dè(?) ....

40. e[nga]r-e mà-a-ra engar-e mà-a-ra engar-e
        a-na mu-un-dirig-ga-àm

41. [ᵈ]en-ki-im-du lú-e-pa₅-apin-ke₄

42. mà-a-ra engar-e a-na mu-un-dirig-ga-àm

43. túg-gíg-ga-ni ha-ma-ab-si-mu

44. engar-ra ganam-gíg-mu mà-e ga-mu-na-ši-ib-si

45. túg-babbar-babbar-ra-ni ha-ma-ab-si-mu

46. engar-ra ganam-babbar-babbar-ra-mu ga-mu-na-ši-ib-si

47. e-ne kaš-sag-gá-ni ha-ma-am-dé-e

48. engar-ra ga-sig₇-a-mu ga-mu-na-ši-in-dé

49. e-ne kaš-sig₅-ni ha-ma-an-dé-e

50. engar-ra ga-ki-si-i[n-mu] ga-mu-na-ši-in-si

---

52 B: −lá-a-ni for −la-na; in B the complex is followed by a gloss reading ṣú(?)-ba-ti-šu na-ap-ši-in.

53 B: −mu− for −mi−.

54 B seems to have a variant complex which reads ....−lá-a-ni; it is followed by a gloss reading: ri-?-? ša ši-pa-ti-šu.

55 B: −ri for −e.

56 B probably inserts −un− after −mu−.

57 B probably has −na− for −a−.

51. *e-ne*⁵⁸ *kaš-sá-gi₄-a-ni*⁵⁹ *ḫa-ma-an-dé-e*

52. *engar-ra ga-BU₅-a-mu ga-mu-na-ši-in-dé*

53. *e-ne kašbir-a-ni ḫa-ma-an-dé-e*

54. *engar-ra mà-e ga-ù-mu ga-mu-na-ši-in-dé*

55. *ḫa-ḫa-la-sig₅-ni*⁶⁰ *ḫa-ma-ab-ší-mu*

56. *engar-ra*⁶¹ *ga-ì-ti-ir-da-mu*⁶² *ga-mu-na-ši-ib-ší*

57. *ninda-sig₅-ni ḫa-ma-ab-ší-mu*

58. *engar-ra ga-ḪU[R-l]d̀-a-mu ga-mu-na-ši-ib-ší*

59. *gù-du₁₃du₁₃-ld-ni ḫa-ma-ab-ší-mu*

60. *engar-ra ga-ḪUR-tur-tur-mu ga-mu-na-ši-ib-ší*

61. *ù-mu-ni-kú*⁶³ *ù-mu-ni-nag-[g]d̀(?)-ta*

62. *id-níg-dirig-ga*⁶⁴ *ga-mu-na-ra-ab-šub*

63. *ga-níg-dirig-ga ga-mu-na-ra-ab-šub*

64. *mà-a-ra engar-e a-na mu-un-dirig-g[a-àm]*⁶⁵

65. *ul àm-te ul àm-te gaba ki-a-a ul àm-te*⁶⁶

66. *ki-a-àm sipad-dè kf̠₆₈d̀[m ul-àm-te]*

67. *sipad-dè ki-a-d̀[m]*⁶⁷*udu na-an-ga-àm-[mi-in-dib]*

68. *sipad-ki-a-a-dib-dib-a-ra*

69. *lù-sipad-ra engar*⁶⁸ *mu-na-ni-[in-te]*⁶⁹

70. *engar-ᵈen-ki-im*⁷⁰*du m[u-na-ni-in-te]*⁷¹

71. *ᵈdumu-zi lugal-e-pa₅-RI....*⁷²

72. *edin-a-na sipad-dè*⁷³ *[edin]-a-na du₁₄ mu-u[n-di-ni-ib-mù-mù]*

58 So C; A omits *e-ne*.
59 C: *-sa-* for *-sá-*.
60 C: *šag₅-ga* for *-sig₅-ni-*.
61. In C *mà-e* follows *engar-ra*.
62 C: *-i-te-* for *-ì-ti-*.
63 B: *-šub* for *-kú*; the complex is followed by the gloss *.i-?-?*.
64 B seems to omit *-ga*; the complex is followed by a gloss ending in *-im*.
65 Line omitted in B.
66 In B, rev. 5-6 correspond to this line; the first legible sign in line 5 is TE; the first legible sign in line 6 is UL (not MI).
66a The traces in B do not point to the reading *ki-*.
67 B: *-a* for *-àm*.
68 B: *engar*(!).
69 B: inserts *-un-* after *mu-*.
70 B: *-im*(!).
71 B: inserts *-un-* after *mu-*.
72 B seems to insert *engar* before *lugal-*.
73 B may have a gloss after *-dè*.

73. [s]u$_8$-ba-^{d}dumu-zi-dè edin-a-na du$_{14}$mu-un-di-ni-ib-mí-mí

74. mà-a za-a-da su$_8$-ba za-a-da su$_8$-ba mí-a za-a-da^{74}

75. a-na-aš mu-da-ab-si$_g$-e-en

76. udu-zu ú-ki-a ḫé-im-mi-kú

77. pa-še-mà udu-zu ḫé-im-mi-dib(?)

78. a-šà-šuba-unu^{ki}-ga še ḫa-ba-ni-in-nag

79. mí(!)-si la$_4$(!)-zu id-U$_4$.NUN-mà a ḫa-ba-ni-in-nag

80. lú-sipad-me-en nam-nita lam-mu-še

81. engar ku-li-mà na-ba-ni-in-tu-ra

82. engar-^{d}en-ki-im-du ku-li-mà engar ku-li-mà

83. na-ba-ni-in-tu-ra-àm

84. gig ga-mu-ra-túm gú ga-mu-ra-túm

85. gú-nunuz-BIR-SIL$_5$-na ga-mu-ra-túm

86. lú-ki-sikil níg-za-a-ra-sì-ga

87. ki-sikil-^{d}inanna še-gín gú-SAL ga-mu-ra-túm

88. sipad-engur-da-a-da-man-dug$_4$-ga

89. ki-sikil-^{d}inanna sà-sa l-zu dùg-ga-àm

90. bal-bal-e-dam

Translation

1. Who is a maid, the stable ....^{75}

2. The maid, Inanna, the sheepfold ....

3. *Kneeling in* the furrows ....

4. Inanna ....

5. *A garment* ....

6. ....

7. .... I am not ....

8. *From* ....

9. .... wife of the shepherd ....

10. Her brother, the hero, the warrior, Utu^{76}

74 In B the traces do not seem to correspond to any of the signs in this line.

75 Lines 1-9 are too fragmentary for a reasonable guess at their contents; the transliteration and translation are based on the more or less obvious readings and renderings, and may of course turn out to be unjustified when the full text is recovered. In line 6, the epithet .in-nín, which superficially seems to be a play on the name of Inanna, is found used not only of Inanna (cf. e.g. SLTN 13:1, PBS X 4 No. 9 obv. 24 (.in(!)-nín); PBS XII 47 obv. 8; ibid. rev. 12 (in-nín(!)); SRT 1 i 16), but also of Ninisinna, cf. SRT 6 ii 32 (= ibid. 7:7).

76 Lines 10-19. A comparison of the new translation with that in SM shows a number of significant changes due primarily to Jacobsen's fruitful efforts, particularly his insight into the grammatical structure of the passage. Thus he noted that ḫé-tuku-tuku, in lines 12 and 16, is a finite verb whose subject follows rather than precedes

11. Says to the pure Inanna:

12. "O my sister, let the shepherd marry thee,

13. O maid Inanna, why art thou unwilling?

14. His fat is good, his milk is good,

15. The shepherd, everything his hand touches is bright,

16. O Inanna, let the shepherd Dumuzi marry thee,

17. O thou who ...., why art thou unwilling?

18. His good fat he will eat with thee,

19. O *protector of* the king, why art thou unwilling?"

10. "[*Me*] the shepherd shall not marry, [77]

21. In his new [*garment*] he shall not *drape* me,

22. *Then I* .... he shall not .. me,

23. Me, the maid, let the farmer marry,

24. The farmer who makes *plants* grow abundantly,

25. The farmer who makes grain grow abundantly,

76 it. Again in lines 20-23 he noted that the final *–en* (*–un, –an*) is the accusative
particle of the *first* person singular added to the third person singular present-
future of the verb. This seems to be contrary to the conclusion reached in *AS* 10:30
where the form *ba–e–dib–bi* "it will seize thee" indicates that the accusative pronominal element when added to a third person singular present future precedes the
root, unless of course we assume that the accusative *second* person singular pronominal
element is treated differently from the accusative *first* person pronominal element.
Note that *ḫé–tuku–tuku* "let (him) marry thee" of lines 12 and 16 when compared with
dè–mu–tuku–tuku–un "let (him) marry me" (line 23) seems to point in the same direction
(perhaps, too, the variant *ḫé–e–* for *ḫé–*, in line 16, is significant, that is, the *–e–*
is the accusative second person singular pronominal element). In line 16 the translation follows Jacobsen in reading *ga* "milk" (as in B) rather than *kaš* "date-wine" (as
in A, where it may be a miscopy); it is milk, not date-wine, which is the shepherd's
major product. On the other hand, it seems preferable to translate *ìa* as "fat" rather
than "butter" since the latter is regularly *ìa–nun*. In line 16 note the rather unexpected Emesal writing for Dumuzi (in A only; B has the Eme-KU form; cf. note 47);
so, too, the writing *sug–ba* for *sipad* in lines 12 and 15 (cf. also lines 73 and 74)
seems unjustified. For the restoration of *unû–* in line 17, cf. e. g. *SRT* 6 ii 29, 33
(*.ibid.* 7:4-8); the meaning of *unû–lá–šuba–lá* which seems to be used here as an epithet
if Inanna (it parallels the *ki–sikil* of line 13 and the *an–dùl–e–lugal–la* of line 19)
is obscure. In line 19, if the translation of *an–dùl–e–lugal–la* proves correct, the
–e– following *–dùl–* is inexplicable.

77.Lines 20-34. In line 21, the translation follows the text in A; the gloss in B is not
clear to me. In line 22, the translation follows the text in A (in *SM* the translation
followed the text in B and assumed that *–gibil–* is to be restored before *–lá–*).
Jacobsen's translation seems to follow the gloss in B (note, however, that only the
word *šipátišu* is certain and that therefore the first sign in B obv. 15 is perhaps to
be restored as *sig*). The verb in line 22 is left untranslated, since there seems to be
no lexicographical indication as to its meaning. In lines 24-5, the translation assumes
that *gùn–gùn–a–da* is the grammatical *gun–gun–ed–àm*; it is to be noted, however, that

2e. ....

(Approximately 7 lines are destroyed.)

34. Me ...."

35. This *matter* ....[78]

36. To the shepherd ....

37. The king of [dyke, ditch, and plow] ....

38. The shepherd Dumuzi ....

39. .... *to speak* ....

40. "The f[arme]r (more) than I, the farmer (more)thar I, the farmer, what has he more
(than I)?[79]

---

77 the particle *–dm* is regularly written in A (cf. e.g. lines 14, 40, 42, etc.). Another
possibility is that the final *–da* is the postposition and that the translation should
therefore read "With the farmer who makes *plants* grow abundantly, With the farmer who
makes grain grow abundantly" (the end of the sentence would then have to be sought in
the broken lines that follow); if so, *gùn–gùn–a–da* is perhaps for grammatical *gùn–
gùn–e(d)–da*. Note finally that in line 24, Jacobsen's translation of *gu* as "beans"
seems to assume that it is synonymous with *gú* of line 59. Line 34, if the restoration
me–e proves correct, is written in the Emesal, and may therefore mark the end of
Inanna's answer to Utu.

78 Lines 35-39. These lines are too fragmentary for constructive comment. Note that line
38 may be written in the Emesal; cf., however, note 76 for evidence that the writings
su$_g$–ba and *^{d}fūmu–z.i* are not conclusive criteria for Emesal orthography, particularly
in the case of A.

79 Lines 40-64. In line 40 (also lines 42 and 64) note the idiomatic use of the postposition *–ra* with the verb *dirig*. For the rendering *e* (line 41) as "dyke" cf.
particularly Thureau-Dangin in *RA* 34:179; *–apin–ke$_4$* is for the grammatical *apin–(a)k–
e*, and might have been expected to be written *apin–na–ke$_4$*. Note that lines 41-2 are
erroneously omitted from the translation in *SM* 102. The new rendering of lines 43ff.
indicates more clearly than the *SM* translation the force of the *ha–* and the *ga–* of
the verbal forms. In lines 44 and 46, Jacobsen's "wool" seems to indicate a misread-
ing *síg* for *ganam*. In line 47, Jacobsen's "prime" for *sag* is preferable to "first"
in *SM*; for the meaning of *kaš*, cf. Poebel in *ZA* 39:146 ff. For the rendering
"stultifying" cf *sá–gi$_4$–a* in line 51, cf. *SL* 261:112; the erroneous translation in
SM is due to a confusion with *ša–gi$_4$–a*. As for the BU$_5$ in *ga–BU$_5$* of line 52, it
might perhaps be expected to have a meaning corresponding to that of *sá–gi$_4$–a* of the
preceding line; the rendering "bubbling" *SM* was a guess based on such equations as
BU$_5$ = *napāḫu*, and should have been indicated as highly doubtful. In Line 55, *ha–ha–la
du$_{19}$–ld* with *gú* while in line 60 *tur–tur* seems to be used with exactly the same
meaning after *ga–ḪUR*. In lines 61-3, note that the new rendering differs considerably
from that in *SM*; it translates *ù–mu–ni–kú* and *ù–mu–ni–nag* as *first* rather than *third*
person verbal forms; still obscure is the nuance intended by the *–ni–* of these forms.
For the meaning of line 61, cf. *kurun–níg–dùg ù–mu–un–nag–eš–[a–ta] kaš–níg–dùg ù–
mu–un–dùg–gi–eš–a–t[a]a–kàr–a–kàr–ra du$_{14}$ mi–ni–ib–mú–m[ú–n]e* "[After] they (i.e.
Laḫar and Ašnan) had drunk the good wine, [af]ter they had .imbibed the good date-
wine, they start a quarrel in the meadows" (cf. *SEM* 55 rev. 10-12+ibid. 57 obv. 3-
5; see also .ibid. 56 obv. 6-8). In lines 62-3, the rendering "leave" for *šub* is
quite uncertain; the rendering "pour" in *SM* is altogether unjustifiable. For the

41. Enkimdu, the man of dyke, ditch, and plow,

42. (More) than I, the farmer, what has he more (than I)?

43. Should he give me his black garment,

44. I would give him, the farmer, my black ewe for it;

45. Should he give me his white garment,

46. I would give him, the farmer, my white ewe for it;

47. Should he pour me his prime date-wine,

48. I would pour him, the farmer, my yellow milk for it;

49. Should he pour me his good date-wine,

50. I would pour him, the farmer, [my] *kisi[m]*-milk for it;

51. Should he pour me his *stultifying* date-wine,

52. I would pour him, the farmer, my .. milk for it;

53. Should he pour me his diluted date-wine,

54. I would pour him, the farmer, my *plant*-milk for it;

55. Should he give me his good *portions,*

56. I would give him, the farmer, my *itirda*-milk for them;

57. Should he give me his good bread,

58. I would give him, the farmer, my *honey*-cheese for it;

59. Should he give me his small beans,

60. I would give him, the farmer, my small cheeses for them;

61. After *I* shall have eaten, shall have drunk,

62. I would *leave* him the extra fat,

63. I would leave him the extra milk;

64. (More) than ·I, the farmer, what has he more (than I)?"

65. He rejoiced, he rejoiced, .. *on* the river-bank rejoiced,[80]

---

79 rendering of lines 61-4, cf. now Falkenstein, *ZA* 45:188ff. where, unfortunately,
   they are treated without regard to the context of the poem as a whole.
80 Lines 65-73. In line 65 *ul—te* (cf. also *TRS* pl. CXXXVII:54') seems to be merely a
   phonetic variant for the more common *ul—ti*; the meaning of *gaba* is altogether uncertain in the context; *ki-a-a* is assumed to be grammatical *ki-a-e*. In line 66 *ki-a-àm*
   is assumed to be grammatical *ki-a(-e)-àm*, but the reason for the introduction of *-àm*
   (B omits it) is not clear; the restoration of the verb is of course uncertain. The
   cause of Dumuzi's rejoicing is unstated in the text, but it seems not unreasonable to
   assume that it was due to a change in Inanna's attitude resulting from his argument;
   that is, *although it is nowhere explictly stated in the text,* we are probably to
   understand that Inanna has now consented to marry Dumuzi, rather than Enkimdu; cf.
   lines 80-83 which point in the same direction. In line 67, the restoration of the
   verbal root *-dib* is based on line 75. The restoration of the verbal root in lines 69
   and 70 is of course quite uncertain, but in any case the verb must be intransitive

66. *On* the river-bank, the shepherd *on* the river-bank [*rejoiced*],

67. The shepherd, moreover, [*led*] the sheep *on* the river-bank.

68. To the shepherd *walking to and fro on* the river-bank,

69. To him who is a shepherd, the farmer [*approached*],

70. The farmer Enkimdu [*approached*],

71. Dumuzi, the farmer, the king of dyke, ditch ....

72. In his plain, the shepherd in his [plain starts] a quarrel with him,

73. The [sh]epherd Dumuzi in his plain starts a quarrel with him.

74. "I against thee, O shepherd, against thee, O shepherd, I against thee[81]

75. Why shall I strive?

76. Let thy sheep eat the grass of the river-bank,

77. In my *meadow land* let thy sheep walk about,

78. In the bright fields of Erech let them eat grain,

79. Let thy *kids* and *lambs* drink the water of my U_4.NUN canal."

80. "As for me, who am a shepherd, at my marriage,[82]

80 since the subject is not followed by the particle *-e*. Line 71 is so fragmentary that it is difficult to fit into the context; it is to be noted, however, that ^{d}*dumu-zi* is not followed by the subject element and that therefore if it is the subject (it may of course be a direct object) the verb must again be intransitive. Note the new renderings for lines 72-3; particularly important is the fact that they are not part of Enkimdu's address as taken in *SM* where the rendering for *edin* was omitted altogether, while *a-na* was assumed to be the interrogative pronoun. For the meaning of line 73, cf. the passage cited toward the end of note 79. Just what the implication of "in his plain" (as opposed to the "river-bank" of the preceding lines) is, is not clear; perhaps the contents of line 71, when restored, may shed some light on the matter.

81 Lines 76-79. These lines contain Enkimdu's placating speech to Dumuzi; Jacobsen's assumption that it is Inanna who speaks these lines is proved erroneous by the fact that they are written in the Eme-KU dialect; Inanna's words, as can be seen from lines 20-26 of our text, would be reproduced in the Emesal. Note the rendering of the verbs in lines 76-79 as precatives even though they are preterit in form; cf. *SS* 1:27, note 56. For the rendering of lines 74-5, cf. *SLTN* 16 rev. 10: *é-me-eš-dumu-mu en-te-en-šeš-zu-ta a-na mu-da-ab*(!)-*si̯-e-en* "Emeš, my son, why dost thou strive against thy brother Enten" (Enlil is speaking). In line 79, the reading *mèš* and *sila₄* for the first two signs (instead of *gú* and *ùr*(?) as in the copy) is based on Jacobsen's insight, as is obvious from his translation of the line; as for U_4.NUN, since it is not followed by the determinative *ki*, it is by no means certain that it is to be read *adab*.

82. Lines 80-83. These lines contain Dumuzi's answer to Enkimdu in which he invites the latter to his marriage, presumably with Inanna. As the reader will note, this new rendering not only differs from that of Jacobsen, who treats it as part of an address by Inanna, but is also the exact opposite of the rendering in *SM*. For here again we find the verbal form introduced by the ambiguous *na-*, and on form alone may be taken either as positive or negative in meaning. The new rendering which takes it as a positive is based on the context and particularly on the following passage in the

81. O farmer, mayest thou be counted as my friend,

82. O farmer Enkimdu, as my friend, O farmer, as my friend,

83. Mayest thou be counted as my friend."

84. "I would bring thee wheat, I would bring thee beans,[83]

85. I would bring thee ....,

86. O thou who art a maid, whatever is .. to thee,

87. O maid Inanna, ... I would bring thee."

88. In the dispute which took place between the shepherd and the farmer,[84]

89. O maid Inanna, thy praise is good.

90. It is a "bal-bal-e."

82. Lugalbanda-Enmerkar poem (cf. PAPS 90:123) in which the IM-DUGUD bird, after finding his young safe in his nest, utters the following lines:

lú g̃ùd-mà ne-eñ ba-e-a-ag
dingir ḫé-me-en inim ga-mu-ra-ab-dug₄
ku-li-mà nam-ba-e-ni-in-tu-ra-àm
lú-lu₆ ḫé-me-en nam ga-mu-ri-ib-tar
kur-r̃i gaba-šu-gar nam-mu-r̃í-in-tuku-tuku
mes-ᵈIM-DUGUD-dè-á-sì-ma ḫé-me-en

"O thou who did *this* in my nest
Be thou a god, I would say a word to thee,
Thou shalt be counted among my friends;
Be thou a man, I would decree thy fate,
The foreign land will not have thy rival,
Verily thou shalt be a hero whom IM-DUGUD has given (his) power."

The texts on which these lines are based are as follows: *SEM* 1 ii 43-7; 2 i 3-end (*SEM* 2 and 4 join); 5 (=*PBS* V 19) ii 3-4; 10 rev. 1-5; 12 rev. 6-10, and the following unpublished texts: UM 29-16-140 (joins *SEM* 1), 29-13-3 (joins *SEM* 7 and 12), 29-16-449 (joins *SEM* 10 and 11), 29-15-356. Among the numerous variants are to be noted *ne-e* for the *ne-en* of the first line, and *-tu-ri-en* for *-tu-ra-àm* in line 3. As the last three lines of our passage seem to show beyond reasonable doubt, IM-DUGUD is offering a reward for a favor rendered him, and *nam-ba-e-ni-in-tu-ra-àm* of the third line must therefore be rendered as a positive (note that if this proves correct, we have in this brief passage one *nam* introducing a positive verbal form, and another, that of line 5, introducing a negative). Finally it is to be noted that *nam-ba-e-ni-tu-ra-àm* (the *-e-* in all probability is due to a pleonastic orthography and is not morphologically significant) might have been expected to end in *tu-r̃i-en-àm*; (that is, the verb is a permansive); this is true also of the verb in lines 81 and 83 of our myth (the omission of *-àm* in line 81 may be a miscopy).

83. Lines 84-87. These lines contain Enkimdu's joyful answer to Dumuzi and, to judge from lines 86-7, to Inanna, who may perhaps be understood to have been present throughout the Dumuzi-Enkimdu dialogue; as a result of the friendly invitation to the wedding, Enkimdu offers to bring them some of the products of his farming. For *gú-nunuz* in line 85, cf. *ŠL* 278:168; for *še-gín* in line 87, cf. *ŠL* 698:243.

84. Lines 88-90. Lines 88-9 contain a comment by the scribe which is typical of this literary genre, cf.*SLTN* 16 rev. 18 ff. and *SEM* 17 rev. 10 ff.; it is rather unfortunate, however, that the line corresponding to *SLTN* 16 rev. 19 and *SEM* 17 rev. 11 is omitted in our case, since that line would have stated who was the victor in the dispute. The last line, *bal-bal-e-dam*, seems to be a variant for the more common *bal-*

The contents of the myth may therefore now be summarized as follows: Following a brief introduction whose contents are largely fragmentary (1-9), we find Utu addressing his sister and urging her to become the wife of the shepherd Dumuzi (10-19). Inanna's answer (20-34?) consists of a flat refusal; she is determined instead to marry the farmer Enkimdu. [85] Following several fragmentary lines of uncertain meaning (35-39), the text continues with a long address of the shepherd directed to Inanna, in which he details his superiority over the farmer (40-64). We then find the shepherd rejoicing on the river bank, probably because his argument had convinced Inanna and induced her to change her mind. [86] There he meets Enkimdu and starts a fight with him (65-73). But Enkimdu refuses to fight and agrees to allow Dumuzi's flocks to pasture anywhere in his territory (74-79). The latter, thus appeased, invites the farmer to his wedding as one of his friends (80-83). Whereupon Enkimdu offers to bring him and Inanna several selected farm-products as a wedding gift (84-87). The scribe then closes the poem with the conventional literary notations.

So much for the first, longest, and most important chapter on the character of speculative thought in ancient Meospotamia, that is, the chapter devoted to the cosmos as a state. In the chapter that follows, entitled "The Function of the State," the reader will find a detailed, lucid, and beautifully analyzed description of the organization of the temple Eninnu in the city-state of Lagash; it is based on a very careful and obviously original study of the texts of the Gudea Cylinders. [87] The chapter then continues with an interesting discussion of the role of kingship in

84 $bal-e$ ^dx(name of deity)$-kam$, cf. e.g. SRT 9 obv. 21; $ibid.$ 23 rev. 28; $SLTN$ 62 rev. 12.

85 Note that there is no introductory statement to indicate who addresses whom in any of the speeches in the poem except the first, Utu's address to Inanna; in all the other cases it is only from the context that we can gather who the speaker is. Helpful in this connection is the dialect in which the speech is reproduced; if the Emesal is used, it is of course Inanna who is speaking.

86 It must be stressed, however, that this is only an inference from the context; it is not expressly stated anywhere in the text.

87 To judge from the statement on p. 189 that "Gudea first noted that something was amiss when the river Tigris, which Ningursu controlled, failed to rise as usual and flood the fields," Jacobsen treats the verbal forms $nam-gi_4$ and nam-DU of Gudea Cyl. I 5, 6, 7, and 9, as negatives. This, unless I am very mistaken, is an error; these verbal forms are in all probability to be taken as positives. That is, the passage refers to a time when Lagash was enjoying a period of prosperity, when Enlil had looked with favorable eye upon Ningirsu, and when, therefore, the Tigris had over-flowed its banks, assuring bounteous crops to the city and its environs. Cf. now Falkenstein, ZA 47.192.

Mesopotamia,[88] and concludes with a very brief analysis of the cult-festivals drama-
tizing the marriage of the gods and their battles, their death and resurrection.

The third and last chapter on Mesopotamia, entitled "The Good Life," begins with
an analysis of the role of obedience as a prime virtue in Mesopotamian life; it is
based largely on new and excellent translations of a number of brief Sumerian "wisdom"
passages.[89] The chapter then takes up several Mesopotamian views with regard to the
problem of justice in the universe, dwelling particularly on Gilgamesh's revolt against
death, on the complaint of the "righteous sufferer," and on the cynical "master-servant"
dialogue which seems to deny all moral values in life.

In conclusion, one cannot praise too highly Mrs. Frankfort's poetical renditions
of the cited Sumerian and Akkadian passages. Largely by means of expert, precise, and
unusually apt selection of her words, she has succeeded in transforming the more
literal and stilted translations of the scholar into flexible and effective poetic
idiom; at the same time her renderings have lost none of the original meaning and none
of its rhythmic flavor. All in all it is a masterful achievement, and sets an example
which future translators, including the present writer, will do well to follow.

88 On p. 192 the statement that Enlil was "commander of the armed forces" is hardly
   justified by the available evidence, for nowhere in the extant texts is it stated
   that Enlil led the gods in   battle. Whenever Enlil has difficulties with foreign
   lands, for example, he sends "heroic" deities such as Ninurta, Nergal, and Ninisinna
   to do battle with his enemies, but there is no indication that Enlil himself ever
   deigns to do the actual fighting.
89 The Sumerian passage translated on p. 202, be it noted, is not part of a "hymn" but
   belongs to a composition known as the "Lamentation Over the Destruction of Nippur"
   (cf. now *SLTN* 33); it is part of the latter half of the composition, which eulogizes
   the delivery of Nippur and its restoration by Išme-Dagan of Isin. To be noted, too,
   is the fact that it is not quite certain whether the Akkadian letter translated on
   pp. 205-6 is actually one addressed to a deity.

University Museum   S. N. Kramer
University of Pennsylvania

MYTH AND THE OLD TESTAMENT

I. Definition of Myth

The initial difficulty in our topic is the definition of myth. The Oxford English Dictionary defines myth as "a purely fictitious narrative usually involving supernatural persons, actions, or events, and embodying some popular idea concerning natural or historical phenomena." This definition does not represent an opinion which is gaining strength in contemporary scholarship. Some deny that it defines the thing to be defined; others regard it as composed *a priori* and too incomplete to be of much value. This scholarly trend is a recent development in philosophy and anthropology. Most contemporary exegetes, it seems, accept the saying of Hermann Gunkel that there is no myth in the OT. Myth, according to Gunkel, was by its nature polytheistic, and it frequently represents the deity in close connection with nature.[1] If this is the proper understanding of myth, then there is no room for further discussion of the topic of this paper.[2] But the question has been raised because of the efforts of philosophers and anthropologists to define myth in such a way as to remove the note of falsehood, which popular opinion places in the very definition; and exegetes ought to face the question.

One cannot review or even mention all the writers who have attacked this problem: but one cannot ignore the work of Ernst Cassirer. Cassirer treated the problem in more than one of his works, but his opinions remained substantially the same in his various writings. He defined myth with art, language, and science as a symbolic form of expression. These four have in common that they are "forces each of which produces and posits a world of its own."[3] The mythic mind is not the abstract analytical mind of discursive thought.[4] Myth is an intuition, not an abstraction or a discourse, and the peculiar quality of mythical intuition is that its object, which is the momentary experience, becomes substantial and permanent.[5] Myth differs from art in that it is an act of belief.[6] It perceives physiognomic, not objective characters; its world is a world of actions, forces, and conflicting powers.[7] To mythical and religious feeling nature becomes one great society, the society of life.[8] For Mircel Eliade myth is an autonomous act of creation of the mind which translates an event

---

[1] *RGG* IV, 381.

[2] Stählin covers myth in the OT and in Judaism on one page (*ThWBNT* IV, 787-788).

[3] *Language and Myth* (translated from the German; New York, 1946) 8.

[4] *Ibid.*, 13.

[5] *Ibid.*, 35.

[6] *Essay on Man* (Garden City, 1956) 101.

[7] *Ibid.*, 102.

[8] *Ibid.*, 110.

into a mode of being.[9] Myth expresses in action and drama what metaphysics and theology express dialectically.[10] Myth is not merely story or tradition, because the object of myth is an archetype, which survives in an eternal Now. Myth is not history but exemplar history, the meaning and value of which lie in its repetition.[11] Johannes Hempel calls myth a form of expression of belief, with no judgment about its veracity implied.[12] Myth claims a correspondence with reality.[13] The element common to all myths, according to Eduard Buess, is that they deal with the knowledge of the unknowable.[14] The unknowable here signifies not the absolutely unknowable or mysterious, but that which is unknowable to man in a given concrete stage of intellectual development. The reality which he perceives but cannot recognize and define is inadequately defined by myth.[15] Ultimately myth reduces all causality to the mysterious divine causality which lies beyond perception.[16] Henri Frankfort distinguished mythical thought from logical thought in this, that where logical thought confronts the world of phenomena as an "It," mythical thought confronts it as a "Thou," and mythical thought is dominated by the "I-Thou" personal relationship. Frankfort defines myth as "a form of poetry which transcends poetry in that it proclaims a truth; a form of reasoning which transcends reasoning in that it wants to bring about the truth it proclaims; a form of action, of ritual behavior, which does not find its fulfilment in the act but must proclaim and elaborate a poetic form of truth."[17] Frankfort, generally following Cassirer, has set forth the characteristics of mythopoeic thought: it does not distinguish the subjective and the objective, reality and appearance, life and death, symbol and reality, part and whole, impersonal and personal causality.[18] Myth is not discursive thought, which operates on general principles and accepted laws of thought and being. Admitting that reality cannot be apprehended adequately by myth, mythical thought accepts the validity of more than one avenue of approach. These avenues may be contradictory in their form of expression, but mythical thought dismisses the contradiction, since reality can be expressed only by manifold images. The contradiction lies not in the manifold images of reality but in reality itself. E. O. James writes: ". . . the conception of myth in popular thought and language cannot be sustained since it is not primarily a fictitious narrative setting forth the exploits of supernatural persons and the unusual and fantastic behaviour of natural phenomena, or of historical occurrences."[19] "The chief purpose of . . . myths has been to stabilize the established order both in nature and in society, to confirm belief, to vouch for the efficacy of the cultus, and to

[9] *Patterns in Comparative Religion* (translated from the French; New York, 1958) 426.
[10] *Ibid.*, 418.
[11] *Ibid.*, 429-430.
[12] *ZAW* 65 (1953) 110.
[13] *Ibid.*, 122.
[14] E. Buess, *Geschichte des mythischen Erkennens* (Munich, 1953) 27.
[15] *Ibid.*, 73.
[16] *Ibid.*, 159-162.
[17] *The Intellectual Adventure of Ancient Man* (Chicago, 1946) 8.
[18] *Ibid.*, 11-19.
[19] *Myth and Ritual in the Ancient Near East* (London, 1958) 279.

maintain traditional behaviour and status by means of supernatural sanctions and precedents."[20] "Myth . . . gave expression to the fundamental experience of a divinely ordered world in which a conflict of supernatural powers and forces was immanent, the one hostile and the other beneficial to their well-being. To fulfil its proper functions it must always be a symbolic representation of the ultimate reality, however this may be conceived and interpreted, concerning the essential meaning and facts of existence and of human destinies. . . . Enshrined in it are the deepest realities, the things by which men live. . . . It is a reality lived. Consequently, every vital religion must have its mythology because myth is the natural language of religion just as ritual is its dramatization in worship."[21] M. Leenhardt describes myth as reality apprehended in images, words, and deeds, and notices that myth and rational knowledge coexist not only in ancient but also in modern society, since neither form of mental operation can do the work of the other nor entirely supplant it.[22] G. van der Leeuw has said: "Doctrine can never completely discard the mythical if it wishes to avoid falling to the level of a mere philosophical thesis."[23]

Millar Burrows has summarized the new view of myth as "a symbolic, approximate expression of truth which the human mind cannot perceive sharply and completely but can only glimpse vaguely, and therefore cannot adequately or accurately express. . . . Myth implies, not falsehood, but truth; not primitive, naive misunderstanding, but an insight more profound than scientific description and logical analysis can ever achieve. The language of myth in this sense is consciously inadequate, being simply the nearest we can come to a formulation of what we see very darkly."[24] And G. Henton Davies writes: "Mythology is a way of thinking and imagining about the divine rather than a thinking or imagining about a number of gods. . . . Myth is a way of thinking, independently of a polytheistic setting."[25] Hence it is legitimate to raise the question of myth and the OT once more. The usual denial of myth in the OT does not touch myth as it is understood in these recent studies. These studies may make it possible to accept myth as a vehicle of truth, and as such it is not by definition excluded from the literary forms of the Bible.

In answering the question of myth in the OT we must remember that the concept of myth in modern scholarship is not strictly univocal. There is no generally accepted definition, and the forms of expression which are covered by the term are too diversified to be easily brought together.

[20] *Ibid.*, 283.

[21] *Ibid.*, 307.

[22] In Brillant and Aigrain, *Histoire des Religions* 1 (Paris, n.d.) 89-90.

[23] G. van der Leeuw, *Religion: Its Essence and Manifestation* (translated from the German; London, 1938) 444.

[24] *An Outline of Biblical Theology* (Philadelphia, 1946) 115-116.

[25] *PEQ* 88 (1956) 88.

Much of the constructive work on mythology has been done by anthropologists. When we deal with the peoples of ancient Mesopotamia and Canaan we are not dealing with primitives. The men who built the cities, the industries, and the commercial networks of the ancient world, wrote its literature and created its art cannot be placed on the same level with the Semangs of the Malay peninsula.

I do not think that the difficulty of elaborating a precise and comprehensive concept of myth makes it impossible to give some answer to the question of myth and the OT. This question touches a definite and known collection of literature which has been closely studied: the myths of Mesopotamia and Canaan. It is to this body of literature that we must turn for the answer to our question. We need not create a philosophy of myth in order to answer it. If we can identify certain patterns of thought and expression in this literature, we should be able to tell whether there is anything in the OT which corresponds to these patterns. What we must avoid is a definition of myth so broad that myth ceases to be a distinct intelligible concept. It seems that one can say with Aage Bentzen that myth is not an independent literary type,[26] hence when I employ the word myth in this discussion, a more precise term would be mythopoeic thought, a phrase which is used by Frankfort.

We find it easier to say what myth is not than to say what it is. Myth is not mere metaphor; myth so understood has no identity of its own.[27] Nor is myth mere poetry, poetic apprehension and expression. Myth is not history, even in the sense in which we use the word history of ancient literature; nor is it the story, popular tradition in the usual sense of the word. It seems most unlikely that the Assyrians would have regarded the story of Ishtar's descent to the underworld as the same type of story which might be told of Sennacherib's victorious campaign in western Asia. It is doubtful that myth should be identified entirely with nature myth, although the connection between myth and nature is very close. Here we do well to remind ourselves that in the ancient Near East there was no concept which corresponds to the modern concept of nature.[28] The world of nature was phenomena: numerous, diverse, and often conflicting, hostile or beneficent to man, exhibiting what we call personal traits and understood as a world of personal beings. But myth was not an allegorical view of nature. Nature deities like Aleyan Baal and Anath represented no particular force or phenomenon of nature, unless one wishes to call such things as life,

---

[26] *Introduction to the Old Testament* (Copenhagen, 1948) I, 241.
[27] Cassirer, *Essay on Man*, 84, 94.
[28] Cf. *CBQ* 14 (1952) 18-24.

death, and sex natural forces or phenomena. But there are in Mesopotamia myths which deal with the relations of man with the gods, and these cannot be classified with nature myths.

Myth is not logical discursive thought; hence it is not strictly true to say that myth is a philosophy or a theology. Neither is myth a substitute or an alternate for discursive thought. It does not really do the work of discursive thought, the work of analysis, organization, and synthesis. Those who employed mythical thought did not employ it because they preferred it to discursive thought, at least for some questions, or because they believed it achieved a deeper insight than discursive thought; they employed it because they had no other mode of thought. When discursive thought arose among the Greeks, the-conflict between discursive thought and myth at first led to a self-conscious employment of myth as poetic ornamentation or allegory, then to a rationalization of myth and a conversion of myth into the terms of discursive thought, and finally to an abandonment of myth in its classical form. The remark of Leenhardt is true of Greece, however, as it is in general; myth continues to coexist with discursive thought even in advanced civilizations.

What is called the myth-ritual pattern school identifies myth as the discourse, the *hieros logos,* which accompanies ritual.[29] Some anthropologists say that the rite comes first and that the myth is added to explain the rite and to determine its validity explicitly. The importance of the ritual myth in the ancient Near East has been indisputably established by modern research; as a universally valid principle to explain the origin of myth it is not so definitely established. There is much Near Eastern mythology for which no place has been found in the cult; until a place has been found for it, it seems that we ought to leave open the possibility that the single explanatory principle of myth, if there be such a principle, is to be sought outside the myth-ritual pattern.

Can we draw up a positive definition of myth as it appears in the ancient Near East, or at least a description? Our discussion up to this point encourages us to go beyond the common popular conception and the dictionary definition if we can. But we ought to note first that the central and essential character of myth cannot lie merely in its opposition to logical discursive thought; this, again, would make its definition so broad that it would comprehend perhaps most of the human ideational process.[30]

[29] The term "school" perhaps imposes a false unity on this group of scholars. Their views were set forth in three collections of essays published by S. H. Hooke: *Myth and Ritual* (Oxford, 1933); *The Labyrinth* (Oxford, 1935); *Myth. Ritual and Kingship* (Oxford, 1958).

[30] It is for this reason that the position of Rudolf Bultmann is not entirely clear

We should note also that while myth seems always to be associated with religious belief and practice, myth should not be so closely associated with religion that the two become identical. If myth is identified simply with polytheism, we shall find it difficult to explain some biblical passages. It is not within the scope of this paper to do that which a generation of scholars has not yet done: to present a philosophy of myth which is organized and comprehensive. I present the remarks which follow as no more than a description of some common traits which emerge in the mythical literature of the ancient Near East and are generally so recognized by the scholars who have studied this literature. I cannot say that this description is complete, or that any single feature is to be regarded as the essence from which the other features are derived as properties.

In the first place, it seems that we must with Cassirer identify myth as symbolic expression. The writers of myth do not pretend to attain and describe as immediately perceived in its concrete existence the reality with which the myth is concerned. They intend to present the reality in a symbolic form. The necessity for symbolic conception arises, as Buess has pointed out, because myth deals with the unknown. To avoid the paradox of knowing the unknowable, we go on to explain that the unknown is recognized as existing and operative; but it escapes definition through the intellectual processes of the myth-making man. The myth is intended,

and consistent. It is curious that the most discussed and debated article in the history of modern exegesis, "Neues Testament und Mythologie" (1941; quoted here from *Kerygma und Mythos*, Hans-Werner Bartsch), defined myth only in a footnote: "Mythologisch ist die Vorstellungsweise, in der das Unweltliche, Göttliche als Weltliches, Menschliches, das Jenseitige als Diesseitiges erscheint. . . . Es ist vom 'Mythos' also nicht in jenem modernen Sinne die Rede, wonach er nichts weiter bedeutet als Ideologie" (*Kerygma und Mythos* I, [1948] 22). Under criticism Bultmann defended his position by modifying it. In response to Julius Schniewind (*ibid.*, 122) he wrote that myth is a *Denk- und Redensweise*, where in his first definition he had called it a *Vorstellungsweise*; these two are not exactly the same, as one can see from the summary of the recent discussion of myth cited above, and it was careless of Bultmann to imply that they are. It is even more curious to find him saying later that he does not think the concept of myth is important (*Kerygma und Mythos* II [1952] 180). He then goes on to place the essence of myth in its opposition to scientific thought; he sets this forth well (*ibid.*, 180-190), but he ends with exactly what he denied he had in his first definition: the concept of myth as an ideology. But B. has committed himself to the position that there is no valid intellectual process except scientific thought; and since this seems to imply that the mythical processes of the NT are not an intuition of truth, it is hard to see how anything can be left after *Entmythologisierung*. But the NT is much more meaningful for B. than this, and hence his lack of consistency. I am tempted to say that if B. had spent as much space on the definition of myth as I have here we should have been deprived of a piquant controversy.

in the words of van der Leeuw, to attain mastery over the external world by endowing it with form—that is, with intelligible form.[31] The unknown remains unknown; but the mythopoeic mind has attained by intuition a fleeting grasp of the unknown reality, and it gives this reality the only expression of which it is capable: the expression of the symbol. The unknown reality which is thus expressed is in general the reality which escapes sense observation and the simple deductions of an intellectual process which has not attained the skill of logical discourse or does not know how to apply this skill to the unknown reality.

If we give this reality definition we remove it from the area of myth; hence it is not strictly accurate to say that this reality is the gods, or the divine, or nature, or impersonal force. All such terms give the unknown a definition, the lack of which is precisely what elicits mythopoeic activity. A general term which seems as innocent as any other is transcendental reality. This reality is more than nature, since, as we have observed above, the ancient Near East had no conception of nature as a unified process, a *kosmos*. Now this underlying reality, perceived but unknown and unrecognized, is presented in myth as a personal or a personalized reality. Primitive animism is no longer defended as a theory by contemporary anthropologists even for primitives; it certainly cannot be predicated of the civilized peoples of the ancient Near East. They could distinguish between the "It" and the "Thou." But when they dealt with this unknown reality expressed through mythical symbols, the reality was not identified as an "It." Neither did Near Eastern mythology define this reality as a single personal "Thou": the complexity of reality, the interplay of numerous obviously distinct forces, and the beneficent or maleficent effect of the play of these forces on man suggested to them the presence of a personal activity like the unpredictable activity of human beings. In this reality were rooted the phenomena which they observed.

The concept of cause and effect is so different in mythical thinking from what it is in philosophy and science that the terms are almost equivocal.

Cassirer has written: "Isolating abstraction, which singles out a specific factor in a total complex as a 'condition,' is alien to mythical thinking. Here every simultaneity, every spatial coexistence and contact, provide a real causal 'sequence.' It has even been called a principle of mythical causality and of the 'physics' based on it that one take every contact in time and space as an immediate relation of cause and effect. The principles of *post hoc, ergo propter hoc* and *juxta hoc, ergo propter hoc* are characteristic of mythical thinking."[32]

[31] *Op. cit.*, 552-553.
[32] *The Philosophy of Symbolic Forms II: Mythical Thought* (translated from the German; New Haven, 1955) 43.

"Whereas empirical thinking speaks of 'change' and seeks to understand it on the basis of a universal rule, mythical thinking knows only a simple metamorphosis. . . . When scientific thinking considers the fact of change, it is not essentially concerned with the transformation of a single given *thing* into another: on the contrary, it regards this transformation as possible and admissible only insofar as a universal law is expressed in it, insofar as it is based on certain functional relations and determinations which can be regarded as valid independently of the mere here and now, and of the constellation of things in the here and now. Mythical 'metamorphosis,' on the other hand, is always the record of an individual event—the change from one individual and concrete material form to another."[33] "Science is content if it succeeds in apprehending the individual event in space and time as a special instance of a general law but asks no further 'why' regarding the individualization as such, regarding the here and now. The mythical consciousness, on the other hand, applies its 'why' precisely to the particular and unique. It 'explains' the individual event by postulating individual acts of the will."[34]

Causality in mythical thought is the intuition of a cosmic event which is reflected in the succession of events in the phenomenal world. Without the cosmic event the phenomenal event would not happen or would cease. The succession of phenomena was not governed by the known laws and properties of natural bodies and natural forces; natural bodies and natural forces as such were not known, and no laws of their behavior had been established. The succession of phenomena was achieved by the interplay and sometimes by the conflict of personal wills on a cosmic scale.[35] This does not mean, as I have remarked, that the various personalized forces, whether gods or demons, which the myth-maker saw in the unknown reality were merely allegorical figures of wind, rain, and so forth. The gods are distinguished from the phenomena, and the symbolism is more subtle than the crass allegorism which would identify Hadad with the storm. Were there no Hadad, there would be no storm; were Hadad not a personal being, the storm would not exhibit the capricious behavior which makes it for man both a blessing and a curse. The great seasonal myth of fertility is an expression of the mysterious fact that life as man experiences it comes only from death. Hence the distinction between the two is blurred. The world is annually recreated: were it not for the

---

[33] *Ibid.*, 46-47.

[34] *Ibid.*, 48.

[35] Thorkild Jacobsen has written: "Through and under (the order of nature) he (the Mesopotamian) sensed a multitude of powerful individual wills, potentially divergent, potentially conflicting, fraught with a possibility of anarchy. He confronted in Nature gigantic and wilful individual powers. To the Mesopotamian, accordingly, cosmic *order* did not appear as something given; rather it became something achieved —achieved through a continual integration of the many individual cosmic wills, each so powerful, so frightening" (*The Intellectual Adventure of Ancient Man* 127).

original creation annually renewed, the cycle of fertility would not endure in the world of phenomena, and the monster of chaos would secure lasting dominion. But the gods of fertility are not merely symbols of natural forces; the succession of phenomena depends on the perpetual life-death cycle on a cosmic scale, and these gods make the cycle. Now the concrete cosmic event can be expressed only in the form of a story.[36] Without discursive thought the myth-maker cannot elaborate the abstract universal concept and deduce general principles. Both the story and the concrete cosmic event are removed from time as it is known in the phenomenal world; they become eternally recurrent.

When we say that myth is wider than nature myth, it is necessary to define our extension lest it become unintelligible. Some classifications of myth made independently by several writers will indicate the area covered by the mythopoeic faculty. Paul Tillich distinguishes myth as cosmological, anthropological, soteriological, and eschatological.[37] Johannes Hempel classifies myth as cosmogonic, soteriological, and the revelation myth.[38] René Largement classifies Akkadian and Canaanite myths as myths of origins, myths of the quest of life, and myths of deliverance.[39] There is substantial agreement in these classifications.

The pattern of myth is used to formulate not only the origins of the universe and of man but also the origins of human institutions, the ideals and desires and ambitions of man, and his success or failure in achieving them.[40] In all these the myth ultimately goes to the unknown underlying

[36] Henri Frankfort writes: "The whole man confronts a living 'Thou' in nature; and the whole man—emotional and imaginative as well as intellectual—gives expression to the experience. All experience of 'Thou' is highly individual; and early man does, in fact, view happenings as individual events. An account of such events and also their explanation can be conceived only as action and necessarily take the form of a story. In other words, the ancients told myths instead of presenting an analysis or conclusions" (*ibid.*, 6).

[37] *RGG IV,* 366.

[38] *ZAW* 65 (1953) 120.

[39] In Brillant and Aigrain, *Histoire des religions* 4, 154 ff., 191 ff. On the cultural myth Cassirer said: "(In culture myths) the question of origins shifts more and more from the sphere of *things* to the specifically human sphere: the form of mythical causality serves to explain the origin not so much of the world or particular objects in it as of human cultural achievements. True, in accordance with the style of mythical thinking this explanation stops at the view that these benefits were not created through the power and will of man but were given him. They are regarded not as produced by man but as received by him in a state of completion" (*The Philosophy of Symbolic Forms II: Mythical Thought* 204). It appears that this form cannot be transferred as described to Gn 4,17-22; 9,20-21; but, as we shall see, the Hebrews always transformed mythical patterns.

[40] Cassirer pointed out the social function of myth: ". . . the mythical-religious

reality, whether this reality be explicitly identified as a divine personal being or not. Hence the description of myth as a *Göttergeschichte*, "a story about gods," is not entirely adequate.[41] This pattern of thought and language was intended in the minds of those who employed it not as a vehicle of falsehood or of fiction for the sake of entertainment, but of truth. Does its failure to express truth come from the thought pattern itself or from some other cause working defectively? Is myth so essentially vitiated by the polytheism of the myths which we know that myth cannot be so defined as to exclude polytheism, while the pattern of thought and language remains? Is there any more reason to call myth an essentially defective thought pattern because of its errors than there is to call philosophy an essentially defective thought pattern?

I suggest with the writers cited above that in defining myth in such a way as neither to include polytheism nor to exclude it we do no violence to the mythical literature of the ancient Near East nor to any pattern of thought which logical discourse imposes upon us. If the myth makers were striving for an intuition and an expression of truth, we must give them credit for what they strove to do. Their failure to express the truth about the transcendental reality which lies beyond the phenomenal world is not of necessity to be explained as due to the essential inadequacy of the thought and language processes which they employed. In attempting to tell stories which symbolized the transcendental reality they succeeded only in telling the story of the phenomenal world over again on a larger scale. They did not break through the limits of the observation of phenomena, and their symbols symbolized the unknown without signifying its "wholly other" character. They did not attain the divine; they brought the divine down to their own level, and doubtless they thought they had attained it in reducing it. I submit that they were satisfied with their view of the divine because it was an easier view which made few demands upon them; the ultimate root of their error was not in their thought patterns but in their will.

II. Mythical Patterns in the Old Testament

So much, then, may be said in explanation of one of the two terms of our topic, and it seems necessary to say it. Turning to the other term, we

consciousness does not simply *follow* from the empirical content of the social form but is rather one of the most important *factors* of the feeling of community and social life. Myth itself is one of those spiritual syntheses through which a bond between 'I' and 'Thou' is made possible, through which a definite unity and a definite contrast, a relation of kinship and a relation of tension, are created between the individual and the community" (*ibid.*, 177).

[41] R. A. F. MacKenzie, following Gunkel (*CBQ* 15 [1953] 136).

may state at once and without any need of demonstration that the OT certainly makes extensive use of mythical language, imagery, and conception; this is generally accepted by modern scholars. I treated Gn 2-3 as an original composition of the Yahwist tradition largely made up of fugitive pieces of mythological allusion drawn from various sources.[42] In connection with this passage I also treated Ez 28,12-18 as a variant form of the story of the first man which is likewise an original piece of Hebrew tradition but is more mythical in character.[43]

Hermann Gunkel pointed out as examples of mythical conception and language: the treatment of natural phenomena as the action or the experience of personal beings (Ps 19,6; Is 14,12 ff.; the rainbow, Gn 9,12 ff.); the description of the eschatological period as a return to conditions of the primitive period of creation; etiological stories such as the creation of woman from the rib (Gn 2,21 ff.); the origin of human toil and the pains of childbirth (Gn 3,16 ff.); the union of the sons of God and the daughters of men (Gn 6,4 ff.). In addition Gunkel finds mythical elements in poetry and prophecy: an allusion to the story of the first man (Jb 15,7f.); poetic variations on the creation story; eschatological events such as the world catastrophe, which is a reversal of creation and a return to chaos (Is 24,19; 17,12 ff.); the sword and judgment of Yahweh upon the nations (Is 34,5); the return to chaos (Jer 4,23 ff.); the golden age (Is 11,6 ff.); the imagery of prophetic visions, such as the enthroned Yahweh (Is 6) and the chariot of Yahweh (Ez 1).[44] Johannes Hempel has adverted to what he calls the historicization of myth, by which he means the use of mythical conception and imagery to describe a historic event, such as the fall of the great king represented as a descent into Sheol (Is 14,5-15); Israel as the bride of Yahweh, a response to the myth of fertility (Os 2; Yahweh has no divine spouse, He has chosen Israel; cf. also Is 62,1-5). Hempel also sees mythical language and conception in eschatology, especially in such features as the Day of Yahweh (Jl 2,10 ff.; 3,3 ff.) and the final victory of Yahweh over His enemies (Is 51,9-13; 1,21-27) and in particular in the tension between history and eschatology in the prophets, which frequently permits them to describe contemporary events in terms of the Day of Yahweh.[45] Edmond Jacob also has adverted to the historicization of myth.[46] In this conception the mythical event, the importance of which lay originally in its character as "exemplar history" (Eliade) and its eternal Now by which it sustains the succession of phenomena, loses its transfiguration and becomes important as a single event. Geo Widengren alleges the assembly of the holy ones (Ps 89,18; 16,3; Dn 8,13; Ex 15,11; Ps 82); the identification of Jerusalem with the mountain of the north, the mountain of assembly (Ps 48,3);

---

[42] *TS* 15 (1954) 541-572.

[43] *JBL* 75 (1956) 322-327.

[44] *RGG IV*, 382-383, 387-388.

[45] *ZAW* 65 (1953) 111-135. For this tension in the prophets S. B. Frost cites Is 29,1-2; 2,10-17; Am 5,18 ff. (*VT 2* [1952] 70-80).

[46] E. Jacob, *Theology of the Old Testament* (translated from the French; London, 1958) 197-201.

Gn 2-3 and Ez 28; the imagery of the theophanies (Ex 19; 33.19-23; Jgs 5,4-5; 3 Kgs 19,9-18; Hb 3).[47] Evidently these instances are not all of equal value, and the scope of this paper does not permit an analysis of each pattern. Equally evidently, however, some of them do bear the stamp of the mythopoeic pattern; cf. my own treatment of some of these passages cited in notes 42, 43, 47, 48.

In some instances the mythical character of the thought and language is evident. The conception of creation as a victory of Yahweh occurs in several passages.[48] Edmond Jacob says that these passages reflect a history of creation, not a myth of creation; the characteristics of myth, especially repetition, he finds absent.[49] It is true that the passages appear to be no more than echoes of the creation myth of the Near East. But Jacob has not defined the characteristics of myth; and not all of the characteristics which I have outlined above are absent from these passages. I am now no longer ready to accept these passages as mere poetic imagery and embellishment; I would rather say that Hebrew religious belief was broad enough to admit more than one symbolic form in which the belief in creation could be expressed.[50] One, which is found only in fragments in the OT, is the victory of Yahweh over the monster of chaos; the other and more reflective account appears in Gn 1, but this passage too has a relation to myth. The creative combat includes a characteristic of mythical thinking which is rarely verified elsewhere in the OT: the conception of the event as eternally recurring. The creative victory is constantly achieved anew. Yahweh continually slays the monster, but in some passages he keeps it under restraint; thus He removes the perpetual danger that it may break loose and the world may return to *tohu wabohu*. Creation is thus a continuing achievement.

Besides these instances of mythical conception, we are able by comparison of the OT with extant literature to see how the Hebrews could revise an existing myth. It is quite impossible to suppose that Gn has any source of the story of the deluge besides the Mesopotamian myth. By this I do not mean that Gn knew precisely the myth in the literary form in which we know it, but that it possessed the same source in tradition and no other. The use of the tradition in Gn gives it no more and no less historical value than it had in Mesopotamian tradition. The Hebrew here was not dealing

[47] In S. H. Hooke, *Myth, Ritual and Kingship* 159-176. On the theophanies cf. also Otto Eissfeldt, *Einleitung in das Alte Testament* (Tübingen, 1956) 37-38, and my own remarks in *CBQ* 14 (1952) 35-39.

[48] I collected these passages in *TS* 11 (1950) 275-282. For a more recent treatment cf. Widengren in *Myth, Ritual and Kingship* 170-173.

[49] *Op. cit.*, 138.

[50] Thus reversing an opinion expressed in *TS* 11 (1950) 282.

with history. Now what did Hebrew literary art do with this myth? It removed the gods of Mesopotamia and with them the dissension among the gods which was the moving factor in the myth. As a motive of the deluge it replaced the capricious anger of Enlil with the righteous anger of Yahweh aroused by the deep and total guilt of all mankind. It omitted the passage in which Ea rebuked Enlil for inflicting a punishment which exceeded the guilt. Both the Mesopotamian and the Hebrew faced the problem of destructive natural catastrophes. In common they sought an explanation of these disasters not in the operations of natural forces according to physical laws but in the will of a personal being behind the phenomena. For the Mesopotamian this being was divine—not supreme, but powerful enough to impose his will upon his associates. His will—and this is important—is like the human will in this, that its movements sometimes defy a reasonable explanation, and man is ultimately the victim of catastrophe because he cannot be altogether certain of what the will of the gods may be; like him, the gods may act unreasonably and he suffers their anger without knowing why. For the Hebrews this view of divinity was intolerable. If God exhibits anger it must be reasonably motivated, and there is no reasonable motivation of His anger except the sin of man. When men sin, He punishes them through the operations of nature. The Hebrew neither affirmed nor denied the historical character of the deluge of Mesopotamian myth. What he affirmed was that, if such a catastrophe occurred, it had an adequate motivation. In the world of experience in which the Hebrews lived such cosmic catastrophes did not occur, and this he attributed to the kindliness of God, who spared man the extreme punishment which his rebellion might well deserve.

The creation account of Gn 1 is another example of a re-treatment of a known myth. Here, however, the writer has excised the mythical elements more radically; he has written an explicit polemic against the creation myth.[51] Polytheism is removed, and with it the theogony and the theomachy which are so vital in the Mesopotamian form of the myth. Even the creative combat is removed, and the author has very little left of the myth except the structure of the universe, which is not strictly a mythical concept. The act of creation is achieved in entire tranquillity, and it is achieved simply by the creative word—an element which is paralleled in the Memphite theology of Egypt.[52]

Now what are we to call such compositions as the creation account of

[51] Cf. Hempel in *ZAW* 65 (1953) 126-128, and my remarks in *CBQ* 14 (1952) 27-28.

[52] Translated by John A. Wilson in *ANET* 4-6.

Gn 1 and the deluge story? The Hebrew did not replace myth with history; it is impossible to suppose that he had historical knowledge of either of these events. He retains too many traces of the myth for us to suppose that he had another source on which to draw. Some might wish to call the Hebrew version a theological reconstruction or interpretation. Theology, however, is logical discourse: a synthesis of abstract concepts which are obtained by the analysis of phenomena. Discursive thought does not appear in the OT, and to call such passages theology is to use the term improperly. It may be necessary to use some term improperly, but why should it be theology? Actually, the Hebrews displaced the objectionable story only by telling another story; and whether this other story is to be called myth depends ultimately on the definition of myth.

Extending the question to other passages where mythical thought and language appear, we may ask whether the Hebrews chose deliberately to portray the unknown reality with embellishments drawn from the wealth of mythical imagery, although they were able, if they wished, to describe the reality in more sober and less figured language. We have no right to say that they proceeded in this manner. They had no abstract discursive thought, and I believe we may say of them, as we say of the myths of other ancient peoples, that they regarded such passages as apprehensions of reality. It was not, indeed, a total and immediate apprehension; but they apprehended the unknown reality in single events which were symbols, and single events for them too must take the form of a story. And since no single story, no single intuitional apprehension, can exhaust the unknown reality towards which it strives, the Hebrews, like others, were ready to admit a multiple approach to the unknown reality and to describe it in symbols which were diverse or even contradictory in their imagery. Speculatively viewed, the creation account of Gn 1 and the creative combat of allusions elsewhere in the OT cannot stand together; but the Hebrews did not view them speculatively. They are images, each having its value as an intuition of the reality of creation, neither of which apprehends and describes the reality in its fullness. In the same way we have indications that the story of the fall of man was told in more than one form.

The passages which are cited above all seem to exhibit the features of mythopoeic thought which I have enumerated. They are symbolic representations of a reality which is not otherwise known or expressed. This reality reposes upon a divine background which is represented as personal. This background is apprehended in concrete events on a cosmic scale from which the succession of phenomena arises. This reality is apprehended and described in images, words, and deeds. In the OT we find these forms used of such subjects as cosmogony, soteriology, eschatology, and human origins. · Lest it be thought that I have sketched the characteristics of mythopoeic thought in such a way as to establish my proposition, I wish to say simply that these characteristics do not of themselves define a literary form. If we doubt that myth exists or must exist as an independent literary form, we may be satisfied with saying that Hebrew thought and language, when it deals with questions with which other ancient peoples dealt in mythical compositions, has in common with these compositions certain characteristics which we are accustomed to designate as mythical or mythopoeic. Whether these characteristics are enumerated exhaustively, so that we should apply the term myth without any reservation to the Hebrew pattern, is a question which demands further study.

Some recent writers exhibit an inclination towards an affirmative answer. Adolf Kolping: ". . . darf man nicht übersehen, dass die Aussagekategorien in Israels wie ausserisraelitischen altorientalischen Darstellungen dieselbe Eigenart haben. Wäre das Wort Mythos in unseren Zusammenhängen nicht so stark belastet, könnte man unbedenklich von der gleichen formalmythischen Art reden. . . . Wahrheit eines Satzes besteht bekanntlich in der Übereinstimmung des mittels der Aussagekategorien ausgedrückten Aussageinhaltes mit der objektiven Wirklichkeit. . . . Der inspirierte Autor des Pentateuch hat die alten Erzählungen in der Eigenart ihrer unreflektierten Einheit von anschaulichem Aussagemittel und intendiertem Aussageinhalt in die Genesis aufgenommen. Hier fand er die Gedanken vorgedacht und vorformuliert, die dem entsprechen, was er ausdrücken will."[53] A.-M. Dubarle: "Ces considérations diverses conduisent à admettre que le récit de l'Éden, et plus largement l'ensemble de l'histoire primitive, proviennent de la foi d'Israel par le moyen d'activités mentales qui, dans les religions moins nettement liées à l'histoire et n'ayant pas la même connaissance du vrai Dieu, ont abouti à des récits mythiques. Cette solution, qui admet l'union étroite, dans l'esprit de l'écrivain sacré, du fond et de la forme, reconnaît dans ces chapitres un genre littéraire très largement symbolique, sans avoir à distinguer des parties historiques et des parties fictives . . . (Cette histoire biblique) atteint les faits dans des productions littérairement apparentées aux mythes, mais dans lesquelles le contenu et l'orientation de la pensée mythique avaient déjà été profondément modifiés par le foi historique d'Israël."[54] M. Leenhardt: ". . . le rationalisme n'a jamais pu chasser des préoccupations humaines la pensée religieuse. Celle-ci concerne des réalités humaines que seule la connaissance mythique permet d'appréhender." The same writer explains his application of the term myth to the fall of Adam and the redemption in these words: "Il va de soi que le mot 'mythe' est employé ici dans le sens même d'événement circonscrit indiqué dans ces pages, mode d'appréhension pour saisir une réalité qui échappe aux sens."[55] J. Henninger: "On voit ainsi comment la révélation, qui n'est pas un événement mythique,

---

[53] In *Alttestamentliche Studien* (Bonn, 1950) 147-149.
[54] *Le péché originel dans l'Écriture* (Paris, 1958) 52-53.
[55] In Brillant and Aigrain, *Histoire des religions* 1, 90-91.

mais un événement historique precis, a pu utiliser, elle aussi, le langage du mythe, étant donné que c'était le mode le plus adéquat pour une pédagogie divine d'atteindre l'homme. On voit aussi que les tendances les plus profondes de l'attitude mythique, à savoir entre autres l'actualisation des événements primordiaux, pouvaient trouver leur accomplissement et leur sublimation dans le christianisme."[56] H. Cazelles: "Quelque transcendant que soit le message biblique, il plonge trop dans le milieu littéraire oriental pour ne pas s'être exprimé dans les formes utilisées par ce milieu. . . . Le mythe est la forme littéraire qui exprime le besoin qu'a l'homme de connaitre la divinité, non pas sous une forme abstraite et métaphysique, mais de manière personnelle et concrète . . . le mythe exprime le caractère personnel des forces qui s'exercent sur l'homme dans et par la nature. Or la religion biblique restera toujours une religion où l'homme est en rapports personnels avec Dieu, le connaissant comme volonté et esprit."[57] Cazelles would limit the word to the earliest portions of Hebrew literature.

It should be stated emphatically that no one who has followed the recent discussions of myth and mythical thinking will be in danger of placing the biblical conception of these things on the same level with the myths of ancient peoples, against which Pius XII warned in *Humani Generis*.[58] The recent literature on the subject, viewed *in globo*, brings out more sharply the difference between the Hebrew treatment of the material of myth from the treatment of other ancient peoples.

Eduard Buess places the difference in the idea of God, which is the unique feature of the Bible.[59] The Yahweh of the OT is not a form posited by mythical thinking; the mythical thinking of the Near East, as far as we know it, showed itself incapable of producing any such form. The unique character of this God is so evident that it needs no discussion. Is the concept so unique that it shatters myth beyond repair? Certainly not to the extent that mythical patterns of thought and language are entirely excluded from the Bible, as we have seen. But the conception of God affects very seriously one of the characteristics of mythopoeic thought which I have enumerated; for God is the unknown reality recognized as unknown and symbolized by mythological forms, the divine background which is conceived as personal. Hebrew religion is unique precisely in that the unknown is not totally unknown. In their own belief the character of this God was known through His revelation of Himself. Their treatment of mythical pieces such as the deluge and the creative combat is to remove anything which is out of character with the God who revealed

[56] *DBS VI*, 245-246.
[57] *Ibid.*, 252.
[58] *AAS* 42 (1950) 577.
[59] *Op. cit.*, 189-192.

Himself to them. This knowledge of God through the revelation of Himself they possessed. But the unknown remained unknown and mysterious; man was incapable of a total revelation. When the Hebrews touched upon the questions of the relations of God with nature, with man, and with society, what resources were available to them to give expression to the impact of this mysterious reality upon phenomena and upon their own minds? They had no logical discourse of science and philosophy through which they could express these relations. It is not a tenable view that God in revealing Himself also revealed directly and in detail the truth about such things as creation and the fall of man; the very presence of so many mythical elements in their traditions is enough to eliminate such a view. All they could do was to represent through symbolic forms the action of the unknown reality which they perceived mystically, not mythically, through His revelation of Himself.

III. Conclusion

Whether this Hebrew representation of reality is to be called mythopoeic may appear to be merely a question of terminology. Since the recent discussions of myth are known only in the world of scholars, and not even throughout that world, the application of the terms myth, mythical, and mythopoeic to the OT will certainly be misunderstood. My colleague R. A. F. MacKenzie has suggested the term "religious prehistory" to designate the material of Gn 1-11.[60] This term is probably an echo of the term "primitive history" coined by Père Lagrange in 1902. I am doubtful that this term is altogether acceptable. If history must in some sense mean a human witness of past events, the application of the term to this material stretches the term at least as far as it will go. The term is not applicable at all to the mythical patterns of eschatological passages or to the creative combat. These passages have such a distinctive character that it is very difficult to classify them with any recognized literary forms. I remarked above that perhaps some term must be improperly applied: if it is not to be theology or history, why should it not be myth? And is not myth a less improper term than these others? No doubt something should be added to distinguish these passages from the myths to which the name has so long been exclusively applied. Tentatively and as no more than a step in the right direction I suggest that mythopoeic pieces be classified under the general heading of wisdom rather than history; this has already been suggested by A.-M. Dubarle for the Paradise story.[61]

[60] *CBQ* 15 (1953) 140.
[61] *Les sages d'Israël* (Paris, 1946) 9.

But the question is perhaps deeper than terminology; it may even be a question of the honesty and integrity of scholarship. The studies of the last generation have brought all exegetes to a realization of the kinship of Israel with the ancient Near East in civilization and literature. The theological and religious significance of the OT, we know, has gained, not lost, by this broadening of perspective; this is less well known and realized outside of professional circles. Certainly we have an imperative duty to make this truth better known. Our studies of the Near East have taught us to understand the language of Israel better, to enter its mind and to share its experience. The more deeply we share its experience and its cultural milieu, the more overwhelming becomes our awareness that Israel's experience of God was like nothing else in the ancient world. Surely there now ought to be little room for timidity and misunderstanding if we call Hebrew literature in some passages mythical, or wisdom discourses couched in mythopoeic patterns. Even if the rigorous ethics of scholarship do not clearly demand the adoption of this terminology, they do demand the recognition of Israel's community with the ancient Near East in patterns of thought and language. We shall never understand the OT unless we learn to read its language. To make it speak our own language is ultimately necessary if we are to make it intelligible; but we cannot do this unless we have first apprehended its meaning in its own literary, cultural, and historical *Sitz im Leben.* The Hebrew intuition of the ineffable reality which revealed itself to man as the personal reality behind the succession of phenomena, the agent of the great cosmic event which we call creation, the reality from which all things came, in which they exist, and to which they must return, was not the creation of mythical form or of logical discourse, but a direct and personal experience of God as the "Thou" to whom the human "I" must respond. But they had no media through which they could enunciate the ineffable reality except the patterns of thought and speech which they inherited from their civilization.

JOHN L. MCKENZIE, S.J.
West Baden College,
West Baden Springs, Indiana

METHOD IN THE STUDY OF NEAR EASTERN MYTHS

R. A. Oden Jr

There can be few areas within the study of religion which
have witnessed ethnographic advances in this century
equivalent to those achieved in the study of Near Eastern
myths. This is particularly true with regard to the
discovery and increasingly accurate translation of ancient,
primary documents. The number of Mesopotamian, Egyptian,
and, especially, Syrian myths available to scholars today
is simply far greater than the number available a century,
or even a few decades, ago. Unfortunately, however, these
ethnographic advances have not been coincident with any
increasing sophistication in the area of the interpretative
frameworks which are brought to bear upon the bulging corpus
of Near Eastern myths. Indeed, it is not to exaggerate to
claim that those methods which are used most widely today are
not just out of fashion, though they are surely that too,
but are regarded as demonstrably fallacious or inadequate by
theoreticians of mythology.

It is perhaps best to state here, at the outset of the
present study, that a concern for method in the study of
Near Eastern myths is often seen as a diversion from the
primary task before one - as something of a red herring.
This view was understandable, perhaps even laudable, in the
initial stages of the analysis of Near Eastern myths, when
so much fundamental work needed to be done - when texts
required preliminary translations, and when historical
contexts needed to be reconstructed. However, the implicit
claims for theoretical autonomy which this view makes can
no longer be maintained. If the study of Near Eastern myths
is to make any claims for scientific validity, then it needs

Religion   Volume 9   Autumn 1979
© RKP 1979 0048-721X/79/0902-0182 $1.50/1
182

to submit itself to the same rigours of examination,
empirical and theoretical, to which other disciplines must
submit themselves (1). Informed eclecticism has about it a
certain charm; but there comes a time when methodological
choices have to be made. The same point, it seems, is made
by Lévi-Strauss: 'It is a healthy attitude, at certain stages
of scientific investigation, to believe that, in the present
state of knowledge, two interpretations of the same facts
are equally valid....The error consists, not in recognizing
this state of affairs when it exists, but in being satisfied
with it and in not seeking to transcend it' (2).

Of the potential pitfalls into which a student of Near
Eastern myths fall, two stand out. The first is the adoption
of what one might fairly call a classic functionalist mode
of analysis. The second is the assumption that there is a
one-for-one correspondence between the social background of a
mythical narrative and the empirical institutions of the
society which produced the myth. It is rarely the case
that either the assumption of such a one-for-one correspondence
or the use of a functional analysis is explicitly defended.
Rather, both of these theoretical constructs are regarded
as intuitively correct, and therefore not requiring any
defence. It is the case, however, that as theoretical
constructs both of these assumptions need careful scrutiny.

Functionalism is, according to I.C. Jarvie, 'a method
of explaining social events and institutions by specifying
the *function* they perform' (3). Its aim is, in the
predictably precise formulation of Carl Hempel, 'to understand a behavior pattern or a sociocultural institution by
determining the role it plays in keeping the given system
in proper working order or maintaining it as a going
concern' (4). Historically, functionalism is associated
above all with the work of Malinowski, and Malinowski
offers functional explanations of totemism, of religion, and
of myths. Thus, for Malinowski, totemism is 'a system of
magical co-operation, a number of practical cults, each with
its own social basis but all having one common end: The
supply of the tribe with abundance' (5). Religion, in turn,
'establishes, fixes, and enhances all valuable mental
attitudes, such as reverence for tradition, harmony with environment, courage and confidence in the struggle with
difficulties and at the prospect of death' (6). And finally,
for Malinowski, 'myth fulfills in primitive culture an
indispensable function: it expresses, enhances, and codifies
belief; it safeguards and enforces morality; it vouches
for the efficiency of ritual and contains practical rules
for the guidance of man....[It is] a pragmatic charter of
primitive faith and moral wisdom' (7).

Now, it hardly needs saying that functionalism is a method in disrepute today, though it is of course true that a method's having fallen out of fashion is hardly sufficient reason for the abandonment of that method. For example, though Leach apparently continues to feel some fondness for the method, he correctly notes that functionalism is 'an oversimplified mechanistic style of sociological theorising now generally viewed with some contempt' (8). Similarly, Jarvie concludes that 'the criticisms of functionalism are so serious that it must be renounced as an ideology: it has practical and logical limitations which are most serious' (9). Here, I want to discuss three of these limitations. First, there are those examples, now numerous, when empirical data conflict with the claims of functionalism. This is perhaps most easily demonstrated in the case of those so-called totemistic species which are *not* useful, feared, or dangerous: 'that there is not, in fact, a one-for-one correspondence between useful fruits and vegetables and the totemic system is enough to bring a utilitarian explanation, such as that of Malinowski or Firth, crashing down in logical ruins' (10).

Secondly, there is with functionalism as a method of explanation the problem of what one might call, with some understatement, a lack of economy. That is, there is a striking disparity between the end to be achieved and the means utilized to achieve this end. This problem has been articulated most clearly by Sperber:

> This disproportion between means and end, clear in the case of mythology, becomes truly exorbitant in the case of ritual. When we think of the time, the tension, the passion, and the expense necessary to put on the smallest ritual, how can we believe that the uncertain attribution of a semantic interpretation - one therefore paraphrasable in ordinary language at a comparatively non-existent expense of energy - can account in any fashion for the nature of the phenomenon? (11).

This problem of disproportion is seen most vividly in the case of a Malinowskian interpretation of a myth as a charter. A myth as a charter for a particular social institution meets the presumptive need for such a charter most indirectly, if not obscurely, and at an expense far in excess of a simple statement that some social institution is in fact desirable (12).

The third critique of functionalism is one of such power that the previous two seem minor if not trivial by comparison. I refer to Hempel's 'The logic of functional

analysis' (13). If the two previous attacks upon functional
explanations are essentially attempts to demonstrate that
functionalism has practical limitations, Hempel's argument
is one which goes to the very heart of functionalism as a
method of explanation. There is certainly not space, and
perhaps there is no need, to provide here an elaborate
description of Hempel's argument. Hempel describes a typical
functional explanation, and concludes that such an explanation
is fallacious in that it affirms the consequent with regard
to one of its premises. That is, functionalists argue, almost
always implicitly, that a given society functions well if a
certain trait (for example, a given myth) is present in that
society. However, it is precisely this trait which we want
to explain; and we have not explained why this trait, rather
than a host of others, is present in the society. The
argument can be revised by affirming that a society functions
well *only if* a certain trait is present. Thus revised, the
argument is valid. But the revised argument is an argument
which one can hardly conceive anyone using: who is willing
to claim that a given Near Eastern society is a going concern
only because of the existence there of a particular myth?
Alternatively, one can revise the argument so that a given
trait (in this case, a myth) is one of a group of traits
which keeps the society on an even keel. This revision also
yields a valid argument. However, to say that a myth is one
of a group of traits which keeps a society functioning is to
abandon the quest to differentiate myth from other societal
traits; and yet myths plainly are not to be identified with
any and all aspects of society (14).

        Any one of these three criticisms of functionalism
(and surely the three criticisms together) is sufficient
demonstration of this method's limitations to cast serious
doubt upon its continued application. The lesson would
therefore seem to be that functionalism, which is so
intuitively satisfying, is a method to be used, if at all,
with great care and with a clear awareness of its limitations.
Despite this conclusion, Near Eastern myths continue to be
explained, by nearly all interpreters, within the confines
of a fairly straightforward functionalist framework.

        The second basic presupposition upon which nearly all
students of Near Eastern myths rely is, it will be remembered,
the assumption that there is a one-for-one correspondence
between the social background of a mythical narrative and
the empirical institutions of the society which produced
the myth. This assumption is, again, intuitively satisfactory; but it too proves to be problematic. Since there
is so much in any mythical narrative which does not reflect

ordinary experience, one has little basis for assuming that
a myth's social background does reflect this experience.
That is to say, in the corpus of Near Eastern myths we read,
for example, of a man cursing and breaking the wing of the
South Wind, of two young heroes slaying the bull of heaven,
of women conceiving at a very advanced age, of an emasculated
young man becoming a pine cone, and then a bull, a tree, and
a sliver of wood. None of these events correspond to
empirical reality. Given the lack of correspondence in this
area, why need we assume that a given social setting in a
myth - say, a social setting of dynastic kingship and
cross-cousin marriages - does correspond to the empirical
reality of social institutions?

The questioning of this one-for-one correspondence
assumption does not demand that one adopt a structuralist
stance; but it is true that Lévi-Strauss has spoken with the
greatest clarity on this issue. It is, Lévi-Strauss argues,
'naïve to suppose that there is always and in all circumstances
a simple correlation between mythological imagery and social
structures....The mythological system is relatively autonomous when compared with the other manifestations of the
life and thought of the group' (15). Lévi-Strauss then
proceeds to demonstrate this lack of correspondence, most
clearly in 'The story of Asdiwal' (16) and in 'Four Winnebago
myths' (17). In the latter, Lévi-Strauss discusses a
Winnebago myth which is set within a highly stratified
society. This setting had bothered previous interpreters
of the myth, because Winnebago society itself is not so
structured; and these interpreters had then argued, in a
fairly predictable response to this dilemma, that the
stratified society in this particular myth must be a
reflection of a Winnebago social structure which existed in
the hoary past. There is, however, simply no evidence for
such a stratified society in any era. Rather, Lévi-Strauss
argues that 'the society of the myth appears stratified,
only because the two heroes are conceived as a pair of
opposites....Thus the so-called stratified society should
be interpreted, not as a sociological vestige, but as a
projection on some imaginary social order of a logical
structure' (18). Many, of course, will want to question
this assertion that myths reflect logical structures, as
they will want to dispute other aspects of structuralist
analysis. However, I am here interested only in Lévi-
Strauss's repeated demonstration that the relationship
between actual institutions and those portrayed in myths is
a complex and unpredictable one.

II

I want now to turn from this theoretical discussion to an examination of the methodological assumptions operating today in the study of Near Eastern myths, selecting one interpreter from each of three ancient Near Eastern cultures: Mesopotamia, Syria, and Egypt. Lest I be accused of doing battle with straw men, in each case I will discuss the work of a scholar who is generally recognized to have done some of the most useful interpretative work in that area. Thus, for example, I will not, in discussing the interpretation of Syrian mythology, talk about the work of Gaster, since, although some of his work is of undoubted brilliance, Gaster relies consistently upon a myth-ritual scheme which is increasingly difficult to defend.

If proof be needed that I do not propose to take on straw men, let me begin with an examination of one aspect of the work of Thorkild Jacobsen. It is generally, and, I would argue, correctly agreed that Jacobsen is among the most sensitive of all students of Near Eastern myths. Despite this consensus, there is much in the work of Jacobsen which may need some revision (19). I want to concentrate here upon one of Jacobsen's most influential reconstructions, that of his notion of primitive democracy. The classic statement of this notion is as follows:

> Our material seems to preserve indications that pre-
> historic Mesopotamia was organized politically along
> democratic lines, not, as was historic Mesopotamia,
> along autocratic. The indications which we have,
> point to a form of government in which the normal
> run of public affairs was handled by a council of
> elders but ultimate sovereignty resided in a general
> assembly comprising all members - or, perhaps better,
> all adult free men - of the community (20).

Among the indications to which Jacobsen points are some preserved in mythic materials (21). As he says, 'our sources for the earliest political forms in Mesopotamia are the ancient myths, stories about the gods and their exploits' (22). Jacobsen prudently recognizes that this is an assumption which requires some discussion, even if the assumption is one made with some regularity; and he therefore defends the assumption as follows:

> Since it is difficult to conceive that the original
> myth-makers could have depicted as setting for their
> stories a society quite outside their experience and
> unrelated to anything they or their listeners knew,
> and since furthermore the myths of a people usually
> constitute the oldest layer of its tradition, one

must assume that a political setting such as occurs
in these tales once existed in Mesopotamia and was
later replaced by more developed political forms (23).
The adequacy of this defence, however, is just what we are
questioning here. We have just seen that one need not
assume that a myth's political setting once actually existed,
and that there are cases in which a myth's political setting
bears a complex and perhaps inverse relationship to actual
social institutions. We are not arguing that mythic settings
are 'unrelated to anything' known in a given society; but we
are arguing that this relationship is often something other
than direct replication.

Jacobsen's reconstruction of prehistoric Mesopotamia,
including this notion of primitive democracy, continues to
receive widespread support, most especially among biblical
scholars (24). To cite here but one example, writing in
1967 Nels Bailkey claims that Jacobsen 'has demonstrated
persuasively that the tyranny of historical times was
preceded by primitive monarchy (or what he more aptly terms
"primitive democracy")' (25). I would certainly not claim
that in pointing out a potential weakness in Jacobsen's
reconstruction I have thereby proved that prehistoric
Mesopotamia was not, or could not have been, organized as
a primitive democracy. I would, however, argue that in so
far as Jacobsen's model rests upon the assumption that the
social structure related in various Mesopotamian myth is the
same as some actual social structure in ancient Mesopotamia,
this model rests upon something less than a reliable
foundation. If the past generation's studies in mythology
have demonstrated anything, it is that myths can be used as
sources for the reconstruction of ancient social institutions
only with a great deal of care and with the addition of
considerable controls from other sources (26). There is,
in addition, a sense in which Jacobsen's reasoning here is
somewhat circular: he assumes that social institutions
produce myths; he then uses myths to argue for the
existence of specific social institutions.

I have spent a fair amount of time with the theoretical
presuppositions of this notion of primitive democracy
because Jacobsen's is such a widely, and deservedly, respected
voice, and because among some, and again this is particularly
true among biblical scholars, the primitive democracy
reconstruction has achieved the status of a proved fact of
Mesopotamian life. I will be less comprehensive with the
following examples. Let us move, then, from Mesopotamia to
Syria, and to a discussion of John Gray's interpretation of
Ugaritic mythology. As with our first example, it is again

the case that Gray's work is characterized by care and
thoroughness; and it is easily demonstrable that his two
lengthiest, technical treatments of the Ugaritic myths and
legends have been widely influential (27). Gray readily
assumes that myths provide one with a documentary source for
the reconstruction of an ancient society. For example,
Gray writes of the Tale of Aqhat that this text is 'of
foremost significance for our understanding of certain
social values among the primitive Canaanites' (28). However,
as this quotation already indicates, it is primarily Gray's
consistent use of a functional analysis which I want to
emphasize here. Again, given functionalism's long popularity
in anthropology, Gray is hardly exceptional in his
utilization of functional explanations. Indeed, it is
probably fair to say that such explanations are the norm in
the study of Near Eastern myths.

Having said that, it is true that few use functional
analysis as often or as boldly as does Gray. For example,
of the purpose of myth and ritual in general Gray writes,
'the actualization in myth and ritual of the initial
establishment of Order against the menace of Chaos was at
once a means of preserving the *status quo* and a provision
for the future with the effect of relieving the emotional
tension of men and of assuring them of the future' (29).
This statement is a virtual catalogue of functionalist presuppositions. It speaks of direct needs, in this case the
maintenance of the existing social order, and also of derived
needs, in this case the relaxing of emotional tension.
Whether he speaks of direct needs or of derived needs,
however, Gray implicitly commits the logical error of
affirming the consequent in the course of his argument; and,
it will be remembered, this was Hempel's chief criticism of
functional analysis. Gray does so in his affirmations that
the conditions which gave rise to the Ugaritic myths were
such that the existing social order needed preserving, that
emotional tension needed to be relieved, and, since Ugaritic
society was a going concern, that Ugaritic myths met these
two needs. That is, even if one expands the second premise
of a functional explanation so that the necessary conditions
to be satisfied are both direct and derived needs, one still
commits the logical fallacy which Hempel has described.
Nor is it only in summary statements about Ugaritic
mythology generally that Gray proceeds in this manner.
Particularly relevant here is Gray's interpretation of
the Keret text: 'this text, we maintain, was, no less
than the pure myths, functional. The text, that is to say,
was not an aesthetic exercise, but served a practical purpose
in the community where it was current, to achieve some desired
end or to conserve certain accepted values' (30).

As with our discussion of the work of Jacobsen, I
would not wish to deny that the work of Gray has yielded
real insights for our understanding of Syrian mythology.
However, Gray's interpretive framework is so overtly
functionalist that his general analyses of Ugaritic myths
are wholly dependent upon the adequacy of this method.
Appropriate here is a comment from Leach's *Rethinking
Anthropology*: 'In the heyday of functionalism simple cause
and effect relationship were all that were sought for in the
way of explanation....If an institutionalized arrangement
could be shown to "satisfy a need", it was not considered
necessary to look further' (31). Particularly striking is
Leach's assumption that the 'heyday of functionalism'
resides in some bygone era. Many students of Near Eastern
myths plainly remain embedded in that age.

Finally, and to complete this abbreviated tour of the
Near East, I want to turn to Egypt and to some comments of
J. Gwyn Griffiths with regard to the Egyptian myth of Horus
and Seth. I can perhaps speak most briefly here since I
have discussed 'The contendings of Horus and Seth', and
Griffiths's analysis of it, at length elsewhere (32).
Griffiths's comments are most relevant in the context of the
present discussion, for his interpretation of this myth is
fundamentally grounded in the two presuppositions under
investigation here. Of the origin of the conflict between
Horus and Seth, Griffiths writes that the conflict 'is
political and historical in origin' and 'reflects tribal
struggles preceding the political union of Egypt under
Menes' (33). Of the myth's purpose, he argues that 'the
litigation of the Horus-Seth feud was a myth which obviously
gave theological sanction to the principle of rightful patri-
linear succession in the Egyptian kingship' (34). The
problematic assumptions in these two statements are perhaps
clear by this point in our discussion. Griffiths's first
statement holds true only if one can assume that there is
a one-for-one correspondence between the social background
of the Horus-Seth myth and the realities of Egyptian social
structure and history. His second statement holds true
only if one utilizes an explicitly causal functional explanation. These assumptions are, of course, made with great
regularity by students of Near Eastern myths more generally.
Yet it is precisely the adequacy and continued usefulness of
such assumptions that the present study wishes to question.

III

This survey of some of the methodological assumptions made,

though rarely defended, by the majority of those analysing
Near Eastern myths is a survey whose judgements are largely
negative. This critical tone seems justified, given the
disparity between the conclusions of those who have devoted
themselves to the theoretical discussion of mythical
interpretation and the interpretative framework regularly
utilized by students of Near Eastern myths. We might
therefore conclude by noting that there is available a method
of analysis which departs radically from the various
functionalist methods in common use. This method is
structuralism. It is chiefly the structuralists, several
of whom have been cited above, who have pointed out some of
the prevalent errors in many standard analyses of myths.
Moreover, neither of the arguably inadequate methodological
assumptions described and criticized above is utilized by
one who works from within a structuralist framework. The
reason why structuralism naturally avoids these errors, if
so they be, is, as Boon and Schneider have stated as clearly
as anyone, that structuralism demonstrates 'how domains of
a cultural semantic field can be liberated from socio-
functional prerequisites and reveal an autonomous integrity
analysable in its own right' (35). 'Mythology', Lévi-
Strauss claims with typical boldness, 'has no obvious
practical function' (36). The codes which myths use are,
to be sure, drawn *from the world*. However, these codes are
used in such a way that myths cease to speak *about the world*.
It is just here that the analysis of Near Eastern myths has
gone astray: it has consistently mistaken the code for the
message. Only by making such a mistake could students of
Near Eastern myths assume that these myths can be used as
documentary sources for the reconstruction of a given
ancient society.

NOTES

1 In thus arguing that the study of Near Eastern myths
   must cease to claim for itself a special and protected
   status, I am saying something about this discipline very
   similar to what Lévi-Strauss writes about the study of
   religion generally: 'If it is maintained that religion
   constitutes an autonomous order, requiring a special
   kind of investigation, it has to be removed from the
   common fate of objects of science. Religion...will
   inevitably appear, in the eyes of science, to be distinguished as no more than a sphere of confused ideas....
   Conversely, if religious ideas are accorded the same
   value as any other conceptual system, as giving access
   to the mechanism of thought, the procedures of religious

anthropology will acquire validity' (Claùde Lévi-Strauss,
Totemism, trans. Rodney Needham, Harmondsworth: Penguin
University Books 1973, p. 177). There have, of course,
been some methodological investigations into the study
of the Near Eastern myths, especially in the past few
years. I might mention here G.S. Kirk's *Myth: Its
Meaning and Functions in Ancient and Other Cultures*,
Cambridge: Cambridge University Press 1971, a volume
remarkable both for its judiciousness and for its
boldness, though I cannot assent to Kirk's ultimately
eclectic methods. Also to be noted is a recent study
entitled 'Northwest Semitic religion: A study of
relational structures', by David L. Petersen and Mark
Woodward, *Ugarit Forschungen*, 9 (1977), pp. 233-48.
This latter study mentions many of the same criticisms
of functionalism which I note below.

2   Claude Lévi-Strauss, *Structural Anthropology*, trans.
Claire Jacobson and Brooke Grundfest Schoepf, New York:
Basic Books 1963, pp. 88-9.

3   I.C. Jarvie, 'Limits of functionalism and alternatives
to it in anthropology', in Don Martindale, ed.,
Functionalism in the Social Sciences (American Academy
of Political and Social Science Monographs, 5),
Philadelphia: American Academy of Political and Social
Science 1965, p. 19. For a lengthy and ultimately quite
positive assessment of functionalism, see now Wilbert
E. Moore, 'Functionalism', in Tom Bottomore and Robert
Nisbet, eds, *A History of Sociological Analysis*, New
York: Basic Books 1978, pp. 321-61.

4   Carl G. Hempel, 'The logic of functional analysis', in
Aspects of Scientific Explanation, New York: Free Press
1965, p. 305.

5   Bronislaw Malinowski, *Magic, Science and Religion*,
Garden City: Doubleday Anchor 1954, p. 46.

6   Ibid., p. 89.

7. Ibid., p. 101.

8   Edmund Leach, *Lévi-Strauss*, revised edition, Glasgow:
Fontana/Collins 1974, p. 8. For a similar summary
statement of the present assessment of functionalism,
see Kirk, *Myth,* op. cit., pp. 6-7. Again, it is because
the criticisms of functionalism, some of which are
reviewed below, are convincing, and not because
functionalism is unfashionable, that the method needs
to be either modified considerably or abandoned. That
is to say, there are good reasons for the present low
regard for this method.

9   Jarvie, 'Limits of functionalism', op.cit., p. 31.

10 Robert C. Poole, 'Introduction', to Lévi-Strauss,
Totemism, op. cit., p. 40. This whole area of discussion,

including that of the functionalists' resort to 'anxiety',
is covered by Lévi-Strauss in *Totemism*, pp. 126-42.

11 Dan Sperber, *Rethinking Symbolism*, trans. Alice L. Morton
(Cambridge Studies in Social Anthropology), Cambridge:
Cambridge University Press 1975, pp. 8-9. Cf. Sperber's
statement of a similar problem with regard to a functionalist interpretation of myth on p. 6. Kirk (*Myth*, pp. 12-31)
offers a clear account of the discussion of the relationship between myth and ritual. Briefly, the boldest
statements of the myth-ritual school are regarded today
both as impossible to substantiate, and, more significantly, as not carrying with them anything of explanatory
significance.

12 Cf. Percy S. Cohen's objection that 'the chief weakness
of most sociological theories of myth is that they do
not really explain why the social function of myth should
be performed by myth and not by some other device':
'Theories of myth', *Man*, NS 4 (1969), p. 345. The
observations of both Sperber and Cohen here were antici-
·pated by Lévi-Strauss: 'Some claim that human societies
merely express, through their mythology, fundamental
feelings common to the whole of mankind....But why
should these societies do it in such elaborate and
devious ways, when all of them are also acquainted with
empirical explanations?' (*Structural Anthropology*, p. 207).

13 Hempel, 'The logic of functional analysis', pp. 297-330.

14 Ibid., p. 310. Hempel's account of functional explanations is as follows:
  (a) At *t*, *s* functions adequately in a setting of kind
      c (characterized by specific internal and external
      conditions)
  (b) *s* functions adequately in setting of kind *c* only if
      a certain necessary condition, *n*, is satisfied
  (c) If *i* were present in *s*, then, as an effect, condition
      n would be satisfied
  (d) (Hence), at *t*, trait *i* is present in *s*
This explanation 'involves the fallacy of affirming the
consequent in regard to premise (*c*)', and it 'fails to
explain why the trait *i* rather than one of its alternatives
is present in *s* at *t*' (p. 310). For a clear description
of Hempel's argument, and a comprehensive discussion of
the attempts to revise the argument, see Hans H. Penner,
'Creating a *Brahman*: A structural approach to religion',
in Robert D. Baird, ed., *Methodological Issues in
Religious Studies*, Chico, California: New Horizon Press
1975, pp. 55-9. Anyone familiar with Penner's article
will recognize my heavy reliance upon it in the above
paragraph.

15 Claude Lévi-Strauss, *The Raw and the Cooked: Introduction*

to a *Science of Mythology: I,* trans. John and Doreen
Weightman, New York: Harper Colophon 1975, p. 332.

16   Claude Lévi-Strauss, 'The story of Asdiwal', in Edmund
Leach, ed., *The Structural Study of Myth and Totemism*
(A.S.A. Monographs, 4), London: Tavistock 1967, pp.' 10-11
and 29-30 (=Claude Lévi-Strauss, *Structural Anthropology:
Volume II,* trans. Monique Layton, New York: Basic Books
1976, pp. 155-6 and 172-3).   The most extensive critique
of Lévi-Strauss's 'The Story of Asdiwal' is that of
L.L. Thomas, J.Z. Kronenfeld and D.B. Kronenfeld, 'Asdiwal
crumbles: a critique of Lévi-Straussian myth analysis',
American Ethnologist, 3 (1976), 147-73.   There is hardly
opportunity here for a lengthy discussion of this
critique.   However, it might be noted briefly that
Thomas, Kronenfeld and Kronenfeld are wrong in their
implicit assumption that a system of kinship is, for
Lévi-Strauss, a system of actual behaviour.   For a
structuralist, as James A. Boon and David M. Schneider
note, 'societies do not *have* patrilateral or matrilateral
systems;   rather groups or parts of groups reveal ideas
of such marriages which might be carried out to various
extents...marriage rules are not laws, rather norms.
And norms are normative, not actual'.   'Kinship vis-à-vis
myth: Contrasts in Lévi-Strauss' approaches to cross-
cultural comparison', *American Anthropologist,* 76 (1974),
p. 810.   For an excellent, and critical, theoretical
discussion of Lévi-Strauss, see Ivan Strenski, 'Falsifying
deep structures', *Man,* NS 9 (1974), pp. 571-84.

17   *Structural Anthropology: II,* pp. 198-210.

18   Ibid., p. 207.

19   An example may be Jacobsen's continued utilization of
the terminology of Otto, even in his recent works: see
Thorkild Jacobsen, *The Treasures of Darkness: A History
of Mesopotamian Religion,* New Haven and London: Yale
University Press 1976, p. 3.   The best description of
Otto's position with which I am familiar is that of
Helfer: 'This stance constitutes a Protestant polemic
against all forms of religious knowledge and experience
which do not, in content as well as structure, recapitulate
Otto's own....His position is the *reductio ad absurdum*
of methodologically solipsistic apriorism':   James S.
Helfer, ed., *On Method in the History of Religions
(History and Theory,* Beiheft 8), Middletown, Conn.:
Wesleyan University Press 1968, p. 4.

20   Thorkild Jacobsen, 'Primitive democracy in ancient
Mesopotamia', in *Toward the Image of Tammuz,* ed., William
L. Moran (Harvard Semitic Series, 21), Cambridge, Mass.:
Harvard University Press 1970, p. 169 - originally
published in *Journal of Near Eastern Studies,* 2 (1943),
159-72.

21 Jacobsen himself is much too wise to rely solely upon
    myths for his reconstruction of primitive democracy,
    though the same cannot be said for many who have utilized
    this model in subsequent discussions. See Jacobsen's
    fuller discussion of this model in 'Primitive democracy
    in ancient Mesopotamia' and in the study referred to in
    the following note.
22 Thorkild Jacobsen, 'Early political development in
    Mesopotamia', in *Toward the Image of Tammuz,* p. 137 -
    originally published in *Zeitschrift für Assyriologie,*
    52 (1957), 91-140.
23 'Early political development in Mesopotamia', op. cit.,
    p. 137.
24 For examples of the continued reference to Jacobsen's
    primitive democracy model, see Geoffrey Evans, 'Ancient
    Mesopotamian assemblies', *JAOS,* 78 (1958), 1, or William
    W. Hallo and William Kelly Simpson, *The Ancient Near
    East: A History,* New York: Harcourt, Brace, Jovanovich
    1971, pp. 42-3. (in this latter work there is the
    recognition that the model is 'reconstructed in part
    from later mythology'). Georges Roux argues that there
    are problems with the model, but accurately observes
    that the theory is 'still widely accepted in the United
    States': *Ancient Iraq,* Harmondsworth: Penguin 1976,
    p. 105. As noted above, this is much more the case
    among biblical scholars than it is among Assyriologists.
25 'Early Mesopotamian constitutional development',
    American Historical Review, 72 (1967), 1213.
26 Cf. Lévi-Strauss, 'The story of Asdiwal', op. cit., p. 30
    (=*Structural Anthropology: II,* p. 173).
27 I refer to his *The Legacy of Canaan,* 2d edition *(SVT* 5),
    Leiden: E.J. Brill 1965, and to *The Krt Text in the
    Literature of Ras Shamra: A Social Myth of Ancient
    Canaan,* 2d edition, Leiden: E.J. Brill 1964. Note the
    subtitle of the latter work. Gray, in common with many
    others, does attempt to make some distinction between
    saga or legend and myth (see, e.g., *The Krt Text,* pp. 4-5).
    However, I would argue that in the present state of the
    discussion of this issue, we are on the firmest ground
    in labelling as a myth any traditional narrative which
    deals with the activities of superhuman beings, and thus
    that the Keret tale, like the tales of Baal or Aqhat, is
    a myth. Cf. the definition of myth formulated by Joseph
    Fontenrose, *The Ritual Theory of Myth* (University of
    California Folklore Studies, 18), Berkeley: University
    of California Press 1966, pp. 54-5, and the discussion
    of myths and folktales in Kirk, *Myth,* pp. 31-41.
28 *The Legacy of Canaan,* p. 18.
29 Ibid., p. 13. A fine and critical discussion of Gray's

functionalism, which bears upon the statement of Gray just cited, is Islwyn Blythin's 'Magic and Methodology', *Numen*, 17 (1970), pp. 45-59. A particular virtue of Blythin's study is his observation that some of the views of earlier anthropologists, especially Frazer, have become 'deeply entrenched in Old Testament study' (p. 53).

30   John Gray, *The Krt Text,* op. cit., p. 4. Cf. Gray's similar statement about the Keret tale in *The Legacy of Canaan,* op. cit., p. 17.

31   E.R. Leach, *Rethinking Anthropology* (London School of Economics Monographs on Social Anthropology, 22), London: Athlone Press 1961, p. 65.

32   Robert A. Oden, Jr,'"The contendings of Horus and Seth" (Pap. Chester Beatty I): A structural interpretation', *History of Religions,* 18 (Spring, 1979).

33   J. Gwyn Griffiths, *The Conflict of Horus and Seth, from Egyptian and Classical Sources* (Liverpool Monographs in Archaeology and Oriental Studies), Liverpool: Liverpool University Press 1960, p. vii.

34   Ibid., p. 68.

35   Boon and Schneider, 'Kinship vis-à-vis myth', op. cit., p. 814;   cf. Lévi-Strauss's own similar statement, cited above (note 15).

36   Lévi-Strauss, *The Raw and the Cooked,* op. cit., p. 10.

R.A. ODEN, Jr is an Assistant Professor of Religion at Dartmouth College. Among his publications are editions of (pseudo-) Lucian's *Syrian Goddess* and Philo Byblius' *Phoenician History,* as well as studies in the areas of Semitic philology and of method in the study of religion.

Prof. R.A. Oden, Jr, Dept of Religion, Dartmouth College, Hanover, New Hampshire 03755, USA.

WENDY DONIGER O'FLAHERTY

Inside and Outside the Mouth of God:
The Boundary between Myth and Reality

1. Introduction

Do MYTHS REMIND US of passionate moments in life, or are those moments compelling because they remind us of myths? This is no longer a burning question in the study of mythology, in part because we despair of ever answering it and in part because it has gone out of fashion. For, ever since the massive takeover of mythology by the social science cartel, myths have been set to work at practical rather than spiritual tasks, while, on the other hand, contemporary theologians in their intellectual mufti are embarrassed by a formulation that cuts so close to the bone of ontology, to the question of whether or not there really is anything "out there," and, if so, what it is.

But *within* the myths this has always been, and still is, an issue of great moment, and it has fascinated a line of scholars that extends from Plato through Jung to Eliade. In returning to this basic question about the nature of mythology, I will both challenge and stretch the insights of these scholars, while locking horns, *en passant*, with the social scientists and their theory of the function of myth as social charter. Moreover, I hope to show that even those who (like Freud) have denied the validity or value of myth, or who (like Claude Lévi-Strauss) see its function in logical rather than irrational constructions of reality, can contribute greatly to our understanding of the irrational truth of myth. Finally, it is my contention that recent speculations by natural scientists about what is "out there," as well as about the mechanism of memory in the human brain (i.e., "in here"), allow us to take seriously the assertion of myths not only that there is indeed something out there, but that it may be far more "there" (in the sense that, as Gertrude Stein remarked about Oakland, there is no "there" there) than what is normally referred to as reality.[1]

There are as many definitions of myth as there are mythologists, and as many definitions of reality as philosophers, and I do not intend to pick a fight with any of them at this point. In this essay I will make use of several overlapping but not, I think, contradictory definitions of myth and reality; definitions of myth, like myth variants, build up a composite image of something that cannot be said once and for all.[2] Moreover, since the very point of many of the texts I will be using is that one is forced to modify radically one's definitions of myth and reality in midstream, I will often use the terms in one sense at the beginning of a passage and in a very different sense at the end. I hope the context will guide the reader when the ambiguities become dizzying, and if I stretch the words beyond their normal usages, I will, like Humpty Dumpty, try to pay them extra.[3]

If we cannot pin down our definitions of myth and reality, we can at least indicate the general area in which the terms vibrate, like a group in set theory or the atoms of a table in the theory of indeterminacy. Reality, also known as material or historical existence (*"Wie es eigentlich gewesen ist"*), generally refers to the phenomenal physical world that is the hunting ground of the natural sciences (though myth often poaches on it[4]). It is also roughly equivalent to common sense, "common" in that it is agreed upon by most sane people, and "sense" in that it is rationally apprehended by sight, touch, and so forth, and can be measured or mapped in standard units of time and space. Reality to each of us is the span of existence that we live through and perceive. Though myth, too, is "common" in that it uses recurrent, traditional, shared imagery (and may in fact provide the most reliable link between individual perceptions of reality[5]), it is both "uncommon" and "non-sense" in that it draws upon highly personal (albeit universal) experiences and expresses them through a medium that is neither rational nor methodical but rather imaginary or metaphysical. Where memory and science have been described as cognitive maps (of the "real world"),[6] myth is a cosmic map of the intersecting territories of reality and fantasy.[7]

Just as it is possible to find a linguistic prototype by tracing back historic lines until they converge,[8] so too we may seek the realm of myth by following certain convergent lines. That we attempt to translate myths from one culture to another implies the presupposition of a common core not only of experience, but also of the symbolic system to express that experience. We map out one territory from the study of symbolic systems (poetry, ritual, theatre) and another from our awareness of human experience (our own and what we learn from history, psychology, anthropology), and where they intersect is the land of which myth is the map.

It is not necessary, I think, to postulate a collective unconscious in order to explain the uncanny recurrence of certain figures in this landscape, enduring motifs for which "archetypes" is probably as good a word as any, and one hallowed by a usage stretching back beyond Plotinus. It is, however, necessary to understand the ways in which myth and reality intersect, or, rather, to understand the ways in which we presuppose that myth arises from a common understanding or experience of reality.

Archetypes are not myths; they are elements within myths, and they occur in other symbolic modes as well, particularly in those that aspire to achieve what myths often achieve. In our secular world, the myths that express our fusion of fantasy and reality are found not only in the remains of ancient sacred scriptures, but also in dreams, the theatre, films, in stories told to children, in works of art, and, most of all, in our own actual experience.[9] One might view these various expressions as being ranged on a continuum of common sense or agreed criteria of validity, between reality and imagination, spanning (from the "hard" end) science, history, and anthropology, through drama, ritual, film, and literature, to (at the "soft" end) dreams and personal fantasy. Myth and personal experience are incorporated to greater or lesser degrees in all these forms of cognition.

My analysis of myth turns on the question of limits (the pivot of all the articles in the present symposium) in two ways. "Limit" may be construed as a barrier to human understanding or as a borderline between two adjacent territories. By defining myth in the second of these senses, as a boundary line where fantasy and reality meet, I hope to show how it may be used in the first sense, as a place where an apparent barrier to human understanding may be forded or breached by the translation of one person's reality into another's through the mediation of myth.[10] To this end, I have selected from the great variety of myths a few that deal explicitly and self-consciously with the question of intersecting levels of myth and reality. Though I will limit myself primarily to the Indian, Greek, and Shakespearean myths that I know best, the reader will surely recall his own favorites that tell a very similar tale; that resonance is precisely the point of this essay.

2. The Unreality of Reality: Myths of the Mouth of God

Myths that apply "scientific," common sense criteria to apparently mythic, imaginary phenomena and myths that lay bare the magical nerve in apparently everyday phenomena are two complementary genres. We will begin with the second type, that peels back the cover from ostensibly "real" experience, and progress from there to the reality of ostensibly "mythic" experience.

Myths of the second type often make use of the image of entering the mouth of God. Such a myth is the story of Krishna and Yashodha:

> One day when the children were playing, they reported to Yashodha, the mother of Krishna (who was an incarnation of the god Vishnu), "Krishna has eaten dirt!" Yashodha took Krishna by the hand and scolded him and said, "You naughty boy, why have you eaten dirt?" "I haven't," said Krishna. "All the boys are lying. If you believe them instead of me, look at my mouth yourself." "Then, open up," she said to the god, who had in sport taken the form of a human child, and he opened his mouth.

> Then she saw in his mouth the whole universe, with the far corners of the sky, and the wind, and lightning, and the orb of the earth with its mountains and oceans, and the moon and stars, and space itself; and she saw her own village and herself. She became frightened and confused, thinking, Is this a dream or an illusion fabricated by God? Or is it a delusion in my own mind? Or is it a portent of the powers of this little boy, my son? For God's power of delusion inspires in me such false beliefs as "I exist," "This is my husband," "This is my son." When she had come to understand true reality in this way, God spread his magic illusion in the form of maternal love. Instantly Yashodha lost her memory of what had occurred. She took her son on her lap and was as she had been before, but her heart was flooded with even greater love for God, whom she regarded as her son.[11]

Hindu myths of this sort pull the carpet out from under reality by lifting the barrier expressed by the image of the mouth of God. On the narrative level of myth, in which gods participate as dramatis personae, the world of events occurring outside the mouth of God is regarded as real, a common sense world with one moon and one sun in the sky. But we do not remain on this level for long. When the myth of Yashodha opens, we think we know what reality is; it is the life of a harried mother with her mischievous child. Then, suddenly, when she glances into the mouth of the child, we learn that the child is God, and that inside his mouth there is a world that appears to be mythical or at least unreal (since it replicates the world that we have assumed to be uniquely real). Yashodha cannot sustain the vision of that world; she cannot bear the idea that *that* might be reality. She thinks it may be a dream or a hallucination of her own making, or an illusion or portent sent by God. We who read the myth know it is the fourth of these options, as well as an inversion of the third: the *rest* of her life is an illusion, as she herself realizes while gazing inside the mouth of God. This illusion is *maya*, the divine magic that makes the phenomenal world seem real to us when, in the view of classical Hindu philosophy, it is not. Out of pity for her in her fear and confusion, Krishna erases the vision of reality and substitutes for it the illusion that he is not God but merely her son. This illusion is made of maternal love. [12]

The child plays an important role in another myth about the mouth of God:

> After Vishnu burnt the universe to ashes at doomsday and then flooded it with water, he slept in the midst of the cosmic ocean. The sage Markandeya had been swallowed by the god and roamed inside his belly for many thousands of years, visiting the sacred places on earth. One day he slipped out of the god's mouth and saw the world and the ocean shrouded in darkness. He did not recognize himself there, because of God's illusion, and he became terrified. Then he saw the sleeping god, and he was amazed, wondering, Am I crazy, or dreaming? I must be imagining that the world has disappeared, for such a calamity could never really happen. Then he was swallowed again, and as soon as he was back in the belly of the god, he thought his vision had been a dream.
>
> So, as before, he roamed the earth for hundreds of years, and then again he slipped out of Vishnu's mouth. This time he saw a little boy hidden in the branches of a banyan tree, a boy who blazed so like the sun that Markandeya could not bear to look at him. I think I have seen this once before, mused the sage. I think I'm being fooled by the illusion of God. In confusion and terror, Markandeya began to swim away, but Vishnu said, "Do not be afraid, my son. Come here. I am your father." Markandeya bowed to him with love, and Vishnu taught him His true nature and commanded him to return inside His belly. Then Vishnu swallowed Markandeya once more, and the sage lived there in peace, longing to hear again the true nature of God. [13]

Like Yashodha, Markandeya at first thinks that some sort of illusion is being foisted upon him, and, like her, he gets it backwards: when he falls out of the mouth he feels he has entered an illusion, not knowing he has just escaped from the illusion. Both Markandeya and Yashodha think that God is a child and that they themselves may be dreaming or crazy.

But the myth of Markandeya goes on to develop a view that is the inverse of the myth of Yashodha. Ultimately, Markandeya understands the truth of the vision and becomes identified with the enlightened narrator of the myth. As the myth progresses, the protagonist is gradually released from his delusions; he discovers that God is not (or not merely) a child, whereas the persistent belief that God is her child continues to ensnare Yashodha. For her, the experience of the real hierophany takes place inside the mouth; for him, it takes place outside the mouth. The actual starting point is arbitrary, for the point of the enlightenment is the transition, the motion across the threshold—in either direction. But Markandeya continues to move back and forth between the two worlds until he ends up with the double image of both at once, while Yashodha's momentary experience of a new reality is never repeated, and she rejects it permanently.

Since she is a woman, and a mother, she cannot live for long on the plane of metaphysics but lapses back into emotional involvement; since he is a man and a sage, he cannot live for long on any level other than the metaphysical.[14]

The myth attempts within the frame of the story what the text attempts in the culture: to teach the philosophical doctrine of illusion to nonphilosophical worldly Hindus who dwell in the common sense world of materialism and science, the world in which reality is defined by normal, social, conventional human existence ("This is my husband," "This is my son"). Within the myth of Yashodha, this lesson is a failure: she does not change her view of what reality is. Outside the myth, however, the situation is the reverse: the reader (or hearer) does change his view; he is moved to redefine his concept of reality. The persuasive power of the vision in the myth is not logical but irrational and emotional; it dismantles our rational disbelief even while it fails to overcome Yashodha's combination of rationality (in clinging to the phenomenal world) and irrationality (in backsliding from her moment of pellucid enlightenment into the comfortable, familiar maternal love of the god). The myth of Markandeya, on the other hand, works in the opposite way: Markandeya *does* change his view of what reality is, and he does this by being shocked into a state of metaphysical rationality and a philosophically grounded love of the god. Doubtless, many readers of the text would follow him on this path, and others would not.

Both Yashodha and Markandeya mediate between two points of view, that of the omniscient narrator or enlightened sage (who knows that reality is on the other side of the mouth of God) and that of the blinkered participant in the drama (the other villagers or inhabitants of Vishnu's stomach, who think that reality is on this side of the mouth of God). For us, as readers of the myth, several options are presented: one could play the role of Yashodha or the role of Markandeya, for each of us must find the level on which he prefers to live—or, rather, the level on which he was meant to live. In any case, the myth jars us out of simply accepting the level on which we happened to be before we encountered the myth.

The androcentrism inherent in the Hindu pattern of saved males and doomed females[15] is somewhat mitigated—and perhaps explained—by the thinly veiled female gender of the divinity who swallows the protagonist. For, inside the mouth of God is not merely his belly, but his womb. The demonic sage Shukra is swallowed by the god Shiva and then emitted through Shiva's phallus in the form of seed; the divine sage Kaca is in turn swallowed by Shukra and emitted through his side.[16] Each of these sages emerges with the secret of immortality and is, in addition, made immortal by becoming the child of the god who gives birth to him; in this he enacts the "true" perception of reality appropriate to the enlightened male sage (Markandeya, Jesus), in contrast with the deluded woman's view of god as her child (Yashodha, Mary). The symbolic femaleness of the swallowing god becomes literal in a final variant in this series, in which Shukra is seized by a female demon who has teeth and eyes in her vagina; she swallows him not with her upper mouth but with her lower, the *vagina dentata*.[17]

Shukra is merely one Indian example of the hero who journeys through the gates of hell or through the jaws of the dragon who guards the gates of hell. Odysseus survives a number of encounters with such devouring females with their "hollow caves" and toothy mouths; Scylla is the most blatant of these, with her hollow cave in the middle of her body, lined with teeth full of black death,[18] but she is followed hotly by Charybdis, Circe, Calypso, the Sirens, and Clytaemnestra. In Euripides' *Bacchae* the worshipers of Dionysus devour him ritually by devouring the animals in whom he dwells (primarily cattle); Pentheus, who rejects the god by steadfastly refusing to acknowledge the way in which the myth has taken over his reality, is dismembered by the god's human instruments, the mediating women, the Bacchae. Dionysus (who is androgynous in his birth as well as in his form) proves his existence to the skeptical Pentheus by using him as the sacrificial victim in place of the god himself or of the usual surrogates. The god draws Pentheus helplessly and hypnotically into the whirlpool of the myth that he denies, by transposing the myth from the ancient past *(in illo tempore)*, where Pentheus thinks it belongs, into the present moment, collapsing profane and mythic time together,[19] as ritual so often does. That Pentheus is forced to behave like a child and is then killed by his own mother has further significance in the context of the myths of Shukra and Kaca (who are devoured by gods who then give birth to them from male wombs).

On the psychological level, one could gloss this corpus of myths as expressions of a deep and widespread fear of being devoured by the mother (a projection of oral aggression) or by the whore (the myth of *vagina dentata*).[20] Indeed, the universality of the experience of being fed milk at the breast (and the subsequent correlative experience of feeding semen to the vagina) may well explain why this particular corporeal image is so often unconsciously chosen to express so abstract a concept as the transition from the physical to the metaphysical world. To this extent, the Freudian hypothesis does help us to understand the processes of creative thought.

But the truth or falsehood of the Freudian gloss in no way diminishes the role of the myth in jarring us into a reassessment of the nature of the reality of the world. For the myth sets out explicitly to dramatize the fact that the boundary between myth and reality is highly mobile: though it may appear to be firm and permanent, it is ultimately arbitrary and elusive.

3. Levels of Reality in Dreams and the Theatre: The Last Visible Dog

Within the myths characters often believe (mistakenly) they are dreaming, while other, wiser observers suggest that, on the contrary, people who think they are dreaming often perceive (rightly) that they are participating in a myth—that is, that they have actually crossed over to the other side of the mouth of God. And mythologists suggest both that dreams incorporate into personal fantasy elements of traditional, shared mythology, and that mythology is built up out of shared elements pooled from individual dreams. This is not the occasion to review the extensive literature on myths and dreams, nor to assess the oft-challenged hypothesis that the universality of the vocabulary of dreams may be the basis of the universality of the vocabulary of myths.[21] Eliade puts the case well: "The unconscious displays the structure of a private mythology. . . . It can even be said that modern man's only real contact with cosmic sacrality is effected by the unconscious, whether in his dreams and his imaginative life or in the creations that arise out of the unconscious (poetry, games, spectacles, etc.)."[22] Stories about dreams, like stories about myths, often deliberately obfuscate the understructure of common sense in such a way as to leave the reader uncertain which is the "real" level, like the victim of a practical joke who wakes up after a drunken night to find himself in a room in which the rugs and chairs have been affixed to the ceiling and the chandelier appears to grow out of the ground. A famous example of such obfuscation is the story of the Chinese philosopher Chuang Tsu:

> Once upon a time Chuang Tsu dreamed that he was a butterfly, a butterfly fluttering about enjoying itself. It did not know that it was Chuang Tsu. Suddenly he awoke with a start and he was Chuang Tsu again. But he did not know whether he was Chuang Tsu who had dreamed that he was a butterfly, or whether he was a butterfly dreaming he was Chuang Tsu.[23]

Stories of this sort, perhaps imported from India or China, were known and loved in classical antiquity.[24]

A delightful modern variant of the Chinese myth of the dream is the work of Woody Allen:

> The Emperor Ho Sin had a dream in which he beheld a palace greater than his for half the rent. Stepping through the portals of the edifice, Ho Sin suddenly found that his body became young again, although his head remained somewhere between sixty-five and seventy.[25] Opening a door, he found another door, which led to another; soon he realized he had entered a hundred doors and was now out in the backyard. . . . When the Emperor awoke he was in a cold sweat and couldn't recall if he dreamed the dream or was now in a dream being dreamt by his bail bondsman.[26]

Despite the characteristically Allenesque incongruities, the myth emerges as a myth through its classical mixture of the magical and the banal, the dream/reality reversal, and the doors beyond doors.

A famous literary example of the dream turned inside out is the episode of the Red King in *Through the Looking Glass*, in which Alice tries to prove that she is real by pointing out that she is crying, an appeal to the emotional truth of myth but one that is wasted on Tweedledum, who simply remarks, in a tone of great contempt, "I hope you don't suppose those are *real* tears?" At the end of the book it appears that Alice has dreamed that the Red King dreamed that Alice saw him dreaming of her, but Lewis Carroll will not let us solve the riddle so easily: "Let's consider who it was that dreamed it all. This is a serious question. . . . He was part of my dream, of course—but then I was part of his dream, too! . . . Which do *you* think it was?"[27]

One device that Carroll uses to blur the boundaries is a variant of the traditional technique of the Chinese box narrative, the tale within the tale within the tale, or the doors within doors. The twist comes when Carroll reverses the position of two of the narrators in the chain (Alice and the Red King), further challenging the reader's assumption that he is on the very outside of the box— the last one in the line of listeners—rather than part of the story being told to yet someone else.

Myths often imply that there is no end to the boxes, sketching an infinitely receding image that may be represented visually, as on the Dutch Cleanser can: a woman holding a Dutch Cleanser can with a picture of a woman holding a

Dutch Cleanser can with a picture of a woman . . . Velasquez's painting that makes use of this device (a man with a mirror) is ingeniously hung in the Prado on a wall facing a mirror, so that the observer can trace the images inside the painting and then outside it again, with himself as the pivotal level of "reality." The metaphysical implications of this *mise en abîme* make use of that peculiar juxtaposition of the banal and sublime (the "incongruity" of myth[28]) that serves Woody Allen's humor (as it served Benchley and Perelman before him, and the narrators of comic myths centuries before them), but also serves a far more serious purpose. In Russell Hoban's book for children, the "last visible dog" on a can of dogfood, illustrated like the Dutch Cleanser can, becomes a symbol for heaven, for the place where the protagonists find a release from the hell of their reality.[29]

The locus classicus for this onion-layer technique of storytelling is the play within the play, which often carries with it the implication that the audience witnessing the play, within which there is a play, is itself part of a play — perhaps part of a play within another (metaphysical) play. Of all literary forms, drama best reproduces the effects of myth, most powerfully through the catharsis of the tragic drama, but also in the surreal humor of great comedy such as Aristophanes' *The Frogs*.[30] In our day, drama (or film) often takes the place of the communal ritual that was a frequent (though certainly not inevitable) complement to the traditional myth.[31] Drama built upon archetypes functions as the enactment of a myth.

Shakespeare is the supreme master of the play within the play, not merely in his explicit use of the device, as in *Hamlet* and *A Midsummer Night's Dream*, but in the depiction of historical characters conscious of their roles as actors. Richard II acts out a play that he constantly rewrites and plays as an alternative, personal reality competing with the reality based on historical facts[32] (a reality that is, in its turn, merely another myth,[33] somewhat closer to the common sense end of the continuum between reality and fantasy, but hardly the photographic representation of "*Wie es eigentlich gewesen ist*" that the nineteenth century historians thought they had snapped). But Richard II is not merely acting out a play; he is playing a myth — or, rather, playing two myths. Richard is making his own life into a myth by selecting classical fragments that correspond to the actual events of his life and constructing a dramatic truth out of them. Yet he also perceives, in a less specific way, an entire myth to which his inner tragedy corresponds. By comparing himself to Christ betrayed by Judas, "Richard is finding his supporting script. He is finding the fragments of the myth, the outline to carry his purified emotion through the scene he is about to act — and create. He is Christ again in the holiness which is violated — but he is particularly Christ in the infidelity around him."[34] Richard does not merely *make* the myth he lives; he also *finds* it.

4. The Chain Reaction between Reality and Myth

Hindu literature is self-conscious about the role of the audience in the play within the play. The use of aesthetic experience in salvation was the subject of much discussion; by seeing, and therefore participating in, the enactment of the myth of Krishna, one was led unconsciously into the proper stance of the devotee. Moreover, the viewer was not merely inspired to decide what role in the cosmic drama he wished to play (mother, lover, brother, or friend of Krishna); like Richard II, he was inspired to discover what role he *was* playing, had been playing all along, without knowing it.[35]

This assumption is implicit in the argument in Aristophanes' *The Frogs*, a play within a play whose protagonists are playwrights. In answer to Aeschylus's accusation that Euripides had put "unholy matings" on the stage—in particular by depicting the incestuous passion of Phaedra with Hippolytus, Bellerophon with Stheneboia, and anonymous women who go to bed with their brothers— and that Euripides had called Oedipus a happy man,[36] Euripides replies that his depictions were harmless. To this Aeschylus objects, saying that married women took hemlock out of shame because of Euripides' depiction of the love of Stheneboia for her stepson Bellerophon. Here Aeschylus blurs the permeable fourth wall between theatre and reality: the audience becomes part of the drama by reacting to it. Euripides is being judged not only for the actions of "his" Bellerophon and Stheneboia, but for the actions of the "real" women who took hemlock as a result of seeing the play.

Euripides counters this with a claim that mythic drama and reality do in fact intersect, but on a different plane, and one that justifies rather than condemns his depiction of the myth: "The story I told about Phaedra was true, wasn't it?" he argues, and Aeschylus does not deny this.[37] But Aeschylus's final rebuttal takes yet another tack: he says that even true stories, when immoral, should not be put on the stage, since poets speak to young men (in the world of the theatre) as the schoolmaster speaks to children (in the world of reality). Thus Aeschylus accepts the assertion that real events do lead to myths about real events (that the story of Phaedra was true), but turns around and asserts that the myths, in their turn, produce real events (forming the character of young men as the school-master instructs children), for better or for worse.

This very Greek line of reasoning is also found in Plato, who says that the tyrant enacts what haunts us in dreams when *logos* fails us; these thoughts, suppressed even in sleep, are present in everyone (an early argument for the universality of the dream/myth): someone will lie with his mother or with a god or an animal, or commit murder or eat forbidden things (a possible reference to cannibalism), and so on. Eros is the tyrant in all of us, but, Plato warns, we must not tell stories like that about the gods to children even if they are *true*.[38] Like Aristophanes, Plato affirms the power of myths to grow out of reality and to *make* reality, in turn. The individual could, like Richard II, both find his myth and make his myth, and Plato fears that people will find a bad myth, and use it to construct an evil reality.

For a vivid Greek example of the unconsious play within the play used as a device to prove the reality of myth, one need look no farther than Sophocles' *Oedipus Rex*, where, with grotesque irony, Sophocles has Iocasta assure Oedipus that he need not worry about the prediction that he would sleep with his mother, since everyone knows that that is something that men always dream about (as Plato pointed out) but never do.[39] Penelope advances a similar argument when Odysseus, in disguise, tells her that her dream of an eagle killing the geese in the house means that her husband (Odysseus) will return to kill the suitors. She says that dreams that pass through the gates of horn come true, but those that pass through the gates of ivory do not, and she thinks that her dream was not from the gates of horn.[40] She is, of course, as wrong as Iocasta was. That Oedipus is fooled into mistaking a true myth (that is, a myth that is his reality, a dream from the gates of horn) for a "mere dream" (from the gates of ivory) is an illusion (like those that Markandeya and Yashodha *thought* they were experiencing). This illusion is raised to yet another level by the next frame of the myth: for we, the audience, know the reality not only of Oedipus's incest but of our own, an insight clear as day to the Greeks 2,500 years before Sigmund Freud made it a canon.

The assumption that the myth in the theatre expresses a human truth shared by the audience is implicit in Aeschylus's accusation of Euripides: the effect of the myth of Stheneboia and Bellerophon was not to establish a social law ("Don't commit incest.") or to reinforce an already existing social law ("Aren't you glad you don't commit incest!"), nor to inspire antisocial behavior ("How about committing incest?" arguing on the lines that violence on television causes children to grow up violent), but to reveal an already existing reality, one that was masked and unconsciously denied. It made women commit suicide out of shame at the sudden realization of their own incestuous impulses, by showing them that they were already participating in the myth of Stheneboia by virtue of their erotic relationships with their sons.[41] This is reinforced by Aristophanes' equation of the audience with the sinners in hell, a motley group who include sexual miscreants.[42]

The myth/drama in *Hamlet* has the same effect on Claudius that the myth of Stheneboia had on the Greek wives: it makes him face not only the fact that his guilt is known but even the fact that he is guilty; the play within the play precipitates him directly into the episode of (unsuccessful) repentant prayer. For, to the extent that (as Shaw pointed out) conscience is the fear of being caught, the public experience of mythic truth through the drama is the instrument of conscience—not of social conscience, but of cumulative individual conscience.

5. Myth as the Inverse of Social Charter

Myths of the mouth of God are the opposite of social charters. The social charter theory has an impeccable Durkheimian pedigree and remains canonical for most anthropologists today, as well as for Eliade, who cites Malinowski's straightforward definition: "These stories . . . are to the natives a statement of a primeval, greater, and more relevant reality, by which the present life, fates, and activities of mankind are determined, the knowledge of which supplies man with the motive for ritual and moral actions, as well as with indications as to how to perform them."[43] This description, of course, applies to many myths; indeed, it is even applicable to certain aspects of the myths of the mouth of God, for often the one who is swallowed is not a dégagé sage but a very much engagé hero, who emerges from the liminal jaws to give birth to a culture and to establish its ritual forms[44] (including, of course, the ritual of initiation for which the myth provides the archetypal model). Athena, swallowed by Zeus and then reborn to teach the Greeks their crafts, is an example of such a combination of motifs.[45] The myth as social charter is also manifest in the "moral primer" function of the myth of history.[46]

But many myths ultimately depart from the limitations of the social charter. They do indeed reveal a "more relevant reality" that inspires certain action; they inspire "archaic man," in Eliade's formulation, to reenact certain rituals; they inspire the witness of the mythic drama to reassess his view of reality or even to act in a different way; and they are "social" in the sense that they may be shared or cumulative experiences of moral conscience as well as common bodies of traditional knowledge. But they are not social charters.

Aristophanes and Plato disapproved of myths precisely because they did *not* teach people the right way to behave; on the contrary, the myths showed how inevitable "bad" behavior was, an insight that is at the heart of the tragic drama. The element of cumulative individual conscience might indeed inspire action, and to that extent it might be regarded as prescriptive, but it inspired *bad* actions: Greek women to drink hemlock, and Claudius to have Hamlet shanghaied. Lévi-Strauss has pointed out that myth imagines certain impossible situations in order to show that they *are* impossible, to allow us to go on living with an insoluble paradox.[47] Repressed Hindus rejoice in myths of extreme forms of ascetic yogic mortification and erotic Tantric orgiasticism; these mythologies provide fantasies that establish the boundaries of the real Hindu world, making it possible to totter on the brink without actually falling into it, and then to come back to the realm of the possible, now a world whose bounds have been extended, if only by a little.[48] The myth supplies an ideal no less useful for being unreal. It is a target (positive or negative) that establishes the full range of the scale, like the paradox of Achilles and the tortoise: you never reach the shore, but you measure all your leaps in terms of the distance by which you reduce the gap between you and the shore. The mythic drama serves vicariously not only as an escape valve to release intolerable tensions, but also to allow its witness to experience at one remove what it is actually like to translate fantasy into reality; the drama is more real than fantasy, less real (and hence less costly[49]) than reality.

Myth in this limited function as social touchstone exercises a complex interrelationship with society that could be described as cybernetic, symbiotic, synergistic, or simply chicken-and-egg. Myths told to children influence how they grow up; children grow up with certain cultural preoccupations that lead them to tell certain kinds of myths to their children. Thus, anthropologists and psychologists speak of shared "nuclear fantasies" transmitted in India from mother to child and later modified by individual experience; the myth of the decapitating goddess is based on the child's overabrupt weaning. In this view, the actual experience precedes and determines the myth. But it is also suggested that the shared fantasy of the demonic goddess inhibits the sexual activity of young married men in India. In this view, the myth is not a reflection of behavior but a cause of it.[50] Clearly, there is some truth, and some falsehood, in both views. To the extent that myth arises out of reality and has an effect on reality, there can be no particular starting point or end point: it is a cycle.[51]

Myth has been defined as "a cosmic map of an unknown country, where each piece of the landscape is recognized as totally familiar when you get there, only it does not tell you how to get there, or how to act when you do."[52] In this, myths are quite different from paradigms; the myth of Christ's Passion did not tell Richard II what to do, only how to understand what he was doing anyway. This is why, as Lévi-Strauss points out, myth is never an answer to the problems it allows us to state;[53] it merely lets us recognize those problems as mythic.

For the myth does not tell us what to do; it makes us realize that it is not as simple as we thought it was (or as our lawmakers told us it was) to figure out what to do. Yet, myth tells us that we must do *something*. Rilke's description of the effect of viewing a statue of Apollo speaks of this: *"Du muss dein Leben ändern."*[54] The myth achieves this effect not through logic or example (positive or negative) but by activating our emotions as it punctures our assumptive world. In our everyday life we cling to our private cosmologies long after they have outlived their power to sustain us, patching them up as scientists patch their theories with epicycles, as a child patches a disintegrating Teddy bear; we make minor or major alterations in the superstructure of our lives—a bigger house, a different job, a younger wife—until the whole jerry-built construction topples down under its own weight. In the end, we are forced to realize that the world remains the same, despite our manipulations; but the myth offers a transforming change of perspective.

6. Truth Criteria for Myths

The positive or negative moral effect of myth on its audience led to a reassessment of the truth or "reality" of myth in the Western world. We have seen the way in which the myths of the mouth of God attempt to undermine one's confidence in the reality of apparently real phenomena (on this side of the mouth of God). The obverse of this process is the attempt to establish the reality of apparently mythic phenomena (on the other side of the mouth of God).

At first, Aristophanes and Plato argued that, although myths might be true (though Plato also implied that they might *not* be), they were immoral (and therefore were not to serve as social charters). Later it was argued that, because the myths (or the gods who were the subject of myth) were immoral, they could not be true (or real):

> The target of the rationalists' attacks was primarily the adventures and arbitrary decisions of the Gods, their capricious and unjust behavior, their "immorality.". . . This thesis—more particularly the objection that the divine myths as presented by the poets cannot be true—triumphed, at first among the Greek intellectual elites and finally, after the victory of Christianity, everywhere in the Greco-Roman world.[55]

Xenophanes argued that the stories told by Homer and Hesiod about the gods could not be true, because in these works "the gods do all manner of things which men would consider disgraceful: adultery, stealing, deceiving each other."[56] In other words, the gods could not be both immoral and immortal.[57] Although it is in fact possible to believe in the myths without believing in the gods, or the reverse, Plato and Xenophanes condemned them both.

That the good and the true are one and the same is part of our heavy legacy from Plato; in India, too, the ideas merge so completely that one Sanskrit word (*sat*, related to our own "is") means not only what is true, and what is good, but what is *real*. The myths, by depicting the shameful things that Aeschylus objected to (though he, at least, did not deny that they were *true*), came to be defined as quintessentially unreal: "If in every European language the word 'myth' denotes a 'fiction,' it is because the Greeks proclaimed it to be such twenty-five centuries ago."[58]

Most "civilized" people assume that myths are not true. But this assumption is not shared by traditional or archaic cultures: "In societies where myth is still alive the natives carefully distinguish myths—'true' stories—from fables or tales, which they call 'false stories.' "[59] And in the course of defending themselves against the rationalists, mythmaking cultures have often attempted to beat the realists at their own game, to *prove* the reality of myths in "scientific" terms.

There are many Indian and Tibetan tales in which a man steps somehow over the threshold into the world of myth and lives there for many years before returning to his own world, where he reappears only a split second after his departure (in the time scale of the people of that world); he then produces some sort of physical proof that he has been in another world, proof that is accepted by his amazed family and friends.[60] Japanese myths present a dislocation of time in the opposite direction: the hero returns after his mythic journey to find that everyone in his village has aged terribly; the proof of his experience is the proof of his own identity (when he reveals knowledge or characteristics that no one but he would have, and that are accepted as "historically true" by the surviving villagers) and the fact that he has not aged (as he would have done had he stayed in this world). That the hero wins the secret of immortality and the secret of his own identity is usually regarded as the metaphysical point of the mythic journey; here, it is the physical point, the evidence of the reality of the myth.

In one Hindu story of this type, a king disappears from his court and materializes in a village of Outcastes; he lives there for many years, marrying and begetting children, until, during a famine, he commits suicide by entering a fire (being swallowed by the jaws of hell), disappearing from the village and reappearing at court, which he has, apparently, never left during the brief time that the courtiers think has elapsed. The king eventually verifies his story by producing the wife, children, and friends that he had in the Outcaste village. The text uses this story to prove that, since all is illusory, one person's private illusion is just as real as any other part of reality: "The illusion in the king's mind having reflected itself on the minds of the outcastes as though it were a reality . . . becomes objectivized in the physical world."[61]

This view that, since all that is real is the mind, everything that exists is merely a mental projection, may perhaps be regarded as extreme when applied to physical reality, but it is certainly true of myth. Lévi-Strauss maintains that mythology is simply the mind talking about the mind, rather than the mind talking about "reality," and he regards the task of the mythologist as the search for the "constraining structures of the mind," an enterprise that he regards as "Kantism without a transcendental subject." That is, since the mythology of atheism is not looking for a truth basis "out there," it finds it "in here." This makes the mythical pattern an "autonomous object," and Lévi-Strauss describes it in terms not unlike those of the Hindu text: "I believe that mythology, more than anything else, makes it possible to illustrate such objectified thought and to provide empirical proof of its reality."[62]

Now, the transformations in time and space described in the Hindu text are strikingly similar to certain features of the hologram,[63] which exists outside of time and space and thus can reverse time, like the quark that appears to move from here to there but arrives there before it has left here. The image in the king's mind is broken down and rebuilt in another place (the "inverse Fourier transformation"); the king's memory becomes a hologram. Such dislocations of time and space are also the basis of the myths of the mouth of God. Mystic and mythic texts redefine time just as Einstein did; certain myths and certain scientific theories use the same metaphor to explain the way in which the brain uses images to map space and time.

7. The Common Sense of Magic

Attempts to establish the reality of myth through "scientific" common sense evidence are legion in world mythology. When Homer tells us that Athene spoke to Telemachus in a dream, or by taking the form of Mentor, one might think he was allowing his audience the option (which the post-Homeric rationalist Greeks so often took) of interpreting this allegorically or psychologically: Telemachus was inspired (on his own). But Homer does not leave it there; he insists on meeting the realists on their home territory. We are told that Athene in the form of Mentor accompanied Telemachus on his voyage to Nestor and conversed with Nestor; later, Noemon tells the suitors about a disquieting rip in the fabric of reality: "I noted Mentor going on board Telemachus's ship as leader—or else it was a god who resembled Mentor in all ways. But this is what I wonder at: I saw noble Mentor here, yesterday morning, but at that other time he went aboard the ship for Pylus."[64] The suitors' reaction to this cognitive dissonance[65] is to ignore it; they think (wrongly, as we know and they later find out to their peril) that it has no reality for their story, and we may assume that they shrugged it off with some rationalization such as, "Perhaps Noemon did not see properly," or "Perhaps Mentor did not remain on board after all." So, too, when Odysseus returns and Athene speaks to him, he recognizes her as Athene (though he addresses her as Mentor), but the suitors think she is Mentor; they rebuke her and then say, "Mentor has gone away," even when she turns into a swallow and flies up to the roof.[66] Like Yashodha and Pentheus, they reject the theophany.

But the man who does "wonder" at it is the most matter-of-fact of men, Noemon. Noemon doesn't care about Athene; he just wants Telemachus to come back with the ship he borrowed from Noemon, who wants to sail it to Elis to see his twelve brood mares and to break in a mule; Noemon worries that some sort of divine monkey business is going on with *his ship*. This plain man mediates between the evil suitors who do not believe (or, worse, do not care) that Athene was on the ship, and the good people who do believe—Homer, his audience, and (within the story) Telemachus and Nestor. The latter two first "wonder" like Noemon, and then immediately realize that the pseudo-Mentor is a goddess.[67] Nestor at once makes elaborate plans to inlay the horns of a heifer with gold and sacrifice it, evidence that he does not normally hobnob with the gods but is able immediately to assimilate this extraordinary event within the range of his ideas about what is possible. The reasonableness of mythic experience is made convincing through the use of the banal detail of Noemon's mule or the mud in Krishna's mouth.

When Athene makes her penultimate appearance in the ambiguous form of Mentor/swallow, the bard Medon reports, "I myself saw an immortal god who stood close beside Odysseus and resembled Mentor in all ways. But then he appeared before Odysseus as an immortal god. . . ."[68] Medon uses the same phrase that Noemon had used to describe Athene/Mentor, but he recognizes that she is a goddess. For, as a poet — the narrator of the tale within the tale — he alone has one foot in the world of myth and the other in the world of reality. Indeed, Medon's argument has a crucial effect on the actual events of the *Odyssey:* though the suitors are apparently impervious to theophany, their friends and relations (to whom Medon speaks in this passage) are persuaded that there is, in fact, a goddess standing beside Odysseus, and they turn back without exacting the revenge on which they had been intent before the intervention of Medon. Thus the poet's testimony to the *deus ex machina* has the effect of an actual *deus ex machina;* the myth, when believed, changes reality.

One common sense test to see whether or not you are living a myth is laid out explicitly in several Sanskrit texts. If you are in doubt as to whether your companion is a mortal or a god, look for these telltale signs: gods do not blink or sweat; their garlands never wither, nor does dust settle on them; and their feet rest ever so slightly above the ground, like a "hovercraft."[69] Significantly, the myths in which these rules appear present them as a means by which one can *avoid* close encounters with gods, avoid the theophany and the dangerous transition to the other side of the barrier[70] (the intercourse with the gods that Plato listed as tantamount to incest or bestiality). The fear of theophany, the desire *not* to be drawn across the border from reality into myth, is manifest in the figure who resists the myth: Oedipus, Pentheus, Yashodha, the suitors in the *Odyssey,* as well as in Clark Gable's distrust of the flimsy barrier in *It Happened One Night.*[71]

Sometimes the very vehemence with which the myth is denied on one level is testimony to its insidious power on another. As archy the cockroach remarks, "you want to know / whether i believe in ghosts / of course i do not believe in them / if you had known / as many of them as i have / you would not / believe in them either."[72] But generally, in our skeptical times, the theophany is simply not believed. Although from time to time hard proofs are still sought, they are never culturally validated. Almost always the witness is a child, who is of course not believed by adults. A notable exception to this pattern is the film *Miracle on 34th Street,* in which the existence of Santa Claus (who is literally on trial) is finally established not by any sacred authority, but by the epitome of temporal, banal authority: the U.S. Postal Service. Usually, however, the physical proof of the reality of the myth either vanishes or is judged too ambiguous to be persuasive. Thus, when Dorothy returns from the Land of Oz (in the film *The Wizard of Oz*), she discovers that the magic red shoes that would have proved her adventure to be true (and not merely a dream, as it appeared to her Kansas friends) have fallen off on the way back across the barrier. When the

Banks children return from a magic tea party with Mary Poppins (a classic combination of the mythic and the banal), *they* know that the crumbs on the rim of Mary's hat can only be explained by the fact that she had tea while suspended upside down by magic, but they know better than to try to explain that to their parents.[73] For, as the starling in the book explains, Mary Poppins is the only grown-up who retains knowledge of the mythic world, a knowledge that all infants have but that disappears when the child learns to speak.[74]

8. The Problem of the Pregnant Male

Hindu myths often play cat-and-mouse with the demand made by myth for the suspension of common sense criteria of reality; common sense wanders in and out of the myth like a bit player. Stories about pregnant males are often liminal in this way, straddling the threshold between the worlds of reality and myth. We have already alluded to the myths of Shukra, who is swallowed and given rebirth by the god Shiva, and Kaca, who is swallowed and given rebirth by Shukra. These stories of the mouth of God are often told without challenge. But some texts pollute the myths with common sense:

> The wife of a certain demigod was too great with child to attend a party she wanted to go to. She asked her husband to take the embryo so that she could attend, and out of affection and kindness he did so, for he had the magic power to assume any shape. With her beautiful figure restored, she went to the party, where, enjoying the pleasures of the flesh with another young demigod who took her fancy, and recalling the pains of childbirth, she decided not to return. Her husband suffered for the full nine months as the embryo grew, and finally, unable to find a passage for the delivery, he died in agony.[75]

The myth leads the reader down the garden path, luring him into a suspension of disbelief, and then suddenly bringing him up short with a reminder that of course a man can't *really* give birth to a child. Other male pregnancies have less tragic but equally hard-nosed consequences: one king became pregnant and gave birth without any labor pains, and the latter fact, but not the former, was regarded as "a great miracle"; he had trouble, however, in breast-feeding the child, and so he invoked a male god to produce milk from his (the god's) thumb.[76] Again, the latter was regarded as reasonably likely to happen, while no one apparently expected the king to be able to lactate.[77] The distinction is not simply a matter of the different powers of mortals and gods, for other Hindu gods do not mind becoming pregnant, but draw the line when they begin to lactate and therefore, only then, become a laughingstock in heaven.[78] One ricochets back and forth between physical and metaphysical standards of what is possible.

Where the Hindu myths degenerate into common sense, the North American Trickster cycle moves in the opposite direction, from common sense to myth. The Trickster, who is always hungry, wishes to marry a chief's son in order to eat the wedding banquet. He makes a vulva out of an elk's liver, and breasts out of an elk's kidneys, and he tricks the chief into accepting him as a woman and marrying him to his son. So far, we are still in the world of common sense, of bawdy humor and events that are physically possible.[79] We are therefore taken off balance when the text goes on to tell us that the Trickster became pregnant and gave birth to three boys.[80]

294

These traditional stories fight against great odds to maintain the underlying belief in the pregnant male, because it expresses an essential and useful truth. The Freudians reveal its truth basis in male pregnancy envy and in sublimation through anal creation;[81] the androcentric mythmakers use it as an effective metaphor for the socially convenient idea that men can do anything that women can do. The mythic truth of the pregnant male extends into the broader corpus of myths in which the hero achieves rebirth by being swallowed and released by a male god who plays the role of a goddess, a primeval androgyne.[82] But the stories that challenge these myths are part of an uneasy world in which the line between myth and reality is still rigidly defined, so that the attempt to bridge the gap must come about not by blurring the line, nor by undermining reality, but by trying to drag the myth to the other side, to the side of reason and science.

9. The Science of Myth: The Constraint of Elegance

This rapprochement between myth and science has recently received a boost from an unexpected ally: the natural sciences themselves. It is increasingly apparent that both science and myth are essentially committed to the belief that there is order in the universe. The religious basis of this belief emerges from such statements as Einstein's much-quoted remark that God does not play dice with the universe (though in Hindu mythology he not only plays dice, but cheats as well[83]) and in J. Robert Oppenheimer's invocation of the doomsday epiphany of the *Bhagavad Gita* —the jaws of the God[84]—when he witnessed the detonation of the first atomic bomb. Our underlying biological directive to see patterns, to jump to conclusions, has high survival value if in fact the world is ordered.[85] These patterns are the archetypal elements of myth, and the evolutionary advantage of jumping to conclusions substantiates the pragmatic validity of believing in what cannot be logically or rationally proved.

This thirst for order fuels the prime criteria for both a scientific theory and a myth: elegance and repetition. An established theory is abandoned (or regarded as inadequate) not merely upon the discovery of new facts (for cherished theories generate epicycles and corollaries almost beyond endurance in order to accommodate contradictory data; this is the function of cognitive dissonance), but upon the creation of a more elegant theory.[86] The aesthetic value of elegance also affects the artist's manipulation of myth, [87] but scientists jettison a theory only when cumulated data are accommodated by a new theory that is both more elegant and logically more persuasive. Myths persuade us with their emotional beauty, not only to restructure our assumptions about the real world (as scientific theories do), but even to abandon our assumption that the world is real at all.

There are, nevertheless, significant differences between the processes of scientific and mythic conversion. "Elegance" in scientific terms generally refers to simplicity, to Occam's razor: one wishes to account for as many facts as possible with as few theorems as possible. Elegance in myth, by contrast, is extravagant: the high value placed on repetition of the theme and variations tends to produce a myth that accounts for as little data as possible with as many theorems as possible. Laplace boasted that he did not "need" the hypothesis of God; it is unfashionable to believe in things that science no longer finds necessary to men-

295

tion in its theories.[88] But need is irrelevant to the economics of mythmakers, who are on the side of King Lear: "Allow not nature more than nature needs, Man's life is cheap as beast's."[89] Science's laboratories are Bauhaus; the palace of myth is baroque and rococo. Indeed, Occam's razor is merely one of a number of constraints of logic or reality that science must apply to the "melange of the various actual or created elements of our memory,"[90] while fantasy must not.

But the arbitrary nature of these scientific constraints serves once again to join myth and science in a common enterprise. Common sense, as Einstein once remarked, is what we are taught by the age of six (while certain Jesuits allowed one more year for a similar indoctrination); that is, common sense is an attribute of culture, not of nature, a part of myth rather than a part of reality. As scientists become more adventurous in restructuring their reality (and most revolutionary discoveries are made by young scientists, as close as possible to the six-year-old's Eden not yet invaded by the serpent of common sense), common sense is thrust unceremoniously into a dusty old attic along with the astrolabes and the perpetual motion machines. We learn from the special and general theories of relativity and quantum and nuclear mechanics that

> the laws that relate to us the nature of the macrouniverse . . . and those that relate the nature of the microuniverse . . . provide a somewhat similar conception of reality. This reality, highly mathematical in nature, departs considerably from ordinary sensory experience.[91]

One must beware, however, of implying that both science and myth prove that the universe obeys certain disquieting laws of time and space, that science and myth substantiate each other's more outlandish claims, like two drunks holding each other up. The point is, rather, that their ways of looking at the universe are more similar than has previously been supposed, though in fact it ought not to surprise us, since both scientists and mythmakers are human beings using the same mental equipment to map the same universe.

The value of myth for science lies in providing a change of metaphor that creates a fresh focus, a new set of terms for dealing with intellectual material, and thus serving both to explode mental logjams and to provide a source of creativity in the search for answers. Solutions to scientific problems often require metaphors that may not yet be conceptualized;[92] the lack of such metaphors is another sort of "constraint" that works upon science but not upon myth, to the detriment of science and the advantage of myth. Mythmakers, like the White Queen, have had more practice than scientists in believing impossible things ("half an hour a day").[93]

Finally, it is worth noting that the two systems, when they do conflict, are not necessarily incompatible; here, too, cognitive dissonance comes into play. The "maps" are not mutually exclusive. New Yorkers who recognize the truth in Saul Steinberg's brilliant map of the planet as seen from 9th Avenue (with Jersey a mere brown blob, and China and Russia as vague streaks on the horizon beyond the isolated points that are Los Angeles and Chicago) are also perfectly capable of finding their way around with the aid of conventional street maps. We choose our maps according to what universe we wish to move in at any given time.

10. The Recognition of Myth in Life

At certain crucial moments, we seem to follow two maps at once, as if two celluloid overlays were placed upon the same page; here again myth and reality intersect. There are times when we confront an actual experience and respond to it as we would respond to the confrontation of a myth. We recognize the myth in moments of real life because we recognize certain archetypal elements common to myth and life; and, as the banality of myth demonstrates, this happens to everyone, even to the "plain man" like Noemon. Jung remarked that "myth is not fiction: it consists of facts that are continually repeated and can be observed over and over again. It is something that happens to man, and men have mythical fates just as much as the Greek heroes do."[94] Richard II recognized two myths at once: the shared, tragic myth of Christ, which he found, and the myth of his own particular character, which he constructed out of smaller mythic moments. These moments include, but are not limited to, those formalized in rites of passage: the experience of birth (ours or our childrens'), suddenly changing from child to adult, falling in love, marriage, death (ours and our parents'). The same feeling overcomes us in moments of more modern and banal tragedy—news of failure or desertion, an accident, a mugging, being sentenced to prison. We encounter these primal echoes also in classical occasions of joy—plunging into the ocean, galloping on a young horse, climbing mountains, watching geese fly south, lying out under the stars, listening to sublime music, watching the sunrise or sunset.

These passionate encounters with life are so classical that they often border on the trite, like something out of a cheap novel or a Hollywood-sent dream; they may embarrass us to the point where we hesitate to acknowledge their genuine power over us. Their juxtaposition with the everyday quality of the rest of our lives makes them seem overblown, even as this banality forges the essential bond with the reality of the myth. But these experiences momentarily lift the artificial barrier that we have imposed between myth and reality, so that we gaze back suddenly upon the myth that we had unknowingly entered. All at once, in retrospect, we realize that we have not been alive until now; that, by comparison, all that has gone before has not been real. The film *The Wizard of Oz* goes along for a quarter of an hour until Dorothy arrives in the land of Oz, opens the door, and looks out into a world in glorious technicolor; and only then do we realize that we have been accepting the convention of filming in black and white, that we had not *missed* the true colors. This is how mythic moments in life retroactively transfigure our frame of reference.

Eliade tells how, when one "lives" the myth, "one is seized by the sacred, exalting power of the events."[95] He is speaking of "archaic man" and of particular ritual events; but what of ourselves? Do we find myths or make myths in our lives—or both, like Richard II? The argument for the former is the argument for the archetype: most deep passions and the matrix of circumstances in which they appear make immediate contact with what underlies the great myths. These evocative passions often sweep along in their flood the solid, banal details that are the flotsam and jetsam of human nature and human culture—particular colors, particular animals, particular geographical places—the grey pony on the Irish coast in *Riders to the Sea*.[96] Seemingly neutral, these things are highly charged with evocative detail to which we are helplessly drawn by a kind of centripetal force, just as Richard II experienced "the emotional surrender to a pre-conceived pattern of fictive passion."[97]

These patterns are archetypal, but they are not merely archetypal; they are colored with culturally specific and personally specific "manifestations."[98] The phallus may well be archetypal (for Jungians as well as Freudians, let alone the rank-and-file), producing an archetypal and instinctive response in real life as well as in myth; but it is always *someone's* phallus, someone with manifestations (a tone of voice, a taste for Beaujolais) or (to switch from the Jungians to the structuralists) someone structured within a context (a past, a social role). These are the banal details that, like Noemon's mule, make the myth real and also our own. The purely archetypal phallus does appear in some myths (the castrated, disembodied phallus that the Trickster keeps in a box until he needs it,[99] or the anonymous instrument of Erica Jong's "zipless fuck"[100]), but even here one has the details of the frame (what kind of a box, what kind of zipper?).

Shakespeare uses actual historical details to link myth with history, details that "remind us of the accidental objects which are there all the time for us to stub our toes against. . . . Paradoxically, the more actual the history . . . the more it becomes a kind of mythology with almost magic properties."[101] Herodotus did it too. In narrating the birth of Cyrus, he makes use of the standard archetypal motifs of the birth of the hero: the slaughter of the innocents, the highborn child secretly transferred to shepherd stepparents, and the death of the shepherd child as a sacrificial substitute for the future king. But then Herodotus vividly imagines the state of the mind of the shepherd mother whose own child had been stillborn:

> When she saw the child so big as it was, and so beautiful, she burst into tears, and taking her man's knees begged him by no means to expose the child. . . . "For you shall not be caught wronging your masters, nor shall we have laid our plans ill. Our dead child will receive a royal burial, and the child that survives will not lose its life."[102]

This human insight, like Yashodha's tenderness toward the child-god Krishna, makes the myth true for us, makes it both more mythic and more persuasive.

Even when we feel that we are finding a myth with all its details right in our lives, we are also making the myth by framing it with nonarchetypal details in order to see it, just as films about invisible people have to put clothes or paint on them so we can tell they are *not* there. But because we know how the myth goes, we then ignore those details in selecting the mythic elements of the event as the ones that are real. And we select elements that can be naturally structured in a pattern that is mythic, a pattern of repetitions and irony and paradox, as we focus on the events and details and patterns that are such stuff as myths are made on.

Some people, the kind we often refer to as self-dramatizing, regard every moment in an apparently ordinary life as mythical; but other people really do seem to have mythical lives, just as some paranoids really are surrounded by malicious enemies. Shakespeare paints Richard II as self-consciously aware of the fact that he is acting out a myth. To some extent he has this thrust upon him (as a figure of great political power and personal charisma); but he also achieves "myth-hood" by his own perception of his life and his ability to project this perception into the minds of the people around him, as the Wizard of Oz made everyone in the Emerald City wear green-tinted glasses so that it *became* the Emerald City. Mythic events seem to happen more often to people who believe in the mythic dimension, who seek it out and allow it to break in on them; or perhaps people who live through many such events become converted, even against their own common sense, to a belief in the reality of myth. Though the myth does not tell us what to do in such situations, it does at least enable us to recognize them, to value them, and ultimately, as Rilke says, to let them change our lives.

Because, or in spite, of our conscious attempts to live a myth, or to live against a myth, mythical patterns lay hold on us when our passions reach the spot at which the myth originally asserted itself. "Archaic man"—the man who lives his myths—is an endangered but not yet extinct species. Eliade writes: "At a certain moment in history—especially in Greece and India but also in Egypt— an elite begins to lose interest in this divine history and arrives (as in Greece) at the point of no longer believing in the *myths* while claiming still to believe in the *Gods.*"[103] The problem for us now is quite the reverse: we no longer have the gods, but we still sense the truth of the myths. There is a second way in which the new "archaic" man differs from the Eliadean prototype: *in illo tempore*, the man who lived the myth lived it in a group and in a shared, traditional ritual; now, as the myths of the inversion of social charter demonstrate, one must live the myth *against* the group, surrendering to disturbing and totally personal emotions that often threaten one's existence as a social creature or one's common sense as the creature of realism and materialism. Ours is a lonely mythology of atheism and solipsism; we find it not in churches but in films, comics, and our own experience.

Myth in this sense is both solitary and communal: solitary, in that the mythic experiences are among the most private and highly personal; communal, in that they are experienced by all of us. Lévi-Strauss describes the paradox in somewhat different terms:

> It is a consequence of the irrational relation between the circumstances of the creation of the myth, which are collective, and the particular manner in which it is experienced by the individual. Myths are anonymous: from the moment they are seen as myths, and whatever their real origins, they exist only as elements embodied in a tradition. When the myth is repeated, the individual listeners are receiving a message that, properly speaking, is coming from nowhere; this is why it is credited with a supernatural origin.[104]

We have seen that Lévi-Strauss's denial of a "there" anywhere but in the human mind leads him to objectify myth within the individual. Here he allows it to be drawn out into the community, with the result that the individual feels (wrongly, as Lévi-Strauss implies) that it is in fact coming from "out there." The communal role of the myth that has become absorbed in this way makes it into sacred history. Myth is "democratic history" transformed from tedious statistical generalization into a detailed history at once universal and personal —though it is, of course, a timeless history and hence hardly history at all in the usual sense of the word. Mythic man as I have defined him is remarkably similar to the nineteenth century Romanticist, the individual who stands apart from the group in his innocence and inspiration, and in his need to transcend limits;[105] but mythic man as Eliade defines him cannot exist except in a sacred community.

The loss of community has changed the role of myth in life. Many canonical stories no longer set in a sacred context are no longer taken seriously; the crucifixion has lost its power as a shocking mythic image. Meanwhile, where myth was once, for the rational Greeks and their heirs, a mere story, it is now regaining its meaning (at least for the secular individual); theology, by contrast, is losing its meaning for the individual outside the special ranks of sacred communities. Myth is now our secular, personal theology; we have nothing left to build our myths with but our own lives. In the Epilogue to Shaw's *Saint Joan*, when Charles dreams of meeting Joan after she has been burnt at the stake, he dreams that the chaplain apologizes for what has happened and says that, had he (the chaplain) actually seen it, as he has now, he never would have acted as he did. Pierre Cauchon replies, "Must then a Christ perish in torment in every age to save those that have no imagination?"[106]

We lack the imagination to be shocked by our own myths and are forced to learn mythic truths the hard way, by living through them. Yet, we can still be shocked by the myths of other people; hence, the truth of the old story, lovingly repeated by Martin Buber and Heinrich Zimmer, about finding your own treasure in the home of a stranger in a foreign land.[107] Within the myth, characters experience the mythic shock of recognition (Yashodha, Markandeya, Penelope), but we, the readers, see it coming and take it in our stride. (The myths of "common sense"—the pregnant male and the Trickster—are an exception to this, but they surprise us not through their insights but by moving outside of the conventional frame of reference of the myth.) The myth shocks the characters inside it because it is *about* shock; it narrates the shock, however, in totally familiar terms, and it narrates the same shock over and over again. Shock and recognition play at tug of war within the myth.

In traditional societies, as we have seen, the ritual functions as a physical, experiential complement to the myth, and these rituals do in fact subject the initiate to various shocks—physical torture (fasting, sleeplessness, mutilation), fear, and the symbolic experience of being swallowed and reborn. This is what the myth is about, the experience for which the myth has prepared not only the initiate but the community that shares vicariously in the ritual. In our world, where myth is bereft of ritual and has become a mere story—a religion deprived of a congregation—it has once again begun to draw to itself a kind of ritual and community, through the theatre and, less powerfully perhaps but certainly far more frequently, through film and "cult." Yet, the main arena in which the mythic shock of recognition takes place is in our own lives.

11. The Art of Myth: Bricolage

Sometimes personal myths are constructed piecemeal out of the evocative bits of archetypal flotsam and jetsam. These are in themselves self-selecting fragments: out of the many things that might happen in myths, remarkably few occur over and over. These recurrent fragments are what Lévi-Strauss has termed "mythemes," in recognition of the way they function like the phonemes in a language (or "my-themes" in life) or the atoms in a molecule: they are the building-blocks out of which any myth will be constructed. This process is also known as *bricolage*, since the mythmaker, like the French handyman of that name, works with the materials he is given, and must ingeniously construct any new item from the fragments of the old. Thus, when we make our lives into myths by censoring out the nonmythic materials and focusing on the mythemes, we are simply doing what the authors of the myths did in the first place; but now the elements with which we build are not words but "real" elements, the facts of our lives as *objets trouvés*.

These leftover scraps are curiously akin to the building blocks of animal life itself, not merely in terms of the metaphor of the atom, but also in the actual historical development of the elements. For evolution from time to time throws up nonadaptive scraps that have no purpose or survival value, that are not "necessary" in Laplace's (or Lear's) terms, and hence can be used extravagantly, *ars gratia artis*.[108] On another scientific plane, the Fourier transformations break down and reconstruct three-dimensional forms as the *bricoleur* breaks down a bicycle's seat and handlebars to make the head of a bull. And in the theatre we have seen Richard II building his abdication out of mythic scraps inherited from Christ, even as Shakespeare built his play on scraps from Holinshed.

Why are these fragments so limited in number? Why do we make use of such a small part of the available vocabulary, just as the snail forms his shell in so few of the shapes he might make? Wittgenstein maintained that, although logic is limited, emotion is limitless; but this seems to be untrue when applied to the emotional content of myth, in which (as in music) the number of archetypes is limited, perhaps because they are all general types and hence, by definition, absorb within themselves all minor variations (the manifestations).[109] Moreover, the discarded elements "are always present in latent fashion, behind those that have been singled out."[110]

These limitations apply to art as well as to myth. The artist mediates between the official mythmakers and our instinctive or self-conscious myth-construction in our lives. He is a *bricoleur* who builds out of the mythemes of his culture and his own individual genius a kind of metamyth; responding truly and artistically to patterns in the myths, tossed up by some fertilizing influence in his own experience, he creates out of a true symbiosis of his personal theme and some depth of meaning that he has discovered in the myth. Since the myth arises in the first place as a spontaneous growth in the human consciousness, shaped by the basic artistic impulse, the instinct of the great artist is merely a later stage of the same process, strengthening and extending the life of the myth. The Greek tragedians have been accused of having had a sinecure in inheriting the myths full-blown;[111] but all artists inherit myths and rework them to greater or lesser degrees, explicitly and creatively (as Shakespeare does, or Yeats) or subconsciously and, often, tritely (as do many hack novelists and writers of science fiction).

We have seen how the bard in the *Odyssey* weaves the elements of his life (as an actor in the episode of the suitors' revenge) together with his traditional art (as the narrator of the tale). In the Indian epic, too, the sage Vyasa both tells the story and plays a key part in it (begetting several of the protagonists and performing rituals that turn the tide of affairs). On the other side of the barrier, Kekulé's "enlightenment" about the circular molecular structure of benzene was a combination of the traditional, mythic meaning of the snake biting its tale and certain events of his own life. The artist or inspired scientist must cross over the barrier into both his own unconscious and the traditional archetype, entering the dangerous jaws of the devouring muse in order to bring back the prize he seeks.[112] The painter or musician builds out of the old archetypes, extending them into new realms, tinkering with the elements of *bricolage* as nature itself does in the process of evolution.

But the differences between the creative processes of scientists and myth-makers apply as strongly to individual fantasists and great artists, though here it is primarily a difference in the use of repetition and recognition. The critic may complain that archetypes in their raw state "are what children learn when they tediously reiterate nursery rhymes, intone tiresome chants, and make visual images that only fond parents delight in, psychiatrists regard as interesting, and Wordsworthian Romantics find profound."[113] One may perhaps question whether the raw archetypes are in fact so tedious to any but the most jaded tastes, but still one must admit that the true artist does use archetypes in a very special way.

"Genius all over the world stands hand in hand, and one shock of recognition runs the whole circle round."[114] For most people, the shock of recognition consists precisely in the inexplicable familiarity of the episode; for artists, the shock is both that and the shock of seeing the familiar in a totally new way, the aesthetic shock of surprise coupled with the personal shock of recognition. Personal fantasy, especially when obsessively neurotic, is sterile and mind-numbing in its repetition;[115] artistic fantasy is unique, infinitely various in the manifestations that it creates from the limited archetypes. Myth, midway between them, frames the archetype with just enough banal detail to make it real and to shock us with its familiarity, but aesthetic grace or originality is not essential to the persuasive power of myth. Lévi-Strauss has said that, while poetry is what is lost in translation, myth is what survives even the worst translation. This argument for the "artlessness" of mythology is somewhat more refined in Lévi-Strauss's assertion that myth is not so much opposed to poetry as able to mediate between the two opposed sign systems of music and articulate speech. In this model, though not everyone is a poet, "the vehicle of poetry is articulate speech, which is common property." Music, by contrast, depends on special gifts; and Lévi-Strauss has developed at great length the analogy between music and mythology. Thus, to the extent that mythology is "cultural," like music, it is artful; to the extent that mythology is "natural," like the colors present "naturally" before they are used by the painter, it transcends art.[116] On my continuum, mythology is precisely the point where nature and culture intersect, but to the extent that the natural or "real" element predominates, it is artless.

Myths, like the people we love, do not have to be beautiful or original in order to move us; the power of myth depends on the purity of the vision rather than the complexity of the words or painted lines that express the vision. The artist makes use of this power and his own creative powers of transformation: "The more original his work, the more imperiously recognizable it will be."[117]

12. Remembering the Myth

We have been talking about *how* myths affect us; now we can no longer avoid the question of *why* myths affect us. What is it that we are reminded of when we recognize the country of myth? This brings us back to the question with which we began: do myths remind us of passionate moments in life, or are those moments compelling because they remind us of myths? Which side of the mouth of God is reality on?

Inevitably, we find ourselves bumping into Plato, as Alice kept finding herself walking back in at the garden door in Wonderland. Despite Plato's profound distrust of the power of myth, he is largely responsible for the survival of the theoretical structure in which myths are accepted as real. C. S. Lewis's Narnia is the land of Platonic forms:

> Our own world, England and all, is only a shadow or copy of something in Aslan's real world. . . . And of course it is different; as different as a real thing is from a shadow or as waking life is from a dream. . . . This is the land I have been looking for all my life, though I never knew it till now. The reason why we loved the old Narnia is that it sometimes looked a little like this.[118]

And, as Lewis has the grace to have the old professor remark, "It's all in Plato, all in Plato: bless me, what *do* they teach them at these schools!"[119]

If one is not willing to go all the way with Plato (that is, if one does not really believe in the existence of a world of ideal forms, in the existence of something "out there"), one is likely to be thrown back upon Jung. The idea of a collective unconscious transmitted like genetic information in the brain is no longer quite so fatuous as it once seemed; the brain does in fact appear to be able to hand down simple archetypes, though not complex ones (another point in favor of the fragmentary mythemes),[120] and the Jungians may turn out to be right when they suggest that "we all have the same kind of dragons in our psyche, just as we all have the same kind of heart and lungs in our body,"[121] though there is still no "scientific" evidence that this is so. A more modest likelihood is that, out of a universal biology and a universal experience on the planet Earth, we all generate again and again the same dragons (the variations in dragons corresponding to the considerable variations in biology and experience).

However, one is then left with the problem of explaining why we *feel* that we are being reminded of something when in fact there is nothing "there" to be reminded of. As Markandeya says when he falls out of Vishnu's mouth, "I think I have seen this before." He has, of course; this is the second time he has fallen out of Vishnu's mouth, though he forgot the first experience (as Yashodha forgets hers). What he finds inside Vishnu's mouth is his memory of the first time. The mythic hero wins his memory of the past by being swallowed by the God(dess), by entering the womb-jaws of hell; this is the treasure guarded by the dragon at the barrier.

In Eliade's view, the hero journeys to win the memory of the past so that we may reenact that past in recreating the myths. For Eliade, what we "remember" is the ancient time when the myth was first made real, rather than a world of ideal forms or a racial memory: "Myth assures man that what he is about to do *has already been done*." In his view, this is a collective journey, and a collective memory is won by it (the traditional, archaic model of myth). But a different, individual journey, a kind of concrete journey into the past to retrieve memory, is the object of the psychoanalytic trip. Eliade compares Freud's belief that through memory, or a "going back," one can relive certain traumatic incidents of early childhood with the collective "going back" into the primordial events of myths: "Psychoanalytic technique makes possible an individual return to the Time of the origin."[122] This, too, is an individual journey that may involve the rejection of a social charter—the rebellion against the imprint given by one's parents.

Both Eliade and Freud seek for the memory of actual, lived events: Eliade, for those lived traditionally and culturally and preserved in ritual; Freud, for those actually lived by the individual doing the remembering. Yet, Eliade in his own life sees the two memories inextricably tangled. He concludes his memoirs with a reflection on the nature of the autobiographical journey, "a journey which takes place across different landscapes, forms, and colors, arouses a series of associations just as precious for the secret history of the soul as are, in Jungian analysis, the associations brought about by hearing certain words, names, legends, or myths, or as is the contemplation of certain paintings or drawings."[123] For the myths speak of a different kind of remembering, the recognition of a country where neither the individual nor the group has ever been before. Mythic memory, unlike "normal" memory, can remember things that have not yet happened, like the two-way memory of the White Queen, who remarks, "It's a poor sort of memory that only works backwards."[124]

The sense of *déja vu* haunts the uncanny osmosis between myth and reality. If one wishes to make it canny, to expose it to the criteria of common sense, one might call upon neurophysiology, from which we learn, first of all, that *all* thought is memory and the patterning of memory. Moreover, because memory is distributed throughout the brain, "in some circumstances a distributed memory might be 'confused' in the sense that it will respond to new events as if they were seen before, if the new event is similar to ones that have been previously seen. It will 'recognize' and 'associate' events never, in fact, seen or associated before."[125] *Déja vu* is thus somewhat akin to the setting off of a burglar alarm when a cat steps on a wired surface; the "I remember" system is activated by an experience that should properly be shunted into the "I am seeing this for the first time" department. This explains, perhaps, the power of *personal* manifestations of *déja vu* (triggered by mechanisms such as Proust's *madeleines*), but it does not explain why certain archetypes that are rarely viewed (the grey pony by the sea) "confuse the distributed memory" in so many of us, while other images encountered far more frequently (a cocker spaniel on a sofa) do not.

The structure of myths reinforces the mental rhythms of memory, for we *have* heard the story before (over and over, in a traditional culture); as A. K. Ramanujan remarks of the Indian epic, "No Indian ever hears the *Mahabharata* for the first time."[126] Moreover, we have heard the episode before in earlier, parallel episodes of the same myth (the slightly varied leitmotivs of the adventures of each of seven brothers), and, on the most basic level, we have heard the same words before (in the formulaic structure of ritual speech).

Repetition is what makes the myth real, by setting up a pattern at variance with, but ultimately parallel to (and hence able to replace), the repetitions given by experience. Though crude repetition is poison to art and superfluous to science, artful repetition is the lifeblood of art and the security blanket of science. "A child seems willing to accept any connection, marvelous or trivial, if it is repeated and part of his world," even such a marvelous fact as the push of a button producing talking images on a television screen.[127] In personal fantasy, too, the enduring patterns are not merely the pleasant and the traumatic, but those that are repeated over and over, regardless of their content.[128] In myth, as in science and fantasy, or as in the Bellman's statements about the Snark, "what I tell you three times is true."[129] This "illogical but magically compelling repetition"[130] does not become tedious in myth; it becomes sacred.[131] Indeed, only when we meet it for the second time is it sacred, retroactively, the first time.

Charles H. Long's definition of myth is illuminating in this regard: Myth is the attempt to experience again what we never experienced in the first place.[132] We have the feeling of doing something for the second time—in life, as in myth—when we confront for the first time something that speaks to a special core of passion and understanding. People who live a substantial part of their lives in contact with that core seem to bypass many of the first times, like bright children who skip first grade and begin in second without missing anything. People who are familiar with myths recognize mythic moments in life when they encounter them for the first time, and people who have experienced and understood passion in their lives are not surprised by the things that happen in myths.

13. Myth as Child's Play

Given this pervasive quality of memory and recognition in myths, how can we explain the equally pervasive presence of children in them—for children are the ones to whom everything happens for the first time. Children appear in myths all the time: they experience the theophany that is denied to adults, and they are the (real) counterpart of the audience of the (mythic) theatre of Aristophanes; gods appear as children in myths; and the world of children is the one sought by the psychoanalytic journey. Myth has always been associated with children, though for different reasons at different times: in the ancient world, children were regarded as the pure medium through which religious ideas became manifest ("out of the mouths of babes"); in our time, though we still pay lip service to this idea, children are generally regarded as the only people foolish enough to believe in fairy tales and superheroes (the last survivals in the mythology of atheism).

The myth would thus seem to be an inversion of reality, as is often the case: in real life, children do *not* recognize recurrent experiences (since, to them, such experiences have not yet occurred for the first time), and in myth they do. To have a child see the first time as the second time is a logical paradox, like calling World War I by that name in 1918. The child's freshness of vision is a function of the fact that everything is new to him.

But this vision is, in its own way, also a quality of the mythic world, for it emphasizes the "shock" aspect of the shock/recognition tension. Most people gradually adjust to successive, repeated sound stimuli (the rhythmic ringing of a bell, for example), so that the pattern of brain waves, disturbed at first by each stimulus, gradually subsides and ignores subsequent stimuli; but certain Zen masters continue to react to each ringing of the bell with the change in brain-wave pattern characteristic of the first stimulus; to the Zen master, the second time is just like the first time.[133] This is the time frame of the child, who is truly shocked by the story that has come to be second nature to adult society.

But the myths are not composed and transmitted by children; they are the work of adults, who frame the child's view with their own, in a complex series of Chinese boxes: cynical adults tell myths to children, whom they regard as naively gullible, and these myths are about children who experience true myth-ic realities that are foolishly ignored by the adults in the story. The adult view-ing the myth of the child (or viewing his own child experiencing a mythic event—seeing the ocean for the first time, falling in love for the first time, or hearing the myths that the adult loved as a child) experiences a kind of temporal double-exposure: he feels the event as the first time for the child, and as the second time for himself. This double exposure is closely akin to the sensation of *déja vu:* the adult recognizes what shocks the child.

The child, in myth or reality, cannot respond to the hierophany with "com-mon sense" or with a memory of actual events; he can only accept it on its own terms. Thus, perhaps the final reason for the importance of children as keepers of the mythic vision is our belief that they have not yet ineradicably inked in the boundaries in their map of myth and reality, that they have not yet learned to point out portions of experience as Not Possible or Not Important or, finally, Not Real.

14. The Translation of Reality into Reality and Myth into Myth

We say that children understand the language of myth, and in *Mary Poppins* the children cease to understand the mythic world, the language of sunbeams and starlings, as soon as they learn to speak a "real" language. In many ways, myth is the opposite of language, despite the etymological basis of the word we use to describe it in English and other European languages (from the Greek *mythos,* "speech"). Lévi-Strauss's remark about the ability of myth to survive bad translations supports our contention that myth takes place on a level of experience where words are both inadequate and superfluous, where logic and reason are misleading rather than revealing. Though this appears to fly in the face of Lévi-Strauss's description of myth as an instrument of logic, it is quite compatible with his analogy between myth and music. For, though he shows us that myths are "good to think with," this does not rule out the function that we have seen in the myths of the mouth of God: that myths are also good to *feel* with. Myth is a way of expressing inexpressible paradoxes, says Lévi-Strauss.[134] Myth is a way of expressing the ineffable.

Yet we can best understand our own myths, and those of other people, by translating them into other myths,[135] by drawing them back into that internal hub where our own reality, our own nature, intersects with the myths pre-served by tradition, by culture. This provides, in passing, a way of translating myths, but it also provides a means of addressing the far more serious problem of translating reality, of establishing a vocabulary with which to understand what goes on in the heads of other people. Properly understood, myths provide a conceptual system through which we may understand and thereby construct a universal reality, a roundhouse where we can move from the track of one person's reality to another's, passing through the myth that expresses them all.

We cannot communicate the manifestation, but we may move back through it to the archetype. If you fall in love and introduce the man to your parents, they may hate him, but if they can remember how it felt to be in love, they can share your private myth. If you read a book that changes your life and you give it to your friends, they may be baffled or bored by it, but it might remind them of the books that changed *their* lives. We share the structures on this level, and on another we share the fragments, the mythemes, with which the structures are built. The scientist may argue that "existential understanding is essentially private, while scientific understanding is essentially and eminently shareable,"[136] but we have seen that neither of these propositions is entirely true; existential (mythic) experience and scientific (common sense, real) experience have both the same limits and the same ability to transcend limits of communication. It all depends on what one is looking for. The Jungian assumption that "we all have the same kind of dragons in our psyche" leads to the hope that "we can communicate, that alienation isn't the final human condition, since there is a vast common ground on which we can meet, not only rationally, but aesthetically, intuitively, emotionally."[137] Lévi-Strauss says that his ambition is "to discover the conditions in which systems of truths become mutually convertible and therefore simultaneously acceptable to several different subjects."[138]

Even without the assumption that there is something "in there" (let alone "out there"), myth can be an instrument for the translation of reality into reality. The myths of the mouth of God provide a mirror image of conventional social evaluations of what is real and what is not real, denying not only the claims of society but even those of *soi-disant* physical reality as defined by Newtonian science. The historians have demonstrated that there is no such thing as an even theoretically impartial observer, and the anthropologists have cynically undermined our hopes of getting inside the heads of other cultures, relativistically or otherwise.[139] The linguists and philosophers have, finally, hopelessly defamed the character of language as a possible vehicle for mutual understanding.

So we are stripped down to our naked myths, the bare bones of human experience. They are, perhaps, our last hope for a nonlanguage that can free us from these cognitive snares, a means of flying so low, so close to the ground of the human heart, that they can scuttle underneath the devastating radar of the physical and social sciences. Indeed, the same growing skepticism that has tended to disqualify these sciences as arbiters of reality has, as we have seen, begun to make peace between the rational Establishment and the irrational guerrilla enclaves of myth that have so often raided scientific territory. For now that we have been challenged to relax our stranglehold on inherited Enlightenment maps of reality on this side of the mouth of God, we may be able to make use of mythic maps that chart a very different kind of enlightenment on the other side. Better yet, we may pull back the illusory curtain between them once and for all.

REFERENCES

[1]These and other generalizations in this essay can be supported not only by the few examples I have mustered here, but by numerous specific examples from the larger corpus of studies in mythology I have published elsewhere, particularly in *Asceticism and Eroticism in the Mythology of Śiva* (New

York: Oxford University Press, 1973); *Hindu Myths* (Harmondsworth: Penguin, 1975); and *The Origins of Evil in Hindu Mythology* (Berkeley: University of California Press, 1976). Many of the perceptions reproduced here as my own arose out of tactful but sharp criticisms of early drafts of this paper by the other participants in this symposium and by friends, colleagues, and students, particularly William K. Mahony, Brian K. Smith, and David Grene.

[2]Claude Lévi-Strauss, *Structural Anthropology* (New York: Basic Books, 1963), p. 229; *The Savage Mind* (London: Weidenfield and Nicolson, 1966), p. 22; *The Raw and the Cooked* (New York: Harper & Row, 1969), pp. 340-1.

[3]Lewis Carroll, *Through the Looking-Glass and What Alice Found There* (London: 1872), ch. 6.

[4]See below, sections 7-9.

[5]See below, section 14.

[6]See the essay by Leon Cooper in this volume.

[7]Problems that arise from the definition of myth as map are alluded to by Jonathan Z. Smith in "Map Is Not Territory," pp. 289-309, in his volume of essays by the same title (Leiden: E. J. Brill, 1978).

[8]This is the standard operating procedure for the reconstruction of hypothetical proto-Indo-European language and culture.

[9]For dreams and the theatre, see below, section 3; for children's books, section 13; for art, section 11; for experience, section 10.

[10]See below, section 14.

[11]*Bhagavata Purana* 10. 8. 21-45. Here and throughout this essay I have summarized rather than translated in full. The complete text of this myth appears in O'Flaherty, *Hindu Myths*, pp. 218-21.

[12]A similar episode is described in the *Bhagavad Gita* (11. 7-30 and 41-44), when Arjuna sees within Krishna's mouth a doomsday fire that swallows up the gods, crushing them between his jaws; in abject terror, Arjuna begs Krishna to return to his usual form, to be like a father with a son.

[13]*Matsya Purana* 167-8. A full translation of this myth appears in *Classical Hindu Mythology* by Cornelia Dimmitt and J. A. B. van Buitenen (Philadelphia: Temple University Press, 1978), pp. 253-6.

[14]Though Arjuna is male, he ends up outside Krishna and, like Yashodha, forgets the vision of being swallowed, for he must go on being involved in the world of action; this is the whole point of the *Bhagavad Gita*.

[15]For doomed females, see, for example, *Kalika Purana* 49-54, translated and discussed in O'Flaherty, *Asceticism and Eroticism*, pp. 205-9, and O'Flaherty, *Women, Androgynes, and Other Mythical Beasts* (Chicago: University of Chicago Press, 1980), pp. 93-96. For saved males, see the analysis of this tale of Vishnu and Markandeya in Heinrich Zimmer's *Myths and Symbols in Indian Art and Civilization* (New York: Pantheon, 1946), pp. 35-53, and the tale of Indra and the ants (in which Indra, like Arjuna, backslides at the end), also told by Zimmer (Ibid., pp. 1-11).

[16]*Mahabharata* 12. 278. 1-38 and 1. 71-72. These texts are translated, the first briefly, the second in full, in O'Flaherty, *Hindu Myths*, pp. 297, 280-9, and discussed in O'Flaherty, *Women, Androgynes*, pp. 264-72.

[17]*Padma Purana* 6. 18. 82-90. Also discussed in O'Flaherty, *Women, Androgynes*, pp. 267-8.

[18]*Odyssey* 12. 91-93 for Scylla. For other examples, see Mircea Eliade, *Rites and Symbols of Initiation: The Mysteries of Birth and Rebirth*, Willard R. Trask (tr.) (New York: Harper, 1958; Torchback, 1975), pp. 35-36 and 51-52.

[19]I am indebted to James Redfield for this insight into the *Bacchae*.

[20]See O'Flaherty, *Women, Androgynes*, passim.

[21]See numerous articles by Jung and Eliade, as well as Dorothy Eggan, "The Personal Use of Myth in Dreams," in *Myth: A Symposium*, Thomas Sebeok (ed.), (Bloomington, Ind.: Indiana University Press, 1958), pp. 67-75, and *Myths, Dreams, and Religion*, Joseph Campbell (ed.) (New York: Dutton, 1970). See also the cyclic relationship between personal fantasy and collective myth discussed by Meredith Skura in this volume.

[22]Mircea Eliade, *Myth and Reality* (New York: Harper & Row, 1963), p. 77 n.

[23]Chuang Tsu, ch. 2, "The Equality of Things and Opinions," 2. 1. 2. 11.

[24]St. Augustine tells such a story in chapter 18 of *The City of God*. A philosopher appears to a man in a dream and expounds to him certain Platonic passages. When the two meet later, the philosopher tells the man that he (the philosopher) had merely dreamt that he had explained the passages to the man.

[25]This matter-of-fact modification of the traditional mythical beast is a Woody Allen speciality: "The great roe is a mythological beast with the head of a lion and the body of a lion, though not the same lion." Woody Allen, *Without Feathers* (New York: Warner Books, 1976), "Fabulous Tales and Mythical Beasts" (first published in *The New Republic*), p. 193.

[26]Ibid., pp. 192-3.

[27]Carroll, *Through the Looking Glass*, ch. 4 ("Tweedledum and Tweedledee") and ch. 12 ("Which dreamed it?").

[28]Jonathan Z. Smith discusses this "incongruity" as a function of the intersecting territories in a myth in "Map Is Not Territory."

[29]Russell Hoban, *The Mouse and His Child* (London: Faber and Faber, 1969), pp. 34-35, 67-80 (where "The Last Visible Dog" is a play that satirizes Becket), 120-6 (where the mouse child uses the image as a yantra to meditate on nothing and infinity), and 190-200 (where it is used as a symbol for the final resting place).

[30]See below, section 4.

[31]See below, section 12.

[32]David Grene, *Messenger Lectures*. I am grateful to Professor Grene for permission to see and cite the manuscript of his expanded Messenger Lectures, now in press under the title *Shakespeare: Theatre and the World of Politics*.

[33]See the discussion by Judith Shklar in this volume. As Lévi-Strauss remarks in *The Raw and the Cooked* (p. 13) "History . . . can never completely divest itself of myth."

[34]Grene, *Shakespeare: Theatre and the World of Politics*.

[35]Rupagosvamin's *Bhaktirasamritasindhu* 2. 27. I am indebted to David Haberman for this source. See also my discussion of it in *Women, Androgynes*, pp. 87-88, and cf. also *Bhagavata Purana* 3. 25. 34.

[36]*The Frogs*, 1194. Aeschylus seems to pity Oedipus as much for taking to bed an *old* woman as for the fact that she happened to be his mother.

[37]Euripides may be implying a contrast between the story of Stheneboia, which was not true and therefore drove women to commit a real act of self-destruction, and the story of Phaedra, which was true and therefore either did not lead to such an act or would have been justified even if it did.

[38]Plato, *The Republic*, 571 d., 573 b., 378 a.

[39]Sophocles, *Oedipus Rex*, 981-3.

[40]*Odyssey* 15. 560-5.

[41]For evidence that Greek mothers and sons did in fact wrestle with this problem, see Philip Slater, *The Glory of Hera* (Boston: Beacon Press, 1968).

[42]Aristophanes, *The Frogs*, 141, 149, 274.

[43]Bronislaw Malinowski, "Myth in Primitive Psychology," published in 1926 and reprinted in *Magic, Science, and Religion* (New York: Doubleday, 1954), p. 108.

[44]I am indebted to Judith Shklar for this realization.

[45]See H. J. Rose, *A Handbook of Greek Mythology* (New York: Dutton, 1959), p. 108. So, too, Arjuna returns, after being "swallowed" by Krishna in the *Gita* epiphany, to function as the Hindu hero par excellence.

[46]See the discussion of this function of history by Judith Shklar in this volume.

[47]Claude Lévi-Strauss, "The Story of Asdiwal," in *The Structural Study of Myth and Totemism*, Edmund R. Leach, (ed.) (London: Tavistock, 1967), pp. 29-30; and Edmund R. Leach, *Lévi-Strauss* (New York: Viking Press, 1970), p. 57.

[48]O'Flaherty, *Women, Androgynes*, pp. 271-2.

[49]See below, section 10.

[50]G. Morris Carstairs, *The Twice-Born* (Bloomington, Ind.: Indiana University Press, 1958), pp. 156-67. Also, O'Flaherty, *Women, Androgynes*, pp. 114-5.

[51]See the article by Meredith Skura in this volume.

[52]David Grene, personal communication, August 4, 1979.

[53]Lévi-Strauss, *Structural Anthropology*, p. 229; *The Savage Mind*, p. 22.

[54]Rainer Maria Rilke, "Archaïscher Torso Apollos," *Neue Gedichte: Anderer Teil* (Leipzig: Insel Verlag, 1908). Ursula K. Le Guin also applies this line to the function of myth in *The Language of the Night: Essays on Fantasy and Science Fiction* (New York: Putnam, 1979), pp. 77-78. The chapter "Myth and Archetype in Science Fiction" first appeared in *Parabola* I (1976): 4.

[55]Eliade, *Myth and Reality*, p. 149.

[56]Xenophanes B 11-12, Jaeger translation. Cf. also Plato, *Republic*, 377 b-d.

[57]This is the tip of the iceberg of the Greek approach to the problem of evil or theodicy. For a comparison with the Indian view, see O'Flaherty, *The Origins of Evil in Hindu Mythology*, and for an analysis of the Greek view, see Paul Ricoeur, *The Symbolism of Evil* (Boston: Beacon Press, 1969).

[58]Eliade, *Myth and Reality*, p. 148. I was caught up in this degraded use of the word "myth" when a Hindu (K. S. Narayana Rao) reviewing my *Hindu Myths* (in *Books Abroad*, 1976, p. 474) began by taking me to task thus: "The title is offensive. To the Hindu, the stories of his sacred literature are not myths; they are as much a reality and are as sacred as are the stories of the miracles of Christ or of Adam and Eve and Noah to the Christians."

[59]Eliade, *Myth and Reality*, p. 8.

[60]Cf. Zimmer, *Myths and Symbols*, pp. 35-53. For examples of attempted proofs of the reality of previous incarnations, see O'Flaherty, *Karma and Rebirth in Classical Indian Traditions* (Berkeley: University of California Press, 1980). For the Japanese story, see Richard M. Dorson, *Folk Legends of Japan* (Tokyo and Rutland, Vt.: C. E. Tuttle Co., 1961 and 1962).

[61] The *Yoga-Vasistha-Maha-Ramayana*, attributed to Valmiki (2 volumes, Bombay: Nirnaya Sagara Press, 1918), 3. 104-22. Quotation from Sir Thomas W. Arnold's catalogue of the Indian miniatures in the Chester Beatty collection (revised and edited by J. V. S. Wilkinson, 3 volumes, Oxford: Oxford University Press, 1936, p. 24), which has an illustrated manuscript of this text.

[62] Lévi-Strauss, *The Raw and the Cooked*, pp. 10-11 and 341.

[63] See the essays by Karl Pribram and Leon Cooper in this volume.

[64] *Odyssey* 2. 330-70; 4. 653-6.

[65] The term was coined by Leon Festinger in *A Theory of Cognitive Dissonance* (Palo Alto: Stanford University Press, 1957) to refer to the way in which people continue to maintain essential beliefs even when these are flatly contradicted by the failure of their predictions, a close analogy to the way that people hang on to myths in the face of the lack of supporting physical evidence.

[66] *Odyssey* 22. 205-38.

[67] *Odyssey* 1. 323; 3. 371-464.

[68] *Odyssey* 24. 438.

[69] *Mahabharata* 3. 54. 20-24.

[70] Cf. O'Flaherty, *Women, Androgynes*, pp. 95-96.

[71] See the essay by Stanley Cavell in this volume.

[72] Don Marquis, *archy and mehitabel* (New York: Doubleday, 1930), "xxxiii. ghosts," p. 135.

[73] P. L. Travers, *Mary Poppins Comes Back* (New York: Harcourt, Brace and Co., 1945), pp. 108-9.

[74] P. L. Travers, *Mary Poppins* (New York: Harcourt, Brace and Co., 1934), pp. 139-42.

[75] *Tantropakhyana* 10. Text and translation by George T. Artola, *Adyar Library Bulletin* 29 (Madras: 1965), 1-4; cf. the Tamil version, pp. 113-4 of the same issue.

[76] *Mahabharata* 3. 126. 1-26.

[77] For these and other unchallenged myths of male pregnancies, see O'Flaherty, *Origins of Evil*, pp. 342-4, and *Women, Androgynes*, pp. 299-326.

[78] *Saura Purana* 62. 5-12.

[79] The story up to this point is very similar to a Tibetan tale in which the Trickster figure constructs a vagina out of the lung of a sheep and uses it successfully to have sexual intercourse with a rich man's son. See *Tales of Uncle Tompa*, compiled and translated by Rinjing Dorje (San Rafael: Dorje Ling, 1975), pp. 24-27.

[80] Paul Radin, *The Trickster* (New York: Schocken Books, 1972), pp. 22-23.

[81] Alan Dundes, "Earth Diver: Creation of the Mythopoeic Male," *American Anthropologist*, 64 (1962), pp. 1032-1105. Reprinted in Alan Dundes, *Analytical Essays in Folklore* (The Hague: Mouton, 1975), pp. 130-45.

[82] O'Flaherty, *Women, Androgynes*, pp. 264-73.

[83] O'Flaherty, *Asceticism and Eroticism*, p. 223.

[84] See Reference 12, above.

[85] See the essay by Leon Cooper in this volume.

[86] Thomas Kuhn, *The Structure of Scientific Revolutions* (Chicago: University of Chicago Press, 1970).

[87] See below, section 11.

[88] From an earlier version of the article by Leon Cooper that appears in this volume. That scientists do, in fact, believe in things that are not "necessary" is brilliantly mocked in Hilaire Belloc's poem about the microbe, said to have seven tufted tails and other detailed characteristics, including "eyebrows of a tender green;/ All these have never yet been seen—/ But Scientists, who ought to know,/ Assure us that they must be so./ Oh! Let us never, never doubt/ What nobody is sure about!" (Hilaire Belloc, *More Beasts for Worse Children*, "The Microbe," London: 1898; Harmondsworth: Puffin Books, 1964, p. 96).

[89] Shakespears, *King Lear*, II. iv. 267.

[90] See ret. 14 of Leon Cooper's essay in this volume.

[91] See the essay by Karl Pribram in this volume, and cf. also Fritjof Capra, *The Tao of Physics* (London: Wildwood House, 1975).

[92] See the essay by Stephen Jay Gould in this volume.

[93] Lewis Carroll, *Through the Looking Glass*, ch. 5 ("Wool and Water").

[94] C. G. Jung, *Answer to Job* R. F. C. Hull (tr.) (London: Routledge and Kegan Paul, 1954), p. 75.

[95] Eliade, *Myth and Reality*, p. 19.

[96] John M. Synge, *Riders to the Sea* (New York: Random House, 1935).

[97] Grene, *Shakespeare*.

[98] Adolphe Bastion's terms (*Elementargedanken* and *Volkergedanken*) were taken over and modified by Jung.

[99] Radin, *The Trickster*, pp. 18-20. Cf. Uncle Tompa, pp. 9-16.

[100] Erica Jong, *Fear of Flying* (New York: Holt, Rinehart and Winston, 1973), p. 11, in which she refers to her "fantasy of the Zipless Fuck. The zipless fuck was more than a fuck. It was a platonic ideal."

101Grene, *Shakespeare*.

102Herodotus 1. 107-12. I am indebted to David Grene for this text and for the translation, which is his own.

103Eliade, *Myth and Reality*, p. 111.

104Lévi-Strauss, *The Raw and the Cooked*, p. 18.

105See the essays by Judith Shklar and Leonard Meyer in this volume.

106George Bernard Shaw, *Saint Joan* (Baltimore: Penguin, 1966), p. 154.

107Zimmer, *Myths and Symbols*, pp. 219-21.

108See the essay by Stephen Jay Gould in this volume.

109See the essay by Leonard Meyer in this volume.

110Lévi-Strauss, *The Raw and the Cooked*, p. 341

111F. M. Cornford, *The Unwritten Philosophy and Other Essays* (Cambridge: Cambridge University Press, 1950).

112On this point and also Kekulé's discovery, see the essay by Meredith Skura in this volume.

113See the essay by Leonard Meyer in this volume.

114Herman Melville, "Hawthorne and his Mosses," in *Collected Poems* (Chicago: Chicago University Press, 1947). The term "the shock of recognition" was used by Edmund Wilson for the title of his book on American literature.

115See the essay by Meredith Skura in this volume.

116Lévi-Strauss, *Structural Anthropology*, p. 210; *The Raw and the Cooked*, pp. 18, 27.

117Le Guin, *The Language of the Night*, p. 79.

118C. S. Lewis, *The Last Battle* (Harmondsworth: Penguin, 1964), pp. 153-5.

119Ibid., p. 154.

120Personal communication from Stephen Jay Gould.

121Le Guin, *The Language of the Night*, p. 79.

122Eliade, *Myth and Reality*, pp. 141, 78.

123*Mircea Eliade, No Souvenirs: Journal, 1957-1969*, Fred H. Johnson, Jr., (tr.) (New York: Harper & Row, 1977), p. 327.

124Lewis Carroll, *Through the Looking Glass*, ch. 5 ("Wool and Water").

125See the essay by Leon Cooper in this volume.

126Personal communication from A. K. Ramanujan.

127See the essay by Leon Cooper in this volume.

128See the essay by Meredith Skura in this volume.

129Lewis Carroll, *The Hunting of the Snark*, Fit the First, vol. 2. In *The Annotated Snark*, Martin Gardner (ed.) (Harmondsworth: Penguin, 1962), p. 46. Gardner points out that Norbert Wiener in *Cybernetics* discusses the duplication of neuronal mechanisms (as in distributive memory [see below, section 12]) and remarks, "Like the computing machine, the brain probably works on a variant of the famous principle expounded by Lewis Carroll in *The Hunting of the Snark*: 'What I tell you three times is true.' "

130See the essay by Meredith Skura in this volume.

131See the discussion of repetition and the sacred in S. G. F. Brandon, *History, Time, and Deity* (Manchester: Manchester University Press, 1965).

132Personal communication from Charles H. Long.

133Charles T. Tart, *Altered States of Consciousness* (New York: Wiley & Sons, 1969).

134Lévi-Strauss, *Structural Anthropology*, p. 229.

135"Conversations with Lévi-Strauss," by George Steiner, *Encounter* 27 (10) (April 1966): 38.

136See the essay by Karl Pribram in this volume.

137Le Guin, *The Language of the Night*, p. 79.

138Lévi-Strauss, *The Raw and the Cooked*, p. 11.

139See the essay by James Boon in this volume.

II

THE TRUTH OF MYTH *)

Myth, in the usual acceptation of the word, belongs to the realm of the imagination, which as such is distinct from, even opposed to, the world of reality. The gods, who are the characters in myth, are for us fabulous beings in whom we do not believe. Criticism of myth goes back to pagan antiquity, to those first Greek thinkers, such as Theagenes and Xenophanes, who lived in the sixth century B.C. and already found the anthropomorphism of the Homeric gods incompatible with the ideal of deity. But myth is older than Homer and belongs to a world which did believe in the gods. This faith in myth, this religious reality of myths, which is already overshadowed in Homer, is on the contrary very much alive in primitive mythology, and the myths themselves are the proof of it, while explicit confirmation is provided by a number of testimonies furnished by the natives themselves.

The Pawnee, a North American tribe of Caddo speech, differentiate "true stories" from "false stories", and include among the "true" stories in the first place all those which deal with the beginnings of the world; in these the actors are divine beings, supernatural, heavenly or astral. Next come those tales which relate the marvellous adventures of the national hero, a youth of humble birth who became the saviour of his people, freeing them from monsters, delivering them from famine and other disasters, and performing other noble and beneficent deeds. Last come the stories which have to do with the world of the medicine-men and explain how such-and-such a sorcerer got his superhuman powers, how such-and-such an association of shamans originated, and so on. The "false" stories are those which tell of the far from edifying adventures and exploits of Coyote, the prairie-wolf [1]). Thus in the "true" stories we have to deal with the holy and the supernatural,

---

*) Originally published in *SMSR* xxi (1947-48), pp. 104-16; title *Verità del mito*. Abbreviated German version in *Paideuma* iv (1950), pp. 1-10; title *Die Wahrheit des Mythos*.

1) G. A. Dorsey, *The Pawnee: Mythology* (Pt. i), Washington 1906, pp. 10, 13, 141, 428.

while the "false" ones on the other hand are of profane content, for Coyote is extremely popular in this and other North American mythologies in the character of a trickster, deceiver, sleight-of-hand expert and accomplished rogue [2]).

In this connexion there is a story from the Wichita, who also speak Caddo and are akin to the Pawnee, which is full of significance. It tells of a contest between Coyote and an opponent as to which knew most, i.e., which knew more stories [3]). The contest takes place at night, and the two opponents, sitting beside the fire, tell each a story in turn. At a certain point, Coyote's opponent begins to show signs of fatigue, and is slower and slower at finding a new tale to match that told by Coyote, while the latter goes on without stopping or hesitating, as if his repertory were limitless. At last the opponent owns himself beaten, and is killed. Why does Coyote win? Because, says the tale, his stories are "false", i.e., invented and therefore indefinitely many, while those of his opponent, who, we should note, is a falling star, are "true", that is, they tell of things which have really happened, and consequently are as many as they are, no more. The tales of Coyote, who appears here, as usual, as a breaker of his word, a violator of women, and so forth, would seem probably to be accounts of his imaginary adventures, easily to be multiplied at will on the model of his real ones. Certainly the Wichita themselves differentiate "old" tales, which have to do with the beginnings and the first age of the history of the world, from "new" ones, which treat of the present age, and it is only the former which are "true stories" for them [4]).

Similarly, the Oglala Dakota, a tribe of the Western Sioux family in North America, distinguish "tales of the tribe", that is of historical events which really took place, which are considered as "true tales", and "funny stories", mere inventions having no real substance, such as are above all the adventures of Iktomi, a figure corresponding to Coyote [5]). Analogously, the Cherokee, who are Iroquois, distinguish

---

2) E.g., among the Crow, see FR. B. LINDERMAN, *Old Man Coyote* (New York 1931).

3) G. A. DORSEY, *Mythology of the Wichita* (Washington 1904), 252 foll.

4) DORSEY, *op.c.*, 20-22.

5) MARTHA W. BECKWITH, *Mythology of the Oglala Dakota*, in J(ournal of) A(merican) F(olk-) L(ore) xliii (1930), 339. On the legendary cycle of Iktomi (*Inktomi* among the Assiniboin, *Isginki* among the Iowa, *Istinike* among the Ponca and Omaha) see also J. R. WALKER, *The Sun Dance and other Cere-*

between sacred myths (of the beginnings of the world, the creation of the heavenly bodies, the origin of death) and profane tales whose object is, for instance, to give an explanation, often a humorous one, of the more outstanding anatomical and physiological peculiarities of certain animals 6).

In Australia also, among the Karadjeri tribe of Lagrange Bay on the north-west coast, the sacred traditions dealing with the mythical age, and in particular those of cosmogonic contents, which are taught the novices during their initiation, are known as "true" 7).

In Africa, among the Herero, the tales which tell of the beginnings of the different groups into which the tribe is divided are supposed to be historically true, and consequently are distinguished from the many more or less comic tales which have no foundation in fact 8). The Negroes of Togoland, again, think of their stories of beginnings as "absolutely real" 9). Similarly, the Haussa distinguish between sagas or historical narratives and fanciful tales concerning human beings or the lower animals 10).

Now it is precisely the tales of beginnings, the cosmogonies, theogonies and legends of superhuman beings who brought things into existence and founded institutions, which are myths. And yet we see that for those who have and tell these tales, they are "true", and as such quite clearly distinguished from "false" stories; and the difference is not merely in their content, but affects the very nature of myth, showing itself likewise in conspicuous external signs.

Indeed, among the Pawnee and the Wichita, the tales of beginnings, including those of the associations of shamans, are recited in the course of certain cult-ceremonials, during the intervals between one rite and the next, which is not done with the false tales 11). Furthermore, the

---

monies of the Oglala Division of the Teton Dakota, in *Anthropological Papers of the American Museum of Natural History,* xvi, 2 (New York 1917), pag. 164 foll.

6) J. MOONEY, *Myths of the Cherokee* (19th Annual Report of the Bureau of American Ethnology, Pt. 1, Washington 1900), 229 foll.

7) R. PIDDINGTON, *Totemic System of the Karadjeri Tribe,* in *Oceania* ii (1932), 374, 393; *Karadjeri Initiation, ibid.* iii (1932), 46 foll.

8) G. VIEHE, in *Mitt. des Seminars f. orientalische Sprachen zu Berlin* v (1902), iii. Abteilung, p. 112.

9) A. W. CARDINALL, *Tales from Togoland* (London 1931), 9.

10) C. K. MEEK, *The Northern Tribes of Nigeria* ii (Oxford 1925), 147.

11) DORSEY, *op. cit. (supra, n. 1),* 13, 141; SAME, *op. cit. (supra, n. 3),* 16.

true tales, in contrast to the false, are not common property; among the Cherokee the stories of the creation, of the heavenly bodies, and the like were told (at night) in the presence of a small gathering [12]). Among the Pima, who live between California and New Mexico and speak a language of the Uto-Aztecan family, the myths were not told if women were present; only a few experts knew them thoroughly, and to them the boys were intrusted for four consecutive nights, to be taught how the world was made, whence the Pima had come, and of their conflicts with demons, monsters and fierce beasts [13]). Finally, while the false tales may be recited indifferently and with impunity at all times and in all places, it is not so with the "true" stories, which are told almost exclusively in winter or autumn, and only exceptionally in summer [14]), but in any case never in the day, but always at night or in the evening [15]).

Among the Tinguian of Luzon (see F. C. COLE, *Traditions of the Tinguian, a Study in Philippine Folk-Lore,* Field Museum Pub. 180, Chicago 1915, p. 6), the medicine-men's tales are told only during the preparations for the sacrifice of a beast or other offering to the gods.

12) MOONEY, *op. cit (supra, n. 6),* 229.

13) FR. RUSSELL, *The Pima Indians* (26th Annual Report of the Bur. of Am. Eth., Washington 1908), 206. Among the Berbers on the other hand it is the (old) women who tell the tales, and men are never among the listeners, see H. BASSET, *Essai sur la littérature des Berbères* (Algiers 1920), 101.

14) Among the Berbers the tales are told in summer and in winter, but not by day (BASSET, *op. cit.* 103). Among the Yavapai of Arizona, the myths are told in summer, by night, and to tell them in winter is to run the risk of raising a great storm. This, however, is the custom only of the south-eastern Yavapai, see E. W. GIFFORD, *The South-Eastern Yavapai,* Univ. of Calif. Pubs. in Am. Archaeology and Ethnology xxix, 3 (1932), 212. On the contrary, among the other Yavapai, those of the west and north-east, the myths are told (by old men, at night) in autumn or winter, by the fire (GIFFORD, *North-eastern and Western Yavapai Myths,* in J.A.F.L. xlvi, 1933, 347). Among the Tinguian of Luzon tales of the mythical era are generally told during the dry season, Cole, *op. c.* p. 5.

15) Among the Bukaua (Papuans of New Guinea), the tales are told in the evening during the season in which tubers and grains ripen, see NEUHAUSS, *Deutsch Neu-Guinea* iii, 479 foll., quoted in LÉVY-BRUHL, *La mythologie primitive* (Paris 1935), 116. Among the coastal Yuki in California, myths are called "night stories", because told only during the nights (of winter), while to tell them or even to think of them during the day is to risk becoming hump-backed (E. W. GIFFORD, *Coast Yuki Myths,* in J.A.F.L. 1937, 116). Among the Californian Miwok, myths are told (by old men) in the season which follows the first winter rains, and always at night, see C. MERRIAM, *The Dawn of the World* (Cleveland 1910), 15, cited by VAN DEURSEN, *Der Heilbringer,* (Groningen 1931) 28-30. Among the Thonga, who are southern

It is thus evident that the myth is not pure fiction; it is not fable but history, a "true story" and not a "false" one. It is a true story because of its contents, which are an account of events that really took place, starting from those impressive happenings which belong to the beginnings of things, the origin of the world and of mankind, that of life and death, of the animal and vegetable species, of hunting and of tilling the soil, of worship, of initiation-rites, of the associations of medicine-men and of their powers of healing. All these events are far removed in time, and from them our present life had its beginning and its foundation, from them came the present structure of society, which still depends on them. The divine or other superhuman persons who play their parts in the myth, their remarkable exploits and surprising adventures, all this world of wonders is a transcendent reality which may not be doubted, because it is the antecedent, the *sine qua non* of present reality.

Myth is true history because it is sacred history, not only by reason of its contents but also because of the concrete sacral forces which it sets going. The recital of myths of beginnings is incorporated in cult because it is cult itself and contributes to the ends for which cult is celebrated, these being the preservation and increase of life. Among various peoples of Australia, during the initiation-ceremonies the stories of the mythical age are told, the endless journeyings of the totemic ancestors who were the progenitors of the individual clans, because these recitals, apart from keeping alive and reinforcing the tribal traditions, promote the increase of the various totemic species. To tell of the creation of the world helps to preserve the world; to tell

---

Bantu, stories are not told by day, but only in the evening, and anyone who tells them in the daytime will go bald (H. A. Junod, *The Life of a South African Tribe*, ed. 2, London 1927, ii, 211). Among the hunting peoples of Siberia and those of the Altai, the tales are told in the evening at that time of year when hunting-parties go out; among the Ostiaks of Yenissei it is forbidden to tell tales in summer, until the streams begin to freeze; among the Abkhases and other peoples of the Caucasus, and also among some other nomadic Iranian peoples, the prohibition against telling them by day is in force, see Zelenin, *Die religiöse Funktion der Volksmärchen*, in *Internat. Archiv f. Ethnographie* xxxi (1910), 21 foll. The same customs and prohibitions are in force for the recital of legends both in the Mediterranean countries and elsewhere in Europe. Thus, an Irishwoman who was a story-teller would not hear of telling her tales in the daytime, because it brings ill-luck, see Bolte-Polivka, *Anmerkungen zu den Kinder- und Hausmärchen der Brüder Grimm* iv, p. 5.

of the beginnings of the human race helps to keep mankind in being, that is to say the community or tribal group. The recital of the institution of the initiation-rites and shamanistic practices has power to ensure their efficacy and their duration in time. Thus in ancient Mesopotamia, to recite the "Creation-epic" at the *akītu* or New Year festival was as it were to repeat the creative act; it was as though the world began again, and thus the year was truly inaugurated in the best manner, as a new cycle of time initiated by a new act of creation [16]).

That is why myths are true stories and cannot be false stories. Their truth has no origin in logic, nor is it of a historical kind; it is above all of a religious and more especially a magical order. The efficacy of the myth for the ends of cult, the preservation of the world and of life, lies in the magic of the word, in its evocative power, the power of *mythos* in its oldest sense, of the *fa-bula* not as a "fabulous" narrative but as a secret and potent force, akin, as its very etymology shows, to the power of *fa-tum* [17]). "It is said that it is so and therefore it is so"; that was the sentence in which an Eskimo of the Netsilik tribe expressed forcefully the magical truth, that is the power to make real which the spoken word possesses. He was referring especially to the Netsilik narratives, which "are both their real history and the source of all their religious ideas" [18]).

This evocative power of myth is reflected likewise in certain practices which often accompany its telling. Among the south-eastern Yavapai of Arizona, anyone listening to the story of the dying god [19])

—— · —— · ——

16) Cf. the chapter *Babilonia* in my *Confessione dei peccati* ii (Bologna 1935), 91 foll., also my art. *Der babylonische Ritus des Akitu und das Gedicht der Weltschöpfung*, in *Eranos-Jahrbuch* xix (1951), 404-30.

17) A thought of the invariability prescribed for magical formulae arises when one reads that among the coastal Yuki of California the teller of a tale must recite every word of it without the smallest variation (GIFFORD in *J.A.F.L.*, 1937, 116). Among the Miwok of California, the myths which make up the religious history of the people are handed down from generation to generation by word of mouth with no omissions nor additions (MERRIAM, *The Dawn of the World*, p. 15). Among the Haussa of the Sudan, if the teller of the tale introduces a variation into the text of it, even of an insignificant word, the listeners correct him (MEEK, *The Northern Tribes of Nigeria*, ii, 153).

18) Knut RASMUSSEN, *The Netsilik Eskimos* (Copenhagen 1931), 207, 363.

19) The myth of the god or hero who dies (and rises again) is common to sundry peoples of south California, as the Luiseño, Diegueño, Mohave and others. See Constance GODDARD DU BOIS, *The Religion of the Luiseño Indians*, in Univ. of Cal. Pubs. in Am. Arch. and Ethnol. viii, 3 (Berkeley 1908), 145; T. T. WA-

ran the risk of falling ill, with the result that when the narrative was ended every listener would get up, stretch and shake himself, with the intention of freeing himself in this way, as he believed he could, from the besetting malady [20]). Among the western and north-western Yavapai, when the elder has finished telling a story (at night), he says to the young people, boys and girls, who have listened to him, "Now get up, and before the dawn appears, run to the river to wash your faces, because this is a 'great story', and if you do not, you will go lame" [21]). Analogously, among the Cherokee, when anyone had been present at night at the telling of the myth of Kanati and Selu, that is of the origin of corn and of game (therefore a sacred legend, a "true story"), with all the explanations and comments belonging to it, he must "go to water" at dawn, before eating, in other words bathe in running water, while the medicine-man occupied himself with certain of his ritual performances on the bank [22]). Or, according to a parallel testimony [23]), after spending the night in hearing stories,

At daybreak the whole party went down to the running stream, where the pupils or hearers of myths stripped themselves, and were scratched upon the naked skin with a bone-tooth comb in the hands of the priest, after which they waded out, facing the rising sun, and dipped seven times under the water, while the priest recited prayers upon the bank.

This shaking, washing and blood-letting were all processes of riddance, having in view the same end, namely to free the hearer from the harmful influences which he had contracted while listening to, in other words during the evocation of, those imposing or even sinister events, such as the death of the god among the Yavapai, which, thus evoked, might by sympathetic potency bring about the death of the listener.

Riddance is also the aim of certain formulae often employed at the

TERMAN, *The Religious Practices of the Diegueño Indians,* ibid. viii, 6 (1910), 338 foll.; A. L. KROEBER, *Two Myths of the Mission Indians of California,* in *J.A.F.L.* xix (1906), 314; R. PETTAZZONI, *Miti e Leggende* iii (Turin 1953), 201 foll.

20) E. W. GIFFORD, *The South-eastern Yavapai,* 242.

21) SAME, in *J.A.F.L.* xlvi (1933), 347.

22) J. MOONEY, *Myths of the Cherokees,* in *J.A.F.L.* i (1888), 98; R. PETTAZZONI, *Miti e Leggende* iii, 490.

23) MOONEY, *Myths of the Cherokee* (19th Annual Report of Bur. of Am. Ethnol., Pt. i, Washington 1900), 229 foll.

end of the narration. Among the Thonga, a Bantu people, the narrator
is accustomed to end his story with these words, addressed to the
story itself, "Run away, go to Gwambe and Dzabana!" This is as much
as to say, "Depart to the spirit-world", for Gwambe and Dzabana are
the first man and the first woman, who as ancestors of the human race
are the rulers of the realm of the dead, the country of spirits [24]).
Among the Berbers also, narratives begin and end with formulae, which
vary from tribe to tribe, but generally speaking, the introductory ones
have a propitiatory force ("may God give us good and death to our
enemies!"), the concluding formulae have an apotropaic meaning intended to transfer the evil influences to some animal, for instance the
jackal, or to some character of the story itself [25]).

The same principle of an utterance intended to cause a riddance governs the
confession of sin, which indeed is, in its elementary forms, also associated with
acts of riddance, such as washing, stripping, burning, drawing blood, vomiting
and spitting. With all these, the sinner means to put the sin away, or take it out
of himself, or shake it off his back, and for this reason also he confesses it,
because by doing so, that is by putting it into words, he evokes it, "expresses
it" in the most literal sense, and so expels it from his own person [26]). The same
principle holds good also for a dream, which often leaves the dreamer under the
oppression of its phantasms and the influence of its boding apparitions. To drive
these away, according to the ancients, it was useful to wash, especially in sea-
water [27]), as the enchantress Kirke does in the *Argonautica* of Apollonios
of Rhodes (iv, 663, 670) [28]). But another beneficial process was to tell the drawn
in the open air [29]) and in the sunlight, as we are informed in a scholion on the
Electra of Sophokles à *propos* of Klytaimestra's dream related by Chrysothemis
(*El.* 424 foll., cf. 644 foll.). The ancients, says the annotator, "were accustomed,
as a rite of riddance, to tell their dreams to the sun." The intention is still the
same, to rid the person in question of the residual influence of the ghosts and
spectres seen in the dream, nightly phantoms which the sun scattered and drove
back to their own realms of darkness.

---

24) H. A. JUNOD, *The Life of a South African Tribe,* ed. 2, London 1929,
ii, 211, 349.

25) H. BASSET, *op. cit.* (*supra*, n. 13), 104.

26) See my *Confessione dei peccati* i-iii (Bologna 1929-36) and i-ii (Paris
1931-32), also No. V, p. 49 of this volume.

27) Aeschylus, *Persae* 201 foll.; Aristophanes, *Frogs* 1340, with the scholiast
there.

28) The natives of Morocco spit when they awake from a bad dream (E.
DOUTTÉ, *Magie et religion dans l'Afrique du Nord,* Paris 1909, 408). Among
the Akamba, who are Hamitised Bantu of East Africa, if anyone has had a bad
dream, he takes a burning brand, puts it out and throws it away, saying, "May
my ugly dream go away like this brand". (See G. LINBLOM, *The Akamba,*
Uppsala 1919-20, 212).

29) Eurip. *Iphig. Taur.,* 43.

It is not without cause that among peoples who live by hunting myths and tales of beasts are told on the occasion of hunting-parties. Thus among the Pawnee the tales already mentioned, the "true stories", of the mythical hero who saved his people from hunger by slaughtering buffaloes, used to be recited by hunters taking part in an expedition, because this remarkable "bag" in the myth, by the very fact of being told, that is spoken aloud, and therefore evoked, had the power to assure good success to the actual hunting [30]). Analogously, the Korwa, who are Kolarians of Chota Nagpur in east-central India, before they go to hunt, are accustomed to tell each other stories of hunting, assured that this contributes to the better success of the enterprise [31]). Among sundry people of Siberia, as the Buriats and others, and of the Altai, hunters are wont to tell stories in the evening in the communal hut, because, as they say, the spirits of the wood, who are the natural protectors of the beasts, are so fond of hearing them that they immediately crowd in and stay there invisible until the end, forgetting their protégés, which being thus left to themselves fall a prey more easily to the hunters [32]). This however is a secondary rationalistic motivation, which misses the real meaning of the narratives. These must originally have been told to attract, not the spirits, but the beasts themselves, of which the guardian spirits who watch over single species are after a fashion a transfiguration, an animistic hypostasis [33]).

The fact is that the tales told by the hunters of Siberia and the Altai are nothing else than tales of animals, as indeed the myths of the Bushmen, who are still more primitive hunters, are mostly stories of beasts. The rock-paintings of these same Bushmen also represent for the most part figures of animals and hunting-scenes, for the same magical principle is at work in these representations as in the recital of the myths; the picture is credited with a sympathetic potency fitted to promote the reproduction of the thing portrayed, that is the multiplication of the animal in question or the repetition of an equally pro-

---

30) DORSEY, op. cit. (supra, n. 1), 141.

31) R. V. RUSSELL, The Tribes and Castes of the Central Provinces of India iii (London 1916), 577.

32) D. ZELENIN, op. cit. (supra, n. 15), 21 foll., cf. K. MENGES, Jägerglaube u. -gebräuche bei Altajischen Türken, in Muséon, 1932, 85.

33) Cf. UNO HARVA, Die religiösen Vorstellungen der Altaischen Völker, (Helsinki 1938) 391 foll.

ductive hunt, and the like. For in the sphere of magic the picture that is drawn or painted has the same power as the word that is spoken, and anyone who possesses the effigy of a person has that person himself at his mercy, like him who knows his name; and anyone acquainted with the myth of the origin of an animal or vegetable species has in his power all the individuals of that species [34]), as anyone who can draw the capture of a bison on a rock is master of all bisons.

And this is equally true of prehistoric epochs and for the oldest rock-paintings of palaeolithic, mesolithic and neolithic huntsmen, for these pictures are mostly figures of animals and hunting scenes. And as these are for us the oldest monuments of graphic art, it has been thought [35]) that correspondingly the beast-tale, from the Bushman myths to Aesop's fables and beyond, represents the oldest form of human story-telling, since both the art of those distant days and this primitive "literature" go back to the rudimentary culture of hunting and food-gathering, and both come from the spirit of magic, which is the spirit properly belonging to that ancient humanity, as yet sunk in animalism, always uncertain of to-morrow, always at the mercy of the unknown, always awaiting lucky happenings, such as a fortunate capture of game or the discovery of fruit-bearing bushes.

But this primitive humanity was already, for all its magic, a religious humanity. There never was, as Frazer supposed, a magic epoch earlier than religion, as there never was a religious epoch earlier than magic. Assuredly, the myths of beginnings with their great figures of creative Beings, Creators of the world and of the human race, of life and of death, are nearer to what *we* mean by religion. But the idea of a Supreme Being who creates, as a purely logical concept of pre-mythical thought, such as W. Schmidt postulates, is a wholly arbitrary construction. A pre-mythical stage is no more and no less an abstraction than the pre-logical stage of L. Lévy-Bruhl; human thought is mythical and logical at the same time. Neither is religion pure rational thinking

---

34) Among the Cuna of the Isthmus of Panama, a formula alluding to the origin of a given species confers the power of attracting the creautres of that species; to know the origin of a plant is the necessary and sufficient condition for the success of its medicinal action (ERL. NORDENSKIÖLD, *La conception de l'âme chez les Indiens Cuna de l'Isthme de Panama*, in *Journ. de la Société des Américanistes*, 1932, pp. 6, 15, 24).

35) Cf. ZELENIN, *op. cit. (supra, n. 15)*, 28 foll.

which knows nothing of myth, as Andrew Lang supposed. Like magic, so also myth is already religion. The idea of the creative Supreme Being among primitive peoples is nothing but a form of the myth of beginnings and as such shares in the character of myth, at once magical and religious [36]). This character is, as we have said, the very truth of myth, an absolute truth because a truth of faith, and truth of faith because a truth of life. The myth is true and cannot but be true, because it is the charter of the tribe's life, the foundation of a world which cannot continue without that myth. On the other hand, the myth cannot continue without this world, of which it forms an organic part, as the "explanation" of its beginnings, as its original *raison d'être*, its "prologue in heaven" [37]). The life of myth, which is at the same time its "truth", is the very life of its natal world of formation and incubation. Apart from this, the myth can indeed survive, but a surviving myth is no longer true, because no longer living; it has ceased to be a "true" story and become a "false" one.

As already stated, the tales of Coyote, the prairie wolf, among sundry peoples of North America, are "false". They form an extensive cycle of narratives concerning his adventures, which are far from edifying, since they consist of frauds, practical jokes, intrigues, lies, traps, swindles, deceits, thefts, love-makings, fornications and vulgarities of every kind, in sharp contrast to the loftiness, seriousness, dignity and impressiveness of the myths of beginnings, which are "true stories". But the figure of Coyote has not only these despicable attributes; Coyote appears frequently as a sort of demiurge, the benefactor of humanity, the lawgiver, the founder of institutions, and sometimes even as Creator, subordinate and in opposition to the Supreme Being [38]).

The complex and contradictory nature of Coyote's aspects results from the composite process which gave rise to his figure. Originally, Coyote clearly goes back to that primitive world of hunters in which life depends above all on hunting, and the good result of a hunt

---

36) See No. III, pp. 26-27 of this volume.

37) [The reference is to the famous scene with which the action of Goethe's *Faust*, Pt. i, begins. — TRANS.]

38) So among the (north-eastern) Maidu of California, see R. B. DIXON, *Maidu Texts* (1912), 4 foll., cf. his *System and Sequence in Maidu Mythology*, in *J.A.F.L.* xvi (1903), 32 foll.; R. DANGEL, *Der Schöpferglaube der Nordcentralcalifornier*, in *S.M.S.R.* iii (1937), 31 foll.

depends on the beasts, and in the first place on the Lord of Beasts who has them in his power. That is what Coyote was to begin with. As such, he was a rudimentary Supreme Being, as is, in other North American mythologies, the Hare or the Crow, as in Africa the praying mantis among the Bushmen, the spider or the elephant elsewhere, and such he remained as long as that primitive world from which he sprang lasted and continued. But when that world passes, its Supreme Being passes with it, that is to say the Lord of beasts, or Lord of the bush and of the game in it [39]). Then Coyote yielded up his place to another Supreme Being, the Creator, and survived only as the Creator's opponent and implacable adversary, a figure without dignity, a "false" figure confronted with the "truth" of the new Supreme Being, as his legends henceforth are false in face of the truth of the creation-myth.

A day will come when the myths of beginnings too will lose their "truth" and become "false stories" in their turn, in other words fabulous. This will occur when their world, built up on the ruins of the first one, collapses in its turn to give place to a later and different structure. This indeed is how history proceeds, in a series of disintegrations and reintegrations, dissolutions and rebirths, in the everlasting alternation of life and death. And when, by reason of internal degeneration or overpowering external forces, a world breaks up and another rises on its ruins, when one form of culture fades, to be replaced by another, the organic relationship of its constituent parts comes to an end. Disintegrated, disjointed, sundered, they lose all cohesion and fall a prey to dispersing centrifugal forces. Then the myths too, fragments among the fragments, stripped now of their genuine religious character and constitutionally foreign to the new structure, which has an ideology of its own, are thrust to the margins of the new life, until, utterly severed from their matrix and with every bond that held them loosened, they go on the ways of the world, passing from mouth to mouth as mere sport and amusement.

This does not mean that all profane tales are ancient myths desacralised. Many, and perhaps from the literary point of view the most interesting, were profane from the beginning, pure inventions and

---

39) H. BAUMANN, *Afrikanische Wild- und Buschgeister,* in *Zeitschr. f. Ethnologie* lxx (1938 [1939]), 208-39; cf. A. DIRR, *Der kaukasische Wild- und Jagdgott,* in *Anthropos* xx (1925), 139. See further my forthcoming book, *The Allknowing God* (London 1955), Epilogue.

fictions, "false stories" which never had been "true stories". But by the side of these are others, of more remote origin, which from having been myths, that is to say "true" stories, as they were to start with, have become fabulous, "false stories", tales to laugh at, "a theme of laughter and of sport" [40]). By this same process Coyote, from being a rudimentary demiurge and afterwards the adversary of the Creator, a distant forerunner of Satan, of the Devil, the "Spirit that still denies", degenerated into a sacrilegious buffoon, a jesting cheater, a vulgar harlequin. It was the same procedure by which another literary *genre*, the drama, which was once a liturgical performance, changed into a secular entertainment, the same through which, in another department, pictorial art got free, as an end in itself, from the primordial magico-religious paintings of prehistoric caves, and in yet another, the mystic bull-roarer of primitive initiation-mysteries degenerated into the ludicrous function of a plaything for little children [41]), and an ancient holy rite founded upon the course of the sun ended by becoming a ball-game [42]).

------

40) [*Argomento di riso e di trastullo,* a line from a well-known poem of Giacomo Leopardi. — TRANS.]

41) Cf. Chap. i of my book *I Misteri* (Bologna 1924).

42) Cf. ALICE C. FLETCHER and FR. LA FLESCHE, *The Omaha Tribe* (27th. Ann. Report of the Bureau of Am. Ethnol., Washington 1911), 197; Father P. H. MEYER, *Wunekau, oder Sonnenverehrung in Neuguinea,* in *Anthropos,* 1932, 427; W. KRICKEBERG, *Das mittelamerikanische Ballspiel u. seine religiöse Symbolik,* in *Paideuma* iii, 3-5 (1948), p. 118 foll.

Introduction: The Symbolic Function of Myths

1. FROM THE PRIMARY SYMBOLS TO MYTHS

UP TO THE PRESENT we have been trying to "re-enact" in imagination and sympathetically the *experience* of fault. Have we really reached, under the name of experience, an immediate datum? Not at all. What is experienced as defilement, as sin, as guilt, requires the mediation of a specific language, the language of symbols. Without the help of that language, the experience would remain mute, obscure, and shut up in its implicit contradictions (thus defilement is expressed as something that infects from without, and sin as a ruptured relation and as a power, etc.). These elementary symbols, in their turn, have been reached only at the price of an abstraction that has uprooted them from the rich world of myths. In order to attempt a purely semantic exegesis of the expressions that best reveal the experience of fault (stain and defilement, deviation, revolt, transgression, straying, etc.), we have had to bracket the second-degree symbols which are the medium for the primary symbols, which are themselves the medium for the living experience of defilement, of sin, and of guilt.

This new level of expression embarrasses the modern man. In one sense, he alone can recognize the myth as myth, because he alone has reached the point where history and myth become separate. This "crisis," this decision, after which myth and history are dissociated, may signify the loss of the mythical dimension:

because mythical time can no longer be co-ordinated with the time of events that are "historical" in the sense required by historical method and historical criticism, because mythical space can no longer be co-ordinated with the places of our geography, we are tempted to give ourselves up to a radical demythization of all our thinking. But another possibility offers itself to us: precisely because we are living and thinking after the separation of myth and history, the demythization of our history can become the other side of an understanding of myth as myth, and the conquest, for the first time in the history of culture, of the mythical dimension. That is why we never speak here of demythization, but strictly of demythologization, it being well understood that what is lost is the pseudo-knowledge, the false logos of the myth, such as we find expressed, for example, in the etiological function of myths. But when we lose the myth as immediate logos, we rediscover it as myth. Only at the price and by the roundabout way of philosophical exegesis and understanding, can the myth create a new *peripeteia* of the logos.

This conquest of myth as myth is only one aspect of the recognition of symbols and their power to reveal. To understand the myth as myth is to understand what the myth, with its time, its space, its events, its personages, its drama, adds to the revelatory function of the primary symbols worked out above.

Without pretending to give here a general theory of symbols and myths, and limiting ourselves voluntarily and systematically to that group of mythical symbols which concern human evil, we can set forth in the following terms our working hypothesis, which is to be employed in the whole course of our analysis and verified in the performance:

1. The first function of the myths of evil is to embrace mankind as a whole in one ideal history. By means of a time that represents all times, "man" is manifested as a concrete universal; Adam signifies man. "In" Adam, says Saint Paul, we have all sinned. Thus experience escapes its singularity; it is transmuted in its own "archetype." Through the figure of the hero, the ancestor, the Titan, the first man, the demigod, experience is put on the track of existential structures: one can now *say* man, existence, human

being, because in the myth the human type is recapitulated, summed up.

2. The universality of man, manifested through the myths, gets its concrete character from the *movement* which is introduced into human experience by narration; in recounting the *Beginning* and the *End* of fault, the myth confers upon this experience an orientation, a character, a tension. Experience is no longer reduced to a present experience; this present was only an instantaneous cross-section in an evolution stretching from an origin to a fulfillment, from a "Genesis" to an "Apocalypse." Thanks to the myth, experience is traversed by the essential history of the perdition and the salvation of man.

3. Still more fundamentally, the myth tries to get at the enigma of human existence, namely, the discordance between the fundamental reality—state of innocence, status of a creature, essential being—and the actual modality of man, as defiled, sinful, guilty. The myth accounts for this transition by means of a narration. But it is a narration precisely because there is no deduction, no logical transition, between the fundamental reality of man and his present existence, between his ontological status as a being created good and destined for happiness and his existential or historical status, experienced under the sign of alienation. Thus the myth has an ontological bearing: it points to the relation—that is to say, both the leap and the passage, the cut and the suture—between the essential being of man and his historical existence.

In all these ways, the myth makes the experience of fault the center of a whole, the center of a world: the world of fault.

It can already be guessed how far we are from a purely allegorical interpretation of the myth. An allegory can always be *translated* into a text that can be understood by itself; once this better text has been made out, the allegory falls away like a useless garment; what the allegory showed, while concealing it, can be said in a direct discourse that replaces the allegory. By its triple function of concrete universality, temporal orientation, and finally ontological exploration, the myth has a way of *revealing* things that is not reducible to any translation from a language in cipher to a clear language. As Schelling has shown in his *Philosophy of*

Mythology, the myth is autonomous and immediate; it means what it says.[1]

It is essential, therefore, for a critical understanding of the myth to respect its irreducibility to the allegory.

2. MYTH AND GNOSIS: THE SYMBOLIC FUNCTION OF THE NARRATION

For a critical understanding of the myth it is first necessary that the myth be entirely divorced from the "etiological" function with which it appears to be identified. This distinction is fundamental for a philosophical handling of the myth; for the principal objection that philosophy addresses to myth is that the mythical explanation is incompatible with the rationality discovered or invented by the Pre-Socratics; from that time on, it represents the simulacrum of rationality.

The distinction between rationality and its imitation is, in fact, as decisive as that between history and myth. Indeed, it is the foundation of the latter; for history is history only because its search for "causes" leans upon the *Epistêmê* of the geometers and the physicists, even when it is distinguished from it. If, then, the myth is to survive this double distinction of history and myth as well as of explanation and myth, the myth must not be either history, happening in a definite time and place, or explanation.

My working hypothesis is that criticism of the pseudo-rational is fatal not to myth, but to gnosis. It is in gnosis that the simulacrum of reason attains realization. Gnosis is what seizes upon and develops the etiological element in myths. The gnosis of evil in particular takes its stand on the ground of reason; as the word itself makes clear, gnosis tries to be "knowledge." Between gnosis

[1] As the third book of this work will show, the refusal to reduce the myth to an allegory that can be translated into an intelligible language does not exclude all "interpretation" of myths. We shall propose a type of "interpretation" that is not a "translation"; let us say, to be brief, that the very process of discovery of the field of experience *opened up* by the myth can constitute an *existential verification* comparable to the transcendental deduction of the categories of the understanding. Cf. the final chaper of the second book: "The Symbol Gives Rise to Thought."

and reason a choice must be made. But perhaps there is a way of recovering the myth as myth, before it slipped into gnosis, in the nakedness and poverty of a symbol that is not an explanation but an opening up and a disclosure. Our whole effort will be directed toward dissociating myth and gnosis.

We are encouraged in this attempt by the great example of Plato. Plato inserts myths into his philosophy; he adopts them as myths, in their natural state, so to speak, without trying to disguise them as explanations; they are there in his discourse, full of enigmas; they are there as myths, without any possibility of confusing them with Knowledge.

It is true that the myth is in itself an invitation to gnosis. Furthermore, the problem of evil seems to be the principal occasion of this passage from myth to gnosis. We already know what a powerful incitement to questioning springs from suffering and sin: "How long, O Lord?" "Have I sinned against some divinity?" "Was my act pure?" One might say that the problem of evil offers at the same time the most considerable challenge to think and the most deceptive invitation to talk nonsense, as if evil were an always premature problem where the ends of reason always exceed its means. Long before nature made reason rave and threw it into the transcendental illusion, the contradiction felt between the destination of man, projected in the image of primordial innocence and final perfection, and the actual situation of man, acknowledged and confessed, gave rise to a gigantic "Why?" at the center of the experience of existing. Hence, the greatest explanatory ravings, which compose the considerable literature of gnosis, came into being in connection with that "question."

What, then, was the myth prior to its "etiological" pretensions? What is myth if it is not gnosis? Once more we are brought back to the function of the symbol. The symbol, we have said, opens up and discloses a dimension of experience that, without it, would remain closed and hidden. We must show, then, in what sense the myth is a second-degree function of the primary symbols that we have been exploring up to the present.

For that purpose we must rediscover this function of opening up and disclosing—which we here set in opposition to the explanatory function of gnosis—right down to the most specific traits that distinguish the myth from the primary symbols. Now, it is the *narration* that adds a new stage of meaning to that of the primary symbols.

How can the narration *mean* in a symbolic and non-etiological mode?

We shall have recourse here to the interpretation of the mythical consciousness proposed by the phenomenology of religion (Van der Leeuw, Leenhardt, Eliade). At first glance, that interpretation seems to dissolve the myth-narration in an undivided consciousness that consists less in telling stories, making myths, than in relating itself affectively and practically to the whole of things. What is essential for us here is to understand why ·that consciousness, structured lower than any narration, any fable or legend, nevertheless breaks out into language under the form of narration. If the phenomenologists of religion have been more concerned to go back from the narration to the pre-narrative root of the myth, we shall follow the opposite course from the pre-narrative conscious- ness to the mythical narration. It is in this transition that the whole enigma of the symbolic function of myths is centered.

There are two characteristics of the myth for which we must account: that it is an expression in language and that in it the symbol takes the form of narration.

Let us transport ourselves behind the myth. According to the phenomenology of religion, the myth-narration is only the verbal envelope of a form of life, felt and lived before being formulated; this form of life expresses itself first in an inclusive mode of be- havior relative to the whole of things; it is in the rite rather than in the narration that this behavior is expressed most completely, and the language of the myth is only the verbal segment of this total action.[2] Still more fundamentally, ritual action and mythical

---

[2] "It is necessary to accustom oneself," says Eliade, "to dissociating the notion of myth from the notions of speech and fable, in order to relate it to the notions of sacred action and significant gesture. The mythical includes not only everything that is told about certain events that happened and certain personages who lived *in illo tempore*, but also everything that is

language, taken together, point beyond themselves to a model, an archetype, which they imitate or repeat; imitation in gestures and verbal repetition are only the broken expressions of a living participation in an original Act which is the common exemplar of the rite and of the myth.

There is no doubt that the phenomenology of religion has profoundly affected the problem of myths by thus going back to a mythical structure which would be the matrix of all the images and all the particular narrations peculiar to this or that mythology, and relating to this diffuse mythical structure the fundamental categories of the myth: participation, relation to the Sacred, etc.

It is this mythical structure itself that leads to the diversity of myths. What, in fact, is the ultimate significance of this mythical structure? It indicates, we are told, the intimate accord of the man of cult and myth with the whole of being; it signifies an indivisible plenitude, in which the supernatural, the natural, and the psychological are not yet torn apart. But *how* does the myth signify this plenitude? The essential fact is that this intuition of a cosmic whole, from which man is not separated, and this undivided plenitude, anterior to the division into supernatural, natural, and human, are not *given,* but simply *aimed at.* It is only in intention that the myth restores some wholeness; it is because he himself has lost that wholeness that man re-enacts and imitates it in myth and rite. The primitive man is already a man of division. Hence the myth can only be an intentional restoration or reinstatement and in this sense already symbolical.

This distance between experience and intention has been recognized by all the authors who have attributed to the myth a biological role of protection against anxiety. If myth-making is an antidote to distress, that is because the man of myths is already an unhappy consciousness;[3] for him, unity, conciliation, and recon-

---

related directly or indirectly to such events and to the primordial personages" (*Traité d'Histoire des Religions,* p. 355).

[3] One cannot hold at the same time, as G. Gusdorf does in *Mythe et Métaphysique* (Paris, 1953), that the myth has a biological, protective role (pp. 12, 21) and that it is "the spontaneous form of being in the world." All the excessive overestimations of the mythical consciousness come from

ciliation are things to be *spoken of* and *acted out,* precisely because
they are not *given.* Myth-making is primordial, contemporaneous
with the mythical structure, since participation is signified rather
than experienced.

Now, in manifesting the purely symbolic character of the relation of man to the lost totality, the myth is condemned from the
beginning to division into multiple cycles. There does not exist, in
fact, any act of signifying that is equal to its aim. As the study
of the primary symbols of fault has already suggested, it is always
with something that plays the role of analogon as starting point
that the symbol symbolizes; the multiplicity of the symbols is the
immediate consequence of their subservience to a stock of analoga,
which altogether are necessarily limited in extension and individually are equally limited in comprehension.

Lévi-Strauss has insisted strongly on the initial discrepancy
between the limitation of experience and the totality signified by
the myth: "The Universe," he writes,[4] "signified long before man
began to know what it signified . . . ; it signified from the beginning the totality of what humanity might expect to know about
it"; "man has at his disposal from the beginning an integrality
in the *significans,* about which he is greatly perplexed as to how
to allocate it to a *significatum,* given as such without, however,
being known." This totality, thus signified but so little experienced,
becomes available only when it is condensed in sacred beings and
objects which become the privileged signs of the significant whole.
Hence the primordial diversification of symbols. In fact, there does
not exist anywhere in the world a civilization in which this surplus
of signification is aimed at apart from any mythical form or definite ritual. The Sacred takes contingent forms precisely because it
is "floating"; and so it cannot be divined except through the

---

this forgetfulness of the distance between experienced conciliation and
aimed-at reconciliation. If it is true that "the primitive man is still the man
of conciliation and reconciliation, the man of plenitude," and that he
preserves the mark of "that concordance of reality and value that primitive
mankind found without difficulty in the myth," one can no longer understand why the mythical consciousness gives itself up to the tale, to the
image, and, in general, to significant speech.

[4] Quoted by G. Gusdorf, *op. cit.,* p. 45.

indefinite diversity of mythologies and rituals. The chaotic and arbitrary aspect of the world of myths is thus the exact counterpart of the discrepancy between the purely symbolic plenitude and the finiteness of the experience that furnishes man with "analogues" of that which is signified. Narrations and rites, then, are needed to consecrate the contour of the signs of the sacred: holy places and sacred objects, epochs and feasts, are other aspects of the contingency that we find in the narration. If the plenitude were experienced, it would be everywhere in space and time; but because it is only aimed at symbolically, it requires special signs and a discourse on the signs; their heterogeneity bears witness to the significant whole by its contingent outcroppings. Hence, the myth has the function of guarding the finite contours of the signs which, in their turn, refer to the plenitude that man aims at rather than experiences. That is why, although the primitive civilizations have in common almost the same mythical structure, this undifferentiated structure exists nowhere without a diversity of myths; the polarity of the one mythical structure and the many myths is a consequence of the *symbolic* character of the totality and the plenitude that myths and rites reproduce. Because it is symbolized and not lived, the sacred is broken up into a multiplicity of myths.

But why does the myth, when it is broken up, take the form of narration? What we have to understand now is why the original model, in which the myth and the rite lead us to participate, itself affects the character of a drama. It is, in fact, because that which is ultimately signified by every myth is itself in the form of a drama that the narrations in which the mythical consciousness is fragmented are themselves woven of happenings and personages; because its paradigm is dramatic, the myth itself is a tissue of events and is found nowhere except in the plastic form of narration. But why does the narration-myth refer symbolically to a drama?

It is because the mythical consciousness not only does not experience the plenitude, but does not even indicate it except at the beginning or the end of a fundamental *History*. The plenitude that the myth points to symbolically is established, lost, and reestablished dangerously, painfully. Thus it is not given, not only because it is signified and not experienced, but because it is signified through a combat. The myth, as well as the rite, receives from this primordial drama the mode of discourse peculiar to narration. The plastic character of the myth, with its images and events, results, then, both from the necessity of providing contingent signs for a purely symbolic Sacred and from the dramatic character of the primordial time. Thus the time of the myth is diversified from the beginning by the primordial drama.

The myths concerning the origin and the end of evil that we are now going to study constitute only a limited sector of myths and furnish only a partial verification of the working hypothesis set forth in this introduction. At least they give us direct access to the primordially dramatic structure of the world of myths. We recall the three fundamental characteristics ascribed above to the myths of evil: the concrete universality conferred upon human experience by means of archetypal personages, the tension of an ideal history oriented from a Beginning toward an End, and finally the transition from an essential nature to an alienated history; these three functions of the myths of evil are three aspects of one and the same dramatic structure. Hence, the narrative form is neither secondary nor accidental, but primitive and essential. The myth performs its symbolic function by the specific means of narration because what it wants to express is already a drama. It is this primordial drama that opens up and discloses the hidden meaning of human experience; and so the myth that recounts it assumes the irreplaceable function of narration.

The two characteristics of myths that we have just emphasized are fundamental for our investigation of the world of fault.

In the first place, the surplus of signification, the "floating *significans*," constituted by the Sacred, attests that the experience of fault, as we have described it in Part I, is from its origin in relation or in tension with a totality of meaning, with an all-inclusive meaning of the universe. The relation, or the tension, is an integral part of the experience; or, rather, the experience subsists only in connection with *symbols* that place fault in a totality which is not perceived, not experienced, but signified, aimed at, conjured up. The language of the confession of sins, then, is only a fragment of a vaster language that indicates mythically the origin and the end of fault, and the totality in which it arose. If we detach the living experience from the symbol, we take away from the experience that which completes its meaning. Now, it is the myth as narration that puts the present experience of fault into relation with the totality of meaning.

On the other hand, this total meaning, which is the background of fault, is linked to the primordial drama by the mythical consciousness. The fundamental symbols that impregnate the experience of fault are the symbols of the distress, the struggle, and the victory which, once upon a time, marked the foundation of the world. Totality of meaning and cosmic drama are the two keys that will help us unlock the myths of the Beginning and the End.

3. Toward a "Typology" of the Myths of the Beginning and the End of Evil

But if the mythical consciousness in primitive civilizations remains very much *like itself,* and if, on the other hand, mythologies are *unlimited in number,* how shall we make our way between the One and the Many? How shall we escape getting lost, either in a vague phenomenology of the mythical consciousness which finds "mana" and repetition and participation everywhere, or in an indefinitely diversified comparative mythology? We shall try to follow the counsel of Plato in the *Philebus,* when he tells us not to imitate the "eristics," who make "one too quickly and many too quickly," but always to seek an intermediate number that "multiplicity realizes in the interval between the Infinite and the One"; regard for these intermediate numbers, said Plato, "is what distinguishes the dialectic method in our discussions from the eristic method."

This "numbered multiplicity," intermediate between an undifferentiated mythical consciousness and the too much differentiated mythologies, must be sought by means of a "typology." The "types" which we propose are at the same time *a priori,* permitting us to go to the encounter with experience with a key for deciphering it in our hands and to orient ourselves in the labyrinth of the mythologies of evil, and *a posteriori,* always subject to correction and amendment through contact with experience. I should like to think, as Cl. Lévi-Strauss does in *Tristes Tropiques,* that the images which the myth-making imagination and the institutional activity of man can produce are not infinite in number, and that it is possible to work out, at least as a working hypothesis, a sort of morphology of the principal images.

We shall consider here four mythical "types" of representation concerning the origin and the end of evil.

1. According to the first, which we call the drama of creation, the origin of evil is coextensive with the origin of things; it is the *"chaos" with which the creative act of the god struggles.* The counterpart of this view of things is that *salvation is identical with creation itself;* the act that founds the world is at the same time the liberating act. We shall verify this in the structure of the cult that corresponds to this "type" of the origin and end of evil; the cult can only be a *ritual re-enactment* of the combats at the origin of the world. The identity of evil and "chaos," and the identity of salvation with "creation," have seemed to us to constitute the two fundamental traits of this first type. The other traits will be corollaries of these dominant traits.

2. It has seemed to us that there is a change of type with the idea of a "fall" of man that arises as an irrational event in a *creation already completed;* and consequently we shall try to show that the dramas of creation *exclude* the idea of a "fall" of man. Any indication of a doctrine of the "fall"—if there be any— within the dramas of creation is held in check by the whole of the interpretation and heralds the transition to another "type"; and, inversely, the idea of a "fall" of man becomes fully developed only in a cosmology from which any creation-drama has been eliminated. The counterpart of a schema based on the notion of a "fall" is that salvation is a new peripeteia in relation to the primordial creation; salvation unrolls a new and open history on the basis of a creation already completed and, in that sense, closed.

Thus the cleavage effected, with the second type, between the irrational event of the fall and the ancient drama of creation provokes a parallel cleavage between the theme of salvation, which becomes eminently historical, and the theme of creation, which recedes to the position of "cosmological" background for the *temporal* drama played in the foreground of the world. Salvation, understood as the sum of the initiatives of the divinity and of the believer tending toward the elimination of evil, aims henceforth at a specific end distinct from the end of creation. That specific end, around which gravitate the "eschatological" representations, can no longer be identified with the end of creation, and we arrive at a strange tension between two representations: that of a creation brought to a close with the "rest on the seventh day," and that of a work of salvation still pending, until the "Last Day." The separation of the problematics of evil from the problematics of creation is carried out along the whole line, beginning with the idea of a fall that supervened upon a perfect creation. It is, then, the event of the fall that carries the whole weight of this mythology, like the point of an inverted pyramid.

3. Between the myth of chaos, belonging to the creation-drama, and the myth of the fall, we shall insert an intermediate type that may be called "tragic," because it attains its full manifestation all at once in Greek tragedy. Behind the tragic vision of man we shall look for an implicit, and perhaps unavowable, theology: the tragic theology of the god who tempts, blinds, leads astray. Here the fault appears to be indistinguishable from the very existence of the tragic hero; he does not commit the fault, he is guilty. What, then, can salvation be? Not the "remission of sins," for there is no pardon for an inevitable fault. Nevertheless, there is a tragic salvation, which consists in a sort of aesthetic deliverance issuing from the tragic spectacle itself, internalized in the depths of existence and converted into pity with respect to oneself. Salvation of this sort makes freedom coincide with understood necessity.

Between the chaos of the drama of creation, the inevitable fault of the tragic hero, and the fall of the primeval man there are complex relations of exclusion and inclusion, which we shall try to understand and to recapture in ourselves; but even the relation of exclusion occurs within a common space, thanks to which these three myths have a common fate.

4. Altogether marginal to this triad of myths, there is a solitary myth that has played a considerable part in our Western culture, because it presided, if not over the birth, at least over the growth of Greek philosophy. This myth, which we shall call "the *myth of the exiled soul,*" differs from all the others in that it divides man into *soul* and *body* and concentrates on the destiny of the soul, which it depicts as coming from elsewhere and straying here below, while the cosmogonic, or theogonic, background of the other myths receives little emphasis. One test of our typology— and that not the least—will be to understand why the myth of the exiled soul and the myth of the fault of a primeval man could sometimes merge and blend their influences in an indistinct myth of the fall, although these two myths are profoundly heterogeneous, and the secret affinities of the Biblical myth of the fall carry it toward the myth of chaos and the tragic myth rather than toward the myth of the exiled soul.

Thus our "typology" ought not to be confined to an attempt at classification; we must go beyond the statics of classification to a dynamics that has as its task the discovery of the latent life of the myths and the play of their secret affinities. It is this dynamics that must prepare the way for a philosophic recapture of the myth.

ELISEO VIVAS

Myth: Some Philosophical Problems

I

THE REMARKS that follow are based on a number of assumptions some of which, it would seem, it is too late in our century
to question.

Today it is generally agreed that myth making is a permanent
activity of all men, an activity that apparently men cannot live without.
Whether a contemporary of the painters of Altamira or of the writer
or writers of Genesis, or of Einstein and Bohr, man has always lived
in and by myth. And this holds for us today whether we are educated
or illiterate. To say man lives in myth is to say that the picture of the
world within which he lives is at least in part mythical; to say that he
lives by myth is to say that he uses that picture for living.

It is also usually held that the sharp distinction once accepted by
some anthropologists between primitive mentality—whether the mentality of archaic man or of our contemporaries the savages—and ours,
is a false distinction.

Another assumption held today, although not universally, is that
myths are the product of the human mind working in its own right.

89

Cassirer would say that myths have their own formative laws. If the pedantry be permitted, we could say that myths are autotelic and autonomous. Myth seems to have its own way of being; and it can be said of it that it seeks, so to speak, its own ends; thus it can be distinguished, if not separated, from other products of human activity.

This latter assumption raises a number of difficult questions that it would be most interesting to investigate. For instance, the similarities and differences between myth and literature—or, as I prefer to call it, poetry. Another would seek light on the distinction between myths and *Weltanschauungen*. Still another, of vast theoretical and practical importance, would ask about the unity of experience. But I cannot deal with all of them in one essay, or with any one of them in a sufficiently detailed manner to offer a satisfactory analysis of it.

I do not intend to justify these assumptions but it is desirable to dwell on them briefly.

As regards the distinction between the mind of the primitive and that of the civilized man, so brilliantly expounded by Lévy-Bruhl, I know of no one today whose opinion deserves attention who takes it to be valid. It is my impression that it was never seriously held by American anthropologists since Boas. In any case, Lévi-Strauss confirms a hunch I have long entertained. He tells us that it was in neolithic times that man gained his dominion over the great arts of civilization: ceramics, weaving, agriculture, and the domestication of animals. And he goes on to assert that no one today would dare explain these immense conquests as the fortuitous accumulation of a series of chance findings. He adds that each one of these techniques presupposes centuries of active and methodic observation, of daring and controlled hypotheses to be rejected or accepted by means of tireless and repeated experiences. We need not go along with Lévi-Strauss's notion of the science of the concrete to see that archaic man achieved his technological conquests because he was capable of thinking as Watts, Morse, and Edison thought. Involved in the rejection of the distinction between primitive and civilized mentality is the insight that myth is not necessarily the exclusive possession of the dark mind of savages, whether in Neolithic times

90

or today, and that the mind of civilized man is, or can be, free from what the rationalist takes to be the wearying incubus of myth.

The assumption that man can live without myth is one of the precious "truths" of village atheists and vestigial eighteenth-century rationalists living in our mid-century, and it seems to be supported by our widespread belief in social evolution. For this reason, this point deserves a few words of comment. The extrapolation from biological evolution to social evolution, and the more or less systematic identification of evolution and progress, once explicitly and widely held by the educated (and today still held by many of us but in a more or less hidden manner) seems to put beyond doubt the conviction that at an earlier period of man's development he was immersed in darkness, superstition, and terror, from which he has gradually liberated himself. Whether that liberation has taken place by continuous process or by well-defined states we do not know, but we still find it difficult to believe that intellectual as well as technological progress has not taken place. The denial of progress not only seems to contradict the facts—the amelioration of living, the increase in knowledge; it seems to involve the denial of biological evolution.

This is not the occasion on which to sketch the fortunes of theories of social evolution. We all know that prior to Boas and Goldenweiser they were generally accepted and that the great anthropologist and his disciple not only demolished them as hypotheses, but virtually stopped almost altogether their fabrication. But in fact, whatever its history, social evolutionism was never really given up, since any other theory but an evolutionary one seems inconceivable to modern educated man. The theory of social evolution assumes that there was a time when the animal that was to become man—Hominid, as the experts call him—did not have the mental equipment that he finally came to possess. When he acquired it, he became human. The advance from those early years, it is imagined, has been on the whole continuous. And the advance has involved the attainment of a greater and more widespread employment of reason. The next step in the speculative chain is easy to take and is relevant to our theme: With the rise of the sun of reason, the

91

343

thick fogs of illusion and superstition are dispelled. The final step is the proclamation that illusions have no future. Or at least, that they should have none.

II

But while there are some men who believe that myth can be left behind, or has already been left behind, it is not difficult to show that all men can do is to abandon one myth for the sake of another. This is what Mircea Eliade has shown in *The Sacred and the Profane*. Modern non-religious man, he writes, *"makes himself,* and he only makes himself completely in proportion as he desacralizes himself in the world . . . . He will become himself only when he is totally demysticized."

But this is the myth of the man without myth, for as Eliade points out in the same chapter, (the italics are his), "non-religious man in *the pure state* is a comparatively rare phenomenon, even in the most desacralized of modern societies." And he adds: "A whole volume could be written on the myths of modern man, on the mythologies camouflaged in the plays he enjoys, in the books he reads." And he concludes:

> In short, the majority of men "without religion" still hold to pseudo-religions and degenerate mythologies. There is nothing surprising in this, for, as we saw, profane man is the descendant of *homus religiosus* and he cannot wipe out his own history—that is, the behavior of his religious ancestors that has made him what he is today. This is all the more true because the great part of his existence is fed by the impulses that come to him from the depths of his being, from the zone that has been called the "unconscious." A purely rational man is an abstraction; he is never found in real life.

What Eliade is saying may be very old hat to all of us. It is to me, and was before I ever heard of Eliade. The idea that myth plays an important role in human living has been around for quite some time. It was put forth by Nietzsche under the label of the vital lie. What Eliade has done is confirm Nietzsche's brilliant insight with an impressive amount of erudite evidence. About the importance of the rôle of myth, then, there is no question. What is in question is what is the nature of the rôle.

The assumption about the autonomic and autotelic nature of myth also calls for a few words of comment. It contradicts the obsolete idea that myth is a primitive explanation of the world or an embryonic philosophy. I do not know whether anyone who deserves serious attention today still holds this interpretation of myth. But there are writers who deserve our most serious attention, who hold that myth has cognitive value. Thus, in their Introduction to *The Intellectual Adventure of Ancient Man*, Mr. and Mrs. Henri Frankfort write:

> The imagery of myth is therefore by no means allegory. It is nothing less than a carefully chosen cloak for abstract thought. The imagery is inseparable from the thought. It represents the form in which the experience has become conscious. Myth, then, is to be taken seriously, because it reveals a significant, if unverifiable truth—we might say a metaphysical truth. But myth has not the universality and lucidity of theoretical statement. It is concrete, though it claims to be unassailable in its validity. It claims recognition by the faithful; it does not pretend justification before the critical.

Myth is, of course, to be taken seriously. But I do not believe that it reveals metaphysical or any other kind of truth.

III

If myth has no cognitive content, what relation does it have to knowledge? For surely Eliade is right when he writes that in primitive and archaic societies in which myth happens to be the very foundation of social life and culture "myth is thought to express the *absolute truth*, because it narrates *sacred history*; that is the transhuman revelation that took place at the dawn of the Great Time, in the holy time of the beginning (in *illo tempore*)."

There is no question that men believe their myths to be true; perhaps they always believed them to be absolutely true. As late as Bishop Wilberforce in 1860, and in Dayton, Tennessee, sixty-five years later, to put it in round numbers, men still believed the story of Genesis to be true and the Darwinian hypothesis to be error, and sacrilegious error at that. But an important qualification is necessary. For the idea of truth conceived by mythic man and our idea of truth are quite different. When he believed his myths to be true he was not saying of them what we say

93

of a hypothesis we take to be true. When the primitive or archaic mind asserts that his myth is the absolute truth we must take his asseveration in his own philosophical context, or more precisely, in the lack of philosophical context from which he speaks. Whatever the word "truth" means to him, we use the word in a very different sense. We are more demanding. We distinguish notions he lumps together and that he does not know that he lumps. To put it briefly he confuses belief, conviction, the psychological accompaniment of some statements, with their truth. He fails to distinguish the affective component of his response to the myth from what we usually call the logical aspect of it.

But moving beyond the primitive and the archaic minds and their beliefs, I do not mean to assert that the function of myth is altogether unrelated to knowledge and hence to truth. I mean to deny that it conveys knowledge. And therefore I deny that it can have truth value in any rigorous contemporary sense of "truth." Before we can proceed we must make certain that we understand what I am trying to say.

I intend to use the word "knowledge" for a chain of statements that claim truth. This is to say that the chain asserts something about a state of affairs and the assertion can be certified or rejected. Even at this late date the usage bears iteration. The word "knowledge" is used when the truth or falsehood that the chain of statements asserts or claims to assert, can in principle be challenged. This is the reason I call myself a post-Carnapian.

On the post-Carnapian usage, then, of truth, the Frankforts' metaphysical truths, significant if unverifiable, are no doubt statements or stories of great significance. This I know, although the term "significance" is one of those terms I call "harlot words," which is to say, words that work any street in which they can get away with it, offering themselves to any man or boy that passes without discrimination. It would have to be examined before we can fall back on it with confidence. But whatever mythic stories are, true they are not—not in the post-Carnapian sense of the word. Indeed a great many of them we know to be false, since they are not coherent with known facts or established hypotheses. I am not much of a biblical scholar but on the usage of the word "true"

94

stipulated above, the Bible seems to me to be full of stories that are false and incredible, beginning with the first one.

The question of the significance of "significance" need not be broached here because it will have answered itself in passing when I explain how I use the word "myth." And I put it in this way to avoid the onerous job of sorting out the various meanings of the harlot word, "myth," and to indicate explicitly that no effort to define the term will be made, if definition is taken in a responsible logical sense.

Let me stipulate the way in which I use the word. "Myth" is to be used for stories that organize the primary data of experience, and I shall use the term "religious myth" for stories that organize the data when men respond to it in the religious mode. The position can be simplified as follows: Religious myths are stories that symbolize religious experience. But following Cassirer, we must distinguish "sign" from "symbol." Strictly speaking, these stories are neither true nor false; they are pictures of the world within which and by which men live. It is assertions about the world pictured in them that can be true or false. This does not mean that these pictures are equally adequate, as will be discussed below.

The word "story" is not intended in a pejorative sense and there is no circularity in this usage, since the religious mode of response can be differentiated from the other three basic modes of response into which I take the totality of human experience to be classifiable—the moral, the cognitive, and the aesthetic. The full meaning I give the word "myth" can be ascertained by referring to Cassirer's *Philosophy of Symbolic Forms*, according to which the mind is constitutive in the act of perception, and the constitution it achieves is expressed in symbols as distinct from signs. Symbols are the product of a synthesis of our intuitions or impressions, received by the mind, selected and added to in order to achieve informed substance that is present to it as experience. Prior to information of the matter for experience there is no substance and there is no experience. It is convenient to call what there is "matter for experience." Before the newborn's mind this matter consists of uninformed intuitions deriving from his sensory responses to the external world. But these responses make no sense to him. As his mind develops, the "matter for"

95

is trans-substanced as it is informed. The product is the informed substance of experience.

It is this informed substance that the mind grasps and calls its world. It should be observed that the expression "informed substance" is pleonastic, since there is no substance without form or form without substance, for us, in perception. But I find the pleonasm useful in order to underline the fact that substance and form are inseparable in perception and can only be conceived as separate from one another for the purposes of analysis by an act of abstraction. I do not mean, however, to suggest that form and substance, conceived independently of their conjunction, have no status in being whatever: I am no nominalist. But that is another problem. Ordinarily we say that form and substance are organically related. I have no objection to the expression. For what is important is to understand with a modicum of clarity the Kantian, or rather, neo-Kantian, doctrine that there is no world, out there or inside, for us, unless it has been constituted by the mind.

Let us take one more step. The word "experience" can legitimately refer to the relational complex [s - R - o], which is to say, subject in relation to an object, outward or inward; or it may refer to the object in the relational complex, the object of experience or the experienced object. But this object is there, present to the mind, and as merely present it is neither true nor false. Statements about it, interpretations of it, deductions from it, alleged entailments—these are either true or false, and our ascription of truthfulness or falsehood to them depends on our certification of them. But as to the world itself, the question of its truth or falseness does not arise until I wonder about its reality or, in the legal phrase of Bacon, put it to the question. If I bump against an object I have not noticed, I look to see what I ran into. But usually I neither affirm nor question the world within which I move.

IV

It is time to turn to the object of religious myth, the gods or God. For primitive and for archaic man stones are sacred—Hermes, he of the stones—and brooks, trees, mountains, the lingam, animals, and food.

96

If Rudolph Otto is right about the highly developed religions of the world, and I believe that with some important qualifications he is, I see no reason we should not extend the analysis of the religious response to stones, brooks, trees, animals, the lingam, food, which elicit from some peoples, although not from us, the kind of response our gods do from us.

Let us move upwards beyond stones and brooks and all other idols which man has worshipped, and consider the object of response of the great Western religions. And I limit it parochially because an ignorant man has enough trouble handling the little he knows and would make a fool of himself if he discussed things he is ignorant of. The religions of the East I exclude from consideration because I know nothing about them. But as regards the great religions of the West I am confident that Otto's analysis is adequate so long as we keep it at the psychological level and do not jump as quickly as he does to the ontological level.

For the religious mode of response, the object of experience is present, as Otto emphatically asserts, as objective, as outside the self. And it is apprehended as a tremendous mystery, in relation to which we recognize ourselves as creatures. A complex and strong rush of affectivity is elicited by it when our response to it is fresh and not merely stereotyped. Liturgy is intended to keep, and often does keep, the response fresh. But sometimes it furthers its slow death, and the result is what happens to a Tibetan monk mumbling his beads in a semicomatose condition.

I know of no better analysis, let me iterate, of the rush of fresh affectivity than Rudolph Otto's: Dread, awe, eeriness, fascination, horror, mystery. The object of religious response both attracts and repels; it sanctifies and defiles.

The reader cannot have failed to perceive that I have not used two key terms in Otto's analysis: the word "numen," and the phrase, "the wholly other." The reason is that if the numinous and "wholly other" object is an object that reveals itself to the religious mind immediately as a supernatural object (which is to say that its disclosure to the mind does not involve interpretation, yet announces itself as ontologically different from other objects of experience), I am afraid that with great reluctance I must reject the contention. Reflection and my own philo-

97

sophical commitments force me to deny, reluctantly but unambiguously, that what presents itself to men in the religious response is or can be immediately apprehended as supernatural. The operative word in the assertion is, of course, "immediately." For I hold that we can, and for many good reasons we must, assert that the object that discloses itself to the religious mode of apprehension is best interpreted as supernatural and transcendent. But the supernatural nature of God is arrived at by inference, by interpretation of the apprehended object in a wider context than the experience itself, by construction or hypothesis, and not in the immediacy of the religious experience itself. I hold as confidently as one can when considering topics on which confidence is not circumspect but reckless, that nothing presents itself to men immediately in experience except empirical, which is to say, natural, objects. I have to go farther in my post-Carnapian obtuseness and assert that those who claim to transcend experience seem to me to be doing nothing of the kind. What they are doing is interpreting and extrapolating.

Granting this point, at least for the sake of permitting me to proceed, two of the many questions that arise must be faced. One may have suggested itself earlier when I asserted that the object of the symbolic process, the symbol in which experience is embodied, or rather, in which the matter for experience is turned into informed substance, cannot be said to be true or false, but that it is only what we say about it that can be characterized in this manner. I already answered this question when I pointed out that the symbolic process constitutes experience, and that its objects are neither true nor false for the symbolizing mind. The other is one of the great questions for men interested in our subject, namely, "What can we mean by the word *God*?" Otherwise stated, we men of today who cannot find the sacred in stones, in the lingam, in mountains, or in trees, where do we find it? Where do we find God?

But before turning to that question, let me indicate that we are in a position to grasp with greater clarity than I have so far managed to impart, the nature and role of myth. I shall broach the subject by indirection. In Volume II of *The Philosophy of Symbolic Forms*, Cassirer makes a statement that, for our purpose, it is fruitful to dwell upon. He writes:

98

Whenever philosophy sought to establish a theoretical view of the world, it was confronted not so much by immediate reality as by the mythical transformation of that reality. It did not find "nature" in the form which it acquired (not without the decisive contribution of philosophical reflection) in a later period characterized by a highly developed consciousness of experience; on the contrary, the whole material world appeared shrouded in mythical thinking and mythical fantasy. It was these which gave its objects their form, color, and specific character.

Cassirer is telling us, as I have already suggested hastily above, that phylogenetically man starts to know the world from a previously constructed mythic view of it. In his earliest human gropings he was not confronted with "phenomenal reality," in the sense that the educated heirs of Thales or Galileo were. But Cassirer seems to hesitate, for in *Language and Myth* he allows to each of the two agencies roles in the creation of the picture of the world men achieve. He writes:

> . . . it is evident that myth and language play similar roles in the evolution of thought from momentary experience to enduring conceptions, from sense impression to formulation, and that their respective functions are mutually conditioned, together and in combination they prepare the soil for the great syntheses from which our mental creation, our unified vision of the cosmos, springs.

Because it is not advisable to go off into a detailed examination of Cassirer's thought on this problem, four hasty observations will be entered here. The first is that it seems correct to distinguish myth from language, however closely interrelated they may be in the mind of archaic man. The second is that the sweeping historical generalizations which I have indulgently offered would not be, nor are they expected to be, acceptable to those who want history as it actually is. These generalizations are themselves quasi-historical myths. Or, if you prefer, historical quasi-myths. Note also that the term "phenomenal reality" is not for Cassirer a contradiction in terms. Phenomena, appearances, can be real or not, since some of them can be, and are, merely subjective, while others are satisfactorily objective. And finally, let us understand clearly that "phenomenal reality" is not fixed once for all. The mythic world has gradually become demythologized; and the *Weltanschauungen* of a philosophic or

99

quasi-philosophic nature that have taken its place were not reared, so to speak, with newly baked bricks and beams shaped from newly felled trees: many old bricks and beams went into their making and still do.

The time came when men substituted for dominantly mythic pictures of the world more or less systematic philosophical pictures, *Weltanschauungen*. These pictures perform the same tasks as myths. They are the means by which men organize the several modes of experience and thus they are the intellectual structures of their cultures. Philosophical *Weltanschauungen* interrelate and bring to coherence the diverse human activities within a culture in which they are operative. But they have a function mythic pictures lack. They satisfy the need for truth in the narrower sense. Claiming truth, they are amenable to criticism and correction. They are cognitive pictures. But to suppose that these philosophical structures, however carefully reared, are free from mythic components is quite erroneous. Think of the Platonic world picture, or that of Empedocles.

"Scientific" pictures are indeed in some respects more adequate—and adequate in two senses of the word: They are closer to the nature of things as they are disclosed by science; and adequate in a pragmatic sense, since they are more comprehensive and thus more responsive to the needs of civilized man than a thoroughly mythic picture of the world could possibly be. The savage, whose cognitive needs go no farther than the demands of his technology, can live in the imaginative constructions he rears. We could not. But I am convinced that this is not a question of either a world picture that is "phenomenally real" or a totally mythic picture. And it is not, because no philosophical picture is totally positivistic and because the world picture of contemporary savages and of archaic man is one to which his practical knowledge, knowledge derived from his technological achievements, contributes.

We cannot avoid myths: they are either totally mythic constructions or *Weltanschauungen* that have been subjected to more or less rigorous philosophical discipline. In *The Sacred and the Profane*, Eliade tells us that the religious man feels the need always to exist in a total and organized world, in a cosmos. Whether the need arises from man's religious faculty or not, the need no doubt is there in all of us, although it seems

100

to make itself felt with different urgency in different men and in different cultures. Let us assume that Eliade is right. The need was felt by archaic men who made vast imaginative constructions. In Greece the poets subjected the myths to a degree of organization. And when philosophy began in Ionia, the philosophers inherited the myths, borrowed elements of them for their constructions, transcribed them into language they found more acceptable, and passed them on to the Romans and the barbarians. From antiquity, processed by restless minds gifted with powerful acuity, they were transmitted to the Franciscans of Oxford, who began the development that in the course of time was to lead to Galileo. Thus, new conceptions of order have arisen by continuous process in the course of our civilization.

In response to a need for order, for a cosmos, our knowledge tends to become more secure, more reliable. But the knowledge is kneaded back into the objects of experience produced by the symbolic process. These structures, the objects of experience, are then the product of the symbolizing process and of the knowledge of the objects of the process we constitute. But as the objects thus presented to us in experience they are neither true nor false: they are objects of apprehension or perception which for the curious mind soon give rise to questions leading to increased knowledge. But they need not lead to knowledge. They may become for another mind, taking another stance towards them, objects of intransitive apprehension, which is to say, aesthetic objects; or they may become objects that elicit the religious response or objects in which we discern moral value.

If the reader should now ask on what grounds are men justified in calling stones, brooks, trees, and fountains sacred, the answer is that the mind that responds to them in the religious mode of experience discerns in them their sacred quality or nature. But they are not sacred in themselves, are they? The answer is that in themselves, all they are is matter for the diverse modes of experience. Nor are they sacred for us. For we have somehow gone beyond the primitive and the archaic minds and can no longer respond to these objects in the religious mode.

At this point these ruminations threaten to become unmanageable and I must simplify, compress, and summarize. Let me ask, "What, in

101

the experience of modern man, elicits in him the religious mode of response?" I answer in one sentence and without much hesitation, "The mysterious creativity of the whole and of its parts." Of the whole, that appears to us replete with creative energy—appears, that is, if by good fortune we were not fitted or did not fit ourselves with scientistic blinkers in our adolescence, or if by a lesser good fortune we tore them off later in life. Of the whole, of unimaginable vastness the thought of which dwarfs us and makes us shudder today even as it did Pascal: a whole that is stupendous, awful, weird, of unimaginable grandeur, of impenetrable mystery, abounding with creativity. Of this whole that ultimately remains as impenetrable as it was to the first human mind who looked upon it and shuddered. When we look upon it without scientistic blinkers we easily grasp the fact that about the whole we are not much better off today than was the writer or writers of Genesis. Deeply moved by the wonder of his world, awed, let me imagine, and fascinated by the tremendous mystery that it is, and of course in need, as human beings have always been, of shaping his experience, of expressing the chaos of his responses—which is to say in my *papiamento* of turning the matter for experience into the informed substance of experience—he found his need fully met when it occurred to him that in the beginning the earth was without form and void; and darkness was upon the face of the deep, and that the Spirit of God moved upon the face of the waters, and that God said, "Let there be light"; and there was light, and that he saw that the light was good.

Let me expose my naïveté. I have long thought that here, in the last sentence, was informed ontological matter of high value. "And God saw the light, that it was good." It was not until some four thousand years later, by the pre-Darwinian calendar, that old Hobbes corrected the writer of Genesis. The light was not in itself good. God merely thought it was good, because the light was an object of his appetite or desire. I submit that the biblical myth is considerably more adequate to the actuality of our experience of values than the lucubrations of old Hobbes.

But from our experience the parts also elicit the religious response. For they too are pregnant with the mysterious creativity, as mysterious

102

354

a creativity as that of the whole. In the last thirty to forty years biology has taken gigantic steps; and I have heard rumors of the Astrophysicists and their bangs and their monstrous condensations of energy that appear from nowhere here and there in the universe. But for all these wonderful advances the mystery remains and it is creative. Let them talk of the synthesis of life by a conjunction of elements in an atmosphere of ammonium. What do we know then? The mysterious potencies that it and they are is what men have chosen to call God.

MYTH IN GREEK HISTORIOGRAPHY[1]

The value of myth and the mythical[2] was one of the major problems raised in the development of Greek historical writing. A large part of available material, both oral and written, was mythical in kind; it consisted of genealogies and stories about the time when gods and men were on closer terms.[3] Many such 'facts' were accessible in Homer and Hesiod.[4] There were, too, numerous local traditions, dealing with such topics as the founding of cities, anecdotes related by local guides and preserved out of patriotic satisfaction. As historians came to concentrate on their own times, or the recent past, making use of oral sources and personal observations,[5] they discovered that their own enquiries were often in conflict with the versions of myth. Not surprisingly, mythical and historical came to be considered as opposites, and mythical, in the sense of 'untrue', became almost a by-word.[6] Myth seemed likely to be rejected from all historical work; but since the material was abundant and the stories well known, critics and historians continued to discuss the place of myth in history. This paper is an attempt to illustrate the ways in which Greek writers tried to save myth for history; and to indicate briefly the validity of myth in historical writing as compared to its validity in philosophy and rhetoric.

Both Herodotus and Thucydides, in their different ways, held the view that myth was unsatisfactory. The word 'myth'[7] occurs twice in Herodotus, and both passages show that history, in the sense of Herodotean enquiry, has almost put myth out of business. In ii. 23 Herodotus is writing about the rea-

---

[1] I am indebted to Professor A. D. Momigliano and Mr. J. B. Trapp for advice and discussion about this paper.

[2] The terminology is flexible; usually we find μῦθος or τὸ μυθῶδες, but quite often λόγοι. Cf. Hecataeus, F. Gr. Hist. 1 F 1a .. λόγοι πολλοί τε καὶ γελοῖοι... and 1b Ἑκαταῖος Μιλήσιος ὧδε μυθεῖται. See Nenci, Hecataei Milesii Fragmenta, Firenze, 1954, p. xxiii f. For the terminology of Aesopean fable (below n. 63) see Chambry, Esope, (Budé 1927) p. xxxii f.; and for a distinction between Märchen and Mythus see Aly, Volksmärchen, Sage und Novelle bei Herodot. p. 7, 238.

[3] Cf. e. g. Plato, Hippias Maior, 285 D. περὶ τῶν γενῶν, ὦ Σώκρατες, τῶν τε ἡρώων καὶ τῶν ἀνθρώπων, καὶ τῶν κατοικίσεων ... and see n. 40.

[4] The locus classicus is Herodotus ii 53. οὗτοι δέ εἰσι οἱ ποιήσαντες θεογονίην Ἕλλησι κτλ.

[5] The distinction between ὄψις and ἀκοή is common in Herodotus. Cf. e. g. ii. 99 and the claim of an armchair historian parodied by Lucian, Quomodo historia sit conscribenda, 29; Γράφω τοίνυν ἃ εἶδον, οὐχ ἃ ἤκουσα.

[6] Cf. Josephus, c. Ap. i. 25, where τὸ μυθολογεῖν is joined with panegyric and malevolent criticism as an enemy of truth.

[7] Powell, Lexicon to Herodotus, 1938.

26*

sons for the Nile rising in summer.[8] One of the versions he gives (of which he says ἀνεπιστημονεστέρη μέν ἐστι τῆς λελεγμένης, λόγῳ δὲ εἰπεῖν θωμασιωτέρη) accounts for the phenomenon by the alleged fact that the Nile has its source in the Ocean which encircles the whole earth. In criticism of this view Herodotus says: "the λόγος about the Ocean refers the story (μῦθος) to something unseen and is not verifiable. I at any rate know of no river Ocean. I think that Homer or an earlier poet invented the name and introduced it into his work." Myth here is a story which cannot be corroborated by personal observations or enquiry. Much of Herodotus' work is based on two methods; seeing with his own eyes[9] and asking questions of people who had themselves been eyewitnesses, whether the facts deal with remote parts or events earlier in time. Since myth cannot be checked by observations, it loses status, especially when compared with Herodotean enquiry.

In another passage (ii. 45) Herodotus gives a Greek story (μῦθος) about Heracles.[10] According to this version, Heracles arrived in Egypt and was dressed for sacrifice. He allowed the procession to take place, but on reaching the altar became violent and killed all the Egyptians within reach. The story is criticized on two grounds. In the first place it shows extreme ignorance of Egyptian customs; it would be absurd to find human sacrifice in a country where even animal sacrifice was limited to a few kinds. Secondly, how could a single individual dispose of many thousands, particularly when the event falls within the period, not of his divinity, but of his manhood? The point of the criticism is similar to the remark about the Ocean, since this story too is rejected on the grounds of inconsistency with experience and observation. It is at variance with the observed behaviour of Egyptians; and our own experience suggests that individuals do not stand much chance against a crowd.

Thucydides' remarks[11] in his introduction also helped to weaken the position of myth: 'Perhaps the non-mythical aspect of my work will appear less attractive ....; but it will be sufficient if those who want to know exactly what happened .... decide that it is useful.' *The functions[12] of myth and history are sharply distinguished.* Myth produces entertainment, while history, through aiming at truth, will ultimately be a service; if not to the public, at any rate for the minority who want to know what happened. Since the pattern of events will probably recur, Thucydides' work will help posterity to follow the history of their own times. It would not be unreasonable to claim that

[8] See How and Wells, *Commentary, ad loc.* Also Sourdille, *La durée et l' étendue du voyage d' Hérodote en Egypte,* 1910. ch. i.

[9] Cf. Jacoby, *RE*, Herodotos, 247f. Herodots Reisen.

[10] For further references see How and Wells, *Commentary, ad loc.*

[11] Thuc. i. 22. 4. See Gomme, *Commentary, Book i.*

[12] Cf. Cic. *de fin.* v. 19. Nec vero sum inscius, esse utilitatem in historia, non modo voluptatem. Quid cum fictas fabulas, e quibus utilitas nulla duci potest, cum voluptate legimus?

Herodotus stressed the nature of historical method, while Thucydides, though perfectly aware of the importance of the right method, had his eye on distinguishing knowledge from amusement as the goal of history. Both men contributed to understanding the correct place of myth. But it so happened that Herodotus' remarks were overlooked in antiquity. It was thought that Thucydides, in excluding the mythical, was probably making a silent criticism of Herodotus for incorporating stories about 'Candaules and Gyges, Croesus and Adrestos, Polykrates and his ring, Xerxes' dream before the sailing of the armada and Hippias' dream before Marathon'.[13] These stories are not mythical in the same way as the story about Heracles; they contain marvellous, exotic elements, strange coincidences, and deal with the recent past or foreign parts. They do not raise problems about antiquity, e. g. as to when the heroic period began to shade into the merely historical. In view of this interpretation of Thucydides, and in view of the number of stories in Herodotus, it was easy to forget what he had said about myth elsewhere, and to ignore the fact that he did not necessarily believe all the stories he told.[14]

Herodotus' reputation suffered considerably from his many ancient critics.[15] They fell into two main groups. The smaller group, represented for us in the 'De Herodoti malignitate', accused Herodotus of pro-barbarian prejudice and hostility to Greek local traditions.[16] The others[17] accused him of being a vulgar entertainer, exploiting the mythical merely to amuse, with little regard for the truth. A later theorist[18] put it tersely: 'ὁ δὲ Ἡρόδοτος μύθοις ὑποκλέπτων ἀεὶ τὴν ἀλήθειαν ἀπιστεῖται καὶ τέρπει.' Thucydides on the other hand is credited by his scholiast[19] with only one myth, the Tereus passage[20] in ii. 29, and another critic described even this myth as something *necessitated* by the narrative – ἐξ ἀνάγκης.[21] Myth, it seems, should be almost intrinsic to the narra-

[13] Cf. Gomme's note *ad loc.* and add the scholiast's remark on i. xxii. 4: τὸ μὴ μυθῶδες: πάλιν πρὸς Ἡρόδοτον. See *Scholia in Thuc.*, ed. Hude.

[14] Cf. vii. 152. 3. ἐγὼ δὲ ὀφείλω λέγειν τὰ λεγόμενα, πείθεσθαί γε μὲν οὐ παντάπασιν ὀφείλω, καί μοι τοῦτο τὸ ἔπος ἐχέτω ἐς πάντα λόγον.

[15] For refs. see Schmid-Stählin, Gesch. d. gr. Lit. 1. 2. p. 668.

[16] Cf. Schmid-Stählin, *loc. cit.*: Der einzige, der seinen Tadel nicht auf harmlose Fabeleien beschränkt, ... ist Plutarchos.

[17] Cf. Jos. *c. Ap.* i. 16 Ἡρόδοτον δὲ πάντες (sc. ψευδόμενον ἀποδεικνύουσιν). F. Gr. Hist. 264 F 3 πρὸς τούτοις καταγινώσκουσιν Ἡροδότου οἱ τὰ περὶ μάγων γράψαντες. Cic. de leg. i. 5. Quamquam et apud Herodotum, patrem historiae, et Theopompum, sunt innumerabiles fabulae. See esp. A. D. Momigliano, *History*, xiii, 1958, p. 1–13.

[18] Romanus Sophista, *Rhet. Gr.* xiii (ed. Camphausen). The passage is important because the author continues with observations on Thucydides (below) and Plato.

[19] See Gomme, *Commentary*, on ii. 29. 3. The scholiast comments: σημείωσαι ὅτι ἐνταῦθα μόνον μῦθον εἰσάγει ἐν τῇ ἱστορίᾳ, καὶ τοῦτον διστάζων.

[20] The passage appears to be polemical, as though Thuc. were contesting an identification made for propaganda purposes. For another myth see ii. 102. 5.

[21] Romanus Sophista, *Rhet. Gr.* xiii (Camphausen) ... ὁ δὲ Θουκυδίδης καὶ Πλάτων αὐτὸς ὁ μὲν ἐξ ἀνάγκης ἀπεικάζει Τηρέα Τήρῃ ...

tive, just as Aristotle prefers those plots[22] (μῦθοι) where the conclusion is a necessary or probable development from the beginning.

In spite of the fact that Herodotus' part was misrepresented, the effect of his work and of Thucydides' preface was to push myth to the edge of historical writing. It was possible to justify myth as a digression, serving a definite structural function in the whole history. It will be convenient to start an account of 'myth as a digression' with Theopompus.

Theopompus had probably had some practice in discovering what to omit. He abridged[23] Herodotus and cut him down to two books, presumably leaving out many of the stories and concentrating on the events which led to the defeat of Persia. However, his own work on Philip II offered even more scope for surgery. A later king of Macedon, Philip V, performed a radical operation on Theopompus and had his work reduced from 58 books to 16.[24] The exploits of Philip were connected by the epitomator and the digressions excised.

It is fairly clear from the evidence about Theopompus, as well as from the fragments, that plenty of space in digressions was given to mythical subjects.[25] A whole section of the *Philippika* contained Mirabilia,[26] or Thaumasia as Servius calls them. Aelian[27] gives a story about Silenus, which he found in Theopompus, and concludes by saying: "people can believe this if they find Theopompus credible in the matter. My own view is that he is a δεινὸς μυθόλογος not only with regard to this story, but elsewhere too!" The example can be paralleled by others, and it is plain that Theopompus made considerable use of myth in digressions. It is instructive to see how far the performance was justified by historians and critics.

Some people considered that Theopompus overdid it. In contrast to Philistus,[28] who apparently never digressed, Theopompus used these excursuses on the grand scale, since pages went by without even a mention of Philip or the Macedonians.[29] Our authority for this, Theon of Smyrna, makes it plain that Theopompus was overdoing a good thing. The whole point of digressions, with their mythical apparatus, was to give the reader a rest. Theory had it that he deserved some rest by the way, so that he could then turn refreshed to the

---

[22] For the meaning of the word in Aristotle see Else, *Aristotle's Poetics*, 1957, p. 242-244 and esp. n. 81. Myth clearly has one meaning in history, another in tragedy; but the same closeness of exposition is expected both from the historian and from the tragedian.

[23] See *F. Gr. Hist.* 115 T 1 and F 1–4.

[24] For the number of books see *F. Gr. Hist.* 115 T 17–18; and for the reduction, T 31, where Photius says that all the digressions (παρεκτροπαί) were removed.

[25] See F. Gr. Hist. 115 F 31, 70.   [26] The VIIIth book of the *Philippika*. F. 64–76.

[27] Aelian, *Varia Historia*, iii. 18 = *F. Gr. Hist.* 115 F 75c.

[28] Cf. *F. Gr. Hist.* 115 T 30. οὐ γὰρ ἁπλῶς χρὴ πᾶσαν (sc. παρέκβασιν) παραιτεῖσθαι, καθάπερ ὁ Φίλιστος ... For his concise style cf. *F. Gr. Hist.* 556 T 17 and 21.

[29] Cf. *F. Gr. Hist.* 115 T 30 δύο γάρ που καὶ τρεῖς καὶ πλείους ἱστορίας ὅλας κατὰ παρέκβασιν εὑρίσκομεν.

study of events. Polybius[30] notices the practice and the reason for it; he too has to justify digressions and says that the reader needs a respite. 'This is why earlier writers pause over digressions. Some make use of myths and stories, while others have digressions about events'. The connected narrative can be interrupted by myth or by an account of contemporary events in other theatres.[31] The whole point of such digressions was to give the reader a brief relaxation.

The fear of abusing a concession appears to be exemplified in the work of Diodorus. His excursus on Palike (xi. 89) is a case in point. The subject is presented fairly quickly, as though Diodorus were uneasily aware of some theorist looking over his shoulder and calculating the length of the digression. At the end he talks apologetically of "getting back to the subject" and heads his reader back to the connected story. There are other noteworthy digressions[32] which are best treated as panegyrics (ἔπαινοι) and ἀρχαιολογίαι, however we are to translate the term. But there too his treatment of the subject is rapid, his manner defensive and the apology indicates that the episode is now closing. He clearly knew that digressions ought to be limited and tried to obey the rules. We should probably allow that even the maligned Diodorus has been successful here.

We have already seen that some writers considered that Theopompus digressed too much. On the other side the critic[33] Dionysius of Halicarnassus has nothing but praise for the man whose name soon earned a reputation for malice. He begins by commending Theopompus for reasons which Thucydides himself would have approved. Many of the events described were part of his personal experience, and he was also in personal contact with many eminent politicians and generals of the day. These were undoubted qualifications. When Dionysius goes on to describe the variety of the contents,[34] he divides them into three groups: (1) foundations of cities and origins of peoples; (2) lives and characters of kings; (3) marvellous or unusual products of countries. Both (1) and (3) cover items which would be at least partly mythical. The former could include legends connected with a foundation, and the latter embraces the sort of quasi-geographical[35] information for which, for example, Cleitarchus[36] was scorned as a 'mythical' writer. We are then told that the purpose of Theopompus' work is not merely to entertain (ψυχαγωγία). This material is immensely

[30] xxxviii 6. The passage may be conveniently consulted in F. Gr. Hist. 115 T 29.

[31] Or about earlier events. A good example is Thuc. i. 97 ... τὴν ἐκβολὴν τοῦ λόγου.

[32] E. g. xiii. 35 and 83 (ἔπαινοι); xiii. 90 (ἀρχαιολογία); xiv. 76 (didactic). The note of apology is frequent.

[33] F. Gr. Hist. 115 T 20a. = ep. ad Pompeium 6.

[34] τὸ πολύμορφον τῆς γραφῆς.

[35] For mythical geography see Thomson, History of Ancient Geography, 1948, esp. p. 33–43.

[36] See F. Gr. Hist. 137 T 7 = Cic. Brutus, 42.

useful, since 'philosophical rhetoric' (as Dionysius calls it) has to draw on the widest possible varieties of human experience. We begin to see that the truth sought by history is no longer sought for its own sake, or subordinate to the training of politicians. It has become subordinate to the needs of the ideal orator, whose subject is superior to philosophy and history and uses their results.[37]

Rhetoricians then could think of myth as useful (ὠφέλιμον), and just as serviceable as the truth of 'pragmatic' history. We must point out that the standards of rhetoric as "queen of the arts" were extremely lax; and prefer the view of those critics and historians who chose to use myth as an amusing digression. There could be no compromise between the two views; and history, on the whole, has been on the right side. This is probably how we should interpret the remarks of Plutarch:[38] "digressions in history are reserved mainly for myths, ἀρχαιολογίαι and panegyrics." Such digressions can be amusing but do not have historical truth as their objective.

Myth in the strict sense dealt with events of the remote past. This raises a different problem; so far we have been considering historians who wrote about events within or near their own lifetime, or later writers who used the works of such historians. It is easy to see that myth could only be incidental to the main theme. But when writers approached the remote past, with a view to constructing history, they found myth at the centre of their subject.[39] These myths had to be converted, if possible, into history; and this is why ἀρχαιολογίαι and myths are not exclusive of each other, as the passage from Plutarch might suggest, but myths, as well as being independent, are also to be included in ἀρχαιολογίαι. This is clear from a passage in Plato,[40] where the term covers subjects like the deeds of heroes and city-foundations, as well as from Strabo, who uses the word of a story about Jason and Armenos.[41]

According to Diodorus,[42] Ephorus "passed over the old stories (μυθολογίαι) and started his work with the Return of the Heracleidae".[43] The implication is that most of the mythical was excluded by Ephorus, even though he was

---

[37] See e.g. the *Brutus*, 25f.   [38] Plutarch, *de Herodoti malignitate*, 855 D.

[39] Cf. the division made by Romanus Sophista, τὸ δὲ ἱστορικὸν γένος ... διαιρεῖται εἰς τε συγγραφικὸν-μήτε πρὸς χάριν μήτ' ἀπεχθῶς, περὶ νεωτέρων πραγμάτων — καὶ ἱστορικὸν ὁμώνυμον, ἐν ᾧ τοῦ μύθου δεῖ, περὶ παλαιοτέρων.

[40] *Hippias Maior* 285 D. See above n. 3. The verb occurs at Thuc. vii. 69, where it seems to cover remarks about ancestors. See also Josephus, *BJ*. pref. 6., D. H. *A.R.* i. 74.

[41] Strabo xi. 14. 12. Other examples at Diodorus, ii. 46, Dionysius Hal., *A.R.* i. 74.

[42] D. S. iv. 1. 3. He adds that Callisthenes and Theopompus similarly ἀπέστησαν τῶν παλαιῶν μύθων.

[43] See Barber, *The Historian Ephorus*, 1935 p. 22 and esp. Appendix ii. According to Schwartz, *RE*, Ephoros (= Griechische Geschichtschreiber, p. 20), the starting-point was conditioned by geography — "da nach der Überlieferung mit diesem Ereignis die Verteilung der hellenischen Stämme in ihre historischen Wohnsitze beginnt".

dealing with the remote past. It may be correct here to see the influence of Herodotus' criticisms still at work. Diodorus gives his own reasons for Ephorus' choice. The facts of the earlier period were difficult to discover because of their remoteness in time; the chronology could not be accurately tested; the large number of heroes and demi-gods made an exhaustive treatment difficult; and the disagreements of mythographers had brought the whole subject into disrepute. Diodorus[44] and Dionysius of Halicarnassus, who certainly thought of themselves as historians, were both obliged to build on myth as a foundation for their narrative; it is instructive to see how they went about their task.

From Diodorus one gets the impression that earlier writers had shrunk from the sheer labour of compilation. His own work begins explicitly with the μυθολογούμενα of Greeks and barbarians and he proposes to test the tradition (τὰ ... ἱστορούμενα)[45] as far as possible. For the most part, however, he repeats the traditions, without criticizing them. Dionysius gives a better idea of how this material should be treated. He too is conscious that his predecessors had not worked as thoroughly as they ought to have done.[46] His own work is a thorough-going investigation into the history of early Rome.

It is clear that he thought his subject non-mythical in the sense that there was a chronology with which to work. He[47] distinguishes five great powers in the history of mankind; Assyria, Media, Persia, Macedonia, and Rome. He describes the Assyrian ἀρχή as παλαιά τις οὖσα καὶ εἰς τοὺς μυθικοὺς ἀναγομένη χρόνους. By this he clearly means an absence of chronology, since his remarks on the greatness of the succeeding four empires all have some chronological data, whether they are based on generations or years. But as he began with the 'oldest myths' he found himself dealing with accounts which sometimes differed considerably and often challenged his credulity. Some examples will show his approach.

When he discusses the Aborigines, the ancestors of the Romans, he says that the best Roman writers favoured a Greek origin. These writers had used a Greek myth to support their view, but gave no authority for it. But if they are right, he continues, and the Aborigines were in fact Greeks, they will have been Arcadians, since Oenotrus the Arcadian was the first Greek to cross to Italy. In the absence of a definite date in his source — οὐκέτι μέντοι διορίζουσιν οὔτε φῦλον Ἑλληνικὸν οὗ μετεῖχον οὔτε χρόνον οὔθ' ἡγεμόνα κτλ.[48] — he works by a kind of εἰκός or probability. A still better illustration of this method

[44] It is worth noticing that Diodorus claimed to have travelled widely (i. 4), and was not therefore just an armchair historian.

[45] The term weakened from its meaning in Herodotus. Dion. Hal., A R. lxi. 3 speaks of μυθικῶν ἱστορημάτων and Plutarch, Sertorius ix, calls Juba ἱστορικώτατος when a myth is being discussed.

[46] A.R. i. 5. f. He criticizes others for using τὰ ἐπιτυχόντα ἀκούσματα.   [47] A.R i. 2.

[48] A.R. i. 13. Notice that he warns the readers against accepting another version out of impatience with this tradition.

comes in his treatment of the death of Romulus.[49] The rival versions are quite clearly distinguished. Some give a 'rather mythical account' when they say that Romulus was taken up to heaven; and others, who say that Romulus was murdered by his own people, write τὰ πιθανώτερα (? πιθανώτατα). Here the method is clearly that of probability; and the result is to reject the myth in favour of a version consonant with experience. An earlier passage,[50] referring to Numitor and Rhea, runs as follows: μέχρι μὲν δὴ τούτων οἱ πλεῖστοι τῶν συγγραφέων τὰ αὐτὰ ἢ μικρὸν παραλλάττοντες, οἱ μὲν ἐπὶ τὸ μυθωδέστερον οἱ δ' ἐπὶ τὸ τῇ ἀληθείᾳ ἐοικὸς μᾶλλον, ἀποφαίνουσι ... The effect is to reject[51] myth in favour of probability. Probability is, as it were, the genre of the method, and the species of it consists in such ideas as comparing chronologies, or testing by human experience.

The same method can be observed in those Lives of Plutarch which deal mainly with the mythical period e. g. the Theseus, the Numa, and the Romulus. The general nature is stated in the Theseus;[52] by using λόγος and εἰκός on mythical subjects we can arrive at a sight of history (ἱστορίας ὄψιν). Particular problems show how τὸ εἰκός has set to work; the story that Romulus was taken up to heaven is contrary to τὸ εἰκός, not because it is against human experience, but because it violates the correct notion that the body is mortal, only the soul being immortal. A writer could include in the idea of τὸ εἰκός any belief which he held to be true; if it were in conflict with the myth, so much the worse for the myth. Dionysius' way of treating the Romulus story is paralleled in Plutarch by the passage (Theseus xv. 2) which deals with the youths and maidens sent to Crete. The version that the Minotaur devoured them is ὁ τραγικώτατος[53] μῦθος, and is contrasted with the account of Philochorus, which held that the young were employed in funeral games.

Similar questions occur when a writer is confronted with 'the mythical' in treating the events of the historical period. Plutarch, for instance, found a story that a statue erected by the Romans not only spoke, but repeated its statement: θεοφιλεῖ μὲ θεσμῷ γυναῖκες δεδώκατε. (Coriolanus, xxxvii). After continuing ταύτην καὶ δὶς γενέσθαι τὴν φωνὴν μυθολογοῦσι Plutarch ex-

---

[49] A.R. ii. 56. See also Plutarch, Romulus, xxviii.   [50] A.R. i. 79.

[51] A.R. i. 78 is worth consulting, where τὸ μυθευόμενον γένος (δαίμονες) is said to be a subject best left for philosophers. Plutarch occasionally lets a myth stand as a kind of monument; ἀνακεῖσθαι. See Sertorius, ix, where a myth taken from Juba is allowed to stand as a mark of honour to Juba's historical interests; and de genio Socratis 593 A τὸν λόγον ... ἀνακεῖσθαί φημι τῷ θεῷ χρῆναι ...

[52] Theseus i. esp. ὅπου δ'ἂν αὐθαδῶς τοῦ πιθανοῦ περιφρονῇ (sc. τὸ μυθῶδες) καὶ μὴ δέχηται τὴν πρὸς τὸ εἰκὸς μῖξιν, εὐγνωμόνων ἀκροατῶν δεησόμεθα καὶ πράως τὴν ἀρχαιολογίαν προσδεχομένων.

[53] For tragedy as a pejorative term, and the relation between History and Tragedy, see B. L. Ullmann, TA PhA 73, 1942, p. 23 f., Giovanni, Phil. 2., 22, 1942, p. 308 f., P. de Lacy, A J Ph 73, 1952, p. 159, E. Gabba. Athenaeum, 35, 1957, p. 3 and 193, F. W. Walbank, Bulletin of Inst. Class. Studies, 2, 1955, p. 4 f.

amines the possibility. There is no obstacle to statues appearing to sweat or weep. He has a 'scientific' explanation which will account for that and for changes of colour produced by the atmosphere. Such phenomena, though open to scientific explanation, can still be acting as the signs of heaven — οἷς ἔνια σημαίνειν τὸ δαιμόνιον οὐδὲν ἂν δόξειε κωλύειν. But it is difficult to accept a story of the inanimate speaking, since even god has to have a body for this purpose. That seems to be Plutarch's own view, though he goes on to say that the strongest argument for those who are anxious to defend the tradition is the supreme majesty of god's power. Any paradox or absurdity can be justified on this view, out of good-will towards heaven. From the historian's point of view it would be an ἀργὸς λόγος, putting a stop to enquiry, even though an enquiry conducted by probability.

These bookish writers of the Augustan Age and the early Empire did not invent the method for themselves. Something like it had already been tried by Thucydides, who makes use of τὸ εἰκός on several occasions in his preface.[54] For this reason, probably, the title ἀρχαιολογία[55] is often applied to Thucydides' first twenty-three chapters. However, his method appears to have one important difference from, for example, the Dionysian. Thucydides does not use τὸ εἰκός to reconstruct events out of myth, or to contrast the more likely explanations with the mythical. Instead he works on traditions which he accepts – like Minos' sea-power – and uses them in order to compare the magnitude of power in earlier times with his own day. He wants to show that the Peloponnesian War is the greatest so far; and so he does not write a history of events of the earlier period, but guesses at the power of earlier states.

There were then two principal ways in which the mythical could be justified. One group of writers was able to use myth as legitimate digression. Whether this was for amusement or truth would depend on the writer, though we have seen that the historians and the historically minded critics preferred the former. In another sense myth and the mythical had to be sifted to arrive at the truth about early times. Even here, however, there was a tendency to consider that mythical meant untrue, and to accept the version of a story which put the least difficulty in the way of belief. To put the matter in another way, we may assert that myth as a *method* had been ousted by personal enquiry, the practice of those historians whose subject was the history of their own times; such writers had to choose between tradition and enquiry, and rightly preferred the latter. On the other hand myth as content was to be treated by the method of probability, the critical weapon of writers who selected the mythical period. The "contemporary" historian, in rejecting myth, was announcing a change

[54] Cf. Gomme, *Commentary on Bk. i*, p. 40f.

[55] Cf. Gomme, *loc. cit.* p. 40, quoting Wilamowitz; and Mme. de Romilly, *Thucydide*, Budé edn., vol. i. p. iv.

of method, whereas the bookish writer spoke as the critic of a tradition on which he built.

To some extent history was at a disadvantage as compared with philosophy and rhetoric. Both of these subjects had a much freer hand where myth was concerned; whereas historians, particularly if they chose the early period, were continually forced to measure myth by likelihood and experience, with a considerable risk of being taken for liars. Some examples will show how philosophy and rhetoric were more favourably placed.

To take philosophy first. Superficially it might seem as though myth was treated contemptuously by Plato.[56] The myths of the poets are rejected for being lies about the true nature of human behaviour, or lies about the gods. But the fact that there are false myths does not prevent the philosopher from discovering or inventing true ones. These are used, as in the *Phaedo*,[57] partly to let the reader rest after the λόγος, but mainly to illustrate the truth in a poetic way. Myth is in the service of truth, and is not just an idle amusement. The practice was continued by later writers, as by the Platonist Plutarch in his *de genio Socratis*.[58] Although myth is often opposed to λόγος,[59] in the sense of false to true, there is also a sense in which myth can help to complete λόγος.

Rhetoric, as can be seen from Dionysius,[60] was even more favourably placed. The usage here can be illustrated from actual speeches and from rhetorical theory. Isocrates,[61] for example, in telling the story of Demeter in Attica, says: 'even if it is mythical it is fitting for it to be told now'. Why fitting? Because it illustrates an important conviction cherished by the Athenians – that they were the founders of agriculture and the benefactors of mankind in religion and law. Even if the incident did not actually happen, it does correspond to a true state of affairs, since Athenians *rightly* believe that they are the benefactors of the world in material and spiritual prosperity.

Some of the theorists[62] devote a section of their treatises to myth, by which

---

[56] Cf. the remarks at *Rep.* 364 B.

[57] Beginning at 108 D. Cf. Frutiger, *Les Mythes de Platon.*

[58] See Plutarch, *Moralia* 589 f. καὶ γὰρ εἰ μὴ λίαν ἀκριβῶς, ἀλλ' ἔστιν ὅπη ψαύει τῆς ἀληθείας καὶ τὸ μυθῶδες. The myth is studied by Hamilton, *C. Q.* xxviii. 1934 p. 175 f. *Moralia*, 614 B shows that μῦθος can end in λόγους ἐπιεικεῖς καὶ πρέποντας. Plato, he says, ὑγροτέροις λήμμασι καὶ παραδείγμασι καὶ μυθολογίαις προσάγεται τοὺς ἄνδρας.

[59] Cf. *Moralia*, 669 F and 1124 B. οὐ μῦθος ἀλλὰ λόγος.	[60] See above p. 407 and n. 33.

[61] Isocrates, iv. 28. For a story from the historical period see Lycurgus, 95. Gomme's remarks (*commentary* i. 149) ignore the function of myth in rhetoric. There are useful observations in Jost, *Beispiel und Vorbild usw.*, Paderborn, 1936. See esp. p. 128 on Isocrates, and contrast Demosthenes, p. 167 – "Im Unterschiede zu Isokrates kennt er das mythologische Exemplum so gut wie gar nicht." Jost emphasizes (p. 53) that the orators had a preference for "die wirklich historischen Paradeigmata".

[62] See *Rhet. Gr.* (Spengel 1853–56), for the treatises of Theon, Hermogenes and Aphthonius. Note the remark of Theon, Προγυμνάσματα, 178; ... αὐτὸς ὁ μυθόλογος ὁμολογεῖ καὶ ψευδῆ καὶ ἀδύνατα συγγράφειν, πιθανὰ δὲ καὶ ὠφέλιμα.

they mean, for the most part, animal fable.[63] Myth is defined as λόγος ψευδὴς εἰκονίζων ἀλήθειαν,[64] and the chief representative of the kind is Aesop. The myth is false in the sense of impossible, since animals do not speak; but it represents the truth by amplifying in a picturesque way the simple statements of the διήγησις. The fable [65]attributed to Demosthenes is perhaps an example. Fable as a genre may have acquired some *cachet* from Socrates' versifying;[66] at any rate the popularity of the genre can be gathered from the treatises and from remarks in Julian.[67]

Clearly, therefore, philosophers and rhetoricians could make freer use of myth in order to illustrate the truths they had advanced by argument or narrative (λόγος or διήγησις). The historian was much worse off, since the best practice and theory tended to exclude myth or restrict its use as a formal recreation. The temptations to use myth were immense, since a large number of myths had a quasi-historical slant, being designed to explain a local custom or to account for contemporary pride. A writer who dealt with too many myths would risk the charge of being called an entertainer; and the later bookish writers who exploited myth for the history of the early period were not first-hand historians like Thucydides. It seems fair to suppose that historians envied their rivals, philosophers and rhetoricians, for whom myth was still a serviceable tool. The prestige of myth in these subjects[68] was probably more harmful to historical writing than the 'substantialism' to which Collingwood[69] attributed some of the defects of the ancient historians.

University of Reading   A. E. WARDMAN

[63] Hence mostly Aesopean; and known as αἶνος; see e. g. the introduction to Aphthonius' manual.

[64] Theon, 147. Aptitude for a μῦθος or a διήγησις will also be useful for a history – καλῶς καὶ ἱστορίαν συνθήσει.

[65] Cf. Plutarch, *Demosthenes*, xxiii ... τὸν περὶ τῶν προβάτων λόγον .... Also Julian, vii, 2278, ... σὺ δὲ οὐδὲ τὸν Δημοσθένους ἀκήκοας μῦθον ...

[66] See the *Phaedo*, 61B. And cf. Plutarch, *Moralia*, 16c, where the episode is referred to. Aesop was popular at Athens; see the introduction in Chambry's edn. n. 2. above.

[67] See esp. or vii, *passim*. Sallustius wrote an account of the five kinds of myth; see A. D. Nock, *Sallustius*, 1926, p. xl–lv, with valuable notes and references.

[68] The parody of myth in comedy – Schmid-Stählin, i. iv, 54, and *RE*, xi, 1240 – is outside the scope of this paper.

[69] R. G. Collingwood, *The Idea of History*, p. 43.

THE SEMANTIC APPROACH TO MYTH

By Philip Wheelwright

AS an initial definition of myth I am content to borrow the one recently published by Alan W. Watts: "Myth is to be defined as a complex of stories—some no doubt fact, and some fantasy—which, for various reasons, human beings regard as demonstrations of the inner meaning of the universe and of human life."[1] This definition has the negative advantage of avoiding any connotation of "untrue" or "unhistorical" as a necessary part of the meaning, and the positive advantages of stressing both the narrative character and the transcendent reference of myth. These two latter properties, however, need to be qualified with some care, lest they involve us in undue limitations of the myth concept.

Regarding the narrative aspect of myth, we may take our bearings by two rather extreme and contrary views. The one, represented by Cassirer, treats myth as primarily a matter of perspective, and in this vein Cassirer speaks of "transposing the Kantian principle"—that all knowledge involves, at the instant of its reception, a synthesizing activity of the mind—"into the key of myth."[2] Myth here becomes a synonym of the mythopoeic mode of consciousness—a view that is reflected or at least adumbrated, I should think, both in Lévy-Bruhl's theory of participation and in Susanne Langer's treatment of myth as a primary type of human expression, parallel to, but distinct from, those two other primary types, language and art.[3] At the opposite extreme from this view, which defines "myth" without any necessary implication of "narrative" (although recognizing that mythic envisagement may, in fact, have a strong tendency to develop into narrative forms), we may place the view, lately revived in Richard Chase's Quest for Myth, that "myth is literature and must be considered as an aesthetic creation of the human imagination";[4] in other words, that the earliest mythologizers were individual poets—or, by modern analogy, novelists—constructing out of their especially sensitive imaginations tall tales characterized by a peculiar complication "of brilliant excitement, of the terrific play of the forces natural and human," and eventuating in some deeply desired and socially sharable feeling of reconciliation among those forces.

In any such controversy as this, concerning what myth "is," there is danger of confusing questions of fact with questions of definition. While questions of fact are the terminally important ones, we can behold them steadily only if we first settle the question of definition on an accurately relevant basis. It is pretty obvious that Chase, who takes myth as a species of literature, and Langer, who follows Cassirer in distinguishing between myth and art as separate categories, are not working from the

[1] Alan W. Watts, Myth and Ritual in Christianity (London, 1953), p. 7.

[2] Ernst Cassirer, Die Philosophie der symbolischen Formen, Vol. II: Mythisches Denken (Berlin, 1923-1929).

[3] Lucien Lévy-Bruhl, How Natives Think (London, 1926), chap. 2. Susanne Langer, Philosophy in a New Key (Cambridge, Mass., 1942), chap. 7.

[4] Richard Chase, Quest for Myth (Baton Rouge, 1949), p. 73; cf. p. 110, et passim.

same initial definition. Without wishing to claim anything like finality in the matter I would offer, as a tentative classificatory principle, a threefold conception of myth; or (as it may be regarded) a theory of three main ways in which "myth" has been, and may legitimately be, conceived. For convenience I shall call them *primary* myth, *romantic* myth, and *consummatory* myth. Of course in any particular mythic instance we must be prepared to expect some overlapping.

Briefly (since I have not yet focused down to the main point of my paper) I would say that Cassirer and Langer are dealing with myth in the primary sense, as a basis, and even perhaps in some instances as a pre-linguistic tendency, of human envisagement; whereas Chase is taking myth in the romantic sense (as connoting *le roman,* or deliberately contrived story), although with rumblings of universality which never become quite explicit. (I hope it will be recognized that I intend nothing pejorative in reviving this now slightly soiled word "romantic".) The consummatory myth, as I conceive it, is a product of a somewhat late and sophisticated stage of cultural development: a post-romantic attempt to recapture the lost innocence of the primitive mythopoeic attitude by transcending the narrative, logical, and linguistic forms which romantic mythologizing accepts and utilizes. Admittedly the line between the romantic and the consummatory is wavering and obscure; nevertheless we can hardly deny a significant difference of tone, technique, and quality of insight as we pass from the bright epic-Olympian story-forms of Homer to the utilization of symbols and patterned imagery in Aeschylus and Pindar, or from the faery-fantasy of *A Midsummer Night's Dream* to Shakespeare's utilization in *The Tempest* of neo-Platonic symbols to throw open the vision of a brave new world of peculiar values and destinies, or from the straightforward storytelling of any typical nineteenth century novel (or its stunted descendant, the television drama) to such a charting of unknown seas as in Kafka's *The Castle*. Indeed, I tend to think that the idea of consummatory myth offers a clue to the mysteries of much modern art—perhaps even to what is most authentic in all modern art, of which Picasso's *Guernica,* with its agonized repudiation of hitherto acceptable forms of construction and its single-pointed insistence upon the reality of dislocation, enormity, and pain, might stand as an eminent representative.

My purpose in distinguishing these three meanings, or modes, or (it may be) stages of myth has been to separate out the first of them for clearer analysis. For myth in its primary aspect bears a special relationship to language, and the exploration of this relationship strikes me as a particularly useful way of discovering something about the nature of myth and language alike. Unfortunately, that towering nineteenth century scholar, Friedrich Max Müller, has muddied the waters of this particular stream by his too provocative remark that myth is a "disease" of language, and by the subsequent eddies of doubt as to whether his etymological examples were sufficiently representative. For even though disease may have its creative side—as the pearl in the oyster and the last quartets of the deaf Beethoven attest—the word implies a derogatory valuation which is quite arbitrary with respect to the evidence. Accordingly, I propose that we reconsider the basic relationship between primary myth and the linguistic function without the use of shock-tactics and relying more upon semantic analysis and the known meanings of certain mythic symbols than upon the sometimes risky hypotheses of philology.

To clarify the question before us I am obliged to repeat, in brief summary, a distinction which I have developed at some length elsewhere:[5] the distinction between *steno-language* (the language of plain sense and exact denotation) and *expressive language* (such as is found to varying degree in poetry, religion, myth, and the more heightened moments of prose and of daily conversation). These two complementary and interpenetrating uses of language are the outgrowth, by and large, of two complementary semantic needs: to designate clearly as a means to efficient and assured communication, and to express with maximum fullness. The two are not always in actual conflict, to be sure; for many of the everyday ideas that we need to communicate have only a limited *relevant* fullness. But the criteria of relevance are altered by context, circumstance, and intention, and there are occasions when a writer or speaker cannot avoid the choice of whether to put primary emphasis upon wide-scale communicability or upon associative fullness and depth.

Myth in its first phase, the primitive, generally arises in an age before steno-language has been evolved to any marked extent, and consequently when some kind of expressive language is still the widely current medium of linguistic encounter. Or it may be that certain characteristics of steno-language have been developed for secular, everyday practical use, whereas expressive language is employed in that wide area which may be designated "sacred," and which doubtless includes those forms of story-making that have enough transcendental reference to be properly classified as "myth." Consequently, in order to estimate what effect language may have had upon the early growth and character of myth, it will be desirable to survey certain main characteristics of expressive language.

First, then, into what, if any, components can expressive language be analyzed for the sake of inspecting its modes of operation more minutely? In steno-language the basic elements are easy to identify: they are the *term*—which is non-assertorial: it simply means, but does not declare; and the *proposition*—which is an assertorial relation between terms. That is to say, a proposition ("The dog barks") can be meaningfully affirmed or denied, whereas a term ("dog") cannot. In expressive language, on the other hand, no such tidy distinction can be maintained. For terms and propositions, in their strict logical signification, are the products of a considerable logical and linguistic evolution, and their analogues in expressive language do not ordinarily show such clear-cut outlines and differences. Nevertheless, such analogues do exist even in the most fluid, exalted, and emotively charged language. A rough distinction can still be found between its non-assertible and its assertible or quasi-assertible elements; and for purpose of easy reference I shall call these elements by the names *diaphor* and *sentence* respectively.

By "diaphor" (a word coined by Friedrich Max Müller) I mean approximately what the term "metaphor" has come to mean in some contemporary writing, according to Herbert Read's definition of it as "the expression of a complex idea, not by analysis, not by direct statement, but by the sudden perception of an objective relation."[6] But since the older definition of metaphor, as "the transference (*epi-phora*) of a name from the thing which it properly denotes to some other thing,"[7] is still widely current, we can better avoid ambiguity by using the less familiar, more neutral

[5] Philip Wheelwright, *The Burning Fountain: A Study in the Language of Symbolism* (Bloomington, Ind., 1954), chaps. 2, 4, et passim.

[6] Herbert Read, *English Prose Style,* rev. ed. (New York, 1952).

[7] Aristotle, *Poetics,* chap. 21.

term. *Meta-phora* connotes motion—i.e., what may be figuratively conceived as a semantic motion, or the production of meaning—away from the already settled meaning of a term to an unusual or contextually special meaning: as when a man of filthy habits is called a pig. But such metaphoric transfer is possible only where certain terms with already settled meanings are available as starting-points; it is, therefore, more characteristic of the romantic phase of myth than of the primitive. There is a prior semantic movement which operates, often pre-consciously, by bringing raw elements of experience—qualities, capabilities, emotionally charged suggestibilities, and whatever else—into the specious unity of being represented by a certain symbol. Such primitive meanings are formed by a kind of semantic "motion" (*phora*) through (*dia*) a number of experiential elements, related in the first instance, no doubt, by a sort of vague but highly charged and tribally infectious emotive congruity, and then gradually formalized into a tribal tradition. Such a semantic motion seems to be indicated, for instance, by the Sioux Chief Standing Bear's explanation of the multiple yet unified significance of the pipe for his people: "The pipe was a tangible, visible link that joined man to Wakan Tanka and every puff of smoke that ascended in prayer unfailingly reached His presence. With it faith was upheld, ceremony sanctified, and the being consecrated. All the meanings of moral duty, ethics, religious and spiritual conceptions were symbolized in the pipe. It signified brotherhood, peace, and the perfection of Wakan Tanka, and to the Lakota [Dakota?] the pipe stood for that which the Bible, Church, State, and Flag, all combined, represented in the mind of the white man."[8]

Of course any such catalogue of diaphoric meanings is a cutting of the cloth into retail lengths. In the mythopoeic mode of consciousness there is a strong tendency of the different experiential elements to blend and fuse in a non-logical way. And not only that, but the selfhood of the worshiper tends to blend with them; that is to say, he becomes a full participant, not a mere observer. Finally, there is a blending, or partial blending, of worshiper and sacred objects and ceremonial acts with certain transcendent Presences—such as, for the Sioux, the Four Winds and the great spirit Wakan Tanka.

The last of these dimensions of the participative law points to a most important aspect of much diaphoric language: namely, its concrete universality, or archetypal character. I would suggest (although I am not sure how far the generalization will carry) that the most forceful archetypes are likely to arise out of a diaphoric situation where at least two of the diaphorically related elements represent human functions or interests of a deep-going and pertinently associated sort. Thus to the ancient Egyptians the scarab, or dung-beetle, was a symbol which conjoined diaphorically such diverse themes as the visible motion of pushing a ball (since it could be seen rolling a pellet of dung, containing its eggs, along the ground) and the idea of generative potency (since from the invisible eggs new life would mysteriously hatch). Many popular superstitions attached themselves to the dung-beetle too, and the entire mass of such ideas, fused into a general vague notion and attitude, constituted the diaphoric meaning of the symbol for the popular Egyptian consciousness. But the two characteristics I have mentioned played not only a diaphoric but also an archetypal role, since they

---

[8] Chief Standing Bear, *Land of the Spotted Eagle* (Boston, 1933), p. 201. Cf. Hartley Burr Alexander, *The World's Rim: Great Mysteries of the North American Indians* (Lincoln, Neb., 1953), chap. 1, "The Pipe of Peace," where the above passage is also quoted.

applied not only to the lowly dung-beetle, but also to the indispensable and lofty sun. The sun bestows a warmth of generative power, and also the sun appears as a ball being rolled across the sky, no doubt by an invisible celestial beetle. The archetypal meaning becomes further reinforced when, in the process of mummification, a gold scarab is substituted for the dead man's heart; for now the meaning of the symbol is extended to include the idea of spiritual regeneration, as the dead man's *ba* (hieroglyphically indicated as a bird) flies upward to be judged by, and then he mystically united with, Osiris.

Or again, take the ancient Egyptian *tau*. Here, too, was a symbol around which many ideas, superstitions, and ritual observances clustered diaphorically. But two of them had such human importance and such associative vitality as to give the symbol an archetypal character. The *tau* was a plug which held back the waters of the rejuvenated Nile and which, when removed, would release them for the irrigation of the land. The *tau* also, by its shape, carried phallic suggestions. Obviously each of these aspects in its own way implies the archetypal idea of new life. Then, when this fused meaning of the *tau* was already several centuries old, a semantic reinforcement was provided by the Christians of Alexandria, who envisaged the *tau* as the Christian Cross with the top prong broken off, and hence as a symbol of spiritually renewed life from yet another standpoint. (The Scandinavian use of the *tau* as an icon of Thor's hammer is extraneous to the development here described, although historically it did introduce certain later complications.)

What bearing has this curious interaction of diaphoric and archetypal modes of activity on myth? One's answer must be particularized, of course, according to the conditions of each specific culture and the nature of the diaphorically combined ideas. Undoubtedly the existence and character of a myth depend upon a variety of conditioning factors, including early man's love of storytelling, his need to explain odd occurrences, his rationalization of ritual, his moral codes, his techniques of magic, and his readiness to retain almost any sufficiently vivid association. I do not underrate the importance of such factors, although they lie outside the boundaries of the present argument. A semantic approach to the matter is not all-sufficient; it may still be very illuminating, however, provided its results are not spoiled by excessive claims of finality. With the same caution and the same limited claim I now proceed to consider the nature of expressive language from the standpoint of its quasi-assertorial elements— i.e., its typical *sentences*.

Naturally, "sentence" is here to be taken functionally rather than grammatically. The single word "snake" (or the equivalent thereof in some primitive language) may function sententially, and in a variety of ways according to the tones in which it is uttered, the gestures that accompany it, and the context (e.g., whether practical or ritualistic) out of which the utterance arises. Any strictly non-sentential unit (e.g., the word "snake" in the logician's or lexicographer's sense) is a later and more sophisticated construct, abstracted from the actual and living occasions on which a snake has been dreaded, pursued, wondered about, worshipped, and the like. Thus the sentence is a vehicle of concrete meaning, whereas the logical terms which can be analytically discovered in it, together with the logical propositions which are built out of them, are vehicles of abstract meaning. Now the language of terms and propositions is the language of logical analysis and of science. The nature of myth is so stubbornly opposed to the nature of these sterner disciplines as to appear, from the empirio-logical standpoint, arbitrary and false. This is the more understandable because myth sometimes irresponsibly borrows elements of literal language and thus appears to be invading the realm of tidy fact more aggressively than was perhaps deliberately intended. Consider, for example, the mythic statement, "God created the world in six days." The awkward intruder here is the final phrase, which brings a false appearance of scientific precision into an affirmation that is properly mythic in the sense of applying the familiar Craftsman idea to a situation that man's natural wonder spontaneously accepts as transcending the understanding. Of course we cannot be sure how the phrase "in six days" was understood by the ancient Jews who presumably originated the mythos, but in any case it tends to blur the nature of the original mythic sentence by giving it the look of a proposition.

Since I wish to explore the possible relationship between primitive sentence-making and myth, I must first ask what is the nature of a sentence in its pre-logical form. Fortunately, we are none of us logical all day long, and we can discover a good deal by noticing how sentences actually function in our more conversational, everyday, off-guard moments. This is but a special form of the more general question: What is the semantic role of the non-logical in our familiar discourse? Of course there is more than one way of being non-logical. I am not here speaking of the *il*logical (i.e., a using of logical terms without abiding by the rules they impose) nor of the *sub*-logical (as in phatic discourse, the merely perfunctory and vapid), but rather of the expressively *trans*-logical. For in regard to all really important affairs where some degree of valuation and emotional commentary enters, we instinctively recognize the inadequacy of strictly logical forms of speech to do justice to our full intended meanings; and we endeavor by tone of voice, facial expression, and gesture, as well as by choice and arrangement of words, to break through the barriers of prescribed definition and express, no doubt inadequately, the more elusive elements in the situation and in our attitude towards it. Let us call such uses of language "expressive" without any implication that they are therefore to be dismissed as merely subjective and fictional. I am suggesting that in this occasionally spontaneous outreach beyond the conventional and formal properties of language we are perhaps coming somewhat closer to the conditions of primitive utterance (how close we cannot know) than in our more logical declarations and inquiries. Let us, at any rate, accept the possibility as a working hypothesis, and inquire into the nature of *expressive sentences*.

Since there is a good deal of ambivalence in most human attitudes, it will not be surprising if we find that expressive sentences tend to function in terms of certain polarities. Three such polarities seem to me especially prominent and fundamental. An expressive sentence tends to involve, simultaneously but in varying degree, affirmation and questioning, demanding (or hortation) and acceptance, commitment and stylization. Let us look at these three pairs in turn.

In all the larger affirmations that we make about the world there is likely to be a note of questioning; and this is so because such affirmations touch upon the radical mystery of things, which forever eludes our intellectual grasp. There are two ways of affirming such a sentence as "God created the world." It can be affirmed dogmatically, as a declarative without any interrogative aspect; or it can be affirmed with a fitting intellectual modesty, in which case the declarative and the interrogative will be blended as inseparably as the convex and concave aspects of a single curve. For, to assert it as a pure statement is to imply: "There was a question, but the question is now answered, and thus there is no longer a question." But this can be the case only if the sentence, "God created the world," is essentially intelligible—that is, only if "God," "original creation," and "world" carry meanings that we can put the finger on and say, somewhere in experience, "That is it!" And since this condition—the adequate verification of a transcendental idea by the finite evidences of human experience—cannot possibly be met, it is equally impossible that the sentence, "God created the world," should be a pure statement. To assert it as such is therefore self-delusive. On the other hand there is statement resident in the sentence; a believer does not abandon the declarative element. What he does is to fuse something declarative and something interrogative into a single attitude which is a tension between basic faith and deep questioning. Religiously considered, the sentence employs theological terms symbolically in order to express the radical inseparability of meaningfulness and mystery.

The second polarity which expressive sentences tend to involve—a demanding and an acceptance—brings up the question of wishful thinking. There is likely to be some element of the mandatory—an implicit command, "It shall be so," or an implicit supplication or wish—in all expressive thought and utterance. This is the pragmatic element, which William James found to be present in every judgment, religious and secular, idealistic and materialistic alike, so far as it makes any truth-claim beyond the immediately verifiable connections of direct experience. Inasmuch as religious judgments do make such transcendent truth-claims, the presence of a pragmatic element in them is undeniable. But it is equally important to recognize that the pragmatic element is never the whole affair, and that where it becomes unduly dominant the result is fantasy, not religion. In a truly religious judgment the coercive element, the "Let it be so!," plays a strictly limited role, as an expression of loyalty to a certain general way of conceiving and interpreting the world; in each particular respect it is subordinate to an attitude of acceptance, whatever the grounds and occasions of acceptance may be. The sentence, "God exists," if it represents a mytho-religious affirmation and not simply a metaphysical hypothesis, involves both a demand for a certain way of envisaging the world and an acquiescence towards the obligations which that mode of envisaging entails.

An important contribution to the semantic role of acceptance, or acquiescence, in man's primal form of encounter with the world has been made within the last few decades by those continental thinkers (notably Martin Buber, Franz Rosenzweig, Eugene Rosenstock-Huessy, Karl Löwith, Gabriel Marcel, and Julián Marías) who have stressed the priority of the second grammatical person over the third. The logic of science necessarily employs the third person, because its objects must (linguistically) be spoken *about* and (operationally) be manipulated. It is a widespread assumption, in a world of books and research foundations, that the truth about anything can be adequately revealed (in principle at least) by statements made *about* it. The writers just referred to have challenged this assumption. And there is one sphere of experience where the inadequacy of the *I-it* and the indispensability of the *I-thou* relation is universally recognized—namely in our experience of other human persons. Knowledge of one's fellows, to be more than superficial, must grow out of an experience of mutuality, of speaking to them and listening as they speak in return; and according to all of the above writers, this radical dialectic is what primarily distinguishes the *I-thou* relation from the *I-it*. In more primitive societies it seems probable that, to say the least, the lines between spheres where the *I-thou* relationship could be meaningfully adopted and those where it could not were much less sharply drawn than now. A certain readiness to address nature, or the mysterious presences "behind" nature, and to open one's mind and heart to the "signs of address"[9] which are given in return is a recognizable mark of the primitive attitude.

The third of the sentential polarities—truth-commitments vs. stylization—introduces an idea which I have discussed elsewhere.[10] To start with colloquial instances: when we make a conventional remark about the weather, or when we assure our hostess that we have spent an enjoyable evening, how fully do we commit ourselves to the assertorial content of what we are saying? Not altogether, it is obvious; for in making such remarks we are ordinarily less concerned with the strict truth than with what the immediate situation seems to call for. We recognize them as stylizations, to some degree, in a conversational game, and hence as not committing us to full consistency of belief. Nevertheless, stylization is not quite the whole of it; for while we might phatically applaud the virtues of the weather with a good deal of careless latitude, we would hardly be willing to murmur "Nice day!" (unless with conscious irony) in a downpour of rain. Thus, while the assertorial weight of such conventional remarks (cf. "Having a wonderful time"; *"Mi casa es su casa"; "Vous êtes très gentil"*) stands somewhat above the sheer assertorial zero of the purely exclamatory ("Heigh-ho!"), it does not match the full assertorial weight of an intentionally informative sentence ("It is twenty miles to Woodsville") or a deliberate declaration of value ("That is a dastardly scheme").

The casual instances just cited point the way to analogous but more important instances in the linguistic strategies of poetry, religion, and myth. Coleridge's phrase, "suspension of disbelief," and Richards' doctrine of the "pseudo-statement" represent attempts of both critics to explain how it is that although the sentences employed in poetry seem to be making statements of a kind, they often cannot be accepted with anything like full commitment of assent. But as I have argued elsewhere,[11] I believe that Richards errs by making too sharp a dichotomy between "statements" (claimants for exact verification by scientific method) and "pseudo-statements" (word-patterns which look like statements and which serve to organize certain emotive attitudes in the prepared reader, but to which any question of truth or falsity is entirely irrelevant). The most interesting examples of poetic statement fall somewhere between these extremes: they invite some degree of assent, but less than full intellectual commitment.

As we turn from primarily poetic sentences to primarily religious sentences (admitting, of course, a wide area of overlapping) we find that the relation between commitment and stylization is characteristically somewhat different. A genuinely religious believer is one who gives full commitment—not necessarily to the sentences in their literal meanings and in any case not in their literal meanings alone, but to some half-guessed, half-hidden truth which the sentences symbolize. (Let it not be forgotten that the early Fathers of the Church were wont to speak of their articles of faith, in which they certainly "believed," as *symbola*.) The commitment in such a case

[9] The phrase is Martin Buber's. See his *Between Man and Man* (London, 1947), especially Part I, "Dialogue."

[10] Wheelwright, *The Burning Fountain*, pp. 66-70, 274-282.

[11] Wheelwright, *The Burning Fountain*, pp. 33-36, 45-50, 296-298.

does not necessarily diminish as the stylization of liturgy and figurative language is increased (although extreme Protestants have sometimes made the mistake of supposing that it must do so); for the commitment may be given in and through the stylized forms. In short there may be full commitment here, but it is largely commitment by indirection. I say "largely," not "wholly," because a typically religious believer is likely to feel some degree of commitment to the concrete vehicle (e.g., the Virgin Birth, the avatars of Vishnu, the magical connection between pipe smoke and thunder clouds, etc.) as well as to the transcendental tenor (the real but hardly sayable significance of these doctrines for the serious believer). The literal meaning of the vehicle is usually clear and vivid, although perhaps shocking to everyday standards of probability; its transcendental tenor looms darkly behind the scene as something vague, inarticulate, yet firmly intuited and somehow of tremendous, even final, importance and consequentiality. To accept the vehicle in its literal aspect exclusively is the way of superstition; to accept its transcendental references (the tenor) exclusively is the way of allegory. The primitively mytho-religious attitude in its most characteristic forms has tended to settle into some kind of fertile tension between these two extremes without yielding too completely to either of them. So far as the mythic storyteller is half-consciously aware of the tension his narrative may achieve that tone of serious playfulness which characterizes so charmingly much early myth.

The hypothesis with which I now conclude connects the earlier and later parts of my paper, and is offered tentatively, as suggesting certain possibilities of further research. Perhaps the line between the primary and romantic phases of myth, although vague and wavering at best, can be drawn a little more clearly by the aid of such semantic criteria as I have been discussing. Primitive myths may be regarded as the early expressions of man's storytelling urge so far as it is still conditioned by such proto-linguistic tendencies as diaphoric ambiguity and the several kinds of sentential polarity. Later myths, and later retellings of the earlier myths, betray their essentially romantic character by the degree to which such semantic fluidity and plenitude have been exchanged for tidier narratives relying on firmer grammatical, logical, and causal relationships. In its propaedeutic aspect the hypothesis invites a more active liaison between semantics, broadly conceived, and anthropology—a collaboration which might prove to have fruitful consequences for both disciplines.

University of California
Riverside, California

MYTH AND HISTORY
IN ISRAELITE-JEWISH THOUGHT

By George Widengren
UPPSALA UNIVERSITY

History and Myth are almost inextricably mixed.
PIETER GEYL

THE PROBLEM of myth and history in their mutual relation according to Israelite-Jewish thought is of primary importance to the understanding of many questions in the Old Testament and Jewish religion and spiritual life. Thus far, however, this problem has not received a modern, comprehensive treatment in the light of our knowledge of ancient Israelite-Jewish thought in general, and of myth and history especially.[1] Nor does the present article aim at such an ambitious task, which would require much more space than is at my disposal here. The intention is only to present some general views on this difficult complex of ideas, at the same time trying to correct some wrong opinions which have been long accepted in a more or less articulated manner and have thus gained the position of long established scientific truths.

It is quite obvious that we must start with a definition of myth. What is myth? Or rather, what does modern research understand by myth? In Great Britain much effort has been spent on the attempt to give an adequate description of what myth means, and for all practical purposes I think we can accept the definitions given us by the so-called "myth and ritual school," which, it should be pointed out, is no school at all in the traditional, especially the German, meaning of the word but can be more adequately defined as a certain trend in British Old Testament and oriental research work. Professor Hooke, the leader of this "school," has defined myth on many occasions. The following definition is fairly representative and may be adopted here:

The ritual consists of the part which was *done,* for which the Greeks had the name *dromenon,* and the part which was spoken, to which the Greeks gave the name *muthos,* or myth. In the ritual the myth was the spoken part which related the story of what was being done in the acted part, but the story was not told to amuse an audience, it was a word of power; the repetition of the magic word had power to bring about or re-create the situation which they described.[2]

Adopting this definition I should like to emphasize not only the magical but also the *symbolical* aspects of the words of the myth as recited in the actual ritual. Symbolical words and actions were probably no more foreign to the ancients than to us.[3]

Myth, as just stated, was a repetition, a repetition in ritual of what once had happened. Myth accordingly includes both past and present time, but not only that: myth as relating constantly repeated, ever recurring events also includes the future. Time will ultimately bring back what once happened in the beginning, an important aspect of myth that we shall have to consider in the following. With reference to the time aspect then, myth includes both the past, the present, and the future.[4]

The Hebrews did not possess any special word for myth, but the thing was there, for in the beginning of their history in Palestine they had a rich store of myths, as we have tried to show in another connection.[5]

The definition of the term "history" presents greater difficulties, chiefly because our word "history" is taken in various meanings. History means to us what has happened and is happening as well as the knowledge and story of what happened, without any limitations whatsoever to a special subject.[6] But, in a more narrow and articulated sense, the word "history" refers to events in the world of mankind. As it came from the Greek term ἱστορία, the word originally possessed the meaning of inquiry and then of knowledge based upon inquiries, thus the aspect of intellectual curiosity is very prominent.[7] "History" also means the science of history, that department of humanistic research devoted almost exclusively to the investigation of what happened and happens in the world of mankind.[8]

In this article I shall have to deal with history in all these various meanings, but will try to define each time, as far as possible, the particular notion of history which is of concern.

I

As has been correctly observed, the Hebrew language does not possess any indigenous, Semitic name for "history" in our scientific sense of the word.[9] But in this case too the thing was there, as we shall see.

The double meaning of the word "history" has attracted the attention not only of historians but also of Old Testament scholars. Thus an American exegete, when speaking of the religion of the Hebrew prophets, has some very interesting observations to offer. He says:[10]

When we use the word "history" we may mean either events happening in time, or the record of those events. In the former sense, everything that has ever occurred either in nature or in human life is a part of history, but no human mind can ever record or comprehend even a small fraction of that total. Nor is it important that one should. Much of history in this sense is trivial and worthy only of oblivion.

Most of us would surely accept this statement without further comment. But what he then goes on to say is likely to meet opposition in some quarters.

History in the second sense may be either objective or subjective. Objective history is a mere narrative of events as they have occured, with no interpretation of their meaning. In spite of the pretensions of the modern historian, absolutely objective history is extremely rare, if not wholly impossible of attainment, and it is actually of little value and less interest. Subjective history seeks not simply to recover what actually occurred but to explain why it occurred and its meaning for man. Subjective history is internal history, remembered events bound together by a thread of interpretation. It may include tradition, and tradition often is of deeper meaning for man than purely objective history. We should not think, however, that when one is concerned with history all critical faculties must be suspended. Everyone interested in the writing and interpretation of history must, because of the compelling curiosity of the human mind, search for objectivity; but he must remember that objective fact alone is of little value.

I do not in this place intend to enter upon a discussion of the principles of historical research; I wish only to point out that the declaration just quoted runs counter to the main principle of all historical investigation since the days of the great Leopold von Ranke, who declared its aim to be to ascertain "wie es eigentlich gewesen ist."[11]

Of course all historians—and I myself write here as an historian—are grateful for the permission granted us to make use of some critical faculties. At the same time, all professional historians would probably claim the right to use as many critical faculties as possible and they would also most probably contend that even if in some cases objectivity obviously is difficult to attain, the situation isn't as bad as our American colleague wants us to believe. Further, the fact that objectivity is hard to reach does not liberate us from the duty to do our research work in the most objective way possible. "That objective fact alone is of little value" is also a sentence the truth of which is not easily seen, because history as a science recording events in the world of mankind is wholly dependent upon the conscientious recording of single objective facts.[12]

Still more interesting is the position taken by our American colleague when treating of the time aspect of history, for now he says:

We have thus far considered history as if it included only past occurrences. But an adequate definition of history must include both present and future as well as past. The past is only a small fragment of time, and history cannot contain a sense of destiny and purpose unless the present and future are comprehended within its scope . . . to some degree the future is latent within the past and the fleeting present to him who has eyes to see.

The last sentence is taken over from Berdyaev's well-known work on the meaning of history.[13]

Leaving aside some doubtful contentions, such as the one that to this author history as a science also ought to possess a sense of destiny and purpose—a contention likely to meet with a most violent opposition, e.g., among Scandinavian historians[14]—we turn our attention to that special idea of history advocated by our American authority. The quotations given to illustrate his position afford us excellent examples of what may be called a prescientific, nonscientific, or mythic view of history. For this American conception of history can well serve as a modern illustration of the ancient Hebrew notion of history.

The conception of history among the Hebrews, indeed, had nothing to do with modern, scientific ideas of history as they are accepted by all real scholars occupied with research in various historical subjects. When the modern American scholar just quoted—who, however, is no historian—and Berdyaev, Toynbee, and a few other people take a different view they exhibit a most remarkable agreement with the view taken by the ancient Hebrews. The reasons for this rather astonishing agreement cannot be dwelt upon here.[15] We wish only to point to *one* single important factor: the idea of time, for we remember the striking statement that "to some degree the future is latent within the past and the fleeting present to him who has eyes to see." Here the historical past, the present wherein we live, and the future yet to come are fused into a mystic totality. Let us see then what the aspect of time has to teach us about the Hebrew notion of history, for it goes without saying that for our understanding of the meaning of history among the Israelites and Jews it is necessary to know what the notion of time meant to Israel.

Then it should first of all be noted that time to the Hebrews was no abstract idea, not "a neutral and abstract frame of reference but rather a succession of recurring phases, each charged with a peculiar value and significance" as H. and H. A. Frankfort once put it.[16] Now, it should be expressly stated that this insight is due above all to Pedersen, whose name is casually mentioned in a note to the passage just cited. Actually, Pedersen's words deserve quoting. He says: "For the Israelite time is not merely a form or a frame. Time is charged with substance or, rather, it is identical with its substance; time is the development of the very events."[17]

To the Hebrews, then, time was filled with content. Each epoch possesses its special substance, and vice versa; every thing has its special time, an idea known above all from Ecclesiastes 3.1 ff.: "All things possess their time, all things that are done under the heaven possess their own time . . . God . . . hath made all things good in their time."[18]

Not only that, but time in this manner always is a repetition of what once has passed. As Ecclesiastes says (3.14–15): "I know that whatsoever God doeth, it shall be forever; nothing can be put to it, nor anything taken from it . . . That which happeneth hath been (already), and that which is to be hath (already) been. God establisheth anew that which is past."

Against this background we understand that "times of the same substance are identical." The Israelite can say: "When this time again becomes alive," meaning "at the same time next year."[19] Time is conceived of, then, as an infinite cyclical repetition. The year comes back again in springtime, when the so-called "return of the year" takes place.[20]

Time, accordingly, is felt to be something experienced, not something to be merely measured. You find the same distinction also in modern conceptions of time, where on the one hand you have what the

Germans call "die messbare Zeit," and on the other hand the so-called "erlebte Zeit."[21] The second of these two conceptions corresponds precisely to the Hebrew idea of time.

Time then, according to the Hebrews, was filled by important events, but the peculiar Israelite conception of time with its strong cyclical aspect forbids history as a series of happenings to be conceived of as "a long chain of events, divided into special periods."[22] This does not mean that there was no idea of special periods. On the contrary, there was, and such ideas played an important role in Israelite thought. But characterically enough such a period was no abstract idea. The term used for it was *dōr,* and in Pedersen's definition which is adopted here it denotes "a time with the events distinguishing it, and first and foremost the people who create it and its substance, or, as it is usually rendered: generation."[23]

History, then, is made up of various *dōrōt,* "each with their special stamp."[24] All *dōrōt* together form ʿ*ōlām,* a complex notion, conventionally rendered "eternity" but properly meaning "the most distant time,"[25] and this both in the past and in the future.[26]

When speaking of the Hebrew conception of history we should of course not forget to mention the fact that there also was a Hebrew presentation of history in a sense more akin to our modern, scientific meaning of the word. This Israelite writing of history is famous, as we all know, and deservedly so. But it should nevertheless be noted that the O.T. presentation of history in our scientific meaning of this term does not provide us with a simple account of Hebrew history, but with a peculiar *interpretation* of this history, as has been duly recognized, e.g. by North.[27]

II

In the ancient Near East there was no factual distinction between myth and history as far as quality was concerned. Actually the distinction that immediately presents itself to us as soon as there is a question of the immediate character of reality is not to be found between the spheres of myth and history in the ancient Near East. This has repeatedly been contended by Hempel, and there are very good reasons for doing so.[28] Thus the great historical work in O.T. literature called "conventionally and conveniently" "J," the work of probably the first outstanding Hebrew "historian," started its comprehensive history of Israel not with the oldest period from which real historical traditions were still kept living in memory, but with the creation of the world—an act, according to our way of historical thinking, belonging to the sphere of myth and not to history.[29] That such stories in fact belonged to myths as ritual texts is shown also by the fact that Yahweh's activity as a creator was glorified at the great annual festival, the New Year festival. Moreover, it has been argued with some good reasons that a story of creation, though not that of "J," was read by the priests at the New Year's festival.[30]

Next comes the Flood story, of which we will soon have to speak more. The mythical character of the story of the Great Flood cannot be doubted, for in this case we are able to trace its wanderings back to remote Sumerian times in Mesopotamia where still more of its original mythic character is preserved.[31] Now it also is of considerable interest to see that in the hymns, where Yahweh's deeds are glorified, no distinction is made as to his sphere of activity, be it situated according to our views within the realm of myth or demonstrated in the clear light of history. In fact, his act of creation is associated with his active dealing with his chosen people Israel, e.g. in Psalm 95.5, 8 ff.,[32] where we read:

> To him belongs the sea,
>   for he made it,
> and the dry land
>   which his hands formed.
>
> Harden not your heart as at Meribah,
>   as in the day of Massah in the wilderness.
> When your fathers tempted me,
>   proved me, and even saw my work.

In the same way Yahweh's selection of his servant David (in Psalm 89. 20 ff.) is celebrated against the background of Yahweh's fight with the Powers of Chaos and his act of creation (vv. 10–13). Even if we argue that the hymnal section (vv. 6–19) is an independent poem,[33] we find nevertheless within these verses too the connection of mythical and nonmythical elements, for the thoughts of the poet pass from the great deeds of Yahweh over to his people Israel and its concrete situation: Israel is happy because it knows the cry of jubilation, terū'āh,[34] and walks in the light of Yahweh's face.[35] The word terū'āh alludes to the joy and jubilation at the great festivals when the

385

memory of God's great deeds was kept alive—as we have just stated in the case of the New Year festival when his activity as a creator was celebrated in song.

In this way we meet with a connecting link, joining the great deed of creation in a mythical past with the present state of Yahweh's people and, ultimately, the actual desperate situation of Yahweh's Chosen and Anointed (vv. 39–46). Yahweh's promise to David (vv. 20–38) is given in immediate connection with the preceding sections of the psalm. In that way the introduction of the psalm, with its motif of Yahweh's faithfulness, is taken up in that part where his promise to his servant David is rendered. The psalm is skillfully built, one part meshing with the other. We get also a parallelism of thought: in the beginning Yahweh conquered Rahab and the Powers of Chaos, then he chose his servant David, before whom he will beat down his foes. Exhorting Yahweh not to forget his promise to David, the singer invokes Yahweh not to let the foes of his Anointed scornfully triumph over him and Israel.[36]

In Psalm 136 the poet passes with equal ease from the mythical to the historical sphere of thought. This liturgical hymn, after a short exhortation to thank Yahweh (vv. 1–3), passes to a glorification of Yahweh as the creator of the world (vv. 5–9), then, however, praises his great acts in Egypt and at the Exodus.[37]

The same interaction between Yahweh's mythical and historical deeds is found in Psalm 148, where in a majestic hymn Yahweh's creative activity is glorified by all his creations, nature and man alike. Only in the last verse (v. 14) does the singer pass over to the historical sphere, giving the reason for his exhortation to praise Yahweh: he has exalted the horn of his people.[38]

As we already may be able to see from these few illustrations in Israelite thought, myth in our sense of the word was, so to speak, added to history in our sense of the word. In the psalms just cited Yahweh's activity as a creator was mentioned at the same level as his guidance of the chosen people.

III

Chronology is always said to be the backbone of history. Let us therefore consider the Israelite system of chronology to see how Israel's conception of history works out in its special aspects.

First of all, we should note that the Hebrews possessed an elaborate system of chronology. This chronological system is easily discernible above all in that collection of traditions that literary criticism has labeled "The Priestly Code," abbreviated "P." The chronological scheme found there is intimately linked up with the genealogies of which this collection of traditions is so fond.[39] The key word of "P" actually is *tōledōt,* which may be translated "genealogy." The traditions the "P"-traditionist found before him he brought into a special order by introducing various genealogies.[40] This tendency of his finds its most important expression in the so-called "genealogical tree of Seth" (Genesis 5.1 ff.). Here we find the tradition of the Primeval Patriarchs:

Adam lived	930	years before the Flood
Seth	912	
Enosh	905	
Qenan	910	
Mahalalel	895	
Jered	962	
Henoch	365	
Methuselah	969	
Lamech	777	
Noah	600	

All in all, ten Primeval Patriarchs lived 8,225 years before the Flood.

These ten Primeval Patriarchs of Hebrew tradition long ago were for the first time compared to the ten Primeval Kings of Mesopotamian tradition, at that time known only from the history of Mesopotamia, written at the beginning of the Hellenistic age by the Babylonian priest Berossos,[41] but now found also in original Sumerian documents, the so-called "Kinglists."[42] The points in which both lists actually agree are so many and so striking that the conclusion was inevitable from the outset: Hebrew tradition in this case ultimately can be traced back to Mesopotamian historico-mythical traditions, being taken over from Mesopotamia as part of a complex of traditions, the other two parts of which are the Story of the Flood and the Story of Creation.[43]

In this connection it should be observed that even the chronology of these ten Patriarchs as used in Israel exhibits clear traces of mythical speculation, as is also the case with the Babylonian chronology of the ten Primeval Kings, which was based upon speculations on the great, so-called "world-year."[44]

Now, it cannot be doubted that "P" aimed at establishing a chronological scheme, serving what he imagined to be an historical purpose,
"historical" in this case taken as belonging to the scientific department
of history.[45] The chronological framework of these Patriarchal traditions served the purpose of establishing a chronology of the duration
of the world.[46] For this reason the whole history of mankind from the
First Man to appear on earth, Adam, to the time of the author or
collector of traditions was estimated to comprehend a certain sum of
years. It stands to reason that in this way were combined elements
that we—but not the Hebrews—attribute to two different categories,
i.e. myth and history. Thus the Primeval Patriarchs have nothing to
do with real history; they owe their place in the chronological system
to a Hebrew heritage from Mesopotamian mythical literature.

In order to create, so to speak, a world history, "P" accordingly
mixes mythical and historical elements, seemingly without feeling any
difference whatsoever between myth and history.[47] The same attitude
is found in Mesopotamia.[48] In this connection it should be observed
that genealogy renders immense service by linking up mythical and
truly historical figures together in one single chain.

Next we have to consider the Story of Creation and the Story of
the Flood. From the outset both stories are myths, as modern research
has proved. But they have been adapted by the traditionist to his
chronological scheme of world history. One reason for this inter-
relation of myth and history is to be found in the chronological aspect
of myth, for myth, as we stated, is not only repetition and actualization
of what once happened, in fact it also is a narrative of what happened
at that time. We should not forget *that* very essential aspect of myth,
i.e., to the believer it is a *true* story, it is always held by the community
to relate truly and adequately what once happened.[49] A chronologically
framed history of the world from its beginnings to the time of the
author therefore must include both mythical and historical chronology
—from our point of view.

But we should always remember that our view was not at all that
of the ancient Israelites, because they considered the Story of Creation
and the Story of the Flood as narratives of quite historical events, as
we have stressed here, the word "historical" being taken in our modern
sense of the word. We did hint at the fact that in this regard Israel
was perfectly in agreement with the Mesopotamian manner of looking

upon these things, since the Babylonian Epic of Creation ends its chronological exposition of the story of the beginning by telling how the city of Babel was founded, thus carrying the story from mythical events over to the oldest known real history. *Enūma eliš* accordingly relates not only a myth but also the beginnings of history and these follow immediately after the mythical story of the creation of the world.[50] This fact has been duly emphasized by Hempel.[51]

The collector of the traditions constituting what we are accustomed to call "the Priestly Code" used another principle of arrangement which also possesses a clear mythical background. He introduced four periods in the history of mankind, and of Israel as part of mankind, each period starting with a great bringer of revelation. In this manner we get the epochs of Adam, Noah, Abraham, and Moses, each of whom received from God his own revelation and was given a covenant as a visible sign of his special relation to God.[52] This doctrine of the four periods during which revelation is brought to mankind has an old Near Eastern background and has played a most important role in the history of the religions of the ancient Near East.[53]

The last of the four periods, the period in which Israel actually existed, was introduced by Moses. At this point the true historical period of the life of the Hebrew tribes is linked up with the foregoing —from our scientific point of view—entirely mythical periods. But once more it must be remembered that viewed with Israelite eyes the three foregoing periods were quite as "historical" as the fourth and last one.

Within this last period too we meet with special divisions of time, introduced by important bringers of revelation. When Josephus relates the story of the cult-reformation carried out by Josiah he says:

And when he had done thus in Jerusalem, he came into the country, and utterly destroyed what buildings had been made therein by king Jeroboam, in honour of strange gods; and he burnt the bones of the false prophets upon that altar which Jeroboam first built. And as the prophet Jadon, who came to Jeroboam when he was offering sacrifice, and when all the people heard him, foretold what would come to pass, viz. that a "certain man of the house of David, Josiah by name, should do what is here mentioned." And it happened that those predictions took effect after three hundred and sixty-one years. *Antiq.* X.iv.4 (Loeb Lib. ed.)

However, this chronological observation is entirely wrong; the reformation of Josiah takes place only about 300 years after the accession of Jeroboam. But Josephus wanted to single out Josiah as introducing a new epoch. He—or his source—therefore used the number 361 years, because this number corresponds to that of a "great year," 360 or 361 being a number of mythic-astrological significance in ancient Mesopotamia.[54] Josiah, who in tradition is depicted as a new Moses, concluding a new covenant with his people and bringing a new law as the outward symbol of the divine revelation[55] is in this manner made to introduce a new "great year," a new Aion. Such numerical speculations are indeed highly characteristic of the mythical thought of the ancient Near East.

IV

More specifically characteristic of Israelite thought is the quite astonishing extent to which what we should call a "myth" has been interpreted "historically."

The outstanding example, recognized as such long ago, is the way in which the traditions of the Exodus and the victory over the Egyptians are treated.

The oldest allusion is found in the song of triumph in Exodus 15. 1, 4–5:[56]

> I will sing unto Yahweh for he is elevated,
>   the horse and his chariot hath he thrown into the Sea.
> Pharao's chariots and his host hath he cast into the Sea,
>   and the chosen officers[57] are sunk in the Red Sea.
> The deeps cover them,
>   they went down into the depths like a stone.

This glorification of Yahweh's deeds is kept within the borders of what we call "history," irrespective of how much the original and real event may have been exaggerated in Israelite tradition.[58]

Of great importance, however, is the fact that a text recording an historical event is recited, perhaps even enacted, in the cult.[59] Historical traditions, in this case, take the place of cult myths in the recital of rituals, constituting as it were the "agenda" of the ritual. As the text of the cult, history is the substitute for myth, both "history" and "myth" taken in the modern sense of the terms.

Passing over to psalm literature and prophetic oracles we find, however, another situation. In Psalm 87.4 it is said:

I will mention Rahab and Babel among them that know me,
   behold Philistia, and Tyre, with Ethiopia,
   "this is born there."

The parallelism between Rahab and Babel as well as the following geographical names show that Rahab, which is properly the term for the mythic monster, the Deep or Tehom, in this passage is an enigmatic name for a purely geographical-political entity. How this is to be explained is clear from Isaiah 51.9 f., where the prophet exclaims:[60]

Awake, awake, put on strength,
   oh arm of Yahweh!
Awake as in the ancient days,
   in the generations of primeval times.
Art thou not he that cut asunder Rahab,
   pierced through the Dragon?
Art thou not he that dried up the Sea,
   the waters of the great Deep?
That made the depths of the sea a way
   for the ransomed to pass over?

Because of verse 10b, "That made the depths of the sea a way / for the ransomed to pass over," there can be no doubt about the prophet's thinking of the passing of the Israelites through the Red Sea. The perishing of Pharaoh and his Egyptian army is accordingly seen in the mythical colors of Yahweh's victory over the Primeval Dragon, the Deep of Chaos personified.[61]

In this manner Rahab may be used so to speak as the mythological name of Egypt, as we found in Psalm 87.4. So it is used also by (the first) Isaiah (30.7) when the prophet says:[62]

For Egypt, they shall help with vanity and emptiness,
   therefore I call it:
"Rahab, brought to silence."

Egypt is the Power of Chaos, raging in vain, brought to silence by Yahweh.[63]

It is surely not sufficient to say that in these passages adduced here Egypt has been painted in mythical colors, so that we may speak of a "mythization" of history. No, the wording in Isaiah 51.10 clearly shows that to the prophet Egypt really *was* the Primeval Dragon, the actual representative of the Chaos-Deep, dried up and brought to silence by Yahweh. The Red Sea in this case was the nature symbol,

Pharaoh and his host as it were "the helpers of Rahab," as they are called, the military forces put into action by the Power of Chaos. We may say that Egypt and Pharaoh are the actual historical representatives of the mythical forces let loose in the beginnings, but then we must remember that this is only our own way of looking upon these things, it is *not* the view of the Hebrews. For to them, as we repeatedly tried to make clear, our differentiation of mythical from historical events and persons did not exist. Hence the actual political enemies could be seen as the ever recurring mythical opponents of Yahweh; they were, we might say, the concrete visualization in present history of these foes.

This takes us to the much discussed problem of the enemies in the psalms. Who are these enemies? Political enemies of the ruler, personal enemies of the individual worshipper, or mythical enemies of the sacral king, acting in the ritual as the representative of Yahweh? [64]

Twenty years ago when I was occupied with this problem I tried with the help of Accadian parallel texts to demonstrate how one and the same expression might be applicable to all the three possibilities because of the vagueness of the texts. [65] I was also rather anxious to show how political enemies could be depicted more or less in mythical colors. The fact that they were seen as actual representatives of mythical forces was not altogether neglected by me, but I did not drive home this point with all necessary explicitness. [66] This being the case, I cannot but quote with approval the words of Birkeland, when he says: "Yahweh has once manifested his power through his victory over chaos and enemies, and he shows it again now and ever. The actual powers of chaos, therefore, are the foreign *'elīm* and their worshippers, the *gōyīm*, who disturb order, attacking and oppressing Yahweh's people." When, however, Birkeland argues that *all* enemies mentioned in the psalms must be political enemies of the Israelite ruler it is more difficult to follow him, [67] for in some passages we only find a purely mythical description of the enemies, who are depicted as demoniacal animals attacking the supplicant, e.g. Psalms 22.12–13, and 57.4. [68]

It would seem then, that just as the great Primeval Enemy, Rahab, or Tehom could be mentioned together with political, hostile powers, so also other mythical enemies, demoniacal beings of the Nether World and the like, could be alluded to along with external or internal, political or nonpolitical enemies.[69] This statement does not imply any general opinion on the question of the enemies in the psalms; it deals only with the special aspect we are interested in here.[70]

Before leaving the problem of this so-called "historification of myth" we may note that the prophets sometimes make use of a myth when describing or attacking contemporary persons, powers, or conditions. This is the case with the dirge of Isaiah on the fall of Babel (Isaiah 14), or with Ezekiel's description of the king of Tyre (chap. 28), both poems being written as mythical compositions and based on real myths, as especially emphasized by Hempel.[71]

V

There is another aspect of our main theme that I want to touch upon briefly, namely the importance of the feasts.

Modern research has proved—we may venture to say conclusively—that at least many of the ancient Israelite feasts, being seasonal festivals, originally were intimately associated with a cult myth.[72] So, e.g., the Sukkōt festival (the great annual Feast of Booths) in its Canaanite form obviously was connected from the outset with the marriage between God and Goddess, the leafy hut, *sukkāh,* serving as the place of the *hieros gamos.*[73] But, according to the accepted Israelite-Jewish tradition, this feast was associated with and inspired by the historical memories of the wanderings of the Hebrew tribes during forty years in the desert. Hebrew historical tradition had thus completely shifted the emphasis of this festival, connecting it with the nomad period in the history of the people, whereas popular tradition and custom still kept alive the memory of its original and *truly historical* setting in life within the framework of the Canaanite agricultural system of seasonal festivals, in that way also guarding something at least of its original *mythical* character. From our point of view there is an obvious clash here between myth and history, and I think that the traditionists who tried to connect this festival with the great national memories of Israel really felt something of this clash and were intentionally aiming at a "demythologization" of the annual festival. It must have been a clear intention and purpose behind their effort.[74]

Myth relates events which are repeated cyclically. History, on the contrary, is characterized by what the Germans call *Einmaligkeit,* for history never repeats itself in exactly the same manner.[75] Because of the special Israelite conception of time, however, history "through the annual festival . . . was made something still living and present," as Pedersen puts it, and in this way history was quite like what we call a myth.

History in this case is made a living present, and thus the difference between myth and history is eliminated, a process made possible because history here fulfills the role of myth in ritual. History is thus substituted for myth—according to our modern, scientific views.

VI

Eschatology is both the fulfillment of history and the realization of myth. Eschatology is the doctrine of the last things, *ta éschata*. The last things to happen mark the end of all history and therefore its fulfillment. Eschatology belongs to history, because the last things will happen on this earth, but at the same time it embraces mythical elements, chiefly because the time of end rejoins the time of beginning: end and origin meet each other, the end renewing the time of creation and beginning. As the Germans put it: "Endzeit wird Urzeit." [76] As Yahweh once created the world, so he will now create a new world; he will once more act as a Creator, bringing back the time of paradise. [77] At the same time, however, all eschatological speculation deals with purely historical entities, such as people, countries, political powers. [78]

Apocalyptical speculation about this time of end was much concerned with ideas of the change of time, when the present world period, *hā-ᶜōlām hazzæ,* will be substituted by the world period to come, *hā-ᶜōlām habbā.* But recent research has proved this special notion of ᶜōlām to be entirely foreign to original Israelite thought, and it can easily be shown that we come across in this case one instance of Iranian influence of late Hellenistic age. [79]

We cannot develop here at length the role historical and mythical elements have played in the Israelite-Jewish conception of the figure of Messiah. Suffice it to say that, on the one hand, he is associated with the mythic idea of the returning time of paradise but, on the other hand, as a descendant of David he also belongs to real, human history. [80]

VII

We have found that the Israelite-Jewish conceptions of what we would call myth and history are completely at variance with our Western scientific ideas of what is meant by these two terms. The Israelite notion often seems to move somewhere between myth and history. This is a most conspicuous feature in the so-called patriarchal legends and will perhaps explain our difficulty in interpreting them either as myth or as history. Pedersen, who in some passages speaks of these narratives of the fathers, prefers to define them as "the condensed history of many generations" or as "the history of the people in a condensed form."[81]

But he also prefers this expression when dealing with the special Israelite form of historical outlook. The Israelite people, he says, "still sought their history, so to speak in a condensed form, in the desert. . . . It is understandable that in this way an artificial element must creep into their conception of their history," he continues.[82]

I cannot discuss in this article the expression "condensed history" and its possible value, nor can I take up the idea of Yahweh as the God of history, as he is so often qualified in O. T. modern study, but it goes without saying that, if our viewpoints are correct, the implications in the last mentioned case are of considerable importance.[83]

The quite natural and free way in which to the Israelite mind the ideas and notions pass from a sphere that we call "historical" to what we think a "mythical" sphere and vice versa should warn us not to draw any fixed line of demarcation between myth and history in Israelite-Jewish thought. To Israelite thought Yahweh's interference in the history of Israel is clearly on the same level as his creative activity. For this reason exception is to be taken to the statement of Von Rad à propos Psalm 136: "Hier stehen also Schöpferglaube und Heilsglaube ganz unverbunden nebeneinander."[84] To my mind this is a typical example of the wrong way of interpreting O.T. conceptions, looking at them from the very narrow view of a Christian theologian whose dogmatic training leads him to distinguish sharply between "Schöpferglaube" and "Heilsglaube," and who is unable to place himself in a position subordinate to the texts and to learn how their originators saw things. To the Israelites the great deed of salvation wrought by Yahweh was just his act of creation following his victory over the Chaos Powers. This is really "Heilsglaube," it is the *yēša'* given by Yahweh.

This deed of creation and all other miracles performed by Yahweh, both "mythical" and "historical," were glorified at the great festivals. At these feasts the Israelite in the present time looked back to the past, remembering Yahweh's deeds, but also looked forward, finding in the past a guarantee for the future, exhorting Yahweh to renew his miraculous deeds of old. Clearly the festival is of essential importance to our understanding of the Israelite-Jewish ideas of "history" and "myth." In the festival there is to be found the real forms of the Israelite interpretation of "history." It is here we find the wide range of themes going from the theme of creation to the theme of settlement in Canaan.[85]

As to apocalyptic speculation, Noth has shown that in the Book of Daniel there is a striking mixture of two ideas in the description of the four World Empires, these being conceived of as succeeding empires but, also, as contemporaneous at the world's end. We see here that the time aspect in our modern sense is completely absent. In that moment when the fate of the world is decided by God, the whole course of "history" is present. We can see then that "history" in our sense of the word is not present in these speculations.[86] Thus apocalyptic ideas confirm our views on the relation between myth and history in Israelite-Jewish thought.

APPENDIX

Some Remarks on Myth and History in the Babylonian Epic of Creation

Weiser says concerning the *Enūma eliš*: "Kann man somit an diese Form des Weltschöpfungsmythus eine Geschichte nicht einmal äusserlich anschliessen, so besteht noch weniger hier eine 'innere Verbindung' von Schöpfung und Geschichte, gegen Hempel, Gott und Mensch im Alten Testament."[87] For his opinion he finds support in the words of the concluding hymn on Marduk, where we read:

> May he vanquish Tiamat,   may her life be strait and short.
> Into the future of mankind,   when days have grown old,
> May she recede without cease   and stay away forever.
> Because he created the spaces   and fashioned the firm ground.
>
> *Enūma eliš* VII.132–35

From these words[88] he concludes that the Babylonian Epic of Creation moves within the idea of a cyclical return of events. As he puts it: "Hier ist mit wünschenswerter Deutlichkeit der Weltschöpfungsgötterkampf nicht als Anfang einer 'Geschichte', sondern als 'Anfang und Ende' eines immer widerkehrenden Kreislaufes aufgefasst, der auf dem Boden des natur-mythologischen, kosmischen Denkens entstanden ist und diesen Boden an keinem Punkt verlässt."

In this case Weiser, however, would seem to have overlooked the fact that the epic has as its concluding event the foundation of the town Babel with its sanctuary (*Enūma eliš* VI.47 ff.). Not with the best will in the world can this event be said to be located within the sphere of the ideas of a cyclical return, for the foundation of Babel is not to be repeated every year; it is a fact once for all, and one cannot at all doubt its character of *Einmaligkeit*. Noth[89] and especially Hempel accordingly were quite right in their contention, and not even the most ingenious exegesis would be able to deny the fact that, in the Babylonian Epic of Creation, myth in our sense of the word is followed in the sequence of events by actions belonging to history in our sense of the word. In other words: myth is followed by history, without of course the Babylonians feeling any difference in the character of reality of "myth" and "history."

But even the interpretation of the passage quoted from the *Enūma eliš* needs some qualification. Weiser seems to have overlooked the fact—which is indeed conspicuous everywhere in the Epic but especially in Tablets VI and VII—that the Babylonian Epic of Creation is a cult text, intended to be recited at the New Year festival. The wish that Tiamat may be vanquished forever is of the same kind as that in the hymn in Habakkuk 3.2 ff., when the singer depicts Yahweh triumphantly proceeding to save his Anointed and his people. In the festival the great deeds of Marduk are experienced anew as they were in Israel in the case of Yahweh. We should note the allusion to Marduk's creative activity (*Enūma eliš* 7.135), a motif well known from Israel in connection with Yahweh's fight against the Power of Chaos.

Another viewpoint calls for notice. The Sumerian Kinglist[90] tells us that "when kingship was lowered from heaven, kingship was in Eridu." It then mentions all the kings ruling before "the Flood swept over [the earth]." The kingship again was sent down from heaven, and we get to know all the rulers reigning after that event, i.e. all the postdiluvian kings. Among them are to be found such figures as Etana, Dumuzi, and Gilgamesh, to mention but a few of these mythical rulers. The list then passes over to Mes-Anne-padda, a clearly historical figure because we possess historical inscriptions of his own. Thus the Kinglist passes from the "mythical" to the "historical" sphere with the same ease as we find in Israel. And this fact demonstrates that the same attitude is to be supposed also in *Enūma eliš*, where the creation of the world is linked to the foundation of Babel with its sanctuary.

NOTES

ABBREVIATIONS

ANET   *Ancient Near Eastern Texts Relating to the Old Testament*
BJRL   *Bulletin* of the John Ryland's Library
BZAW   *Zeitschrift für die alttestamentliche Wissenschaft.* Beihefte
ICC   *International Critical Commentary*
JNES   *Journal of Near Eastern Studies*
JSS   *Journal of Semitic Studies*
JThSt   *Journal of Theological Studies*
KAT   *Die Keilinschriften und das Alte Testament*
LUÅ   *Lunds Universitets Årsskrift*
MaR   *Myth and Ritual*, ed. by S. H. Hooke
RGG²   *Die Religion in Geschichte und Gegenwart*, 2d ed.
RHPhR   *Revue d'histoire et de philosophie religieuses*
SMSR   *Studi e Materiale della Storia dei Religioni*
StTh   *Studia Theologica*
UUÅ   *Uppsala Universitets Årsskrift*
ZAW   *Zeitschrift für die alttestamentliche Wissenschaft*

¹ The comprehensive article by Hempel, "Glaube, Mythos und Geschichte im Alten Testament," ZAW, 65:109-67, 1953, which will be quoted several times in the following and which anticipated some of my own conclusions, does not treat of all the aspects of our theme. The present essay is a development of some viewpoints found in my *Religionens värld*, 2d ed. (Stockholm, 1953), pp. 163 f., and reproduces the text of a lecture given at The University College of North Wales in January, 1956. I should like in this connection to thank Professor B. J. Roberts for his invitation and his kind hospitality. I remember also with pleasure my discussions with Professor C. R. North. In the text of my lecture some passages have been slightly expanded, and the notes have been added. I regret that lack of time and space forbids me a more detailed treatment of certain points, but I hope to be able to revert to this interesting theme.

² Hooke, *In the Beginning* (Oxford, 1948), p. 18; see also his *Myth and Ritual*, pp. 3 f.; Widengren, *Religionens värld*, pp. 132 f.

³ The importance of religious symbols has been underlined by Widengren, "Evolutionism and the Origin of Religion," *Ethnos*, 10:90 n. 91, 1945, with reference to Bevan, *Symbolism and Belief* (London, 1938), and Dumézil, *Les dieux des indo-européens* (Paris, 1952), pp. 114-17.

⁴ See Widengren, *Religionens värld*, pp. 149 f., with reference to Lévy-Bruhl, *La mythologie primitive* (Paris, 1935), p. 7.

⁵ Widengren, "Early Hebrew Myths and their Interpretation," in *Myth, Ritual and Kingship*, ed. by Hooke (Oxford, 1958), pp. 149-203. In modern Hebrew the term for "myth" is the Greek loanword מיתוס.

⁶ Bernheim, *Einleitung in die Geschichtswissenschaft*; 4th ed. (Berlin-Leipzig, 1926, p. 5; cf. Kirn, *Einführung in die Geschichtswissenschaft* (Berlin, 1952), p. 8: "1. Geschehen, 2. Darstellung des Geschehenen, 3. Wissenschaft vom Geschehen."

⁷ See Liddell and Scott, *A Greek-English Lexicon*, s.v. ἱστορία, and Powell, *A Lexicon to Herodotus* (Cambridge, 1938), s.v. ἱστορέω and ἱστορίη; see Herodotus VII.96.

[8] Bernheim, *Einleitung*, pp. 58 ff.

[9] Hempel, *Gott und Mensch im Alten Testament*, 2d ed. (Stuttgart, 1936), p. 86: "Dass das A.T. kein Wort für "Geschichte" hat—ebensowenig für "Natur"—, erschwert den Einblick in die Sachlage." In modern Hebrew in this case too we find a loanword, היסטוריה.

[10] Hyatt, *Prophetic Religion* (New York-Nashville, 1947), pp. 77 f.

[11] Ranke, *Geschichte der römischen und germanischen Völker 1495–1534,* Vorwort, in *Gesammelte Werke,* 1 Aufl.

[12] Cf. the weight attached in historical research to the criticism of sources in order to ascertain the objective facts so despised by our American authority; see, for the importance of source criticism, Bernheim, *Einleitung*, pp. 136 ff., and Kirn, *Einführung*, pp. 52 ff. Cf. Bernheim, p. 163: ". . . unwillkürlich begleiten wir die Güter, Ideen, Ziele, die wir für die erstrebenswertesten halten, überall mit unserer Teilnahme, wir bevorzugen die Parteien und Personen, welche für sie eintreten, die Epochen, wo sie herrschen und gedeihen, unwillkürlich vor anderen. Gegen die Einflüsse dieser subjektiven Parteinahme und der ihr zugrunde liegenden *Werturteile* auf unsere Geschichtserkenntnis müssen wir uns mit wissenschaftliche Bewusstsein soweit irgend möglich schützen.

"Wir müssen uns vor allem klarmachen, dass es 'allgemein anerkannte', gleichbleibende Werte, Werturteile in der Wirklichkeit der Geschichte nicht gibt." After developing some principles of method Bernheim then continues, on p. 165: "Durchweg vermögen wir so mit unseren methodischen Hilfsmitteln Objektivität in einem Grade zu erreichen, der von subjektiver Auffassung himmelweit verschieden ist."

From Kirn, p. 85, we may quote the following passage: "Damit haben wir die Forderung anerkannt, dass der Historiker gerecht sei. Wir meinen, er muss auch sachlich sein, d.h. nach der viel umstrittenen *Objektivität* streben. Man drücke sich nicht um die Schwierigkeit mit Hilfe der banalen Behauptung, dass die volle Objektivität nie erreicht werden könne. Es geht ja zunächst darum, ob man sich ihr so weit als möglich nähern soll. Wer dies durch den Hinweis auf die volle Verwirklichung abzutun glaubte, gliche einem Schiffskapitän, der sagte: 'Es ist unmöglich, genau auf der mathematischen Linie des gewählten Kurses quer über den Ozean zu fahren. Also schleudern wir den Kompass ins Meer und steuern wild darauf los!' Die Unmöglichkeit der buchstäblichen Erfüllung eines Gebots entbindet nicht von der Pflicht der bestmöglichen Erfüllung."

Cf. also Geyl, *Use and Abuse of History* (New Haven, 1955), pp. 59 f., on the importance of recording of single objective facts ("specialized pursuits"). Geyl, of course, stresses that "the fact in history cannot be isolated. In itself it is meaningless; it can be made to show different aspects of meaning only as it is related to different parts of the circumstances in which it is embedded" (p. 61). It is obvious that this apparent truth is not what is in the mind of our American colleague who—as far as I am able to understand him—expresses his contempt for the recording of objective facts on which all historical research is based.

[13] Berdyaev, *The Meaning of History* (New York, 1936), p. 41.

[14] Landberg, *Historia* (Stockholm, 1954), pp. 12 ff.; cf. Geyl, *Use and Abuse of History*, p. 70.

[15] It is obvious, however, that the chief factor lies in the substitution of interpretation of history for real historical research. Such is the case especially with Toynbee, who bases his interpretation of history (a) on wrong data, (b) on distorted data, (c) on misinterpreted data. Toynbee's quite fantastic views have been exposed to a trenchant criticism by Geyl, who (as he himself says) "attempted to show

in detail the hollowness to its pretense of being based on empiricism and logical
induction"; see Geyl, *Use and Abuse of History*, p. 65 n. 4, with reference to
Debates with Historians (Groningen, 1955).

[16] See *The Intellectual Adventure of Ancient Man: An Essay on Speculative
Thought in the Ancient Near East* (Chicago, 1946), p. 25, where "early man" in
general is spoken of. I do not know how the Frankforts were able to speak with
such assurance about this rather vague entity, "early man" (who is meant by this
expression? Neanderthal man or people in the *historical* cultures of the ancient
Near East?). It should also be observed that the title "The Intellectual Adventure
of Ancient Man" is singularly misleading, as some critics have noted.

[17] Pedersen, *Israel*, I–II (Copenhagen-London, 1926), 487; see also *Scepticisme
israélite* (Paris, 1931), p. 37: "Si nous ne parlons pas par figures, nous distinguons
nettement entre le temps et les événements qui se passent dans le temps. C'est ce
que ne font pas les anciens Semites. C'est particulièrement évident chez les Arabes.
Naturellement, le temps pour eux représente également des moments et des
périodes, mais toujours de sorte que le temps et son contenu soient identiques.
Le temps est la somme de ce qui se passe." Accordingly, it was not Boman (*Das
hebräische Denken im Vergleich mit dem Griechischen*, 1st ed. [Göttingen, 1952],
pp. 120 ff.) who was the first to find that to the Semites (but in fact the same
holds true also of many other people) the time and its content are identical, as
Hempel would seem to believe (see ZAW, 65:134, 1953).

[18] Pedersen, *Scepticisme israélite*, p. 34f.

[19] Pedersen, *Israel*, I–II, 488.

[20] *Ibid.*, p. 489.

[21] RGG, 2d ed., V, 2090.

[22] Pedersen, *Israel*, I–II, 490.

[23] *Ibid.*, p. 490. When Pedersen (p. 549) says that a connection with Arabic
dahr might be possible he thinks of the near relation between the roots *dwr* and
dhr. See Gesenius and Buhl, *Handwörterbuch*, p. 159a.

The Hebrew word *dōr* belongs to the base *dr*, "surround" or "turn round."
In Hebrew *dōr*, "circle" or "circuit" (of time), assumes the meaning of "generation," the cyclical period from birth to death in the life of an individual (Baumgartner and Köhler, *Lexicon*, p. 206b). In Arabic we have the corresponding word
dawr, "period" (see Driver, *Problems of Hebrew Verbal System* [Edinburgh, 1936],
p. 5, to which we are able to add Accadian *dāru*), which also as the *dawr* of a
planet denotes the cyclical turn the planet makes until it comes back to the same
point (see Dozy, *Supplément aux dictionnaires arabes*, I. 472b). In Arabic the
verb *dāra* of the same root *inter alia* means "to happen," i.e., what comes back
again or what turns around (see Orelli, *Die hebräischen Synonyma der Zeit und
Ewigkeit* [Leipzig, 1871], p. 34). In Accadian we find the words *dāru* and *dūru*,
"eternity," i.e., an ever recurring time cycle, an unlimited period. In Aramaic-
Syriac we find correspondingly *dār*, "circle," "period," "generation," and in
Ethiopic *dār*, "period."

Especially worth noting is the fact that Hebrew *dōr* < *dawr* is exactly formed
as Arabic *dawr*, which denotes not only the period of time but also what it brings
of destiny for man, thus "changed fortune," "fate" (see Driver, JThSt 36:403,
1935).

In view of all these facts, strong exception is to be taken to the following viewpoints of Boman (p. 115). He first admits that it is possible that *dōr* comes from
the same base as *dūr*, "circle," "circuit" (but, as we have seen, there is not the
slightest doubt possible in this case, hence this fact ought to be articulated in a

much more affirmative way). But then he continues: "Damit ist aber nicht bewiesen, dass sich die Hebräer die Generation doch als einen Kreis vorgestellt haben. Es ist nämlich möglich und wahrscheinlich, dass sie umgekehrt den Kreislauf als einen ewigen Rhytmus von Anfang, Fortsetzung und Rückkehr zum Anfang gedacht haben." This supposed "rhythm" is unfortunately a purely gratuitous hypothesis, put forward by the author, who moreover knows from where the Hebrews possessed this rhythm—namely, from their dances in circuit! Here we have definitely left the firm ground of facts and embarked upon the frail ship of pure guesswork. Actually we have been able to ascertain that the Hebrew word for "generation," *dōr*, is entirely connected with the common Semitic base *dr*, "to turn round" and corresponds perfectly to the Arabic term *dawr*, the cyclical period. Hebrew *dōr* then is intimately bound up with the idea of a cyclical return, and means what recurs cyclically.

[24] Pedersen, *Israel*, I–II, 490.

[25] Jenni, *Das Wort 'ōlām im Alten Testament* (Berlin, 1953), esp. p. 50.

[26] *Ibid.*, pp. 44 ff.

[27] North, *The Old Testament Interpretation of History* (London, 1946), p. xi. "The Old Testament in its present form contains, not a straightforward account of Hebrew History, but that history as viewed from the standpoint of the Jewish Church in the period after the Exile."

[28] Hempel, ZAW, 65:121 f.: "Dass zwischen dem, was wir Geschichte nennen, dem menschlich-völkischen Leben, in dem Menschen nach menschlicher Vernunft oder Unvernunft, nach dem, was sie über 'gut' und 'böse' wissen oder wider solche Erkenntnis, nach Gottes Gebot oder in sündiger Lust handeln und ihr Leben zum Guten oder Bösen wenden, und dem, was wir Mythos nennen, dem unmittelbaren Handeln Gottes unter uns Menschen, sei es zum Segen oder zum Fluch—dass zwischen 'Geschichte' und 'Mythos' ein qualitativer Unterschied, ein Unterschied des unmittelbaren Wirklichkeitsgehaltes besteht, ist ein dem antiken Schriftsteller fernliegender Gedanke.... Der Sündenfall ist ihm genau so ein einmaliges 'geschichtliches' Ereignis wie die Arche Noah oder der Turmbau zu Babel oder die Gottesstimme, die Abraham aus Chaldäa rief und in das gelobte Land geleitete." Cf. further Hempel, *Gott und Mensch im Alten Testament*, p. 61 f.; and *Altes Testament und Geschichte* (Gütersloh, 1930), pp. 12 f. I quote what Hempel says in his *Gott und Mensch*, p. 61 f.: "Ich habe in anderem Zusammenhang darauf hingewiesen und muss auch gegenüber neuester Bestreitung daran festhalten, dass die Verknüpfung von Schöpfung und geschichtlichen Grössen an sich noch kein spezifisch israelitischer Gedanke ist. Wie für den Babylonier die Formung der Welt aus den Hälften des erlegten Drachen in der Gründung der Stadt Babel und ihres Tempels gipfelt, so stehen in den Hymnen Deuterojesajas und späteren Texten die Offenbarung der Macht Jahves in der Schöpfung und in der Geschichte *Israels* aufs engste zusammen." The same example was adduced by me in *Religionens värld*, p. 163.

[29] See Hooke, *In the Beginning*, p. 28: "it seems clear that the Jahvist is using for his own purpose a myth which formed part of ancient Hebrew tradition."

[30] See Hooke, p. 36, where he obviously alludes to the article by Humbert, RHPhR 15:1-27, 1935, even though he does not expressly mention Humbert's name.

[31] See my *Early Hebrew Myths*, pp. 162, 164 f., 168, 172 f., 174, 176, etc., for the general observation that myths have come from Mesopotamia to Canaan where they were taken over by the Hebrew tribes after the settlement. For the wandering of the Flood story and the intermediary role played by the Hurrians, see, e.g.,

Rowley, BJRL 32:36 f., 1949. That the Flood story as a living myth has been recited at the great Autumn Festival would seem to be evident from the role played in this feast by the coming of waters; see Pedersen, *Israel*, III–IV (Copenhagen-London, 1940), 749 f., where he refers to Lukianos, *De Dea Syria*, § 13.

[32] Hempel, *Gott und Mensch*, p. 105 with n. 6 (references to Is. 51.9 and to Gunkel and Begrich, *Einleitung in die Psalmen* [Göttingen, 1933], pp. 71 ff.).

[33] Cf. Kittel, *Die Psalmen*, 5th-6th ed. (Leipzig, 1929), p. 296. I cannot understand Kittel when he says: "Sowohl der Anfang, als besonders das Stück 6-19 schliessen sich metrisch und inhaltlich nur lose an das Übrige an." As to the metrical character, we should note that v. 16 has 4 + 4, like the preceding verses, whereas vv. 17–19 have 3 + 3, like the following section. This is quite the opposite of what Kittel alleges.

[34] For this important term see Humbert, *La "terou'a": Analyse d'un rite biblique* (Neuchatel, 1946).

[35] The meaning of באור פניך יהלכון is debated; see the commentaries.

[36] See Kittel, *Die Psalmen*, p. 296; Humbert, *La "terou'a"*, pp. 11, 20, 40 f., 45. Ringgren, in *Psaltarens fromhet* (Stockholm, 1957), p. 152, has been sensible to the interplay of myth and history in this psalm. I find myself in general agreement with him; see below, n. 67.

[37] Von Rad, BZAW, 66:139, 1936, says: "ab v. 10 geht der Psalm in scharfer Wendung zu der Aufzählung der geschichtlichen Grosstaten Jahves über. Hier stehen also Schöpferglaube und Heilsglaube ganz unverbunden nebeneinander." For a criticism of such a view see p. 483.

[38] See also Psalm 114 where, according to the hymnal language of the poet, all nature, the Sea, the Jordan, the mountains, show their compassion in the Exodus of Israel.

[39] See Gunkel, *Genesis*, 3d ed. (Göttingen, 1910), p. xciv.

[40] *Ibid.*, pp. lxxxvi, xciv, 131 ff., 140 f., 152 ff., 262, 385, 493 ff.

[41] See Schnabel, *Berossos und die babylonisch-hellenistische Literatur* (Leipzig-Berlin, 1923), pp. 179 ff.

[42] Jacobsen, *The Sumerian Kinglist* (Chicago, 1939), esp. pp. 70 ff. Hooke (*In the Beginning*, p. 45 f.) referred not only to Berossos but also to the Sumerian kinglists. The older discussion is found in KAT, 3d ed., pp. 530-43.

[43] Gunkel, *Genesis*, p. 132.

[44] See KAT, 3d ed., pp. 538 f., 541 f.

[45] On "P" as an historian, see Millar Burrows, "Ancient Israel," in *The Idea of History in the Ancient Near East* (New Haven, 1955), pp. 124 f.

[46] Gunkel, *Genesis*, p. 133.

[47] Thus we can see how at a given point the exposition passes over from myth to history.

[48] The Mesopotamian kinglists in some cases start with entirely mythical figures like Tammuz or Gilgamesh and pass eventually into the purely historical realm. See Appendix.

[49] That the myth is felt by the worshipers and believers to be a *true* story has been emphasized, e.g., by Pettazzoni, SMSR, 21:104-16, 1947-48. Pettazzoni, however, is of the opinion that the truth of the myths is not of an historical kind. This is correct in so far as the distinction between history and myth is absent on the "mythical" stage. Gaster, in Numen, Vol. I, 1954, contends that Pettazzoni in this case confuses truth with efficacy. If we stick to the fact that myth really is held by its believers to be *true*, to render a truth, no confusion is possible.

[50] The exposition in the mythical epic *Enūma eliš* accordingly corresponds to the passage in genealogy from mythic to historical times.

⁵¹ See also the dictum of Hempel above, n. 28.

⁵² See Gunkel, *Genesis*, pp. 264 f.

⁵³ Widengren, *Religionens värld*, pp. 350 ff., 364 ff. Gunkel (p. 265) was definitely wrong in assuming a Babylonian origin of this typically Indo-Iranian speculation. It is very interesting and important to find it in Israel already in the time of "P".

⁵⁴ We may put the accession of Jeroboam in the year 931 B.C., according to Montgomery, *The Book of Kings*, in ICC, 1951, pp. 58, 63, and the reform of Josiah in the year 621 B.C., also according to the chronology given by Montgomery. Other chronological systems, e.g. those of Albright and Begrich, present small deviations.

The number of 361 years is somewhat puzzling for we would expect 360 years. It may be explained by a special computation taking the actual year after the 360 years and adding it to the real mythical number; or, rather, as a Great Year, 354 years, plus a Great Week, 7 years. On the mythic-astrological number 360, see Meissner, *Babylonien und Assyrien*, II (Heidelberg, 1925), 415.

⁵⁵ Widengren, "King and Covenant," JSS, 2:2-5, 17-19, 29 f., 1957.

⁵⁶ For the poetical form of this song see Albright, *Archaeology of Palestine and the Bible*, pp. 145 f.; *Studies in Old Testament Prophecy*, ed. by Rowley (Edinburgh, 1950, p. 5); Cross and Freedman, JNES, 14:241 ff., 1955.

⁵⁷ For the proper meaning of the term *šālīš* see Baumgartner and Köhler, *Lexicon in Veteris Testamenti libros*, p. 977b; Cross and Freedman, p. 245a. The *šālīš* is the third man standing in the chariot.

⁵⁸ This exaggeration is of course due to the fact that a "mythization" of history in this case has exerted a great influence on the authentic traditions of the event; see, e.g., Pedersen, *Israel*, III–IV, 728: "The object cannot have been to give a correct exposition of ordinary events but, on the contrary, to describe history on a higher plane, mythical exploits which make of the people a great people, nature subordinating itself to this purpose. Östborn, "Yahweh's Words and Deeds," UUÅ, 7:15, 1951, also stresses the mythological traits in the story in Exodus 15.1–18. From the article of Cross and Freedman we may quote the following statements: "It seems most reasonable to suppose that the poetic styles and canons of Canaan have affected strongly the structure, diction, and, on occasion, the actual phraseology of the poem. Certain clichés concerning the anger and might of Yahweh, and conversely, the heaving of the sea, may be derived secondarily from mythological cycles, or rather the lyric poetry and psalmody of Canaan. . . . It seems necessary to conclude that we do not have a mythologically derived conflict here. It is dubious in the extreme to suppose that we have the result of the 'historicizing' of myth . . . Rather we have 'history' shaped by familiar clichés, motifs and literary styles, and even these influences are remarkably restrained" (p. 238a). "The situation, both historically and in regard to the problem of mythological relationships, is far more complex in vss. 16b-18. . . . It is in these verses that we feel the strongest influence of mythological motifs" (p. 240a). We miss, here, however, an insight into the fact that to the Hebrews at this time there was no contrast between history and myth. As to the traditions of the Exodus, I hope to be able to return to this subject, the character of these traditions being a very complex one as is generally recognized.

Hempel, *Gott und Mensch*, p. 65, contends that in Israel history never was mythicized ("in den Bann des Mythus gezogen"), but the Exodus tradition would seem to point in the opposite direction.

⁵⁹ On the Exodus tradition as the cult legend of the Passover, see Pedersen, ZAW, 52:161 ff., 1934. Mowinckel, StTh, 5:66 ff., 1952, has disputed the inter-

pretation of this complex of traditions as given by Pedersen, but he too admits that as we now have it it is built upon traditions possessing a "cult-legendary" character. I cannot enter here upon a discussion of this problem but must postpone it for the future. I shall say only that even Mowinckel does not deny that we are entitled in a way to speak of the Exodus tradition as the cultic myth of the Passover festival: "In diesem Sinne darf man mit Pedersen von der Exodustradition als Kultmythus des Passahfestes sprechen" (p. 86). We should not overlook the fact that still in the Mishnah, Pesachim x.5b, there is a quotation from Exodus 13.8 giving the whole feeling of the festival. The Passover is experienced as an actualizing of the Exodus tradition; see the pertinent remark in Beer, *Pesachim* (Giessen, 1912), pp. 195 f. The Exodus story would accordingly serve the same purpose at the Passover festival as the Flood story at the Autumn festival (leaving aside the major problem of whether the Exodus too may have been associated with the Autumn feast). Hence, even in this case, a perfect parallelism between mythical and "historical" texts.

[60] For the general interpretation see Gunkel, *Schöpfung und Chaos*, 2d ed. (Göttingen, 1921), pp. 30 ff.; Widengren, *Early Hebrew Myths*, pp. 169 ff.

[61] See Gunkel, *Schöpfung*, pp. 31 f.: "Indess bleibt die Frage bestehen, wie denn hier der Untergang Pharaos als die Vertilgung eines grossen Ungeheuers geschildert werden könne. Solche Bilder werden nicht willkürlich erfunden, sondern sie treten nur als eine nachträgliche Umdeutung und Aneignung der Tradition auf,—man beachte, dass Rahab ein Name ist. Das ist hier um so sicherer, als das Bild von Rahabs Zerschmetterung nicht als eine deutliche, vom Dichter erfundene Allegorie begriffen werden kann; denn wer soll Rahab sein— Pharao und Ägypten oder das rote Meer?—Unleugbar ist also, dass hier ein Mythus von Rahabs Überwindung in der Urzeit vorausgesetzt ist, mit dessen Farben an dieser Stelle Pharaos Untergang ausgemalt wird. Das eigentümliche Schillern aber, dass Rahab zuerst Rahab und dann ein Bild für Ägypten ist, ist dem Stile des Dtjes charakteristisch."

[62] For this passage see, in general, *ibid.*, pp. 38-40.

[63] Text: ומצרים הבל וריק יעזרו

לכן קראתי לזאת

רהב המשבת

The interpretation of רהב המשבת as רהב המשבת has been proposed by Gunkel (p. 39 n. 1) with a reference to a proposal advanced by Hensler in Dillmann's commentary on Genesis. All interpreters seem to agree that we have here a clear case of false word division; see, e.g., Delitzsch, *Die Lese- und Schreibfehler im Alten Testament* (Berlin-Leipzig, 1920), p. 4 § 5a (where, however, another reading is adopted). The new MSS from the Dead Sea scrolls in this passage bring the same division of the word as *Textus Masoreticus*. Baumgartner and Köhler, *Lexicon*, p. 947a reads רְהָבָה מָשְׁבָּת. Why?

[64] See Widengren, *The Accadian and Hebrew Psalms of Lamentation as Religious Documents* (Stockholm, 1937), pp. 238 ff.; Birkeland, *Die Feinde des Individuums in der israelitischen Psalmenliteratur* (Oslo, 1933), and *The Evildoers in the Book of Psalms* (Oslo, 1955).

[65] Widengren, *Accadian and Hebrew Psalms*, pp. 197 ff.

[66] *Ibid.*, pp. 208 f., 236 f., 240 f., 242 f. For this reason there is undoubtedly some justification in the criticism directed by Engnell against my position; see *Studies in Divine Kingship in the Ancient Near East* (Uppsala, 1943), p. 49 f. But Engnell in his turn exaggerates the "mythical" interpretation of the actual text of both Accadian and Hebrew psalms of lamentation.

[67] Birkeland, *Evildoers in the Psalms*, pp. 77, 89 f. Ringgren, *Psaltarens fromhet*, p. 179 n. 13, has exploded Birkeland's hypothesis in just four lines.

[68] Widengren, *Accadian and Hebrew Psalms*, pp. 122, 242 f.

[69] Cf. above pp. 479 ff. and note that my conclusions in *Accadian and Hebrew Psalms*, pp. 250 f., ought to be supplemented in a corresponding manner.

[70] It is my intention to treat of the description of misery in the Hebrew psalms in another connection, where I hope to be able to revert to the problem of the enemies in the psalms.

[71] Hempel, ZAW, 65:111-13, 1953.

[72] Widengren, "Early Hebrew Myths," in *Myth, Ritual and Kingship*, pp. 175 f., 178 ff.

[73] *Ibid.*, pp. 181 ff.

[74] It is still valuable to quote what Wellhausen once had to say on the association of festival and history in Israel: "Eine Gegenprobe für die behauptete Denaturierung der Feste im Priesterkodex liegt darin, dass die schon von der jehovistischen Tradition vorbereitete geschichtliche Deutung derselben hier ihre Spitze erreicht hat. Denn sind dieselben ihres ursprünglichen Inhalts verlustig gegangen und zu vorgeschriebenen Formen des Gottesdienstes herabgesunken, so steht nichts im Wege, die leeren Schläuche nach dem Geschmack des Zeitalters neu anzufüllen. So werden nun auch die Laubhütten (Lev. 23) ein historisches Fest, eingesetzt zum Andenken an die Obdächer, unter denen sich das Volk während des vierzigjährigen Wüstenzuges behelfen musste. Bei Ostern wird über die bereits im Deuteronomium und in Exod. 13, 3 ss. sich findende Motivierung durch den Auszug aus Ägypten noch ein Schritt hinaus getan. Im Priesterkodex ist nämlich dies Fest, das gerade wegen seines eminent geschichtlichen Charakters hier als das bei weitem wichtigste von allen gilt, noch mehr als bloss Nachhall einer göttlichen Heilstat, es ist selber Heilstat. Nicht *weil* Jahve die Erstgeburt Ägyptens geschlagen, wird in der Folge das Pascha gefeiert, sondern vorher, im Moment des Auszugs, wird es gestiftet, *damit* er die Erstgeburt Israels verschone. Die Sitte wird also nicht bloss geschichtlich motiviert, sondern in ihrem Anfange selber zu einem geschichtlichen Faktum verdichtet und durch ihren eigenen Anfang begründet.... Einzig beim Pfingstfest zeigt sich noch kein Ansatz zur historischen Deutung; hier ist dieselbe dem späteren Judentume vorbehalten geblieben, welches darin, auf grund der Chronologie des Buches Exodus, eine Erinnerung an die sinaitische Gesetzgebung erkennt. Man sieht aber, wohin der Zug der späteren Zeit geht." *Prolegomena zur Geschichte Israels*, 6th ed. (Berlin, 1905), pp. 97-98. It is highly regrettable that Kraus did not digest these passages in Wellhausen's classical work. His own rather uncritical position takes Old Testament studies back to the pre-Wellhausen period. See Kraus, *Gottesdienst in Israel: Studien zur Geschichte des Laubhüttenfestes* (Munich, 1954).

[75] That history never repeats itself in the same manner is stressed by, e.g., Landberg, *Historia*, pp. 85 f. See further Renier, *History, its Purpose and Method* (London, 1950), pp. 224 f.

[76] Van der Leeuw, *Phänomenologie der Religion*, 1st ed. (Tübingen, 1933), § 87.5; Gunkel, *Schöpfung und Chaos*, pp. 366 ff.; Bousset and Gressmann, *Die Religion des Judentums im späthellenistischen Zeitalter*, 3d ed. (Tübingen, 1926), pp. 283 ff. The German dictum "Endzeit wird Urzeit" is quoted by Frost, *Vetus Testamentum* 2:73, 1952.

[77] Emphasized by Hempel, *Gott und Mensch*, p. 248: "Jahve wird sich abermals als der *Schöpfer* betätigen, die neue Welt schaffen."

[78] *Ibid.*, p. 248: "Die israelitische Religion aber ist so stark geschichtsgebunden,

dass auch dort, wo wirklich der Glaube an die *Endzeit* lebendig wird, die Grössen der *Geschichte*, Volk, Land, Feinde, mitgesetzt sind. Auch die Endzeit rechnet mit *geschichtlichen* und damit mit universellen Grössen." Frost (p. 75) empha- sizes by rights the fact that there was an old Israelite "eschatology in the Old Testament which is not expressed in the terms of myth." By "myth" we under- stand in this case the notion we have defined above in our introduction. But it is not a legitimate method simply to blot out Jeremiah 4.23–26 from the authentic oracles of this prophet (using as his "method" a vicious circle). The same quite gratuitous operations are undertaken (pp. 78 f.) with the prophet Isaiah. For these reasons his conclusions cannot be accepted, for they are based first on the above- mentioned amputations of the texts of the pre-exilic prophets, second on a false assumption of a contrast in Israelite thought of "history" and "myth."

[79] Jenni, *Das Wort 'ōlām*, esp. pp. 86 f. For the idea of the two Aions see Volz, *Die Eschatologie der jüdischen Gemeinde im neutestamentlichen Zeitalter* (Tü- bingen, 1934), and Bousset and Gressmann, *Religion des Judentums*, pp. 243 ff. The hypothesis of Iranian influences in this special case was put forward in Bousset and Gressmann (p. 509), but above all by Reitzenstein, *Das iranische Erlösungsmysterium*, pp. 231 f., and by Von Gall, *Basileia touthrou* (Heidelberg, 1926), p. 275.

[80] For Messiah as associated with the return of paradise, see Gressmann, *Der Messias* (Göttingen, 1929), pp. 149 ff., 278 ff.; for Messiah as a descendant of David, see the material presented by Gressmann on pp. 232 ff. (where, however, the interpretation suffers from the wish of the author to interpret—à tout prix— every Messianic oracle as alluding to the returning David (a highly dubious idea in view of the fact that David may be only the regnal name of the ruler) not to the Davidic king as a sound exegesis demands. The same idea is developed by Schmidt, *Der Mythos vom wiederkehrenden König im Alten Testament* (Giessen, 1933). See also Volz, *Eschatologie der jüdischen Gemeinde*, pp. 203 ff., and Bousset and Gressmann, *Religion des Judentums*, p. 230.

[81] See Pedersen, *Israel*, I-II, 275, 476, 491; III-IV, 656 ff.

[82] *Ibid.*, III-IV, 657.

[83] For the general opinion in this case see Lindblom, LUÅ, 31:43, 55, 72, 1935. In the first of these passages the author says: "Och då för Mose Jahve visat sin makt på historiens område, blev han från den stunden i första hand en historiens levande gud, som såsom personlig vilja handlade i historien, och det efter etiska principer." The second passage reads: "Genom att Jahves verksamhet förlades till historien kom hans egenskap att vara en personlig vilja på ett så dominerande sätt till uttryck att naturbestämdheten i princip övervanns." We should like to ask: on what Old Testament passages are these statements based? It cannot be too strongly emphasized that in this case "history" does not at all mean the same thing as in modern historical research. It is history in the Hebrew sense that we have analyzed above. However, Mowinckel, *Psalmenstudien*, II (Christiania, 1922). 54, would seem to have been sensible to our problem.

[84] See above, n. 37.

[85] The importance of these various themes for the growth of the Pentateuch has been seen in a most meritorius way by Von Rad, *Das Formgeschichtliches Problem des Hexateuchs* (Stuttgart, 1938).

[86] Noth, *Das Geschichtsverständnis der alttestamentlichen Apokalyptik* (Co- logne-Opladen, 1954), pp. 24 ff.

[87] Weiser, *Glaube und Geschichte im Alten Testament* (Stuttgart, 1931), p. 26 n. 86.

[88] It is only fair to observe that Weiser had to rely on a text that was inferior to the recension we possess today, though of course I do not know if he would change his views when confronted with the text quoted above. I have quoted from the translation given by Speiser, ANET, p. 72a.

[89] Noth, "Die Historisierung des Mythus," *Christentum und Wissenschaft* (1928), p. 267.

[90] On the Sumerian Kinglist see above, n. 42.

ACKNOWLEDGMENTS

Aldwinckle, R.F. "Myth and Symbol in Contemporary Philosophy and Theology: The Limits of Demythologizing." *Journal of Religion* 34 (October 1954): 267–79. Reprinted with the permission of the University of Chicago, publisher. Copyright 1954 University of Chicago.

Barr, James. "The Meaning of 'Mythology' in Relation to the Old Testament." *Vetus Testamentum* 9 (January 1959): 1–10. Reprinted with the permission of E.J. Brill.

Barrett, C.K. "Myth and the New Testament: The Greek Word μῦθος." *Expository Times* 68 (1957): 345–48.

Bultmann, Rudolf. "New Testament and Mythology." In Hans-Werner Bartsch, ed., *Kerygma and Myth,* Vol. 1 (London: SPCK, 1953): 1–44. Reprinted with the permission of the Society for Promoting Christian Knowledge.

Cassirer, Ernst. "Judaism and the Modern Political Myths." *Contemporary Jewish Record* 7 (April 1944): 115–26. Reprinted with the permission of the American Jewish Committee.

Dardel, Eric. "The Mythic." *Diogenes,* no. 7 (Summer 1954): 33–51. Reprinted with the permission of UNESCO.

Dörrie, Heinrich. "The Meaning and Function of Myth in Greek and Roman Literature." In Joseph P. Strelka, ed., *Yearbook of Comparative Criticism, Volume IX: Literary Criticism and Myth* (University Park: Pennsylvania State University Press, 1980): 109–31. Copyright 1980 by the Pennsylvania State University Press. Reproduced by permission of the publisher.

Eliade, Mircea. "The Prestige of the Cosmogonic Myth." *Diogenes,* no. 23 (Autumn 1958): 1–13. Reprinted with the permission of UNESCO.

Frankfort, H. and H.A. "Myth and Reality." In H. Frankfort et al., *The Intellectual Adventure of Ancient Man: An Essay on Speculative Thought in the Ancient Near East* (Chicago: University of Chicago Press, 1946): 3–27. Reprinted with the permission of the University of Chicago Press. Copyright 1946 University of Chicago.

Gaster, Theodor H. "Mythic Thought in the Ancient Near East." *Journal of the History of Ideas* 16 (June 1955): 422–26. Reprinted with the permission of the *Journal of the History of Ideas*.

Jacobsen, Thorkild. "Sumerian Mythology: A Review Article." *Journal of Near Eastern Studies* 5 (1946): 128–52. Reprinted with the permission of the University of Chicago Press, publisher. Copyright 1946 University of Chicago.

Kirk, G.S. "Greek Mythology: Some New Perspectives." *Journal of Hellenic Studies* 92 (1972): 74–85. Reprinted with the permission of the Society for the Promotion of Hellenic Studies.

Kramer, S.N. Review of *The Intellectual Adventure of Ancient Man: An Essay on Speculative Thought in the Ancient Near East. Journal of Cuneiform Studies* 2 (1948): 39–70. Reprinted with the permission of Scholars Press.

McKenzie, John L. "Myth and the Old Testament." *Catholic Biblical Quarterly* 21 (July 1959): 265–82. Reprinted with the permission of the Catholic Biblical Association of America.

Oden, R.A. Jr. "Method in the Study of Near Eastern Myths." *Religion* 9 (Autumn 1979): 182–96. Reprinted with the permission of Academic Press, Inc.

O'Flaherty, Wendy Doniger. "Inside and Outside the Mouth of God: The Boundary Between Myth and Reality." *Daedalus* 109 (Spring 1980): 93–125. Reprinted by permission of *Daedalus*, Journal of the American Academy of Arts and Sciences.

Pettazzoni, Raffaele. "The Truth of Myth." In Raffaele Pettazzoni, *Essays on the History of Religions*, Supplements to *Numen*, Vol. 1 (Leiden: Brill, 1954): 11–23. Reprinted with the permission of E.J. Brill.

Ricoeur, Paul. "Introduction: The Symbolic Function of Myths." In Paul Ricoeur, *The Symbolism of Evil* (Boston: Beacon Press, 1969): 161–74. Reprinted with the permission of Harper & Row.

Vivas, Eliseo. "Myth: Some Philosophical Problems." *Southern Review*, n.s., 6 (January 1970): 89–103. Reprinted with the permission of the author.

Wardman, A.E. "Myth in Greek Historiography." *Historia* 9 (October 1960): 403–13.

Wheelwright, Philip. "The Semantic Approach to Myth." *Journal of American Folklore* 68 (1955): 473–81. Reproduced with the permission of the American Folklore Society. Not for further reproduction.

Widengren, George. "Myth and History in Israelite-Jewish Thought." In Stanley Diamond, ed., *Culture in History* (Columbia University Press, 1960): 467–95. Reprinted with the permission of the publisher. Copyright 1960 by Columbia University Press.